ESSENTIALS OF AMERICAN POLITICS AND GOVERNMENT

ESSENTIALS OF AMERICAN POLITICS AND GOVERNMENT

RICHARD M. PIOUS

BARNARD COLLEGE
AND THE GRADUATE FACULTIES
OF COLUMBIA UNIVERSITY

McGRAW-HILL BOOK COMPANY

NEW YORK ST. LOUIS SAN FRANCISCO AUCKLAND BOGOTÁ
HAMBURG JOHANNESBURG LONDON MADRID MEXICO MILAN
MONTREAL NEW DELHI PANAMA PARIS SÃO PAULO
SINGAPORE SYDNEY TOKYO TORONTO

ESSENTIALS OF AMERICAN POLITICS AND GOVERNMENT

Copyright © 1987 by McGraw-Hill, Inc. All rights reserved. Printed in the United States of America. Except as permitted under the United States Copyright Act of 1976, no part of this publication may be reproduced or distributed in any form or by any means, or stored in a data base or retrieval system, without the prior written permission of the publisher. This book is a shorter version of Pious: *American Politics and Government*, copyright © 1986 by McGraw-Hill, Inc.

1 2 3 4 5 6 7 8 9 0   VNHVNH   8 9 4 3 2 1 0 9 8 7

ISBN 0-07-050126-2

This book was set in Zapf Book Light by York Graphic Services, Inc.
The editors were David V. Serbun, James Anker, and Susan Gamer;
the designer was Hermann Strohbach;
the production supervisor was Salvador Gonzales.
The photo editor was Ellen Horan.
The drawings were done by Fine Line Illustrations, Inc.
Von Hoffmann Press, Inc., was printer and binder.
Cover photograph by Mike Mitchell: Photo Researchers.

Library of Congress Cataloging-in-Publication Data

Pious, Richard M.
    Essentials of American politics and government.
    Includes index.
    1. United States—Politics and government.   I. Title.
JK274.P563   1987   320.973   86-27373
ISBN 0-07-050126-2

ABOUT THE AUTHOR   Richard M. Pious graduated from Colby College, where he was editor in chief of the student newspaper and president of the senior honor society, Blue Key. While in college he demonstrated his political talent by losing the election for student body president. Pious received his M.A. and Ph.D degrees from the Department of Public Law and Government of Columbia University, where he was a Harriman Fellow. He began teaching the introductory course in American politics in 1968 at Colby College, then taught at Columbia College and York University (Toronto). He has been the course director for Dynamics of American Politics at Barnard College in New York City since 1973. He is the editor of *Civil Rights and Liberties in the 1970s* (1972); a ten-volume reprint series of classic nineteenth-century books on constitutional, comparative, and international public law (1981); and the centennial volume of the Academy of Political Science, *The Power to Govern* (1983). He is the author of *The American Presidency* (1979) and coauthor (with Christopher Pyle) of *The President, Congress and the Constitution* (1984). He has contributed articles to *Political Science Quarterly*, *Journal of International Affairs*, and *Wisconsin Law Review* and has lectured at many colleges and universities, including Columbia University, Mount Holyoke, New York University, the University of Wisconsin, and the Washington, D.C., program of the Claremont Colleges. He has been a commentator for the Voice of America, several public and network radio and television stations, *Newsday*, and the *Wall Street Journal*; and his op-ed pieces have appeared on the editorial pages of several newspapers. His consulting work has recently included Public Affairs and Research Communications (Washington, D.C.) and the Sloan Foundation. When not teaching or writing, the author enjoys trail bicycling, photography, and tennis.

CONTENTS

PREFACE

In the midst of the American Civil War, President Lincoln called on the American people at Gettysburg to prove to the world not only that our nation could endure, but also that "government of the people, by the people, and for the people, shall not perish from the earth." Today we face the same problems as did those who created our nation in 1787 and forged a stronger union out of the Civil War. How should we provide for our security and prosperity? How can we create a government strong enough to defend us without posing a threat to our freedoms?

If you are a typical reader of this book, you were born in the late 1960s, in years of racial unrest, campus disorders, and political assassinations; and you have grown up with economic uncertainty, political scandals, and increasing skepticism about the ability of government to solve social and economic problems. You began to study civics or social studies just as the Iranian hostage crisis and the Marine casualties in Lebanon were making clear how difficult it is to project American power in the world. You have seen one politician after another campaign on television against the "mess in Washington."

But it is nonsense to say that government causes all our problems and solves none. Politics, in the best sense, is the art of bringing people together to solve problems. Those who would change the way the world works (and I count myself among them) can do no better than to change the way government works or change the leaders of government. In a democracy we have that opportunity. Before making changes, however, it is sensible to learn how the system works, to assess its effectiveness, and to think seriously about how it can be improved.

APPROACH

I wrote this book because I wanted to learn more about American politics and government and then convey my ideas to the generation of Americans who will meet the challenges of our third century of democracy. I followed Paul Samuelson's approach in writing his best-selling economics textbook: give students "nothing unnecessarily hard, but omit nothing essential as being beyond the grasp of the serious student; and above all, present nothing that later must be unlearned as wrong." I hope I have raised the most important political issues that face our nation and provided a comprehensive and balanced discussion to help students draw their own conclusions.

Instead of providing a narrow framework in which to view politics, I offer a broad, eclectic view, which allows instructors to use this book as a teaching tool or supplement that extends their own approach to politics. I take neither a liberal nor a conservative slant; rather, I present several aspects of each issue, hoping that my own iconoclastic stance will encourage readers to question conventional wisdom or their own preconceived notions and to develop skepticism about political rhetoric along with a deeper awareness of the way the game of politics is played.

xi

FEATURES

Special sections in each chapter will help you learn about American politics. Some chapters have an *issue and debate* section which presents the pros and cons of an important issue, such as industrial planning. Many have *close-ups*, short analytical biographies of leaders such as Richard Nixon, Jesse Jackson, David Stockman, and Sandra Day O'Connor, to show the diversity of experiences and viewpoints in American politics. Key topics are examined in *focus* sections. Each chapter closes with a section called *in conclusion*. At the end of each chapter there are references for *further reading*, as well as a *study break*—a guide to films, biographies, and novels about politics which you might enjoy. There are also lists of *organizations* and *useful sources* of information. Near the end of the book there is a *glossary* of important terms (these are set in ***bold italic*** throughout the text). The Constitution of the United States and the Declaration of Independence are given, the former with explanatory notes.

Your instructor may also assign the *study guide* which accompanies this text. It not only will help you review the material but also provides a self-test section on key concepts, data, and terms. The research exercises can also be used to apply some of the concepts and information to practical problems of the kind that political scientists, pollsters, journalists, lobbyists, and government officials routinely deal with.

ORGANIZATION AND CONTENT

Now to specifics. The book is organized in four parts, each with a specific objective. Part One describes the nature and origin of the American political experiment. Chapter 1 defines politics and government and provides you with key concepts. Chapter 2 applies these concepts to a case study: the writing of the Constitution and the creation of our government in 1787. Chapters 3 and 4 discuss two of the key characteristics of our system: its federal structure, making us a nation of diverse states; and its limited powers and guarantees of civil liberties.

Part Two is concerned with the pursuit of power. Chapter 5 discusses voting and nonvoting, because differences in participation help explain who gets elected to office and what those elected do once they get into power. Chapter 6 examines the structure and functions of the Democratic and Republican parties from the local level to the national level. It describes how interest groups and their political action committees (PACS) increased their influence while parties became weaker, and how parties are trying to stage a comeback in the 1980s. Chapters 7 through 9 discuss congressional and presidential nominations and elections and describe campaign finance and organization, the impact of the media and advertisements, voting behavior, and how election results influence both the two-party system and the way the government subsequently works.

Part Three deals with governmental powers and processes. Chapters 10 and 11 deal with the presidency and Congress. They examine the formal and informal "checks and balances" of the Constitution and party system, focusing on the circumstances in which each branch collaborates with or confronts the other. Each chapter also deals with a "power problem": how the President must try to lead Congress without adequate constitutional or political resources; how Congress must represent diverse interests which tend to fragment it, while producing laws which require a majority. Chapter 12 deals with the Supreme Court and other federal courts—the "least dangerous branch"—

and shows how the judiciary has expanded its powers while at the same time remaining strongly influenced by the other two branches. It also discusses the "power problem" of the federal courts: how to balance their responsibility to interpret the law against the reactions of the other branches when they stake out politically unpopular positions. Chapter 13 discusses the "fourth branch," the bureaucracy, and describes how the other three try to control it. The bureaucracy, however, is strongly influenced by interest groups, which are analyzed in terms of "iron triangles" and "issue networks," two concepts which have great implications for the way government really works. Chapter 14, on the budget process, ties much of the preceding analysis together, by showing how the four branches interact with each other to answer one of the fundamental political questions: who gets what, when, and how?

THE FIRST STEP

In his inaugural address to the nation more than twenty-five years ago, President John F. Kennedy set forth his program and then observed, "All this will not be finished in the first hundred days. Nor will it be finished in the first thousand days, nor in the life of this administration, nor even perhaps in our lifetime on this planet. But let us begin." The Chinese philosophers say that every journey, no matter how long, begins with a single step. So it is with the study and practice of politics. I took my first step the month and year President Kennedy gave that inaugural address, when I enrolled in an introductory course in American politics at Colby College. Since then I have taught this course in four different colleges for almost twenty years, as a teaching assistant and professor. Your steps begin today, and I hope that this book helps you in the hundred days of your semester as much as the textbook I used helped me.

ACKNOWLEDGMENTS

I wish to thank the following scholars for their help and advice in reviewing the manuscript of this book: Kristi Andersen, Ohio State University; Gottlieb J. Baer, American River College; Lawrence Baum, Ohio State University; A.M. Burns, III, University of Florida; George F. Cole, University of Connecticut; Howard T. East, Jr., Menlo College; Paul L. Hain, University of New Mexico; Murray C. Havens, Texas Technical University; Richard P. Hiskes, University of Connecticut; Jerome M. Mileur, University of Massachusetts, Amherst; Robert E. Murphy, Florissant Valley Community College; Michael Nelson, Vanderbilt University; Benjamin I. Page, University of Texas; Mark P. Petracca, University of California, Irvine; Palmer C. Pilcher, University of Arkansas; Mavis Mann Reeves, University of Maryland; Donald L. Robinson, Smith College; Robert C. Sahr, Oregon State University; Richard K. Scher, University of Florida; James Sheffield, Wichita State University; Edward I. Sidlow, Miami University; Steven S. Smith, Northwestern University.

I also wish to thank my editors at McGraw-Hill, Eric Munson, David V. Serbun, James Anker, Stephen Wagley, and Susan Gamer; the production supervisor, Leroy Young; the designer, Hermann Strohbach; and the copy editor, Pamela Haskins.

I am grateful for the help of research assistants Sharon Epstein, Susan Kaye, and Cindy Gordon, all Barnard College students; and several Barnard and Columbia College students acknowledged in the footnotes. Melissa Mulliken of Barnard College public relations arranged for my photograph. The librarians at Barnard and Columbia University were, as always, indispensable sources of advice. My colleague Tom Gais provided me with updated data for several tables. Michael Goldstein of Public Affairs Research and Communications gave me access to his extensive files on civil rights politics.

I have benefited from the roundtable discussions of ongoing research conducted by the Political Science Department at Barnard and the Center for the Social Sciences at Columbia University, chaired by Jonathan Cole. The Montauk Seminar on presidential nominating politics, funded by the Sloan Foundation and chaired by Alexander Heard, enabled me to exchange ideas with many of the leading scholars of party and electoral politics. I benefited from the ideas of guest speakers at the YMHA series on the imperial presidency which I chaired in 1984: James MacGregor Burns, William Leuchtenburg, Fred Greenstein, Doris Kearns Goodwin, Robert Caro, and James David Barber.

Friends, colleagues, and acquaintances whose conversations with me involved topics which appear in this book include: Susan Bales, Gerald Benjamin, Richard Brifault, Andre Burgstaller, Demetrios Caraley, John Chambers, Henry S. F. Cooper, Jr., Flora Davidson, Jerry Davis, Louis Fisher, Thomas Franck, Julian Franklin, Ester Fuchs, David Garth, George Gilder, Charles V. Hamilton, Peter Hart, Roger Hilsman, Robert Hirschfield, Dorothy James, Peter Juviler, Ethel Klein, Louis Koenig, Robert Lamb, William McNeil, Lawrence Mead, Robert Mutch, Amy Piro, John Prados, Chris Pyle, Nicholas Rango, Katherine Roome, Hugh Roome, Richard Rubin, Robert Shapiro, Allan Silver, Hilary Silver, Steven Singer, Stephen Solarz, Daniel Traister, Gary Wasserman, Kathryn Yatrakis, and my colleagues at the Barnard Roundtable.

I want to acknowledge the enormous support given to this effort by my mother, Edith Pious; and my mother-in-law, Susan F. C. Weil. Above all else, I acknowledge the help of my wife, Sacha Weil, whose career in high technology gives me insights into the politics of the future.

FINALLY . . .

I welcome any comments students or instructors wish to make about this textbook. Please write to the author at the following address: Department of Political Science, Barnard College, 606 West 120 Street, New York, New York 10027.

Richard M. Pious

ABOUT THIS BOOK

The fourteen chapters in this book were originally published in January 1986 as part of the nineteen-chapter hardcover textbook *American Politics and Government*. Although that text was warmly received by many instructors, others found it too comprehensive for their course needs. Many who teach on quarter and trimester systems find that they have little time to explore questions of public policy, while others prefer to explore public policy through a series of readings rather than relying on textbook chapters. *Essentials of American Politics and Government* has been published to meet their needs.

Essentials of American Politics and Government retains the first fourteen chapters of the hardcover edition, including all the chapters on constitutional and federal issues, parties, elections, and the branches of government. Except for some updating of the text and certain tables, to reflect the results of the 1986 congressional elections and the changes in the tax law, the chapters are unchanged from those in the hardcover edition. The corresponding supplements—the study guide, instructor's manual, test bank, overhead color transparencies, and accompanying book of readings—are unchanged as well.

PART ONE
THE DEMOCRATIC EXPERIMENT

POLITICS: WHO GETS WHAT?

From the election of Andrew Jackson as president in 1828 to Martha Lane Collins's victory in the 1982 Kentucky gubernatorial election, increased democratization has affected the pursuit of power. (Granger Collection; Pat Pfister: Picture Group.)

In the *Devil's Dictionary* the journalist Ambrose Bierce defines politics as "a strife of interests masquerading as a contest of principles. The conduct of public affairs for private advantage." To call people *politicians* or to charge them with "playing politics" on an issue is a serious insult. But politics in the best sense is also, as Ralph Waldo Emerson once said, "the greatest science and service of mankind." This book will explore both aspects of politics: the conduct of public affairs for personal advantage and the effort to solve problems democratically and in the public interest.

Four issues will be considered: the pursuit of power, the uses and abuses of power, the accountability of those who exercise power, and the ends of power. In Part One we will study the formation of the union in 1787 and the ways in which federalism and the Bill of Rights limit governmental power. Part Two discusses how politicians are elected to Congress and the White House and how the parties and interest groups influence the voters' choices. In Part Three we will look at the governing institutions and processes: the three branches of national government (the presidency, Congress, and the judiciary), the bureaucracy (sometimes considered the fourth branch), and the budget process. The book concludes with a section devoted to economic, social, foreign, and military policies.

WHAT IS POLITICS?

To begin, we will consider some definitions and concepts: about politics and government in general and about constitutional and democratic politics and government in particular.

Politics as power and influence

Politics involves ***power:*** a relationship between people in which some get others to obey them, even if they would rather not do so, by means of subtle or overt pressure and even by the use of force. And it involves influence: the ability of people to get others to do what they want them to do by convincing them that it is in their own best interests. Thus politics exists in the classroom, where the college can compel students to take examinations if they wish to pass a course; in the military, where officers can give orders to their subordinates; and in business, where executives can convince the head of a company to make a certain decision.

Politics as the pursuit of position

Politics is about getting power and influence as well as about exercising it. It is about running for public office, becoming an adviser, and getting an appointment to an important government agency. Jockeying for position happens everywhere: academic politics determines who gets to be dean or department chair; corporate politics is played to see who becomes president or chairman of the board; religious politics occurs when a new spiritual leader is elected.

4

Who gets what is often worked out in the corridors of Congress. Lyndon Johnson (then Senate majority leader) makes a point to Senator Theodore Green of Rhode Island. *(George E. Tames: New York Times.)*

The wear and tear of campaigning is evident in Senator Gary Hart's shoe leather—and this was only the first primary of the 1984 season. *(G. Peress: Magnum.)*

Politics as conflict management

"Civilization," as José Ortega y Gasset once wrote, "is nothing else but the attempt to reduce force to being the last resort." Politics is the art of managing conflicts between different individuals or groups by substituting peaceful decision making for brute force. Instead of equating might with right and allowing the strongest to decide, politics settles disputes by means of bargaining, negotiation, and compromise between the parties; through appeals to the customs and laws of the community; by voting on the issues; or by transferring disputes to government agencies or courts. In this sense politics is a *game*, and its rules must be understood by both spectators and participants.

Politics as who gets what, when, and how

Yet another way of thinking about politics is to focus on the score of the game: who wins and who loses, and by how much? Politics sometimes substitutes for other ways of allocating goods and services, such as the marketplace. Samuel Johnson once defined politics as "nothing more than a means of rising in the world," and this is true when politics involves redistributing income and services from the haves to the have-nots, or vice versa, depending on who controls the government.

When a nation makes a decision to establish a system of old-age pensions or public universities, for example, usually the costs are borne by one group

Students are a constituency, too, and at Boston College and elsewhere many sign petitions against proposed cuts in student aid. *(Bruce Flynn: Picture Group.)*

(taxpayers), while the benefits accrue to others (the elderly or students, neither of whom pay much in taxes at the time). This may result in a massive redistribution of wealth from people who work to those who do not. When tariffs are raised or lowered, when defense budgets are increased or cut, and when public works projects are planned or abandoned, different regions win or lose. There is nothing new in these observations. "The art of government consists in taking as much money as possible from one class of citizens to give to the other," Voltaire wrote in the eighteenth century; however cynical, sometimes this statement seems to be true.

Politics as continuity and change

The history, traditions, and customs of a nation—its past political practices and ideas—have a profound impact on its politics. Our separation of church and state, our mistrust of big government and bureaucracy, our reliance on state and local governments for many functions, and our emphasis on individual rights and liberties—these are rooted in hundreds of years of our history. Other nations, just as democratic as our own, like England, France, and Canada, have entirely different traditions of church-state relations, different ways of balancing the responsibilities of central government and local governments, and different ways of safeguarding the civil rights and liberties of their peoples. How a nation conducts its politics today is always based in large measure on how it has acted in the past.

To understand politics fully one must observe how political practices change from one decade to the next and from one century to the next. The rate of political change in a nation is important: in some countries changes occur slowly; other countries have a strong reformist streak and are constantly improvising; and still others alternate between reactionary governments that are unwilling to make needed reforms and revolutionary regimes that make fundamental breaks with the past. Our own tradition is a mixture of institutional reform and dramatic, often violent, revolutionary developments that include our independence from Britain, our expansion across a continent by force of arms against Mexico and the Indians, our consolidation of the union through civil war between the north and the south, and our emergence as a great power through two world wars and several smaller conflicts. In the twentieth century our politics has been transformed by the impact of the industrial and communications revolutions. Our system of party competition is always in flux, our federal-state arrangements have gone through at least five transformations, and the balance of power between the president and Congress constantly changes.

Politics as future shock

Politics is about the future and about how to manage the accelerating pace of economic, scientific, social, and cultural change. Our role in the world economy, for example, has shifted enormously in the past quarter-century; government, working with industry, must devise a strategy to enable the United States to compete in the world marketplace. Scientific changes have enabled people to live longer (requiring changes in social security and medical care programs) but in greater peril (requiring new diplomatic initiatives and defense policies).

"No government can remain stable in an unstable society and unstable world," argued the French prime minister Léon Blum. The world seems more unstable today than at any other time since the end of the Second World War. Does this mean that we are destined to live with unstable government? Can our democracy cope with the crises that we face? How can we best transform it to meet modern challenges?

Politics as ends

"If the people want religion," the British prime minister Harold Macmillan once said, "they should look to their archbishops." But people also look to their politicians, if not for answers to ultimate questions about the meaning of life, then at least for answers to fundamental questions about the larger purposes of civilization. Politics is concerned with more than power and problem solving; it deals with the culture and values of the community and becomes

President Reagan visits a job retraining center in Pittsburgh. What the government should do to combat unemployment remains a divisive issue in American politics. (*Associated Press.*)

the secular equivalent of religion in nations in which church and state are formally separated, as they are in our own. And in much of the world it becomes much more; where it is formally entwined with an established religion, politicians use religion to maintain their power. How a democratic nation manages its religious and cultural politics can ultimately determine whether the people remain united or divide along sectarian lines—whether they remain a community or dissolve into warring tribes.

WHAT IS GOVERNMENT?

A definition

Politics takes place everywhere, but the focus of this text is on politics in government. We have so many governments in our own country—thousands of municipal and county governments—that the Census Bureau had to come up with a definition when counting them so that it would know what to include and what to leave out. Its definition: If an organization can make law or collect a tax, it is a government. Some other characteristics of a government are discussed below.

Government and the monopoly of force

A *government* is the organization that has a monopoly of force over the people in a particular territory. It has armed forces which can put down civil disturbances or attempts to secede from or overthrow the government. It can collect taxes to finance its operations and can compel compliance with its laws.

In reality, no government has a monopoly on force. Organized crime syndicates, guerrilla movements, and terrorists can employ force and can sometimes coerce people into complying with their wishes. But a government has a monopoly over the *lawful* use of force. Only the force it uses (or permits others to use) is lawful, by definition, and the government can regulate or forbid the use of force by others. Those who have power call themselves *the government* and call their force *lawful;* eventually the test of this claim is experiential—either they maintain themselves in power, or they are overthrown and others form a government which makes the same claims.

The "nightwatchman" state

Why should people in any territory allow the government a monopoly on the lawful use of force? Would the people not be better off if they refused to give anyone such a monopoly and kept arms themselves? Historically, many conquered peoples have allowed a government to rule them because it promised to maintain order. It protected them from groups that might tax or coerce them: crime syndicates, religious sects, terrorists, neighboring tribes, warrior hordes, or other countries. Without government, the English philosopher Thomas Hobbes argued, life would be "nasty, brutish and short." People turn to government for protection, from both external and internal threats. The first duty of any government is to act as a *nightwatchman state*—a term derived from the guards who patrolled city streets in the evening centuries ago. Many nations spend more of their money for armaments than for anything else, while local governments usually spend heavily on police protection.

The positive state

In the United States we expect government to do much more than simply take our money by taxing us and provide us with protection in return. We assume that it will take some responsibility for the welfare of the people and for the management of the economy and that it will promote education, the arts, and the sciences. But how much responsibility should government take? How

Liberals have generally favored public housing to replace slums. Conservatives generally prefer free-market solutions or government rent subsidies. *(Burt Glinn: Magnum.)*

much government do we want? Some people, like Tom Paine, argue that government, "even in its best state, is but a necessary evil; in its worst state, an intolerable one." Others, like Andrew Jackson, say that "there are no necessary evils in government. Its evils exist only in its abuses."

Reasonable people disagree about the *role* of government. **Liberals** see government positively, arguing that regulations, services, and benefits free those who are disadvantaged and discriminated against from social and economic burdens and enable them to join the mainstream of economic life. They believe that government must take decisive action to mobilize the resources of society to deal with the complex issues of the modern world. They see danger in weak, indecisive, or ineffective government, for as Franklin Roosevelt warned, "History proves that dictatorships do not grow out of strong and successful governments, but out of weak and helpless ones." **Conservatives** argue that the government has a more limited role, because its programs do not work well and because a government large enough to provide benefits is also a government large enough to take away rights and liberties. They believe that confiding power in the people is dangerous because, as Lord Acton warned, "Power tends to corrupt, and absolute power corrupts absolutely." They believe that people equate government's power with wisdom—a dangerous mistake. "The less government we have, the better," Ralph Waldo Emerson said; "the fewer laws, and the less confided power."

We will be looking at the way in which these disputes have influenced the size, the structure, and the processes of government. Is there a trade-off between the powers of government and the rights and liberties of the people? Do we have to give up some of our freedom to get a more efficient government, or is this a false issue? Does stronger and more effective government, equipped with greater powers, actually increase our freedom? Would weaker government actually lessen it?

**CONSTITUTIONAL
AND DEMOCRATIC
POLITICS:
FIRST PRINCIPLES**

The ancient Greek philosopher Aristotle argued in *Politics* that to be a good person, one had to be a good citizen—one had to participate in politics or else lead an incomplete life. In a democratic government the people are guaranteed the right to participate. That guarantee can be ensured only when the power of government itself is limited—when there is constitutional politics.

Constitutional politics

Characteristics of constitutional government. When people create a government, they usually specify and limit its powers at the outset. To do so they sometimes write a ***constitution,*** which establishes the governmental structure, provides the governing institutions with their formal powers, sets limits on the uses of these powers, and guarantees the people certain specific rights and liberties. Constitutional politics involves the *consent of the governed,* and when the people find the constitution unsatisfactory, they can amend its provisions and change it to their liking—as we have done with our own Constitution many times—or create a new one if necessary.

In many nations rulers exercise virtually unlimited powers, and their constitutions are merely a facade, providing paper guarantees that no one believes will be respected. Having a constitution means nothing unless the political leaders and the people are willing to abide by it, defend it, and fight to preserve it, if necessary.

Limited government and the rule of law. Our Constitution was formed partly to increase the powers and efficiency of government, but also partly to limit these powers and confine them to certain purposes. The Constitution, laws passed by Congress, regulations framed by the bureaucracy, and decisions handed down by federal courts all retain this dual quality: they empower officials to take action, but they also limit them in what they can do. Our government must operate according to the Constitution, laws, and formal procedures, and officials can be challenged in court and often prevented from exceeding their authority. We value the means by which government acts as much as the ends for which it acts.

Geraldine Ferraro, the Democratic vice-presidential nominee, courts black delegates at the Democratic national convention in San Francisco in 1984. *(Gilles Peress: Magnum.)*

Democratic politics are defined by free elections. The Progressive Conservative party leader, Brian Mulroney, votes in his home district in Quebec in the 1984 election that made him prime minister of Canada. *(CP Laserphoto.)*

Democratic politics

Democratic politics involves three principles: (1) that governments are established by and with the consent of the people, almost always by a constitution; (2) that the people choose their leaders in free and fair elections; and (3) that the government and its leaders must ultimately obey the will of a majority of those elected to make laws, except in the case of matters that are specifically exempted from this rule by the constitution. "Democracy is the recurrent suspicion," E. B. White said, "that more than half of the people are right more than half of the time."

Characteristics of democracies. Almost every nation in the world has a written constitution, holds elections, and claims to be a democracy in which the will of the people prevails. Yet few nations are real democracies. How can we distinguish those which are democracies from those in which democratic forms are a sham?

No

COMPETITIVE ELECTIONS. In a democracy there are regularly scheduled elections in which people can compete for office; they have the following characteristics:

- Each citizen votes for each elective office.
- Two or more candidates run for each office.
- Elections are scheduled at or within regular intervals.
- The government does not interfere with the campaigns of opposition candidates.
- The government does not coerce the voters into making a specific choice (though in some nations it requires people to vote).
- The person with the greatest number of votes (the ***plurality***) or more than half the votes (the ***majority***) wins.
- Those who win the elections are not prevented by the government or the military from assuming office.

Most of the time such elections are held in the United States, Canada, western European nations, some nations in Latin America, Australia, New Zealand, Japan, India, and Israel. But few nations in Africa, the middle east, or Asia—and no communist states—hold competitive elections.

MAJORITY RULE. In a democracy the will of the majority ultimately determines government policy. But the people do not resolve every issue. They may have no opinions or may prefer to have elected officials and "experts" make the decisions. When a majority holds a strong opinion, however, this often is translated into public policy. The people may have to wait several years until they can elect new leaders, but they can get their way.

MINORITY RIGHTS. There are some exceptions to the principle of majority rule. The constitution itself may specify certain limitations so that the rights of minorities can be guaranteed against the rule of the majority. Suppose, for example, that the majority wanted to make its own religion the official religion of the nation; the constitution might specifically prohibit the establishment of an official religion.

CONSTITUTIONAL LIMITS. The rules of the game embodied in the constitution may limit the will of the majority. Even if the majority wished to end elections, abolish guarantees of minority rights, or limit freedom of speech, for example, the constitution would prevent it from doing so. Certain rules are necessary for a functioning democracy (each nation determining its own unique set) and may not be changed by rulers who represent transitory majorities.

Direct and indirect democracy. According to our definition of democratic politics, the people must adopt a constitution, elect leaders, and allow the leaders to make policy by majority vote. This is sometimes referred to as **indirect democracy** because policies are made only indirectly by the people, who must entrust most decisions to their elected officials. (We also call this *representative democracy*, and the government that is established a **republic.**)

There is another type of democratic politics, however, in which the people vote directly on decisions without entrusting them to representatives. This is called **direct democracy:** people assemble, discuss the issues and the alternatives, and eventually decide by majority vote what to do about them. They may elect permanent officials to carry out all their decisions, or they may elect

Direct democracy still exists in town meetings like this one in Vermont. *(Magnum.)*

Representative democracy should mean responsive democracy. Edward Brooke, then senator of Massachusetts, discusses problems with a constituent. *(AP Photocolor.)*

temporary officials to implement particular decisions and report back to the assembly.

ADVANTAGES OF DIRECT DEMOCRACY. At first glance direct democracy seems to be a simple and attractive way to conduct politics. Everyone gets to participate and speak his or her mind. It is an educational experience, in which everyone learns more about problems. A consensus may emerge, or at least a compromise position that brings people together. All those involved, even the losers, have the feeling that they made the decisions that affect their lives.

DISADVANTAGES OF DIRECT DEMOCRACY. Direct democracy might work for a college fraternity or sorority, for a faculty meeting, or for a small New England town, but it is impracticable for a large territory containing many people because it would be impossible to get everyone together at one time and in one place. In a small community people know one another, and when they discuss issues, it is not only *what* is said, but also *who* says it, that helps them make up their minds. They listen to people they trust, and they discount the views of others. But in the case of a large community, a meeting would involve hundreds of thousands, or even millions, of people. No nation could pack all its citizens together and expect real deliberation and debate.

SOLVING THE SIZE PROBLEM. Indirect democracy solves the size problem. The people vote for representatives of their choice, who then meet in a much smaller assembly. Indirect democracy allows the people to *recreate* the advantages of direct democracy: the assembly which they elect conducts face-to-face meetings, debates the issues, and reaches a consensus or a compromise so that a majority can decide. Yet when representative institutions are created, they may not truly mirror the views or interests of the people who elected them. They may instead prefer to exercise their own judgment or to substitute their own values for those of their constituents, which may or may not be a bad thing. Special interests may distort the outcomes of elections and reduce the accountability of elected leaders to the people. Representative governments are "more or less" rather than fully democratic.

**Nondemocratic
governments**

A nation is not democratic simply because it holds elections for a president, congress, or parliament. Hitler's Germany had a parliament, but Hitler wrote that the leaders would be free "from the parliamentary principle of decision by the majority" and that decisions would be made only by "responsible persons," which in practice meant himself. In communist countries which call themselves *people's democracies* there are elections to representative bodies, but in almost every case only the Communist Party nominates candidates for office, and the only choice the voter has is to deposit the ballot with the name of the communist nominee or to go into a voting booth and cross off the name in protest. Few people enter a voting booth under such circumstances. A one-party government does not satisfy the conditions for democracy, nor does it provide adequate representation or accountability. "It has been said that democracy is the worst form of government," said Winston Churchill, "except for all those other forms that have been tried from time to time."

Authoritarian government. Some political scientists distinguish two types of nondemocratic government: authoritarian and totalitarian. *Authoritarian* governments base their power solely on brute force rather than the consent of the governed. Their leaders usually come from the ranks of the military or from internal security agencies. They take power in a coup d'état and maintain themselves with rigged elections. Their governments arrest, torture, and kill their political opponents. They tolerate or encourage "goon squads" and "death squads" which support the government by killing or mutilating opponents. Often these regimes justify such use of force in the name of "fighting communism" or "preserving western values" and seek to win public support from democracies by arguing that free elections and a multiparty system are luxuries which they cannot afford while they are putting down their opponents. Their arguments would be more convincing if they did not crush democratic movements and parties that have no connections to communists. They still have no effective answer to Lincoln's question: "Why should there not be a patient confidence in the ultimate justice of the people? Is there any better or equal hope in the world?"

Some authoritarian rulers are little more than thugs, hardly distinguishable from the organized crime figures who prosper under their rule. They may traffic in drugs, smuggle arms, manipulate the currency, divert foreign aid for their own use, and loot the treasury. They run ***gangster states;*** their leaders take power just for the payoffs, and not only can they be bought, but they can also be rented by anyone with a money-making proposition likely to exploit their own people. Recent examples include Cuba under Fulgencio Batista, Haiti under "Papa Doc" Duvalier and his son "Baby Doc," and Uganda under Idi Amin.

Totalitarian governments. As bad, if not worse, are the ***totalitarian*** governments. A governing party, either the communists of the left or the fascists of the right, assumes power from a weak democracy—sometimes by winning an election and sometimes by using force. Imbued with its vision of remolding the people and creating a perfect society, its idealism leads it to excesses. Totalitarians must dominate all groups—religious, social, economic, cultural, and political—and subordinate them to the government. The individual must bow to the will of "the people" (as determined by the ruling party) in all matters. The totalitarian government wishes to control the population in mind and spirit as well as in body.

Totalitarian governments have liquidated millions of people: Nazi Germany sent 12 million people (including 6 million Jews) to death in concentration camps; the Soviet Union under Stalin killed, imprisoned, or exiled millions in its Gulag prisons. For those who live in such countries, there is very little difference between totalitarian and authoritarian regimes.

POLITICAL AUTHORITY AND LEGITIMACY

"Political power," Mao Tse-tung said, "grows out of the barrel of a gun." But people are ruled by more than force, and power is not the only basis of a relationship between rulers and the ruled. **Authority,** which rests on the people's belief in the ruler's capability, and **legitimacy,** which rests on their acceptance of the leader's right to rule, are two important aspects of politics.

Political authority

What is authority?   In everyday speech we might say that a professor is an authority in a field or that a sportscaster is an authority on football; we also put someone down by asking, "What are you, some kind of authority?" Both these examples involve someone who is communicating to other people about a subject. Authority is a relationship which exits when someone sets forth a reasoned elaboration of his or her ideas and this reasoning is accepted by others.

Not all authority is rational. *Traditional* authority depends on magic, superstition, customs, and ritual and might be exercised by a tribal leader, headman, or shaman (witch doctor). *Charismatic* authority involves faith that the personal qualities of the ruler will result in the best policies; the "man on horse-

The authority of government rests in large part on the success and credibility of the laws it makes. Bill-signing ceremonies in the Rose Garden give presidents publicity which helps them lead public opinion. *(Wide World Photos.)*

back" in Latin America is typical, and Indira Gandhi in India, Mao Tse-tung in China, Vladimir Lenin in Russia, and Adolph Hitler in Germany are other examples.

Governments must maintain their authority; people are more likely to obey laws and regulations and to cooperate with the government when they believe that their leaders know what they are doing and are acting in the people's best interests. The politician who loses authority in a democracy is likely to lose the next election.

Authority in the United States. American leaders often find it difficult to maintain their authority. "The Constitution provides for every accidental contingency," Senator Sherman once said about President Buchanan's administration, "except for a vacancy in the mind of the president." In the 1920s Will Rogers made a career out of ridiculing politicians, deadpanning to his audiences, "I don't make jokes, I just watch the government and report the facts." The novelist Saul Bellow says, "Take our politicians, they're a bunch of yo-yos," a sentiment which many Americans share. President Hoover became a laughingstock during the *depression* because of his promises that "prosperity is just around the corner," and Nixon had to tell the American people that "your president is not a crook." Jimmy Carter's authority eroded as a result of the Iranian hostage crisis and the energy crisis, and Reagan lost some public support over the Bitburg incident.

When American politicians lose authority—because they lack the expertise necessary to solve problems, because their forecasts turn out to be incorrect, because their subordinates abuse power, or for any other reason—public support for their programs drops sharply, even when they remain personally popular. It becomes more difficult for them to exert power or influence at home and abroad. Allies reassess their support, while enemies probe for weaknesses. Their party splits into factions and may even challenge the president for renomination, as happened in 1952, 1968, 1976, and 1980. The opposition party keeps up its strong criticism, confident of winning the next election.

It is not always the case that our leaders and our government have little authority. George Washington and his supporters had the confidence of most Americans. Abraham Lincoln actually gained authority during the Civil War. When he entered office, even his own Cabinet and Republican Party leaders, who viewed him as a hopeless frontier politician incapable of leading the nation during a crisis, had little respect for him; at his death he was a major figure, "Father Abraham" to the nation. Franklin Roosevelt's ability as a communicator sustained the authority of the government in the midst of the depression and during the Second World War. "The only thing we have to fear is fear itself," he told the American people at his first inaugural, and they believed him. More recently, presidents Kennedy and Johnson used their authority to preside over a revolution in race relations that secured civil rights for racial minorities. One of the most important tasks in the United States today is that of restoring the government's authority with the people. Ultimately this must involve more effective government, which institutes policies that command wide public support—something easier said than done.

Legitimacy

"The strongest is never strong enough to be always the master," argued the French philosopher Jean-Jacques Rousseau, "unless he transforms strength into right, and obedience into duty." People obey their leaders because they believe that they ought to.

What is legitimacy? By what right does a government exist? By what right do politicians rule? Why should they be obeyed? Each of these questions involves legitimacy. In the most practical sense a government is *legitimate* when other governments concede that it has a right to exercise a monopoly of force over the people in a particular territory and when most of the people it rules concede that it has a right to do so.

To delegitimize an existing government is to raise questions about its right to rule, usually by arguing that, by its very nature, it is unjust or evil. As the philosopher Blaise Pascal said, "Force without justice is tyrannical." When enough people believe that they are living in a society which is fundamentally unjust to them, in which the rulers may abuse their trust without penalty, or in which the rules of the game are rigged against them, that government faces a legitimacy crisis.

Throughout history, rulers have had to legitimize their governments. European kings in the seventeenth century relied on *divine right:* the monarch upheld the authority of an established church (and exempted it from taxation and civil law), and in return the church presided over the coronation and invested the reign with divine sanction. It was a useful arrangement for both church and crown. Other legitimizing principles include **aristocracy** (rule by those suited by birth to govern), **plutocracy** (rule by those who have made money and presumably have demonstrated ability), **technocracy** (rule by those who are scientifically and technically trained to deal with complex problems), and **democracy** (rule by the people, or at least a majority of the people).

Legitimacy in American politics. The American independence movement involved an attack on the right of the British king, George III, to rule over the colonies: the Declaration of Independence is a long list of complaints against the king for his alleged misrule. "The history of the present King of Great Britain," the Declaration says, "is a history of repeated injuries and usurpations, all having in direct object the establishment of an absolute Tyranny over these states." There follow twenty-seven paragraphs, listing in detail all the crimes, abuses of power, and tyrannical acts committed by the king. The Declaration of Independence tried to delegitimize George III so that the rebellion of American subjects against their sovereign could be justified at home and abroad.

We have had other legitimacy crises. In the 1830s, a sectional crisis involving tariffs almost led to the secession of South Carolina. That state argued that any state had a right to *nullify* (that is, to refuse to enforce within its borders) laws passed by Congress. In the 1850s we had a legitimacy crisis between the north and the south over slavery: the north wanted to confine slavery to those states in which it already existed; the south wanted to extend it across the west. Southerners argued that restrictions would be unjust and that if they were imposed, the union was no longer worth maintaining. President Lincoln, in his 1861 inaugural address, pointed out that the Constitution contained no provision for its termination or for the secession of any state. It was a contract between the people of all the states, and it would be illegitimate for a state to

All governments maintain a monopoly of force within the territory they control. Army troops, acting under orders of President Franklin Roosevelt, disperse the "Bonus Army" of unemployed World War I veterans, camped out in the Capital District, during the depression. *(National Archives.)*

leave the union without the consent of all the other states. The south remained unpersuaded, and the Civil War was the result.

We have not had a full-blown legitimacy crisis since the Civil War. The fundamental principles of our government and the right of our elected leaders to govern have not come under sustained attack by a significant part of the nation since 1861. But we have had some close calls. During the great depression of the 1930s, some of the millions of unemployed and desperate men and women turned to communist or fascist movements and parties. But because the New Deal government of President Roosevelt successfully maintained its authority and gave most suffering Americans hope for the future by establishing new government agencies to provide aid, the crisis of legitimacy was confined to only a small minority of the people. In the 1960s, white student radicals and black nationalists also challenged the legitimacy of the system, but their critiques never commanded the support of more than a small fraction of the people, even though many of their specific proposals were incorporated into the reform agenda of the decade.

Legitimacy crises may involve *usurpation* or *abuse* of power. To usurp power is to take the rightful place of another, as when a military strongman institutes a coup and replaces an elected official, suspends civil liberties, and scraps the constitution. To abuse power is to refuse to enforce or follow the laws, to enforce them arbitrarily, or to act completely outside the law. "Nobody has a more sacred obligation to obey the law than those who make the law," the Greek playwright Sophocles wrote, but many politicians cannot seem to get the idea straight. The Watergate crisis of the early 1970s, for example, involved not usurpation of power (Richard Nixon had been reelected president by an overwhelming majority in 1972), but rather abuse of power, since the president conspired not only to ignore certain laws but also to disobey others.

18

Some respected political scientists (such as James MacGregor Burns, a Pulitzer prizewinning presidential biographer) and government practitioners (such as Lloyd Cutler, a former White House counsel) believe that our constitutional arrangements are so antiquated and inefficient that only a complete overhaul will suffice to provide a constitution suited for the third century of democracy in the United States. Other people think that some sort of *world government* should replace nation-states like our own.

Is our Constitution suited to modern conditions? Can it be adapted with minor modifications, or does it need a complete overhaul? Should we try to strengthen our democracy, relying further on the principle of majority rule? Or should we turn over government to a technocracy, to the "experts," and limit the role of the people and their elected representatives? If we still believe, as Churchill did, that although democracy may not be very efficient, it is better than any other form of government, how can we improve our democracy to keep it that way?

PREVIEW

POWER, AUTHORITY, AND LEGITIMACY IN A NEW NATION. Chapter 2 will discuss the pursuit, uses, and ends of power, as well as the accountability of those in power, by examining the politics of the Constitutional Convention of 1787. The events of that year involved politics in the best sense of the word. Crises which threatened the independence and prosperity of the American people reached a climax and were resolved. Analyzing what the convention delegates accomplished

Members of the Continental Congress sign the Declaration of Independence in Philadelphia in 1776. ("*Declaration of Independence,*" *John Trumbull, Yale University Art Gallery.*)

is no sterile exercise in "history," nor does it provide merely "background" knowledge, a preface one must endure before getting to the subject of politics today. Far from it. Chapter 2 is a case study which describes the skills and techniques of professional politicians. You will learn a great deal about practical politics, and you will also gain a useful perspective on some of the problems we face two centuries later, as we continue our experiment in democratic government. For if our system now seems antiquated, there is nothing to stop us from using the same techniques used by the convention delegates to modernize our politics if we choose to do so. That too is what democratic politics is all about.

FURTHER READING

Barnes, James F., Marshall Carter, and Max J. Skidmore: *The World of Politics*, 2d ed., St. Martin's, New York, 1984. The important concepts of politics are summarized and explained, with excellent examples given throughout.

de Tocqueville, Alexis: *Democracy in America*, Vintage Books, New York (first published in 1839). This account by a young French nobleman who was impressed by American society and politics remains one of the most accurate and influential discussions of American politics.

Huntington, Samuel P.: *American Politics: The Promise of Disharmony*, Belknap Press, Harvard University Press, Cambridge, Mass., 1981. A study of the differences between political theory and rhetoric and political practice in American politics.

Lasswell, Harold: *Politics: Who Gets What, When, How*, Meridian Books, New York, 1958. A classic discussion of political power.

Perlmutter, Amos: *Modern Authoritarianism*, Yale University Press, New Haven, Conn., 1984. A discussion of totalitarian and authoritarian states and leaders, from Hitler to Idi Amin.

Rosenau, James M.: *The Dramas of Politics: An Introduction to the Joys of Inquiry*, Little, Brown, Boston, 1973. A highly recommended discussion of ways of approaching political studies, written by a noted political scientist.

Schatschneider, E. E.: *The Semi-Sovereign People*, Holt, New York, 1975. A critique of American politics from the point of view of a political scientist who would like to see greater democratization.

Wolfe, Alan: *The Limits of Legitimacy: Political Contradictions of Contemporary Capitalism*, Free Press, New York, 1977. A radical critique from the point of view of a democratic socialist who believes that this country's class-based and liberal politics is not democratic.

THE STUDY BREAK

Doonesbury. A syndicated comic strip by Garry Trudeau, dealing with students of the 1960s who are now grown-up professionals adapting to the 1980s.

Feiffer, Jules: *Jules Feiffer's America.* A collection of cartoons by a leading liberal, from the 1950s to the present.

Trudeau, Garry: *In Search of Reagan's Brain.* A collection of comic strips by the creator of *Doonesbury*, covering the 1980 election and the early days of the Reagan administration.

1984. A movie based on George Orwell's vision of a totalitarian society, starring Richard Burton.

USEFUL SOURCES

ABC POL-SCI. A monthly compendium (published by ABC-CLIO, in Santa Barbara, California) of the tables of contents of more than 300 journals in political science, international affairs, law, and public policy.

Blum, John N., Edmund S. Morgan, Willie Lee Rose, Arthur M. Schlesinger, Jr., Kenneth M. Stampp, and C. Vann Woodward: *The National Experience: A History of the United States*, Harcourt Brace Jovanovich, New York, 1981. A one-volume history which discusses many of the events mentioned in this textbook.

Degenhardt, Henry W.: *Political Dissent: An International Guide to Dissident, Extra-Parliamentary, Guerilla and Illegal Political Movements*, Gale Research, Detroit, 1983. A discussion of the opponents of sovereign nations in the 1980s.

Handbook of the Nations, 1981, Gale Research, Detroit, 1981. A guide to the economy, government, and defense establishments of 188 nations and other entities.

Holler, Frederick L.: *Information Sources of Political Science*, ABC-CLIO, Santa Barbara, Calif., 1981. A compendium of periodicals, newspapers, and radio and television broadcasts on political topics.

Plano, Jack, Robert E. Riggs, and Helen S. Robin (eds.): *The Dictionary of Political Analysis*, ABC-CLIO, Santa Barbara, Calif., 1982. A useful political dictionary.

Worldwide Government Directory with Inter-Governmental Organizations, 1983, Lambert Publications, Washington, D.C., 1982. A guide to sovereign governments.

CONSTITUTIONAL DEMOCRACY

The ratification of the Constitution was celebrated in New York in 1788. Ever since, it has been amended and adapted to meet new circumstances. One amendment proposed in the 1980s would outlaw abortions. (*Granger Collection; Paul Hosefros: New York Times.*)

They called themselves *regulators*. They were farmers in Massachusetts, many of them veterans of the Revolution, and in the summer of 1786 they faced hard times. Taxes were high, and prices for their crops were low. The lawyers circled around their farms like buzzards, obtaining writs from the courts to take their crops, their livestock, and even their ancestral land in payment for debts.

In the hills of western Massachusetts they held popular conventions and drafted petitions to the state legislature in which they told of their suffering. In Bristol they called for paper money. In Hatfield they asked that the Court of Common Pleas be abolished and that the state stop sending money to Congress. But the state legislature adjourned without heeding the petitions or passing a law which would stay foreclosures.

On August 31 armed men prevented a court from sitting in Northampton, and on September 5 a court meeting in Worcester was disrupted. Crowds would not let cases be tried, and in many places they freed farmers from debtors' prisons. When the state supreme court tried to meet in Springfield, 600 farmers, led by Daniel Shays, who had been a captain in the Revolutionary War, squared off against an equal number of militiamen sent by Governor James Bowdoin, and the judges withdrew to Boston. Mobs prevented courts from sitting in Great Barrington, and judges had to sign pledges that they would not act until the grievances of the people were redressed.

Governor Bowdoin took a hard line. He suspended habeas corpus (which meant that he could hold people without trial), raised a militia with pledges of contributions from the financiers and merchants of Boston who were opposed to paper money, and sent his forces out to crush the farmers. On January 25 Daniel Shays and 1200 followers confronted General William Shepherd and an equal force at the federal arsenal at Springfield. The militia's cannon routed Shays and his men. Some returned home. Others fled through the Berkshires, in deep winter snows over frozen ground, but 4400 fresh militiamen, commanded by General Lincoln, overtook them by surprise at Petersham on February 4, dispersing them and capturing Shays and 150 of his followers.

On March 14 Shays and a dozen other leaders were tried, convicted, and sentenced to death. But Governor Bowdoin, soon to leave office, granted a reprieve, and his successor, John Hancock, pardoned all of them. The legislature, realizing that the farmers had legitimate grievances, decided not to impose a direct tax, lowered court fees, and exempted clothing, household goods, and workers' tools from court judgments.

Shays's rebellion profoundly shocked American political leaders. "For God's sake tell me what is the cause of all these commotions," George Washington said. "Do they proceed from licentiousness, British influence disseminated by the Tories, or real grievances which admit of redress?" To conservatives, like Abigail Adams, wife of John Adams, the American ambassador to London, the rebels were simply "ignorant, wrestless desperadoes, without conscience or principles," acting on "grievances which have no existence but in their imaginations." To Thomas Jefferson, the ambassador to Paris, they were a necessary stimulus to reform. "I like a little rebellion now and then," he wrote to Abigail Adams. "It is like a storm in the atmosphere." Yet everyone knew that Shays's rebellion was not the first of the debtors' rebellions, nor would it be the last, unless some drastic changes were made in the way Americans went about the business of self-government. The troubles in Massachusetts had far more impact than the farmers fleeing in the Berkshire woods could have known. Even then, George Washington and other American political leaders were making plans for a constitutional convention in Philadelphia, one that might be the last chance to preserve democratic government in the states and the nation.

There were strong doubts about the survival of the thirteen state governments and of the Articles of Confederation, which loosely united them. Washington, at his Virginia plantation, feared "the worst consequences from a half-starved, limping government, always moving on crutches and tottering at every step." James Madison received a letter from a friend serving in Congress warning that "if it remains much longer in its present state of imbecility, we shall be one of the most contemptible nations on the face of the earth." In the spring of 1787 Madison himself wrote to Edmund Randolph, the governor of Virginia, saying, "No money comes into the federal treasury, no respect is paid to the federal authority; and people of reflection unanimously agree that the existing confederacy is tottering to its foundation." At the Harvard College commencement of 1787, John Quincy Adams (who later served as the sixth president of the United States) delivered the valedictory address, in which he complained of a people "groaning under the intolerable burden of . . . accumulated evils."[1]

Shays's Rebellion of 1787 in Massachusetts, involving an attack on a federal arsenal at Springfield, demonstrated the weakness of government under the Articles of Confederation. *(Granger Collection.)*

Yet one year later the national mood had changed completely. A constitution, replacing the Articles of Confederation, had created a union of the thirteen states. At the parades held in New York City, Philadelphia, Boston, Charleston, Baltimore, and elsewhere, floats expressed the new optimism: coopers put thirteen staves, each representing a state, into a tremendous barrel symbolizing the union; ship carpenters built huge models of the "ship of state," *Constitution;* chairmakers hung a banner that read, "The Federal States in Union bound, O'er all the world our chairs are found"; and blacksmiths paraded under the slogan, "While industry prevails, We need no foreign nails."[2]

Why had the American spirit changed so completely? And what could a written constitution possibly have contained that would have made Americans so confident about the future of their nation? To answer these questions about the creation of our Constitution is to take up the central problems of politics: authority, legitimacy, and power.

THE BREAKDOWN OF THE OLD POLITICS: THE ARTICLES OF CONFEDERATION

The thirteen colonies declared themselves free and independent from England in 1776 and then won their freedom in the Revolutionary War, which was fought between 1775 and 1781 and was ended by the Treaty of Paris, signed in 1783. Initially, each state was an independent government represented in the ***Continental Congress.***

Government under the Articles

Figure 2-1. Claims of states to lands in the west were a source of potential conflict with European powers and with each other. The British maneuvered against New York and Massachusetts for control of Vermont. The Northern border of Maine remained in dispute. Connecticut and Pennsylvania almost went to war when Connecticut settlers were blocked by the Pennsylvania militia from farming western lands. By 1786 most states had renounced claims to the Northwest Territory, and Congress passed the law providing for its regulation at the same time the Constitutional Convention was meeting in Philadelphia. But unless the states had created a strong central government, other claims would undoubtedly have caused friction in the future.

The thirteen states were allied under the ***Articles of Confederation.*** Drafted in 1777 during the Revolutionary War by the Continental Congress (representatives of each state authorized to fight the war and handle diplomatic relations) and put into effect in 1781, the Articles created a league of friendship rather than a government.

Most Americans mistrusted a strong central government, equating it with the excesses of British rule. They believed that such a government would dominate the states and threaten their individual liberties, as they believed that

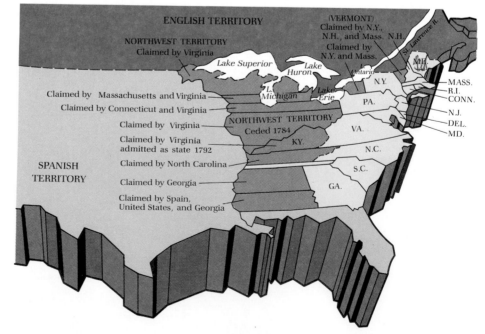

THE ARTICLES OF CONFEDERATION: HOW THINGS LOOKED IN THE 1780S

Features of the government. The state governments have most of the powers. They control commerce with one another and with foreign nations, and they impose duties on imports and taxes on exports. They issue currency and determine which bank notes, coins, and bills from other states are legal tender. They have police and judicial power and their own militia.

Congress has few powers. It decides on matters of war and peace and requisitions funds from the states, but only by unanimous vote. It conducts diplomatic relations and enters into treaties and alliances with other nations. (The states may also enter into treaties with the approval of Congress.) By the vote of seven states, it may issue currency and coins, manage the public debt, run a post office, and arbitrate disputes between states.

Congress has no power to tax. It has no power to raise armed forces directly. It cannot take action against the citizens of the states. It has no police powers and no courts to enforce national law.

National security and foreign relations (Figure 2-1). The British demand payment of their merchants' claims from the Revolutionary War. They use this as a pretext to refuse to evacuate their garrisons in New York and the west. They incite Indian raids against American settlers, encourage Vermont to become a province of Canada, and discriminate against American shipbuilders and merchants. Congress cannot agree on a commerce act to retaliate against the British.

The Spanish close the Mississippi River to American commerce in 1784, putting western settlers at their mercy for trade. They incite Indian raids and claim territory belonging to Georgia—what later became Alabama, Mississippi, Tennessee, and Kentucky.

Indian tribes raid settlements in the Ohio valley in 1786. Congress cannot raise the money to provide protection for western settlers.

Barbary pirates seize American ships in the Mediterranean. Most nations pay a tribute to the pirates to protect their ships, but Congress cannot raise the money for a tribute, and thus American ships and cargoes are put at risk.

Territorial and sectional issues. Settlers in the Northwest Territories threaten to secede. They might ally themselves with the Spanish, who control the Mississippi, their lifeline to the world.

The states have conflicting claims in the Northwest Territories. Some claim lands that belong to others, and there is armed conflict between Connecticut settlers on disputed land (the Wyoming valley) in Pennsylvania. New York and New Hampshire feud over the Green Mountains (later Vermont).

Foreign observers and many Americans believe that the confederation will dissolve into three regional groups, each allied with a different European power.

Economic issues. The states refuse to give the unanimous agreement necessary to pass financial plans drawn up by Congress. Many revenue plans are defeated.

The states refuse to pay their assessments, even though Congress has passed them unanimously.

The states place burdens on interstate commerce by levying duties or erecting trade barriers. They burden foreign commerce with export taxes and import duties.

Congress is unable to raise foreign loans except by borrowing from private bankers at very high rates of interest.

Congress is unable to give soldiers the pensions and bonuses they were promised during the war.

Foreign investors have no confidence in the financial solvency of the government or in its stability, and they hold off on plans to invest in the American economy.

King George and Parliament had done. The states would be the guardians of the "right to life, liberty, and the pursuit of happiness," which Americans had claimed for themselves in the Declaration of Independence.

The Articles guaranteed the sovereignty and independence of the states, which retained vast powers. Congress was limited in what it could do, as "The Articles of Confederation: How Things Looked in the 1780s" indicates. Because it could act only on important matters with extraordinary majorities, it could not solve the most pressing problems: threats to security from foreign powers and Indians, disputes over settlement of western territories, and the payment of debts, the regulation of currencies, and the promotion of commerce.

There was no executive branch. A president of Congress, elected by its members, was the presiding officer and represented the "dignity" of the nation on ceremonial occasions. The powerlessness of this office can best be understood by noting that in the president's absence, a *clerk* was designated to perform his duties. Congress used boards and commissions to transact public business until 1781, when it began to establish departments, each run by a single executive and loosely supervised by congressional committees.

The failure of the Articles

By 1787 most people believed that the Continental Congress had worked better in the 1770s than the Articles of Confederation were working in the 1780s. Americans were of two minds about the Articles. They did not want a strong government, but neither did they respect a weak one. Thus Congress, under the Articles, was intentionally ineffective; it was not given enough power to manage national affairs. Because it had little power, it did not attract the most important politicians, who preferred to serve in state government. There was a high rate of turnover in delegations to Congress, partly because of a provision that prevented anyone from serving for more than three years in any six-year period. Often members did not attend sessions, and it was difficult to keep a quorum of seven states to transact business, much less obtain the approval of nine for important matters.

The drift toward anarchy. The small army was a volatile factor in domestic politics. Peace brought the soldiers and veterans neither the pay nor the pensions they had been promised. In December 1782, a petition from army units in Newburgh, New York, warned Congress that "any further experiments on their patience might have fatal effects." Since Congress refused to bow to pressure, Alexander Hamilton (a former aide of George Washington) encouraged the commanding officer at Newburgh, Thomas Gates, to call a camp meeting, presumably to have the troops march on Philadelphia and pressure Congress. Washington raced to the encampment and called his own meeting. In this tense atmosphere, he took out a speech he had prepared and, fumbling with his spectacles, remarked that "he had grown old and grey in the service of his country, and now he had grown blind as well."[3] Washington called on the men to disavow mutiny, have patience with Congress, and support his own peaceful efforts to secure them their due. The mutiny collapsed. Washington rebuked Hamilton and warned him against conspiracies, though he observed that "no man in the United States is, or can be, more deeply impressed with the necessity of reform in our present Confederation than myself."[4]

Two years later a group of eighty drunken soldiers from a camp near Philadelphia marched into the city, ransacked an arsenal for weapons, took up

Alexander Hamilton, the future Federalist and Secretary of the Treasury, serving as an aide to General Washington during the Revolutionary War. *(Culver Pictures, Inc.)*

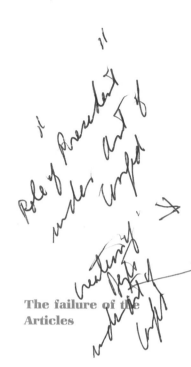

positions near Congress, and, after firing some rounds, forced the legislators to flee to Princeton, New Jersey. The Pennsylvania state militia refused to help Congress, and only after the mutineers threatened to break into the Bank of North America did the state militia chase them out of the city. Between 1784 and 1787 Congress wandered from one town to another, settling temporarily in Princeton, then in Trenton, then in Annapolis, and then in Trenton again, finally coming to rest in New York City, where Benjamin Rush observed that it was "abused, laughed at, pitied, and cursed in every company." The confederation seemed to be drifting toward *anarchy.*

The reaction to Shays's rebellion. Americans were deeply divided, with the most intense conflicts involving debtors against creditors. The latter insisted that the former pay loans off with hard currency, and they foreclosed on property when payments were not made. Enraged debtors, primarily small farmers, won control of the legislatures in some states, and when they did they enacted laws which made paper money legal tender to pay debts, even though such currency quickly depreciated and was almost worthless. Seven states issued such currency in 1786. They also passed "stay laws" that prevented lenders from foreclosing on property.

The situation got out of hand in Rhode Island. The paper money was worth so little that merchants finally decided to close up shop rather than accept it for their goods. Farmers forcibly opened stores and looted them to obtain needed supplies, and they threatened to stop bringing food into towns if merchants stuck to their policy.

The events in Rhode Island, Massachusetts, and other states frightened everyone. The smell of class warfare and revolution was in the air. John Jay, a prominent New York politician (and later the first chief justice of the Supreme Court), wrote to Washington, predicting that "if faction should long bear down Law and Government, Tyranny may raise its head, or the more sober parts of the people may even think of a King." Jay hinted to Washington that the general should consider becoming the American monarch, but Washington responded negatively. It seemed clear to American leaders that if class antagonisms could not be controlled, the fabric of American society, and of the state governments, would be torn to shreds. Disorder, as Jay observed, leads to calls for order, and the choice would then be between tyranny of the masses and a monarchy, with Washington wearing the crown.

It seemed clearer than ever that Congress under the Articles could not maintain order. In the midst of Shays's rebellion, Henry Knox, the secretary of war, informed Congress that the confederation did not have funds to raise and pay troops to put down the insurrection and could not even guard its own arsenal at Springfield, which had almost been captured by Shays's followers.[5]

The crisis and political response

Almost as soon as independence had been won, a few statesmen with vision recognized the need for strong government. Alexander Hamilton in 1781 and James Madison in 1783 proposed that the Articles be amended to strengthen Congress and allow it to regulate commerce and raise taxes. George Washington released a letter in 1783 calling for a stronger government; to avoid any misunderstanding, he pledged that he would "never take any share in public business." But in 1784 and 1786 proposed amendments to the Articles dealing with commerce were rejected.

Alexander Hamilton (a founder of the Bank of New York), Robert Morris, and James Wilson (both cofounders of the Bank of North America in Philadelphia) proposed a national bank which could issue its own currency and manage the national debt for Congress. They thought that a national bank would restore the confidence of property holders and foreign investors in the government. Congress gave a national charter to the Bank of North America in 1781, but its charter to do business in its home state was revoked in 1786 by the Pennsylvania legislature; this put an end to their efforts at commercial and financial reform.

Hamilton and Madison next called for a convention to revise the Articles with regard to commerce. Delegates from only five states showed up at the meeting in Annapolis in 1786 (delegates from several other states were delayed), and so nothing could be done at that meeting, but Hamilton had the group call for a national convention to be held in Philadelphia the following spring. Madison convinced Washington to attend, and twelve states agreed to send delegates.

Such a convention would do more than amend the Articles: leading politicians, especially those in Washington's circle, were upset about events in Massachusetts. If debtors acquired political power, then the prospects of "legal Shaysism" would ensue. Washington was now convinced that only bold steps could end the crisis.

But most Americans continued to mistrust strong government and did not want a national government. They also were opposed to monarchy in any form. There were rumors that the Society of the Cincinnati, a group of former officers who had served with Washington, planned to obtain land grants in the west and fill them with German peasant farmers, thus establishing a feudal system in America. Give Congress the power to tax, some thought, and it would create a monarchy and an aristocracy with an extravagant court life and a large capital city at the expense of country folk.

Prospects for change. Weighed against these difficulties were certain favorable circumstances. Washington was a delegate to the convention. He remained popular with the military—officers and enlisted men alike. He was close to financiers and merchants, was himself a plantation owner and a speculator in western lands, and had ties to northern financial interests. He understood the interests of all regions and of important economic groups. Exasperated by the disorders in Massachusetts, he pressed for fundamental change, not minor reforms.

Above all, Washington reflected the optimism, confidence, and love of experimentation with political forms that spurred Americans to act boldly in crises. The historian David Ramsey caught the spirit of the times in his account of the Revolution, written in 1789, when he observed that the war "gave a spring to the active powers of the inhabitants and set them on thinking, speaking and acting in a line far beyond that to which they had been accustomed. . . . It seemed as if the war not only required but created talents."[6] The same could be said of the crisis that followed.

Limits to change. In hindsight it is obvious that by 1787 a new form of government was needed to replace the Articles. But it was not so obvious at the time to most Americans, who were weary from the war and uninterested in

Within two years of presiding over the Constitutional Convention at Philadelphia in 1787, George Washington became the first president of the United States of America. *(Granger Collection.)*

politics. Most felt that the disturbances in the states would eventually be sorted out and that the economy would improve in the postwar reconstruction.

Most state politicians were willing to support modification of the Articles to improve commerce, but they did not want radical change—especially not change that would reduce their own powers. The convention delegates would be forcing change on a people reluctant to accept it. They would have to convince their colleagues in the states that it was necessary for them to yield power, and always their proposals would be tempered by calculations of what state politicians would accept.

IN CONVENTION ASSEMBLED

From up and down the eastern seaboard delegates chosen by state legislatures to attend the ***Constitutional Convention of 1787*** converged on Philadelphia in the spring of that year. Traveling by coach on muddy turnpikes and post roads or by coastal packets, they were to meet in late May at Independence Hall, where just eleven years earlier another group had signed the Declaration of Independence.

The state delegations

Rhode Island alone among the states refused to send a delegation, realizing that this convention would try to clip the powers of state legislatures. Virginia sent the most prestigious delegation: George Washington, James Madison, Edmund Randolph, and George Mason, all of whom played a major part in the deliberations. Pennsylvania sent a group of eight, six of whom had opposed the state constitution adopted in 1777 because they thought that it was too democratic. They included James Wilson and Robert Morris, cofounders of the Bank of North America, and Gouverneur Morris, a founder of the Bank of New York, as well as Benjamin Franklin, the grand old man of the Revolution and former ambassador to France.

Massachusetts sent a group of seasoned politicians, including the governor, Elbridge Gerry, for whom the *gerrymander* (the drawing of political boundaries to favor one party over another) would later be named. Connecticut and New Jersey sent moderates such as Roger Sherman and William Paterson, who were intent on protecting the rights of the small states. New York sent a curious delegation. Hamilton, who favored a strong national government, was counterbalanced by two delegates, John Lansing and Robert Yates—known as his "chaperones," since they opposed major changes in the Articles and could outvote him.

Overall, the fifty-five delegates represented the cream of American leadership. Over half had received a university education, including nine from Princeton, four each from William and Mary and Yale, and three each from Harvard and Columbia. There were two college presidents, three professors, and several teachers. A dozen were planters or farmers, a dozen were lawyers, and a dozen, including seven governors, held high state office. Forty-six had served in either colonial or state legislatures. Thirty-nine had served in Congress. Twenty had served in, and several had played important roles in, the Revolutionary War. They were young; the average age was the early forties, but five were under 30, and Alexander Hamilton, James Madison, and Gouverneur Morris were all under 36. George Washington himself was only 55. They were, in the words of James MacGregor Burns, "the well read, well fed, well bred, and well wed."[7]

The delegates did not represent a cross section of American political thinking. Most were conservative or moderate. Radicals like Sam Adams of Massachusetts and Tom Paine of Pennsylvania had not been chosen by their states to attend, and Patrick Henry of Virginia refused to serve. Thomas Jefferson and John Adams were abroad serving as ambassadors, and few of the signers of the Declaration of Independence had been chosen as delegates. There were no representatives of debtors, small farmers, western settlers, or societies of mechanics and artisans. Blacks and women had no place. Indians were considered members of sovereign tribes with whom the states had concluded treaties or truces, not citizens who could participate in politics.

We sometimes think of the men who created the Constitution as demigods blessed with infinitely superior wisdom and vision, far removed from the politicians who occupy office today. Nothing could be further from the truth. The Constitution was created by flesh-and-blood politicians. They were first and foremost practical men of affairs. They had founded banks, engaged in commerce, speculated in western lands, and cultivated great plantations and estates. They came together in 1787 as pragmatic experimenters, determined to improve the machinery of government only because the existing machinery had failed them.

Political ideas at the convention

The delegates to the convention were eager to try out some of the new political theories which were being developed both in Europe and in the American states at the end of the eighteenth century.[8] Many corresponded with one another and with Washington in the months before the convention, testing out their ideas. A few belonged to the newly formed Society for Political Inquiry, founded by Madison and Franklin. The delegates—at least the most influential ones—were widely read in history, philosophy, and law, and their ideas informed the convention debates.

Constitutionalism: Limited government by consent. American politicians were familiar with the principles of constitutional government: that a formal compact existed between the people establishing the government; that government rested on the *consent of the people;* that government could exercise only powers delegated to it by the people; and that powers not delegated by the people remained with them and could not be exercised by the government. The first settlers in America established such an agreement—the Mayflower Compact of 1620—even before they set foot on land in America, and American settlers had always claimed the "rights of Englishmen," stemming all the way back to documents such as the Magna Carta of the thirteenth century and the various settlements between Parliament and the crown through the seventeenth century.

The Declaration of Independence embodied these theories of limited government resting on the consent of the people. Now in place of the "rights of Englishmen," the signers had proclaimed: "We hold these truths to be self-evident: That all men are created equal, that they are endowed by their Creator with certain unalienable Rights, that among these are Life, Liberty, and the Pursuit of Happiness. That to secure these rights, Governments are instituted among Men, deriving their just powers from the consent of the governed." Governments were instituted to secure these rights, and "whenever any Form of Government becomes destructive of these ends," the Declaration concluded, "it is the Right of the People to alter or abolish it, and to institute new Government."

After independence each state had written a constitution, most of them providing for strong, popularly elected legislatures, weak executives, and an independent judiciary and most of them recognizing the rights of the people and the limited delegation of power to the government. It was only natural that in establishing a national government, they would also draft a written constitution.

Representative government. Americans agreed that the new government would be based on popular consent. There would be no monarch. Most agreed with Tom Paine's observation that "a thirst for absolute power is the natural disease of monarchy" and his conclusion that "in England a King hath little more to do than to make war and give away places; which in plain terms is to impoverish the nation and set it together by the ears."[9] But direct democracy could not take the place of monarchy: the nation was much too large for that. Some form of indirect democracy or representative government would be required. The convention delegates did *not* believe that any system of representation should simply reflect the social structure: that would allow debtors, the poor, tradespeople and mechanics, and small farmers to dominate the new government. Representative institutions were to operate *for* the people but not consist *of* the people. They would "elevate" the government by creating electoral systems that would keep Congress in the hands of "men of intelligence and uprightness," as James Wilson put it.[10]

The great advantage of a national government, according to James Madison, was that it could be only a representative democracy, and therefore "the public voice, pronounced by the representatives of the people, will be more consonant of the public good than if pronounced by the people themselves, convened for the purpose."[11] Instead of raucous town meetings that might degenerate into more Shays's rebellions, representative government would provide, according to Madison, "the cool and deliberate sense of the community." In a large republic, moreover, there would be many men of talent and virtue, and so it would not be difficult, he reasoned, to fill up political offices with them, thus ensuring that the new government would be off to a good start. In similar words Alexander Hamilton argued that "the Republican principle demands that the deliberate sense of the community should govern the conduct of those to whom they intrust the management of their affairs."[12] There would be regular elections, of course, for as John Adams remarked, "Where the annual elections end, there slavery begins."

Pluralism. What the delegates to the convention worried about most was the possibility of class warfare in America: the have-nots against the haves, the debtors against the creditors, the poor without property against the rich with property. Madison sought to discover a principle that might prevent such conflict and provide for social stability; he believed that he found it in the relationship between federalism and popular government. Madison knew that people would pursue their own interests by combining into *factions*, and he knew that these factions would come into conflict with one another. If the majority-rule principle applies, then the majority with little or no property presumably can band together and govern in their own interest, which will be the antithesis of the interest of the minority with property. Such conflict was occuring in 1787.

One possible solution was to eliminate the cause of factions, which Madison identified as the unequal distribution of property. But to divide up property equally would require so much coercion against the wealthy that it could not be done except by force—and that would mean the end of liberty. If liberty could not be maintained without allowing factions to exist, then the solution would have to involve control, rather than elimination, of factions.

Madison came up with the idea that if the *size* of the republic were extended, so that it comprised all thirteen states, none of the various economic interests would be a majority. People would divide along religious lines (each of the Protestant sects, Catholics, and Jews), occupational interests (small farmers, plantation owners, tradespeople and mechanics, merchants, and professionals), and nationality (for example, those of English, Scotch, German, or Dutch ancestry)—but no one group would have a majority. Factions could not be *eliminated* from politics, Madison argued, but they could be *controlled* by setting one faction against another so that none could establish "the tyranny of the majority." Groups and sects would still clash with one another, but each would be zealous about safeguarding its own liberties and preventing others from transgressing them. The national government, according to Madison, could remain a "disinterested and dispassionate umpire in disputes" between different groups.[13] The result would be **pluralism** in place of majority rule.

Federalism. But how could the size of the republic be extended? At the time of the convention only two kinds of political associations were known: strong, centralized states, with a single government exercising all power and delegating functions to local governments, and leagues and confederacies of states, which allowed councils or congresses to exercise limited authority. The Articles of Confederation had followed the second model and had failed. But no one believed that it would be possible simply to scrap the state governments and replace them with a single national government—even though at various times during the convention both Hamilton and Madison argued for such a course. Neither the state politicians nor the people would support such a change. Americans would have to devise a governmental system that would provide stronger central government while retaining strong state governments. Such a system would have to rest on popular consent and embody democratic principles, and yet up to that time democracy had never been tried on so large a scale. At the time, no model for such a hybrid form of government existed; the delegates would be improvising and experimenting as they went along.

Avoiding tyranny: Separation of powers. "Where might is right there is no right," the playwright Sophocles had his chorus intone in ancient Greece. How to avoid the excesses of unrestrained power had always been a central concern of political theory, and no American government that did not address the problem could be legitimate. Seventeenth- and eighteenth-century political theorists developed the doctrine of *separation of powers* to ensure the rights of people against despotic government. John Locke, the English philosopher, wrote *Two Treatises on Government* after the Glorious Revolution of 1688 had limited the powers of the British monarch; in it he argued that there were three powers of government—legislative, executive, and federative (foreign affairs)—and that free government was best maintained when these powers were entrusted to different institutions. Baron de Montesquieu, in *The Spirit of the Laws*, written a half-century later, held that only when government was separated into executive, legislative, and judicial branches could liberty be ensured. "When the legislative and executive powers are united in the same person, or in the same body of magistracy," he wrote, "there can then be no liberty, because apprehensions may arise, lest the same monarch or senate should enact tyrannical laws, to execute them in a tyrannical manner." Similarly, "if the prince were to have a share in the legislature by the power of enacting, liberty would be lost."[14] William Blackstone's *Commentaries on the Laws of England* also emphasized the doctrine of separation of powers in its analysis of the British constitution. Most state constitutions written after American independence followed the maxim of separation of powers, and many contained clauses that forbade the executive from exercising legislative and judicial power, the judiciary from exercising legislative and executive power, and the legislature from exercising executive and judicial power. By the 1780s both John Adams[15] and Thomas Jefferson[16] had written tracts which defended the state constitutions to skeptical Europeans.

The convention at work: The politics of change

Not only would the delegates to the convention have to create a new form of government, but they would also have to create one that could solve concrete problems and resolve tensions between various sections. How should commerce be regulated? What should be done about the slave trade? How should taxes be collected? What could be done about navigation on the Mississippi? How should large and small states be represented so that all would feel secure in a new union? Political practice, not theory, would solve these problems at the convention.

Preconvention politics. ESTABLISHING AUTHORITY. In the 1780s many Americans thought that economic problems stemmed from postwar conditions and would soon work themselves out. Others thought that debtors were simply shiftless rabble-rousers who would be best dealt with by force. But people like Washington, Hamilton, and Madison recognized the true nature of the economic problems: that they were due in large part to the weakness of political arrangements. From the instability of government came the instability of the currency and the uncertainties about the debt.

The convention called for in 1786 attracted little attention until the Virginia legislature, at Madison's urging, named Washington a delegate. Seven other states then agreed to send delegates, and Congress sanctioned the plan. Washington's prospective participation attracted a roster of other distinguished leaders, twelve of whom had served with him during the war. Twelve others knew him through service in Congress. People like Benjamin Franklin (the president, or governor, of Pennsylvania) and William Johnson (the president-elect of Columbia College) agreed to attend. The presence of such a distinguished group of delegates guaranteed that the convention would have authority.

ENSURING LEGITIMACY. Those who planned on scrapping the Articles of Confederation were proposing a bloodless transfer of power from the states to a new national government. They had to ensure the legitimacy of their efforts, or else they would be accused of usurping power. Washington understood (far

The new Constitution did not gain immediate universal respect. To a pamphleteer of 1792, a national government was a convention of asses. *(Historical Pictures Service.)*

better than Hamilton) that the people would never accept a military takeover, and he understood (far better than Jay) that they would not accept him as their king. Any new plan would have to have popular support.

This did not mean that the people had to be consulted about the Constitution as it was being drafted, or even that the plans had to conform to the wishes of the people. Some delegates argued that the people would never accept a strong central government. Those proposing one argued that it was the duty of the convention to convince the people that such a government was needed.

Madison and Hamilton called for the convention, which was similar to the state constitutional conventions, and arranged to have its meeting endorsed by Congress. Each state would send a delegation, chosen by its state legislature, and would cast a single vote at the convention, arrangements which accorded with the system of representation in Congress. By organizing the convention in terms familiar to the people, the delegates hoped to establish its legitimacy.

CONVENTION ARRANGEMENTS. "Secrecy is the first essential in affairs of state," Cardinal Richelieu pointed out in seventeenth-century France. Politicians must debate candidly, find areas of compromise, and make deals. All this requires frank discussion. To encourage candor, the convention closed its deliberations to the public and the press. Only delegates could attend, and only they could examine the daily journal of proceedings, kept under lock and key by the convention secretary. The delegates agreed that the proceedings would not be made available to the public for fifty years. Thus they could express their opinions without fear of public reaction. They could talk frankly about popular government, sectional disputes, and economic and class interests. Although the deliberations remained secret, the Constitution itself was to be presented to the people as soon as the convention was over. At that time full debate was encouraged by its supporters. Secrecy was a means to obtain consensus on a plan, not a way to thwart the ultimate right of the people to give or withhold their consent to it.

George Washington was elected the presiding officer on the first day. His very presence at the front of the hall was a reminder that the enterprise had a good chance to succeed—especially since most delegates assumed that he would probably head the new government. In fact, during the debates, many of the seemingly abstract discussions about the power of the government (and of the presidency in particular) took place with the realization that those involved were actually discussing powers that *Washington* would exercise.

The art of the possible. "A system must be suited to the habits & genius of the people it is to govern," argued Charles Pinckney, "and must grow out of them."[17] The convention delegates knew their political theories, but they relied primarily on practical experience with colonial government and state governments. "Experience must be our only guide," John Dickinson warned them. "Reason may mislead us."[18] The art of politics is the art of the possible. Pierce Butler reminded the delegates that they "must follow the example of Solon, who gave Athenians not the best Government he could devise, but the best they would receive."[19]

Every provision of the Constitution that was considered or adopted was known from experience with either colonial government or state governments or from observation of English government. For the most part the framers adapted already-existing mechanisms to their own particular circumstances; there were few inventions. Separation of powers was derived from the states. The powers of the president were modeled after those of the governors of New York and Massachusetts. Impeachment was adapted from English practices. Popular elections owed much to the experience of the Virginia House of Burgesses—the state legislature—in which every male Virginian over the age of 21 could vote, but the plantation gentry provided the candidates.[20] This was *deferential politics:* the leading citizens of the nation would run for office and submit themselves to the verdict of their countrymen; this was what most delegates had in mind when they thought of popular government.

Bargaining and compromises.   The convention delegates represented large and small states, northern and southern states, slave and free states, and agricultural and commercial interests. To draft a constitution that would appeal to the entire nation, they would have to compromise.

CONGRESSIONAL REPRESENTATION.   The most important compromise, on which all else turned, was between the large states, which favored the *Virginia Plan,* and the small states, which favored the *New Jersey Plan.* The Virginia Plan, drawn up by Madison with Washington's concurrence and presented early to the convention by Edmund Randolph, the governor of Virginia, conceived of a strong central government with veto power over state actions. The New Jersey Plan, presented by William Paterson of New Jersey, was a modification of the Articles of Confederation that would have added a judiciary, a weak executive, and some new congressional powers. The convention voted to use the Virginia Plan as the basis for its deliberations.

But the convention soon became deadlocked on the most important problem: the apportioning of seats in Congress. "If proportional representation takes place," Ben Franklin wryly observed, "the small States contend that their liberties will be in danger. If an equality of votes is to be put in its place, the large States say their money will be in danger."[21] Madison warned that if the large and the small states had equal representation in Congress, the convention would dissolve, and he hinted that the large states might then form a government by themselves—a veiled threat to the survival of the small states. "The large states dare not dissolve the Confederation," Gunning Bedford responded; "if they do the small ones will find some foreign ally of more honor and good faith, who will take them by the hand and do them justice."[22]

With tempers rising, the large states did not force the issue. Massachusetts, large in population and influence and also a leader of the smaller New England states, supported the equal representation plan. North Carolina, a large state, also shifted to equal representation. The result was the *Connecticut Compromise,* which was adopted on July 16 and which saved the convention from dissolution. Oliver Ellsworth of Connecticut, author of the plan, observed that "we were partly national, partly federal; . . . on this middle ground a compromise would take place."[23] The House of Representatives was to be apportioned on the basis of state population, while each state would have equal representation in the Senate. The members of the House would be chosen by direct elections, while senators would be selected by their state legislatures.

COMPROMISES BETWEEN NORTH AND SOUTH. As an inducement to the south, approval of treaties would require a two-thirds vote; thus the north could not make a treaty with Spain about commerce on the Mississippi River that would harm southern and western interests. The small states also offered a deal involving the Northwest Territories. Congress, at that moment meeting in New York City, was stalled on a plan offered by the south to create states from the territories. The north wanted to hold off on forming states. At the Philadelphia convention, the small states agreed that they would end opposition to the southern plan regarding the territories if the large states agreed to support the Connecticut Compromise. Congress agreed to create three new states from the territories. Three days later the convention agreed to the Connecticut Compromise.[24]

The convention concluded other sectional agreements. The north wanted to end the slave trade. The south opposed any ban. The north wanted Congress to have greater powers over trade and navigation. Again, there was the basis for a deal: the slave trade was permitted to continue for twenty years, fugitive slaves would be returned from the north, and a slave would be counted as three-fifths of a free person for the purposes of apportioning seats in the House of Representatives and levying taxes. Congress was given the power to regulate foreign commerce. Another agreement provided for a national capital district, with the understanding that it would be located between the north and the south, rather than in Philadelphia or New York, the obvious choices.

Techniques for compromise. COMMITTEES. Politicians identify the important issues and refer them to committees. In open debate tempers flare, positions harden, and the temptation is to score points against the opposition rather than to discuss the issues calmly. Committees are small groups, and so conversation rather than posturing is the norm. The setting is conducive to courtesy and cooperation. Committees have the time to think through a problem, to experiment with proposals and language, and to listen to arguments—none of which is easy in large deliberative assemblies. It is easier for people to change their minds and to persuade others to do so in committees. And it is easier to strike complicated agreements and think them through in the relative calm of a small group.

At the convention the Committee of States came up with the Connecticut Compromise; the Committee on Detail expanded the powers of Congress and the president beyond what was proposed in the original draft; the Committee on Postponed Matters adopted a plan for election of the president by an electoral college rather than Congress; the Committee on Style included ambiguous language about the presidency that would later allow for its expanded powers in the final draft. All these committees were dominated by those wanting a strong central government, but they were also skilled in the art of compromise, and so they could develop proposals that the convention would accept. In each case, the committees came up with something more than compromise—they developed new proposals, sometimes departing drastically from plans that the convention had referred to them.

BARGAINING. There are several different ways to bargain. In the *compromise*, each side modifies its position to reach a middle ground. This can usually be done in connection with any issue which can be framed as a "more or less" issue, especially if it involves money or some other quantity. Thus the convention compromised on the requirements to override a presidential veto between those who wanted no override at all and those who wanted an override by a majority: the result was a two-thirds vote. Making a slave equivalent to three-fifths of a free person was a compromise between those who wanted to make a slave fully equivalent (the south) for the purpose of apportioning seats in Congress and those who did not want to count slaves at all (the north). *Logrolling* involves giving up something to get something else, a technique used by the south to preserve the slave trade and by the north to get congressional powers over foreign commerce. The *package deal* is used to consider several related issues at the same time so that the "big picture" can be voted up or down. The delegates did not consider the president's election, term of office, and reeligibility for election as separate matters. Instead, they considered two alternative packages: the weak-president model (election by Congress for a six-year term with no eligibility for reelection) and the strong-president model (election by an electoral college for a four-year term with indefinite eligibility for reelection).[25]

EFFICIENCY NEGOTIATIONS. An agreement in which everyone gains is called an *efficiency negotiation*, and it can be distinguished from a negotiation in which whatever one person gains must come at the expense of another (sometimes called a *zero-sum game*). The convention itself was a gigantic efficiency negotiation conducted between the various regions and different economic interests. More protection against Indian attacks would be good for western settlers, as well as for eastern speculators who had invested in western lands. A navy would be good for southern planters who had crops on ships, as well as for northern boat owners and merchants. A government capable of attracting foreign investment would provide funds for industry in the north and for internal improvements in the south and west. If the states could not pass laws impairing contracts, propertied people everywhere would be more secure and the economy would improve with foreign investment.

POSTPONING CONFLICT. When agreement cannot be reached, a final decision may be postponed. The convention could not decide whether the Supreme Court should have the power to strike down laws passed by Congress. Similarly, no one wished to define precisely what was meant by *direct taxation*. And the question of the land claims of various states was left for the government to determine once the Constitution was adopted. By allowing the slave trade to continue for twenty years but refusing to outlaw slavery, the convention only postponed serious sectional conflicts for a later day.

PURPOSIVE USE OF AMBIGUITY. Sometimes in a negotiation each side agrees to a particular wording, even though the words have no plain meaning and the parties understand them differently. Disagreements can be camouflaged until after the accord has been signed and other provisions have been put into effect. This technique was used at the convention in dealing with the presidency. Those favoring a strong presidency gave the president the "executive power," and made the president commander-in-chief of the armed forces. Because these words lacked precision, they did not engender great controversy at the convention, and the delegates did not take seriously Madison's warning that they should consider ways to "define and confine" the presidency more precisely.

CLOSE-UP

**MADISON, WILSON, AND HAMILTON—
WHAT THE CONVENTION REJECTED.** *James Madison* is considered the father of the Constitution. Yet by the time the convention adjourned, Madison had been defeated on all the following proposals:

- Give Congress the power to veto state laws.
- Base Senate representation on population.
- Increase the size of the House of Representatives.
- Let Congress set suffrage requirements for the states, tax exports, create a national university, incorporate companies and a national bank, and have the power to pardon.
- Give the Senate a share in the presidential power to pardon.
- Give the Supreme Court the power to impeach and a share in the president's veto power.
- Establish a council of state to supervise departments.
- Outlaw the slave trade immediately (rather than in twenty years).
- Provide for ratification of the Constitution by seven states.

James Wilson was one of the most influential of the delegates. He was a strong supporter of popular government. Yet most of his specific proposals were also defeated:

- Treaties to be approved by majority vote.
- The House as well as the Senate to vote on treaties.
- Congress not to be able to override a presidential veto.
- The president to be elected directly by the people.

Alexander Hamilton delivered a speech at the convention which called for the strongest possible central government—a plan, as delegate William Johnson put it, which was "praised by everybody [and] supported by none." Some specifics:

- A supreme governor to be elected for life.
- The governor to have a veto over all laws passed by Congress and the states.
- The governor to have many enumerated powers in a strong central government.
- The governor to appoint the state governors.

Each of these men had strong convictions about his ideal form of government. Each had his most treasured ideas defeated or watered down at the convention. Each had grave reservations about whether the new Constitution, as finally drafted, would work. Yet each strongly supported the plan and fought hard for its ratification, on the premise that half a good constitution is better than none.

James Madison, leading theorist of the Constitution, cofounder (with Thomas Jefferson) of the Anti-Federalist party, and fourth president of the United States. *(Culver Pictures, Inc.)*

RESULTS OF POLITICS: THE CONSTITUTION OF 1787

The triumph of federalism

Our Constitution has four main features, each a uniquely American approach to the art and science of government: federalism, popular government, separation of powers, and checks and balances.

The convention delegates divided into two camps at the outset: a majority believed that they should simply revise the Articles of Confederation to improve commercial relations between the states and that the existing confederacy should be preserved, with its principle that state governments were sovereign. They would strictly define any new powers to be granted to the national Congress. But a minority had other ideas. Madison, Hamilton, Wilson, and others argued that in 1776, when independence had been declared, the American people had transferred their allegiance from King George III to the United States in Congress assembled. Sovereignty, they believed, always had resided in a single American nation, and never completely in the states. Consequently, the convention could act on behalf of the American people to establish a stronger national government with full *sovereign* powers—a government strong enough to solve the existing crisis of authority, and yet legitimate enough to be accepted by the people.

The supremacy clause. Perhaps the most important decision which the convention made early in its work was to accept three principles, proposed jointly by Edmund Randolph and Gouverneur Morris, which stated:

1. That a Union of the States merely federal[26] will not accomplish the objects proposed by the articles of Confederation, namely common defence, security of liberty, & general welfare.
2. That no treaty or treaties among the whole or part of the States, as individual Sovereignties, would be sufficient.
3. That a *national* Government ought to be established consisting of a *supreme* Legislative, Executive, and Judiciary.[27]

These resolutions required the convention to establish a national government whose institutions would be supreme over the states—a common sover-

The Supremacy clause allows the president to use federal troops to uphold laws passed by Congress or enforce judicial orders. *(Danny Lyon: Magnum.)*

To enforce a court order against striking Pullman Company employees, President Grover Cleveland nationalized the Illinois National Guard in 1894. The Guards fired into the strikers. Governor Altgeld of Illinois protested Cleveland's actions. *(Granger Collection.)*

eignty for all Americans. The convention adopted the *supremacy clause*—the most important single provision of the Constitution—which appears as Article VI, Section 2:

> This Constitution, and the Laws of the United States which shall be made in Pursuance thereof; and all Treaties made, or which shall be made, under the Authority of the United States, shall be the Supreme Law of the Land; and the Judges in every State shall be bound thereby, any Thing in the Constitution or Laws of any State to the Contrary notwithstanding.

The supremacy clause established that the national Constitution and laws were supreme over state constitutions and laws. It required state judges to enforce the national Constitution and laws over state constitutions and laws, just as judges of the national government would do. The new Constitution set limits on state governments: neither the national government nor the state governments could take any actions that would violate the Constitution. The supremacy clause established the principle that all actions of the national government and the state governments must be constitutionally sound, for, as Madison argued, "A law violating a constitution established by the people themselves would be considered by the Judges as null and void."[28]

Enforcement of national laws. Under the Articles of Confederation, laws passed by Congress could be enforced only with the consent of the states. If a dispute broke out between Congress and the citizens of a state, Congress had to ask the state government for help. If a state sided with its own citizens, it would weaken the confederacy, and, as Madison argued, such conflicts between Congress and individuals "would look more like a declaration of war, than an infliction of punishment" on a citizen who had violated a law.[29]

Under the new Constitution the national government could enforce laws without asking for cooperation from the states. Disputes between the national government and citizens of states could be settled by state or national judges. State legislatures and governors would not be dragged into these cases. Gouverneur Morris explained that the new government would have "a compleat and *compulsive* operation"—the definition of a sovereign government.[30]

Some delegates could not accept this. Elbridge Gerry, who ultimately refused to sign the Constitution, "warned the Convention against pushing the experiment too far. Some people will support a plan of vigorous Government at every risk. Others of a more democratic cast will oppose it with equal determination, and a Civil War may be produced by the conflict."[31] But others saw things differently. As John Langdon of New Hampshire argued:

> The General & State Governments were not enemies to each other, but different institutions for the good of the people of America. As one of the people he could say, the National Government is mine, the State Government is mine. In transferring power from one to the other, I only take out of my left hand what it can not so well use, and put it into my right hand where it can be better used.[32]

Limitations on state power.   The powers of the states were limited in the new Constitution. The states were prohibited from issuing paper money and from passing laws that would impair contracts, two provisions which would benefit creditors and investors. They were required to give "full Faith and Credit to the Acts, Records, and Judicial Proceedings" of other states, another provision favored by lenders who might want to enforce judgments against debtors who had fled out of state. The states could no longer levy imposts or duties on interstate or foreign commerce. They could make no interstate compacts without the consent of Congress. They could make no treaties and form no alliances with foreign nations.

Maintaining domestic order.   The Constitution guaranteed the people in each state a republican form of government. The national government was required to give military assistance to a state in the event of "domestic violence" (such as another Shays's rebellion) if the state legislature requested such aid (or on application of the governor if the legislature was unable to meet as a result of insurrection). The national government was given the power to call the state militia into its service to "suppress insurrections," in which case it would be directed by national officials rather than by the state governor. If absolutely necessary the national government could suspend the privilege of the *writ of habeas corpus*—a document issued by a judge ordering that anyone holding a person in custody bring that person before the court; it is used by prisoners and their lawyers to question the legality of arrest and detention.

Promoting national security.   By locating sovereign powers in the national government, the convention delegates hoped to convince Europeans that they were serious about maintaining independence. Congress could raise and maintain a navy without asking the states for contributions or personnel. It now had the power to declare war by majority vote, rather than with the unanimity required under the Articles. No longer would European powers be permitted to send ministers to state governments or conclude agreements with them. Henceforth, only the national government could make war and peace, recognize foreign nations, conclude alliances and treaties, and determine trade policy with foreign nations.

With improved commerce and transportation, typified by the Erie Canal (opened by Governor DeWitt Clinton of New York in 1825), the west was opened to development. *(Culver Pictures, Inc.)*

Expanding the powers of Congress. The Constitution added vast new powers to those already granted to Congress by the Articles. In Article I of the Constitution, Congress was given seventeen specific new powers over the economy and the diplomacy of the nation.

Congress was granted, in paragraph 18 of Article I, Section 8, the power "to make all laws which shall be Necessary and Proper for carrying into Execution the foregoing powers, and all other powers vested by this Constitution in the Government of the United States, or in any Department or Officer thereof." This ***necessary and proper clause*** stretched the power of Congress (and for that reason it is also known as the ***elastic clause***). Congress could legislate on any topic involving its own powers or those given to other branches. It could legislate on the means needed to achieve the ends set forth in the Constitution—even if there was no specific language in the Constitution referring to these means. Madison, in arguing for the clause, told the convention delegates that "he should shrink from nothing which should be found essential to such a form of Government as would provide for the safety, liberty, and happiness of the community."[33] To the extent that political leaders could convince the American people that new powers would be needed to deal with problems (that is, if the government could expand its authority), this clause would allow the Constitution to adapt to meet changing conditions.

Majority rule. Under the Articles extraordinary majorities of state delegations were required for important legislation. The Constitution provided instead that each member of the House of Representatives and the Senate would cast an individual vote, with no provision for voting by states. Simple majorities in each chamber (that is, a majority of those present) would be sufficient to pass any bills, including taxes and the declaration of war. Simple rather than extraordinary majorities would decide.

Creation of an executive branch. The convention met to create a more efficient government. Most delegates started by favoring a plural executive, elected by Congress and subject to a recall by a majority of state governors or state legislatures. But some delegates, such as Hamilton, went to the other extreme, calling for a single "supreme governor," elected by the people (or their delegates) and chosen either for life or for a term which could be extended by reelection. The presidential office created by the convention represented a compromise, but one which leaned in the direction of a strong executive.

There was to be a president, elected indirectly by the people through the mechanism of an electoral college (discussed further in Chapter 9) and serving for a fixed term of four years, but eligible for reelection. The president could not be removed from office by state officials, but could be removed only after impeachment by the House and a trial by the Senate in which two-thirds of those present voted for removal.

The president was to have the "executive power of the United States." No council of state or cabinet would share the presidential powers. The president alone would nominate the important civil and military officials, who would assume office if the Senate consented by majority vote. The president was to receive the opinions, in writing, of the principal officers of the departments on matters of presidential interest and was charged with the duty to "see that the laws be faithfully executed" by all government officials. The president was to recommend to Congress such measures as might be deemed expedient and was to report to Congress annually on the state of the union.

The president was to be commander in chief of the armed forces of the United States and of the state militias when called into national service. Other presidential responsibilities were the enforcement of provisions of the supremacy clause against individuals or states and the use of military force if necessary to guarantee the states a republican form of government or to carry out orders of the national courts. The president was given the power to pardon offenses against the Constitution or laws, a useful technique that made it possible to end insurrections and rebellions by offering clemency.

Creation of an independent judiciary. In Article III the Constitution assigned the judicial power of the United States to a Supreme Court and to the lower federal (that is, national) courts that Congress by law would create. Certain original jurisdiction was given to the Supreme Court. Its remaining original and appellate jurisdiction (that is, cases reviewed by higher courts after a trial) was to be determined by law after the Constitution was put into effect.

The supremacy clause provided that national laws, treaties, and the Constitution would be supreme over state laws and state constitutions. Federal or state judges could declare state laws or actions null and void on the grounds that they violated the national Constitution. They could also issue decrees and judgments directly affecting citizens, declaring that their action violated national laws, treaties, or the Constitution.

Justices of the Supreme Court and other federal judges would be nominated by the president and would assume office if approved by a majority of the Senate. They would serve on "good behavior" (that is, for life) and could not be removed by the president; this made the judiciary independent of the executive branch. They could be impeached by the House and removed by the Senate after a trial.

Popular government

The convention delegates rested the legitimacy of the new government on the principle of *popular consent* (Figure 2-2). The preamble to the Constitution expresses the idea.

WE THE PEOPLE of the United States, in Order to form a more perfect Union, establish justice, insure domestic tranquility, provide for the common defence, promote the general welfare, and secure the blessings of Liberty to ourselves and our posterity, do ordain and establish this Constitution for the United States of America.

But some delegates mistrusted popular government (see Figure 2-3). Sherman argued that "the people immediately should have as little to do as may be about the Government. They want [lack] information and are constantly liable to be misled."[34] Gerry, alluding to Massachusetts, argued that "the evils we experience flow from the excess of democracy. The people do not want [lack] virtue, but are the dupes of pretended patriots."[35]

Other delegates insisted that the government be made accountable to the people. George Mason of Virginia, no friend of the common people, was willing to admit that "we had been too democratic, but was afraid we should incautiously run into the opposite extreme. We ought to attend to the rights of every class of the people."[36] James Wilson spoke of "raising the federal pyramid to a

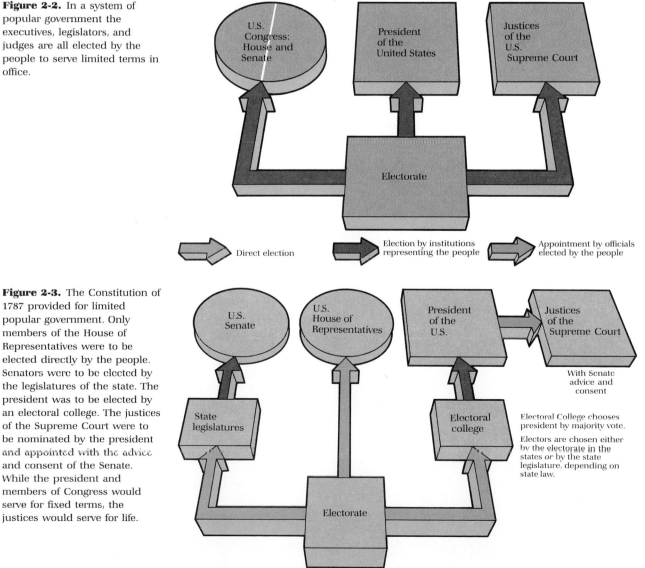

Figure 2-2. In a system of popular government the executives, legislators, and judges are all elected by the people to serve limited terms in office.

Direct election

Election by institutions representing the people

Appointment by officials elected by the people

Figure 2-3. The Constitution of 1787 provided for limited popular government. Only members of the House of Representatives were to be elected directly by the people. Senators were to be elected by the legislatures of the state. The president was to be elected by an electoral college. The justices of the Supreme Court were to be nominated by the president and appointed with the advice and consent of the Senate. While the president and members of Congress would serve for fixed terms, the justices would serve for life.

With Senate advice and consent

Electoral College chooses president by majority vote.

Electors are chosen either by the electorate in the states *or* by the state legislature, depending on state law.

considerable altitude, and for that reason wished to give it as broad a basis as possible. No government could long subsist without the confidence of the people."[37]

It remained for James Madison to fashion the essential compromise shown in Figure 2-3. Direct elections were to be limited to the House of Representatives, which would be the "popular assembly" likely to represent all social classes and interests. Senators would be chosen by state legislatures, and since

---

THE ELECTORAL COLLEGE IN THE CONSTITUTION

Several times a majority of the delegates to the convention voted in favor of having Congress select the president. At first only a few delegates opposed the plan. James Madison, considering it a question of separation of powers, argued that "the appointment of the Executive should either be drawn from some source, or held by some tenure, that will give him a free agency with regard to the Legislature. This could not be done if he was to be appointable from time to time by the Legislature." It would be better, thought James Wilson, to create a mechanism that would bring the people into the decision and keep Congress out. But how could this be done without giving the people the power to elect, which a majority of the delegates opposed?

The answer was an *electoral college.* State legislatures would determine, by state law, how their *electors* (equal in number to their congressional delegation) would be chosen—either by the state legislature itself or by popular vote. Then, in each state capitol, the electors would meet on a date fixed by law to cast two ballots each for president. The results would be sent to Congress, where the outgoing vice president, in the presence of the members of Congress, would count the ballots and announce the name of the next president. The person who received the largest number of votes would be president, and the person who received the next largest number would be vice president.[a]

The electoral college would make it virtually impossible for anyone to fix an election, since there would be so many electors and they would meet in their own states. The electors would be the leading people of character in their states, and they would canvass the states and the nation to choose the best person for the office. At least that was how the delegates hoped the system would work.

The delegates thought that the electoral college would be dominated by electors from the large states. They would vote for someone from their own state, which would result in five leading candidates, none of whom could win the necessary majority. The election for president would then be thrown into the House of Representatives, where each state delegation would cast a single vote for one of the top five contenders.[b] The convention delegates assumed that the electoral college would do the nominating for the presidency, while the House, voting by state delegation, would make the actual selection, thereby giving the states—especially the small states—equal weight in the selection process. Thus, the cumbersome system of a contingency election by the electoral college was actually a compromise between the large and the small states, which is why the convention delegates eventually decided to accept it.

a. The Twelfth Amendment provides for separate ballots to be cast for the president and the vice president; this prevents a tie vote between candidates for the two offices, as occurred in the election of 1800, which had to be decided by the House of Representatives.
b. The Twelfth Amendment restricts the choice of the House to the top three candidates. In the event no candidate for vice president obtains a majority in the electoral college, the vice president is chosen by the Senate, from among the top two candidates, with each senator casting one vote.

there would be only two from each state, they would probably represent the interests of property holders as well as the interests of the state governments. Federal judges would be appointed by the president, not elected by the people. And the president would be chosen by an electoral college, consisting of electors who could be chosen either by the people or by state governments, according to the wishes of each state legislature.

The convention delegates decided that eligibility to vote in national elections would be determined by the states, with only such exceptions or regulations as Congress might provide by law. At the time, all states restricted the vote to white males over the age of 21. Some included further qualifications based on property or instituted voting fees to cut down on eligibility. The Constitution provided that citizens of a state who were eligible to vote for the lower house of the state legislature would also be eligible to vote for members of the House of Representatives. Thus, the extent to which the government would rest on a broad popular base, and therefore the extent to which the national government would be democratic, was left to the individual state governments.

Separation of powers

The convention delegates, like all Americans, were mistrustful of governmental power. Because they were expanding the powers of the national government, especially Congress, and because they were creating a more powerful and efficient government, they concentrated on preventing the abuse of power. There would be what Madison referred to as "auxiliary precautions": governmental mechanisms which would check tyranny. One of these precautions was the separation of powers.

Partial separation of powers. Although Montesquieu, Locke, and other political theorists had argued that separation of powers was necessary to guard against abuse of power, Madison and the convention delegates hit upon an even better approach: the *partial* rather than the *complete* separation of powers. The three branches of government—Congress, the president, and the Supreme Court—would *not* correspond exactly with the legislative, executive, and judicial powers. The Constitution would not provide for a Congress that could exercise all legislative powers and nothing but legislative powers; for a president who functioned as an executive and as nothing but an executive; or for a Supreme Court that operated only with judicial power. It is more accurate to say that the Constitution created separate branches of government which would share in, and compete fiercely for, the various powers. The president could recommend measures to Congress or veto its bills and therefore would share in legislative power. Congress would create and fund the agencies of government, and so it would share in executive power. The courts, in deciding cases, would interpret the law and thus would share in legislative power.

Constitutional ambiguities. The Constitution, by deliberate design of the framers, is silent on some important points, or else ambiguous in its meanings. Often it assigns a duty to a branch without providing expressly for the powers to perform that duty.

The president, for example, is assigned the executive power, and yet nowhere does the Constitution give the president the explicit power to issue orders to department officials or remove them from office. The Supreme Court has the judicial power, but nowhere does the Constitution explicitly give it the power to declare a law of Congress or an action of the president unconstitutional. Congress has all legislative powers, but nowhere does the Constitution specify at what point its powers must give way to executive actions or judicial decisions.

Overlapping grants of power. The new Constitution provided for overlapping grants of power. Congress was given the power to declare war and regulate and fund the armed forces, but the president was commander in chief. The Constitution did not sort out the president's authority to order troops abroad when Congress provided by law that they were to remain at home. It did not specify whether Congress could issue instructions—by law—to military commanders which were at variance with presidential orders. It did not say whether, in the absence of a declaration of war, the president could make war.

Boundary disputes. Ambiguity, overlapping grants of power, and the partial rather than the complete separation of powers all lead to boundary disputes. Either the branches must cooperate and accommodate these claims, or else they must fight constitutional battles. The Constitution is not a blueprint with detailed plans for the workings of government, but rather an arena for conflict. Madison believed that the friction which would inevitably result would be the best safeguard against tyranny, because with branch fighting branch, powers would be limited.

The separation clause. Under the provisions of this clause, members of one branch could not serve simultaneously in another. Members of Congress could not serve in the executive branch, and "no Person holding any Office under the United States, shall be a member of either House during his continuance in office." The *separation clause* distinguished our government from *cabinet government*, which Europeans were just beginning to adopt at the end of the eighteenth century; in a cabinet government, the prime minister and other department heads also hold seats in the legislature. Under the American Constitution, neither the president nor Cabinet officials are members of Congress, and they may not debate or vote. Because the president cannot offer members of Congress any executive office (unless they resign from the legislature), presidential influence with them is lessened.

Checks and balances

To preserve the independence of each branch, the convention delegates relied on ***checks and balances.*** As Madison explained to them:

> Instead therefore of contenting ourselves with laying down the Theory in the Constitution that each department ought to be separate and distinct, it was proposed to add a defensive power to each which should maintain the theory in practice. In so doing we did not blend the departments together. We erected effectual barriers for keeping them separate.[38]

To preserve the three-branch system and prevent tyranny, it would be necessary to give each branch a means to defend itself against the others. In particular, the delegates believed that it would be necessary to prevent encroachment by the legislature, which they viewed as the strongest branch.

Checks on the president. The president could make neither treaties nor appointments to office without the advice and consent of the Senate. The president needed Congress to pass laws to establish, fund, and empower the departments. Presidential choices for Supreme Court justices and for lower court judges had to be approved by the Senate. According to the provision for *impeachment,* the president could be removed from office by Congress for "treason, bribery, and other High Crimes and Misdemeanors."

Checks on Congress. Most of the convention delegates agreed with Madison that "experience had proved a tendency in our governments to throw all power into the Legislative vortex."[39] Madison believed that Congress must be checked by the president. The president was given the responsibility to "faithfully execute the laws" and thus was allowed a certain amount of discretion. All laws and appropriations (funding bills) were subject to a presidential veto, which itself could be nullified by a two-thirds vote of each chamber of Congress. But if the president held the support of just over one-third of the members of either the House or the Senate, the veto attempt would fail.

The Supreme Court could check Congress by interpreting laws in ways which might not gibe exactly with congressional intent. It could strike down laws passed by Congress which it believed were inconsistent with the Constitution itself. (This power, while not specified in the Constitution, was claimed by the Court in the 1790s.)

Checks within Congress. Congress was *bicameral,* or organized into two independent chambers: the House of Representatives and the Senate. Each chamber had a check on the other. Bills, written in identical language, had to pass each chamber before being sent to the president. The House had the sole power to originate revenue bills, but the Senate would have to concur for a measure to become law. The House could vote to impeach officials, but the Senate had the exclusive power to try them. The Senate had the power to consent to presidential treaties and appointments, but often treaty commitments could be carried out only if the House agreed to pass implementing laws or appropriations.

Checks on the judiciary. Supreme Court justices and federal judges were to be appointed by the president with the advice and consent of the Senate. They could be impeached by the House and removed from office after trial by the Senate. Congress was to establish, fund, and determine the jurisdiction of the federal courts, including some of the jurisdiction of the Supreme Court. The courts would not be able to enforce their own decisions in most instances, but would have to rely on national and state officials.

The ultimate check: Constitutional amendments. The convention delegates knew that they could not provide for all circumstances and that periodically the Constitution would have to be modified. They created an amending process (Figure 2-4) which involved Congress, the state legislatures, and the people. According to Article V, amendments could be proposed either by a two-thirds vote of each chamber of Congress or by a national amending convention called by Congress on the application of two-thirds of the states. Amendments were to be ratified either by a vote of three-fourths of the state

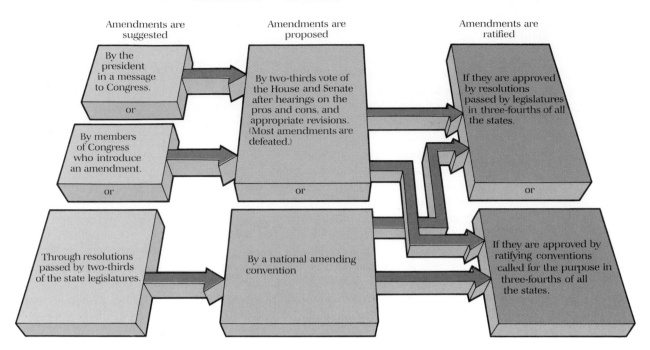

Figure 2-4. There are two ways amendments may be proposed and two ways they may be ratified. No amendment has ever been proposed by a national amending convention as of 1985. Only the Prohibition Amendment has been approved by ratifying conventions called by the states; all others have been approved by state legislatures.

legislatures or by a vote of three-fourths of special conventions called in the states, whose delegates would be elected directly by the people.

The amendment process could be used to make changes in the federal system, modify separation of powers and checks and balances, further democratize the electoral process, and guarantee the liberties of the people, even against the government itself.

THE RATIFICATION CONTROVERSY

When the convention finished its work at the end of a long, hot Philadelphia summer, thirty-nine delegates signed the document. Thirteen were not present or refused to sign, including Edmund Randolph (who had sponsored the original Virginia Plan) and such influential members as Elbridge Gerry and George Mason. Their refusals were based in part on the omission of a bill of rights and on their fears that the president and the Senate would together constitute a monarchy and an aristocracy that would throttle popular government. Their opposition foreshadowed the problems the signers would have in convincing state leaders to accept their plan.

The ratification procedure

The original mandate from Congress provided that the convention was to report back to it and propose a set of amendments to the existing Articles of Confederation, which would have required a unanimous vote in Congress. According to the Constitution, the people would choose delegates to state conventions, which would either ratify or reject the document. The Constitution would go into effect if only nine state conventions ratified it. The very legitimacy of the new government might be put in doubt by this procedure.

Madison argued that the convention could not establish a "firm national government" which would be "adequate to the exigencies of government and the preservation of the Union" (its mandate from Congress in its resolution approving the convention) unless it *disregarded* the procedures of that resolution. To meet the goals of the resolution, he argued, it was necessary to ignore the means. This could be done by recourse to the people. The Constitution was to be considered by more than 1200 popularly elected delegates at state ratifying conventions. "The people were, in fact, the fountain of all power," Madison reassured the delegates in Philadelphia, and "by resorting to them, all difficulties were got over. They could alter constitutions as they pleased."[40]

Bowing to pressure from the convention, which appealed to the people at the expense of Congress and the state legislatures, Congress itself unanimously passed a resolution agreeing to the procedures set forth in the Constitution. The legitimacy crisis had been surmounted.

The Anti-Federalists attack

Supporters of the Constitution took the name *Federalists*—a brilliant strategy, since it implied that their plan was simply an improvement on the existing confederation, rather than a radically different form of government. Opponents let themselves be known as *Anti-Federalists*—an unfortunate decision, since it put them in the position of being against rather than for something.

The distinguishing characteristic of the Anti-Federalists was neither social class nor regional interest—most of their leaders were as distinguished and successful in business and society as the Federalists, and they included such powerful politicians as George Clinton, the governor of New York—but rather an honest doubt that the plan would do what its supporters claimed, coupled with a desire to retain power at the state level. They were "men of little faith," in Cecilia Kenyon's apt phrase.[41] Patrick Henry spoke for many of them at the Virginia convention when he derided the intricate mechanisms that Madison had created to prevent abuses of power. "There will be no checks, no real balances, in this government," he thundered, adding: "What can avail your specious, imaginary balances, your rope-dancing, chain-rattling, ridiculous ideal checks and contrivances?"[42] Instead, Henry and others believed that the national government would soon act to destroy the states. James Monroe argued that the president, at the head of the army, would combine with the Senate and establish a monarchy, leading to a civil war. Tom Paine argued that the proposed Constitution was undemocratic because only the House was directly elected.

The Federalists respond

The Federalists downplayed the vast new powers granted to the national government, and instead they pointed to the similarities between the proposed national government and the existing state governments. They pointed out that Washington, who was sure to become president, had already demonstrated that he had no desire to be a king. They denied that the Senate and the president would combine to create an aristocratic government, pointing out that the Senate was to guarantee the rights of the small states.

The Federalists and the Anti-Federalists sparred in the newspapers. *The Federalist,* a series of newspaper essays by Alexander Hamilton, John Jay, and James Madison, was written to sway public opinion toward the Constitution in New York. It discussed the failures of the existing confederacy, showed how a large republic could end the "tyranny of faction" (an allusion to Shays's rebellion), analyzed the proposed powers of the national government and the state governments and the advantages of a system of separation of powers and checks and balances, and concluded by reassuring the people that the proposed president would not have the power of a British monarch (but would be much more like the governor of New York!) and that the judiciary would not be a threat to the liberties of the people.

The Federalist is the first major commentary on the new Constitution. Although many people consider it an authority on specific provisions, it should be approached with caution. It was primarily a work of political propaganda. Hamilton, in particular, was not above providing interpretations of the Constitution which were at odds with his own understanding of the powers which the president would exercise if the Constitution were adopted. Nevertheless, as a work of American political thought, it ranks among the few classics that this nation has produced. Madison's contributions in *The Federalist*, numbers 10 and 47 to 51 (on pluralism, separation of powers, and checks and balances), and Hamilton's discussion of the presidency in *The Federalist*, numbers 67 to

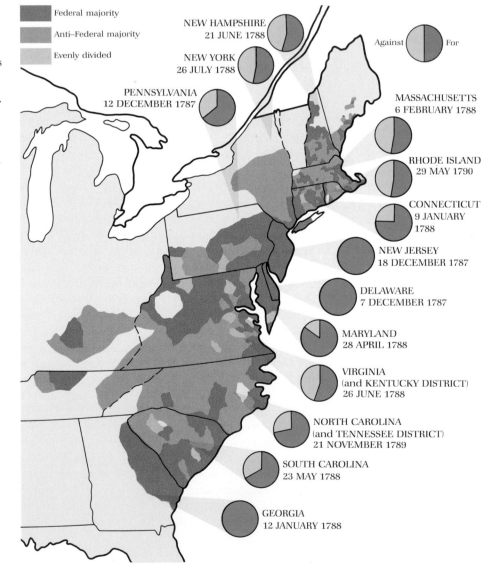

Figure 2-5. The map shows the counties in each state which supported or opposed ratification of the Constitution through their votes for delegates to the state ratifying conventions. The pie charts offshore show the final votes for and against ratification in these conventions.

Federal majority

Anti–Federal majority

Evenly divided

NEW HAMPSHIRE
21 JUNE 1788

NEW YORK
26 JULY 1788

PENNSYLVANIA
12 DECEMBER 1787

Against   For

MASSACHUSETTS
6 FEBRUARY 1788

RHODE ISLAND
29 MAY 1790

CONNECTICUT
9 JANUARY 1788

NEW JERSEY
18 DECEMBER 1787

DELAWARE
7 DECEMBER 1787

MARYLAND
28 APRIL 1788

VIRGINIA
(and KENTUCKY DISTRICT)
26 JUNE 1788

NORTH CAROLINA
(and TENNESSEE DISTRICT)
21 NOVEMBER 1789

SOUTH CAROLINA
23 MAY 1788

GEORGIA
12 JANUARY 1788

77 (describing its expanded powers), deserve reading by every student of politics.

But when the issue remained in doubt in New York after the *Federalist* papers appeared, Hamilton resorted to extreme tactics. He spread the rumor that if New York's convention voted the plan down, New York City would secede and take some downstate counties with it, creating a new state that would join the union. In spite of the opposition of Governor George Clinton and many of the upstate politicians, the Constitution was narrowly approved. In one state after another, a similar combination of argument and maneuver won the day for the Federalists (Figure 2-5).

The call for a bill of rights

The feature of the Constitution that most worried the delegates at the state conventions was the fact that it would enable the new national government to operate directly on the citizens of the states. If Congress could pass laws, to be enforced by federal courts, then the people must have further protections against the possibility of abuse of power.

The Constitution placed few limitations on the power of the national government. Congress could not pass a bill of attainder (a law naming a particular person a criminal and providing punishment) or an ex post facto bill (a law which declares that an action already taken is illegal and which provides punishment for those who have taken it). No religious test could be applied to prospective officeholders. The privilege of the writ of habeas corpus would apply in federal courts unless suspended during a state of emergency. No title of nobility could be granted by the national government. All trials in federal courts would be by jury. Congress, by law, could punish those guilty of treason, but the courts could not convict anyone without the testimony of at least two witnesses to an overt act or without a confession in open court.

Omissions in the Constitution. The Constitution did not provide for freedom of religion, the press, assembly, or speech. It had little to say about judicial procedures. George Mason and Elbridge Gerry wanted the Constitution to provide the same kinds of guarantees of rights and liberties that most state constitutions already provided. Mason observed that "he would sooner chop off his right hand than put it to the Constitution as it now stands." But Gerry's motion for a committee to draft a bill of rights at the convention was handily defeated.

George Washington, James Madison, Alexander Hamilton, and Gouverneur Morris opposed a bill of rights because they believed that it would weaken the new national government. But John Adams in London and Thomas Jefferson in Paris, when they read the provisions of the new Constitution after the convention adjourned, immediately noticed the omission and wrote letters across the Atlantic to their colleagues in protest. Jefferson suggested that the states ratify the Constitution and then use the amending procedures to create a bill of rights. The Federalists realized that they would be defeated in the two states that mattered most—New York and Virginia—unless they agreed to Jefferson's idea.

The Bill of Rights. After the Constitution was adopted, the first Congress passed ten amendments in 1789 which were approved by the necessary number of states in 1791. The ***Bill of Rights*** was based on the theory of the *reserved*

Frederick Kemmelmeyer's "Washington Reviewing the Western Army at Fort Cumberland, Maryland." Washington resigned his commission, establishing a principle of civilian leadership in government. *(Metropolitan Museum of Art.)*

rights of the people: in their compact establishing a national government, the people retained certain rights, some of which were now enumerated in the ten amendments, and others of which remained with the people or the states. The Bill of Rights was to protect people from arbitrary and coercive action by the national government, particularly Congress, just as state declarations or bills of rights protected them from actions of the state governments. (Later the Bill of Rights would also be interpreted by the courts as applying to state governments, but that would not occur until the twentieth century.)

FROM RATIFICATION TO IMPLEMENTATION

By July 1788, almost one year after the convention finished its work, the requisite nine states had agreed to the plan, and soon thereafter Virginia and New York also ratified it. Crucial to the success of the Federalists was the support of artisans and mechanics in the cities and of some of the small farmers in the west, all of whom decided that the economic gains they might reap under a strong national government were more important than safeguarding their power in strong state governments.

After ratification, Congress passed a measure providing for a transition from the old to the new form of government. By law it fixed dates on which electors would be chosen in the states and assemble at the state capitols to choose a president, and it fixed dates on which congressional elections would be held. By the winter of 1788 electors had been chosen, and early in 1789 they chose George Washington as the first president and John Adams as the first vice president. The state legislatures convened and selected members of the Senate. The people voted in elections for the House of Representatives.

According to procedures adopted by the outgoing Congress, the new government assembled in New York City, which was the temporary capital until a new federal district could be established. In March, George Washington entered the city in triumph at the head of a parade of exuberant citizens to take up his duties. In April the new Congress convened. "Our Constitution is in actual operation," Ben Franklin reported to his friends abroad. "Everything appears to promise that it will last; but in this world nothing is certain but death and taxes." The American experiment in constitutional democracy had begun.

FOCUS

PROJECT '87—CELEBRATING THE CONSTITUTION. Project '87, a joint undertaking of the American Historical Association and the American Political Science Association, commemorates the bicentennial of the adoption of the Constitution by promoting public understanding and scholarly appraisal. The project is chaired by the historian Richard B. Morris of Columbia University and by the political scientist James MacGregor Burns of Williams College; Chief Justice Warren Burger serves as honorary chairman of the advisory board.

Research and conferences have been under way for the past several years, and the project has awarded numerous research grants and fellowships and has provided support for five scholarly meetings. It has also funded programs for more effective teaching about the Constitution at the high school and college levels.

Support for Project '87 comes from the William and Flora Hewlett Foundation, with grants for specific programs provided by the National Endowment for the Humanities, the Lilly Endowment, and the Rockefeller, Ford, and Mellon foundations.

Project '87 puts out a quarterly magazine containing articles about its funding programs and research results. For further information, write to: Project '87, 1527 New Hampshire Avenue, N.W., Washington, D.C. 20036.

As part of its efforts to promote the bicentennial of the adoption of the Constitution, Project '87 has made planning and production grants for the following television programs, many of which will be broadcast in 1987 and 1988:

The Living Constitution. National Video Communications, Inc., San Diego, California. Four programs on contemporary issues and how the founders viewed them.

A More Perfect Union. Yale University Media Design Studio. A three-hour television film on the drafting of the Constitution and the Bill of Rights.

To Form a More Perfect Union. WTIF, Philadelphia, Pennsylvania. The history of the Constitution, the Bill of Rights, and the American political party system.

The U.S. Constitution Project. WGBH-TV, Boston, Massachusetts, and the Institute of Politics, Harvard University. An evaluation of the usefulness and the continued vitality of our constitutional system.

Visions of the Constitution. WQED, Pittsburgh, Pennsylvania. Eight half-hour profiles of scholars of the Constitution and their interpretations of it.

We, the People. KQED-TV, San Francisco, California. Seven half-hour documentaries on current issues such as judicial review, federalism, and the First Amendment.

Witnesses at the Creation. Capitol Cities Communication and Lou Reda Productions. Biographies of the writers of the *Federalist* papers.

IN CONCLUSION

The Constitution created in 1787 came about as a result of the failure of the Articles of Confederation to provide for security and prosperity after the Revolutionary War. Calls for reform went unheeded between 1781 and 1786, and Congress was unable to raise taxes to pay its war debts and veterans' pensions, which contributed to instability. Shays's rebellion in 1786–1787 was merely the culmination of several years of disorders between debtors and creditors in many states. It spurred leading state politicians to agree to calls by Washington, Hamilton, Madison, and others for a national convention.

The Philadelphia convention established a new government based on three principles: federalism, popular government, and partial separation of powers. The federal system divided power between a national government and the state governments: a unique American experiment, it was a hybrid of the existing national and confederal models. Popular government meant periodic elections for the House of Representatives. Senators were to be chosen by the state legislators, the president was to be chosen by an electoral college, and the federal judiciary was to be appointed. Partial separation of powers involved three branches—the legislative, the executive, and the judicial—with overlapping jurisdictions and with a system of checks and balances designed to preserve the independence of each branch. The federal principle would promote stability by preventing any single interest or faction from dominating the government. Popular government would keep rulers accountable to the ruled. Partial separation of powers would prevent abuse of power and legislative encroachment on the other branches.

Just as important as the provisions of the Constitution was the politics of the convention. Compromises between the large states and the small states, between the north and the south, and between proponents of different political principles were the key to its success. The convention itself was an efficiency negotiation, in which the compromises and logrolling provided advantages for all participants.

Although the Constitution and its novel ratification arrangements were criticized by the Anti-Federalists, the political skills of the Federalists, combined with a pledge to support a bill of rights, won ratification in the necessary number of states. The new government was instituted in 1789, with George Washington as president, and the Bill of Rights was ratified in 1791.

NOTES

1. Gordon Wood, *The Creation of the American Republic, 1776–1787.* Norton, New York, 1972, p. 393.
2. Robert A. Goldwin and William A. Schambra (eds.), *How Democratic Is the Constitution?* American Enterprise Institute, Washington, D.C., 1980; Alfred F. Young, "Conservatives, the Constitution, and the 'Spirit of Accommodation,'" pp. 145–146.
3. Paul Ford (ed.), *The Writings of George Washington,* Putnam, New York, 1890, vol. 10, p. 170.
4. Richard H. Kohn, "Inside History of the Newburgh Conspiracy," *William and Mary Quarterly,* vol. 28, no. 2, April 1970, pp. 187–220.
5. *Journals of the Continental Congress,* Sept. 28, 1786, pp. 698–699; Oct. 21, 1786, p. 896.
6. Goldwin and Schambra, op. cit.; Young, op. cit., p. 122. See also Daniel Boorstin, "The American Revolution: Revolution without Dogma," in *The Genius of American Politics,* University of Chicago Press, Chicago, 1953, pp. 35–50; and Richard Hofstadter, "The Founding Fathers: An Age of Realism," in *The American Political Tradition,* Knopf, New York, 1948.

7. James MacGregor Burns, *The Vineyard of Liberty*, Knopf, New York, 1982, p. 33.
8. W. B. Gwynn, *The Meaning of the Separation of Powers: An Analysis of the Doctrine from Its Origin to the Adoption of the United States Constitution*, Tulane University Press, New Orleans, 1965. See also Stanley N. Katz, "The Origins of American Constitutional Thought," *Perspectives in American History*, vol. 3, 1969, pp. 474–490; and Edward Corwin, "The Progress of Constitutional Thought between the Declaration of Independence and the Meeting of the Philadelphia Convention," *American Historical Review*, vol. 30, no. 4, 1923, pp. 511–536.
9. Thomas Paine, *Common Sense*, in Moncure D. Conway (ed.), *The Writings of Thomas Paine*, vol. 1, AMS Press, New York, 1894, pp. 67–84.
10. Goldwin and Schambra, op. cit.; Wood, op. cit., p. 13.
11. Joseph M. Bessette, "Deliberative Democracy: The Majority Principle in Republican Government," in Goldwin and Schambra, op. cit., p. 105.
12. Ibid., p. 107.
13. Wood, op. cit., p. 12.
14. Baron de Montesquieu, *The Spirit of the Laws*, 1748.
15. John Adams, *A Defence of the Constitution of the United States of America*, Dilly, London, 1787.
16. Thomas Jefferson, *Notes on the State of Virginia*, in Paul Ford (ed.), *The Writings of Thomas Jefferson*, Putnam, New York, 1892–1899.
17. James Madison, *Notes of Debates in the Federal Convention of 1787*, Ohio University Press, Athens, 1966, p. 185.
18. Ibid., p. 447.
19. Goldwin and Schambra, op. cit.; Young, op. cit., p. 134.
20. Charles S. Sydnor, *American Revolutionaries in the Making*, Free Press, New York, 1965, pp. 60–73.
21. Madison, op. cit., p. 126.
22. Ibid., p. 230.
23. Max Farrand, *The Framing of the Constitution of the United States*, vol. 1, Yale University Press, New Haven, Conn., 1913, pp. 461–462, 468.
24. Calvin Jillson and Thornton Anderson, "Voting Bloc Analysis in the Constitutional Convention," *Western Political Quarterly*, vol. 31, no. 4, December 1978, pp. 535–547.
25. Calvin Jillson, "The Executive in Republican Government: The Case for American Founding," *Presidential Studies Quarterly*, vol. 9, no. 4, fall 1979, pp. 386–401.
26. The word *federal* as it appears in this resolution signifies the existing arrangements under the Articles of Confederation.
27. Madison, op. cit., p. 34.
28. Ibid., p. 353.
29. Ibid., p. 45.
30. Ibid., p. 35.
31. Ibid., p. 516.
32. Ibid., p. 514.
33. Ibid., p. 44.
34. Ibid., p. 39.
35. Ibid.
36. Ibid., p. 40.
37. Ibid.
38. Ibid., p. 340.
39. *The Federalist*, no. 40.
40. Madison, op. cit., p. 564.
41. Cecilia Kenyon, "Men of Little Faith," *William and Mary Quarterly*, 3d Series, no. 12, 1955, pp. 3–43.
42. Jonathan Elliot (ed.), *The Debates of the Several State Conventions*, vol. 2, 2d ed., Franklin, Burt, New York, 1876, p. 54.

FURTHER READING

Beard, Charles A.: *An Economic Interpretation of the Constitution of the United States*, Macmillan, New York, 1913. A study of the framers, emphasizing their desire for personal gain through financial speculation in government debts, which could be secured by a stronger national government.

Becker, Carl: *The Declaration of Independence*, Random House, New York, 1958. A study of the political theory and politics involved in drafting the Declaration.

Burns, James MacGregor: *The Vineyard of Liberty*, Knopf, New York, 1982. A vivid description of the social and economic conditions in early America and of the political leaders of the time.

Farrand, Max: *The Framing of the Constitution of the United States*, Yale University Press, New Haven, Conn., 1913. A narrative account of the work of the convention.

Goldwin, Robert A., and William A. Schambra (eds.): *How Democratic Is the Constitution?* American Enterprise Institute, Washington, D.C., 1980. Essays assessing the motives of those who called for the Constitutional Convention.

————: *How Does the Constitution Secure Rights?* American Enterprise Institute, Washington, D.C., 1985. Essays on the Bill of Rights.

Jensen, Merrill: *The New Nation*, Knopf, New York, 1950. A history of the confederation from 1781 to 1789, written by a historian who is sympathetic to its purposes and generous in his estimation of its success.

Koch, Adrienne: *Power, Morals and the Founding Fathers*, Cornell University Press, Ithaca, N.Y., 1961. Essays on the political thought of Adams, Franklin, Hamilton, Jefferson and Madison.

McDonald, Forrest: *We the People: Economic Origins of the Constitution*, University of Chicago Press, Chicago, 1958. A reexamination of Beard's thesis and a fresh interpretation of the motivations of the framers.

Main, Jackson Turner: *The Anti-Federalists: Critics of the Constitution, 1781–1788*, University of North Carolina Press, Chapel Hill, 1961. An examination of the factions in each state that opposed the Constitution, arguing that they were primarily small farmers and others with no need to promote interstate and foreign commerce.

Rakove, Jack N.: *The Beginnings of National Politics*, Knopf, New York, 1979. An account of the successes and failures of the Continental Congress and of events leading up to the convention of 1787.

Rossiter, Clinton: *1787: The Grand Convention*, Macmillan, New York, 1966. Still the most readable account of the convention and the men who made it.

Rutland, Robert A.: *The Birth of the Bill of Rights, 1776–1791*, Collier, New York, 1962. How the Bill of Rights was framed, proposed, and adopted.

Storing, Herbert J.: *What the Anti-Federalists Were For*, University of Chicago Press, Chicago, 1981. A study of the political principles and programs of those who opposed ratification.

Wood, Gordon S.: *The Creation of the American Republic, 1776–1787*, University of North Carolina Press, Chapel Hill, 1969. A study of the politics of the confederation, emphasizing the weakness of the state governments, and an interpretation of the work of the delegates to the Constitutional Convention.

THE STUDY BREAK

Alexander Hamilton. A movie biography (1931).

The Rebels. In this television movie, a fictional character, Philip Kent, fights in the American Revolution and meets up with some of the founding fathers (1984).

1776. Originally a Broadway musical and later (1972) a movie, starring Howard Da Silva as Ben Franklin.

Vidal, Gore: *Burr.* Random House, New York, 1973. A witty and irreverent view of the founding fathers, written as a novel with a point of view (Aaron Burr's) rather than as objective history.

Washington. A six-part made-for-television series produced by CBS in 1984, emphasizing Washington's love for Martha (his wife) and for Sally Fairfax (his neighbor's wife!).

USEFUL SOURCES

Congressional Research Service, *The Constitution of the United States of America: Analysis and Interpretation,* GPO, Washington, D.C., 1972 (with later supplements). A study of the provisions of the Constitution in the light of 200 years of experience and adaptation.

Elliot, Jonathan (ed.): *The Debates of the Several State Conventions,* 2d ed., Franklin, Burt, New York, 1888–1896. A compilation of debates in the ratifying conventions, shedding light on the interpretations given to particular provisions of the Constitution by key figures.

Farrand, Max (ed.): *The Records of the Federal Convention of 1787,* Yale University Press, New Haven, Conn., 1937 (reprinted in 1966). A four-volume set, including an extensive index, containing notes of Madison, Yates, King, Paterson, Pierce, and Brearley and of the official journal. The most useful source on the debates and reports of the committees at the convention.

Hamilton, Alexander, James Madison, and John Jay: *The Federalist* (first published in 1788 in *The New York Packet* and reprinted in many editions). An interpretation of the Constitution by three prominent supporters.

Levy, Leonard W. (ed.): *The Encyclopedia of the American Constitution,* 4 vols., Macmillan, New York, forthcoming in 1987. Will contain 2000 articles on the history and present state of American constitutional law.

Storing, Herbert J. (ed.): *The Complete Anti-Federalist,* University of Chicago Press, Chicago, 1984. A seven-volume compilation, with commentary and notes, of the essential writings of Anti-Federalist politicians.

This Constitution: A Bicentennial Chronicle. A quarterly magazine published by Project '87 containing articles and documents relating to the Constitution and to proposed constitutional reforms.

ORGANIZATIONS

Federal Bicentennial Commission. 736 Jackson Place, Washington, D.C. A commission created in 1983 to promote and coordinate activities for the commemoration of the adoption of the Constitution. For more information phone 202-456-1414.

Project '87. 1527 New Hampshire Avenue, N.W., Washington, D.C. 20036. An organization of historians, political scientists, constitutional lawyers, and politicians who are conducting research on the Constitution and its relevance to American politics. For more information phone 202-483-2512.

FEDERALISM: A NATION OF STATES

Federal-state and state-to-state governmental relations are both parts of federalism. The twin towers of Manhattan's World Trade Center were built by the Port Authority of New York and New Jersey. State governors are very sensitive to federal budget cuts, such as those proposed by President Reagan. (*Mike Yamashita; Larry Downing.*)

$\mathbf{T}$he American system, Justice Samuel Chase decided at the end of the Civil War, "looks to an indestructible Union composed of indestructible states."[1] But neither the Constitution nor the war provided a definitive answer to the question of what *form* the union would take. Every issue in American politics becomes bound up with the question of federalism. The "when," "why," and "how" of the question, "Who gets what?" are determined in part by federalism, and changing the relations between the national government and the state governments can change the outcomes; thus our federal arrangements are always controversial, always in flux.

Federalism involves the issues of legitimacy and authority. Which government—the national government or a state government—may constitutionally do what? And which would be more effective, more responsive, and more innovative? Some critics say that federalism is an outmoded, inefficient, and cumbersome way to organize American politics—useful in 1787, but not today. Its defenders claim, as Madison did two centuries ago, that federalism offers numerous advantages and that what seem to be complex and inefficient mechanisms are actually the safeguards that make our democracy work.

WHAT IS FEDERALISM?

A federal system divides powers between a national government and smaller territorial units located within the nation's boundaries. (These smaller units are called *provinces*, *republics*, *cantons*, or, in the United States, *states*.) The national government is sovereign over the entire territory and its population, and it conducts foreign affairs and is responsible for national defense. But the states have their own powers, usually guaranteed by a national constitution. Some powers are exercised solely by the national government, some are exercised by the states, and some are exercised concurrently.

Federation versus confederation

In a *__federation__* the national government is fully sovereign; the states may not withdraw without the consent of the national authorities; and the people create both the national government and the state governments, delegate powers to both, and may restrict both through the written constitution. The national government may act directly on the people: it can tax and draft them. In contrast, in a *__confederation__* the states are sovereign: they may join the nation or withdraw from it at will. They delegate specified powers to national institutions and reserve all others to themselves. The national "government" is a creature of the states and can deal only with the states, not directly with their citizens.

Confederation is an ancient form of government; it has bound people together throughout history, from the time of the alliances of the Israelite tribes to the Renaissance and the confederacies which flourished in what is today

> ### POWERS OF THE NATIONAL GOVERNMENT AND THE STATE GOVERNMENTS AS SPECIFIED IN THE CONSTITUTION
>
> ***The national supremacy clause.*** The Constitution, treaties, and laws of the United States are the supreme law of the land. Anything to the contrary in state constitutions or laws is null and void. State officials must enforce national law at the expense of contradictory state laws.
>
> ***Republican form of government.*** The states are guaranteed a republican form of government. No state may have any other type of government.
>
> ***Powers granted exclusively to the national government.*** The national government has power over foreign affairs, military affairs, interstate commerce, commerce with foreign nations, and currency.
>
> ***Powers which the states may not exercise without congressional assent.*** Without the agreement of Congress, the states may not tax imports or exports or foreign shipping, keep armed forces other than a state militia, enter into agreements with other states or foreign nations, or engage in warfare.
>
> ***Powers denied to the states.*** The states may not impair obligations of contracts; deprive anyone of life, liberty, or property without due process of law; or deny anyone equal protection of the law.
>
> ***Obligations of the states to one another.*** The states must give full faith and credit to the judicial proceedings of other states and must grant the citizens of other states the privileges and immunities of their own citizens.
>
> ***Powers exercised concurrently by the national government and the state governments.*** The national government and the state governments concurrently regulate elections, taxation, commerce, spending for the general welfare, and judicial functions.
>
> ***Powers exercised solely by the state governments.*** The Tenth Amendment reserves powers not granted to the national government by the Constitution to the states or the people. Since 1937 that has become a truism: what the national government does not do remains reserved. It is a boundary rather than a limitation on the national government in most instances.

Territories can be admitted to the union by Congress. Once admitted, states can secede only with the consent of Congress. Alaska and Hawaii were the last admitted, in 1959. (*Bettmann Archive.*)

Germany, Italy, the Netherlands, and Switzerland. Federalism is more modern; it was developed first in the United States and later was adopted by one-third of the countries of the world, including the Soviet Union, Brazil, India, Nigeria, Mexico, Switzerland, Yugoslavia, West Germany, Canada, and Australia.

Federal versus unitary government

In a *unitary* system (such as that of the British or the French) the national government develops policies and implements them locally in regions and districts, using its own officials. Today, even nations with unitary systems have modified their constitutions to provide for political autonomy for regions. Great Britain and Spain now have regional legislatures. The Sudan has experimented with autonomy for its religious minorities.

Federalism versus decentralization

In our federal system the powers reserved to the states are specified and guaranteed by the Constitution. State officials are elected by the people, not appointed by the national government, and elected officials run the 3000 counties (smaller territorial units within the states), the 16,700 townships and 19,000 municipalities, and the 28,000 special districts and 15,000 school districts. Only when the states can make their own policies *independently* of the national government—especially their own decisions on taxing and spending and their own economic and social regulations—and only when the right to make these policies is *guaranteed* by the national constitution is there a federal system.

In a unitary system the substantial autonomy that local officials enjoy can be taken away by central authorities. None of their powers are guaranteed by the constitution. They can be removed from office if they do not carry out the instructions of the central government. Occasionally even our national government and our state governments operate as if they were parts of a unitary system. The White House has designated the states as planners for the operations of federal programs and has made the governors "chief federal planning officers" to oversee their implementation. It also has made localities into districts for nationally funded programs, or, in the words of President Carter, into "the delivery mechanisms for most of the actual services the federal government provides."[2] What seems to be federalism, involving cooperation between federal and state officials, is actually decentralization: policies are made at the national level, and the states play an administrative role, however flexible.[3]

THE CHANGING NATURE OF AMERICAN FEDERALISM

American federalism has gone through four distinct phases and in the 1980s is going through a fifth.[4] Each has represented an attempt by politicians to adjust the original constitutional understandings to their own needs.

Phase 1: 1789–1867

The first phase, *classic federalism*, began in 1789 and lasted until the adoption of the Fourteenth Amendment at the end of the Civil War. Members of Congress wanted the national government to serve the states. While some strict constructionists tried to limit the activities of the national government, there was no strict separation between its functions and those of the states.

Administrative collaboration. As a practical matter national officials cooperated closely with their state counterparts: they organized joint stock companies to construct turnpikes and canals and to finance the national bank, with stock held by the United States Treasury, the state governments, and private investors. The national government gave the states land grants, which they used at the end of the Civil War to build the great public universities.[5]

Conflicts over sovereignty. At the level of constitutional theory the issue of sovereignty remained unsettled until the end of the Civil War. The Constitution did not explicitly create a national government with full sovereign powers. It did not claim that the powers of the states were delegated from the national government. And it did not make the states into creatures of the national government by giving Congress a veto power over their laws. Instead, the Constitution granted some powers to the national government, recognized that others were exercised by the state governments, and then forbade the national government to take certain actions and the state governments to take others (and allowed the states to act in some matters only with the permission of Congress). The result was a hybrid government, as Madison suggested in *Federalist* 39, neither fully national nor fully confederal, but partaking of both forms.

The doctrine of national supremacy. The Supreme Court took the first controversial steps toward establishing the supremacy of national law over state law. In *McCulloch v. Maryland* (1819), Chief Justice John Marshall declared that the Constitution was established by the people, not the states, and denied that the states retained any sovereignty. Marshall upheld the power of Congress both to establish a national bank and to prevent the states from taxing the operations of national agencies. He denied that the Tenth Amendment, which reserves all powers not mentioned in the Constitution to the states and the people, could limit the powers of Congress as to the means it could use to implement powers granted to the government by the Constitution.[6] In *Dartmouth College v. Woodward* (1819) the Court upheld a clause in the Constitution forbidding the states to make laws that would impair the validity of contracts.[7] Later, in *Gibbons v. Ogden* (1824), Marshall struck down a New York law giving a company a monopoly on steamboat operations, and in doing so he argued against the notion that a state law and a national law, if in conflict with each other, involved two opposed sovereignties. Instead, he pointed out that Article VI gave supremacy to Congress. The national government was superior and the state governments were subordinate, with the federal courts serving as instruments to implement the policies of Congress.[8]

The doctrine of dual federalism. Counterpoised against the notion of national supremacy was the idea that the Constitution remained a compact of sovereign states which had ceded only limited powers to the national government. State and national authorities faced each other as equals, across a dividing line demarcating their respective powers. In some areas, only the states could act. In others, both the states and the national government could act. Both, for example, had **concurrent power** to control interstate commerce, although the power of the states was limited to matters of local concern.[9] Chief Justice Taney resurrected the Tenth Amendment, arguing that the states were sovereign in certain matters and that the final determination was to be made by the courts—now a neutral arbiter between Congress and the states— "deciding in the peaceful forms of judicial proceeding the angry and irritating controversies between sovereignties, which in other countries have been determined by the arbitrament of force."[10]

The doctrine of nullification. Dual federalism left the issue of sovereignty unsettled. When the Federalists took the nation to war against France in 1798, its majorities in Congress also passed a sedition law, which restricted freedom of speech and of the press. The Anti-Federalists, who were opposed to the conflict, struck back with the Kentucky Resolution and the Virginia Resolution (passed by the legislatures of those states), which declared the law null and void in the two states. This doctrine of **nullification** was later used by the Federalists themselves: during the War of 1812 they refused to heed a call from the Republican-dominated Congress to put the New England state militias into the service of the federal government.

In 1832, when Congress imposed a high tariff, South Carolina declared the law null and void and threatened to secede from the union if the tariff was collected in the port of Charleston by federal officials. President Andrew Jackson issued a proclamation warning the citizens of the state not to violate federal law. He urged antisecessionists to arm themselves and prepare to assist national authorities, and then he warned South Carolina that he would use the army to put down its resistance. Eventually, after Jackson promised to work for a lower tariff law, the state backed down and repealed its ordinance of nullification.

CLOSE-UP

JOHN C. CALHOUN. No other nineteenth-century politician exemplifies the unresolved tensions of American federalism as well as John C. Calhoun. Born in 1782, Calhoun graduated from Yale in 1804 and returned south to practice law. In 1810, after serving a term in the South Carolina legislature (1808), he became a member of Congress. At that time he was a strong nationalist, one of the "war hawks" who pushed the nation into the War of 1812. Later, in 1817, he became secretary of war, and in 1824 he was elected vice president.

In 1828 he was reelected, even though the presidency had shifted from John Quincy Adams to Andrew Jackson. Calhoun and Jackson soon found themselves on opposite sides of the "states' rights" issue. Calhoun believed that the sectional compromises of the 1820s were unfavorable to the south. He thought that the southern minority needed protection against unfavorable laws (having to do with tariffs, banking, and slavery) which might be passed by Congress. In 1832, in pro-

John C. Calhoun. (*New York Public Library.*)

test against a tariff law, Calhoun resigned from the vice presidency, and the South Carolina legislature promptly elected him a United States senator. He was a leader in the attempt by that state to "nullify" the tariff law, an effort which failed when President Jackson made it clear that he would use military force if necessary to collect the duties in southern ports.

While in the Senate, Calhoun proposed to revise the federal system radically. He argued, in his *Disquisition on government,* that the states should be allowed to nullify laws passed by Congress—an argument that had previously been made by the Jeffersonians in the 1790s (during a naval war with France) and by the Federalists in 1812. The states' right not to enforce federal law should be final, he said, except in cases where a new constitutional amendment had been passed. He also proposed a system of concurrent regional majorities to pass laws: only when a majority of northern, southern, and western representatives all voted aye would a bill become a law. If a majority from any region dissented, that would be enough to "veto" the bill.

Calhoun's ideas were not accepted, even in the south. Unionists saw no reason to change the existing system. Moderates believed that threats of secession would induce the north to agree to new compromises on their substantive demands, thus avoiding the need to make changes in the system. Hard-liners were ready to secede if the north did not give in. By 1850 Calhoun was predicting that there would be a civil war within twelve years.[11]

The federal crisis resolved. The Civil War settled the issue of sovereignty. The national government was supreme over the states: Congress, by simple majorities, could make laws which the states were bound to enforce; no state or region could nullify a national law once it was enacted; none could secede from the union to protest policies it opposed; and the president had the power to execute the law, if necessary by the use of armed forces. The north's victory over the south ended any lingering conceptions that the union involved dual sovereignty or should operate according to doctrines of nullification or concurrent majorities; by 1865 there was only one sovereign—the national government.

Phase 2: 1867–1913

Ironically, during the postwar period, when the issue of the union's sovereign *constitutional* powers was settled, the doctrine of ***dual federalism*** flourished: the national government had its responsibilities, the states had theirs, and the national government should stay clear of the business of the states, and vice versa. The courts would make sure that the national government did not overstep its bounds.

Industrial regulation. Dual federalism was a response to the growing industrialization of the nation. A conservative business community and a federal judiciary drawn from the ranks of lawyers that served business wished to limit national regulation of the economy. The courts made a sharp distinction between commerce between the states, which Congress could regulate, and all other commercial, financial, and industrial matters, which they argued were left to the states.[12] The boundaries were far sharper and more restrictive than they had been before the Civil War period, when Congress had used the general welfare clause and the necessary and proper clause for economic regula-

The Supreme Court long struck down federal child labor laws on the ground that they infringed upon states' rights. A 1941 reversal eventually upheld the federal government's regulation of child labor under the interstate commerce clause. (*Lewis Hine: Bettmann Archive.*)

tion. The postwar courts struck down national laws on the grounds that the states had jurisdiction. Antitrust laws were interpreted in such a way as to prevent the national government from interfering with manufacturing combinations.[13]

Substantive due process. The federal courts used the Fourteenth Amendment guarantee of due process of law—a provision enacted at the end of the Civil War primarily to protect the freed slaves in the south—and interpreted it to mean that corporations were "persons" within the meaning of the amendment.[14] Therefore, corporations could not be denied due process of law by the states. The federal courts created a set of protections for corporations known as *substantive due process*, the effect of which was to strike down much (though not all) state regulation of minimum wages, maximum hours, health and safety in the workplace, and the like.[15]

The states were limited in regulating the economy because of substantive due process guarantees to corporations, while Congress was limited in this respect because the courts said that these matters did not involve interstate commerce. Thus neither level of government could act.

The "state" versus the "government." The most noted constitutional lawyers and professors of the day, most of them northerners who had supported a strong union during the Civil War, interpreted the Constitution in a way that reconciled the need for national supremacy with this handcuffing of Congress. They argued that the function of the *union* was equivalent to that of the European state: it was to have all sovereign powers; handle matters of diplomacy, war, and internal security; and remain supreme over the state governments. Meanwhile, the national *government* (which they distinguished from the sovereign state) was to function in limited spheres, with its powers divided among separate, mutually antagonistic branches and with its operations monitored by the judiciary, which would be ever vigilant in protecting the rights of individuals and corporations.[16]

Phase 3: 1913—1941

But the American people wanted more national regulation of the economy. They supported Teddy Roosevelt's "trust-busting" campaign and Woodrow Wilson's "new freedom" program in the presidential election of 1912. Later the depression forced the national government to aid state governments in the relief, welfare, public housing, public employment, and unemployment insurance programs of the New Deal. Funds were provided by the national government, but the programs were also partly funded and fully administered by state and county agencies. Many of these programs were passed by Congress in response to pleas by state officials for help.

The courts at first tried to reaffirm their laissez-faire decisions. They struck down federal laws prohibiting or taxing child labor.[17] Between 1865 and 1937 the Supreme Court struck down seventy-six laws passed by Congress and hundreds passed by states, most regulating the economy. More than 130 state laws were struck down in the 1920s alone. But the Court limited the reach of the due process clause, first by establishing certain exceptions (such as "protective legislation" involving women and children) and then by repudiating substantive due process and allowing the states to regulate corporations.[18] It also expanded the conceptions of the general welfare clause and the necessary and proper clause so that Congress could once again legislate on a large number of social matters, including wages and hours, child labor, social security, and unemployment insurance. It expanded the interpretation of commerce between the states to include manufacturing. It also broadened the definition of interstate commerce to include commerce *within* states that has an effect on commerce *between* states.[19]

Phase 4: 1941—1969

In the next period the focus shifted from the economy to race and poverty. Blacks moved off the land in the south and into the factories of the north during the Second World War. In the postwar period their demands for racial justice profoundly affected the federal system. When the Supreme Court ruled

Federal-state cooperation during the depression led to public housing such as the Whitman Park Project in Philadelphia. (*Department of Housing and Urban Development.*)

in 1954 that public schools must be desegregated because "separate but equal" facilities were inherently unconstitutional, southerners responded with a policy of "massive resistance" and refused to obey court orders to desegregate schools. In some instances this required federal officials to use federal marshals, the FBI, and even federal troops to enforce judicial orders and uphold the Constitution.

Race. Southern politicians responded with claims that their states' rights were at stake and that the southern voters had a right to pass laws and ordinances maintaining racial segregation in public facilities to preserve their "way of life." Meanwhile, blacks and northern liberals argued that only national law could protect the civil rights of minorities and that Congress had the right to pass laws that overrode state and local practices. At times federal troops had to be used to uphold court orders for desegregation involving public schools and state universities. Congress passed the Civil Rights Act of 1964, which desegregated public accommodations involved in interstate commerce; this included most restaurants, hotels, and commercial establishments. The Voting Rights Act of 1965 overrode state election practices such as literacy tests and even provided for federal registrars to take over local functions in certain cases. The Fair Housing Act of 1968 prohibited racial discrimination in the sale or rental of housing, although in practice much discrimination remained.

The national-local relationship. In the 1960s, unlike earlier periods, there was a direct link between national bureaucrats and local officials, especially in the new urban renewal and antipoverty programs. Often the states were bypassed. At times it seemed as if federal and local officials were in alliance against state legislators and governors, who seemed more cautious, more conservative, and even hostile in their attitude toward the new urban-oriented antipoverty, housing, and community development programs. The states felt that they were whipsawed: that they were required to implement national laws and regulations and to fund part of the costs of national programs but were denied adequate input into policy-making and at times were bypassed by the new national-local alliances.

Criticism no longer focused on the right of the national government to act, but rather on how effectively the complex and increasingly costly intergovernmental system was working. Questions of authority had replaced those of legitimacy.

Phase 5: 1969 to the present

Today we are in a fifth phase of American federalism, one which has not yet run its course. It is marked by an increased mistrust of centralized government and by skepticism that "the feds" can solve domestic problems. State governments have become better at solving problems, and many have modernized their antiquated bureaucratic methods. State governments are eager to make policy in areas that have long been controlled by national officials. Meanwhile, the national government, faced with monstrous deficits, has no appetite for new programs and is cutting back or eliminating many old ones. Polls show that more than two-thirds of the public favor granting the states more power and that an overwhelming majority of Americans think that the states understand the needs of the people better than the national government, will administer programs more efficiently, and are less likely to operate corruptly.[20] (See Figure 3-1.)

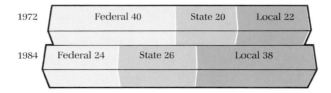

1972	Federal 40	State 20	Local 22

1984	Federal 24	State 26	Local 38

Figure 3-1. "Which level of government—federal, state, or local—is most effective?" The ACIR poll shows a large increase in percentage of respondents who believe that state and local governments, rather than the national government, is most effective in dealing with problems. (Source: Advisory Commission on Intergovernmental Relations, *Significant Features of Fiscal Federalism*, p. 122. *The Washington Post National Weekly Edition*, July 23, 1984, p. 38.)

Unwinding the federal system. The result has been some extreme rhetoric about reviving "state sovereignty" and "unwinding the federal system" so that most functions now handled cooperatively would be assigned exclusively either to the states or to the national government. For example, the states now handle low-level radioactive-waste disposal, and the national government has the exclusive responsibility for high-level radioactive wastes. In part this represents principle, but it is also good politics. Let the states handle difficult or even intractable problems, and let them raise taxes to do so. Meanwhile, national politicians can take the credit for lowering national taxes and reducing the burden of federal regulation.

The reality has been more complex. The existing cooperative mechanisms remain, and state officials fight to keep them rather than unwind the system. But there have been significant cutbacks in funding to the states and attempts to give them greater responsibility.

The new regional issues. Racial and social issues have been displaced in importance by other controversies, often centered on energy, natural resources, and industrial policy. In the west, the so-called sagebrush rebellion involves conflicts between locals and feds over the management of federal lands—parks, forests, grazing lands, and military tracts. The west also challenges federal power to deal with water management and coastal management.[21] In some states there has been intense opposition to plans for basing the MX missile and other strategic nuclear weapons systems. Throughout the nation there have been conflicts over policy involving the construction and operation of nuclear plants, the transportation of nuclear fuel, and the disposal of nuclear wastes. Environmental regulations, toxic-waste disposal,

At times of natural disaster the states move in first. Jim Hunt, then the governor of North Carolina, took charge of relief after a tornado at Faison. The federal government provides disaster relief if the state has difficulty coping. (*AP Laser photo.*)

transportation regulations, and even the issue of speed limits on interstate highways have all become issues in the federal system.

The states continue to resist the power of the national government. Federal civil defense planners call for the evacuation of cities in the event of a nuclear crisis, but local officials refuse to make such plans in Marin County, California; Boulder, Colorado; and Cambridge, Massachusetts. In Connecticut, local officials for a while refused to allow on their interstate highways trucks which exceeded their own standards for weight and bulk, even though federal law permits trucks to travel on such highways.

HOW FEDERALISM WORKS

With all the conflicts over sovereign powers, jurisdictions, and the administration of programs, one might wonder whether federalism is worth it. Why should any nation experiment with such a complicated form of government when a unitary system would be simpler? As it turns out, federalism has some significant advantages; some were understood in 1787, and others have been discovered only in practice.

Checking and balancing power

The framers believed that a federal system would allow national officials to check state officials, and vice versa. The Constitution requires the national government to guarantee each state a republican form of government, which prevents local despotism.

State governments led by the opposition party served to check the excesses of the party in power in Washington in our early history. The first transfer of power between parties, for example, came about in part because the state militia in Virginia served notice in 1800 that it expected the Federalists to turn over the government to the Anti-Federalists or face armed conflict.

Today federalism serves to improve the authority of the government with the public. If national policies are unwise or inadequate, state politicians can be expected to call for a different approach or to demand more power to deal with issues. Likewise, if the states fail to solve their problems, the public may demand that Congress and the president act, and national legislation and programs will supplant those of the states.

Diversity and accountability

A federal system allows different regions and states to pursue different social and economic policies. Voters can compare the programs in their states and regions with those adopted elsewhere and see which are more viable. Since voters elect state officials (and the officials of county and other local governments established by the state), they can make the government responsive to the wishes of local people, even as they change their views about what constitutes intelligent social and economic policy. Some may be permissive, and others restrictive, on issues such as the drinking age, grounds for divorce, gambling, prostitution, use of drugs, the sale of pornography, and punishment for crime. Sometimes allowing states to make social policy can reduce national tensions over an issue and can keep issues out of national politics, especially divisive social issues: drugs, gun control, and child abuse, for example.

Experimentation. A state can experiment, and if an experiment is not successful, others need not adopt the idea. "A mistake in Washington is a mistake for all 50 states," according to Richard Williamson, a Reagan aide, while a

States are often ahead of the national government in social policy. Women voted in the presidential elections in Wyoming in 1888 under state sufferage laws; the federal government did not guarantee women the right to vote until 1920. (*Granger Collection.*)

mistake in one state "only affects that state and they can learn from each other."[22] The states are laboratories which can diffuse innovations to other states or the national government. Wisconsin created unemployment insurance in 1931, and the national government soon followed suit. During the depression other states experimented with legislation for welfare, public works, and collective bargaining before such legislation was adopted by Washington. In the 1940s and 1950s northern states passed fair housing and fair employment laws and established enforcement commissions; the federal government did so in the 1960s. Some western states allowed women to vote in state elections two decades before the suffrage amendment was put in the Constitution. The sun belt tax revolt in the late 1970s was followed by federal tax reductions in 1981 and by tax reform in 1986.

Constraints on experimentation. But federalism also inhibits experimentation. States compete with one another for business investment, and a state must offer a better "business climate" than other states. If personal and corporate taxes are too high and if services are less than adequate, industries and the most productive people will pull up stakes and go elsewhere. States give incentives to industry by reducing taxes and offering credits and exemptions and special depreciation schedules. They spend money on services needed by industry, including convenient transportation, health care, schooling, and job retraining, thus skewing their policies.

A state may not spend as much money as it would like on facilities or services because some will be used by out-of-state citizens who do not pay their share of the costs. States that benefit from the services offered by another state are *free riders*—or, more accurately, *freeloaders*.

One solution to this problem is to have the national government make grants to a state to cover part of the cost of building or operating a facility. The state pays an amount which is proportional to the benefits that will accrue to its own citizens, while the national government pays an amount which is proportional to the benefits that will accrue to citizens of other states.

75

Since air pollution does not stop at state lines, national standards and joint federal-state enforcement efforts are necessary to reduce air pollution and clean up toxic waste dumps. (*Bruce Flynn; George Hall.*)

A state that provides well for its disadvantaged citizens may find that it draws migrants from other states (or foreign nations) who are attracted by the services—the *magnet effect.* If other states do not increase their own services, such a state will wind up with a higher tax burden, a greater level of public expenditure, and inadequate services, because the clientele will have increased enormously. As more poor people move in, the quality of life deteriorates for others, and as their taxes rise, they "vote with their feet" and move elsewhere.

National problem, national action. States and cities may regulate industry in the absence of national regulation, but sometimes they are inhibited by threats that companies will relocate to a more hospitable state. And a state has no incentive to regulate an industry if the benefits (such as maintaining air or water quality) are received by citizens of neighboring states. Nor does a state have any such incentive if regulation would not work unless many other states also acted. It makes little sense for New England states to control their own smokestack emissions if most of the acid rain which pollutes their lakes is caused by smokestacks in the middle west and in Canada. Sometimes the only way to solve a problem is through national action; experimentation by states can be worse than useless because it may delay meaningful efforts.

Going overboard with national action. But the national government, prodded by interest groups and legislators who want to help out financially hard-pressed state and local governments, often takes on more than it needs to: it shares with state governments the responsibility for school security, pothole repair, noise control, arson prevention, snow removal, rat and pest control, jellyfish control, bikeway construction, and car-pool formation. One may wonder what is the point of having state and local officials if they cannot somehow contrive to deal with these issues without involving the national government. Aaron Wildavsky has accurately characterized the present system as *fruitcake* *federalism:* state and local officials compete for grants that they do not need, and they expect the national government to deal with problems and provide funding for all sorts of programs—all without rhyme, reason, or rationale, but simply because it has become a habit to look to Washington for help and to blame Washington for problems that should have been solved locally.[23]

Liberals, conservatives, and states' rights

The standard textbook generalization has it that conservatives favor **state action** because **states' rights** prevent federal regulation of industry and because states and cities are more likely to promote the interests of corporations and to provide a "favorable business climate" through lower taxes and antiunion legislation. Liberals, on the other hand, favor national regulation of industry because it is likely to be stiffer, and they favor national social programs because they are likely to be better funded.

But whether one favors regulation by the national government or by the states depends on the issue. Liberals call for national action on welfare, civil rights, urban reconstruction, and pollution—unless a conservative is in the White House, in which case they look to state governments for innovative programs and more funding.

Conservatives often oppose national programs in principle, but in practice conservative business leaders often prefer a single national law or regulation instead of fifty state laws with which they must comply. They often support national services such as collection of economic statistics, postal services, highway and airport construction, mass transit, freight-rail service, and the bailout of depressed regions. They favor national licensing and regulation of nuclear power plants, while environmentalists and antinuke groups favor state licensing. (The Supreme Court, in a compromise, gave the federal government the exclusive power to regulate safety and environmental issues, and it gave the states the power to regulate the economic aspects of nuclear power.) Conservative politicians in the mountain states line up for national funding for public works, reclamation, and water resource projects; conservatives in the south welcome national funding for canals, power stations, highways, and crop support programs. In sum, whether politicians favor or oppose national action depends less on ideology than on the answer to the question, "Who gets what, when, and how?"

Fiscal federalism

State taxation. In a federal system both the national government and the state governments impose taxes on individuals and corporations. The national government relies primarily on personal income taxes, corporate income taxes, customs duties, alcohol excises, and estate and gift taxes. The states take in most of their revenue from general sales taxes, income taxes (all but nine now have them), automobile registration fees, and excises (taxes on particular goods). Local governments receive most of their revenue from the property tax. Excises on tobacco products and utilities are shared evenly by the national government and the state governments.

The national government accommodates the states' needs for revenue in several ways. Taxpayers who itemize their deductions on federal income tax returns deduct $31 billion worth of state and local income taxes and (until 1987) state sales taxes and thus reduce their tax liability to the national government. Therefore, state and local governments have leeway to raise these taxes without triggering a taxpayers' revolt.

The interest which the national government pays on **bonds** is not taxable by state and local governments, and the $19 billion in interest which state and local governments pay on their bonds is not taxed by the national government. This means that states and cities can offer bonds at lower interest rates than corporations, since the after-tax income that a person receives is the important consideration; in effect, this is a Treasury subsidy to states and cities.

Fiscal crises in the cities. *Fiscal federalism* can help cities whose own resources are insufficient to deal with urban decay and poverty, although national tax policies have hurt the cities. Tax codes have favored new construction, not rehabilitation, which has led industries to build new facilities in the suburbs rather than fix up existing sites. New owner-occupied suburban tract housing was favored over the rehabilitation of rental housing in cities by making the interest on home mortgages and on federally insured mortgages tax-deductible. The interstate highway systems, financed with federal funds, allowed people to move to the country, while urban mass transit fell into disrepair.

The cities' populations are declining, but their elderly, minorities, and immigrants are increasing in number, and most of these people require government services, while few can afford high taxes to pay for them. Municipal unions often escalate wage demands without corresponding increases in productivity. The rehabilitation of bridges, tunnels, harbors, roads, hospitals, and schools requires massive funding. Yet the tax base of many cities has eroded.

Between 1970 and 1980 cities received injections of new money from the national government as direct federal aid to large cities increased by 1500 percent. This money came from urban programs passed by Democrats in Congress. In some large cities up to half the local budgets consisted of federal funds.[24] By 1978, however, federal aid to cities (adjusted for inflation) had begun to decline.

Republican presidents and candidates do not favor direct aid to cities. Reagan did away with job programs and ended a program of antirecessionary fiscal assistance. He also slashed funding for public works and community development. To the extent that funds were made available, they were given to state governments rather than to the big cities. The Reagan administration did propose to use the tax code to target some aid to disadvantaged areas in the big cities. Under this plan, certain depressed areas would have been designated as "urban enterprise zones." Tax breaks for companies locating in these zones would have included credits for capital investment in plant and machinery, no **capital gains taxes** on property sales, a twenty-year period during which business losses could be offset against later profits, and tax credits if young unemployed workers were hired. The Treasury estimated that the cost of these tax breaks would have amounted to $900 million, which is a small commitment, considering the total amount of aid to urban areas, but the program stalled in Congress.

Meanwhile, nineteen states passed their own legislation for enterprise zones. In Camden and Newark, New Jersey, for example, the zones allowed corporations to pay lower state taxes and reduced their taxes by $1500 for each new employee hired who lived in the city and had been jobless for more than ninety days. Sales taxes were also cut or eliminated on goods and services that corporations bought and on any new building or plant expansion in the zone.

BAILING OUT THE BIG APPLE: FEDERAL LOAN GUARANTEES

In 1975 New York City nearly defaulted on loans which a group of banks had made to it. The banks refused to roll over the loans because they did not believe that the city could ever pay the money back. New York came close to declaring bankruptcy. No one could say for certain what that would have meant, but it might have affected the stability of the entire national banking system.

The New York State legislature devised a plan to meet the crisis. City finances were placed under the supervision of an emergency financial control board. It would require the city to balance its budget within three years, and it could reject the city's plans. To refinance existing loans and pay off the banks, the Municipal Assistance Corporation (Big MAC) was created; it had the authority to issue long-term bonds to investors to replace the short-term city notes issued to the banks.

Big MAC found that investors would not buy its bonds, and so Congress, after much lobbying by city officials and the New York State congressional delegation, bailed out the city. It provided $2.3 billion for three years in the form of seasonal loans which the city could draw upon when it needed cash to pay its expenses. Later, in 1978, with its budget not yet balanced, the city returned to Congress to ask for $1.65 billion in loan guarantees for four years. With these guarantees Big MAC was able to market its bonds. By 1985 the city once again could market bonds without federal loans or guarantees.

Those opposing the bailout argued that the city was in trouble because it had lived beyond its means. It provided large welfare and Medicaid benefits, ran a free city university system, broadcast over a municipal radio station, maintained a large free public library system, and so forth. Supporters claimed that the city was in trouble because of the way federalism works: New York City was expected to take care of immigrants who made it their first port of call before moving inland; it had costs associated with the United Nations; and its libraries and cultural facilities were used by visitors but were paid for primarily by residents. They argued that the federal government should increase its aid to the city rather than require it to pay for what were actually national programs to solve national problems.

By the mid-1980s the cities were in greater trouble than ever before. A Joint Economic Committee report revealed that most of the fifty largest cities had raised taxes, cut services, reduced the number of employees, and postponed capital improvements. A survey by the National League of Cities showed that most could not prevent serious deterioration of their facilities.

Fiscal equalization. One of the most important functions of federalism in many countries is to redistribute national income from wealthier regions to poorer ones—*fiscal equalization.* The United States, unlike most other countries with a federal system (such as Australia and Canada), has no explicit goals for fiscal equalization, either in the Constitution or in its laws. Grants made by the federal government to states and cities provide virtually no fiscal equalization because the wealthier states are also those with large concentrations of poor people and with crumbling facilities in need of replacement. Also, the higher-income states in the north spend more on their poor citizens than the low-income states in the south, and so fiscal equalization might actually hurt the poor in the north.[25]

But if one considers *all* federal expenditures in states—such as for defense contracts, military bases, federal offices, and purchases of goods and services—the poorer parts of the country do benefit from federalism. The New England,

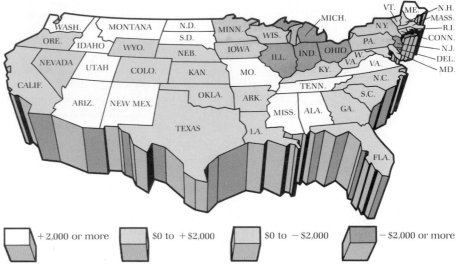

Figure 3-2. The industrial states of the northeast and midwest pay more in taxes per capita than they receive back in federal grants and services. Most southern and western states receive more per capita than their residents pay out. (Source: Advisory Commission on Intergovernmental Relations.)

+ 2,000 or more $0 to + $2,000 $0 to − $2,000   − $2,000 or more

mid-Atlantic, plains, and Great Lakes states pay more in taxes per capita than their citizens receive back in federal expenditures in their states, while the south Atlantic, south central, mountain, and Pacific states receive more in expenditures than their citizens pay in per capita taxes.[26] (See Figure 3-2.)

Redundancy

A simplistic approach to government organization argues that if one unit of government can do something, having two or three different units involved will lead to duplication and waste. There is no reason to have state governments, some critics charge, because the national government at this point has so many duties that keeping the states involved only confuses things.

Paradoxical as it may seem, duplication may lead to more efficient government. This involves the **redundancy principle:** the idea that one should have a "backup" which can take over if something goes wrong. In the *Columbia* space shuttle there are five different computers. When a power cell in the shuttle failed in a 1981 mission, two others provided power, allowing the mission to continue. Having *system redundancy* improves the odds in any operation: if a unit will fail 1 in 10 times, having two units means that the odds are that both will fail only 1 in 100 times.

Load sharing versus system failure.   These principles apply to government. Having two or three different units of government means that if one is not equal to the job, another can take over and carry the load. It also means that if the national government is not carrying out its functions properly, pressure from the states or cities may force it to take a more active role, and vice versa.[27]

During the 1973 energy crisis the national government was supposed to allocate oil supplies. Because it did the job poorly, state energy offices proposed better allocations, which resulted in more efficient distributions. Congress then delegated power to the state governors to allocate fuel, establish conservation measures, and monitor consumption. During the 1979 energy crisis the Department of Energy could not develop efficient rationing plans. Congress refused to pass most of President Carter's energy program. The governors stepped in again; using a combination of national power delegated to them by Congress and their own powers, they installed state rationing systems, provided funds so that the elderly and the poor could pay their oil bills, and allocated fuel to industry. Congress then passed the Emergency Energy Conservation Act of 1979, which allowed the governors to set goals, choose measures to achieve the goals, and implement their own plans rather than those of the Department of Energy.[28]

Taking up the slack. If one level of government reduces its services, another level may increase its commitments. When the states could no longer provide welfare and food to the poor during the depression, the national government stepped in with welfare, job, and housing programs. In the 1980s, as the national government cut back on its commitment to the hungry and the homeless, the cities and states took on a greater role. When President Reagan cut student aid, the states increased their need-based tuition scholarship programs, took over some of the work-study reimbursements, expanded loan programs, and allowed students to transfer to state universities.

Buck-passing. Unfortunately, redundancy systems have their disadvantages. When everyone is responsible for something, sometimes no one is responsible—and nothing happens. Mayors and governors campaign on promises to increase services and cut costs, and then they blame their deteriorating services and facilities on Washington.[29] The feds want the locals to raise taxes and solve problems, while the locals expect Washington to take the political heat for tax increases and to send more money their way. Voters find it increasingly difficult to sort out who is to blame.

INTERGOVERNMENTAL POLITICS

Much of the work of American government is carried out intergovernmentally. Rather than have each level of government run its own programs, a system sometimes called *layer cake federalism*, the modern ***intergovernmental system*** involves each unit in the work of the others. The administration of such programs has been likened to a *marble cake*, characterized by "an inseparable mingling of differently colored ingredients, the colors appearing in vertical and diagonal strands and unexpected whirls."[30] There are no separate levels and there is no hierarchy; instead, there are matrices where clusters of federal, state, and local officials jointly administer programs with the cooperation of private organizations. The marble cake seems complex, with no neat boundaries separating the national government and the state and local governments—and it is.

Intergovernmental cooperation often involves federal funding for part or all of state programs. This may take several forms: categorical grants, project grants, block grants, formula grants, and revenue sharing.

Intergovernmental administration: The grant-in-aid

The federal ***grant-in-aid*** is extremely important to state and local governments; at their peak in 1977, grants-in-aid accounted for more than one-fourth of all state and local expenditures (up from one-tenth in 1950), and in 1985 they accounted for 22 percent, more than 3.4 percent of the gross national product.

Categorical grants. The traditional way to administer programs involves the ***categorical grant.*** The national government grants funds to state and local

President Reagan, along with Governor Mario Cuomo of New York State, Mayor Edward Koch of New York City, Senator Alphonse D'Amato of New York, and a construction worker, dramatizes the joint federal-state interest in developing interstate highways. (*AP Laserphoto.*)

governments for particular services or facilities. States are not required to participate. The federal government may require states to put up *matching funds*—usually between one-tenth and one-half of the federal contribution—and most states do so because participation brings in federal money which otherwise would go elsewhere. In 1862, under one of the first such grants, states were given federal land, which they could sell to get the money to build their public university systems, the great land-grant universities. In 1879 grants were begun to aid the blind, in 1887 to construct agricultural experimentation stations, in 1916 to build state highways, in 1917 to provide vocational education, and in 1920 to aid veterans.

During the depression the national government created the welfare and unemployment insurance systems through categorical grants. Payments were made to individuals by state agencies, with some of the funding coming from the national government.

The peak years for categorical grants were the 1960s and 1970s, when the "new frontier" and "great society" programs established by Democratic presidents Kennedy and Johnson expanded under Republican presidents Nixon and Ford. By 1980 there were close to 600 such programs, transferring about $90 billion from the national government to state and local governments. The Reagan administration cut back these programs sharply: the total amount of funds was reduced by almost half between 1980 and 1984, and many programs were eliminated. (Figure 3-3 shows trends in grant outlays.)

Categorical grants are created by Congress, often as a result of lobbying by governors and mayors who want more aid and by program specialists and interest groups. But sometimes programs are created as a result of presidential, congressional, or departmental insistence that national priorities or standards be imposed on the states—even over the opposition of state and local officials. The federal government created a food stamp program for the poor, even though many of the counties with the largest proportions of malnourished people opposed it.

Project grants. Often money is given by the federal government to help states or cities construct particular facilities. Local officials apply to regional federal offices. In ranking the applications, economists favor the *cost-benefit* approach: costs are divided into the anticipated benefits, and projects with the highest ratios of benefits to costs are funded first. But state politicians and their allies in Congress are not impressed with this approach, especially when their pet projects would cost a great deal and would confer benefits only on particular farmers or business people. In such cases they do not want cost-benefit ranking. They view federal government funds not as part of their costs, but rather as "free goods" for their state.

Politicians rely on *community mobilization:* they get local businesses, labor leaders, bankers, contractors, newspapers, and others who would benefit from a project to support their efforts, and then they get their entire state's congressional delegation to back them.[31] Legislators bargain with other state delegations in Congress and with the White House and department secretaries to win approval for the funding. Thirty states and a number of large cities maintain full-time lobbying offices in Washington to expedite these efforts.

Congressional committees are influential in determining who gets these allocations, although studies have shown that most committee members do not receive a disproportionate share of funds in programs over which they have jurisdiction.[32]

Formula grants. Funds may also be distributed by automatic formula, a system preferred by states and cities. This system, which is designed to end political influence, is used for about one-third of categorical grants. But politics remains: instead of trying to get a particular project grant by changing the rankings, legislators try to change the weighting of the factors in the distribution of the formula. A typical formula for distributing housing funds, for example, might take into account the following: overall population, the percentage

Figure 3-3. Lower line shows amount of money spent by the national government for intergovernmental grants. Note the cutbacks which occurred in 1982. Upper line shows these amounts as the percentage of all state and local expenditures, and it too begins to decline in the 1980s. (Source: Advisory Commission on Intergovernmental Relations.)

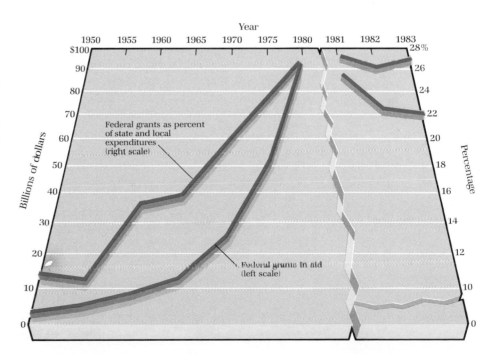

of the population below the poverty level, the tax effort the state makes in funding its own programs, the fiscal capacity of the state to increase its funding by raising taxes, and the number of people in need of the program.

Members of Congress use computer programs to tell exactly how much money their district or state will receive under various versions of the formula. They can then propose a change in the formula which will increase their allocation. Usually a coalition forms, along regional lines, which can impose the formula it wants.

Grants: The view from the states. Governors are not interested in conforming to national standards or meeting national goals. They want the federal government to give them lots of money with very little interference. They want vetoes over any projects in their states that will be funded by the feds. They insist that program funds be routed through state budgets rather than going directly to counties and cities. State legislatures sometimes insist that funds not be spent unless and until they authorize and appropriate the projects or services.

Although state officials consider money from the federal government to be free goods, there is a *diversionary cost*, since state matching funds expended according to national priorities are no longer available for other purposes. In addition, when Congress requires the states to participate in open-ended reimbursement programs like welfare, Medicaid, and unemployment compensation, the states have to pay out funds to all who are eligible, which means that they no longer control their budgets. State officials are subject to federal laws and regulations and to federal court orders interpreting them.

There are at least thirty-seven legal mandates—involving discrimination based on race, sex, or age; access for the handicapped to public places; environmental protection; preservation of historic sites; citizen participation; long-range planning; individual privacy; freedom of information; and the like—which apply to intergovernmental programs. Compliance increases the expenses of states and localities, and the mandates do not take local conditions into account. Sometimes officials refuse to comply, and a case winds up in the federal courts, which are likely to rule for these mandates if issues concerning civil rights or liberties are involved, if the requirement is reasonably related to a

---

THE FEDS VERSUS THE LOCALS: TWO SUPREME COURT CASES

Must a state always comply with federal regulations? In *National League of Cities v. Usury* (1976), the Supreme Court reviewed a law passed by Congress—the Fair Labor Standards Amendments of 1974—which would have applied maximum wage and hour laws to state and local government employees. The Supreme Court struck down the law, ruling that because the states remained a coordinate and not a subordinate part of the constitutional system, they could apply their own wage and hour rules, even in programs partly funded by the national government.

In 1985 the Supreme Court reversed itself. In *Garcia v. San Antonio Metropolitan Transit Authority*, it ruled that the Labor Department could order local transit authorities to abide by national wage and hour regulations. A majority of the Court held that the 1976 approach was unworkable, that national standards could be applied by Congress to state and local employees, and that the states had sufficient influence with their congressional delegations to protect their workers' interests when Congress considered laws to regulate workers.

Congress requires states and cities to provide access to federally funded programs to the handicapped. Near the Capitol, Peter Axelson, a veteran, demonstrates a new bicycle for the handicapped to Bob Edgar (left), then a representative. (*AP Laserphoto.*)

program, and if state participation in the program is voluntary and the state is free to leave. But in several decisions the courts have warned that if national officials *coerce* a state into remaining in a program, they might strike down some of the requirements that interfered with the constitutional powers of the state.

Controls are not as onerous in practice as in theory. Departments do not have enough enforcement personnel. They need more auditors to review financial records and more special investigators to fight corruption. They are lax in holding state and local officials to account in upholding national standards. Members of Congress often pressure department officials to ease up on the local officials. National officials are lax where they should be tough and tough where they should be lax: they insist on compliance with routine paperwork requirements, even though the red tape serves no useful purpose. Yet they rarely cut off funds, even when the local officials are not complying with constitutional or legal guarantees. There is an incentive on both sides to compromise and cooperate.

Grants: The local view. County and city officials want to be free of both national and state controls. "We are sick to death of being an administrative province of the federal government," said Margaret Hance, the mayor of Phoenix, "and we want to avoid becoming administrative provinces of state governments."[33] Local officials want to pick and choose the exact combination of national and state grant programs that suits their needs. They do not want federal aid channeled through, or coordinated by, the states. They think about these grants the way students think about taking courses: while a college tries to impose various requirements concerning majors, distribution of courses, and a core curriculum, students try to fashion programs that suit their own individual needs. If the national government demands lengthy applications or other paperwork from the local officials, they will comply, but like a bored student who wants the credit but thinks that the course requirement (or the teacher) is idiotic, they will produce the paperwork but not make any use of it. This often happens when a local government is supposed to produce a comprehensive plan in order to get a grant.

In the 1970s local officials could shop around because there were so many grants available: seven for highways, twenty-three for pollution control, thirty-six for social services, and seventy-eight for education.[34] Aid was fungible: one program could be substituted for another, and money from a categorical program received by a local government enabled it to transfer its own funds to other programs. Some analysts approved of this, arguing that it enabled localities to create the most flexible mix of programs for their citizens, who in turn would (ideally) have more choices about what kinds of services (public or private, local or national) to accept.[35]

The conversion to block grants

A *block grant* provides funds for a state or local government for a broad functional area (such as education or law enforcement) to be used according to the goals and priorities of the recipient. State officials have long been in favor of converting most categorical grants into block grants.

Lyndon Johnson won congressional approval of two block grants involving health (1966) and law enforcement (1968). Richard Nixon converted thirty-one categorical grants into block grants for health, employment and job training, and community development. They all involved an overall increase in funding to buy congressional support. During the Carter administration, however, no new block grants were created, and block grants accounted for only 10 percent of federal aid.

The Reagan administration proposed another round of consolidations, and Congress responded by converting seventy-three programs into nine block grants in the Omnibus Reconciliation Act of 1981. The following year Congress took other job-training and education programs and created two new block grants: the total number of categorical grants declined from more than 600 to only 441.

Block grants in operation. Congress creates these programs only under presidential pressure, because it prefers categorical grants and the opportunities these grants give it to exert political pressure for the benefit of friends. When Congress creates block grants, it tries to retain some of its influence. Some are really the old categorical grants dressed in new wrappings: four of the block grants created in 1981 consisted of a single former categorical grant. Even when consolidation occurs, Congress may earmark funds for specific purposes or restrict the transfer of funds by the states from one category to another. In some cases, such as the Maternal Health and Childcare grant, there are more restrictions in the block grant than there were in the categorical grant.[36] In some cases block grants may be "recategorized" by administrative regulations to ensure that the money goes for designated purposes.

Once a block grant is in operation, the states pay less attention to national regulations and priorities, and after the funds are received and put into state budgets, it becomes difficult to trace their impact on specific programs and hard to prove or disprove *maintenance of effort:* the requirement that federal funds not be used simply to replace state money which can be diverted to something else. For some grants that requirement has been eliminated, as have rules concerning accounting, auditing, and management by the federal government. Congress has provided that the national government may not establish burdensome reporting requirements.

Conflict over block grants. Conflict occurs between the specialists, who operate the categorical programs, and the generalists—governors, mayors, and state legislators—who want maximum discretion in using federal funds. The generalists win when Republican presidents pressure Congress into transforming categorical grants into block grants. The specialists who operate these programs then pass regulations that have the effect of converting some of them back into categorical programs, in practice if not in form. The generalists then counter with White House pressure to abolish the new regulations or see that exceptions are made.

Conflict also occurs between mayors, county officials, and governors, all of whom want to control federal funds. The governors want the money transferred to their budgets. The county officials and the mayors want *pass-through provisions*, which automatically transfer some of the funds to their jurisdictions. In a 1982 study by the U.S. Conference of Mayors, 70 percent of the city officials surveyed said that they were not fully represented in state decisions on distributing federal money. They wanted advisory committees that would give them input at the state level.

Retrenchment and block grants. In the 1980s the Reagan administration used consolidation as a budget-cutting strategy. Reagan proposed in 1981 to cut intergovernmental expenditures for the programs being converted to block grants by 25 percent, from $8.15 to $6.1 billion. Congress went along with cuts equaling 13 percent. "Block grants are now a tactical budget to cut the federal budget while deputizing governors to hand out the bad news," observed the Democratic governor of Arizona, Bruce Babbit.[37] The Reagan administration argued that the states could make up the difference with savings from less paperwork. In fact, most states reduced services or used their own funds to make up for the cuts.

Reagan's ultimate goal seemed to be to unwind the intergovernmental system and replace it with a traditional conception of federalism that would have each level of government assume the exclusive responsibility for different programs and would give each level the resources to do so. In his 1982 State of the Union address the president put restructuring of the federal system at the top of his agenda. He called for the national government to take over funding for the $18 billion Medicaid health program and for the states to take the sole responsibility for food stamps and welfare, at an estimated cost of $16.5 billion. The national government would transfer $30 billion worth of domestic programs to the states, along with federal tax sources to pay for them. "I dream of a day," Reagan told the National Association of Counties in 1981, "when the federal government can substitute for these, the turning back to local and state governments of the tax sources that we ourselves had preempted here at the federal level, so that you would have the resources."[38] His proposals were undercut by departments, members of Congress from both parties, and many state governors, and they were quickly buried. As Jack Brooks, a Democratic representative from Texas, noted, "New Federalism, New Federalism. What it means is, let's dump our expenses on somebody else and run."

General revenue sharing

Since 1972 the categorical grants and block grants have been supplemented by ***general revenue sharing***—a direct sharing of national revenues with states and cities. First proposed in the 1960s as a means of increasing state funding for social programs, the State and Local Fiscal Assistance Act was passed in 1972 to enable states and cities to substitute national funds for their own funds

President Nixon chose Independence Hall in Philadelphia as the site for signing the "new federalism" revenue-sharing legislation of 1972. (*Wide World Photos.*)

in an effort to keep taxes down while maintaining services. (Most states and cities, as it turned out, preferred to increase operating budgets for new programs, and only one-sixth of the revenues went toward tax reductions.) By the 1980s general revenue sharing was viewed as a form of emergency fiscal relief for hard-pressed local governments reeling under the impact of cuts in categorical and block grants and the impact of a *recession* on their revenues. It accounted for only 8.3 percent of federal grants by 1980.

Revenue sharing has gone through several phases. Between 1972 and 1977 Congress appropriated a total of $30.2 billion to the states, which were required to pass through two-thirds of the funds to local governments. For the period 1977–1980 the program was renewed at the same funding level, but in 1980 Congress provided that all funds would go directly to local governments. In 1982 the states could receive $2.3. billion, but only if they gave up an equivalent amount of categorical aid. Since then, all aid has gone to local governments.

Congress has never been enthusiastic about the program. Support comes from Republicans who are antagonistic to particular categorical grants and responsive to governors and mayors who need operating funds. The attitudes of Democrats are best expressed by John Brademas (a former representative and now the president of New York University), who argued that revenue sharing was "an essential part of a general attempt to diminish the role of Congress" while "increasing the central power of a handful of decision-makers in the executive branch."[39] Congress eliminated the program entirely (effective in 1987) at the request of President Reagan.

Retrenchment politics

Until recently the amount of funds available for intergovernmental programs, in absolute terms and as a proportion of the federal budget and the GNP, has increased annually. Even conservative Republican administrations, committed to cutting back on the functions of the federal government in domestic affairs, did not stop this growth. But by 1978 the ravages of inflation had done what no politician had dared to do: effect the first real cutbacks in many programs. With high inflation and low percentage increases in available funds, intergovernmental funding was reduced—in inflation-adjusted dollars—by 2.7 percent in 1979, by 2.9 percent in 1980, and by 8.3 percent in 1981.[40] (See Figure 3-4.)

To reduce the large deficits, Reagan has called for highly visible and controversial cutbacks. In 1981 he proposed cuts of $13.4 billion from Carter's recommendations, or $8 billion from the existing 1981 program levels. He also proposed additional cuts totaling 32 percent for his first term. Although Reagan did not get all he asked for, his policies did produce some visible results. In 1978 federal aid to state and local governments amounted to $231 for every American; by 1982 that figure had been slashed to $174.

These cuts were aimed at programs benefiting traditionally Democratic constituencies: the poor, minorities, low-income women, and unemployed. Antirecessionary public works programs were eliminated. Urban development grants were frozen. Attempts were made to cut back on social services in the welfare system and to cap expenses for food stamps and medical aid to the poor.

State and local officials, Democrats and Republicans alike, raised strong protests. "This so-called new federalism is a sham and a shame," proclaimed Ed Koch, the mayor of New York. John Gunther, the executive director of the U.S. Conference of Mayors, charged that Reagan had "made it clear that it's his real goal to get rid of federal aid to state and local government." Richard Snelling, the Republican governor of Vermont and the chairman of the National Governors Association, proposed a "summit meeting" between Reagan, the gover-

Figure 3-4. Intergovernmental expenditures, 1972–1982. Expenditures adjusted for the high inflation rates of the late 1970s (constant dollars) show a drop in 1978, although the totals continued to climb until 1982. (Source: Advisory Commission on Intergovernmental Relations.)

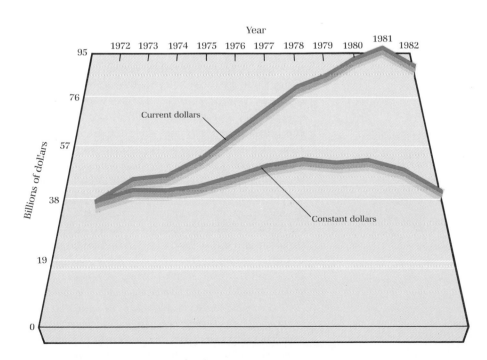

nors, and big-city mayors. The vice chairman of the Republican Governors Association, James Thompson of Illinois, said that the states could not take any more cuts and asked Reagan to cut the defense budget instead. "You cut 'em with a scalpel, you don't use a meataxe" on these programs, advised George Voinovich, the Republican mayor of Cleveland; another Republican, William Hudnut, the mayor of Indianapolis, argued that at some point "cutting becomes gutting."[41]

ISSUE AND DEBATE

MEAT-AX FEDERALISM: Faced with huge and rising budget deficits, President Reagan began his second term by proposing more than $34 billion in spending cuts for the next year. The Reagan meat-ax would cut sharply into domestic programs, especially into grants to state and local governments, which made up more than one-fifth of their budgets. Would such drastic cuts damage the federal system?

The background. Reagan's proposals came in the wake of previous 15 percent cuts in projected spending in 1981 and a reduction from 26 to 22 percent in the percentage which federal funds constitute of state and local budgets. The proposals for 1985 included education; highways; Medicare and Medicaid; food stamps; housing subsidies; welfare for the aged, blind, and disabled; legal services; and block grants. Sewer grants, urban development grants, and federal revenue sharing would be terminated completely.

The revenue proposals offered by the Treasury Department also would affect the states. Ending the deductibility of state and local tax payments from federal income taxes would put pressure on states and cities to reduce their income and sales taxes. Other changes in the federal tax system would depress the real estate market and possibly lower the value of homes and commercial properties, thus reducing the yield from real estate taxes.

As a result, the states seemed to be caught in a double bind: cuts in federal spending would require the states to use their own funds to maintain services, but they would find it impossible to raise or even maintain their current taxes.

The pros. Those in favor of these cuts, like David Stockman, then budget director, and Donald Regan, then secretary of the Treasury, argued that the runaway deficits simply must be brought under control and that necessary sacrifices must be made now, or else the situation will get worse later. They claim that the states will be able to make up the difference with increased revenues coming from the economic prosperity that they foresee in the next decade. Even during the 1982–1983 recession, they say, the states found the money to lessen the impact of the previous rounds of cuts by the federal government. They argue that the most important programs will be maintained, that others will be only frozen rather than increased, and that if all goes well and the deficits are brought under control, it will be possible to restore some programs in the 1990s.

Others, ideologically more conservative, believe that the current deficit crisis provides the opportunity to end or reduce the federal government's participation in domestic programs and give the states back their preeminent role in developing, funding, and administering these programs. Some even argue that if the states cannot fund these programs, it will be no great loss anyway.

The cons. Most state and local officials strongly oppose these cuts. Mayor Voinovich calls them "bad public policy." Democratic mayors and governors have also joined in the criticism. They argue that defense spending should be cut proportionately as well. They believe that the states and cities will not have the huge revenues forecast by the Treasury, especially if parts of Reagan's tax plan pass. They claim that the states have not been able to absorb the last set of cuts. "We've already been pressed to the wall," claims William Bechtel, the director of Wisconsin's lobbying office in Washington, arguing that his state is "reeling and staggering."[42] Democratic mayors and governors believe that these cuts are unfair because they would have the greatest effect on programs aiding the poor and would hurt the northeast and the midwest more than the sun belt states. One official of the National Governors Association says that the governors believe that there should be "no added cuts in basic safety-net programs, such as aid to families with dependent children, food stamps, the social services block grant, child nutrition and Medicaid."[43]

The outlook. President Reagan did not get his 1983 "new federalism" program, and he will get only some of his 1985 meat-ax initiatives. But he has shifted the terms of the debate: no longer is the issue the way in which the federal government will provide more funds and tax assistance to hard-pressed states; instead, it has become how many sacrifices the states can make to help the hard-pressed national government.

IN CONCLUSION

Our federal system was created in 1787 under the Constitution. It involves a sovereign national government, which may act directly on the people and was created by them, and the states, which may exercise powers recognized by the Constitution. Our system has evolved from early attempts at cooperative federalism; to nineteenth-century dual federalism, which protected states' rights and retarded efforts to regulate the economy; into the modern structure of intergovernmental administration of domestic programs.

The advantages of federalism are that it allows diversity, promotes experimentation, checks the power of the national government, and provides redundant safeguards against poor policies. Its disadvantages involve buck-passing, unwieldy administration, and a tendency to provide local solutions to what are actually national problems.

The federal system remains in a state of flux. The important issues no longer involve the legitimacy of regulation by the national government versus regulation by the states, but rather the efficacy of intergovernmental programs. The American people believe that state and local governments are better able to serve them and that they understand their problems better.

In the 1980s, the efforts to unwind the federal system stalled during President Reagan's first term, but his second-term budget-cutting and tax reform proposals would, if adopted by Congress, dramatically reshape the federal system.

NOTES

1. *Texas v. White*, 74 U.S. 700 (1869).
2. Memorandum to the heads of executive departments and agencies, Feb. 25, 1977; see also OMB Circular 95-a, which makes governors the chief executive officers for federal programs.
3. Lewis Kaden, "State Sovereignty," *The Columbia University Law Review*, vol. 79, no. 4, 1979, pp. 869–870; Jane Perry Clark, *The Rise of a New Federalism*, Russell Sage, New York, 1938.
4. Daniel Elazar, "The Evolving Federal System," in Richard M. Pious (ed.), *The Power to Govern*, Academy of Political Science, New York, 1981, pp. 5–19.

5. Daniel Elazar, *The American Partnership*, University of Chicago Press, Chicago, 1962, pp. 297–341.

6. 4 Wheat. 816 (1819).

7. *Dartmouth College v. Woodward*, 4 Wheat. 518 (1819).

8. 9 Wheat. 1 (1824).

9. *Cooley v. Board of Wardens*, 12 How. 299 (1851).

10. *Ableman v. Booth*, 21 How. 506 (1859).

11. Researched by Stacy Burnham.

12. *Wabash R.R. v. Illinois*, 118 U.S. 557 (1886).

13. *U.S. v. E. C. Knight*, 156 U.S. 1 (1895).

14. *The Slaughterhouse Cases*, 16 Wall 36 (1873).

15. *Lochner v. New York*, 198 U.S. 45 (1905).

16. These theories are discussed in Thomas M. Cooley, *The General Principles of Constitutional Law in the United States of America*, Little, Brown, Boston, 1880, pp. 3–54; and Woodrow Wilson, *The State*, Heath, London, 1888, pp. 177–194.

17. *Hammer v. Dagenhart*, 247 U.S. 251 (1918); *Massachusetts v. Mellon, Frothingham v. Mellon*, 262 U.S. 447 (1920).

18. *West Coast Hotel v. Parrish*, 300 U.S. 379 (1936).

19. *NLRB v. Jones and Loughlin*, 301 U.S. 1 (1937); *Seward Machine Co. v. Davis, Helvering v. Davis*, 301 U.S. 548 (1937); *U.S. v. Darby*, 312 U.S. 100 (1941).

20. Advisory Commission on Intergovernmental Relations, *Significant Features of Fiscal Federalism*, GPO, Washington, D.C., 1983, p. 122.

21. Richard Lamm and Michael McCarthy, *The Angry West*, Houghton Mifflin, Boston, 1982.

22. *The New York Times*, Dec. 2, 1981.

23. Aaron Wildavsky, "Birthday Cake Federalism," in Robert B. Hawkins, Jr. (ed.), *American Federalism: A New Partnership for the Republic*, Institute for Contemporary Studies, Berkeley, Calif., 1982, pp. 181–193.

24. Richard Musgrave and Peggy Musgrave, *Public Finance in Theory and Practice*, McGraw-Hill, New York, 1981, pp. 570–571.

25. Ibid., p. 564.

26. Ibid., pp. 576–577; see also Janet R. Pack, "The States Scramble for Federal Funds," *Journal of Policy Analysis and Management*, vol. 1, no. 2, 1982, pp. 175–195.

27. Martin Landau, "Federalism, Redundancy and System Reliability," *Publius*, vol. 3, no. 2, 1970, pp. 173–196; and "Redundancy, Rationality and the Problem of Duplication and Overlap," *Public Administration Review*, vol. 29, no. 4, July–August 1969, pp. 346–357.

28. Alfred R. Light, "Federalism and the Energy Crisis: A View from the States," *Publius*, vol. 9, no. 4, winter 1976, pp. 81–96; and "The Governors Push for Emergency Power," *Publius*, vol. 13, no. 4, winter 1980, pp. 57–67.

29. David Walker, "A New Intergovernmental System in 1977," *Publius*, winter 1978, p. 114.

30. President's Commission on National Goals, *Goals for Americans: Programs for Action in the Sixties*, American Assembly, New York, 1960, p. 265.

31. Morton Grodzins, *The American System*, Rand McNally, Chicago, 1966, especially chap. 9, "Local Mobilization of Public-Private Influence."

32. R. Douglas Arnold, *Congress and the Bureaucracy*, Yale University Press, New Haven, Conn., 1979, pp. 15, 139.

33. *The New York Times*, Sept. 27, 1981.

34. ACIR Information Bulletin 77-2, September 1977, p. 2.

35. Wildavsky, op. cit., pp. 181–193.

36. Richard P. Nathan, "Clearing Up the Confusion over Block Grants," *The Wall Street Journal*, Nov. 3, 1981.

37. Rochelle Stanfield, "For the States, It's Time to Put Up or Shut Up on Federal Block Grants," *The National Journal*, Oct. 10, 1981.

38. ACIR, *Intergovernmental Perspective*, vol. 7, no. 2, spring 1981, p. 4.

39. John Brademas, "Revenue Sharing," *Publius*, vol. 9, no. 3, fall 1976, p. 159.

40. Joseph Pechman, *Setting National Priorities: The 1982 Budget*, Brookings, Washington, D.C., 1981, p. 108.

41. *The New York Times*, Dec. 2, 1981; *Congressional Quarterly Weekly Reports*, Oct. 24, 1981, p. 2047.

42. "Reagan's Proposed Cuts Would Strike Hard at States and Cities," *Washington Post National Weekly Edition*, Dec. 24, 1984, p. 31.

43. Ibid.

FURTHER READING

Elazar, Daniel: *American Federalism: A View from the States*, Crowell, New York, 3d ed., 1984. A comprehensive textbook on the workings of the federal system.

————: *The American Partnership*, University of Chicago Press, Chicago, 1962. A fresh interpretation of the origins and operations of federalism in the nineteenth century, emphasizing the degree of cooperation that existed rather than the separation of functions described by other writers.

Glendening, Parris and Mavis Reeves: *Pragmatic Federalism: An Intergovernmental Review of American Government*, 2d ed., Palisades Publishers, Pacific Palisades, Calif., 1984. An analysis of our intergovernmental system works in theory and in practice.

Goldwin, Robert A. (ed.): *A Nation of States*, 2d ed., Rand McNally, Chicago, 1974. A collection of essays.

Grodzins, Morton: *The American System*, Rand McNally, Chicago, 1966. A collection of articles and case studies which look at all units of government as a single governing system.

Haider, Donald: *When Governments Come to Washington*, Free Press, New York, 1974. A study of the lobbying activities of big-city officials as they fight to obtain federal funds.

Hale, George, and Marian Palley: *The Politics of Federal Grants*, Congressional Quarterly Press, Washington, D.C., 1981. A study of how local officials obtain grants and try to expand the intergovernmental system.

Hamilton, Alexander, James Madison, and John Jay: *The Federalist* (first published in 1788 in *The New York Packet* and reprinted in many editions). Consult numbers 1 to 9, 21 to 23, and 25 on the advantages of a federal republic over a confederacy; see number 39 for a discussion of the federal system. Specific interpretations of the constitutional allocation of power are contained in numbers 32, 41 to 46, and 82. The advantages of a federal system in maintaining social stability are discussed in number 10, a classic of political science.

Hawkins, Robert B., Jr.: *American Federalism: A New Partnership for the Republic*, Institute for Contemporary Studies, Berkeley, Calif., 1982. A presentation of the pros and cons of the new federalism and other recent proposals.

Howitt, Arnold: *Managing Federalism*, Congressional Quarterly Press, Washington, D.C., 1984. An up-to-date account of the intergovernmental system.

Reagan, Michael D., and John F. Stanzone: *The New Federalism*, 2d ed., Oxford University Press, New York, 1981. A comprehensive treatment of developments during the Carter administration.

Walker, David B.: *Toward a Functioning Federalism*, Winthrop, Cambridge, Mass., 1981. The former assistant director of the Advisory Commission on Intergovernmental Relations argues that our intergovernmental system needs some unwinding.

Wright, Deil S.: *Understanding Intergovernmental Relations*, 2d ed., Brooks/Cole, Belmont, Calif., 1982. A comprehensive textbook.

THE STUDY BREAK

Caro, Robert: *The Power Broker: Robert Moses and New York*, Vintage Books, New York, 1975. A biography of the city's master planner and builder, describing how he used the intergovernmental grant system to accomplish his goals. A fascinating account of politics at its best and its worst.

USEFUL SOURCES

The Budget of the United States, GPO, Washington, D.C., annually. Each budget submitted by the president contains statistical information on intergovernmental programs and often recommendations for changes in the system.

Congressional Quarterly Weekly Reports. Reports on new developments in the intergovernmental system, emphasizing congressional politics.

The National Journal. A journal reporting on new developments in the intergovernmental system and emphasizing the politics of the executive branch.

Public Administration Review. A journal containing articles on how intergovernmental programs are funded, implemented, and evaluated.

Publius: The Journal of Federalism. A journal devoted exclusively to issues of federalism.

ORGANIZATIONS

Advisory Commission on Intergovernmental Relations. Suite 2000, Vanguard Bldg., 1111 Twentieth Street, N.W., Washington, D.C. 20006. A government commission that publishes journals, newsletters, special studies, and formal reports on the state of the federal system. For more information phone 202-653-5540.

National Association of Counties. 1735 New York Avenue, N.W., Washington, D.C. 20006. For more information phone 202-783-5113.

National Association of Towns and Townships. 1522 K Street, N.W., Washington, D.C. 20005. For more information phone 202-737-5200.

National Governors Association. 444 North Capitol Street, N.W., Suite 250, Washington, D.C. 20001. For more information phone 202-624-5300.

National League of Cites. 1301 Pennsylvania Avenue, N.W., Washington, D.C. 20004. For more information phone 202-626-3000.

U.S. Conference of Mayors. 1620 I Street, N.W., Washington, D.C. 20006. For more information phone 202-293-7330.

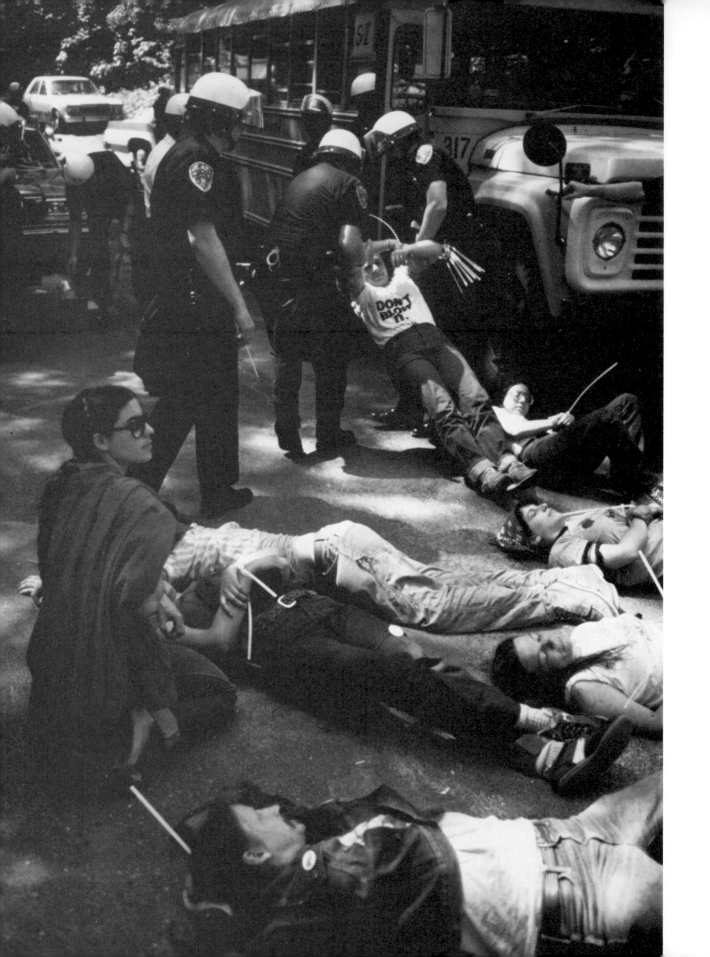

CHAPTER 4
CIVIL LIBERTIES: LIMITED GOVERNMENT AND THE RULE OF LAW

College students (opposite) at a peaceful demonstration against construction of the Shoreham nuclear power plant being removed from the highway leading to the site by state police; June 4, 1983. Right, Senator Jesse Helms (R–N.C.) empties a mailbag which contains some of the more than 500,000 petitions received by Congress in September 1982, supporting voluntary prayer in the public schools. With Helms are Representative Gerald Solomon (R–N.Y.) and Martha Rountree, president of Leadership Action, a group lobbying for a prayer amendment to the Constitution. *(Tannenbaum-Sygma; AP Laserphoto.)*

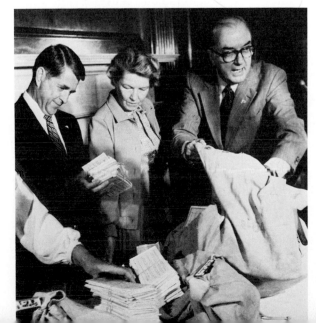

A**ll people are endowed, says the Declaration of Independence, with "certain inalienable rights," among them "Life, Liberty, and the Pursuit of Happiness." The Constitution and the Bill of Rights establish two fundamental principles: (1) that the government must not infringe on the liberties of the people and (2) that the government has an affirmative duty to secure these liberties.

This chapter will define and describe our civil liberties, especially the First Amendment freedoms of religion and conscience, speech and expression, and petition and assembly and the Fifth Amendment guarantees of due process of law. We will look at some struggles between different groups over the role of government in regulating individual behavior, and we will see how judges decide cases involving civil liberties claims.

WHAT ARE CIVIL LIBERTIES?

Civil liberties are those freedoms which allow people to think and speak freely and participate fully in politics without fear of repression. The most important of these liberties are guaranteed by the First Amendment to the Constitution:

> Congress shall make no law respecting an establishment of religion, or prohibiting the free exercise thereof; or abridging the freedom of speech, or of the press; or the right of the people peaceably to assemble, and to petition the Government for a redress of grievances.

Civil liberties also include protections against arbitrary government action. No one may be deprived of life, liberty, or property without due process of law, a protection guaranteed by the Fifth and Fourteenth Amendments.

The establishment clause

The prohibition against an established (that is, state) religion—the ***establishment clause***—means that government officials are subject to no religious law and are not accountable to religious authorities. Laws and policies are based on the will of the majority, expressed by representative institutions, not on the will of a priesthood expounding divine intent. It is neither the right nor the duty of the government to state by law or regulation what the clergy cannot obtain from the people through their consent. "Congress shall never meddle with religion," John Adams predicted, "other than to say their own prayers and to give thanks once a year." Combined with Article VI—"No religious Test shall ever be required as a Qualification to any Office or public Trust under the United States"—the First Amendment creates a wall of separation between church and state. Whatever many Americans think of themselves culturally and historically, *constitutionally* we are not, in spite of the claims of the fundamentalists, a "Christian nation," but a secular one.

But this separation is not absolute. The government puts "In God We Trust" on its currency. Chaplains, paid for by the government, serve the armed forces and Congress, and members of the clergy participate in presidential inaugurations. The courts have upheld the rights of cities to pay for holiday decorations such as a municipal crèche, arguing that the intent is commercial (to bring shoppers to the downtown area during the Christmas season) and that such decorations include cultural and not solely religious symbols. (Thus in New York City the Catholic League for Religious and Civil Rights puts up depictions of the nativity scene in public parks, and the orthodox Jewish Lubavitch Youth Organization displays a menorah on Fifth Avenue.) The White House puts a nativity scene in its Christmas pageant.

The government provides funds to churches and religious schools for textbooks, lunches, teacher training, student testing, and remedial classes. Some states allow taxpayers whose children attend private schools—some of which are religious—to deduct the cost of tuition, textbooks, and transportation. The

Right: There has never been a rigid separation of church and state. National and local politicians greet Archbishop John J. O'Connor on the steps of Saint Patrick's cathedral in New York City during a Columbus Day parade up Fifth Avenue. Ethnic celebrations always bring church and political leaders to the same reviewing stands and podiums. (*AP Laserphoto.*)

Below, left: Recent Supreme Court decisions have made it constitutionally permissible for cities and towns to permit religious symbols—such as the nativity scene at Christmas—on public property. Each December, an Orthodox Jewish organization erects a Hanukkah menorah in Grand Army Plaza in New York. (*Fred R. Conrand: New York Times.*)

By Meyer for San Francisco Chronicle; New York Times Special Features.

A NATION OF WORSHIPERS?

- Forty percent of the public attend a church or synagogue in a typical week.
- Fifty-one percent of Catholics attend mass, compared with thirty-nine percent of Protestants and twenty-two percent of Jews who attend services.

Source: Gallup poll, December 1984.

---

courts, however, insist that such funding must have a completely secular purpose and not promote any particular religion and that it must not involve the government in "excessive entanglements" in religious affairs.[1] But the standard is not rigid. "Not every law that confers an 'indirect,' 'remote,' or 'incidental' benefit upon religious institutions," Justice Lewis Powell decided, "is, for that reason alone, constitutionally invalid."[2]

For many people public morality, as well as private conscience, has its underpinnings in religious belief. The clergy has always played a significant role in public affairs. The abolition of slavery and the underground railroad before the Civil War; the temperance movement, which led to Prohibition; the social gospel movement, which underlay much of the progressive movement's efforts to regulate wages and working conditions in the early 1900s; the civil rights movement of the 1960s; the new right campaigns against abortion and pornography in the 1970s; and the nuclear freeze movement of the 1980s—these were spurred in large measure by members of the clergy and their congregations. While no particular religion has an established place in our government or a particular claim to government support, the combined weight of all religions has a profound influence on our notion of public morality—and on our laws, bureaucratic regulations, and court decisions. It is *religiosity* rather than any particular religion that animates our politicians.

Freedom of religion

The government may not suppress religious freedom or freedom of conscience. "From the beginning," Walter Mondale reminded members of an audience who were quizzing him about religious issues during his 1984 campaign for the presidency, "we told government and the politicians keep your nose out of my own private religion and let me practice my faith."[3] This principle has prevented the violent religious strife that wracked England, France, and Germany in the century before our nation was formed. We have escaped the violence between Protestants and Catholics that still afflicts Ireland, the persecution and mass murder of Jews that stained Germany, and the sectarian conflict that destroyed Lebanon. "I protect my right to be a Catholic by preserving your right to be a Jew, or a Protestant, or a nonbeliever, or anything else you choose," said Mario Cuomo, the governor of New York.[4]

Disputes over the "true word of God" do not dominate our political agenda, though coalitions of religious groups, representing various faiths, often line up against one another on such highly charged issues as abortion, prayer in schools, and aid to parochial schools. These conflicts have not polarized American society along religious lines. Conflicts cross religious boundaries, with some Protestants, Catholics, and Jews in coalition against others.

Regulating religion. Government regulation sometimes infringes on religious beliefs and practices. Mormons may not legally practice polygamy. Old

Order Amish must pay social security taxes. Christian Scientists must obey court orders to hospitalize their sick children. Orthodox Jews in the military must remove their yarmulkes (hats). The Reverend Sun Myung Moon, head of the Unification Church, must pay his taxes as everyone else does or go to jail (which he did). As Chief Justice Warren Burger argued, "The State may justify a limitation on religious liberty by showing that it is essential to accomplish an overriding governmental interest."[5] Thus state laws license church schools, certify their teachers, and require them to follow the state curriculum. All religions must obey the civil and criminal laws. The First Amendment cannot, according to the Supreme Court, "be invoked as protection for the punishment of acts inimical to the peace, good order, and morals of society."[6]

Prayer in schools. In 1962 and 1963 the Supreme Court held that starting the school day with prayer was unconstitutional. The Court banned both prayer and Bible reading as violations of the establishment clause. Polls have shown that an overwhelming majority, about two-thirds of the public, favor voluntary prayer in schools: this includes majorities of liberals and conservatives, Democrats and Republicans, and people in the north, south, and west. President Reagan, recognizing a good political issue, announced during a "national day of prayer" in 1982 that he would introduce a constitutional amendment to permit voluntary prayer in schools. Several versions have been introduced; some would have school officials create a nonsectarian prayer, others would allow students to say any prayer they wished on a voluntary basis, and still others would simply prevent school officials from interfering with the right of students to pray in schools.

In some school districts the Supreme Court's decision has been defied. Some allow spoken prayer, and others permit silent prayer or meditation. The West Virginia state constitution provides for one minute of "contemplation, meditation or prayer." Students, according to state guidelines, may kneel, stand, sit, "or engage in other acts symbolic of their faith," provided they do so silently and without moving around the room. Teachers may not tell students how to pray or meditate "or to whom prayer should be directed," nor may they

Students at the Wilson school in Sayerville, New Jersey, stand for a moment of silence at the beginning of the school day, following provisions of a law enacted by their state legislature. (*James Pozerik: Picture Group.*)

suggest the content of the meditation or prayer. In some school districts another approach is to encourage voluntary prayer groups to form in the classroom just before the start of the "official" school day. Another idea is to have students form a club, such as Students for Voluntary Prayer, and allow the club to use classrooms for a period of voluntary prayer or Bible discussion.

Some parents believe that the issue involves simply the right of their children to pray wherever they wish to: an issue of religious freedom. Other parents believe that their children might be coerced into saying the prayers of the majority or else suffer religious discrimination by their classmates. Some members of the clergy believe that the state should foster a religious attitude in schools by permitting prayer. Others see a great danger if school officials write nonsectarian prayers.

Thus far the proposed constitutional amendments have been defeated in Congress. But in 1984 Congress passed an "equal access" amendment to a federal aid-to-education bill which sanctioned the use of schools for student-initiated religious, political, or philosophical meetings during noninstructional periods. The law cuts off federal aid to schools which do not allow such activities or which allow students to meet for other extracurricular activities but not for religious prayer and discussion. While the Supreme Court has not (as of 1985) ruled on such after-school activities, several federal courts of appeals have barred them in high schools, viewing them as involving a "sponsorship" of religion by the government.

Some religious groups, adamantly opposed to a constitutional amendment permitting or requiring prayer in schools, are just as strongly in favor of permitting extracurricular student-initiated religious activities outside the classroom and after the instructional day.

Freedom of expression

The initial provisions of the First Amendment guarantee freedom of conscience and belief, and the remainder guarantee the freedom to communicate one's beliefs—freedoms without which no democratic society can function. They are essential for free elections. They guarantee a free press and permit interest groups to function independently rather than as quasi-official instruments of the authorities (like trade unions in Poland or the Soviet Union). They guarantee that people can meet, speak their minds, and take political action without being subjected to surveillance, harassment, intimidation, or violence.

The market of ideas. We believe that freedom of expression in a democratic society involves the clash of ideas. "The best test of truth," Justice Oliver Wendell Holmes observed, "is the power of the thought to get itself accepted in the competition of the market."[7] No barriers to this competition can be permitted to obstruct the free workings of the political marketplace. No idea, in and of itself, can be too obnoxious or dangerous to express. We must, said Holmes, grant "freedom for the thoughts we hate."

The democratic creed. A democracy assumes that people can discover the truth by themselves. There is no need for the state to "protect" its citizens by censoring ideas, even if they might be nonsensical. The truth emerges through discussion and debate. Justice Louis Brandeis observed that the framers of the Constitution believed that

An American Nazi standing next to his party's symbol, the swastika. In the United States this symbolic expression of free speech is protected by the First Amendment. In West Germany, Italy, and the Soviet Union, the display of a swastika is a criminal act. (*Jim Anderson: Woodfin Camp.*)

. . . freedom to think as you will and speak as you think are means indispensable to the discovery and spread of political truth; that without free speech and assembly, discussion would be futile; that with them, discussion affords ordinarily adequate protection against the dissemination of noxious doctrine; that the greatest menace to freedom is an inert people; that public discussion is a political duty; and that this should be a fundamental principle of the American government. . . .[8]

Advantages of free expression. Leaders in some developing nations insist that the people are not ready for freedom of expression or that it is a luxury which must wait until economic development has reached higher levels. But societies which guarantee these liberties also provide the best conditions for development. The media can report fully on the activities of government; interest groups can press their demands; and the people can make their grievances known. Incompetent officials are less likely to flourish in such a climate. As Thomas Emerson of Yale Law School argues: "Freedom of expression, far from causing upheaval, is more properly viewed as a leavening process, facilitating necessary social and political change and keeping a society from stultification and decay."[9]

Freedom of expression. The government may not interfere with our thoughts, our conscience, or our personal lives without demonstrating a convincing necessity to the courts. "No official, high or petty, can prescribe what shall be orthodox in politics, nationalism, religion, or other matters of opinion, or force citizens to confess by word or act their faith therein," says Justice Robert Jackson.[10] Freedom of expression, guaranteed by the First Amendment, implies the right *not* to have to say what one *does not* believe. Those who do not wish to recite the pledge of allegiance or salute the flag need not do so.

Symbolic speech. The courts protect *symbolic speech:* actions intended to communicate ideas. These include gesturing or miming, wearing buttons or armbands, holding placards, handing out leaflets, and even burning the American flag or draft registration cards. In a case involving junior high school students in Iowa who wore armbands to protest the Vietnamese war, the Supreme Court held that the students had engaged in symbolic speech, which could not be forbidden by school authorities.[11] When a California college student entered a state courthouse with the words "F____k the draft" (completely spelled out) emblazoned on his jacket, a state judge held him in contempt of court, but the Supreme Court overruled this decision, for, as Justice John Harlan wrote, "While the particular four-letter word being litigated here is perhaps more distasteful than most others of its genre, it is nevertheless often true that one man's vulgarity is another's lyric."[12]

Judicial protection of obscene language or symbolic speech has its limits. If a person addresses "fighting words" to a police officer, the courts will let the resulting arrest stand, and they also uphold convictions for incitement to riot, disturbing the peace, and disorderly conduct based on loud and abusive language. And the courts have little patience with the arguments concerning freedom of speech put forth by proprietors of "head shops" that sell drug paraphernalia such as pipes, clips, and cigarette papers.[13]

Access to the marketplace of ideas

The Constitution and laws guarantee that individuals and groups can present their ideas to the public.

Mails. The government may not censor the mails, and propaganda and pornography are protected along with everything else.[14] But the use of the mails to commit an illegal action (such as securities, bank, or consumer fraud) or to conspire to act illegally (espionage or terrorism) is not free speech and is punishable by the government.

Malls. Groups may assemble and solicit passersby and give them material. But there is no constitutional right to do so on private property, including malls and shopping centers. On the other hand, property owners have no constitutional right to prohibit the actions of such groups. Whether groups can solicit and how they may do so are matters subject to state and city regulations.[15]

Meetings. People may gather in streets and in parks and other public places. But the police may lawfully order unruly crowds to disperse to keep the peace, and they may detain a speaker who incites a crowd to violence.[16] The courts insist that where the state can protect a speaker from a hostile crowd, it must do so, and they often strike down laws giving the police authority to disperse crowds if the laws are too broadly drawn. The government can make reasonable regulations as to when, where, and how speeches are made, but it may not regulate or discriminate against people because of the content of their speeches or ideas.[17]

Media. People have no constitutional right to use the radio or television airwaves or cables or satellite transmission facilities. Since the transmission bands are limited, access is granted by the Federal Communications Commission (FCC), an independent regulatory agency, when it licenses broadcasters and by local authorities who award cable franchises. The FCC's fairness doctrine requires broadcasters to present all significant viewpoints on public issues and a wide variety of spokespersons, but who appears on the air is up to the broadcasters. The FCC has ruled, and the courts have upheld, the principle that no one has a constitutional right to buy airtime, even for political commercials during a campaign.[18]

Freedom of the press

The First Amendment states that Congress shall make no law abridging free-

---

FREEDOM OF ASSOCIATION: THE AMERICAN COMMUNIST PARTY

Should a democratic society permit the operation of political parties which vow to overthrow the government by violent means? Or should it outlaw movements or parties which themselves are nondemocratic? The courts have not formulated consistent answers to these questions.

In 1940 Congress passed the Smith Act, which made it unlawful for anyone knowingly or willingly to "advocate, abet, advise, or teach the duty, necessity, desirability, or propriety of overthrowing or destroying any government in the United States by force or violence" and which made an attempt to commit or conspire to commit such acts a federal crime. The Department of Justice brought indictments against leaders of the American Communist Party. In *Dennis v. U.S.*, 341 U.S. 494 (1951), the Supreme Court affirmed convictions of members of the party. It agreed with the prosecution that the group advocated violent overthrow of the government, and it did not consider the probabilities of their success.

Later the Supreme Court took a different tack. In *Yates v. U.S.*, 354 U.S. 298 (1957), the Court overturned convictions of several party leaders in California. It distinguished between "advocacy" and "action," freeing these leaders because the government had not proved that any actions were about to take place. The Court read *Dennis* to mean that such actions as indoctrination for action or exhortation to immediate action must have taken place to find a conspiracy under the Smith Act. Merely to show that people had advocated, as an abstract proposition, the overthrow of the government (even if by violent action) was not enough for a conviction.

In *Noto v. U.S.*, 367 U.S. 290 (1961), the Supreme Court held that membership in the Communist Party was not in itself evidence of a conspiracy to overthrow the government. In *Scales v. U.S.*, 367 U.S. 203 (1961), the Court interpreted the Internal Security Act of 1950 as requiring not only membership in the party but also "active and purposeful membership, purposive that is as to the organization's criminal ends," in order to convict under the Smith Act. The Court did require the party and other "communist action or front" groups to register with the Department of Justice.

The Communist Party cannot be outlawed under the provisions of the Smith Act, and membership in the party does not in itself constitute evidence of subversive activity. The party need not comply with election laws requiring political parties to disclose the names of campaign contributors because a federal appeals court ruled in 1982 that such disclosure requirements for an "unpopular minority party" might have a chilling effect on potential contributors. The party is constitutionally protected in the rights of association, speech, and privacy, but it remains subject to FBI surveillance and infiltration. To the extent that it acts within the democratic rules of the game, it is given an opportunity to influence electoral politics. But if it steps out of line and conspires to overthrow the government, its members can be prosecuted.

---

dom of the press. People may write and publish what they choose. But these freedoms are not absolute.

Sedition. An early test of the First Amendment occurred during the undeclared naval war with France in 1798. Congress, controlled by the Federalists, passed a ***sedition*** law, which made it illegal to publish "fake, scandalous and malicious writing" that would "bring the government into disrepute" or would "incite against them the hatred of the good people of the United States." The law was directed at the Anti-Federalist faction, and it prompted the state legislatures in Kentucky and Virginia to pass resolutions of nullification, declaring these laws unconstitutional and unenforceable. Public opinion turned against the law, just as it turned against the war, and in 1800, when their opponents won the elections, the Federalists got their comeuppance.

Libel.   Newspaper owners have the freedom to publish what they choose, but they are subject to *libel* suits by people who claim that they have been damaged by untruths. *Time* magazine, for example, was sued by the Israeli general Ariel Sharon after it claimed in a report that he had ordered the massacre of Palestinians in Beirut. CBS was sued by General William Westmoreland for a *Sixty Minutes* documentary which claimed that he falsely inflated "body counts" of enemy soldiers during the Vietnamese war. Neither general won damages from the courts. Public figures are given less protection by the courts on the assumption that by entering the public arena, they have exposed themselves voluntarily to accounts that may be inaccurate. The plaintiff must prove not only that the statements were incorrect, but that they showed malice and a reckless disregard for the truth.[19] Nevertheless, some civil libertarians believe that expensive libel suits can serve as a deterrent to a free press, and they urge Congress to pass legislation preventing public officials from suing for damages.

Temporary injunctions; restraining orders.   The federal courts do not consider freedom of the press to be absolute. They balance this freedom against compelling national interests. In 1971 *The New York Times* published excerpts from a classified multivolume history of the Vietnamese war prepared by Pentagon historians. The history had been copied (without the permission of the government) by Dr. Daniel Ellsberg, a civilian analyst who had worked on them, and given to the *Times*. After publication of the first article, the government went into federal court and obtained an injunction against further publication, the first time in American history that a prepublication injunction had been imposed by a court. The *Times* argued that the government's request for a permanent injunction violated the First Amendment. The government argued that the papers had been stolen, that they involved classified documents and information, and that national security was involved. The Supreme Court ruled in favor of the *Times*, allowing it to print other articles from the Pentagon papers. Six justices held that the government had not shown any compelling justification for prior restraint by the courts.[20]

In 1979 *The Progressive* magazine was ready to print an article entitled "The H-Bomb Secret: How We Got It, Why We're Telling It," which showed how anyone could build a hydrogen bomb using nonclassified sources. The purpose of the article was to demonstrate just how lax government secrecy is and how such secrecy cannot prevent the proliferation of nuclear weapons. The government obtained a temporary order preventing publication from a federal judge alleging that publication would "result in grave, direct, immediate and irreparable harm to the security of the United States and its people." The government based its argument on a loophole which the Supreme Court left in the Pentagon papers case: courts could prevent publication if the government showed "immediate and irreparable damage." The government also claimed that the Atomic Energy Act of 1954 had made it a crime to "communicate, transmit or disclose" certain "restricted data" about the design or manufacture of nuclear weapons. But the statute did not include the word *publish*, leaving it unclear whether it covered this situation. While *The Progressive* argued its case before the court of appeals, several newspapers printed a letter

Myron Farber, a reporter for the *New York Times*, in a Bergen County, New Jersey, jail after being sentenced for contempt of court for failing to provide evidence in a state criminal case on which he had reported. Farber unsuccessfully claimed journalistic privilege to keep his sources confidential. (Eventually he was released by the judge.) (*Wide World.*)

which disclosed most of the "restricted data" that would have appeared in the article. Having failed to prevent publication of the information, the government moved to have the courts dismiss the case. The article appeared in the magazine a few months later.

Enforcing contractual agreements.   Frank Snepp, a former CIA agent, published a book entitled *Decent Interval*, which recounts the agency's activities in Saigon just before the communists took over in 1975. While an employee of the CIA, Snepp had signed an agreement with the agency which permitted it to review and censor, before publication, any manuscript dealing with its activities. Snepp did not submit his book to the CIA, as required by the terms of the agreement, arguing that he did not have to because he had not used any secret information. The CIA sued in federal court to enforce its agreement with Snepp. It asked the court to uphold the agreement and require Snepp to submit future writings, and it sued for damages because the agreement had been violated. The Supreme Court affirmed lower court decisions that required Snepp to turn over all his royalties ($170,000 at the time of the decision) to the government, and it allowed the CIA prepublication clearance and censorship of all his future work.[21]

Reporters and sources.   The courts guarantee everyone a fair trial. Sometimes the right of defendants to cross-examine witnesses and obtain all evidence relevant to their guilt or innocence conflicts with claims made by doctors, lawyers, members of the clergy, and reporters that what people tell them in connection with their professional duties must remain confidential and cannot be revealed, even in a court of law. Journalists argue that they must protect their sources and that they cannot obtain confidential information unless they assure their sources anonymity. But the Supreme Court in 1972 ruled that reporters do not have any right to withhold information about a crime from a grand jury.[22]

Some journalists go to jail for contempt rather than comply with court orders (they are usually let out after sixty days or so). Others comply under protest. Journalists want Congress and the states to pass "shield laws" that would allow them to protect their sources—even people who have committed crimes. Here the balance of competing claims is excruciatingly difficult. What happens if a reporter finds out a fact that has a bearing on the guilt or innocence of someone accused of a serious crime? Which is more important: the right of the accused to everyone's testimony or the right of a reporter trying to protect sources?

Due process of law

The Fifth Amendment (applicable to national officials) and the Fourteenth Amendment (applicable to state officials) require the government to act with ***due process of law*** in depriving people of their lives, liberties, or property. ***Substantive due process*** focuses on the reasonableness of government actions and requires that they be least burdensome to other constitutional rights and liberties. ***Procedural due process*** examines the methods used by officials and requires that these conform to the Constitution and laws and be conducted with fundamental fairness. Due process guarantees are closely related to First Amendment freedoms. Without them, anyone who opposed government policies could be arrested and imprisoned after rigged trials. People would be afraid to exercise their freedoms of speech and association.

A New York City police officer on patrol in Times Square, Manhattan. (*Bernard Pierre Wolff: Magnum.*)

Police patrol. Traditionally the police have emphasized crime control in patrolling neighborhoods: an aggressive search for information that might lead to arrests. People may be stopped and frisked on general suspicion or questioned at length about their presence in a neighborhood (especially if they seem out of place), and those who are considered potential troublemakers may be told to move on. The police control public spaces, threatening to arrest people for vagrancy, loitering, disorderly conduct, failure to move on, and failure to obey a lawful order. They stop people in high-crime areas and make systematic searches or vehicle checks. They search people and cars without warrants, looking for weapons, criminal tools, or stolen property.

What seem to the police to be reasonable efforts at deterrence may be considered harassment by minorities, teenagers, ex-convicts, and others who think that they are being unfairly singled out. Many law-abiding people resent being stopped for no reason at all and asked to give an account of themselves and their presence in a neighborhood. (One Yale Law School professor who was stopped by the New Haven police one evening while jogging even went so far as to write an article for a law review defending his right to refuse to answer such inquiries!)

Civil libertarians try to get the police to institute a due process approach to patrol: the police could not bother anyone unless they had a *reasonable suspicion* that a crime had been, was being, or was about to be committed. People could not be questioned without being advised of their right to remain silent or obtain legal assistance. They could be questioned only if the police suspected them of having committed or witnessed a crime. Anyone who was being investigated for a crime would have to be taken to a station house for questioning and advised of the right to have a lawyer present.[23] Arrests could take place only with *probable cause:* when the facts and circumstances were such that a reasonable person would be justified in believing that a crime had been committed and that the person arrested had committed it. People would not have to identify themselves or account for their presence unless they were being investigated for a crime. They would not have to move on command from the police, and arrests for loitering would not be permitted except where criminal violations were involved. Warrants would be required to search cars unless the search was incidental to an arrest for a crime in progress. Even then, the trunk and the glove compartment could be searched only after a warrant was obtained.

In the past two decades the crime control approach has been challenged in federal and state courts, and many due process elements have been introduced into police practices. Today there is conflict between judges who would extend due process protections even further and those who would cut back on them.

The due process approach is politically unpopular. The aggressive patrol approach and the function of the police in maintaining control of public spaces have the support of the majority, even in many poor neighborhoods that are overrun with drunks, pimps and prostitutes, drug pushers, petty criminals, and "street people." A majority of the public believe that the police have the right to question people and make them account for themselves.[24]

With community support the police sometime evade the decisions of the federal courts. Since it is impossible for a judge to be present in every patrol car, the courts cannot supervise the police and must rely on good-faith implementation. Unconstitutional searches and seizures and questioning still occur.[25] Civil liberties and civil rights groups sometimes sue police departments, alleging brutality or abuse of suspects such as the use of "stun guns" to extract confessions. Civil damages are occasionally awarded. Where police brutality is directed against minorities, the Justice Department has occasionally won decisions on the basis of civil rights statutes (which provide for prison sentences as well as fines).

Criminal procedure. The Federal courts have extended due process guarantees to defendants in state criminal trials. These include the following rights: to be brought before a judicial officer for arraignment within a reasonable time after arrest; to have counsel present after arrest and during police interrogation, at police lineups, and at court-ordered psychiatric examinations; to be furnished with counsel if the defendant cannot afford to pay for it; to present evidence, question friendly witnesses, and cross-examine witnesses for the prosecution; to be tried by a jury of at least six persons who have been selected in a racially nondiscriminatory way; to have a speedy trial; to be furnished a written transcript of the trial for appeals; and to be free of double jeopardy.

In recent years the Supreme Court has cut back on its supervision of the practices of state courts. After being convicted in such courts, prisoners often seek *collateral review* of the procedures by federal courts and a new trial if their constitutional rights have been violated. In 1976 the Supreme Court ruled that state prisoners could not sue in federal courts if they had been given the opportunity to challenge their violation of rights in state courts and had lost.[26] In a 1982 decision, the Court indicated that it would review state cases only if there might be a "miscarriage of justice," not merely technical violations of constitutionally mandated state criminal procedures.[27]

CASE STUDY: THE EXCLUSIONARY RULE. Recent Supreme Court decisions have focused attention on the *exclusionary rule:* the judicial practice of excluding from trials evidence which has been obtained in an unconstitutional or illegal manner; the purpose is to give an incentive to the police and to prosecutors to carry out their functions lawfully. No other rule of law is as controversial. The victims of a crime, the police, prosecutors, and the public are all outraged when courts set aside convictions on the grounds that the evidence was illegally obtained. It seems like a mere technicality and a gross violation of justice. "It just doesn't make sense that just because a police officer made a technical error for the accused to go free [sic]," said Ed Meese, then a White House aide and later attorney general in the Reagan administration.[28] Although a new trial may be ordered, it is often difficult to convict without the "tainted" evidence or to get witnesses to testify a second time. But in spite of complaints by the police, the exclusionary rule has not hampered most prosecutions. In slightly more than 1 percent of federal prosecutions evidence is excluded, and in half of these cases the defendants are convicted anyway.

The courts need the rule to uphold judicial power: it is a procedural instrument which regulates access to the courts, and it is a way to compel the police and prosecutors to comply with judicial supervision. It is the only practical sanction that the courts can impose on law enforcement personnel who act illegally. Other remedies, such as private lawsuits for violation of a defendant's rights, are ineffective: juries are reluctant to award damages against the police or prosecutors. In any event, state or local governments could indemnify these officials and protect them against suits.

As the crime rate soared, law enforcement officials pressed their attack against the exclusionary rule. The courts have backed away from a broad application (1) by limiting its application to give the police and prosecutors more latitude in introducing illegally obtained evidence if the violation was inadvertent and the search was conducted "in good faith" by police officers who believed that their actions were legal (that their search warrant was not defective); (2) by allowing evidence if it would have been inevitably obtained in the course of the arrest, even if it was obtained illegally or with a defective warrant; (3) by refusing to overturn convictions when the evidence was not central to the issue of guilt or innocence; and (4) by limiting the collateral review of the federal courts and relying on state courts instead. While the exclusionary rule remains in reserve for serious abused of due process rights, it has become less of an inhibition to the police and prosecutors, reflecting the hardening of public attitudes toward crime control.

CIVIL LIBERTIES: THE POLITICAL CONTEXT

Most Americans strongly support the freedoms of religion, conscience, and expression and the due process guarantees of the Constitution. But one person's pursuit of happiness may be an affront to someone else. The due process rights of a defendant may seem excessive to victims of crime. Free speech may shade into political activity, such as street demonstrations, which must be regulated. Often civil liberties conflicts involve not the good guys against the bad guys, but competing claims involving important social values.

Group conflicts

Most civil liberties conflicts involve interest groups, which try to educate the public, lobby Congress and state legislatures to pass laws, and negotiate with executive officials about government actions. They try to elect candidates who favor their cause, and they fund research institutes, lobbying offices in Washington and state capitals, and litigating units to try to score judicial victories.

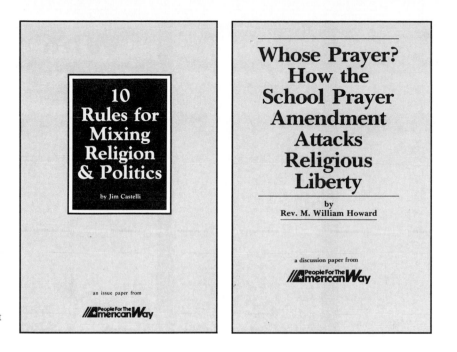

Pamphlets published by People for the American Way, a civil liberties group which strongly opposes any prayer in public schools. Two members of its board of directors are Protestant ministers.

The litigating units are sometimes referred to as *private attorneys general* because they act on behalf of individuals who believe that they have been wronged by a state action, much as a state attorney general brings cases on behalf of persons who have been wronged by criminals.

The oldest and most important group is the American Civil Liberties Union (ACLU), founded in the 1920s. It has a national staff of more than 400 located in New York City, and it has fifty state chapters with more than 275,000 members and 5000 volunteer attorneys; it handles over 7000 cases annually. The ACLU litigates on behalf of every conceivable group, including the poor, minorities, women, the handicapped, mental patients, and politically unpopular groups such as the American Nazi Party, defending freedom of expression for all.

Another important group is People for the American Way, organized by Norman Lear (the television producer responsible for such programs as *All in the Family*). It was formed in 1980 to educate the American public about its First Amendment freedoms. It sponsors and produces television specials, and it combats efforts at book censorship in schools and libraries, especially by right-wing political and religious organizations.

Many other groups are concerned about separation of church and state, abortion, prayer in schools, gun control, pornography, censorship, and other issues, and they litigate in cases involving their interests. Below we consider three examples of groups that are trying to define the permissible limits of government regulation.

Gun control and the National Rifle Association (NRA). The NRA has over 2 million members in more than 11,000 clubs. It sponsors programs aimed at the safety of hunters and the safe use of firearms. It lobbies states for laws making it easy to own handguns and rifles, and it opposes all efforts at gun control sponsored by the National Coalition to Ban Handguns and by police departments. According to the NRA, polls show that 80 percent of the public oppose bans on handguns, although Gallup polls in the early 1980s showed a narrower margin against handgun control, more like 54 against to 41 in favor—

The National Rifle Association runs an extensive public relations and education program, which includes the distribution of these and other pamphlets.

with those in favor of regulation getting more and more support—compared with polls in the 1970s, which showed that fewer than one-third favored gun control. The NRA claims that possession of a gun is a right guaranteed by the Second Amendment, which states that "a well regulated Militia, being necessary to the security of a free State, the right of the people to keep and bear arms, shall not be infringed." Gun control groups argue that the Second Amendment prevents only Congress, not the states, from regulating and prohibiting arms and that it protects only militias and does not grant individuals the right to bear arms.

These issues are far from settled. The federal courts have allowed the states to regulate weapons, and the Supreme Court has allowed Congress to ban sawed-off shotguns.[29] Some states and cities have passed strict gun control measures and have banned handguns altogether; in Massachusetts, for example, possession of a handgun means a mandatory year in jail. Meanwhile, the NRA litigates against these measures in court. It brings cases against the federal government's Bureau of Alcohol, Tobacco, and Firearms (BATF), which enforces bans on cheap handguns, claiming that BATF agents beat, abuse, and harass gun dealers and obtain evidence for prosecutions by violating due process guarantees. The NRA's Institute for Legislative Action lobbies states to head off new laws. In spite of polls showing public support for new measures, it manages a successful rearguard action.

Book banners. Many schools and libraries are pressured by community organizations to remove certain books from their shelves or not use them in courses. In the 1960s most such cases involved charges that the books were racist or sexist, but in the 1980s most of the action has come from religious and "profamily" groups on the political right, which claim that some books are unpatriotic, immoral, or antifamily. In this decade more than 250 book titles have been challenged in more than 400 public schools, while the American

Norma Gabler, a Texas homemaker, brings her battle against textbooks that depart from "traditional values" to the Texas Textbook Committee hearings in August 1982. Mrs. Gabler and her husband Mel have influenced school boards throughout the nation. (*AP Laserphoto.*)

THE BOOK BANNERS AND THEIR NONREADING LISTS

Book banners on the right include the Moral Majority, Mel and Norma Gabler's Educational Research Analysts (which distributes lists of books that should be removed from school library shelves), and Phyllis Schlafly's Eagle Forum. Other groups (liberal and left) protest against books on the grounds that they portray religious or racial groups unfairly.

Some of the titles banned by various schools and libraries around the nation include the following: *The American Heritage Dictionary*, John Steinbeck's *Grapes of Wrath*, Mario Puzo's *Godfather*, Ernest Hemingway's *Farewell to Arms*, F. Scott Fitzgerald's *Great Gatsby*, J. D. Salinger's *Catcher in the Rye*, and William Shakespeare's *Merchant of Venice*.

But the book-banning prize goes to the Mark Twain Middle School in Virginia, whose principal banned *Huckleberry Finn*, written by Mark Twain, on the grounds that it portrays blacks unfavorably—which isn't even true.

Book Banners are opposed by the National Coalition against Censorship, which includes the American Library Association's Office for Intellectual Freedom, the National Council of Teachers of English, the National Education Association, the Writers Guild of America, the Association of American Publishers (Freedom to Read Committee), and People for the American Way (Schools and Libraries Project and National Resource Center on Censorship).

Library Association reports more than 1000 complaints involving public libraries each year.[30]

Conflicts between book banners and anticensorship groups sometimes wind up in court. The Supreme Court decided *Pico v. Island Trees School District*, which involved a school board's 1976 decision to remove nine books from its library.[31] The board called the books "anti-American, anti-Christian, anti-Semitic, and just plain filthy." The ACLU represented five students who objected to the removal of books such as *Slaughterhouse Five*, by Kurt Vonnegut; *The Fixer*, by Bernard Malamud; and *Best Short Stories of Negro Writers*, edited by Langston Hughes. The Supreme Court ordered a federal district court to conduct a trial and consider the motives of the school board, ruling that the lower court could limit the discretion of the school board if it had intended to limit "access to ideas," although the Supreme Court indicated that it would uphold the school board if it was removing books merely because they were vulgar or lacked educational content. In 1983, the school board decided to allow the books back on the shelves.

"Censorship in a Free Society" poster. An advertisement from People for the American Way attacking library and textbook censorship.

CENSORSHIP IN A FREE SOCIETY.
IT'S A BAD MATCH.

Censorship is the greatest tragedy in American literature. It constricts the mind, teaches fear and leaves only ignorance and ashes.

Today, all over the country, books are being banned, burned and censored. Teachers, students, librarians, and book and magazine publishers are being harassed.

The attacks of these self-appointed censors are endorsed by our silence. The freedom to read is one of our most precious rights. Do something to protect it.

Contact:
People For The American Way, P.O. Box 18900, Washington, D.C. 20036 or call 202/822-9450.

People For The American Way

THE FBI AND MARTIN LUTHER KING

The national government and the state governments have the constitutional and legal power to thwart conspiracies which involve treason, bombing, kidnapping, assassination, or other criminal actions. But agencies responsible for counterespionage and counterintelligence may themselves commit excesses. What prevents the government from using these security organizations to stifle legitimate dissent? How do we prevent police agencies from creating a *police state*—a government in which the police influence partisan politics? The relationship between the Federal Bureau of Investigation (FBI) and Dr. Martin Luther King, Jr., the most influential black civil rights leader of the 1960s, demonstrates some of the problems involved in political surveillance.

The FBI became interested in Dr. King as a result of an operation known as COMINFIL (aimed at infiltration of communist organizations). An FBI informant in the Communist Party claimed that one of King's closest associates, Stanley Levison, had been a member of the party in the 1950s. The FBI put Levison under surveillance to see whether he was still a member and found nothing. But the FBI leaked documents to Congress showing Levison's influence on King and, by inference, the influence of communists on the civil rights movement. J. Edgar Hoover, the chief of the FBI, did this because he opposed civil rights bills being considered by Congress.

Because King believed that Levison had severed his connection with the communists, he kept him on as an adviser. Because Levison remained an adviser, Attorney General Robert Kennedy thought that King might be a communist dupe or sympathizer. Hoover convinced Kennedy to allow the FBI to place wiretaps in King's Atlanta and New York City offices and in his hotel rooms when he led civil rights demonstrations.

These FBI taps indicated that King and his associates often made negative (and sometimes graphically explicit) remarks about various government leaders. By invading King's privacy, the FBI obtained information which had no bearing on his possible connection with communists. It chose to use this information to damage King. The FBI provided President Lyndon Johnson with some of the tapes, and Johnson asked the agency to find out what King's plans for the presidential contest of 1964 were, particularly his attitude toward an attempt by blacks in Mississippi to unseat the regular state delegation to the Democratic convention and replace it with a black group. Johnson asked for the wiretapping to obtain political intelligence involving his party, not for reasons of national security.

Meanwhile, William Sullivan, director of the FBI Division Five (domestic intelligence), used the tapes for his own "dirty tricks." He was outraged that King might have been in the company of women other than his wife when he was on the road. He sent King's wife copies of some of the FBI tapes, together with a letter in which he threatened to release them publicly if King accepted the Nobel peace prize that he had just been awarded. And he hinted that King should consider committing suicide! The FBI even tried to get the local police to raid an apartment in Atlanta to catch King with a woman companion.

These tactics did not destroy King's marriage or dampen his resolve to continue his civil rights efforts. King accepted the Nobel prize, and the FBI did not release any tapes. But until his assassination in 1968, King remained under surveillance by the FBI, which developed political intelligence on his "poor people's campaign" and his activities in opposition to the Vietnamese war. The FBI never found any information confirming that King or his movement was controlled or influenced by communists or that the movement represented any threat to national security.

The FBI's conduct in this matter raises the most serious questions about the uses of surveillance. Hoover used tapes to try to sidetrack a congressional bill; his deputy tried to destroy King's marriage and lead him to suicide; and President Johnson used the surveillance to keep himself informed about domestic politics. Each of them violated King's civil rights as well as his own public trust.

Source: Based on David J. Garrow, *The FBI and Martin Luther King, Jr.*, Norton, New York, 1981 .

Political surveillance. How to keep the police effective in their mission against terrorism and subversion, and yet safe for a democracy, is a problem that defies easy solution. It may be necessary to place individuals or groups under surveillance, but once surveillance begins, it almost inevitably leads to abuses. Civil liberties groups propose that surveillance be strictly limited by Congress and the courts. They claim that it violates the First Amendment rights of free speech and association, the Fourth Amendment ban on unreasonable searches and seizures, the Fifth Amendment ban on self-incrimination, and the Ninth Amendment guarantee of the right to privacy. They say that surveillance constitutes a *general warrant*, which is banned by the Constitution—a fishing license for investigators who hope that "something will turn up—rather than a specific warrant that says exactly what crime is being investigated and what evidence is being searched for.

Civil libertarians would restrict surveillance to circumstances in which there is probable cause to believe that someone is planning or engaging in serious illegal acts, for which ordinary after-the-fact criminal prosecution would be insufficient to protect the public interest. The police would have to obtain a judicial warrant, and the courts would supervise the operation by granting warrants only for a limited time and for specific criminal investigations.

The courts have decided many surveillance cases against the FBI and against the state and local police. *U.S. v. U.S. District Court* held that domestic organizations cannot be put under surveillance without a warrant if criminal prosecution is to be sustained by the courts. The case also decided that in national security investigations of organizations involving foreign agents or funding, warrants are not required to sustain a later prosecution.[32]

An important consideration for the courts is the ***chilling effect*** of government surveillance: are people inhibited from joining a group and speaking their minds if they know that the organization is likely to be watched by the

The Reverend Martin Luther King and his wife, Coretta Scott King, leading a voting rights demonstration in Selma Alabama in 1965. Marches like these were directly responsible for passage of the Voting Rights Act of 1965. (*Bruce Davidson: Magnum Photos, Inc.*)

police? The leading case is *Dombroski v. Pfister,* in which Louisiana's law dealing with subversive activities was found to be unconstitutional because it might have a chilling effect on freedom of association.[33] Later the Court sought to strike a balance, indicating that the good or bad faith of the government would determine the constitutionality of surveillance.

Public opinion and civil liberties

Through the 1920s a restrictive view of civil liberties, rather than an expansive view, commanded public support. Severe restrictions on political expression were upheld, especially against unorthodox fringe groups. Prosecutors in criminal cases were heavily advantaged over defendants. But since 1937 the Supreme Court and the lower federal courts have turned their attention to civil liberties issues, especially those dealing with claims against state governments. Their decisions upholding the rights of defendants in criminal cases and of unpopular political groups have run ahead of public opinion, leaving the courts vulnerable to political counterattack. Yet as the pace of such attacks increased in the 1980s, public opinion surveys demonstrated greater support than in earlier decades for civil liberties claims, possibly indicating that the Court had successfully educated the public.

Tolerance for unpopular groups has increased. As Figure 4-1 shows, support for the rights of atheists and communists to speak and teach has increased. Surveys have shown that 71 percent of the public in the 1980s were proudest of the "freedom and liberty" enjoyed in the United States. They believed that they "fully and completely" enjoyed freedom of religion (97 percent), the freedom to travel anywhere (95 percent), a free press (90 percent), the freedom to vote for a candidate of their choice (84 percent), the freedom to lead their lives as they saw fit (78 percent), and privacy in their personal lives (63 percent).

Support for civil liberties claims is weakest under the following circumstances: when the group itself is controversial, such as Nazis, the Ku Klux Klan, or communists; when the action to be protected offends most of the community, such as flag burning, homosexual activity, or the sale of pornography; and when the action to be prohibited is strongly supported by the community, such as prayer in schools.

A Ku Klux Klan rally held in Danbury, Connecticut, in August 1982. Even hate groups that espouse racial or religious discrimination are protected by the First Amendment freedoms of speech and assembly. (*Steve Silk: Picture Group.*)

Figure 4-1. Civil liberties for unpopular groups. Between 1954 and 1977 support (blue) for the civil liberties of unpopular groups increased sharply. (Source: *Public Opinion*, December-January, 1980, using data from National Opinion Research Center.)

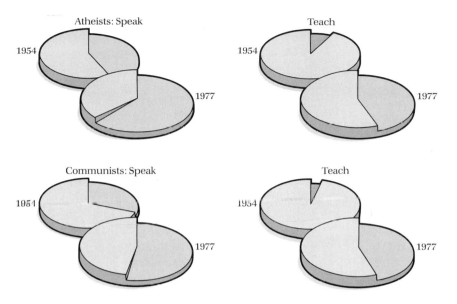

The problem for the courts

It is precisely when the majority wants to suppress the liberties of an unpopular group that the courts become vulnerable. People may agree with the local official, faced with an invasion of cultists, who remarked: "When the Founding Fathers gave us religious freedom, they didn't have these people in mind." But the courts cannot permit an abridgment of freedom based on the popularity of the group involved. As Justice Frankfurter says, "The safeguards of liberty have been forged in controversies involving not very nice people."[34]

The validity of a judicial decision never rests on its popularity with the public. In civil liberties cases the courts are required to act as instruments of constitutional government rather than of democratic rule. Judges are granted life tenure so that they will have the backbone to stand up to community pressure. As Justice Robert Jackson points out, "One's right to life, liberty and property, to free speech, a free press, freedom of worship and assembly, and other fundamental rights, may not be submitted to vote; they depend on the outcome of no election."[35]

Public disapproval of court decisions may even be taken as evidence that the courts are doing their job. Yet such decisions may weaken the authority of the courts with the majority and ultimately weaken the legitimacy of judges cho-

© *Jules Feiffer; by permission of The Village Voice.*

sen for life (and not even elected to federal courts), leading to charges of "government by the judiciary."

The courts balance competing claims, and sometimes they extend and sometimes retreat from civil libertarian positions. In the late 1930s they extended liberties, but in the late 1950s, faced with congressional opposition to several decisions involving members of the Communist Party, the courts began to rule in favor of the government on some free-speech regulations. In the 1960s the rights of criminal defendants were extended, but by the late 1970s a Supreme Court with a majority of the justices committed to "law and order" had begun to cut back on some of these rights, a situation which continued in the 1980s, as the Justice Department argued that some civil liberties decisions were unwise intrusions on the powers of the legislative and executive branches.

In the 1980s right-wing groups—spearheaded by the Moral Majority, Citizens for the Republic, the Committee for the Survival of a Free Congress, the National Conservative PAC, and the Congressional Club—have used the media to defeat members of Congress who do not agree with their positions on social issues. After the 1980 elections, when seven liberal senators were replaced by conservatives as a result of such media campaigns, the civil liberties groups counterattacked. People for the American Way presented a two-hour television special, *I Love Liberty*, broadcast in 1982, with former president Ford, Walter Cronkite, and Lady Bird Johnson as hosts and with such media stars as Jane Fonda, Burt Lancaster, Mary Tyler Moore, and Christopher Reeves. The fundamentalists and the civil libertarians had taken their disagreements from the nation's courtrooms and put them into the nation's living rooms.

CIVIL LIBERTIES CASES: HOW FEDERAL COURTS DECIDE

The federal judges and the Supreme Court justices must consider two issues in most civil liberties cases. One involves *federalism:* the power of the national courts to issue orders to state and local officials. The other is the role of the judiciary when dealing with elected executives and legislators: to what extent should judges be activists, and to what extent should they accept the authority of these officials?

The federal issue

The Bill of Rights was originally intended to safeguard the people against actions of the national government, particularly Congress. The First Amendment refers to Congress, while other amendments deal with the federal courts, the military, and the executive branch—but none mention or seem to apply to the state governments. Yet most civil liberties cases decided by the federal courts involve actions of state officials or laws passed by state legislatures. How can the federal courts apply the Bill of Rights to the states? How far should protections originally intended to apply to the national government be applied to the states?

Dual citizenship. During the nineteenth century the Supreme Court embraced the doctrine of dual citizenship. Chief Justice John Marshall, in *Barron v. Baltimore,* restricted the application of the Bill of Rights to the national government. "These amendments contain no expression indicating an intention to apply them to state governments," he observed, concluding that "this court cannot so apply them."[36] In a post-Civil War case Justice Samuel Miller held that "there is a citizenship of the United States, and a citizenship of the state, which are distinct from each other, and which depend on different characteristics or circumstances in the individual."[37] By the turn of the century the prevailing doctrine was summarized by Justice Brewer, who concluded that the first ten amendments "contain no restrictions on the powers of the state, but were intended to operate solely on the federal government."[38]

Applying the Bill of Rights to the states. In this century the Bill of Rights has been applied to state governments, and therefore the federal courts can hold unconstitutional the actions of state officials and private individuals.[39]

The change began when the Fourteenth Amendment was adopted in 1868; it provided in part that no state could deprive anyone of life, liberty, or property without due process of law. This language echoed the due process clause of the Fifth Amendment, which applied to the national government; now the states were under the same restrictions. But what is due process of law? According to *strict-constructionist* judges, it refers to the rules designed to ensure a fair trial. The federal courts could review state trials only if, in the words of Justice Frankfurter, their proceedings would "shock the conscience." Torture, extreme forms of interrogation, intimidation of witnesses, and other methods of gaining an unfair advantage for the prosecution during a trial would be held unconstitutional by the federal courts, but otherwise the federal judges would stand aside.

Other judges argued that the Fourteenth Amendment incorporated some of the fundamental guarantees of the original Bill of Rights—not only the right to a fair trial—which could now be applied to the states. Justice Sanford began the process of incorporating the Bill of Rights into the Fourteenth Amendment in *Gitlow v. New York*, a 1925 case, in which he decided:

> For present purposes we may and do assume that freedom of speech and of the press which are protected by the First Amendment from abridgment by Congress are among the fundamental personal rights and liberties protected by the due process clause of the Fourteenth Amendment from impairment by the States.[40]

Six years later, in *Near v. Minnesota*, freedom of the press was protected against state laws. *DeJonge v. Oregon* incorporated freedom to assemble six years after that. In *Hamilton v. Board of Regents*, freedom of religion was incorporated.[41]

FULL VERSUS PARTIAL INCORPORATION. Some justices argued that the judiciary should complete the **incorporation** of all ten amendments. As Justice Hugo Black argued, the purpose of the Fourteenth Amendment was "to extend to all the people of the nation the complete protection of the Bill of Rights. To hold that this court can determine what, if any, provisions of the Bill of Rights will be enforced [against the states] and if so, to what degree, is to frustrate the great design of a written Constitution."[42]

With few exceptions the full-incorporationist view has prevailed. Just about everything in the Bill of Rights now applies to the states, with the following minor exceptions: the right to bear arms, which the states may regulate through gun control laws; the protection against quartering troops in houses in peacetime; indictment by jury in major criminal cases (the states may use other methods to indict); and the right to a jury trial in civil cases involving amounts over $20 (the states may hold nonjury civil trials in cases involving larger amounts).

INCORPORATION PLUS. The due process clause of the Fourteenth Amendment not only incorporates most of the Bill of Rights but also may include liberties not mentioned in the first ten amendments, through the "incorporation-plus" doctrine. Justice Benjamin Cardozo argued that certain liberties are "the very essence of a scheme of ordered liberty" because they involve "those fundamental principles of liberty and justice which lie at the base of all our civil and political institutions."[43] As Justice Murphy noted, "Occasions may arise where a [state] proceeding falls so far short of conforming to fundamental standards of procedure as to warrant constitutional condemnation in terms of lack of due process despite the absence of a specific provision in the Bill of Rights."[44] Or as Justice Goldberg put it, "The Framers of the Constitution believed there are additional fundamental rights, protected from governmental infringements, which exist alongside those fundamental rights mentioned in the first eight constitutional amendments."[45]

CIVIL LIBERTIES AND STATE JUDICIARIES. In recent decades the state judiciaries have developed their own civil liberties protections, based on the state constitutions and laws, and often these go beyond the rights and liberties recognized by the federal courts. At least thirty-nine state constitutions provide greater protection of freedom of speech than the Bill of Rights.[46] A state court decision based on the state's own constitution is insulated from review by the federal courts, which lack jurisdiction over decisions made on grounds independent of the national Constitution. In the 1980s, as the federal courts have allowed the police and prosecutors more leeway, civil liberties groups and defense attorneys have looked to the state courts for safeguards for defendants. The state courts also have pioneered in extending rights to privacy, especially rights involving sexual behavior, the "right to die" for the severely ill, and freedom of speech and of the press.

Some state courts have rejected the reasoning of the Supreme Court in interpreting language in state constitutions which is similar to that in the national Constitution, such as due process of law and equal protection of the laws. Some have ruled that women have a right to public funding for abortions, which is opposite to the ruling of the Supreme Court. Justice William Brennan approvingly noted that the supreme court of Hawaii went beyond the United States Supreme Court in one case, and he claimed that "while this results in a divergence of meaning between words which are the same in both federal and state constitutions, the system of federalism envisaged by the United States Constitution tolerates such divergence where the result is greater protection of individual rights under state law. . . ."[47]

Most experts in constitutional law see state civil liberties protections as part of a redundant system of judicial power. As Laurence Tribe explains, "There is a reciprocal relationship between the U.S. Supreme Court and the state courts. As the Supreme Court's own energy flags or it reaches the limits of appropriate federal judicial activity, it may nonetheless have marked the path that creative state jurists will want to follow." He adds that "in the long view of history, most of the truly creative developments in American law have come from the states."[48] As the Supreme Court has backtracked on civil liberties protections, some states have moved forward in response.

The role of the judiciary

The extent to which the federal courts will decide cases that have civil liberties dimensions involves not only issues of federalism but also conceptions of the proper role of the judiciary in dealing with other branches and levels of government.

Self-restraint versus close scrutiny. In many kinds of cases judges prefer to assume that legislators and executives have acted rationally, lawfully, and constitutionally, putting the burden of proof on those with complaints who must demonstrate otherwise. But this principle of *self-restraint*, applied to such matters as presidential powers in foreign affairs or laws regulating the economy passed by Congress, is not the principle by which justices operate in civil liberties cases. Instead, they rely on *close scrutiny*: actions of officials are considered suspect, and the burden of proof is on the government, which must demonstrate that limitations or restraints serve a public purpose. This principle was articulated in the most famous footnote ever to appear in a Supreme Court case, written by Justice Harlan Fiske Stone in *United States v. Carolene Products Co.*, in which he argued that there was little or no presumption of constitutionality for any law "which restricts those political processes which can ordinarily be expected to bring about repeal of undesirable legislation."[49] Justice Benjamin Cardozo similarly identified for close scrutiny anything that infringed upon First Amendment rights, which he said were "the matrix, the indispensable condition, of nearly every form of freedom."[50] The courts must protect these freedoms and give them the benefit of the doubt against any form of government regulation precisely because these freedoms are at the core of the workings of the entire system of government.

Preferred freedoms. The courts have developed a set of **preferred freedoms** (First Amendment freedoms) to which they apply the rule of close scrutiny. They will not uphold regulations which define or limit in any way the type of person or group which is protected by the First Amendment, but they may uphold a law or regulation, applied to everyone, which reasonably regulates when, how, and where speech or assembly may occur. The courts uphold laws punishing people who joke about planting bombs on airplanes or who shout "Fire!" in a crowded theater. They allow bans on the sale of pornography involving children. They permit communities to establish regulations governing the use of loudspeakers.

Ruling for the government. The courts do not always rule against the government in case involving freedom of expression; indeed, many of the ringing defenses of civil liberties quoted thus far were written as part of dissenting opinions or were majority opinions upholding a government prosecution. CLEAR AND PRESENT DANGER. The toughest test is that of demonstrating a *clear and present danger* to public order. The government must prove that a regulation or law which it passed or that an action which it took was necessary to eliminate or prevent such a danger. As formulated by Justice Holmes in a World War I case involving the conviction of an antiwar protestor who passed out leaflets, "The question in every case is whether the words used are in such circumstances and are of such a nature as to create a clear and present danger that they will bring about the substantive evils that Congress has a right to prevent."[51] Holmes insisted that a danger had to be clear and imminent because he thought that in most circumstances, even if the danger was great, a democratic society could tolerate speech. As justices Brandeis and Holmes argued in their dissent in another case:

> No danger flowing from speech can be deemed clear and present, unless the incidence of the evil apprehended is so imminent that it may befall before there is opportunity for full discussion. If there be time to expose through discussion the falsehood and fallacies, to avert the evil by the processes of education, the remedy to be applied is more speech, not enforced silence.[52]

In more recent cases the courts have extended this argument to consider the likelihood that an action will succeed. Even if a danger is imminent, there must be a substantial probability that it will occur before the government is justified in intervening.[53]

CLOSE-UP

JUSTICE OLIVER WENDELL HOLMES, JR. One of the greatest Supreme Court justices, Oliver Wendell Holmes, Jr., played an important role in strengthening the First Amendment guarantees of freedom of expression. Holmes went to Harvard College and became acquainted with Henry Wadsworth Longfellow, William James, and Ralph Waldo Emerson. The same year in which he received the honor of class poet, Holmes enlisted in Company G to fight in the Civil War, reaching the rank of captain after being wounded three times.

Holmes attended Harvard Law School, taught at Harvard, and was appointed to the Supreme Judicial Court of Massachusetts in 1882. He became chief justice of that court in 1899. His legal scholarship put him in the first rank of American jurists. He took a sociological rather than narrowly legalistic approach to the law. "The life of the law has not been logic," he wrote in his book *The Common Law,* "it has been experience." He tried to adjust legal doctrines to the realities of life, believing that the law was meant to adapt.

President Theodore Roosevelt appointed Holmes to the Supreme Court in 1902. Holmes's decisions and dissents often followed the principles of the progressive movement. He favored state regulation of working hours and a minimum wage for women and children, he opposed child labor ("If there is any matter upon

Associate Justice Oliver Wendell Holmes, Jr. (*Bettmann Archive.*)

which civilized countries have agreed," he wrote in a dissent, "it is the evil of premature and excessive child labor"), and he wanted to hold employers responsible for injuries sustained in the workplace. Holmes did not always vote the White House line, however. When Roosevelt had the Northern Securities Company prosecuted for alleged restraint of trade, Holmes dissented, along with the chief justice and two other judges, against the president's policy (beginning his opinion with the words, "Great cases like hard cases make bad law,"), arguing that the size of the company did not make it illegal. His opinion outraged Roosevelt, who told his friends, "I could carve out of a banana a judge with more backbone than that!"

Holmes was a defender of personal freedom and consistently dissented against a conservative-dominated court, often in tandem with Justice Louis Brandeis. True, he wrote the majority opinion which sent the socialist Eugene Debs to prison, but he did that because Debs had taken illegal actions—he had tried to obstruct military recruitment for the war. But in 1919 the Court upheld convictions under the Espionage Act of men who had distributed pro-Soviet pamphlets. Holmes dissented, arguing that they were being prosecuted solely for their beliefs. "Congress," Holmes said, "certainly cannot forbid all effort to change the mind of the country." In 1925 the Court upheld the conviction of Benjamin Gitlow for publishing a manifesto that was illegal under the Criminal Anarchy act. Holmes dissented because in his view Gitlow had not incited anarchy, but had simply put forth his ideas. In 1928 the Court held that wiretapping did not violate the Fourth Amendment guarantees against unreasonable search because there had been "only listening" and no search, seizure, or entry. Holmes again dissented, calling wiretapping a "dirty business" and arguing that it was "less an evil that some criminals should escape than that the Government should play an ignoble part."

Holmes was called "the great dissenter" because of these and other opinions (he dissented in about one-tenth of the cases brought before him). In his time he was respected more for the grace and clarity of his opinions than for his influence on the law. But today we recognize his immense influence on civil liberties: his "clear and present danger" test, his distinction between thought and action, and his insistence that wiretapping must require a judicial warrant are all ideas which have been accepted by the courts and Congress.[54]

LEAST-MEANS TEST. Any restriction on First Amendment freedom has to pass the least-means test: the government must limit its infringement as much as possible, doing only that which is necessary to prevent danger. It must not take advantage of any situation to substantially weaken freedom of expression. The courts will strike down laws or regulations for *vagueness* and *overbreadth* if they go beyond a particular situation and could be applied to other situations. Thus an ordinance that prevents people from marching in uniforms, designed to discourage the Nazi Party, for example, will be struck down because it could also apply to members of high school marching bands.

SPARK THEORY. The courts also have doctrines which favor the government. One focuses on the content of free speech. If people advocate the violent overthrow of the government, there is no need, according to this doctrine, to prove that the danger is clear, imminent, or likely to occur. Justice Sanford argued instead that "a single revolutionary spark may kindle a fire that, smoldering for a time, may burst into a sweeping and destructive conflagration." Therefore, he continued, the state may "extinguish the spark" at the outset.[55] Along with this doctrine there is the *bad-tendency test*, which has to do with speech that is "inimical to the public welfare" as well as incitement to crime, disturbing the peace, and threatening to overthrow the government. For some justices, speech is a form of action because it incites criminal conduct. The government does not regulate speech, but rather *illegal actions taking the form of speech.*

The courts are more likely to distinguish between the advocacy of ideas and a conspiracy to act. Justice Brandeis, for example, would not uphold a lower court conviction unless the government could show "either that immediate serious violence was to be expected or was advocated, or that the past conduct furnished reason to believe that such advocacy was then contemplated."[56]

BALANCING TESTS. Many justices prefer neither restrictive nor permissive doctrines. They take the approach of Chief Justice Vinson, who argued that the balance would involve "whether the gravity of the 'evil' discounted by its improbability, justifies such invasion of free speech as is necessary to avoid the danger." Similarly, justices Frankfurter and Harlan were great balancers; Frankfurter claimed that he approached each case with a "candid and informed weighing of the competing interests involved."

This balancing approach infuriated Justice Black, a constitutional absolutist who thought that no conceivable government interference with free speech could be justified. "I do not believe that any federal agencies, including Congress and this Court, have power or authority to subordinate speech and press to what they think are 'more important interests,'" Black said in a dissent.[57] Yet even Black, faced with a case in which civil rights demonstrators marched around and around a state courthouse while a trial was pending, reacted sharply to what he viewed as attempts to pressure the courts, and he upheld convictions of the demonstrators for violating a statute prohibiting such demonstrations.

ISSUE AND DEBATE

RIGHT TO LIFE VERSUS FREEDOM OF CHOICE. *The background.* Until a century ago neither the state governments nor the national government legislated about abortion. Between the 1870s and the turn of the century doctors convinced the states to outlaw most abortions. Most states prohibited abortion unless the life of the mother was at stake; this resulted in many illegal abortions and consequent injury to, and death of, mothers as well as fetuses. In 1973 the Supreme Court ruled, in *Roe v. Wade*, 410 U.S. 113 (1973), that state laws prohibiting abortion in the first trimester of pregnancy were unconstitutional violations of the Ninth Amendment guarantee of the right to privacy. No other civil liberties decision of the Court has evoked so much controversy. A coalition of Roman Catholic and Protestant fundamentalist clergymen and clergywomen bitterly attacked it, and the pro-life movement was born. The Republican Party platforms of 1980 and 1984 opposed the decision, while the Democrats remained deeply divided. Conservative organizations have embraced the "right-to-life" cause, and it is the top priority on the new right's social agenda. Congress has responded to pressure from antiabortion groups and has prohibited the expenditure of federal health care funds for abortions. This provision was upheld by the Supreme Court in *Harris v. McRae*, 100 S. Ct. 2671 (1980).

Pro-life groups in state legislatures have proposed or passed laws which would cut off state funding for abortions for the poor, disallow abortions after the first trimester, and make them difficult to obtain. The Justice Department, in several cases that reached the Supreme Court in 1983 and 1984, asked the justices to give "heavy deference" to these laws, arguing that it is for the states and not federal judges to make policy.

Many politicians are caught in the middle. The Catholic church and many Protestant fundamentalist groups, believe that abortion is murder. Yet most politicians wish to maintain a distinction between their personal beliefs and morality and their obligations to the entire community. Geraldine Ferrarro, the democratic vice presidential nominee, and the governor of New York, Mario Cuomo (a potential presidential candidate), have both tangled with New York's Cardinal O'Connor, who has called on Catholic politicians to heed the teachings of the church. Vice President Bush, in the 1984 debates, embraced the pro-life position of his party's conservative wing, but other moderate Republicans have not done so.

Public opinion. Public opinion polls show that the nation is sharply divided on the issue of abortion; a 56 to 44 majority agreed with the statement in a 1982 Gallup poll that "every woman who wants an abortion should be able to have one." An October 1984 survey by the National Opinion Research Center indicated that 90 percent of those surveyed believed in abortion if the woman's health was endangered, 80 percent if the baby would have birth defects or if the woman had been raped, 46 percent if she could not afford more children, 44 percent if she was unmarried and did not want to marry the father, and 43 percent if she did not want more children. There is little difference between Protestants and Catholics in such surveys, which do show a stronger pro-life position among blacks than among whites.

The proposed constitutional amendment. Several different versions of anti-abortion amendments to the Constitution have been proposed. One would simply ban all abortions, while others would make exceptions if the life of the mother was in danger. None has been seriously considered by Congress. Instead, the Life Amendment Political Action Committee, the Right to Life Committee, and the Ad Hoc Committee in Defense of Life have proposed a constitutional amendment (the Hatch Amendment, named for its sponsor in the senate) which would declare the fetus a human being endowed with constitutional liberties and would permit states to ban abortion, making such laws unreviewable by the Supreme Court. Policy would then be made at the state level rather than by the national government. The amendment passed the Senate Judiciary Committee in 1982. Pro-choice groups such as Planned Parenthood, the National Organization of Women, the National Abortion Rights Action League, and Friends of Family Planning joined in a coalition to defeat the amendment in the House. Three-fourths of respondents in Gallup polls taken at the time opposed amending the Constitution to outlaw abortion.

The pros. Supporters of the Hatch Amendment believe that it is a sensible compromise. By returning the issue to the states, it would allow diverse social policy. Given the mobility of the American people, most pregnant women who wished to have abortions would still be able to obtain them in states that permitted them. Meanwhile, in states with large antiabortion majorities, the will of the state legislature would not be obstructed by the courts.

Supporters of amendments banning some or all types of abortion believe that all abortion is murder, that it violates divine law, and that it must be outlawed. Given the Supreme Court decision upholding the right to an abortion, the only way to prevent abortion, they believe, is through a constitutional amendment.

The cons. Opponents of the Hatch Amendment believe that returning the issue to the states would allow abortions to continue but would unfairly discriminate against women who did not have the money to travel to states where abortions were legal. The back-alley practitioners who perform illegal abortions would endanger the lives of these women.

Opponents of a constitutional amendment banning abortion argue that it would embed social policy (and an unenforceable one at that) in the Constitution. It would be similar to Prohibition: it would not prevent abortions from taking place, just as prohibition did not prevent the sale and consumption of alcoholic beverages, and it would create a disrespect for the Constitution among the millions of women who would obtain abortions. Opponents believe that the opinion of the Supreme Court should be respected and that no other burdens should be placed by Congress or the states on the right of women to make their own choices. Those who believe that abortions are morally wrong, they argue, should work privately to prevent them, through counseling expectant mothers to give birth voluntarily, rather than relying on the coercive power of the state to force childbirth on them.

IN CONCLUSION

Civil liberties are guaranteed by the Bill of Rights, the first ten amendments to the Constitution. Almost all have been incorporated into the due process clause of the Fourteenth Amendment and also apply to the states. The most important First Amendment rights involve a ban on establishing a state religion and a guarantee of freedom of religion, making the United States a secular nation (albeit with a religious dimension to its public morality), as well as freedoms of speech, petition, assembly, and the press. The other important provisions guarantee that the government cannot take life, liberty, or property without due process of law, and they specify certain police and criminal procedures. These prevent the United States from becoming a police state.

Since 1937, federal judges have given greater weight to the protection of civil liberties than to other actions of the national government and the state governments. They have elevated civil liberties to a preferred position and have given state action closer scrutiny in these matters than in others. Nevertheless, no liberties are absolute: judges often weigh and balance competing claims, and many decisions favor the government. In recent years freedom of speech and freedom of religious practice have been extended, while the police have, in the past decade, won a number of cases that have restored some of their "crime control" model of patrol and arrest. The outlook is for most civil liberties protections to remain intact, mirroring recent developments in public opinion, but for the courts to reconsider and possibly modify their positions on abortion and prayer in schools.

NOTES

1. *Walz v. Tax Commission*, 397 U.S. 664 (1970); *Lemon v. Kurtzman*, 403 U.S. 602 (1971).
2. *Committee for Public Education and Religious Liberty v. Nyquist*, 413 U.S. 756 (1973).
3. *The New York Times*, Sept. 14, 1984.
4. Ibid.
5. *Lee v. United States*, 457 U.S. 1122 (1982).
6. *Reynolds v. United States*, 98 U.S. 145 (1879).
7. *Abrams v. United States*, 250 U.S. 616 (1919), p. 630.
8. *Whitney v. California*, 274 U.S. 357 (1927), p. 375.
9. Thomas Emerson, *The System of Freedom of Expression*, Random House, New York, 1970, p. 7.

10. *West Virginia Board of Education v. Barnette*, 319 U.S. 629 (1943), p. 638.
11. *Tinker v. Des Moines School District*, 393 U.S. 503 (1969).
12. *Cohen v. California*, 403 U.S. 15 (1971).
13. *Hoffman Estates v. Flipside*, 456 U.S. 950 (1982).
14. *Bolger v. Youngs Drug Product Corp.*, 77 L. Ed. 2d, 469 (1983).
15. *Pruneyard Shopping Center v. Robins*, 447 U.S. 74 (1980).
16. *Feiner v. New York*, 340 U.S. 315 (1951).
17. *United States v. Mary T. Grace*, 75 L. Ed. 2d, 736 (1983).
18. *Red Lion Broadcasting Co. v. FCC*, 395 U.S. 367 (1969).
19. *New York Times v. Sullivan*, 376 U.S. 255 (1964).
20. *New York Times v. United States*, 403 U.S. 713 (1971).
21. *Snepp v. United States*, 444 U.S. 507 (1980).
22. *Branzburg v. Hayes*, 408 U.S. 665 (1972).
23. *Miranda v. Arizona*, 384 U.S. 436 (1966).
24. James Q. Wilson, and George L. Kelling, "Broken Windows" *The Atlantic Monthly*, March, 1982, pp. 29–38.
25. Lawrence Baum, *The Supreme Court*, Congressional Quarterly Press, Washington, D.C., 1981, pp. 187–188.
26. *Stone v. Powell*, 428 U.S. 465 (1976).
27. *Rose v. Lundy*, 455 U.S. 509 (1981).
28. *The New York Times*, June 14, 1982.
29. *United States v. Miller*, 307 U.S. 174 (1939).
30. *The New York Times*, Apr. 5, 1982.
31. *Pico v. Island Trees School District*, 455 U.S. 903 (1982).
32. *United States v. U.S. District Court*, 407 U.S. 297 (1972).
33. *Dombrowski v. Pfister*, 380 U.S. 479 (1965).
34. *United States v. Rabinowitz*, 339 U.S. 56 (1950), p. 69.
35. *West Virginia Board of Education v. Barnette*, 319 U.S. 629 (1943), p. 642.
36. *Barron v. Baltimore*, 32 U.S. 243 (1833), p. 250.
37. *The Slaughterhouse Cases*, 16 Wallace 36 (1873), p. 74.
38. *Brown v. New Jersey*, 175 U.S. 1972, p. 174.
39. Richard C. Cortner, *The Supreme Court and the Second Bill Rights*, University of Wisconsin Press, Madison, 1981.
40. *Gitlow v. New York*, 268 U.S. 652 (1925).
41. *Near v. Minnesota*, 283 U.S. 679 (1931); *DeJonge v. Oregon*, 299 U.S. 353 (1937); *Hamilton v. Board of Regents*, 293 U.S. 245 (1934).
42. *Adamson v. California*, 332 U.S. 46 (1947), p. 89.
43. *Palko v. Connecticut*, 302 U.S. 319 (1937), p. 325; also *Hebert v. Louisiana*, 272 U.S. 312 (1926).
44. *Adamson v. California*, 332 U.S. 46 (1947), p. 124.
45. *Griswold v. Connecticut*, 381 U.S. 479 (1965), p. 488
46. David Margolick, "State Judiciaries Are Shaping Law That Goes Far Beyond Supreme Court," *The New York Times*, May 19, 1982, pp. 1, B-8.
47. William J. Brennan, Jr., "State Constitutions and the Protection of Individual Rights," *Harvard Law Review*, vol. 90, no. 489, 1977, p. 500.
48. Margolick, op. cit.
49. *United States v. Carolene Products Co.*, 304 U.S. 144 (1938), p. 152.
50. *Palko v. Connecticut*, 302 U.S. 319 (1937), p. 327.
51. *Schenck v. United States*, 249 U.S. 47 (1919).
52. *Whitney v. California*, 274 U.S. 357 (1927), p. 377.
53. *Brandenberg v. Ohio*, 395 U.S. 444 (1969).
54. Researched by Maurice Suh, Columbia College.
55. *Gitlow v. New York*, 268 U.S. 652 (1925), p. 669.
56. *Whitney v. California*, 274 U.S. 357 (1927), p. 376.
57. *Dennis v. United States*, 341 U.S. 494 (1951).

FURTHER READING

Abraham, Henry J.: *Freedom and the Court*, 3d ed., Oxford University Press, New York, 1977. A comprehensive textbook on civil liberties.

Barker, Lucius J., and Twiley W. Barker: *Civil Liberties and the Constitution*, Prentice-Hall, Englewood Cliffs, N.J., 1981. A study of leading civil liberties cases.

Berns, Walter: *The First Amendment and the Future of American Democracy*, Basic Books, New York, 1976. A conservative view of the reach and limits of First Amendment freedoms.

Brant, Irving: *The Bill of Rights*, Bobb-Merrill, Indianapolis, 1965. A treatment of the adoption and subsequent application of the Bill of Rights, including incorporation into the Fourteenth Amendment.

Chaffee, Zechariah, Jr.: *Free Speech in the United States*, Harvard University Press, Cambridge, Mass., 1941. A classic treatise on First Amendment freedoms.

Cox, Archibald J.: *Freedom of Expression*, Harvard University Press, Cambridge, Mass., 1981. An update on civil liberties decisions of the Burger Court.

Emerson, Thomas: *The System of Freedom of Expression*, Random House, New York, 1970. A comprehensive discussion of First Amendment freedoms.

Friendly, Fred: *The Good Guys, the Bad Guys, and the First Amendment*, Random House, New York, 1977. An account of the news media and the government.

Garrow, David: *The FBI and Martin Luther King, Jr.*, Norton, New York, 1982. A vivid account of FBI harassment of this civil rights leader.

Hayes, Arthur G.: *Let Freedom Ring*, Boni and Liveright, New York, 1928. Accounts of some of the most controversial cases involving freedom of expression in the early twentieth century, including the Scopes "monkey trial" in Tennessee and the Sacco and Vanzetti trial in Massachusetts.

Hentoff, Nat: *The First Freedom*, Delacorte Press, New York, 1980. A discussion of some of the important post-World-War II First Amendment cases.

Levy, Leonard: *Legacy of Suppression*, Harvard University Press, Cambridge, Mass., 1960. An account of the early struggles for civil liberties.

Lewis, Anthony: *Gideon's Trumpet*, Random House, New York, 1964. A case study of a landmark Supreme Court criminal justice decision.

Markham, Charles L.: *The Noblest Cry*, St. Martin's, New York, 1965. An account of the history and accomplishments of the American Civil Liberties Union.

Morgan, Richard: *The Supreme Court and Religion*, Free Press, New York, 1973. A survey of church-state issues as decided by the Supreme Court.

Schwartz, Bernard: *The Great Rights of Mankind: A History of the American Bill of Rights*, Oxford University Press, New York, 1977. A study of the historical evolution of civil liberties and rights.

Shapiro, Martin: *The Pentagon Papers and the Courts*, Chandler, San Francisco, 1972. A study of a case involving freedom of the press decided by the Supreme Court.

THE STUDY BREAK

Lenny. Stars Dustin Hoffman. A movie about Lenny Bruce, a comedian who ran afoul of local antiobscenity ordinances, and the events that eventually led to his suicide (1974).

Roth, Philip. *Our Gang*, Random House, New York, 1971. A fictionalized satire of President Nixon's commitment to civil liberties.

USEFUL SOURCES

Brownlie, Ian (ed.): *Basic Documents on Human Rights, 2d ed.*, Oxford University Press, New York, 1981.

Emerson, Thomas, David Haber, and Norman Dorsen: *Political and Civil Rights in the United States*, 2 vols., 3d. ed., Boston, Little, Brown, 1967. Leading court cases and commentary.

Kelly, Alfred H. (ed.): *Foundations of Freedom in the American Constitution*, Harper & Row, New York, 1958. Articles on civil liberties.

ORGANIZATIONS

American Civil Liberties Union. 132 West 43d Street, New York, N.Y. 10036. For more information phone 212-944-9800.

American Enterprise Institute. 1150 17th Street, N.W. Washington, D.C. 20036. Useful polls from many sources on public support for civil liberties protections are reprinted in its magazine, *Public Opinion*. For more information phone 202-862-5800.

Moral Majority. 499 South Capitol Street, Washington, D.C. 20003. Publishes *Moral Majority Report*. For more information phone 202-484-7511.

People for the American Way. 1424 16th St., N.W., Suite 601, Washington, D.C. 20036. Publishes *Quarterly Report*. For more information phone 202-462-4777.

POLITICAL PARTICIPATION: WHO VOTES?

Legal barriers against women, minorities, and the poor restricted the suffrage for much of American history. Today these restrictions have been abolished, but turnout rates have fallen. (*Bettmann Archive; Shepard Sherbell: Picture Group.*)

It was to be the biggest mobilization of voters in the twentieth century, and it would bring about a fundamental change in American politics—at least that was the feeling during the spring and summer before the 1984 presidential election. Close to 60 million eligible Americans were not registered to vote, and if past practices were any indication, close to half the total of 174 million eligible voters would not show up at the polls. But what would happen if large numbers of people did register and vote? That was the joker in the electoral deck, the wild card that could upset all the pundits' calculations.

The Democrats announced a drive to register more than 10 million new voters; then the Republicans countered with a goal of 2 million. Jesse Jackson's Rainbow Coalition coordinated voter registration drives in the black churches of the nation and urged the congregations to register and vote in the Democratic primaries. The National Organization of Women sponsored a drive which it said resulted in the registration of 250,000 new voters; the Southwest Voter Registration Project, active among Hispanics and Indians, claimed more than 200,000 new registrants in Texas. The Voter Education Project spurred the effort in the south, while the NAACP organized "overground railroad" marches to publicize its campaign among black voters in the midwest. The U.S. Students Association and the National Student Educational Fund sponsored Freedom Summer '84, the purpose of which was to register black voters in Mississippi. The American Coalition for Traditional Values, a group of 100,000 conservative ministers, sponsored a drive to register 2 million fundamentalist Christians.

Other drives were nonpartisan. The National NonPartisan Voter Registration Campaign encouraged officials to set up telephone numbers so that people could dial VOTER-84, leave their names and addresses on an answering machine, and receive voter registration forms by mail. Nineteen foundations donated money to the Advertising Council of America, which sponsored a "get out the vote" series of print and television commercials. The Ad Hoc Funders Committee for Voter Registration and Education coordinated more than $4 million in foundation donations to nonpartisan voter registration groups. The National Student Campaign on Voter Registration helped campus "get out the vote" groups, and their activities reached a peak on October 1, which was proclaimed National Student Voter Registration Day.

Did all this effort change the course of American politics? Not really. In 1980, 115 million people were registered—69.8 percent of those eligible. In 1984, the number rose to 125 million, but since the population had also increased, the percent of those eligible rose to only 71.8 percent. And there was just a 1 percent increase in voting in the 1984 elections—almost half the eligible voters stayed away from the polls, just as they have done in every presidential election year since 1972.

Each party wants to increase voter registration and turnout. Neither seems able to make the breakthrough that would reshape the political map. Each has experimented with new ways to mobilize nonvoters; thus far these efforts have amounted to treading water. Ways to increase registration would be the super-weapon of American politics; the inability to do so remains its great mystery.

CITIZEN OR SUBJECT?

"If liberty and equality, as is thought by some, are chiefly to be found in de-mocracy," the Greek philosopher Aristotle argued thousands of years ago, "they will be best attained when all persons alike share in the government to the utmost."[1] But not all American citizens share in the government. Those who vote for Democratic and Republican candidates are far outnumbered by those who vote for no one; the "nonvoter" party attracts almost half of all those eligible to vote in presidential elections, and each of the two major parties manages to win the votes of slightly more than one-fourth of the people.

Does democratic government require that most of the people vote most of the time? Would it make any difference if they did? Some people believe that low rates of voting enhance the stability of democracies. They think that most nonvoters are satisfied with their leaders and that nonvoting is a rational re-sponse for citizens when the costs of voting (that is, the inconvenience of registering, learning about issues and candidates, and going to the polls) are not justified by any conceivable benefits which they could obtain by choosing new leaders. The political scientist Everett Ladd argues that the overall record of western democracies fits this linkage of "low turnout to relative voter satis-faction."[2] Sam Ervin, a former senator, recalled the nineteenth-century tradi-tion which restricted voting to those who deserved the privilege when he said, "I don't believe in making it easy for lazy, apathetic people. I'd be extremely happy if nobody in the United States voted except for the people who thought about the issues and made up their own minds and wanted to vote."[3]

But others believe that nonvoting is a symptom of deep-seated problems. "The legitimacy of a democratic leadership and the health of the democratic process depend squarely on the informed and active participation of the elec-torate," argues Curtis Gans, the director of the Committee for the Study of the American Electorate, a group which monitors low turnouts.[4] In ancient de-mocracies a distinction was made between the good person and the good citizen. To be merely the former, personally honest and obedient to the gov-ernment, was to be a good subject—but that was not good enough. "We regard the man who takes no part in public affairs not as easygoing and sensible," the Athenian leader Pericles observed, "but as worthless and foul."[5]

Voter turnout is the key to political power. Candidates for office devote most of their campaign efforts to bringing their supporters to the polls. Anyone who wants to influence politics—by helping in a campaign, running for office, or lobbying politicians for change—learns that getting out the vote is the way to do it.

In this chapter we begin our study of campaigns and elections by studying **registration** and **turnout rates.** Who are the voters, and how do they differ from nonvoters? How might turnout rates be increased? We will consider the American experience in historical and comparative perspective, and we will look for an explanation of the central paradox in Americans' voting behavior: as the constitutional and legal requirements for voting have been eased and as the people have become better educated about, and more interested in, poli-tics, the percentage of the eligible population that votes has declined.

Direct democracy

In a *direct democracy* the majority of the people decide on the policies of the government. At a **town meeting** the whole community meets in one place, discusses matters, and then votes. But such meetings are limited to communities in which all citizens can gather in one place at one time.

On a larger scale, direct democracy relies on the **plebiscite,** or issue election.[6] The community need not meet in one place at one time, and the election does not follow right after any particular meeting or discussion.

In the United States there are two types of plebiscites: the *initiative,* which allows anyone to put a proposal on the ballot if enough people sign petitions to do so (usually 1 to 2 percent of the voters), and the *referendum,* which is a proposal submitted to the people by the state legislature. Twenty-three states now use initiatives, and all provide for the referendum. As yet there is no form of direct democracy for the national government, making the United States one of the few democratic nations that do not use such procedures.

Indirect democracy

The main problem with any plebiscite is that there is no way to improve a proposal by discussing and amending it, as could be done at a town meeting. The public has to accept or reject it and cannot shape it once it has been put on the ballot. Effective democracy requires indirect methods: a way for representatives of the people to recreate the advantages of the town meeting—its discussion, and debate.

In representative democracies the people choose the representatives who decide the issues. There is only an indirect relationship between candidates and issues: candidates make pledges during a campaign and, if elected, hold themselves most accountable to those who voted for them and try to translate these voters' preferences into public policy. Elections provide clues as to the wishes of the voters, and politicians "read the returns" accordingly.

**WHO VOTES?
TURNOUT RATES**

In our *political culture* (our beliefs about what should and what should not be done and about what is and what is not legitimate) we think that the good citizen is one who votes. Perhaps this is why, when people are asked whether they vote in elections, there is significant overreporting—as if people were ashamed to tell pollsters that they do not bother to go to the polls. In 1984 the Census Bureau found that its national sample of 66,000 households overreported their rate of voting by almost 10 percent, and a sample of voters questioned by the Survey Researcher Center of the University of Michigan (the leading academic center studying voting behavior) overreported by up to 15 percent.[7] When the Gallup poll asked people in 1984 whether they were registered, about 4 percent falsely reported yes. In spite of our political culture, what we say is quite different from what we do.

Calculating turnouts

To determine voting rates in any election, we need to know two things: the number of adults who are eligible to vote (the voting-age population, or VAP) and the number of people who actually voted (the turnout). The voting-age population consists of American citizens age 18 and older who are not in prison or mental institutions. We can obtain reasonably good estimates of the VAP from the Census Bureau, which two years after the end of every decade (for example, in 1972 and 1982), publishes a report on the size of the VAP, as well as the number of people who registered and who voted for president and

---

TURNOUTS AND DIRECT DEMOCRACY

Would turnouts be higher if there were more direct votes on the issues? In a Gallup poll 48 percent of the respondents who had not voted in the 1980 presidential election said that they would be more likely to vote, and only 2 percent said that they would be less likely to vote, in issue elections. In another Gallup survey 52 percent favored and 23 percent opposed national referendums.

Before we decide that such elections would increase turnouts, we should examine the experience of states in which they are held. In 1978 the average turnout rate was only 40 percent, and in 1980 it rose to 52.1 percent—slightly less than the turnout rate for candidate elections.[a]

Even intensely debated issues do not bring majorities to the polls. Consider Proposition 13, a 1978 California initiative to cut property taxes and state spending and a battle which began the great tax revolt of the past decade. The turnout rate was only 43 percent. Turnout rates in the 1982 nuclear freeze referendums held in nine states ranged from 32 percent in Arizona to 49 percent in Oregon.

Issue elections of the past decade have not attracted more voters to the polls than candidate elections. They have not stimulated interest in voting or prevented the decline in turnout rates.[b] In fact, in nonsouthern states in 1980 the turnouts were lower in states that held issue elections than in states that did not.

a. *Public Opinion*, vol. 42, no. 4, November–December 1978, pp. 26–28; *Public Opinion*, vol. 45, no. 1, February–March 1981, p. 40.
b. David Everson, "The Effects of Initiatives on Voter Turnout," *Western Political Quarterly*, vol. 34, no. 3, 1981, pp. 415–425.

---

for representatives in each state. For the 1984 elections there were 174 million people in the voting-age population. By dividing the turnout in each presidential and congressional election by the voting-age population for that election, we can calculate past turnouts (Figure 5-1).

Figure 5-1. Turnout rates, 1856–1984. There is higher turnout in presidential election years than in midterm election years (shown here since 1922). The turnout rate in 1986 was 37 percent. (Sources: *Historical Statistics of the United States*, Washington, D.C., Government Printing Office, 1975; U.S. Bureau of the Census, *Statistical Abstract of the United States*, Washington, D.C., Government Printing Office, 1984.)

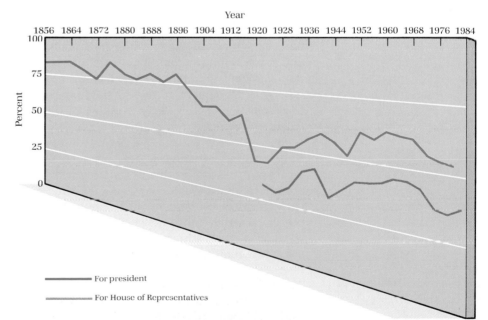

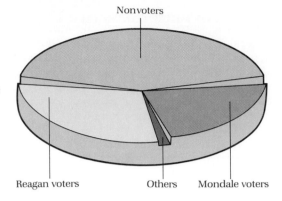

Nonvoters

Reagan voters   Others   Mondale voters

Figure 5-2. Turnout and choice in the presidential election of 1984. Of approximately 178 million Americans eligible to vote in 1984, 96 million did so, giving Ronald Reagan a landslide reelection share of 31.5 percent of the electorate.

National turnouts. Turnout rates vary for different kinds of elections. In presidential elections recent rates have varied from 63 to 53 percent. Of the voting-age population, the largest number, almost a majority, choose not to vote at all. The winning presidential candidate receives votes from only 26 to 35 percent of the VAP (Figure 5-2).

If all these nonvoters suddenly turned up at the polls, would it change the results? Most nonvoters have weak ties to the major parties (although the Democrats have a small lead in this regard), and many are independents. If they voted, they would probably support the presidential candidate who was going to win anyway, simply adding to the margin of victory. In 1956, for example, 72 percent of the nonvoters favored the winning candidate, Dwight Eisenhower; in 1960 John Kennedy had the support of 57 percent of the nonvoters; and in 1964 Lyndon Johnson was favored by 77 percent of those who did not vote. In 1972, 1976, and 1984 the margins of victory of Nixon, Carter, and Reagan also would have been increased if nonvoters had gone to the polls. The only election in which nonvoters would have made a difference was that held in 1968: the nonvoters favored Humphrey over Nixon by a small margin, but their support could have been crucial in the close race.[8]

Turnouts for congressional elections vary enormously. In presidential election years (for example, 1980 and 1984) slightly fewer votes are cast for senators and representatives than for president, while in off years (for example, 1978 and 1982) considerably fewer votes are cast. In the 1982 congressional elections only 38 percent of the VAP chose to vote. On the average, the winners in these elections received the support of slightly more than one-fifth of those eligible to vote.

State and local turnouts. The turnout rates are even lower in most state and local contests. In part this is a matter of timing, since most of these elections are not held in presidential election years. Turnout rates vary; in some states they approach 60 percent, and in others they plunge to 20 percent or lower, but usually they range between 30 and 50 percent of the VAP in elections for state legislators, governors, mayors, and city council members. The typical state officeholder is elected with the support of only one-fifth of the VAP.

Turnouts in historical perspective

Turnouts today are neither the highest nor the lowest in our history. Between 1856 (the first year for which accurate statistics are available) and 1896, a period which was marked by extensive corruption and mediocre leadership and during which neither major party focused on the issues, turnout rates were the highest they have ever been. This was due in part to the close two-party competition for the presidency, in part to relaxed registration requirements (that is, all white males over the age of 21 were eligible to vote), and in part to massive vote fraud, which inflated the totals. Between 1900 and 1916 the progressive movement encouraged measures such as issue elections, petitions to recall public officials, and party primaries that gave voters a chance to participate in nominations, and elections were fought on the issues. Yet the turnout rates slumped as more stringent registration requirements were introduced and as the Democrats dominated the south and the Republicans dominated the north, thus lessening two-party competition: they declined by an average of 2.9 percent in each election. Although more people voted after 1920, when women were given the right to vote, the rate of voting declined sharply.

In the 1930s, when the economy was in dire straits and the very survival of our economic and political institutions seemed at stake, voting rates began to climb dramatically, breaking the previous pattern of low interest–high turnout and high interest–low turnout: the Democrats mobilized new constituencies, while the Republican Party fought to maintain its status as a major party. Between 1960 and 1980, as it became easier for the young, the poor, and minorities to register and vote, we went back to the old pattern, and turnout rates dropped 10 percent in those two decades.[9] In the 1980s turnout rates began once again to increase: there was a 3 percent rise between the 1978 and the 1982 midterm congressional elections, followed by a 1 percent rise between the 1980 and the 1984 presidential elections.

Turnouts in comparative perspective

In most nations with democratic governments the turnout rates are higher than they are in the United States. In western European democracies 85 to 95

Besides electing candidates to office, voters are frequently asked to pass on referendums as well. No nation gives its voters as many issues to decide or candidates to elect as the United States. (*Tony Karody: Sygma.*)

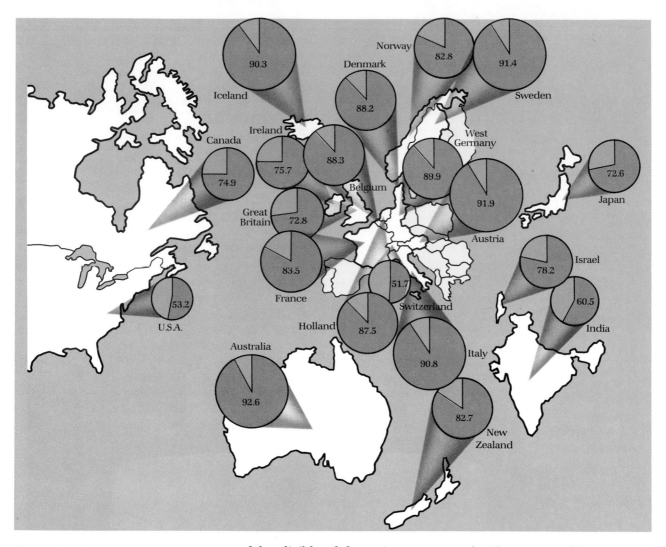

Figure 5-3. Turnout in selected democratic nations.

percent of the eligible adults register, compared with our rate of 72 percent in 1984 (Figure 5-3).

Do these turnout rates mean that the United States is less democratic than other nations? Not necessarily. Most other countries hold only a national election (every four to seven years) to choose the members of parliament and local elections for mayors and city council members. In the United States there are dozens of elections every year: in presidential election years for president, senators, and representatives; in off years for senators and representatives; and in odd or off years for state governors, state senators, and state representatives (and in some states for judges). There are also county elections for sheriffs, judges, and executives and local elections for mayors, city council members, judges, school board members, etc. In addition, we have a large number of ***primary elections*** (in which voters choose the nominees of their party to run in the general elections—a practice almost unknown in other countries) and referendums and initiatives. In no other nation are voters kept so busy or called upon to make up their minds on so many candidates and issues: the United States has more than 450,000 elected officials, far more per capita than any other nation in the world.

LEGAL FACTORS: REGISTERING TO VOTE

Explanations for the fluctuations in turnouts focus on the constitutional and legal factors which encourage or inhibit voting, on the characteristics of the population, and on the political environment. This section considers legal factors involving registration.

Voter registration was introduced in many states at the turn of the century as a progressive measure designed to improve the quality of the electorate and prevent vote fraud. In the nineteenth century, any male, even a noncitizen, could go to the polls on election day and vote; but the new registration laws required that local officials record the names and addresses of people who intended to vote, often well in advance of an election. State laws also required that in order to be accepted by the registrars, one had to be a citizen, to have resided in the community for a specified period of time, and to meet certain other requirements, such as literacy in English. By enforcing such requirements in an unfair or discriminatory manner, local political leaders could use them to encourage some people to vote and discourage others. To keep immigrants from voting, for example, a law might require residency of one year and proof of an eighth grade reading knowledge of English. Some states required periodic reregistration and purged the rolls of those who had not voted in previous elections (almost all still do so).

Registration and racial discrimination

Millions of blacks were disenfranchised in eleven southern states between 1890 and 1910, when registration procedures were introduced. At the time, poor blacks and whites, represented by the Populist movement, were challenging entrenched interests for control of state governments. Conservative whites, who controlled local newspapers, tried to turn whites against blacks by describing in lurid detail crimes supposedly committed by black men against white women. They called for the separation of the races in all public facilities. Race politics, based on mutual suspicion, soon supplanted class politics, and the white Populists embraced white supremacy. In state after state, constitutional conventions or the state legislatures used the following means to purge blacks from the registration lists:

1. *Literacy tests,* administered unfairly by local registrars, which kept even black college graduates from voting.
2. *Poll taxes,* payment of which was required in order to register and vote; these also discouraged poor whites from voting.
3. *Good-character tests,* which required prospective registrants to get two people already on the rolls to vouch for them. Once blacks were removed from the rolls, no white voter would help them get back on.

Because many low-income and poorly educated whites could not meet the stringent new requirements, some states adopted *grandfather clauses:* anyone whose grandfather had been eligible to vote would not have to meet these new requirements. Since only the grandfathers of whites had voted (the grandfathers of blacks had all been slaves), this satisfied whites. But in 1915 the Supreme Court, in *Guinn v. United States,* ruled that this provision was unconstitutional and struck it down; as a result, many uneducated whites were eliminated from the rolls.[10] Through the 1920s, it was not uncommon in parts of the south for turnout rates to remain as low as 10 percent.

The civil rights movement in the 1960s completely transformed the registration systems of the southern states. Before 1965 fewer than one-third of eligible blacks had managed to register in the region. As a result of the efforts of civil

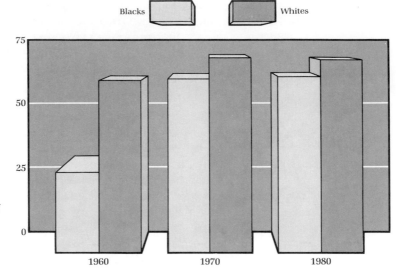

Figure 5-4. Registration rates in the south, 1960–1980. The registration rate for blacks increased markedly after passage of the Civil Rights Act of 1965. Rates for whites also increased as state literacy tests were suspended. (Source: U.S. Commission on Civil Rights.)

rights groups and of a coalition of liberal Democrats, labor unionists, religious groups, and moderate Republicans, Congress passed the Voting Rights Act (VRA) of 1965, which provided that in counties in which the turnout rate in presidential elections was less than 50 percent, literacy tests would be suspended. Federal registrars would register blacks who encountered serious obstacles from local registrars. Discrimination based on race or color was made a federal crime. The Justice Department was given the right to review any changes in state or local election laws to make sure that they did not discriminate against blacks. In 1970 an amendment to the VRA suspended the application of literacy tests throughout the nation. Registration rates for blacks and uneducated whites rose dramatically in the south, as Figure 5-4 indicates.

Although much has been done to end discrimination, as late as 1982 the United States Commission on Civil Rights reported that in some parts of the south discrimination and even threats of violence still affected registration and voter turnout among blacks.[11] And in 1984 the House Judiciary Subcommittee on Civil and Constitutional Rights reported that artificial and arbitrary barriers to registration were still being used against minorities, including inconvenient locations and hours to register, failure to appoint minority registrars, bans on door-to-door registration, and the requirement that mail registration forms be notarized. But today racists must violate national and state laws to actually keep minorities from registering, even though they can still make it inconvenient for them to do so.

Registration and language barriers

In the north and west, barriers were put up against newly arrived immigrants by groups that were already in control of state politics. Under the *Americanization doctrine*, developed between 1910 and 1920, immigrants would not be able to register until they assimilated the language and political values of Americans. They would have to prove that they had done so by becoming citizens and then demonstrating their literacy in English, according to the provisions of some state constitutions (like New York's constitution of 1915) or election laws. There is something to be said for assimilating people into the culture of the majority and having them learn the language, since this promotes national unity, facilitates communication, and speeds the social and economic progress of immigrants. But the politicians who instituted these requirements did so to disenfranchise their opponents; when immigrants supported the party in power, the laws were disregarded.

Most of the requirements for literacy in the English language have been eliminated. The VRA provided in 1965 that Puerto Rican citizens could vote if they had attended an "American flag" school through the sixth grade in Puerto Rico, even though their education might have been in Spanish. The 1970 amendment, which suspended all literacy tests, eased voting for millions of Hispanics in the southwest and in Florida as well. Amendments to the VRA in 1975 and 1982 provided for bilingual registration materials and ballots and for interpreters for many different groups—including Hispanics, Asians, American Indians, and native Alaskans—in counties in which the Census Bureau determines that these groups make up more than 5 percent of the population and in which their illiteracy rates are above the national average.

Easing registration

Poll taxes for national elections imposed by the states were abolished by the Twenty-Fourth Amendment, ratified in 1964. Two years later the Supreme Court, in *Harper v. Virginia State Board of Elections*, abolished poll taxes for state elections as well.[12] The 1970 amendments to the VRA lowered the voting age for national and state elections from 21 to 18, but the Supreme Court ruled that the law could apply only to national elections. In 1971 the Twenty-Sixth Amendment lowered the voting age for both national and state elections to 18. The 1970 VRA amendments provided that people who live in a state for thirty days before a federal election may vote in that election, no matter what the state residency requirements are.

Almost all states have now dropped periodic reregistration in favor of permanent registration. Most states now allow people to vote in state as well as national elections if they have lived in the state for thirty days, and some states allow registration on election day. Hours for registration have been lengthened, offices are kept open on weekends and are in convenient locations, and many states allow candidates, parties, and grass-roots organizations to provide deputy registrars who can register people in their homes as well as in shopping malls, banks, and other, similar locations. Some states also permit registration by mail.

Local ***registrars*** still discriminate against college students. Some election boards claim that students who live in dormitories do not have a legal residence and refuse to register them. Students have won cases against such decisions in the federal courts; for example, a 1984 decision in New York allowed hundreds of thousands of students to register for the election. But in other states they still find it difficult to vote. Nevertheless, more than a quarter of a million college students registered to vote from their campuses in 1984.

Some changes in registration laws have had a enormous impact on registration and voter turnout, as the data for the south between 1960 and 1980 indicate. But political scientists disagree on whether further easing of requirements—which makes fraud easier and increases costs—would increase turnouts. Raymond Wolfinger and Steven Rosenstone speak for those who think that easing requirements would bring more people to the polls when they argue that "if every state had had registration laws in 1972 as permissive as those in the most permissive states, turnout would have been about 9 percentage points higher in the presidential election."[13] Reformers believe that states could eliminate the thirty-day residency requirement and permit (as a few states do) election-day registration; simplify absentee registration and voting for the sick, the disabled, the handicapped, and those who are away from home; and institute a nationally funded system of postcard registration.[14] They also suggest that election day be made a national holiday and that states end the practice of purging the rolls of nonvoters after two or four years, as most of them do. Congress has refused to enact postcard registration (proposed by President Carter in 1977) or any of the other suggested reforms.

More skeptical political scientists argue that further easing of registration is not likely to increase turnouts. They point out that while many states did change their laws in the 1970s, their turnouts diminished or remained the same, and often there was no difference in turnout in adjoining states, one of which had eased requirements, while the other had not.

More could be done to ensure that the 2 million Americans who live overseas can register and vote in their home states. Many states require them to file early in an election year and then mail ballots to them too late, failing to process the forms or even count the ballots which are sent back. The Defense Department could encourage voting in the military, where the rates are 15 percent lower than the rates in the civilian population in presidential elections and as much as 25 percent lower in off-year congressional elections.

ISSUE AND DEBATE

SHOULD VOTERS BE REGISTERED IN GOVERNMENT OFFICES? *The background.* For the 1984 elections a number of states—including Texas, Ohio, Michigan, and New York—allowed their residents to obtain voter registration forms or assistance at state agencies, either from state workers or from volunteer "get out the vote" groups. In Michigan, people who are renewing a boat, car, or driver's license are asked whether they are registered, and more than 4.6 million voters have filled out voter registration forms in government offices. In New York State, five agencies (labor, motor vehicles, social services, and workers' compensation) were ordered to conduct voter registration projects and help citizens fill out mail registration forms. Drivers who were renewing their licenses were routinely invited to register to vote by clerks at the counters. In Ohio, state laws require that government officials ask citizens whether they would like to register and that each high school have a designated registrar so that 18-year-old students can sign up. In West Virginia and New Mexico, on the other hand, people must ask for registration forms before assistance can be given to them, although signs are posted announcing that aid is available. Various private organizations, such as Project Vote and Human SERVE, set up shop in government buildings and register low-income citizens who are waiting in agencies that handle welfare, unemployment insurance, food stamps, disability payments, and day care.

In 1982, after Project Vote's first major effort resulted in the registration of more than 100,000 people in nine states, four Republican governors barred registrations in unemployment offices. Project Vote sued in federal court, and these bans were overturned as violations of the First Amendment guarantees of freedom of speech and freedom to petition the government. But whether state employees could be directed to conduct such registration drives remained a separate issue. Was it a proper activity for state employees?

The arguments for. Those in favor, such as the League of Women Voters, the

AFL-CIO, the nonpartisan registration groups, and the Democratic Party, argue that making it easier for prospective voters to register is the most important factor in increasing the turnout rate. They believe that most state election laws can be interpreted to require that registration forms be distributed as widely and freely as possible, including at state agencies. They believe that state employees can be trusted to conduct such drives in a fair and nonpartisan manner, and they point to Governor Cuomo's order which requires that state officials in New York "shall maintain a position of strict neutrality with respect to a person's party enrollment."

The arguments against. Republican politicians have argued that in most states registration is already easy, that state election laws should be interpreted strictly and do not now permit state officials to conduct registration drives, and that state employees, especially those affiliated with the human services employees' unions, are likely to conduct such drives to benefit the Democrats.

Critics also point out that regulations prohibit federal employees from using their official authority for the purpose of interfering with, or affecting the results of, an election. The White House Office of Personnel Management threatened three Democratic governors with cutoffs of some federal funds unless they could demonstrate that their orders did not violate these federal regulations. In response, the Democrats charged that the administration was using blackmail and pressure tactics.

Resolving the issues. The state and federal courts will eventually resolve this dispute. After Governor Cuomo issued his Executive Order 43 in New York, the Republican Party filed suit in the state court to block its implementation. A lower court judge agreed, arguing that "it is a use of state funds for purposes not authorized by law," and that it violated a provision of the state constitution requiring bipartisan control of registration. The court insisted that such actions must be authorized by the legislature before being put into effect by the governor, and the state's high court extended the ban for a year while the case was being considered.

THE NONVOTERS: WHO ARE THEY?

In modern times it has become easier to register and vote than at any other time in our history, and yet the percentage of eligible adults who choose to register has declined from approximately 85 percent in the 1950s to around 70 percent in the 1980s, while the percentage of people who vote has declined from about 63 percent to about 53 percent.

The image of the nonvoter, Arthur Hadley points out, is that of "Boobus Americanus," whom he describes as a "young lunkhead, bombed on beer or stoned on pot, a high school dropout, perhaps a motorcycle-revving white or jiving black, living in the rural South or Northern city slum, dirty, poor, alienated, undereducated, and alone."[15] While some nonvoters fit this description, the fact is that most do not.

Nonregistrants

Younger, poorer, less well educated, more mobile, and single people are more likely not to register. Members of racial and linguistic minority groups are less likely to register than white English-speaking Americans, as Figure 5-5 shows.

These figures must be approached with caution. It is not true that all minorities and all poor, young, and uneducated people do not register, but it is true that they are less likely to register than wealthier, older, better-educated people. High *rates* should not be confused with large *numbers of voters:* Jews, who

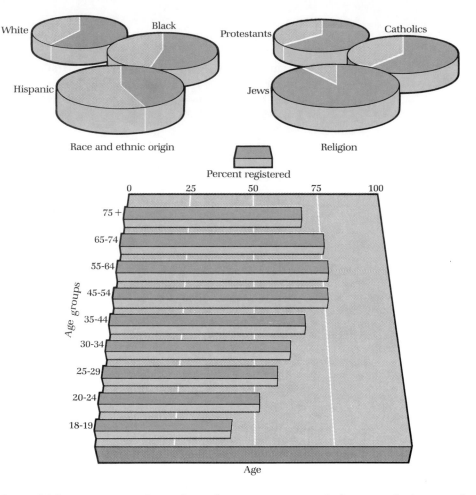

Figure 5-5. Registration rates for selected categories: race and ethnic origin, age, and religion. Whites have the highest voting rates, followed by blacks and Hispanics. Young voters, 18–29, have the lowest rates of any age group. (Sources: For race and ethnic origin and age: U.S. Bureau of the Census, *Voting and Registration in the Election of November 1980*, Current Population Reports, Series P-20, no. 370; for religion: *Gallup Opinion Index*, September 1979, p. 271.)

have high rates, constitute less than 3 percent of the population, and the number of Jewish voters is far smaller than the number of Hispanic or black voters—even though Hispanics and blacks have much lower registration rates.

Registrants: Core and peripheral voters

The decision to register or not to register is the major determinant of voting or not voting. But even among those who register, approximately one-fifth will not vote in presidential elections, and almost half will not vote in off-year congressional elections. Between one-half and three-fourths of those who are registered will not vote in off-year state and local elections.

How do we explain the dropouts? The *core-peripheral* explanation argues that most registrants vote most of the time but that some vote very little; thus there are significant differences between the core and the peripheral electorate.[16] A core, consisting of about 40 percent of the VAP—60 percent of the registered voters—vote in most elections. A group of peripheral voters vote occasionally; they constitute about 20 percent of the VAP and about 30 percent of the registered voters. Those who have voted in the past are likely to vote in future elections, while those who have voted only occasionally in the past (or not at all) are likely not to vote in forthcoming elections.[17] The key in any election is to get larger numbers of peripheral voters into the voting booths.

DO COLLEGE STUDENTS VOTE IN CAMPUS ELECTIONS?

The turnout rates in student elections on most college campuses are quite low. At the University of Texas the students abolished their students' association in 1978, and in a vote to reestablish it in 1982, only 3905 students voted out of a total enrollment of 45,825. At the University of Kentucky only 2112 of the 23,000 students voted for a president of the student body in 1982. At Columbia College the 1983 elections for class president produced a turnout of less than 7 percent, while at Barnard College in 1984 a similar percentage voted for president of the freshman class.

How does your college compare?

Socioeconomic and demographic factors influencing participation

The most important **socioeconomic factors** influencing political participation are education, income, and occupation. The most important **demographic factors** are age, gender, race, ethnicity and language, and class.

Education. The key factor is education. Figure 5-6 shows the relationship between years of school completed and turnout rates in the 1980 presidential election. Note that as the number of years of school completed increases, the voting rates rise. Schools emphasize a citizen's obligation to vote, and they impart information which makes people feel more confident about participating in public affairs.

But an increase in the educational levels of the entire population has not led to an increase in turnouts; in fact, just the reverse occurred in the 1960s and 1970s. As the educational levels rose, turnouts fell. Clearly, other factors must have worked to drive turnouts down.

Figure 5-6. Education and turnout, 1980. Turnouts are higher among people who have completed more years of schooling. (Source: U.S. Bureau of the Census, *Current Population Reports*, Series P-20, no. 370.)

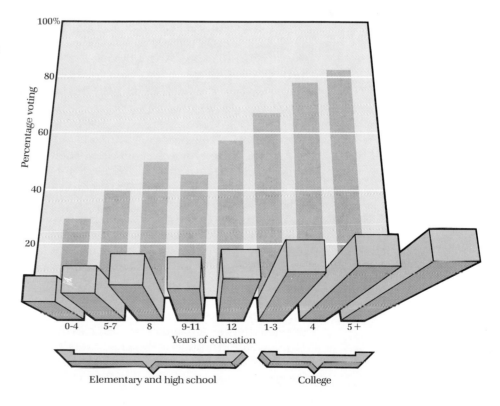

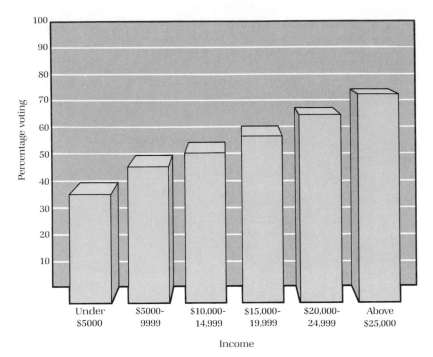

Figure 5-7. Income and turnout, 1980. Turnouts are higher among people with more income. (Source: U.S. Bureau of the Census, *Current Population Reports*, Series P-20, no. 370.)

Income. Higher income levels are associated with sharply increased rates of voting, as Figure 5-7 shows. This is due in part to the fact that more years of school completed are associated with higher income, and it is the schooling, rather than the income level, that is the important factor. People who have finished college vote at high rates no matter what their income.

Yet just as with education, increased income does not lead to larger turnouts. As the per capita wealth of the population increased in the past two decades, turnouts fell. And although real income had fallen for several years, turnouts in the 1982 congressional elections increased. This mirrors the dramatic rise in turnouts in the 1930s, when economic misery rather than prosperity brought people to the polls.

Occupation. Professionals and executives have the highest rates; managers and white-collar workers come next. They are followed by farmers; clerical, skilled, and service workers; unskilled workers; and farm laborers. The lower the occupation, the less education completed and the lower the income, all of which reinforces nonvoting.

Turnouts are especially low among those who have recently been laid off from work, a result of the blow to their self-esteem. The higher the short-term unemployment rate, the lower the turnout. In the 1980 elections only 50 percent of those who were unemployed reported registering, and only 41 percent reported voting—and it is likely that the actual voting rates were lower. Sometimes those who are most affected by worsening economic conditions are least likely to make their presence felt in elections.[18] At other times, such as during the great depression and in the 1982 congressional elections, the jobless have a respectable turnout (only 3 percent less than the employed in 1982).

Unionized workers vote at higher rates than nonunionized workers. Since the early 1970s union members have made up a declining proportion of the labor force, now constituting less than one-fifth. This could account for millions of dropouts in the past decade, since formerly unionized workers and nonunionized entrants into the labor force are not mobilized to vote by union shop stewards.

Recent transformations in the American economy may also affect turnout. Workers in thriving industries in the 1960s had a sense of job security and relative affluence. But in the 1970s, as their industries declined, many of these workers became insecure. New entrants to the work force could not obtain these good industrial jobs. Many found nonunion, lower-paying, seasonal, service employment, which requires lower levels of skill but involves higher levels of stress. Lower-paid workers who are seasonally unemployed are less likely to vote than higher-paid workers with steady jobs.

Age. Turnouts are much lower among younger people than among older people. In 1972, when those between the ages of 18 and 21 were given the vote, 11 million people entered the electorate. Their initial registration and voting rates were the lowest of any age group; only 48 percent voted in 1972, and in every subsequent election a lower percentage of people in this age group have registered and voted. In 1980 only 35 percent voted, and in 1984 only half even bothered to register. The young are less likely to vote because they are highly mobile; three-fifths of them move every two years, and they have few ties to their communities. But in the near future voting rates may increase: between 1987 and 1993 the number of people between ages of 18 and 31 will decline from 57 million to 53.5 million, and meanwhile the number between the ages of 32 and 38 will increase from 26.5 million to 29.5 million—which means that the population is aging and, other things being equal, older people are more likely to vote.

Gender. Turnouts were lower among women than among men until recently. Women were socialized to believe that politics was "men's business" or were discouraged from voting by their husbands or fathers. Times have changed, and gradually the turnout rates of men and women have converged. As Figure 5-8 shows, by 1972 women had just about ended the gender gap, and by 1980

Figure 5-8. Age and sex and turnout, 1980. Turnout rates are higher for women than men. The only exception is among women over 60, some of whom may not vote because they were brought up to believe that politics is "for men only." In another decade it is likely that women of all age groups will have higher turnout rates than men. (Source: U.S. Bureau of the Census, *Current Population Reports,* Series P-20, no. 370.)

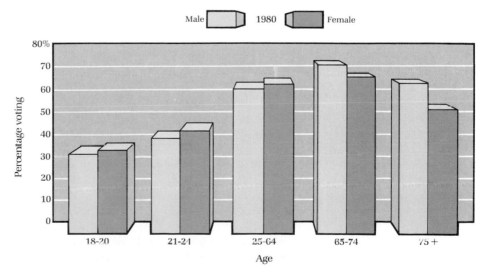

women under 65 were voting at higher rates than men, giving women a higher overall turnout rate than men for the first time in American history. Since there are approximately 6 million more women than men in the eligible electorate, for the foreseeable future women will constitute a majority of those voting.

Still, many women do not vote, especially women who are members of minority groups, poor women, and working women (although the rates of women under 45 are higher than those of men under 45); only 30.4 percent of Hispanic women and 52 percent of black women voted in 1980. In the 1984 elections, the Women's Vote Project was organized by sixty-five national women's organizations to conduct a nonpartisan drive to register 1.5 million women and concentrate on lower-income working women and minorities.

Race. Because of the constitutional and legal barriers erected by southern states against blacks, until the 1970s their registration and turnout rates were far lower than those of the white majority. Since then the gap has narrowed, especially in the south, where participation of blacks equals or exceeds that of whites. In the remainder of the nation it is a different story. Turnouts among blacks decreased after 1968, to a low of 43.5 percent in 1980. But the increase in numbers is impressive: from 4 million registered in 1966 to 8 million in 1980. The successful mayoral candidacies of blacks in Chicago, Philadelphia, and other big cities in the 1980s—including Los Angeles, Detroit, New Orleans, Atlanta, Oakland, Newark, Birmingham, Richmond, and the District of Columbia—and the presidential primary campaign of Reverend Jesse Jackson in 1984 reversed the decade-long trend. Black registration increased by 573,000 between 1980 and 1982, by 600,000 in 1983, and by another 2 million in 1984.[19]

Turnouts have also increased because the Voting Rights Act, as amended in 1982 and subsequently interpreted by the courts, voided certain ways of organizing elections that made it unlikely that black candidates could win. These included at-large, multiple-slate, and other winner-take-all systems which allowed white majorities to shut out black minorities from political power. Instead, systems which created districts that black candidates could win in local and congressional elections (drawn to maximize the number of black voters) encouraged large turnouts among blacks, and these systems were increasingly in use in the 1980s.

Ethnicity and language. Studies have shown that among people whose native language is not English, a greater facility in reading and understanding English is associated with a greater likelihood of voting.[20] There are more than 15 million Hispanics in the United States, which makes them the second largest, and the fastest-growing, minority group in the nation. About 60 percent are of Mexican origin and are concentrated in the southwest; the remainder consist of Cubans in Florida, Central Americans in California and Texas, and Puerto Ricans in the northeast.

Hispanics have a median age of 23, compared with a median age of 25 for blacks and of 30 for whites. Their median family income in 1982 was $16,401, compared with $23,517 for whites and $13,266 for blacks. They have fewer years of schooling, and some have less facility in English. Many have chosen not to become citizens. Not surprisingly, these socioeconomic and demographic characteristics are associated with low rates of voting. Only 44 percent of Hispanics, or 6.6 million, are even eligible to vote.

Immediately following their naturalization at Miami's Orange Bowl in 1984, 10,000 new citizens register to vote. (*AP Worldwide Photos.*)

For the 1984 elections Hispanic organizations mounted registration drives in Texas, Florida, and California. The Republicans registered Cuban Americans in Dade County, Florida, where surveys show that 57 percent are Republicans and that only 16 percent are Democrats. Mexican-American mayors in Denver and San Antonio and a Puerto Rican mayor in Miami spurred voter registration drives. The Southwest Voter Education Project and the Midwest Voter Registration Project conducted a $2 million drive to register Hispanics in the west, hoping to increase the total to 4.4 million registered and more than 3.6 million voting. As the proportion of Hispanics who are citizens, speak English well, are married and settled, and have completed high school increases greatly in this decade, the number of Hispanics who vote will also increase markedly. By the year 2000 there will be 30 million Hispanics in the United States, about 12 percent of the total population, and as they show up at the polls in larger numbers, they will transform the politics of the southwest, just as voting by blacks has changed the politics of the south and of the cities of the north.

Class. Between 1960 and 1980 as many as 15 million white middle-class and working-class people dropped out of the electorate or decided to vote only occasionally; thus a new group of peripheral voters emerged. Most of these voters are concentrated in the large northern industrial states.[21] This shift from the core to the periphery of the electorate increased *class polarization* among white voters: the tendency to divide along *class* lines. Increasingly, voters were the affluent and well educated, and nonvoters were the less affluent and less well educated. In 1980 people who described themselves as "working-class" voted at a 40 percent rate, while self-identified members of the "upper middle class" voted at a 70 percent rate.[22]

Some observers have pointed out that class polarization in the 1970s was no greater than it was in the 1950s and that it was sharply reduced in the mid-1980s; thus these changes from one decade to the next should be put in perspective. Also, as some working-class whites dropped out of the core electorate, their places were taken by blacks and Hispanics.

Socioeconomic and demographic factors: A caution. The data presented thus far show that people with different characteristics—race, income, education, occupation, and age—have different rates of registration and voting. There is nothing inevitable about these rates. There is no natural or sociological "law" which says that some kinds of people will always participate less than others. In New York City, two-thirds of the Puerto Ricans are unregistered, while in Puerto Rico the turnout rates among all groups exceed those on the mainland. In Miami when a Puerto Rican mayor ran for reelection in 1981, the turnout of Hispanics exceeded that of whites. In Atlanta in 1981 the turnout of blacks was equal to that of whites when Andrew Young, a black candidate, ran successfully for mayor. Black turnout rates in primaries exceeded those of whites in many states in 1984, when Jesse Jackson ran for president. Socioeconomic correlations can describe rates of voting among different people, but they cannot tell us why rates differ or when rates will change.

Political factors influencing participation

Deciding to vote or not to vote, to register or not to register, is political behavior, and it is shaped by attitudes toward politics. Nonvoters have somewhat different political attitudes from those of voters; these include party identification and conservative versus liberal attitudes toward government policies.

Party identification. The stronger a person's identification with a major political party, the more likely that person is to vote. The people who are most likely to vote are strong Republicans, followed by weak Republicans and independents who lean toward the Republican Party. Strong, weak, and independent Democrats are less likely to vote. People who claim to be independent of the parties and have no identification with them are least likely to vote. The data are summarized in Figure 5-9.

Figure 5-9. Party identification and turnout, 1980. Strong Republicans and Democrats have the highest turnout rates, followed by weak and independent Republicans, then by weak and independent Democrats. Pure independents have the lowest turnout rates. (Source: Center for Political Studies of the Institute for Social Research, University of Michigan.)

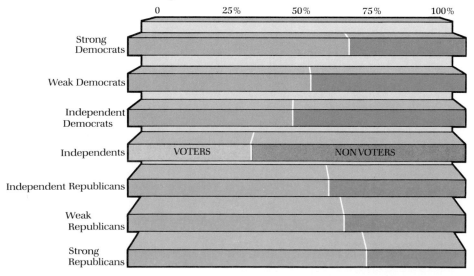

Of those who vote, Republicans are more likely than Democrats to remain in the core electorate. A 1976 survey indicated that 68 percent of the Democrats, compared with 79 percent of the Republicans, reported voting in all or most presidential elections, while 18 percent of the Democrats reported voting in some elections, compared with 14 percent of the Republicans.[23]

A common misconception is that most nonvoters are Democrats. Democrats hold a slight margin among unregistered men (38 to 43 percent) and a greater margin among unregistered women (31 to 48 percent), but the lead is not overwhelming, and it decreased shortly before the 1984 elections. Most youthful voters, again contrary to popular belief, are not Democrats: among the 14 million unregistered people between the ages of 18 and 24, Republicans hold a slight edge (42 to 41 percent). Again, among the 4 million unregistered college graduates, Republicans hold their own against Democrats (44 to 44 percent). Republicans therefore concentrate their voter registration drives on young men, especially those with good jobs and a college education. Democrats are more likely to gain among women, minorities, and those without a college education.

Liberalism versus conservatism. Most voters consider themselves liberal (favoring a large role for government and innovation in policy-making), conservative (favoring a smaller role for government and more traditional policies), or moderate. Self-described liberals and conservatives have the same voting rate, which is somewhat higher than that of moderates or of those who describe themselves as "very conservative." From a sample of unregistered people who were asked to describe their orientation, we can project that, among all the unregistered, 9 million are liberals, 16 million are moderates, and 13 million are conservatives.[24]

Conservatives have often argued that if the millions of nonvoters could be mobilized for a cause, their side would benefit. Liberals have made the same argument for their side. But the data indicate that if all the nonvoters did register and vote, there would be little change in the moderate to conservative politics of American life. Polls have shown little difference between voters and nonvoters on the issues of abortion, taxes, defense spending, and the Equal Rights Amendment. Major change would occur, however, if a party or cause registered its supporters, while other nonvoters remained unregistered.

EXPLAINING THE TURNOUT RATES

Thus far this chapter has discussed registration and turnout rates in historical and comparative perspective and has described in socioeconomic and political terms the characteristics of voters and nonvoters. But such *descriptions* are not *analysis:* we know who votes and who does not vote, but not why; and we do not know why rates rise and fall. To analyze voting and nonvoting, we need to isolate differences in attitudes between voters and nonvoters. For anyone interested in political office or power, an explanation of these differences offers the possibility of new strategies and tactics to mobilize supporters.

Is the electorate disillusioned?

People may feel negatively about politics: they may believe that "the system" is rigged and corrupt and benefits other people or groups at their expense, and if they decide that the system is no longer legitimate, they become alienated from it. Or they may lose trust in politicians, considering them corrupt, incom-

A casual observer at this New York polling place might conclude that turnout is heavy, but antiquated procedures can snarl even a short line. (*Richard Hackett.*)

petent, or evil, which erodes the authority relationship. They may believe in the system and in their leaders, but oppose some of the policies of the government. They may lose interest in politics and become apathetic.

The alienated: Mistrust of government. Mistrust of government and politicians has increased until the 1980s.[25] Figure 5-10 shows that this mistrust was paralleled by a loss of confidence in most other institutions.

It would be misleading to assume from these data that such attitudes directly affect registration and turnouts. Studies conducted by the National Opinion Research Center in 1977 and 1978 found few differences between voters and nonvoters (Figure 5-11). Nonvoters were more likely than voters to agree that "people running the country do not care what happens to you" (60

Figure 5-10. The decline of confidence in institutions, 1966, 1971–1981. In 1966 and from 1971 to 1981, the Harris survey used the following question to poll opinion about major institutions of American society: "As far as people in charge of running _____ are concerned, would you say you have a great deal of confidence, only some confidence, or hardly any confidence at all in them?" Results for four of the institutions are shown here. (Source: Data from Harris survey, 22 October 1981, no. 85; used with permission of Chicago Tribune-New York News Syndicate.)

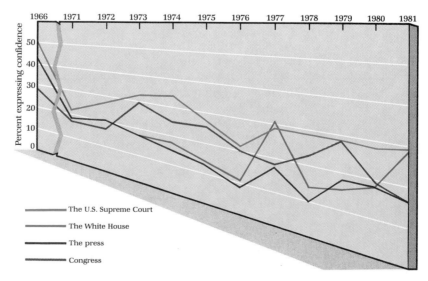

Figure 5-11. Increase in suspicion of government, 1964–1980. People were polled in election year on the following questions: (1) "Would you say the government is pretty much run by a few big interests looking out for themselves or that it is run for the benefit of all the people?" (2) "How much of the time do you think you can trust the government in Washington to do what is right—just about always, most of the time, or only some of the time?" (3) "Do you feel that almost all of the people running the government are smart people, or do you think that quite a few of them don't seem to know what they are doing?" (Source: Surveys by Center for Political Studies of the Institute for Social Research, University of Michigan Election Studies, latest that of April 1980; graph adapted from *Public Opinion*, June/July 1981.)

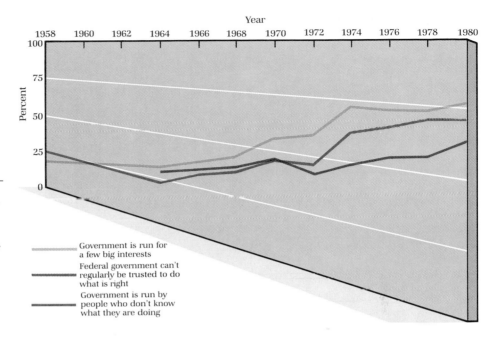

Government is run for a few big interests

Federal government can't regularly be trusted to do what is right

Government is run by people who don't know what they are doing

to 50 percent), and they were more likely to agree that "public officials are not interested in problems facing the average person" (72 to 62 percent). But on most other questions, such as "people in Washington are out of touch with the rest of the country," there were hardly any differences between the two groups. Similarly, Louis Harris Associates found virtually no difference between voters and nonvoters in levels of confidence or in the leaders of major institutions.

The apathetic: No enthusiasm for candidates. Low turnouts might be due to lack of enthusiasm for the candidates. The 1980 Census Bureau survey of nonvoters, for example, found that 47 percent did not prefer a candidate or were not interested in the election and that 27 percent of those who were registered but did not vote also felt that way. Such apathy could account for as many as 21 million nonvoters.[26] Since 1952 the Gallup organization has polled voters in the summer of each presidential election year. Its interviewers hand respondents a "scalometer" card with ten boxes, numbered from +5 on the top to 0 in the middle and down to −5 at the bottom. The respondent marks +5 to indicate the highest opinion of a candidate and −5 to indicate the lowest opinion. For every election between 1952 and 1980, with the exception of that in 1976, the trend has been downward, as Figure 5-12 makes clear.

Again, we should not conclude that apathy about candidates causes low turnouts. The Census Bureau survey shows that only one-ninth of the registered nonvoters had no preference among candidates. Some studies have shown that there is little or no difference between voters and nonvoters in terms of their feelings about candidates.[27]

The dissatisfied: Disagreement with policies. Some people may leave the core electorate or become nonvoters because they disagree with government policies. Minorities and the poor may think that government favors the white working class and middle class; the white working class and middle class may

Figure 5-12. Perceptions of presidential candidates, 1952–1980: percentage of respondents to the Gallup Poll giving highly favorable ratings to presidential candidates. (Source: *The New York Times*, 31 October 1980.)

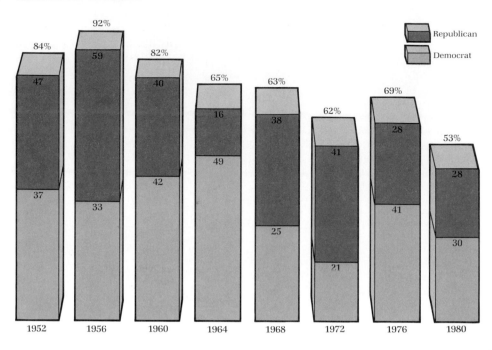

think that government is oriented toward minorities and the poor. Hawks may want the government to take a stronger stand against communism; doves may oppose any American interventions in foreign countries. Profamily groups and religious fundamentalists may believe that the government's policies favor the side of those whose views are more humanist and secular, and vice versa.

But again, there seems to be little difference between voters and nonvoters here. And there is little difference between the poor and minorities who choose to vote and those who do not or between white core voters who have dropped out of the electorate and those who have not. One could also argue that dissatisfaction with government policies can just as easily lead to larger turnouts and a protest vote as to smaller turnouts—something that seemed true in the 1984 presidential election.

Mobilizing large numbers of nonvoters around dissatisfaction with issues seems to be the Holy Grail of presidential politics. Conservatives like Barry Goldwater in 1964 argued that there were millions of disaffected people just waiting for a conservative presidential candidate; he expected them to come out of the woodwork and propel him to victory, but they never appeared and he was crushed in the election. George McGovern in 1972 thought that there were millions of disaffected liberals who were eagerly awaiting his candidacy to come back to the polls; he expected to get 60 percent of the young people (who he thought were antiwar liberals and radicals) to vote and to get at least 60 percent of their vote. Instead, only 40 percent turned out, and of these, only 40 percent voted for him. In the 1980s the religious and conservative groups of the new right argued that millions of religious fundamentalists could be mobilized to vote for right-wing candidates for the presidency and Congress, while social welfare activists on the liberal and left radical end of the political spectrum believed that millions of the poor would go to the polls in protest against

Reaganomics and completely reshape public priorities, from the military to social welfare. Both groups were disappointed.

Social scientists find little evidence to support such assumptions. On most issues, either nonvoters hold opinions that are virtually identical to those of voters, or they have weak opinions or no opinions at all.[28] Sometimes voters are more liberal than nonvoters and sometimes they are more conservative, depending on the issue. On most issues voters represent the attitudes of the entire population. Surveys taken in the 1970s, when participation was declining, show that there was little difference of opinion between voters and nonvoters. Yet it may well be that in the 1980s, after years of cutbacks, retrenchment, and conservative domestic and foreign policies, the poor and minority nonvoters have a quite different political agenda from that of the majority of voters.

The cynical: Voting does not matter. Some people believe that voting is meaningless. Arthur Hadley labels these people *refrainers* and argues that they are disgusted with politics and politicians because they believe that their own values and ethics are not reflected in a corrupt system. Most of these people are white, are middle-class, and have strong ethical or religious values.[29] In 1984 many of them were mobilized by fundamentalist religious leaders, and more than 2 million registered to vote for the first time—most in the Republican Party.

The powerless: Loss of efficacy. Some voters and nonvoters differ significantly in their feelings of *efficacy:* their belief that they can successfully influence politicians. The Survey Research Center asked a national sample questions which measured feelings of efficacy, and it found that since 1960 the trend has been downward for the entire population.

The greatest declines in feelings of efficacy are associated with the movement from core to peripheral voting and with dropping out of the electorate. One study showed that a decrease in feelings of efficacy accounts for 30 percent of the drop in turnout since 1960.[30] The way to get more people to the polls is to convince them that they can make a difference and that politicians will have to respond to their needs. An increase in feelings of efficacy can be promoted by candidates for office, as Franklin Roosevelt managed to do with his coalition of religious minorities, the poor, and the unemployed in the 1930s and as Jesse Jackson did with racial and ethnic minorities in 1984, with his ''I am somebody'' slogan.

The mass media: Impact on participation

The two-way flow of political communication—between leaders and the electorate—may also offer a partial explanation for fluctuations in turnouts.

Communicating to voters. The American people have changed their reading and viewing habits in the past two decades. Surveys have shown that people who rely on newspapers or news magazines obtain more factual information than those who rely on thirty minutes of televised network or local news. A front-page article in a serious newspaper contains 10 to 20 times as much information as a one-minute feature on the nightly news.

The print and the broadcast media present political events differently: the print media emphasize issues and try to put events into context and give them

Computerized direct-mail techniques can reach millions of voters, as shown by Richard Viguerie, who handles conservative candidates and causes. (*David Burnett: Contact.*)

larger meaning. They offer editorial opinion and comment by columnists. The better papers have op-ed pages that feature contributions from politicians, civic leaders, and academics. Broadcasts give a brief summary of the day's events, often without providing any context, background, or comparative perspective. They emphasize visual excitement and personalities, but often they leave the viewer with an emotional rather than a reasoned response to a story and with the impression that politics involves a series of random, disconnected, and violent events with little meaning.

More than two-thirds of the public rely primarily on news broadcasts for information or politics. Studies indicate that as much as 20 percent of the decline in voter turnout can be attributed to the changeover from reading to viewing, presumably because the broadcast media provide less information than the print media and leave people more confused.[31]

Communicating with politicians. Campaigning has always been a form of entertainment. Once it involved face-to-face contact between voters and candidates. Parades, marches, ballgames, and picnics were organized by parties. Local party workers passed around ribbons, buttons, and leaflets to people in their neighborhoods. They asked people to vote for candidates, and they were in the neighborhoods on election day to make sure that their friends went to the polls. Today candidates use political commercials, phone banks, and direct mail to communicate with voters; face-to-face communication has disappeared. It is easier to drop out of the electorate when there is no one to answer to. It is easier to believe that "no one cares" when politicians are just images on the screen—when their messages are no different from advertisements for soap or sodas.

Studies have shown that turnouts in poorer neighborhoods in the early twentieth century were high because these neighborhoods were organized by strong local parties. At the Joint Center for Political Studies, researchers have found that registration campaigns among black voters were most effective when they were controlled by party groups which could follow up with election-day efforts to pull voters to the polls.

Chloroforming the electorate. Some efforts at communication involve attempts to keep voters away from the polls. "Some of the tactics we use in political campaigns do very much suppress the vote," admitted Robert Squier, a consultant for the Democratic Party.[32] Commercials may try to play on voters' apathy, alienation, or feelings of inefficacy in an effort to reduce turnout in opposition strongholds. The key to such efforts at communication is to use commercials which cast doubt on the character and integrity of opposition candidates or which try to weaken the party loyalty of opposition voters.

THINGS TO COME

COMPUTER DEMOCRACY. Turnouts are once again increasing, as we saw in the congressional elections of 1982 and the presidential election of 1984. The development of new campaign technologies should maintain this trend.

Media "narrowcasting." The proliferation of radio and cable and of low-power and satellite television stations means that more stations appeal to narrow segments of the community. There are stations for minorities (known as *urban contemporary* or *inner-city* stations), for suburbanites, for immigrants, and for non-English-speaking minorities. Often these stations put on "get out the vote" drives, and increasingly these are being sponsored by major corporations. Modern advertising techniques applied to voter registration have the potential to increase turnouts among young voters.

"Merge and purge" computerized drives. Many organizations that are interested in issues have sponsored voter registration drives. The traditional "shoe leather" approach involves canvassing neighborhoods or setting up booths where pedestrian traffic is heavy; the Republican Party's "Reagan roundups" of potential voters in 1984 are an example. New computerized technology is aiding these efforts. A local group can obtain lists of registered voters. It can match these lists against car registrations, magazine subscription lists, new utility hookups in suburban developments, and census tracts. The various lists are "merged and purged," and everyone who is already registered is removed. The remaining nonvoters can be sorted by neighborhood, income, race, religion, ethnicity, occupation, and social class; this enables each party to concentrate on those who are most likely to support its candidates. The computer can then automatically dial a number and connect a party worker with one of these nonvoters, simultaneously displaying information about the person on the monitor. Or it can play a recorded "get out the vote" pitch or even a recorded message from a prominent politician. In 1984 computerized drives worked very effectively for the Republican Party, which dominated new registrations in important sun belt states.[33]

Interactive media. In the next two decades other technological changes in the area of **interactive media** have the potential to transform our electoral processes dramatically. From the ballot box of the past to the modern voting machine, we have relied on primitive mechanical methods of registering voters and counting votes. In the future it will be possible to register voters by using telephone links to central computers or by using a home computer or a "two-way" cable television hookup (which permits a viewer to send a message to a central computer).

Interactive communication. A crucial change will come when interactive television becomes a familiar household amenity. By pushing buttons, viewers can shop, bank, make plane or theater reservations, and even take college courses—all in their own homes. The implications of interactive television were noted as early as 1961, when Buckminster Fuller (an inventor best known for the geodesic dome) argued that "with two-way TV, constant referendum of democracy will be

The next century may well see "push-button voting." Already Warner Communications' QUBE system conducts public opinion polls for local cablecasters. (*Michael Abramson: © Warner Amex Cable Communications.*)

manifest, and democracy will become the most practical form of industrial and space-age government by all people, for all people."

Warner Communications has developed the QUBE system for cable television. Viewers press buttons on their hand-held consoles, and their opinions on any subject are recorded by the studio's central computer. Within minutes, the results of an opinion poll can be flashed onto the television screen, and viewers can see how everyone else responded—and so can pollsters and politicians. In Columbus, Ohio, local officials used the station to conduct a poll that determined the city's snow-removal plans; the viewers told the mayor that they did not want to pay higher city taxes just to get the streets cleared sooner.

Push-button voting? Interactive systems could be used for election-day voting. The ballot could appear on television, and the votes could be transmitted over telephone or cable lines to a central computer. People could use special identifying codes (much as they safeguard themselves when using a bank money machine or a long-distance telephone service), which they would be given when they registered to vote.

Before we assume that electronic registration and voting are just around the corner, we should recognize some of the problems. First, the cable technologies are expensive—the push-button mechanisms and cable boxes cost as much as $300, and two-way cable services cost $50 or more per month. Unless the government decided to give them to everyone (which could cost as much as $1000 per household, or $70 billion), access would be limited to those who could afford them. We would then have a two-tier system: home voting by the affluent and voting at the polls by the poor. Other problems include fraud by people voting at home, stealing elections by tampering with the central computers, and ways to preserve privacy and prevent any pressuring of voters at home. If these problems can be surmounted, interactive media could transform registration and voting, leading to much higher rates of voting (especially among the elderly and disabled and those who are away from home). But these changes are not likely to occur before the year 2000, and a national system of home voting is probably least likely. It is more likely that politicians will use nonbinding public opinion polls on a regular basis to gather information; yet if such systems are instituted in the next two decades, they will in effect become "votes" that influence politics just as much as the real votes that elect people to office.[34]

IN CONCLUSION

A small majority of eligible Americans vote for president, and the percentage of eligible voters who vote for candidates for other offices is even lower. Of all the western democracies, the United States holds the most elections, asks the most of its voters—and has the lowest rates of registration and turnout.

Those who register and vote often differ significantly from those who vote infrequently or have dropped out of the electorate. Better-educated, wealthier, older people have higher voting rates, as do women, whites, and those who are strongly identified with a party (especially Republicans). Minorities, the young, the unemployed, and nonunionized workers have the lowest rates of voting. Alienation and apathy, although widespread, do not distinguish voters from nonvoters; voters, however, believe that they can act effectively in politics and nonvoters do not.

The outlook for mass participation by the electorate in the near future is improving. Massive voter registration drives, aided by computer technologies, the aging of the electorate, and the elimination of remaining discriminatory practices, led to the increases in turnout in the 1982 and 1984 national elections. In the more distant future, new technological developments may dramatically transform the entire election process and lead to much higher rates of participation and a renewed emphasis on direct democracy.

NOTES

1. Aristotle, *Politics*, Clarendon Press, Oxford, 1948, book 4, chap. 2, pp. 262–267.
2. *Public Opinion*, vol. 44, April–May 1980, p. 32; see also Seymour Martin Lipset, *Political Man*, Doubleday, Garden City, N.Y., 1960, part 2.
3. Arthur T. Hadley, *The Empty Polling Booth*, Prentice-Hall, Englewood Cliffs, N.J., 1978, p. 106; see also E. E. Schattschneider, *The Semi-Sovereign People*, Holt, New York, 1960.
4. Curtis B. Gans, "The Empty Ballot Box," *Public Opinion*, September–October 1978, p. 34.
5. Pericles, "Funeral Oration," in Thucydides, *The Peloponnesian Wars*.
6. David B. Magleby, *Direct Legislation: Voting on Ballot Propositions in the United States*, Johns Hopkins, Baltimore, 1984.
7. Lee Sigelman, "The Nonvoting Voter in Voting Research," *American Journal of Political Science*, vol. 26, no. 1, February 1982, pp. 47–55.
8. *Public Opinion*, vol. 44, April–May 1980, p. 33; see also John R. Petrocik, "Voter Turnout and Electoral Oscillation," *American Politics Quarterly*, vol. 9, no. 2, April 1981, pp. 161–180.
9. Richard W. Boyd, "Decline of U.S. Voter Turnout," *American Politics Quarterly*, vol. 9, no. 2, April 1981, pp. 133–136.
10. *Guinn v. United States*, 238 U.S. 347 (1915).
11. U.S. Commission on Civil Rights, *The Voting Rights Act: Unfinished Goals*, GPO, Washington, D.C., 1982, pp. 22–37.
12. *Harper v. Virginia State Board of Elections*, 383 U.S. 663 (1966).
13. Raymond Wolfinger and Steven Rosenstone, *Who Votes?* Yale University Press, New Haven, Conn., 1980, p. 88.
14. Steven Rosenstone and Raymond Wolfinger, "The Effect of Registration Laws on Voter Turnouts," *American Political Science Review*, vol. 72, March 1978, p. 33.
15. Hadley, op. cit., p. 17.
16. This concept was developed in Boyd, op. cit.
17. Michael W. Traugott and Clyde Tucker, "Strategies for Predicting whether a Citizen Will Vote and Estimation of Electoral Outcomes," *Public Opinion Quarterly*, vol. 48, no. 1, spring 1984, pp. 332–334.
18. Steven J. Rosenstone, "Economic Adversity and Voter Turnout," *American Journal of Political Science*, vol. 26, no. 1, February 1982, p. 438.

19. Data from Joint Center for Political Studies.

20. Carlos Arce, *Language Proficiency and Other Correlates of Voting by Mexican Origin Citizens,* University of Michigan, Survey Research Center, Ann Arbor, 1982.

21. Howard L. Reiter, "Why Is Turnout Down?" *Public Opinion Quarterly,* vol. 43, no. 3, fall 1979, pp. 297–311.

22. Data from William A. Crotty, *American Parties in Decline,* 2d ed., Little, Brown, Boston, 1984, table 1.4, p. 14.

23. Data from University of Michigan, Survey Research Center, Ann Arbor.

24. Data from Crotty, op. cit., and New York Times/CBS polls, 1983–1984.

25. Seymour Martin Lipset, *The Confidence Gap,* Free Press, New York, 1984, p. 15.

26. Bureau of the Census, "Voting and Registration in the Election of 1980," ser. P-20, no. 359, p. 113.

27. William Maddox, "Candidate Images among Voters and Non-Voters in 1976," *American Politics Quarterly,* vol. 18, no. 2, April 1980, pp. 209–220.

28. Wolfinger and Rosenstone, op. cit., p. 109.

29. Hadley, op. cit.

30. Stephen D. Shaeffer, "A Multivariate Explanation of Decreasing Turnout in Presidential Elections, 1960–1976," *American Journal of Political Science,* vol. 25, no. 1, February 1981, pp. 68–93.

31. Ibid.

32. Thomas Edsall, "How to Keep Voters Away from the Polls," *Washington Post National Weekly Edition,* May 14, 1984.

33. Thomas Edsall, "The GOP's Registration Coup," *Washington Post National Weekly Edition,* Oct. 1, 1984.

34. Susan D. Weil and Richard M. Pious, "Emerging New Technologies: Political Applications," report to the Sloan Foundation Commission on the Presidential Selection Process, Sept. 30, 1983.

FURTHER READING

Amundsen, Kirsten: *A New Look at the Silenced Majority,* Prentice-Hall, Englewood Cliffs, N.J., 1977. A study of nonvoting.

Hadley, Arthur T.: *The Empty Polling Booth,* Prentice-Hall, Englewood Cliffs, N.J., 1978. Ideas on what makes nonvoters tick.

Kimball, Penn: *The Disconnected,* Columbia University Press, New York, 1972. A pioneering study of nonvoters in urban centers.

Lane, Robert E.: *Political Life,* Free Press, New York, 1959. A historical analysis of turnouts in the United States and other democracies, with useful comments on the role of the media.

Lipset, Seymour Martin: *Political Man,* Doubleday, Garden City, N.Y., 1960. A consideration of political behavior. Part 2 compares the United States with other democracies and argues that larger turnouts might lead to political instability.

Scott, Anne F., and Andrew M. Scott (eds.): *One-Half the People,* University of Illinois Press, Urbana, 1983. A study of the fight for women's suffrage.

U.S. Commission on Civil Rights: *The Voting Rights Act: Unfinished Goals,* GPO, Washington, D.C., 1982. A discussion of racial discrimination and its effects on turnouts in the 1980s.

Wolfinger, Raymond, and Steven Rosenstone: *Who Votes?* Yale University Press, New Haven, Conn., 1980. A consideration of voting behavior, debunking many social science theories about the causes of low turnouts and describing the impact of changes in registration laws in the 1970s.

USEFUL SOURCES

Burnham, Walter Dean: *Presidential Ballots, 1836–1892,* Johns Hopkins, Baltimore, 1955. Statistics on the popular vote and the electoral vote.

Kinnell, Susan, et al.: *The American Electorate: A Historical Bibliography,* ABC-CLIO Information Services, Santa Barbara, Calif., 1984. Lists sources on suffrage and turnout.

Robinson, E. E.: *The Presidential Vote: 1896–1932,* Stanford University Press, Stanford, Calif., 1947. Statistics on the popular vote and the electoral vote.

Scammon, Richard: *America at the Polls,* Governmental Affairs Institute, Washington, D.C., 1920–1964. Election statistics.

————et al. (eds.): *America Votes: A Handbook of Contemporary American Election Statistics,* Congressional Quarterly Press, Washington, D.C., biannually. Statistics on national elections, useful for calculating turnouts.

U.S. Bureau of the Census: *Voting and Registration in the Election of November 1984,* issued after each presidential election.

ORGANIZATIONS

Committee for the Study of the American Electorate. 421 New Jersey Avenue, S.E., Washington, D.C. 20003. For more information phone 202-471-1539.

Project Vote. 1200 Fifteenth Street, N.W., Suite 201, Washington, D.C. 20005. A coalition of groups that conduct nonpartisan voter registration drives. For more information phone 202-293-3933.

Southwest Voter Registration and Education Project. 201 N. St. Mary, Suite 501, San Antonio, Texas 78205. Reports on minority voting in the southwest. For more information phone 512-222-0224.

Voter Education Project. 52 Fairlie St., N.W., Atlanta, Georgia 30303. Reports on minority voting in the south. For more information telephone 404-522-7495.

From Cook County's Democratic organization
to the Republican National convention of
1984, there are many ways to participate in
party politics. (*D. Goldberg: Sygma; Kevin
Horan: Picture Group.*)

CHAPTER 6

PARTIES AND PACS: FROM OLD POLITICS TO NEW

mericans have always been ambivalent about political parties. "A good party is better than the best man that ever lived," said Thomas Reed, the Speaker of the House, at the end of the nineteenth century; but George Washington, in his farewell address to the nation, had warned of "the baneful effect of the spirit of party," and an antiparty spirit has been with us ever since.[1]

The Constitution makes no mention of parties. But the constitutional arrangements which preclude parties in theory almost require them in fact. Without them, how could a majority form in the electoral college to choose a president? How could Congress form majorities to pass legislation? Washington himself did nothing to discourage his followers from creating the Federalist Party, and James Madison, who in the Federal papers had written so eloquently of "curing the mischief of faction" (that is, party spirit), was one of the founders of the Anti-Federalist Party. Even those who have opposed parties in theory have found them indispensable in practice.

PARTIES: DEFINITIONS AND CHARACTERISTICS

A *political party* is an organization whose goal is to elect its members to public office. In the United States it is a private association, although it performs public functions. It differs from an *interest group* (which is also a private association) in that the goal of the latter is to affect policy, and to do this it elects its friends to office. The goal of a party is to win elections, and its means of accomplishing this involve policy.

Parties differ from *campaign organizations*, such as polling or advertising agencies: parties are organized to contest elections in a particular area—a city, a county, or a state—while professional campaign organizations go anywhere they are hired to go in order to help candidates win elections.

The people in parties

A party consists of three parts: the party-in-government, the party-in-the-electorate, and the party organization.

The *party-in-government* is made up of the elected or appointed officials who hold public office and belong to the party—the president and the Cabinet, other top administration appointees, members of Congress, state governors, state legislators, mayors, members of city councils, and the like. There are about 3000 elected and appointed officials in the national government and 600,000 or so in the state and local governments.

The *party-in-the-electorate* consists of voters who are identified with the party and (depending on state law) who are registered as party members. Of the 174 million people who were eligible to vote in 1984, about 125 million registered, and most identified themselves as Democrats or Republicans. Parties have open membership: the voter decides whether to join when registering to vote and cannot be kept out by party officials. The party cannot drop anyone from membership. It does not limit participation in party affairs or votes in party elections to an elite group, and in this respect American parties differ from most foreign parties, which set stiff membership requirements and can "purge" members who do not follow the party line.

Table 6-1. Activity of the electorate, 1980

Voted	53.2%
Attended political meetings, rallies, etc.	7%
Worked for a party or a candidate	4%
Gave money to a presidential candidate	6%

Source: Center for Political Studies.

The **_party organization_** consists of people who campaign and help candidates win elections but who usually do *not* themselves hold public office. As of 1980 only 3 percent of the public had ever belonged to a political party organization.[2] Table 6-1 summarizes other party activities.

We are a nation of joiners, but not when it comes to parties. Fewer than 1 percent of us currently belong to a party organization, compared with the 30 to 40 percent of voters who join community and civic organizations.

Functions of parties

Parties recruit people to run for public office. They limit the number of serious candidates to those nominated by the two major parties, which simplifies the choice for voters. They set priorities in elections by emphasizing some issues and ignoring others. The party in power holds itself accountable to voters for its conduct in office, while the opposition party gives voters an alternative: they can replace the incumbents with the challengers.

Parties provide a link between voters and the government by giving people the opportunity to voice their discontent to party workers. They mobilize voters and help increase turnouts. They organize the government to bridge the formal separation of powers, making it possible for party members to work together even though they are in different branches.

Responsible parties. There are two ways in which parties can perform these functions. One is for each party to be organized around a set of principles, develop its program from them, and offer a clear alternative to voters. The party should be prepared to implement the program in its entirety if it wins.[3]

Coalition parties. American parties rarely organize around consistent principles. Instead, they create coalitions from a variety of racial, religious, ethnic, sectional, cultural, and occupational constituencies. Coalition parties often embrace groups with competing interests, which requires them to put principles in second place. The New Deal coalition, organized by the Democrats in the 1930s, contained white racists and blacks, antiunion businesspeople and union members, conservatives opposing and liberals favoring regulation of business and greater expenditures for social welfare, and those favoring and those opposing a greater role for the national government. Republicans since the 1930s have included Main Street businesspeople who want low interest rates and Wall Street bankers who accept higher rates; sun belt and snow belt politicians who are competing for the same defense contracts and public works; and supply-siders who want tax cuts and fiscal conservatives who want tax increases.

CONVERGENCE. To keep a coalition intact, principles must be compromised, extreme positions moderated, and divisive issues submerged. Our parties span a continent and must appeal to a majority coalition fashioned from more than 180 million people of voting age. They usually win by appealing to a broad middle ground, although the Republicans move toward the center from a conservative position, and the Democrats move toward the center from a liberal one. Even when parties make appeals to principles, once they are in office, they are likely to depart from them. In the last two decades, supposedly liberal Democratic administrations increased defense spending, became involved in foreign wars, cut taxes for businesses and increased their subsidies, and by 1978 called for retrenchment in spending for social welfare. Supposedly conservative Republican administrations in the 1970s ended the Vietnamese war, cut the size of the military, negotiated arms agreements with the Soviets, made diplomatic overtures to communist China, and imposed wage-price controls on the economy, while presiding over a massive increase in spending for social welfare. In the 1980s the most conservative Republican administration in modern times ran up the largest deficits in history and got Congress to enact major tax cuts.[4]

DIVERGENCE. But convergence has its limits. The Republicans remain positioned to the right of center, and the Democrats to the left of center, and since 1980 they have diverged rather than converged. Thirty years ago the Democratic party-in-the-electorate was spread equally among all income groups; in the 1980s it has become increasingly the party of lower-income people, families with a female head of household, minorities, and liberals. In the same period the Republican party-in-the-electorate has gone from being only slightly skewed to upper-income families to a situation in which more than half of its membership consists of families whose income puts them in the top third. The changes in the parties' constituencies give them incentives to propose different economic and social policies.

Party structure: Key principles

American parties mirror the formal structure of government: they are federalized, decentralized, and split into legislative, executive, and judicial wings. These structural arrangements prevent the party organization from controlling the party-in-government.

Federal structure. The national parties are coalitions of fifty state parties, which in turn are coalitions of county and local parties.[5] Historically, the national party, as one local leader put it, "meets as infrequently as possible, decides as little as possible, establishes no public policy whatsoever, but does manage to hold a convention every four years."[6] Parties are organized horizontally rather than vertically: there are no "higher" or "lower" units. On most matters the national party cannot give orders to state parties, and state parties cannot give orders to county and local parties. All units of the party are autonomous and can deal with other units as equals—and so can their leaders.[7]

Executive, legislative, and judicial parties. The parties are organized around the major institutions of the national government and the state governments. The president, governors, and mayors—and their key appointees—form the "executive party," the members of Congress and state legislatures form the "legislative party," and candidates for state and local judgeships form the "judicial party."[8]

State and local party organization

The two national parties are organized from the bottom up rather than from the top down, in ***party committees*** which compete for public office. Those in villages, towns, townships, and cities compete for mayoral and city council posts. The members of county committees compete for county executive and legislative posts, for state judgeships, and for positions as prosecutors and sheriffs. The members of state committees compete for the offices of governor, lieutenant governor, attorney general, treasurer, and other statewide positions (including United States senator). The members of congressional district committees compete for seats in the House.

Choosing candidates for the party-in-government. There are three ways in which a *candidate* is chosen, depending on the state election laws: *designation* by a party committee, nomination by a *convention* to which registered party voters have chosen delegates, and nomination by a *primary* in which registered party voters (and sometimes independents) have participated.

Selecting the party organization. The members of these party committees are chosen in party elections, at conventions, or by the designation of other party committees. Party elections are organized in precincts (known in some states as *election districts*); a *precinct* is a small geographic area containing close to 1000 voters (nationwide there are 188,432 precincts). Each holds elections for party and public office, and each has a ballot box or voting machine, a list of registered voters, and election officials. The party's registered voters in each precinct choose a precinct committeeman and a precinct committeewoman (depending on state law, the names of these positions may differ) to represent the precinct on the party's county committee. (Nationwide there are 3041 counties, about sixty in each state.) That committee, in turn, elects a county leader. Either the precincts or the county committee selects members to serve on other party committees (unless state law requires a primary).

MACHINES AND RINGS

Between 1840 and 1960 machines and rings dominated party politics. They were controlled by party bosses, without formal education, who went into politics because they had few other opportunities. They were neighborhood leaders with followings in the streets. They gained control of one or more precincts and formed alliances with others like them to dominate city and county party committees.

The machine had precinct workers and a **precinct captain,** who could bring out the vote. In rural areas they would report directly to the county leader; in urban areas the district leader or ward leader (whose area comprised about ten to thirty precincts that elected a member of the state legislature or city council) controlled the precinct captains. Together the leaders and the precinct captains constituted the **urban machine** or **county courthouse ring:** they were interested as much in the gain from politics as in the game of politics—in living off politics rather than for it.

The machine nominated candidates for public office, or if conventions did the nominating, it made sure that its people were elected to the convention. If a primary was used, the machine would bring its supporters to the polls. Machines rigged party and general elections in the nineteenth century. They paid "venal voters," and, as James Michael Curley, the mayor of Boston, observed, "Some of the bosses also made sure that the men exercised their voting prerogative as frequently as possible. Men who were in jail, in hospitals, out of town or peacefully reposing in a cemetery often swung elections."[a]

The machine offered voters benefits in exchange for their support. It helped them

a. As quoted in *The New York Times*, Dec. 26, 1982.

(Continued.)

The death of Richard Daley, Chicago's mayor and Cook County Democratic chairman for nearly two decades, was the beginning of the end for the strongest of the big-city political machines. (*Cornell Capa: Magnum.*)

Daley's successor as mayor, Michael Bilandic, never achieved control of the organization. (*UPI; Bettmann Archive.*)

Defeating Bilandic, Jane Byrne served a term as mayor, only to be defeated in an election that polarized black and white voters, ending the black alliance with the county organization. (*Jeff Lowenthal: Woodfin Camp.*)

get jobs, brought them food baskets and coal in hard times, and clothed and housed them after fires. It could fix traffic tickets, get people out of jury duty, and arrange for the release of people who had been arrested by the police for assault or drunkenness. It gave free legal advice and made bail for its supporters.

Precinct captains were rewarded with lower-level government jobs: as street sweepers, sanitation workers, police officers, fire fighters, transit workers, water workers, inspectors, and clerks. This does not sound like much today, but for youngsters in poor neighborhoods at the time, these jobs were hard to get, and they offered opportunities for payoffs. Ward and district leaders got jobs as sheriffs and city marshalls, performing duties for the courts in return for high fees. They became law secretaries to judges—powerful positions in which they influenced the courts to benefit their friends in return for other favors or money. They became commissioners or deputy commissioners in city or county agencies. Anyone who received such a job was expected to contribute between 1 and 2 percent of his or her salary to the party each year, usually by buying tickets to picnics, dances, or party banquets. Those nominated to high public office, such as judges, were expected to contribute the equivalent of one year's salary to the party.

Machines thrived on corruption, permitting party and public officials to misuse their offices for personal gain. Members could be *bribed* to make decisions. They might grant delays, exemptions, or variances from local laws or administrative codes, especially those involving health, safety, sanitation, zoning, waste disposal, construction, and fire hazards. They could propose special-situation laws to benefit particular companies. Or they might *extort* funds by threatening to withhold city services or permits, proposing ordinances or laws that would harm businesspeople unless they paid up, or threatening to enforce existing laws in ways that would

Harold Washington, Chicago's first black mayor, presides over a factionalized city government. (*John Picara: Woodfin Camp.*)

Alderman Edward Vrdolyak squares off against Mayor Washington in a struggle for control of the city council. (*AP Laserphoto/John Swart.*)

impose extra costs on local businesses. The machine could receive *kickbacks:* contributions from companies that had been awarded government contracts. When a party organization held its annual dinner, those who had been given government contracts would buy blocks of tickets and also put paid "advertisements" in the party's yearbook.

Party workers set up businesses which received government contracts: companies involved in construction, maintenance, painting, building supplies, janitorial services, furniture and fixtures, cafeteria services, security services, and insurance. Their contracts, negotiated with people they had put into office, ensured them excessive profits. The employees of these businesses could be counted on to back the machine in elections, since their jobs depended on the machine's control of government.

Machines and rings were not an unalloyed evil. They helped immigrants assimilate, become citizens, and then voters. They helped the poor, the uneducated, and the unconnected. They gave the natural leaders of the community a chance to advance. As Richard Daley, the mayor of Chicago, argued: "The party permits ordinary people to get ahead. Without the party I couldn't be Mayor. The rich guys can get elected on their money, but somebody like me, an ordinary person, needs the party. Without the party only the rich would be elected to office."[b]

But many activities of machines and rings were indefensible. While some stayed within the letter of the law, most did not. They put the government up for auction to the highest bidders. They lined their own pockets with bribes and kickbacks. They rigged elections. They corrupted the police, prosecutors, and judges. The worst of them cooperated with organized crime.

b. Mike Royko, *Boss!* New American Library, New York, 1971, p. 84.

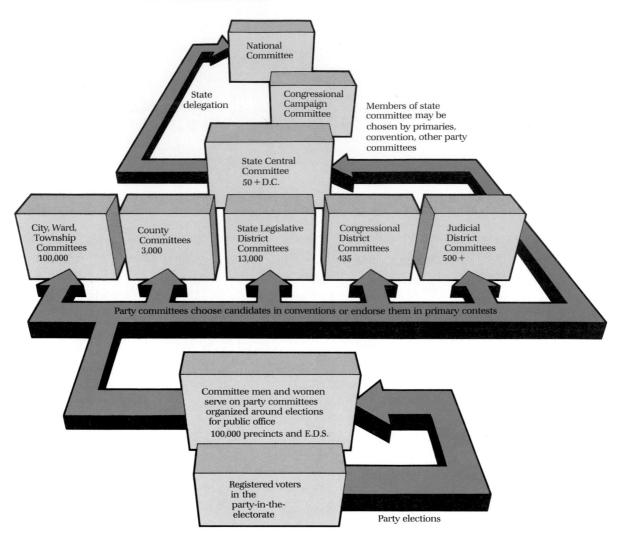

Figure 6-1. Party structure. There are thousands of party committees at the local level and fifty state parties. Each unit is autonomous, and its relationships with others depends on influence, persuasion, bargaining, and negotiation. The party structure is not hierarchical. In a hierarchy, commands are issued at the top and carried out by subordinate units. But the national committee does not control the state parties, and the state parties do not control the county or local parties. There are only a limited number of national party rules, designed to regulate the presidential nominating contest.

The state committees are usually composed of all the county committeemen and committeewomen (Figure 6-1).

Most voters know nothing about these organizations, and they do not turn out for elections to choose members of party committees (unless these elections are held at the same time as high-turnout presidential contests). Otherwise, only about 5 percent might turn out, and so a small number of voters can control the party committees. Even in general elections few voters have any idea whom to choose for such strange jobs as "state committeewoman" or "delegate to the nominating convention for the state committee," and often voters decide not to cast ballots for them. The party organization gets its own supporters to the polls and instructs them whom to vote for, which ensures its control of these positions.

National party organization

The national party consists of representatives of each of the state parties, organized into a *national committee* with the following functions:

- Prepare for the national convention (which meets every four years to nominate a presidential candidate) by deciding on the place and date and handling arrangements for thousands of delegates and reporters.
- Ensure compliance of the state party with the rules of the presidential nominating contest agreed to at the previous national convention.
- Ensure compliance of the state party with all rules of the national party.
- Recommend new party rules to the national convention.
- Raise funds for presidential and congressional elections.
- Give campaign assistance to state and local parties and their candidates.
- Fill any vacancies that might arise on the presidential ticket between the end of the convention and the election.

The national committee has very little power. It cannot tell state and local parties what to do, determine their candidates for office (including candidates for seats in the House and Senate), or establish candidates' positions on the issues. It cannot nominate candidates or determine the party platform or rules (this is done by the national convention). It does not manage election campaigns (the candidates themselves do this). It does not speak or act authoritatively for the party-in-government or set its policies.

Each national party has congressional and senatorial campaign committees which provide services (and funds) for the legislative party. These are discussed in Chapter 7.

MEDIA POLITICS

For more than a century—from 1830 to 1960—political power was exercised by strong party organizations at the local and state levels. They chose the party-in-government and influenced what it did. But power has shifted in modern times to the party-in-government, which no longer needs the state or local party to get nominated or elected to public office. Parties no longer have a monopoly on recruiting potential candidates for office, on financing and running their campaigns, on mobilizing voters, or on providing a link between the party-in-government and the party-in-the-electorate. All these functions are now shared with the candidates' own campaign organizations and political action committees.

Candidate-centered politics

Since the early 1960s *party* organizations have been displaced by *candidate* organizations. Candidates who run for office can communicate directly with voters. As Pat Caddell, a campaign consultant who helped Jimmy Carter win the presidency in 1976, explained:

> What we've done with media, what we've done with polling, and what we've done with direct organizational techniques is that we've provided candidates who have the resources (and that's the important thing, the resources), the ability to reach the voters and have a direct contact with the electorate without regard to party or party organization.[9]

Traditional party politics has given way to some extent to ***media politics.***

Candidates communicate directly with voters without using the party organization. They use radio and television (because the average American watches more than three hours of television daily); in the era of new politics the amounts spent on advertising have skyrocketed: from $24.6 million in 1972 to more than $150 million in 1984. Direct mailings and phone banks cost an equal amount.

Candidates who can afford this advertising can run for office without the support of the party leaders, and sometimes against their wishes. The consultant Bob Goodman, who has helped elect a number of Republican senators, says, "We have enabled people to come into a party or call themselves independent Democrats or Republicans and run for office without having to pay the dues of being a party member in a feudal way."[10] The loser of a Democratic primary for governor of Pennsylvania says, "You can't rely any more on political organizations. They don't work anymore."[11]

People who want to enter politics figure that the easy way to get to the top is to start there. Wealthy businesspeople, athletes, and movie celebrities can run for Congress or the Senate or for governorships without serving apprenticeships, provided they can put together their own campaign organization (Figure 6-2).

The new campaign organization

To run a media politics campaign, the candidate must raise money, create an image, communicate this image to potential voters, and then mobilize the electorate.

Fund-raising. The campaign techniques of media politics are expensive. The candidate must raise money and cannot rely on the party for funds. This restricts the field to the wealthy and to those who are adept at fund-raising. The initial funds come from the candidate's family and friends. This campaign chest allows the candidate to open an office, hire a manager, and poll voters. It also permits the candidate to hire a direct-mail fund-raising firm, which prepares a letter (on the basis of poll results), designs the envelope (there is an art involved in getting recipients to open a letter rather than toss it away), and sends the letter to likely contributors.

Getting a good mailing list of potential contributors is the key to fund-raising. There are several kinds of lists:

- House lists, owned by the firm, which may generate a positive reply of as high as 20 percent
- Past-contributor lists—lists of people who have donated to previous campaigns
- Borrow lists, owned by other politicians, who give them to newcomers they like
- Membership lists—lists of people who belong to organizations or who subscribe to magazines which make it likely that they will agree with the candidate's stance on the issues

The funds collected, minus the considerable expenses involved in raising them, are used to enlarge the campaign organization. The candidate hires a consulting firm, which manages the campaign and creates the media image, subcontracting out much of the work of actually making commercials to specialists.

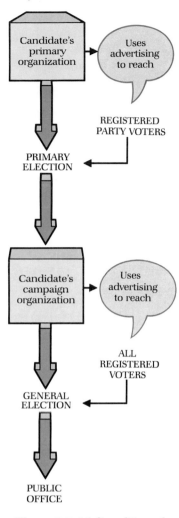

Figure 6-2. Media politics—the road to public office. The media politics candidate relies on his or her own organization to win the primary contest, making heavy use of campaign advertising.

MEDIA POLITICS CAMPAIGN ORGANIZATION

The inner circle

> The campaign manager: in charge of overall strategy and tactics and supervision of campaign workers
> Family, friends, and close advisers
> Mentors and financial backers
> Speech writer
> Pollster
> Media adviser: in charge of production and placement of political advertising
> Director of press and media relations

Headquarters staff

> Office manager (conversant with communications and computer technologies)
> Lawyer (familiar with campaign finance and election laws)
> Campaign treasurer and comptroller
> Secretaries and volunteer assistants

Research

> Polling organization, hired either by the candidate or by the state or national party
> Issues research: on the opponent's record and votes
> Position research: to develop stands on issues
> Precinct targeting: to decide where to allocate field-workers
> Direct-mail targeting: to decide which voters to send information

Image making

> Media adviser: in charge of the overall operation and the hiring of other media professionals
> Producer-director and copywriter of television and radio advertisements
> Producer and copywriter for outdoor and print advertisements
> Time buyer for advertisements
> Graphics designer
> Packaging designer for direct mail
> Producer and copywriter for direct mail

Media coaching

> Speech coach
> Television coach
> Wardrobe consultant
> Makeup person

Field operations

> Candidate advance: prepares site and obtains audience for the candidate
> Security coordinator: works with local security and the police
> Coordinator of volunteer operations
> Coordinator of the voter registration drive
> Coordinator for phone canvassing
> Coordinator for field canvassing and election-day turnout drive
> Liaison with the party and other local organizations

Image making. The purpose of creating an organization and raising funds is to get the candidate's name and message across to voters. The agency that produces the first set of advertisements tries to give the candidate *name recognition* with voters. The next set *positions* the candidate so that voters think that their beliefs and values are the same as the candidate's. The purpose is to give voters not only information but also an emotional reason to identify with the candidacy and support it.

The media consultant is central to the whole operation. Hiring a good consultant in itself establishes the credibility of a candidacy and helps raise funds. To some extent the best media consultants call the shots: they audition candidates and take on only the ones they like, and they insist on control of the entire campaign. Far from being hired hands, they have become the major political strategists in modern politics.

The consultant oversees the production of thirty- or sixty-second "spot" commercials for television and radio. "You play his song and write his movie," says Robert Goodman, a media advisor.[12] Commercials use the following techniques to maintain the audience's interest:

- *Personalize:* The candidate is a warm, concerned, committed person who cares about people, listens to them, and tries to help them. The candidate is competent and compassionate, knows how to get things done, and has new ideas. He or she has been successful in other careers and has entered politics to advance the public interest.
- *Characterize:* The candidate is pragmatic, progressive, and a dynamic liberal or a responsible conservative. But the opponent is a radical or a reactionary, too idealistic or too cynical, and out of touch with the people. The candidate is either a newcomer with energy and fresh ideas or a seasoned and experienced public official; the opponent is an inexperienced novice or else a worn-out incumbent who should be replaced.
- *Dramatize:* The commercials show the candidate doing something—listening to voters on the street or in a factory, confronting a heckler in the audience, responding to a reporter at a news conference, jogging on the beach, or even parachuting to a rally.
- *Visualize:* Since viewers are turned off by a "talking head" that fills the television screen, the commercial features dramatic visual images rather than the candidate's face, such as a city skyline, an "action shot" of crime or arson, or a missile taking off or a nuclear bomb exploding.
- *Thematize:* Each commercial concludes with a slogan that sums up the campaign. "Experience that money can't buy" works against a rich newcomer. "He (or she) is fresh and everyone else is tired" helps a challenger against an incumbent. "Leadership that works" helps an incumbent. "Send them a message" is an appeal for a protest vote.

Media consultants like David Garth argue that a series of thirty-second spot commercials can provide voters with adequate information about candidates. Garth has created an hour-long videotape presentation of his campaign advertisements for Tom Bradley, the mayor of Los Angeles, designed to convince skeptics that his work provides voters with what they need to know to make an informed decision. Studies by political scientists show that spot commercials provide more information than local television news broadcasts.[13]

Critics, especially those who are involved in more traditional party politics, agree with Edward Costikyan, a former county leader, who described spot

As party organizations decline, political consultants like David Garth have moved to fill the vacuum with media-based campaigns. (*Burt Glinn: Magnum.*)

Barney Frank's mother in a thirty-second spot appeals for votes for her son's tight congressional race. (*Photo by Barry S. Surman from "The Spot: The Rise of Political Advertising on Television," M.I.T. Press.*)

commercials as "simple words which oversimplify even simplistic thoughts."[14] Former congresswoman Millicent Fenwick observed that Alphone D'Amato, a senator from New York, had conducted a study after he was elected senator to find out why he had won and "found it owing to a commercial in which his dear mother held a bag of groceries and implored viewers to vote for her son, Al. Well, my dear," Fenwick concluded, "I cannot help thinking that is not quite what Thomas Jefferson had in mind."[15]

Mobilizing voters: Phone and field canvassing. During the closing weeks of any campaign the candidate must try to create the kind of precinct organization which parties used to provide for their candidates.

The party organization may help a media politics candidate who agrees not to try to take over the organization or interfere in its party elections. Many candidates strike such deals with the party leaders after they have won a primary against a candidate who was backed by the organization. Unions, professional organizations, trade associations, corporations, neighborhood improvement groups, environmentalists, and civil rights groups can get their members to work in the precincts for a favored candidate.

The candidate can create his or her own *field organization*. The local phone company sells reverse-list directories, which list subscribers by street address; thus lists of voters for each precinct can be compiled. Telephone canvassers call every voter in each precinct to determine those who support the candidate, those who are opposed, and those who are undecided. A phone bank can be used to create an *instant precinct organization*. Campaign workers call people and ask whether they would like to volunteer to become precinct captains just for the last week of the campaign. Those who agree can be brought to campaign headquarters and trained to canvass their neighborhoods. They visit the people who have been listed as "undecided" by the phone canvassers.

Just like a traditional party campaign, a media politics campaign must "pull" its supporters to the polls on election day. The phone and field canvassers provide volunteers at headquarters with lists of all their supporters, precinct by precinct. On election day the campaign assigns a *poll watcher* to each precinct. As each person votes, the poll watcher, armed with the list for that precinct, checks his or her name off the list. In the late afternoon, a runner takes the list back to campaign headquarters, where phone canvassers call those who have not yet voted; then field canvassers ring their doorbells—the end of the campaign.

Media politics:
An assessment

The methods of media politics work. Even public officials who started out as party-oriented politicians admit that public opinion polls, direct mailing, and spot commercials are effective, and parties now routinely make use of them.

Media politics has improved the quality of elected officials. People can enter public life without consorting with machine politicians and becoming party hacks. Professional men and women who are skilled at raising and managing money, creating and running organizations, and communicating and motivating people are drawn into political life; one would expect that, as a result, the government would be not only less corrupt but also more effective. And it is.

But there is another side to the coin. The public can be manipulated by slick media appeals. As Edward Costikyan puts it, media politics "rewards the performer, the actor, the electronic personality, the simplifier of complex problems into thirty-second commercials."[16] Media politics appeals to people whose egos need massaging in the media and who can pay for a campaign ego trip. In the film *The Candidate*, Robert Redford, playing such a person, wins the election. He turns to his media managers and asks, "What do we do now?" Larry Sabato concludes that these managers "have sought candidates who fit their technologies more than the requirements of office and have given an extra boost to candidates who are more skilled at electioneering than governing."[17]

Media politics has become a game for the wealthy, the educated, and the urban professionals. As they dominate, if not monopolize, the paths to elective office, one may ask how the less affluent and the less well educated are to participate in politics. Are they merely to become an audience for electronic advertisements? Are their interests adequately represented by today's media politicians?

Although officials elected through the techniques of media politics are a cut above their party predecessors in terms of personal honesty, they may govern in ways which are subtly corrupting and injurious to the public welfare. To understand why this might be so, it is necessary to examine further the role of interest groups in elections; for as the power of the parties has declined, the importance of these groups has increased, and their intersection with media politics campaigns has transformed American politics.

PAC POLITICS:
THE CHALLENGE
TO PARTIES

When local and state parties had a monopoly on nominations to office, groups that were interested in certain policies would finance campaigns through the parties in return for access to the party-in-government. But the virtual evaporation of strong parties since the 1960s has left a vacuum: no longer can interest groups maintain access to public officeholders by financing campaigns through the parties. Instead, they must contribute directly to the candidate-centered campaigns.

PACs: What are they?

Interest groups have established their own committees, which legally collect and distribute funds in campaigns; these are known as ***political action committees*** (PACs). PACs have gone far beyond the traditional (and often corrupt) relationships which have always existed between politicians and interest groups. PACs now operate within the law, but the law is skewed in their favor. Not only do they help finance campaigns, but as parties have disintegrated, they also have taken on some of their functions: they recruit candidates, finance and help manage candidates' campaigns, select candidates' media consultants, and influence public debate through their advertising.

PACs are now regulated according to the 1971 and 1974 campaign finance laws passed by Congress; although some labor and business PACs have been in existence since the 1940s, it is only in the past ten years that PACs have proliferated, as Figure 6-3 makes clear. As of 1985 there were more than 1500 corporate PACs, 650 trade association PACs, 400 labor PACs, and 940 other PACs.

Not all organized interest groups form PACs. The smaller ones find it too expensive in terms of administrative costs and compliance with federal election regulations. A group of political scientists found that only 17 percent of the interest groups it surveyed had formed PACs. Those most likely to do so are corporate interest groups, especially those with adequate funds, which think that legislative lobbying is important and are involved in conflict with other

Figure 6-3. Growth of PACs. A decade ago there were few PACs, and the majority were organized by labor unions. Since then their number has soared, with most created by corporations, trade and professional associations, and other nonlabor organizations. (Source: U.S. Federal Elections Commission.)

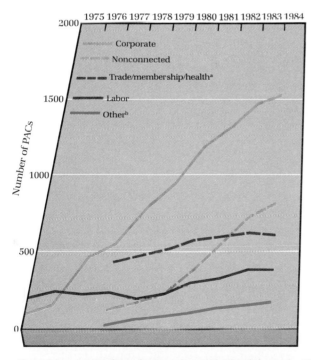

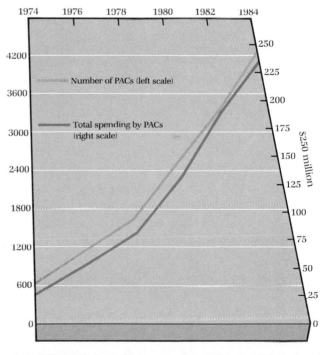

a. From January 1975 through December 1976, FEC did not identify categories of PACs other than corporate and labor PACs. Therefore, numbers are not available for trade/membership/health PACs or nonconnected PACS.

b. Includes PACs formed by corporations without capital stock and cooperatives. Numbers are not available for these categories of PACs from January 1975 through December 1976.

interest groups over significant public policies. Those which favor the status quo or believe that it is likely to be maintained in the near future have less incentive to form PACs.[18]

Corporations, unions, trade associations, and national banks may not spend their own funds in federal elections, according to laws dating back to 1907 (though in some states they can contribute to state and local elections). But they can establish PACs called *separate segregated funds* (SSFs), which may receive contributions from their own employees, stockholders, or members, and they can make contributions from these funds to candidates. Their expenses can be carried by their parent organization, and so all their receipts go directly to campaigns. Twice a year these SSFs can solicit the general public for contributions. Some of the most active groups include the National Association of Realtors, the National Association of Home Builders, the American Medical Association, the American Dental Association, the Attorneys Congressional Campaign Trust, the United Auto Workers, the Machinists and Aerospace Workers, the SeaFarer's Union, the National Education Association, the American Bankers Association, the Association of Milk Producers, the Auto and Truck Dealers Association, and the AFL-CIO.

Issue-oriented groups, such as those dealing with gun control, abortion, civil rights, the environment, and energy, may also create PACS. These differ from SSFs because they must pay their own expenses, but they can solicit funds from the public whenever they like.

There are also ideological organizations, some affiliated with parties and some independent, which contribute to conservative or liberal candidates. The most important are:

- *Democrats for the '80s,* founded by Pamela Harriman in 1980 and composed of moderate Democrats who have served in high positions, mostly in connection with matters of national security. It focuses on economic and defense issues and aids centrist Democrats.
- *National Committee for an Effective Congress* (NCEC), founded in 1948 by Eleanor Roosevelt and other liberal Democrats. It aids approximately 100 Democrats and a handful of moderate Republicans during each congressional election.
- *Independent Action,* founded by Morris Udall in 1980 and composed mostly of neoliberals who mistrust big bureaucracy and of holdovers from John Anderson's 1980 presidential campaign. It makes contributions in House elections to Democrats and will back a few Republican moderates against conservatives in their primaries.
- *Progressive Political Action Committee* (PROPAC), founded in 1982. It runs negative campaigns against right-wing candidates and is closely affiliated with the AFL-CIO.
- *Congressional Club,* organized in 1978 by Jesse Helms, the Republican senator from North Carolina. It makes contributions to right-wing Republican candidates for Congress and the Senate, mostly in the south.
- *National Conservative Political Action Committee* (NCPAC), founded in 1978. It runs negative campaigns against liberals.
- *Committee for the Survival of a Free Congress* (CSFC), founded in 1978 as a counterweight to the NCEC. It emphasizes a conservative stance on social issues and contributes to Republican candidates for the House.

President Ronald Reagan addresses a conference of conservative PAC leaders early in the 1984 presidential election campaign. (*AP: Wide World.*)

The contributors to the most liberal PACs are most likely to be professionals from urban areas who are younger and better educated than rank-and-file members of the Democratic Party. They have weak identifications with the Democratic Party and mistrust the party leadership; one survey showed that only 15 percent trusted their party on the issues. Contributors to the most conservative PACs, in contrast, are more likely to be in small business, to come from rural areas, and to be more interested in family and social issues than rank-and-file Republicans. Fewer than half (40 percent) have great confidence in their party leadership. Thus the impact of these PACs is to pull the two parties further apart on social issues and foreign policy.[19]

PAC Funding

What PACs may spend and receive according to law is indicated in Table 6-2.

PACs can evade limitations in three ways. First, they can act as a *clearinghouse* for contributions to a candidate: they solicit checks made out directly to the campaign (not the PAC) and forward these checks to the candidate, thus helping to raise much more than $5000. Second, PACs can donate up to $20,000 to each party's national committee, senatorial campaign committee, and congressional campaign committee, with the understanding that these committees will spend the money on behalf of particular candidates. Third, PACs may give money to state and local parties for voter education and registration drives, supposedly not for particular candidates; in practice, however, such contributions directly benefit candidates in national elections by getting out the vote for them.

Most PACs invest in campaigns of incumbents to guarantee their access to these officials after they are reelected; this has led critics to call PAC financing

Table 6-2. Receiving and contributing PAC funds

Donor	Recipient		
	National party committee	**PAC**	**Candidates for federal offices**
Individuals[a]	$20,000 total	$5000 per PAC	$1000 to each candidate in any primary or election
PACS[b]	$15,000	$5,000 to any other PAC	$5000 to each candidate in any primary or election
Party	$20,000 from state party committee to national party committee		National parties may give $5000 to House candidates and $17,500 to Senate candidates, plus $40,000 in uncoordinated expenditures in House races and $80,000 to $1 million in Senate contests
Candidates			$5,000 each to any other candidate

a. Individuals may contribute no more than $25,000 to all types of election committees in any two-year election cycle.
b. PACs may contribute in state contests according to applicable state laws. They may also contribute soft money for state party building (that is, voter registration) which does not come under the limits for federal campaigns, although these activities may directly benefit candidates for federal office.

the "incumbent protection system." But some contribute to challengers who have a reasonable chance of defeating the people they oppose. And as some of these challengers win, other incumbents start to believe that PAC money made the difference. The result is that both challengers and incumbents begin a mad scramble for PAC funds: the challengers to mount a serious media campaign, and the incumbents to raise so much money so early that anyone thinking of mounting a challenge to them will be scared off. As Elizabeth Drew, an observer of Washington politics, noted, politicians "are signed up on a systematic basis by interests that wish to enjoy influence over their official conduct."[20]

PACs and campaigns

Choosing campaigns. How do PACs know which campaigns to fund? They get their most important clues from a few PACs that seem to know which incumbents are in trouble and which challengers could use the money effectively: BIPAC (a business group), the Chamber of Commerce listing of "Opportunity Races," and *The PAC Manager,* published by the National Association of Manufacturers, are used by business and trade PACs. Labor PACs pay attention to the AFL-CIO Committee on Political Education (COPE).

What PACs do in campaigns. PACs have taken over many of the functions of political parties: they recruit candidates and provide important campaign assistance.

RECRUITMENT. Some of the liberal, conservative, and issue-oriented PACs recruit candidates directly. All these groups rely heavily on scare tactics (if the other side wins, the republic will come to an end) and on direct-mail appeals for funds, taking their war chests to potential candidates who share their views.

CAMPAIGN ASSISTANCE. PACs help candidates by conducting polls at their own expense and then "leaking" the results to the newspapers so that candidates can make use of them. (They cannot give campaigns the results directly because that is considered a contribution in excess of their $5000 limit.) PACs can introduce potential candidates to media consultants. They may supply campaign workers. They can help campaigns obtain good direct-mail services and can make their own lists available.

INDEPENDENT EXPENDITURES. In federal elections PACs may contribute no more than $5000 to a primary or election campaign (although they can contribute more if they take advantage of legal loopholes or violate the law); however, as a result of the Supreme Court's decision in *Buckley v. Valeo,* they may legally spend unlimited amounts to help candidates, provided that they do not coordinate their efforts with a candidate's campaign. These are called ***independent expenditures.***

NEGATIVE CAMPAIGNS. Some PACs run ***negative campaigns:*** they attack the character, the honesty, and even the patriotism of officeholders whom they oppose, sometimes years before anyone runs against them. They try to "soften up" voters and erode the incumbent's support, which will encourage someone to make the challenge in the next election. PACs can also intimidate officeholders by threatening to run such campaigns unless they change their positions.

Negative campaigns have been attacked by leaders of both parties. They go against the "Eleventh Commandment" of the Republicans—"Thou shalt not speak ill of fellow Republicans"—because some PACs threaten to run negative campaigns to unseat moderate Republicans in primaries and replace them with hard-line conservatives. They also go against the code of ethics of the American Association of Advertising Agencies, and most reputable campaign firms stay away from such tactics.

SHAPING PUBLIC OPINION. There are no legal limits on the amounts that PACs may spend to present their views on the issues. They do so even outside the campaign season, to create a climate of public opinion that influences whoever is in office. When candidates poll voters, they will find that they agree with the PACs on the issues, and the candidates will then take the same positions in their campaigns—at least so the PACs hope. And if the government's policies harm a PAC's interests, it can sponsor an initiative and allow the voters to settle the issues. The federal courts have ruled that any limits on the noncampaign spending of PACs would violate the freedom of speech of those who contribute to them.

The Federal Communications Commission balances PAC spending through the *Cullman doctrine*—its 1963 ruling—which requires radio and television stations that broadcast advertisements expressing controversial views to give free time (though not necessarily equal time) to others to present contrasting opinions. Some stations refuse to air PAC commercials because of this "free time" provision, and PACs have initiated lawsuits in federal courts arguing that this unconstitutionally restricts their access to the people.

Assessing PAC politics

PACs focus attention on issues and interests. They provide a useful corrective to campaigns which otherwise would deal mostly with personality and party loyalty. They can educate voters and get them thinking about fundamental policies. But PAC politics is *unbalanced:* there are many more business-oriented PACs than PACs favoring labor or consumers or PACs concerned about the environment. PAC politics (like party politics) offers no chance for unorganized interests or individuals to express themselves effectively.

PACs contribute to the weakening of the parties, which paradoxically means that PACs themselves cannot get what they want from the party-in-government. The problem, as Elizabeth Drew says, is that "a candidate entering politics now must systematically make the rounds of the interest groups and win

A DECLARATION OF WAR

The time has come to draw the line. Political Action Committees (PACs) have put Congress on the take. And *you're* being taken for a ride. Consider your health: PAC money from doctors helped convince Congress *not* to pass a bill that would help keep your hospital costs from skyrocketing. Consider your protection from fraud: PAC money from auto dealers helped convince Congress *not* to pass a bill that would require used car dealers to tell you what's wrong with the second-hand car you're buying. Consider your savings: PAC money from the dairy industry has helped to convince Congress, year after year, *not* to make needed cuts in dairy subsidies, which artificially inflate the price of the milk, butter and cheese you buy. Consider yourself *mute*. Your voice is being *drowned out* by the ringing of PAC cash registers in Congress.

Senator Robert Dole, Chairman of the Senate tax writing committee, says, "When these PACs give money, they expect something in return other than good government." These are contributions with a purpose—a legislative purpose. And the PAC system works according to the golden rule, says former Congressman Henry Reuss: "Those who have the gold make the rules."

We're not talking about illegal campaign contributions of the sort that ten years ago created a national scandal called Watergate. We're talking about $80 million in campaign contributions that are *perfectly legal*, creating a new national scandal corrupting our democracy. And *that* is a crime.

Unless we change our system for financing Congressional campaigns and change it soon, our representative system of government will be gone. We will be left with a government of, by and for the PACs.

We can't let that happen. We *won't* let that happen. Common Cause has declared war — a war on PACs. Ours has always been a government of, by and for the *people*. We must keep it that way.   Common Cause.

As the influence of PACs increases, so do efforts to regulate them, such as this ad campaign mounted by Common Cause in 1983. (*New York Times*, Feb. 6, 1983.)

their approval, and their money, by declaring himself, usually in very specific terms, in favor of the legislative goals they seek."[21] Some people in office end up doing little more than running errands for the interest groups that helped elect them. This makes politics more issue-oriented, but when everyone is pursuing his or her own agenda, the result is chaos. If the party structure evaporates, so does the organization which can set the government agenda, determine priorities, promote compromise, and create coalitions that can pass programs. The result is a government that seems to have no conception of the public interest and offers no coherent policies. All it offers is favors to those who invested in it; ultimately, that is not enough to retain its authority.

Party politicians oppose PAC politics. Because PACs focus on narrow issues, they make coalition building and compromise difficult. Politicians find it harder to build centrist majorities when the emotions of voters have been aroused by media techniques. They believe that PACs, in the words of Bill Brock, a former chairman of the Republican National Committee (RNC), "reduce the quality" of public officials, and that PACs engage in "all kinds of mischief," as another chairman of the RNC, Richard Richards, has said. Candidates recruited by PACs are less experienced in government and often do not have the skills or temperament necessary to make compromises. The negative campaigns that got them into office alienate potential colleagues from both parties. By 1982 Republican Party leaders were trying (unsuccessfully) to get PACs to agree not to run independent or negative campaigns in areas where local leaders opposed them—a symptom of the growing rift between pragmatic party professionals and right-wing zealots.

PACs compete with the parties for funds. "I can't believe that draining our resources is helpful," Brock argued. It is no wonder that Paul Weyrich, the executive director of the Committee for the Survival of a Free Congress (one of the more conservative PACs), says, "Both parties would have an all-night celebration if we were to go out of business."[22]

ISSUE AND DEBATE

PAC POLITICS. "The nation's capital is awash with cash," the vice president for federal relations of the Dana Corporation reported to his company. "It sloshes, ebbs and flows through the K Street canyon of corporations, trade associations, union headquarters and exquisitely appointed suites of special-interest law firms, around the embassies of Kalorama Road, through the pale drawing rooms of Georgetown, past the White House and, defying all laws of gravity, alternately seeps and gurgles its way uphill to the Capitol."[23]

Campaign financing by PACs has become a major issue. Some critics charge that it has led to "the best government money can buy," saying that things are now so bad that politicians can be not only bought but also rented by the special-interest groups. "Votes are given in exchange for contributions," charged William Brodhead, a former Republican representative, explaining why he had decided to retire from Congress. But Sam Melcher, a Republican senator, scoffs at these charges, claiming that contributions are small because of federal laws that prohibit PACs from contributing more than 1 percent of a candidate's campaign funds; he concludes that "no one is going to buy me for 1 percent."[24]

Do PACs corrupt the political process? Do they affect the competitiveness of elections because they give overwhelmingly to incumbents rather than to challengers? Should PACs be prohibited from contributing funds in state and national elections, or should the amounts they can give be limited? Should there be a limit on the percentage of a candidate's campaign funds which can come from PACs?

The background. Both the number of PACs and the size of their contributions have increased dramatically since the 1971 Federal Election Campaign Act and its 1974 amendments began to regulate them. In 1974 spending in congressional campaigns totaled $74 million, and PACs contributed only $12.5 million of that amount. By 1982 total spending had reached $343 million, of which PACs contributed $83.1 million. The number of PACs increased in that same period from 608 to more than 3400. Overall, PACs raised more than $189 million for state elections and federal elections in 1982, and by 1984 the total had reached well over $200 million.

The case against PACS. Critics of PACs—like Common Cause's People Against PACs, the bipartisan Citizens Against PACs, LASTPAC (a PAC whose goal is to eliminate PACs), and many concerned public officials—argue that they threaten representative government. "Poor people don't make campaign contributions," observed Robert Dole, a Republican senator, adding that "you might get a different result if there were a Poor-PAC up here."[25] PACs benefit contributors from the corporate and professional worlds and from labor at the expense of the public. Officeholders become accountable to PACs, not to the voters. Critics see a direct correlation between campaign contributions and votes, pointing to the 286 members of Congress who voted to strike down a Federal Trade Commission rule requiring used-car dealers to list each car's defects: those voting with the car dealers against the rule had previously received $742,371 in contributions from them. Critics also point to the seven companies which were affected by environmental regulations and which gave $767,000 to the members of the House Energy and Commerce Committee, as well as to the energy PACs, which contributed more than $500,000 to the members of these committees.

Critics claim that PAC contributions are investments, made to protect the interests of a PAC, not to elect the best candidate to office. Many candidates receive most of their PAC contributions from committees that represent the interests of people far away from their own constituents. In 1974, only 28 percent of House members got one-third or more of their funds from PACs outside their districts, but by 1984 over 70 percent did so.[26] Because honest politicians do not want to mortgage their votes to PACs, they must go into debt or risk being defeated by well-financed opponents. Many decide to retire from office instead. Those who win elections today may have spent so much on their campaigns that they need PACs just to retire their debts. The system "virtually forces members to go around begging for money," charges Tom Eagleton, Democratic senator.[27] Not only can politicians who play ball with PACs get money for their campaigns, but those who were first elected before January 1980 may transfer funds from their campaigns to their own bank accounts after they leave office—even if they collected hundreds of thousands of dollars after 1980!

The case for PACs. Supporters of PACs argue that they are part of a broad increase in individual participation in politics and grass-roots organizing which started in the 1960s. They claim that in the 1950s and 1960s, when labor PACs were dominant and contributed most of their funds to liberal Democrats, the critics never complained; now, when corporate and trade association PACs are countering the contributions of labor PACs, and are making slightly more than half their contributions to Republicans, PACs have suddenly become an issue. Supporters claim that only since 1980, when corporate PACs began to make their contributions to Republican challengers rather than to Democratic incumbents, have PAC contributions dominated the liberal agenda.

Supporters of PACs argue that the funds do not buy votes—they simply help officeholders and challengers explain their positions in the campaigns, which actually promotes rather than destroys accountability. PACs help challengers overcome the advantages of incumbents. Since PACs have come into existence, turnover in Congress and state legislatures has increased. Voters are always free to reject a candidate and his or her position, and PACs give them better-financed candidates from which to choose.

The PAC system is legal, provides for full disclosure of contributors, and makes it relatively easy to see which officeholders are taking contributions from which PACs. "Today campaign finance is cleaner than it's ever been. We know who gave and who got. And we have the broadest base of political giving in our history," argues Richard Armstrong, the president of the Public Affairs Council (a nonpartisan organization of corporate public affairs executives).[28] This, defenders argue, is much better than surreptitious and illegal contributions, made by lobbyists behind closed doors, which are more likely to involve direct vote buying. Without PACs, defenders argue, candidates would have to finance their campaigns out of their own pockets or rely on "fat cat" donors. With PACs, candidates can concentrate on issues and get money from voters who care about them. Far from eroding responsibility to the people, in this view PACs make parties and candidates more responsive to voters' concerns.

Defenders of PACs argue that PAC spending does not give politics a corporate bias. All PAC contributions combined (including the contributions of labor PACs) amount to less than one-fourth of giving in federal elections. Corporate PACs provide less than 10 percent of total giving. The average contribution of a corporate PAC to a candidate for national office in 1981–1982 was $657, and 97 percent of all gifts are under $2500. This, the defenders say, cannot buy very much access, and in any event, getting access is not the same as buying votes. Richard Armstrong concludes that "by comparison with what went on in politics 15 years ago, PAC's are the Little Sisters of the Poor."[29]

PACs do favor incumbents, their defenders concede, but that is only natural: so do all other campaign contributors. Corporate PACs, in fact, are more likely to favor challengers than other types of PACs or large individual donors, and this opens up the system. And although corporate PACs are likely to favor Republicans, labor PACs are overwhelmingly Democratic; thus PAC giving reinforces tendencies toward a responsible party system rather than suppressing them.

Proponents of PACs argue that to regulate or restrict them would deny people their freedom of speech and assembly and would stifle full debate about the issues. They argue that allowing officeholders to pass laws which restrict the public's ability to fund groups that communicate to voters through the mass media would set a dangerous precedent. They believe that special interests are a condition of democratic politics and that PACs, by bringing their contributions into the open, do the best they can to promote accountable government. Considering the wide variety of PACs which contribute money, they say, the pluralism of American politics is enhanced by them rather than diminished.

Finally, defenders of PACs have public opinion on their side. A 1983 survey by Civic Services, Inc., of 1503 voters in precincts across the nation indicated that almost two-thirds of the public knew what PACs were and that a small majority (53 percent approved of their contributing to federal elections, while only 33 percent disapproved.[30] (See Figure 6-4.)

Proposed reforms. Some of the proposed changes in campaign laws include the following:

- Reducing the maximum amount of PAC contributions, from $5000 to $1000.
- Limiting the amount of money that a campaign may accept in PAC contributions (Common Cause would limit it to $90,000 in House elections) or limiting the percentage of total campaign funds that such contributions may constitute.

Figure 6-4. Attitudes toward PACs. Public opinion toward PACs depends on the type: women's and environmental PACs are strongly favored, while business and labor PACs are seen as a negative influence. The public says it opposes candidates' accepting PAC funds—yet most incumbents who do are reelected handily. (Source: Harris Survey, no. 1, January 3, 1983.)

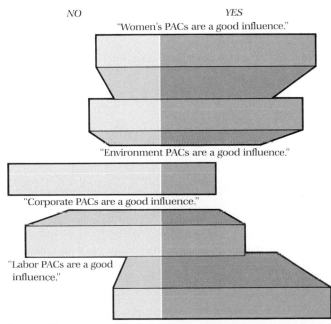

NO   YES

"Women's PACs are a good influence."

"Environment PACs are a good influence."

"Corporate PACs are a good influence."

"Labor PACs are a good influence."

". . . would oppose candidates for federal office who accept PAC funds."

- Allowing PACs to contribute only to state or national party committees, rather than to candidates, with an increase in the amounts permitted.

Critics of these reforms believe that Congress will not adopt public financing of campaigns. They think that such measures would benefit incumbents, making it more difficult for challengers to spend enough to communicate with voters. And they believe that limits on PAC expenditures would not reduce their influence in politics, since PACs could always mount their own noncoordinated campaigns.

Supporters of PACs believe that the best way to minimize any undue influence of PACs would be to allow them to contribute more, not less, to campaigns. They would like to see higher limits on individual campaign contributions and more tax deductibility to spur such donations. They would end all limits on spending by party committees on behalf of candidates and would eliminate limits on individual contributions to parties. These and similar measures, they believe, would increase the diversity of funding sources and make it even less likely that PACs could exert undue influence.[31]

PARTY RENEWAL IN THE 1980s

National and state parties remain weak, but they have tried hard in the 1980s to rebuild themselves in an effort to regain ground lost as a result of both the candidate-centered media politics and the interest-centered PAC politics of the preceding decade. They are better organized and better financed, and they provide more services to candidates.

State and local parties

Machines and rings have disappeared almost entirely. Elections are usually honest. Civil service has eliminated most machine patronage. Unions of government employees protect workers who refuse to contribute to parties. As a result of the Supreme Court decision in *Elrod v. Burns*,[32] the winning party cannot dismiss lower-level civil servants and replace them with its own supporters. The federal courts even require cities like Chicago to file plans on how they will end politically motivated hirings, dismissals, and harassment in the public work force.

Nevertheless, while remaining within the letter of the law, modern parties still compete for prizes in the game of politics: the high salaries and fringe benefits of public office and the appointments to state and city commissionerships and judgeships and to boards of public corporations that run everything from sports complexes to transit systems to airports. Elected and appointed officials in turn hire politically connected firms and consultants to provide professional services: law, architecture, engineering, accounting, management, labor relations, advertising, insurance, travel arrangements, and even market research and television commercials for state agencies (such as those dealing with tourism and industrial development).

The new patronage. Paying firms to provide these services constitutes the *new patronage* that has replaced capital construction and maintenance kickbacks, which fueled the old-time machines. The new patronage does not use extortion or bribery, and no one violates the laws.[33] Instead, professionals in these firms work for the parties as volunteers in ways that are hardly different from most civic and community improvement activity. They help elect their friends to office, and in return their friends give them the opportunity to provide professional services for large fees.

Parties and bureaucracies. Parties no longer provide goods and services directly to voters in exchange for their support. They now help constituents obtain government benefits by cutting through the red tape, explaining procedures, and providing legal advice. They become active in community development by working with local groups to obtain government grants.[34] The remaining corruption—and there is still quite a lot—is usually not organized by the party itself. Instead, most cases now involve individuals who take it upon themselves, without the sanction of the local party, to extort funds and demand kickbacks or bribes. After all, with so much legal opportunity to make money providing services to government or obtaining government contracts, only greedy or stupid people or lower-level workers will risk committing criminal acts.

Party workers. The modern party attracts different kinds of people from those who were attracted by the machines. Studies in Detroit and Los Angeles show a decline in the percentage of workers without a college education, as blue-collar workers are being replaced by white collar professionals. The majority of workers today are concerned more with issues than with personal gain, they do not need the patronage of a machine, and they are likely to enter party politics as an outgrowth of their work with community organizations.[35]

Parties and community groups. The traditional local party has evaporated over the past quarter-century. Many are now paper organizations: their precincts are not covered by captains, and they do little or nothing in the community between elections.[36] The control of such organizations has passed to mayors, county executives, and others in the party-in-government, who recruit party workers to fill seats on committees to fulfill the requirements of state election laws; thus the party organization serves as an appendage to the party-in-government.

The tasks of recruiting candidates and financing and managing campaigns are now shared with local community and civic groups: owners of newspapers and television stations, corporate and labor leaders, religious congregations, merchants' associations, neighborhood improvement groups, veterans' associations, ethnic organizations, and civil rights groups. Candidates for office are recruited by them—or they recruit themselves.[37] The support or endorsement of a party committee means less to candidates than the support of a newspaper, a union leader, or a civic association, and often the former follows the latter, as parties react to the initiatives of others. These days the *real* local and state parties are the group coalitions whose leaders recruit candidates.

The national Democratic Party

The Democrats began to transform their national party organization in the 1960s, when civil rights workers, college students, women, and activists against the Vietnamese war demanded that the party open its doors to them. Battles centered on rules for presidential nominations resulted in significant reforms between 1968 and 1976:

- *Affirmative action* programs to increase participation by women, minorities, and young people in party affairs at both the national and state levels. This put an end to overt race and sex discrimination in state and local parties.
- Women to constitute half the national committee and half the delegates to the national convention.

- The national party to be supreme over the state parties in making and enforcing these and other party rules.

The national charter. In the late 1970s the Democrats changed their party structure. They approved a charter and bylaws, in effect their first national "constitution." The Supreme Court, in *Cousins v. Wigoda*, ruled that a national party could enforce its rules on the state parties—even if state laws mandated different procedures. The Court has also decided that national party rules take precedence over state party rules.[38]

The charter and subsequent actions by the Democratic National Committee (DNC) led to the creation of the following new units within the national party:

- Judicial Council, to resolve disputes between the state parties and groups claiming discrimination or other violations of rules
- National Finance Council, to improve fund-raising
- Business Council, open to people who contribute $10,000 or more
- Labor Council, to give unions an important voice
- Equal Rights Amendment Advisory Committee, to give women's groups a greater role in the party
- Strategy Council, consisting of sixty party officials, to promote coordination of national and state campaigns
- National Education and Training Council, to improve management in local and state campaigns
- Center for Democratic Policy, to develop new policy initiatives for the national party-in-government

The midterm conventions. In 1974 the Democrats held their first *midterm convention.* That year it was used to attack the Republicans for burglarizing the DNC headquarters and committing other Watergate-related crimes. In 1978, with Jimmy Carter in the White House, the convention became a battleground for his supporters and those of Edward Kennedy, as the two sides fought over the policies of the government. In 1982 party leaders scaled down its size (from 1600 to 900 delegates), and the convention focused on issues that Democrats could run on in the upcoming congressional campaign—unemployment and the recession. It also became a forum for presidential hopefuls, who campaigned among the delegates representing local party organizations. The Democrats eliminated the midterm convention in 1986.

Aiding the state parties. In the 1980s the focus of party reform has shifted away from regulating the state parties and toward rebuilding them. The Democratic Party's National Training Academy, opened in 1981, ran three-day sessions on campaign management for candidates and campaign managers. Its talent scout program recruited candidates for local office. Funding for voter registration drives was increased. In 1982 the party started making direct financial contributions to Democrats in Congress who faced strong Republican challengers. It sponsored several issue-training conferences to brief its candidates on national economic issues. A program begun in 1981, with the unlikely name of State Party Works, trained state party officials in fund-raising, polling, and advertising.

Emulating the PACs. In the 1980s the DNC started to use the same techniques as the PACs. It spent millions of dollars upgrading its direct-mail list of potential contributors. Beginning in 1982, the party mailed out millions of pieces, including:

- The Critical Issues Survey, in which Charles Manatt, the chairman of the DNC, invited contributors to express their "personal views on what is troubling our nation" and promised to "share your views with the very highest level of the Democratic Party leadership."
- Invitations to potential contributors to join the Convention Club (for $5000), the Business Council (for $10,000), the Senate Democratic Leadership Circle (for $15,000), the Democratic National Finance Council (for $5000), and the Speakers Club (for $5000) and to become card-carrying members of the Democratic Party by making contributions of $100 or more.
- "Telegrams," targeted at senior citizens, setting forth the Democrats' program to defend social security and inviting contributions to the party.
- Direct mailings, some signed by Tip O'Neill, the Speaker of the House, beginning a drive to defeat the Republicans.

By 1984 the national Democratic Party was operating as a super-PAC. By running negative campaigns against Republican candidates, it solicited funds even before the campaigns were launched. It used funds to upgrade its mailing list and to expand its direct mailings, on the sound principle that to make money one must spend money. It took out newspaper advertisements and made television commercials. It even put out slick televised responses to President Reagan's State of the Union addresses in 1983 and 1984, a far cry from its past efforts, which had put most viewers to sleep. For the 1984 elections the DNC organized "Americans for Mondale" committees as subsidiaries of each state party to raise $25 million for further party-building activities.

Although the Democrats had accomplished much, Charles Manatt, in comparing his party with the Republican party in the aftermath of the 1980 elections, admitted: "We have been out-conceptualized, out-organized, out-televised, out-coordinated, out-financed, and out-worked."[39]

**The national
Republican Party**

The Republicans' efforts to rebuild the party began in the aftermath of the *Watergate* scandal of 1973–1974. The party made a disastrous showing in the 1974 midterm congressional elections and then lost the White House in 1976. Looking toward the 1978 contests, the party controlled only one-third of the seats in the House and the Senate and slightly less than one-third of the seats in state legislatures, and it had only twelve governors. Many commentators began to talk of a "one-and-a-half-party system" as the Republicans hit bottom. Yet by 1984, the reporter Thomas Edsell noted, "The Republican Party has become the most sophisticated and potent national political organization in this century, and probably in the history of the United States."[40]

Party finance. In the late 1970s the Republicans invested in a completely new direct-mail operation, which by 1979 provided them with a list of more than 2 million donors, up from 450,000 in 1976.[41] At the base of the pyramid were 1.6 million "sustaining members" who each contributed between $25 and $500 annually. Because they provided almost one-third of the party's funds, by 1982 the Republican National Committee (RNC) began organizing regional share-

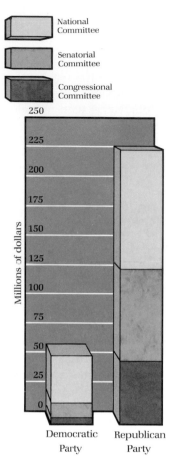

National Committee

Senatorial Committee

Congressional Committee

Figure 6-5. Financing the Republican National Committee in the 1980s. The RNC receives most of its funds from small contributors, PACs, and wealthy "friends of the party." In turn it provides funds to state and local parties and candidates and encourages PACs and wealthy contributors to give to them directly. The DNC lags behind the Republicans and raises one-tenth of the funds raised by the RNC. (Source: U.S. Federal Elections Commission.)

holders' conventions; like the national conventions, they were held in big-city convention halls and attracted 10,000 contributors for briefings by top party officials.

There were the Major Donors ($500 to $999), the Associates ($1000 to $9999), and, at the summit, the Eagles ($10,000 to the legal maximum of $20,000 that an individual may donate to a party committee in a two-year election cycle). The RNC maintained a staff of four "Eagle representatives" to give the Eagles access to top officials in the Reagan White House. For $10,000 contributors could join the Senatorial Trust; for $5000, the Vice President's Club; or for $2500, the Republican Congressional Leadership Council.

The RNC encouraged PACs to contribute their legal maximum of $20,000 to the party. It told PACs, corporations, and wealthy individuals who wanted to do more that they could make unlimited contributions to Republican state and local parties for "party-building activities"—a loophole in the federal election laws. Moreover, the RNC coordinated efforts to raise these funds for state and local parties (referred to as **soft money,** to distinguish it from the more closely regulated *hard-money* contributions to the national party and candidates for national office). Funds supposedly used for registration drives or state campaigns would obviously benefit congressional and presidential candidates as well, and so soft money became an essential part of Republican national fund-raising. Its "unity dinners," attended by candidates Reagan and Bush during the 1980 campaigns, raised more than $9 million for the state parties, a reversal from the usual practice: most of the time party dinners are held to raise money at the local level and transfer it to the national party. In 1984 the national ticket helped raise more than $16.8 million for the state party-building efforts.

Hard-money contributions increased dramatically. The RNC, the Republican Senatorial Campaign Committee, and the Republican Congressional Campaign Committee raised $111 million in 1980, compared with only $18.8 million raised by the three comparable Democratic committees. By 1982 the Republican groups had raised $191 million, compared with $32 million raised by the Democrats, and in 1984 they raised $246 million, compared with $59 million raised by the Democrats. Because many Democratic candidates raised their own campaign funds, these figures do not mean that the Democrats were outspent, but merely that the national Republican Party could give more help than the national Democratic Party (Figure 6-5).

Campaign assistance. The national party also provided campaign services for the state parties, especially in the area of new campaign techniques. Since 1977 its Local Elections Division has spent more than $2 million annually on contests for state legislatures. It finances state polls which can be used by candidates for all state offices, thus avoiding unnecessary duplication. Its research and issues staff provides information on the records of vulnerable Democrats. It provides up-to-date information on the votes on Democratic state legislators and members of Congress through computer links between the national party headquarters and the state party headquarters and local campaigns. The RNC Campaign Management School trains professional campaign managers and then places them in local campaigns. The national party then contributes toward their salaries. The ultimate goal (not yet achieved) is to place in each congressional district a salaried party agent who will recruit candidates and manage their campaigns.

Local organization. "There is no alternative to building up local party organization, county by county," according to the master blueprint for the 1980s, "A Republican Party Strategy for Controlling Government in America in This Century." Accordingly, the Republicans adopted a trickle-up theory: strengthening the party at the local level would enable it to become the majority party nationally. In 1983 Frank Fahrenkopf, the chairman of the RNC, announced plans for a buildup of local Republican organizations in the 1100 counties where they had been weak or nonexistent.

State organization. With national help in fund-raising, most state Republican parties restructured their operations.[42] They moved into permanent headquarters, hired full-time chairpersons and executive directors, and expanded their staffing. They even organized statewide advertising campaigns and beefed up their polling and direct-mail operations.

National organization. The national party completely revamped its own operations. By 1976 it had provided for a full-time paid chair and co-chair and had established eight vice chairs—one man and one woman for each of the four regions. By 1978 they were augmented by thirteen regional political directors who worked with the state parties. Regional finance directors had put the soft-money system into place by 1980. The RNC expanded its staff into several units, each designed to help local and state parties raise money, manage campaigns, and develop media images.

Candidate recruitment. For the first time in the history of the Republican Party, the regional officials directly recruited candidates to run in party primaries. They did so to counteract the influences of PACs and new politics, discouraging both issue extremists and wealthy but inexperienced newcomers from entering the races and instead encouraging seasoned and attractive politicians to run for higher office. Local mayors, city council members, and county legislators were asked to run for the state legislature; the best of the latter group were encouraged to make statewide races or to try for Congress.[43]

The Republicans' control of the White House helped them recruit good candidates. At the request of the RNC, President Reagan promised each state chair that he or she could have five "must-hire" recommendations to the White House Personnel Office, and he promised 100 jobs for Republican candidates for Congress who were defeated in the general elections. The RNC could offer candidates a package deal: a fund-raiser with personal appearances by a top-level official (possibly a Cabinet member or Vice President Bush), a televised "message from the president" to be used as a campaign ad, professional campaign management, a computerized link to Republican headquarters for research on issues, and help in preparing the media campaign. The party hired advertising agencies to develop commercials for local candidates and to run a series of ads for the entire party on network television. The White House political aides, through the "assets and priorities" group, channeled RNC and PAC contributions to candidates in "winnable" contests. Losing candidates would receive help from the RNC in obtaining one of the federal jobs that the White House had reserved for them.

THINGS TO COME

NATIONALIZED PARTIES OR SUPER-PACs? The two parties have reversed their tendencies toward decentralization. In the future, if the national parties and their agents can recruit most local candidates and create a "career ladder" for them to climb, then the preconditions for responsible parties will exist, and PAC politics and media politics will no longer dominate the parties-in-government. The parties will be able to force members to adhere to the party line on issues by threatening them with loss of funds and campaign assistance in the next election (or even competition in the primaries) unless they do so.

But there is no reason to believe that party nationalization is the inevitable outcome of revitalization. The Democrats have maintained the same freewheeling style that once prompted Will Rogers to remark, "I'm a member of no organized political party; I'm a Democrat." Their state and local parties challenge attempts by the national party to impose rules on them. Their factionalism weakens their presidents and their presidential candidates, prevents coherent policy-making, and allows the Republicans to exploit their disunity in Congress.

The Republicans are ahead in terms of party modernization and nationalization, but that does not always translate into success at the polls. As Republican candidates are recruited and are provided with funds and services by the national party, their inclination to stray from the party line in order to appeal to their local constituencies may decrease. But only locally tailored campaigns can win the support of voters. The Democrats, with their looser ties to national party committees, are freer to follow their own political instincts. The Democratic Party remains more localized, and hence more responsive, and the Democrats win many more elections than their opponents. As of 1985 they had a 4 to 3 lead in state legislators, a 2 to 1 lead in governors, and a 4 to 3 lead in the House of Representatives.

Figure 6-6. Party and PAC politics in the 1980s. Groups in politics are either party- or candidate-oriented, and ideological or coalitional in nature.

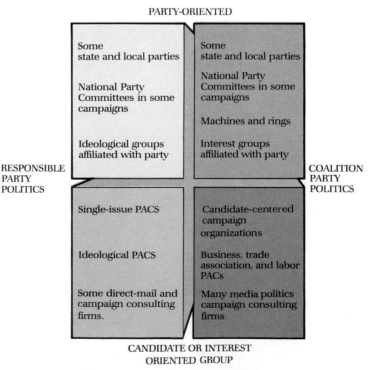

PARTY-ORIENTED

Some state and local parties National Party Committees in some campaigns Ideological groups affiliated with party	Some state and local parties National Party Committees in some campaigns Machines and rings Interest groups affiliated with party
Single-issue PACS Ideological PACS Some direct-mail and campaign consulting firms.	Candidate-centered campaign organizations Business, trade association, and labor PACs Many media politics campaign consulting firms

RESPONSIBLE PARTY POLITICS

COALITION PARTY POLITICS

CANDIDATE OR INTEREST ORIENTED GROUP

To understand the transformation of party politics, we must return to two distinctions made earlier in this chapter: (1) the distinction between responsible and coalition parties (that is, parties which take a principled stand on issues, as opposed to those which concentrate on creating a majority coalition) and (2) the distinction between party politics and media politics. Figure 6-6 diagrams political organizations according to these distinctions: the extent to which they are coalitional, centrist, and pragmatic, as opposed to being principled, extreme, and issue-oriented, and the extent to which they are geographically based party organizations or antiparty operations, like PACs.

What kind of organization will predominate in the future depends in large measure on two factors: how existing organizations adapt to changing technologies and which style seems most likely to help candidates win elections. The new developments in television and radio would seem to give the edge to any organization that can reach an audience and motivate it to give money and listen to its message. This would seem to favor PACs (or perhaps **super-PACs**), which have experience in appealing to narrow constituencies and raising funds from them.

IN CONCLUSION

For more than a century, machines and courthouse rings dominated traditional party politics. In the past quarter-century their monopoly on the recruitment of candidates and the funding and management of campaigns has been challenged by candidate-centered campaign organizations and by political action committees. No one kind of organization, and no one style of politics, now predominates.

The erosion of party politics provides a greater opportunity for people to run for office using the methods of media politics, but by and large this has favored the wealthy. PACs have taken advantage of campaign finance laws (and loopholes), which tends to bias the system toward the interests of business.

The restructuring of the two national parties and the modernization of the state and local parties have given women and minorities more opportunities to participate in party affairs, raised the caliber of those running for office, ended much of the bribery and extortion that characterized traditional party politics, and increased party discipline and cohesion, especially in the Republican Party, although it remains to be seen whether greater centralization will help win elections.

The long-term outlook is for PACs to continue to flourish, because they help the party-in-government run effective new politics campaigns, but for the parties to adopt more sophisticated fund-raising and campaign techniques and try to counter the influence of PACs. The predominant organization of the future will be the one that politicians find most useful in winning elections.

NOTES

1. James D. Richardson, *Messages and Papers of the Presidents of the United States, 1789–1897*, vol. 1, Bureau of National Literature and Art, Washington, D.C., 1898, p. 219.
2. Samuel Eldersveld, *Political Parties in American Society*, Basic Books, New York, 1982, p. 85.
3. Austin Ranney, *The Doctrine of Responsible Party Government*, University of Illinois Press, Urbana, 1954.
4. On convergence theory see Anthony Downs, *An Economic Theory of Democracy*, Harper and Row, New York, 1957, p. 28.
5. David Truman, "Federalism and the Party System," in Arthur MacMahon (ed.), *Federalism: Mature and Emergent*, Doubleday, Garden City, N.Y., 1955.

6. Edward Costikyan, *Behind Closed Doors*, Harcourt, Brace and World, New York, 1966, p. 153.
7. Eldersveld, op. cit., p. 99.
8. James MacGregor Burns, *The Deadlock of Democracy*, Prentice-Hall, Englewood Cliffs, N.J., 1956.
9. Larry Sabato, *The Rise of Political Consultants*, Basic Books, New York, 1982, p. 286.
10. Ibid., p. 288.
11. Frank Sorauf, *Party Politics in America*, 4th ed., Little, Brown, Boston, 1982, p. 234.
12. Dom Bonafede, "Are You Planning to Run for Office?" *The National Journal*, Jan. 16, 1982, p. 104.
13. Thomas Patterson and James McClure, *The Unseeing Eye: The Myth of Television Power in National Politics*, Putnam, New York, 1976.
14. Edward Costikyan, *How to Win Votes*, Harcourt Brace Jovanovich, New York, 1980, p. 93.
15. William Geist, "Millicent Fenwick: Marching to Her Own Drum," *The New York Times Magazine*, June 27, 1982.
16. Costikyan, *How to Win Votes*, Harcourt, New York, 1980, p. 142.
17. Sabato, op. cit., p. 7.
18. Thomas Gais, "On the Scope and Bias of Interest Group Involvement in Elections," paper delivered at the annual convention of the American Political Science Association, 1983.
19. John C. Green and James Guh, "The Party Irregulars," *Psychology Today*, vol. 18, October 1984, pp. 46–50.
20. Elizabeth Drew, "Politics and Money," *The New Yorker*, Dec. 6, 1982, p. 54.
21. Drew, op. cit., p. 147.
22. Sabato, op. cit., p. 274.
23. As reported by Al Hunt, *The Wall Street Journal*, July 15, 1984.
24. Ibid.
25. Ibid.
26. Phillip M. Stern, "Pronounce PACs 'POX,'" *The New York Times*, Mar. 13, 1984.
27. *The New York Times*, Feb. 3, 1983.
28. Richard A. Armstrong, "Election Finance and Free Speech," *Newsweek*, July 18, 1983, p. 5.
29. Ibid.
30. *Attitudes toward Campaign Financing*, Civic Services, Washington, D.C., February 1983, p. 9.
31. For the anti-PAC position, see *People against PACs*, Common Cause, Washington, D.C., 1983; for a defense of PACs, see Herbert E. Alexander, *The Case for PACs*, Public Affairs Council, Washington, D.C., 1983.
32. *Elrod v. Burns*, 427 U.S. 347 (1976).
33. Costikyan, *How to Win Votes*, pp. 16–17.
34. Raymond Wolfinger, "Why Political Machines Have Not Withered Away and Other Revisionist Thoughts," *Journal of Politics*, vol. 34, no. 3, 1972, pp. 365–398.
35. Eldersveld, op. cit., p. 171.
36. Robert Agranoff, *The Management of Election Campaigns*, Holbrook Press, Boston, 1976, p. 103.
37. Frank Sorauf, "Political Parties and Political Analysis," in William Chambers and Walter Burnham (eds.), *The American Party Systems*, Oxford University Press, New York, 1967.
38. *Cousins v. Wigoda*, 419 U.S. 477 (1974).
39. *The New York Times*, Feb. 28, 1981.
40. *Washington Post National Weekly Edition*, Sept. 10, 1984, p. 23.
41. F. Christopher Arterton, "Political Money and Party Strength," in Joel L. Fleishman (ed.), *The Future of American Political Parties*, American Assembly, New York, 1982, pp. 101–139.

42. Robert Huckshorn and John Bibby, "State Parties in an Era of Political Change," in Fleishman, op. cit., pp. 70–100.

43. John F. Bibby, "Political Parties and Federalism: The Republican National Committee Involvement in Gubernatorial and Legislative Elections," *Publius*, vol. 12, winter 1979, pp. 229–236.

FURTHER READING

Agranoff, Robert: *The Management of Election Campaigns*, Holbrook Press, Boston, 1976. A nuts-and-bolts discussion of how to manage a media politics campaign.

Diamond, Edwin, and Stephen Bates: *The Spot: The Rise of Political Advertising on Television*, M.I.T., Cambridge, Mass., 1984. An illustrated history.

Fleishman, Joel (ed.): *The Future of American Political Parties*, American Assembly, New York, 1982. Essays on the relationship between the party organization and the party-in-government.

Handler, Edward: *Business in Politics*, Lexington Books, Lexington, Ky., 1982. A discussion of how business PACs work.

Pomper, Gerald (ed.): *Party Renewal in America*, Praeger, New York, 1980. Essays on party modernization.

Royko, Mike: *Boss!* New American Library, New York, 1971. An account of how Mayor Daley's Democratic machine ran Chicago.

Sabato, Larry J.: *The Rise of Political Consultants*, Basic Books, New York, 1982. A description and critique of campaign consulting firms and their work.

Sabato, Larry J.: *PAC Power*, Norton, New York, 1984. How PACs influence elections and officeholders.

THE STUDY BREAK

Burdick, Eugene: *The Ninth Wave*. Houghton-Mifflin, Boston, 1956. A novel (written by a political scientist) about a media politics entrepreneur named Mike Freeman and what happens to him in California politics. The plot mixes politics with romance and some surfing.

The Candidate. A movie starring Robert Redford as a man who knows how to win a media politics election (1972).

The Last Hurrah. A movie about a media politics candidate who runs against the incumbent mayor of Boston—a party regular who finds that he has become antiquated in the era of television (1958). Spencer Tracy plays the mayor.

Riordon, W. L.: *Plunkitt of Tammany Hall*, Dutton, New York, 1963. Reminiscences of a New York City politician at the turn of the century.

Shapley, R. E.: *Solid for Mulhooley*, Carleton, New York, 1881. A book about how ward politics was played in the old days.

USEFUL SOURCES

Campaigns and Elections. A Journal of campaign management.

Kinnell, Susan (ed.): *The Democratic and Republican Parties in America: A Historical Bibliography*, ABC-CLIO Information Services, Santa Barbara, Calif., 1983.

Roeder, Edward: *PACs Americana*, Sunshine Services, Washington, D.C., 1982. A directory of PACs.

Weinberger, Marvin: *The PAC Directory*, Ballinger, Cambridge, Mass., 1982. A guide to PAC support of candidates and parties.

ORGANIZATIONS

Democratic National Committee. 1625 Massachusetts Avenue, N.W., Washington, D.C. 20036. For more information phone 202-792-5900.

Federal Elections Commission, Office of Public Communications. 1325 K Street, N.W. Washington, D.C. 20463. For more information phone 800-424-9530.

PACs and Lobbies. 1512 Pennsylvania Avenue, SE., Washington, D.C. 20003. For more information phone 202-544-1141.

Republican National Committee. 310 First Street, S.E., Washington, D.C. 20003. For more information phone 202-863-8500.

The need to get to the people and get out the vote has never changed—only the methods have. The nineteenth century emphasized stump speaking, but today mastery of television is crucial. (*George Caleb Bingham, "Stump Speaking," Boatman's National Bank of St. Louis; AP Laserphoto.*)

CHAPTER 7

CONGRESSIONAL ELECTIONS: CLIMBING CAPITOL HILL

Every two years Americans elect 435 voting (and three nonvoting) members of the House of Representatives and one-third of the 100 members of the Senate. These elections shape the course of government: presidents emerge either with a cooperative Congress or with one that opposes their programs, ignores their priorities, and sets its own agenda. It is no wonder that candidates pour more than $400 million into these elections or that hundreds of thousands of people work in their campaigns. Neither is it any wonder that in the 1982 midterm elections, Tip O'Neill, the Democratic Speaker of the House, appealed for funds to hundreds of thousands of Democrats, warning: "The White House and Senate have fallen. The battle for the House is the last stand." Nor should we be surprised that Ronald Reagan wrote a letter to his backers, claiming that their "vote would decide whether or not we will continue on this new course to economic prosperity, or revert back to the discredited ideas that almost led us to national bankruptcy."[1]

Who runs for Congress, and how are candidates' campaigns organized and financed? What are the roles of parties, and of PACs, in the era of new politics? Who gets elected? Answering these questions will help us understand how Congress works, because how legislators climb Capitol Hill has a great deal to do with what happens once they get there.

RUNNING FOR CONGRESS

To be elected to Congress, one must be constitutionally eligible, legally qualified, and politically viable. Certain kinds of occupational and political experience also help candidates get elected.

Constitutional eligibility

To be elected to Congress, one must be an American citizen (for at least seven years for election to the House and for nine years for election to the Senate). A member of the House must be 25 years of age at the time the oath is taken; a senator must be 30 years of age. Both must be residents of the state. A representative need not reside in the district that he or she represents, and about 100 members of the House currently do not maintain permanent homes in their districts, although almost all have a legal residence there for political reasons. The Constitution bars any religious qualifications for office.

The separation clause states that "no Person holding any Office under the United States, shall be a member of either House during his continuance in Office." Anyone holding an executive or judicial office must give it up to take a seat in Congress. Conversely, a member of Congress must give up his or her seat to accept an executive or judicial appointment. It is easier for the president to appoint *defeated* congressional candidates to the administration than winners. Thus George Bush, after being defeated in a Senate race by Texas voters, received high-level appointments in the Nixon and Ford administrations (CIA director, ambassador to the United Nations, and emissary to the People's Republic of China).

George Bush has climbed the ladder. After serving in the House and then losing a Texas senatorial election, Bush was appointed ambassador to the United Nations, director of the CIA, and head of the liaison office in Peking before his election as vice president on the Republican tickets of 1980 and 1984. (*Office of the Vice President.*)

Legal qualifications

The states regulate congressional elections subject only to federal laws, regulations of the Federal Elections Commission (FEC), and federal court decisions. Requirements to qualify for the ballot—such as filing fees and the number of signatures on nominating petitions—differ from state to state. Candidates must comply with state party rules to enter a nominating primary, in which registered party voters (and sometimes independent voters) select the party nominee. In some states one needs only a plurality to win the nomination, but in many a majority is required, which means that a *runoff primary* between the top two vote-getters may be necessary. Runoffs work against extremist candidates who may obtain a plurality but lose to a more moderate member of the party in the second round. Some minority politicians claim that such runoffs discriminate against them: in a district in which close to half the voters are black or Hispanic, in the first round a minority contender may receive the plurality, but in the second round, if everyone votes on racial lines, the white candidate will win a majority.

Political viability

Nomination by a major party. Almost all serious candidates for Congress are nominated by one of the two major parties. So far, not a single member of a minor party has been elected, although in the past, several small parties—most notably the Populist Party and the Progressive Party between 1880 and 1920—achieved some representation.

Gender. Most members of Congress are male. A few wives of congressmen and senators have filled the vacancies when their husbands died. In the case of the Senate, they were appointed by the governor to fill out the term, while in the House they were chosen by local party leaders to run in special elections. These "congressional widows" were expected to keep the seat warm for other local politicians until the next election, and often they had to fight for renomination against the local party leadership.[2]

In the past twenty years women have found ways to get to Congress other than over their husbands' dead bodies, and the number of women in the House has increased from ten in 1969 to twenty-two in 1985 (of sixty-five who ran). There are more than 1000 women in state legislatures (holding around 11 percent of statewide executive offices), two woman governors and several woman lieutenant governors, 1700 woman mayors, and a total of 17,000 elected woman officials; thus there is a large and experienced pool of woman politicians who can run for Congress. At the present rate it will take 400 years for women to constitute half of the House and Senate; clearly some breakthrough is needed if women are to have their demographic share of legislative positions.

Minorities.   Many blacks were elected to Congress in the aftermath of the Civil War; this was the result of Reconstruction policies enforced at the point of the bayonet by victorious union armies, but once these troops were withdrawn, the representation of blacks diminished, and it ended completely when southern blacks were disenfranchised in the period 1890–1910. In modern times most districts which elect blacks are urban with an average black population of 62 percent. Many districts which are 40 to 60 percent black are still represented by whites, and only two blacks were elected in the sixty-three districts in which blacks constitute between 20 and 40 percent of the voters. Black voters are willing to support white incumbents and to cross over and vote for a white against a black on issues—as some in a district with a black

Freed blacks were added to the electorate in 1867, although federal officials were needed to protect them at the polls. (*Granger Collection.*)

majority did in a 1984 Mississippi contest in which a white right-to-life candidate defeated a black pro-choice candidate. Representation of blacks in the House increased from nine in 1969 to twenty in 1985. There are approximately 6000 black elected officials in the nation, including almost 400 state legislators, and blacks make up 11 percent of the electorate; hence their underrepresentation in the House (and their lack of representation in the Senate) is due primarily to their inability to represent nonminority districts—to the unwillingness of white voters to cross racial lines and vote for blacks.

Hispanics also find it difficult to win nominations or elections except in heavily Hispanic areas. In California, Texas, New Mexico, and New York one or more "Hispanic districts" are created by the state legislature. No Hispanics were elected in the thirty-four districts in which they constitute 20 to 40 percent of the voters. There were ten voting Hispanics (and one nonvoting representative from Puerto Rico) in the House in 1985, and thus they are underrepresented in proportion to the percentage of Hispanics in the population (close to 10 percent). Overall, there are more than 3200 Hispanic officeholders.

Asian Americans do somewhat better in appealing to non-Asian voters. In 1985, two of the three in the House represented districts with an Asian-American population of less than 10 percent.

Religion. Protestants, who constitute the vast majority of the members of the House and Senate, are usually elected from districts or states with disproportionate concentrations of their denominations: the Baptists tend to come from the south, the Lutherans from the midwest, the Episcopalians from the eastern seaboard, and so on. The more evangelical sects are underrepresented, while the relatively few (but socially and economically advantaged) Episcopalians, Congregationalists, and Presbyterians are overrepresented in proportion to their numbers in the population, with more than 100 representatives and thirty-four Senators. The more numerous Baptists, Lutherans, and Methodists come next, with a total of 118 in the House and thirty in the Senate. Other Protestant groups have far fewer members in Congress. Slightly more than one-fourth of the members of the House and one-fifth of the members of the Senate are Roman Catholic, which is in rough proportion to the percentage of Catholics in the population (22.6 percent). In contrast, there are thirty Jews in the House and eight in the Senate, which is somewhat greater than the percentage of Jews in the population (2.6 percent).

Demographics. Increasingly, unmarried, divorced, and young politicians have been elected to office. (No longer need most members of Congress be happily married white males with two children.) The average age of members of the House has dropped from 50 to 47 in the past decade, and the average age of senators is just over 50. Close to 100 representatives and ten senators are under 42. The number of unmarried, widowed, or divorced members of the House has gone from twenty-nine in 1969 to close to 100 today.

Occupational and political experience

The occupational structure of our legislatures is narrow compared with those of most other western democracies. The halls of Congress are filled with lawyers and self-made business entrepreneurs; absent are the scientists, engineers, corporate executives, union leaders, novelists, poets, journalists, doctors, ministers, and blue-collar workers that one finds in other countries. In

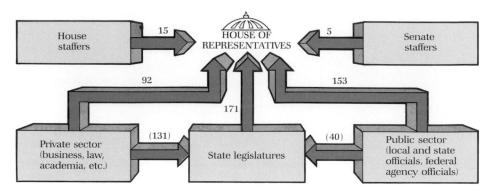

Figure 7-1. Previous careers of members of the House, 1981–1982. How do people make the climb up Capitol Hill? People in business, advertising, banking, building, and college teaching usually serve first in state legislatures or other local and state positions before winning election to Congress. Lawyers, farmers, accountants, insurance brokers, and other teachers usually start even further down the ladder: first winning a job in city and county government, then moving to state government, and finally running for Congress. Blue-collar workers, social workers, journalists, and engineers typically require three job changes in the private and public sectors before they make it to Congress. (Source: *Congressional Directory*, 98th Congress, U.S. Government Printing Office, 1983.)

European parliamentary systems, often the party of management is pitted against the party of labor, or parties are divided along religious, linguistic, or ideological lines. Our legislators are brokers between competing interests rather than direct representatives of classes, religions, ethnic groups, or ideologies.

Occupations. In the past, the vast majority of members of both the House and the Senate were lawyers, but in the last two decades their share of seats has diminished markedly, down in 1985 to 43 percent in the House and 61 percent in the Senate. In that same year 144 representatives and thirty senators had had prior business or banking careers; thirty-seven in the House and ten in the Senate had been in education; twenty-four in the House and seven in the Senate were in farming; twenty-one in the House and seven in the Senate were in journalism; and there was a smattering of engineers, doctors, athletes, pilots, astronauts, former military personnel, and members of the clergy. Surprisingly, in our media-dominated age, there are few television producers, on-air broadcast personalities, movie stars, or people from advertising, lobbying, or public relations (Figure 7-1).

Political experience. One-fourth of the members of the House have no prior political experience. Of these, one-third are businesspeople, one-third are lawyers, and one-sixth are college professors and teachers; the rest come from the fields of banking, insurance, real estate, and the professions. These men and women are highly successful and respected in their communities—and often they are bored stiff with their roles, which is why sometime in their late thirties or early forties they decide to devote themselves to public service. Some are recruited by party leaders, but most are recruited by their bathroom mirrors.

But the other three-fourths of the members of the House, and most of the senators, are career politicians. Focusing on their occupations is misleading; they list themselves as farmers, lawyers, bankers, and the like, but rarely do they practice their professions once they are in Congress. Some get to Capitol Hill by moving up through the party organization and getting its backing, entering Congress as "ambassadors" from the party and intent on helping the organization get patronage and whatever else is to be had from the government. But local and county party jurisdictions are not coterminous with congressional district boundaries and today are not much interested in congressional nominations. Even party-oriented politicians find that the jump from a state legislature (in which help from the party organization is crucial) to Congress means abandoning the party organization and creating a candidate-centered one.[3]

Interest groups are interested in and can affect nominating contests: corporate and trade associations, labor unions, and single-issue groups (such as those for or against abortion, gun control, or prayer in schools) all get involved. They may recruit, and in effect "sponsor," a potential candidate in the primaries.

The majority of those who get to Congress are experienced vote-getters. About one-third of the members of the House come directly from state legislatures, and most are well versed in local party affairs. Another third come directly from jobs with county and city governments or with state or federal agencies and also have close ties to the parties. About twenty come directly from Capitol Hill as staffers. Not only do they have local party contacts, but they also are connected to interest groups which may urge them to run.

RUNNING FOR THE HOUSE OF REPRESENTATIVES

Incumbents and challengers

It is almost impossible for an ***incumbent*** to lose a primary contest for renomination—fewer than 2 percent did so between 1956 and 1982, and only three were defeated in 1984. It is also highly unlikely that an incumbent will lose in the general election—fewer than 10 percent did so in those same years, and only seventeen lost in 1984. Elections which involve incumbents are quite different from open-seat contests, which do not.

Incumbents. In any House election approximately 4 percent of the members decide to retire, 4 percent seek higher office, and death or disability claims 7 percent. The remaining 350 to 370 incumbents will try to win renomination and reelection, and approximately 90 percent will do so, as Table 7-1 makes clear.

Not only will incumbents win, they will win big (see Table 7-2). Before 1966 about two-thirds of the incumbents won with 60 percent or more of the two-party vote, and since then 75 percent have done so. The number of *marginal seats*—those in which the incumbent won by less than 5 percent—declined from one-fifth in 1964 to around one-eighth in 1972 (and in 1984 to only 12.9

Table 7-1. Turnover in House elections, 1966 to 1986

Year	Seeking reelection	Defeated in primary	Defeated in election	Percent reelected
1966	411	8	41	88.1
1968	409	4	9	96.8
1970	401	10	12	94.5
1972	390	12	13	93.6
1974	391	8	40	87.7
1976	384	3	13	95.8
1978	382	5	19	93.7
1980	388	6	31	90.7
1982	371	10	29	89.5
1984	392	3	17	90.1
1986	394	2	6	97.9

Source: John F. Bibby, Thomas E. Mann, and Norman Ornstein, *Vital Statistics on Congress, 1980,* American Enterprise Institute, Washington, D.C., 1980, table 1-7.

Table 7-2. Landslide victories in House elections, 1972 to 1986

Year	Democrats	Republicans	House, percent
1972	185	123	70.8
1974	209	52	60.0
1976	208	89	68.2
1978	195	105	68.9
1980	173	121	67.5
1982	199	95	67.5
1984	182	140	74.0
1986	219	132	77.9

Note: A landslide is defined as anything more than 60 percent of the total vote. This table gives the number and percentages of districts in which landslides occurred. A century ago only one-fourth of House seats were won by landslides; the number increased to two-thirds in the period 1960–1980.

percent) and has remained at that level.[4] These data are surprising because the public has little respect for Congress as an institution and yet seems to reelect most of its members.[5] Why should this be so?

INCUMBENTS' ADVANTAGES. "No Congressman who gets elected and who minds his business should ever be beaten," the former chairman of the House Democratic Campaign Committee once said. "Everything is there for him to use if he'll only keep his nose to the grindstone and use what is offered."[6] And what is offered to an incumbent amounts to approximately $1 million in staff and campaign resources, all paid for out of congressional funds. The members can make up to thirty-two free trips home each year. They are provided with funds for district offices, mobile offices, trailers, and vans so that they can help their constituents (known as *casework*) deal with government agencies (state and local as well as federal); for example, they inquire about social security eligibility, give advice on Medicare, help college students fill out loan forms, and handle problems of immigrants. Studies have shown that most voters believe that they have been helped by their representatives and view them favorably—even if they did not get what they wanted from the bureaucracy. Incumbents are often supported by such people, even voters from the opposition party.[7]

Recently elected members and those who are worried about reelection make heavy use of the House television and recording studios, which produce "news releases" about their activities for district radio and television stations. They can use the congressional frank to send out newsletters free until sixty days before an election; the cost of these newsletters (approximately 860 million pieces of mail in 1984) exceeds $250,000 per member, or more than $110 million annually. They have free WATS telephone lines that they can use to call people in their districts.[8]

Local media coverage benefits incumbents, who often help journalists from their area with features and get them access to Washington news sources. Most of the coverage by the local press is favorable, and the local media are likely to use the "canned" press releases, videotapes, and audiotapes that are sent to them, often portraying these as news coverage rather than as prepackaged material. Most incumbents are not covered by the national newsweeklies or television networks, which might be more critical of their performance.[9]

People in the districts know their representatives, and by a 3 to 1 margin in most instances they view them favorably. In contrast, most voters at the beginning of a campaign have no idea who is running against an incumbent in the primaries or the general election, do not recognize challengers' names, and do not view them positively.[10] Even by the end of a campaign, less than half the voters report having had any contact (even through newspaper articles or television coverage) with the challenger.[11]

House members claim the credit for government programs in their districts, even if they had no hand in obtaining them.[12] "Rivers Delivers" was the campaign slogan used by L. Mendell Rivers, the chair of the House Armed Services Committee, after obtaining so many military bases and hospitals that local voters in Charleston, South Carolina, joked that the city would sink below sea level. A large majority of voters think that House members care about getting the district its fair share of federal programs.[13]

How important is incumbency? We can quantify its advantages in two ways.

Geraldine Ferraro, then a representative from Queens, New York, handing out campaign literature to her constituents in 1982. (*David Burnett: Contact Stock Images.*)

First, we can compare the margin of victory in the first term with margins in subsequent terms. There is a **sophomore surge:** between 1970 and 1978 the average margin of victory between the first and second terms increased from 5.8 to 7.5 percent. In 1982 it was 2 percent for Republicans and 12.3 percent for Democrats who were reelected to second terms, and in 1984 it was 3.9 percent and 10 percent, respectively. Second, we can compare the margin of victory achieved by an incumbent in his or her last election with the margin gained by a successor of the same party in the following election—known as the **retirement slump.** The decrease in the margin of victory is usually between 6 and 11 percent.[14]

VULNERABLE INCUMBENTS. Incumbents *can* be defeated: in 1985, one-fourth of the members of Congress had beaten an incumbent to get to Capitol Hill. The odds are fairly good that an incumbent will eventually be defeated—even if the odds are low in any particular election.[15] This is so because congressional careers often follow a pattern: a close initial election victory, then vulnerability for the succeeding two elections (when the other party tries to recapture the seat), and then a constituency-building phase during which the incumbent works energetically to build support in the district. This is followed by a period in which the incumbent concentrates more on influencing decisions in Congress and forgets to cultivate the folks at home, eventually losing some support and entering another vulnerability phase, in which lower margins of victory give strong challengers an incentive to run.[16] A large number of losing incumbents slip in the previous election and win with less than 55 percent of the vote. Often a weakened incumbent faces a rematch and must run against a strong challenger from the previous election who is better known than a complete newcomer.

Corruption and scandal can be the kiss of death: twenty-six members of Congress were *convicted* of crimes between 1972 and 1982; some resigned as a result, and others were defeated. Of eighty members facing *charges* of corruption between 1968 and 1978, sixty-five ran for reelection and sixteen were defeated.[17]

207

Districting and redistricting. The Constitution apportions representation in the House among the states on the basis of their population. After each census some states gain and some lose House seats, since the size of the House has been fixed by law at 435 voting members since 1911. As a result of the Supreme Court decision in *Wesberry v. Sanders*, each district must have the same number of people.[18] Even in states that do not lose or win seats as a result of interstate reapportionment, changes in intrastate population distribution usually require new district lines after each census.

The Constitution does *not* require election to the House by districts, and before 1842 (when Congress itself prohibited it) some states elected a few members-at-large to represent the whole state. Every state legislature draws up district lines (except for six states whose population is so small that they have only one representative), and each district elects a single member by a winner-take-all plurality vote. The shape of these districts can have a substantial effect on election results, usually benefiting incumbents.

REDISTRICTING AND RACE. According to the Voting Rights Act (VRA) of 1965 and its amendments in 1982, the states cannot draw district lines to discriminate against minorities. In practice the Justice Department interprets this provision to mean that the proportion of minority voters in a district cannot be substantially reduced and that predominantly black or Hispanic districts may be created. The Supreme Court, in *Mississippi Republican Committee v. Brooks* (1984), upheld a lower court decision which held that in some circumstances, in a state with a past history of racial discrimination, the VRA could require the creation of a district with a majority of black voters.[19] In other words, in an area in which there were large concentrations of minority voters, it would be discriminatory to create two districts in which they constituted 45 percent of the voters, rather than one district in which they constituted 55 percent and another in which they constituted 35 percent—an actual issue in the *Mississippi*

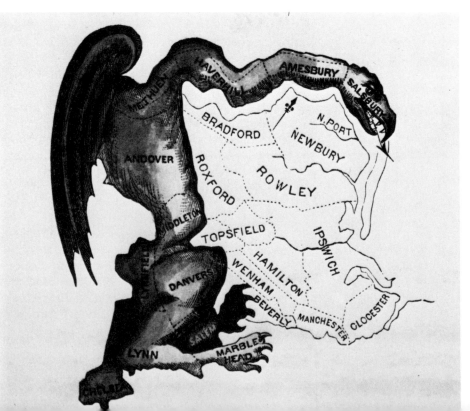

Governor Elbridge Gerry's map of a congressional district in Massachusetts so resembled a salamander that the term *gerrymander* still designates artificial, politically motivated districting. (*Historical Pictures Service.*)

Figure 7-2. A gerrymandered district in California. Democrats redrew the district lines somewhat to exclude some Republican areas. They extended the district to include white working-class, black blue-collar, and Hispanic areas. The forty-fifth district, on the other hand, was created to give the Republicans a safe seat. One part, Coronado, contains many retired military people who are conservative and decidedly Republican. Another part includes the suburbs of San Diego, also solidly Republican. By making the Democratic district even more Democratic and doing the same for the Republican district, the gerrymandered lines drawn by the Democratic legislature produced the desired result: the House seat in the forty-fourth was captured by a Democrat in 1982 with an overwhelming 65 percent of the vote; the forty-fifth was taken by a Republican with 69 percent. (Source: *Congressional Districts in the 1980s*, Washington, D.C., Congressional Quarterly, 1983.)

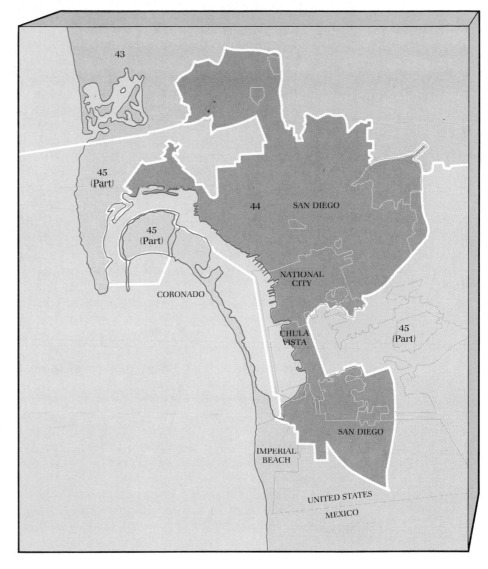

case. The creation of a few solidly minority districts benefits minority incumbents. It also benefits most white politicians, who have less to fear from minority challengers. The only politicians who suffer are minority challengers, since there are fewer districts in which minority voters form a substantial part of the electorate.

REDISTRICTING AND PARTY. Drawing district lines to benefit a party is known as *gerrymandering* (after Elbridge Gerry, an eighteenth-century governor of Massachusetts). When done on racial grounds to discriminate against minorities, it is unconstitutional, but when done by one party against another, or in collusion by both, it has not been ruled unconstitutional by the courts (Figure 7-2).

There are two ways to gerrymander. *Packing* a district means creating one in which the opposition party has total support. While that party wins the seat with just about 100 percent of the vote, every vote over 50 percent is a wasted vote. Meanwhile, the other party keeps an edge in all the other districts, winning them with few wasted votes. The net result is that the second party wins more seats. *Cracking* a district means breaking up opposition party voters and putting them into other districts so that in each one they total less than 50 percent of the vote—and all their votes are wasted, since they win no seats.

State legislatures often gerrymander districts. The Republican National Committee (RNC) helps state parties with its Redistricting Division's $1 million computerized facilities, which are used to determine the optimum district lines for state and national elections. The Democrats, who have overwhelming majorities in state legislatures, however, rely on their political advantages to overcome the Republicans' technology.

Incumbents benefit from *collusive redistricting:* the two parties agree on a plan to preserve the maximum number of incumbents by minimizing party competition in every district. (This also has the effect of lowering turnouts.) Although redistricting helps incumbents, there is little evidence that it is a significant factor. In both gerrymandered and nongerrymandered districts in the 1970s, incumbents' margins of victory increased at about the same rate.[20]

New and open seats. Candidates have their best chances in contests for new and ***open seats.*** In five of the last eight elections, more party turnover occurred in open-seat races than in races against incumbents, although in 1984 fourteen new members defeated incumbents, while only seven won open seats. About half the members of Congress in 1985 had first won their seats when an incumbent retired.

CENSUS REAPPORTIONMENT. Some states gain new seats as a result of the census; after 1980 the northeastern and midwestern states lost seventeen seats, which went to the southwest and the south. In theory the new seats should benefit the Republicans—partly because an open seat always gives the minority party in the House a better chance and partly because new seats are created in the sunbelt, where the Republicans have been doing well in recent elections and where Democratic identification among voters have been weakening. Although the Republicans expected big gains in 1982, the Democrats won more new seats. They did so as a result of advantageous redistricting in states where they controlled the legislature. In California, for example, they "stole" three seats in Los Angeles by clever gerrymandering.[21] They also used gerrymanders well in New Jersey, Illinois, Missouri, and Minnesota. The Republicans turned the tables on them in Pennsylvania and Indiana; on balance, however, the Democrats came out ahead.

OPEN SEATS. Around twenty to fifty members retire each session; this is about triple the rate of the 1960s, but it is small in comparison with turnover in the nineteenth century, when one-third of the House members retired each session.[22] Older members and those in poor health are likely to retire, especially if faced with strong potential challengers in a primary or an election. More recently younger men and women, in the prime of their careers, are leaving Congress. Many are dissatisfied with the strains of holding office— burned out by the work and by commuting to and from their districts. They think that restrictions on their outside income are unfair (since they maintain two homes and many have private school or college tuition to pay). In recent years about three-fifths of the retirees have held leadership positions; seemingly some of the best are bowing out. Most won previous elections handily

Typifying a growing trend to retire early from Capitol Hill, Representative Barbara Jordan announced her decision not to run in 1978. (*David Burnett: Press Images.*)

and could have remained in office.[23] Few members resigned in 1984, however, which may mean the beginning of a low-turnover pattern.

Each session between five and twenty members of the House quit to run for higher office. They are the brave ones: most representatives never try this because the risk is too great.[24] Their odds of winning a Senate seat or a governorship are about 1 in 3. The cumulative effect of these contests is that only five or six governors, but almost one-third of senators, have served in the House.

In open-seat contests the Democrats usually hold an open primary and let the winner of this free for all carry the party banner.[25] The Republicans operate differently. Their state and local parties consult with the national party organization, hoping to unite around a strong politician—usually someone with experience at the state or county level. If at all possible, local parties are encouraged to avoid divisive primaries. Sometimes the national party intervenes early and supports one of the contenders, hoping to get others to dropout.

Gender plays a role in determining who gets to run in an open-seat contest. When a party has a good chance of winning, white males usually run; when the opposition looks like a shoo-in, a woman or a member of a minority group often makes the race. In 1984, for example, forty-one women (twenty-four Republicans and seventeen Democrats) had to run against incumbents, and none won; only two Republican and two Democratic women ran in the more desirable open-seat contests. As more women become state and local party leaders (there were more than a dozen in the Republican Party in 1985, for example), fewer women should be relegated to unwinnable races.

UNCONTESTED RACES. When the south was solidly Democratic, close to 100 representatives and twenty-two senators faced no opposition in the general elections. More recently, as Republicans have built strong southern parties, most seats have been contested. Today, about 12 percent of House seats remain without two-party competition and are held by a few remaining entrenched southern Democrats and a few popular northerners who sometimes can get endorsements from the opposition.

The challengers. There is no shortage of challengers to run against incum-

Table 7-3. Seats lost in off-year elections, 1966 to 1986

Year	Party winning presidency	Seats gained in House in presidential election year	Seats lost in House in off-year election	Incumbents defeated from president's party
1964	Democrats	37		5
1966			48	39
1968	Republicans	5		0
1970			12	9
1972	Republicans	12		3
1974			48	36
1976	Democrats	1		7
1978			16	14
1980	Republicans	33		3
1982			26	26
1984	Republicans	14		3
1986			5	5

bents, even though the odds are poor. In 1982 there were only fifty-eight open-seat contests and in 1984 there were only twenty-seven such contests, and so everyone else had to buck the greater odds of unseating an incumbent. Most challengers are five to seven years younger than incumbents, have less experience (only one-fifth have held elective office before), and have less funding and fewer resources.[26] How can each party recruit *strong* challengers and help them finance respectable races when the odds suggest that their best prospects are to wait for new or open seats?

PRIMARIES.   One way is to defeat an incumbent in the primaries. This can be done when the incumbent is involved in a scandal, is in poor health, or has cast a particularly controversial vote. Otherwise, although one-third of the Democratic members and one-eighth of the Republican members are likely to face challengers, almost all will survive. Challengers find that it is hard to get name recognition, impossible to get news coverage in such low-key contests, and difficult to raise funds. Incumbents benefit from low turnouts in which their supporters are more likely to vote.

RECRUITING STRONG CHALLENGERS.   There are good and bad nominations. In perhaps 40 contests the challenger has a real shot at the seat; in the other races the opposition party is going through the motions. When a party hack, a factional leader, or an oddball wins a nomination, it is a sign that no serious politician thought that it was worth having. But there is no difficulty in recruiting against a vulnerable incumbent; the problem is to narrow the field. The strongest challengers are those who have name recognition in the district, political experience, proven vote-getting ability, and the support of grass-roots organizations in the community.

Strong challengers give themselves better odds if they run in off-year elections against an incumbent of the president's party. In every election held in the twentieth century except that in 1934, the president's party has lost seats in the next midterm election. Off-year losses for the president's party average twelve seats in the first term (although the Republicans lost twenty-seven in 1982); in the second term losses average over twenty seats, as Table 7-3 indicates.

Financing House elections

"There are four parts to any campaign," according to Tip O'Neill, the Speaker of the House: "The candidate, the issues of the candidate, the campaign organization, and the money to run the campaign with. Without the money, you can forget the other three."[27] Rich Bond, former deputy chairman of the Republican National Committee, quotes Lee Atwater, a White House aide, as saying, "You can't buy a district, but you can sure buy 2 percent," and 2 percent of the voters may be all that is necessary to win twenty or thirty close races.[28] In 1982, according to Tony Coelho, the chairman of the Democratic Congressional Campaign Committee, massive spending by the Republicans "saved them from an overwhelming, embarrassing defeat," an assessment shared by Republican Party officials.[29] Yet in 1984 the same spending resulted in meager gains, in spite of a Reagan landslide. Clearly money is important, but it is not decisive.

The costs of campaigning. In 1982 winners of House seats raised $124.4 million, or an average of $181,748 for each race, and losers raised $60.7 million, or an average of $101,178 per race. Money talks in House elections, although candidates need not outspend their opponents. All candidates must do is raise enough money to run a good race (that is, get themselves known and considered by most voters), whether that is more than the opposition spends or not (Figure 7-3).

The role of political action committees. PACs provide a significant amount of money for House campaigns. Winners received 26 percent of their contributions from PACs in 1976, 35 percent in 1982, and close to 40 percent in 1984. Total PAC contributions in congressional races rose from $8.5 million in 1971–1972, to $62.2 million in 1981–1982, and to close to $100 million in 1984. By 1982 PACs had displaced the small contributor as the primary source of funds for House campaigns.

Incumbents receive the lion's share of PAC funds, which means that Democrats in the House get more money than Republicans: in 1982 Democratic

Figure 7-3. The high cost of politicking. Campaign costs for primary and general elections for the Senate and House in the past decade. These costs have increased far faster than the cost of living. In 1986 total spending for House races was $187 million, and total spending for Senate races was $155 million. (Sources: Citizens Research Foundation; Federal Elections Commission.)

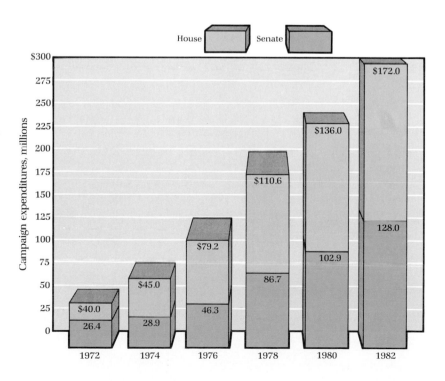

incumbents received 43 percent of their funds from PACs, while Republicans received 32 percent of their funds from this source. Incumbents in 1982 received 65.9 percent of all PAC contributions, while challengers received 13.3 percent and open-seat contestants got 14.8 percent.

Labor PACs favor Democratic candidates, while corporate and trade and professional association PACs seem to favor Republican candidates but give to Democratic incumbents as a form of "insurance" to guarantee access to them if they are reelected. In 1982 labor PACs gave 94 percent of their $20.8 million to Democrats, corporate PACs gave 66 percent of their $29.3 million to Republicans, and trade and professional association PACs gave 57 percent of their $22.8 million to Republicans. In 1984 business PACs gave 43 percent of their funds to Democrats, in response to a coordinated drive by the Democratic Congressional Campaign Committee. When funding challengers, nonlabor PACs give 9 times more to Republicans than to Democrats.

Liberal and conservative PACs play an important role in congressional races, targeting opponents for negative campaigns and providing direct contributions or services to those they favor. *Democrats for the 80s*, for example, spent $575,000 in 135 Democratic races in 1982. The *National Committee for an Effective Congress* used its Campaign Services Project that year to provide precinct targeting, polling, direct-mail, consulting, and research services, valued at $342,000, to liberal House candidates. The National Conservative PAC and other conservative PACs also spend millions, mostly on their own noncoordinated campaigns, and give little directly to House candidates.

National party finance. The national parties have become major contributors in House elections, with Republicans leading the way. Each national party committee may contribute up to $10,000 to offset the primary and general election expenses of each candidate, and each campaign may receive funds for "coordinated expenses"—party services such as polling, direct mailings, and television commercials. Figure 7-4 shows that Republican candidates have taken advantage of these provisions.

THE REPUBLICANS. The National Republican Congressional Committee has a list of more than 1.1 million donors, each of whom makes an average annual

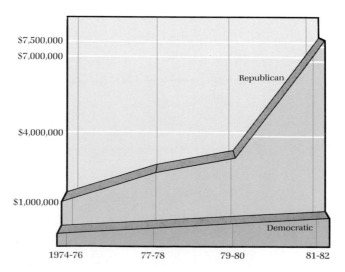

Figure 7-4. Spending by congressional campaign committees. The Republican Party's congressional campaign committee spends far more on its candidates for election to the House than the Democratic Party's committee. This has not yet resulted in significant electoral successes in the House, since Democratic incumbents have been able to outspend their Republican challengers by raising money themselves. (Source: Federal Elections Commission, *Reports*, vol. 9, no. 6, June 1983.)

CONGRESSIONAL CAMPAIGN FINANCE LAWS

Sources of funds. It is illegal for national banks and corporations (Tillman Act, 1907), federal employees (Hatch Act, 1940), and labor unions (Taft-Hartley Act, 1947) to contribute funds to congressional candidates.

Corporations and unions may establish separate segregated funds (SSFs), which may solicit contributions from stockholders, executives, and administrative personnel (corporate SSFs) or from union members and their families (union SSFs). The sponsoring organizations may pay administrative expenses. Contributions are determined by the governing boards of the SSFs (Federal Election Campaign Act, [FECA], 1971).

Disclosing sources of funds. House and Senate campaign committees must report to the Federal Election Commission (FEC) at specified times, listing all individual and PAC contributions. The FEC issues interim, quarterly, and annual reports. Computerized files permit the data to be arranged by contributor donations or by candidates (FECA election campaign amendments, 1974).

Limitations on individual contributions. In the past, individuals could contribute no more than $5000 to congressional campaign committees (Federal Corrupt Practices Act, 1925), but candidates evaded this limitation by setting up several committees. Today, individual contributions are limited to $1000 in each primary, $1000 in each runoff primary, and $1000 in each general election contest in any two-year congressional election cycle (FECA election campaign amendments).

Individuals may contribute up to $20,000 in a two-year election cycle to national political party committees (FECA election campaign amendments). These funds may be used for congressional candidates.

Individuals may contribute no more than $5000 to any multicandidate PAC (FECA election campaign amendments).

Individuals may contribute up to $1000 in volunteer expenses for candidates (FECA election campaign amendments).

Individuals may contribute no more than $25,000 to all candidates, party committees, and PACs in a two-year election cycle (FECA election campaign amendments).

Limitations on PAC contributions. PACs may contribute no more than $5000 to each House and Senate primary, $5000 to each runoff, and $5000 to each general election contest. (FECA election campaign amendments).

Limitations on party contributions. National and state parties may contribute no more than $5000 per candidate in each primary, runoff, or general election to the House. They may contribute up to $14,720 in coordinated services in House contests. They may contribute $17,500 per candidate in Senate contests and up to 2 cents per registered voter in each state (figures as of 1980, with subsequent limits adjusted for inflation; FECA election campaign amendments).

The national party may act as the agent of a state party in collecting funds (the so-called agency agreement), which are then donated by the state party to the House or Senate candidate.

Public funding of campaigns. There are no provisions for public funding of congressional campaigns. Taxpayers may claim a $50 credit or a $100 deduction for contributions to a political campaign.

Limitations on spending. The FECA election campaign amendments of 1974 permitted candidates for the House to spend no more than $25,000 of their own funds. This provision was ruled unconstitutional in *Buckley v. Valeo*, and candidates now may spend as much of their own money as they wish in House and Senate elections.

The FECA amendments limited House campaign expenditures to $94,000 and Senate campaign expenditures to a formula based on the number of registered voters in the state. This was ruled unconstitutional in *Buckley v. Valeo*, and today there are no limitations on spending.

PACs may spend unlimited amounts, provided that their expenditures are uncoordinated and are independent of a candidate's own efforts.

contribution of $25. Republicans who are running for the House receive close to the maximum party contribution and the maximum in funds for coordinated expenses. The National Republican Congressional Committee (NRCC) handles the House campaigns for the national party. Its activities are coordinated with those of the Republican National Committee and the White House Political Affairs Office. Its priorities are (1) to protect Republicans from Democratic challengers, (2) to win open-seat contests, and (3) to assist Republican challengers in close races. It also tries to gain back seats lost to Democrats in a previous election, while new members are still vulnerable. The committee has been most successful in defeating some representatives from the liberal wing of the Democratic Party and least successful in protecting Republican incumbents and in winning open-seat contests.

Although all Republican candidates receive the maximum in party funds, the real work of the NRCC involves recruiting attractive candidates, even before the primary season; getting PACs to contribute to their campaigns; providing the close races with polling services, advertising services, and other campaign assistance; and sending in outside speakers to stump the district with the candidate (the "surrogate" program). The RNC sends "generic" direct mail to targeted House districts urging independent voters to become Republicans. In 1984 the Reagan-Bush Committee shared with House candidates the results of its phone canvasses: lists of Democrats and independents who supported the president. And it used state "party-building funds" to send canvassers to more than 4 million homes with party literature. The Republican Party also channels funds into very tight races, sometimes by taking money from races in which its candidates are strong.[30]

THE DEMOCRATS. Democratic candidates received an average of $5000 from their national committee for the 1984 elections; the national committees preferred to use their money to counter the Republican media blitz. The Democrats now have a direct-mail campaign organized through the Democratic National Campaign Committee (DNCC), which has created a national media center, but they have not yet been able to provide much assistance to most House candidates.

Other funding. Candidates typically pay for about one-tenth of their own campaign costs, but that figure varies: some wealthy self-recruited candidates can finance the entire cost of their campaigns, while some entrenched incumbents pay next to nothing and coast to victory. Individual contributions under $500 account for almost half the funds raised in House races, while contributions over $500 account for one-tenth of these funds. Republicans get a greater share of the small contributions, usually obtained by direct-mail appeals to members of single-issue groups; Democrats rely more on dinners, brunches, and cocktail parties and on wealthier givers, and so a larger proportion of their contributions is in amounts over $500.

The party that controls the White House has an advantage when it comes to fund-raising. A visit to a congressional district by the president, the vice president, or a Cabinet secretary, timed to coincide with a big fundraising event, can provide needed cash for House races. The president can encourage individuals to give money to close campaigns. In 1982 and 1984 "teleconferences," transmitted by satellite, allowed President Reagan to talk informally about the congressional elections with thousands of contributors in dozens of cities.

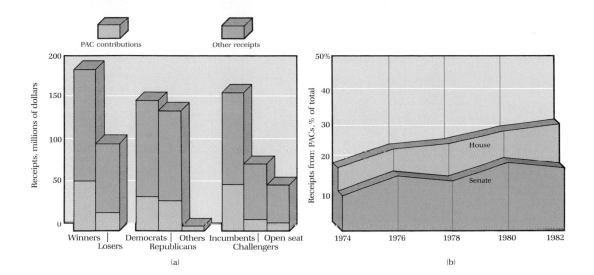

(a)

(b)

Figure 7-5. Campaign receipts in congressional elections. (a) In House elections, winners do significantly better than losers and receive far more PAC contributions. Incumbents, most likely to win, far outstrip their challengers. Democrats receive more funds than their Republican rivals, but only marginally. (Source: Federal Elections Commission, *Reports*, vol. 9, no. 6, June 1983.) (b) Percentage of contributions from PACs in general elections, for both the House and the Senate, from 1974 to 1982. (Source: Data from Michael J. Malbin, ed., *Money and Politics in the United States*, American Enterprise Institute and Chatham House, Washington, D.C., 1984, app. table A.7, pp. 288–289.)

Spending by incumbents and challengers. Incumbents have an advantage in terms of spending. As Figure 7-5 shows, incumbents raise far more money than either challengers or candidates for open seats. Since most incumbents are reelected, this advantage also shows up in two other ways: winners raise and spend far more than losers, and Democrats raise and spend more than Republicans.

Incumbents sometimes can discourage challengers by raising large war chests even before their next election. In 1985 incumbents were busy lining up support from PACs and holding fund-raisers in their districts to build up their coffers for 1986 and raise the ante on potential challengers.

Weak challengers are unable to raise, even with assistance from the national party, the $150,000 or so necessary to make a serious challenge. Thus incumbents who face such opponents need not raise or spend much while coasting to victory. (See Figure 7-6.)

But if a strong challenger can raise money, the picture changes completely. The campaign becomes a *focal point* in the national politics: the media may assign the local race some significance, saying that it is a signal about the mood of the voters, and the parties or ideological PACs may raise the ante. Out-of-state contributors may be solicited by direct mail, and the candidate may fly off to the "money centers"—such as New York City, Los Angeles, Chicago, Atlanta, Boston, Denver, and San Francisco—to meet with PAC managers and individual contributors. People who have given once in response to direct-mail appeals will give again to keep the challenger strong, and the closer the contest, the more likely they are to do so.

The incumbent then must organize a serious campaign and raise funds. But having to raise lots of money is a sign of weakness. Every dollar spent by the challenger gives him or her greater name recognition and viability. Every dollar raised by the incumbent goes toward defending his or her record and refuting charges. The more incumbents spend on House elections, the worse they do against their opponents. This is not a cause-and-effect situation; extra spending by an incumbent is a symptom of an already close race.[31]

In close races both the incumbent and the challenger are likely to spend so much money that they wind up in considerable debt. The national parties assist the winners, especially new members in Congress. After each election there is a debt-retirement party, organized by each congressional campaign

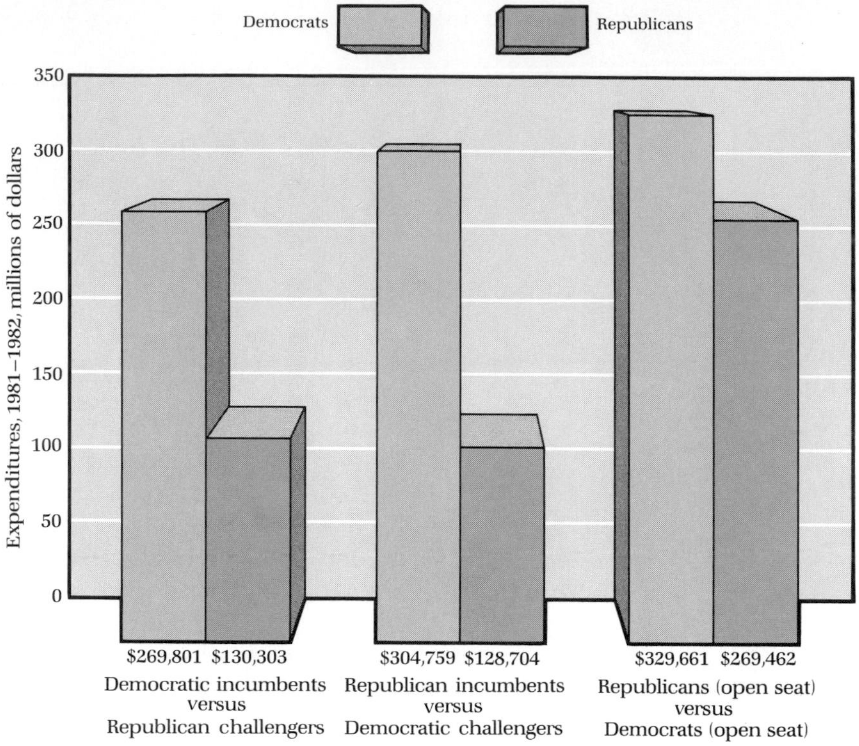

Figure 7-6. Campaign expenditures in House elections, 1981–1982. Democratic and Republican incumbents far outspend their challengers. Republicans spend more in open-seat contests than Democrats, though in 1982 more Democrats were elected to open seats. (Source: Federal Elections Commission, *Reports*, vol. 9, no. 6, June 1983.)

committee even before the new House convenes, at which time members of Congress meet PAC managers who are eager to make contributions to their previous campaign.

How much is enough? Some critics argue that we spend too much on congressional elections and that such spending forces candidates to mortgage their politics to PACs. Some comparisons may be helpful. In the United States, congressional candidates spent approximately $1.51, and presidential candidates spent about $1.75, per voter in 1980, for a total of $3.75 per voter. This compares with the figures for West Germany ($3.20 in 1983), Ireland ($3.93 in 1981), Israel ($4.34 in 1977), and Venezuela ($26 in 1983). Moreover, the figures for the United States include the costs of primary contests and PAC expenditures, while no comparable expenditures are included in the figures for the other countries.

In a system in which incumbents have so many advantages, it is necessary for challengers to spend a great deal to unseat their opponents. If we want to make elections more competitive and increase accountability in Congress, we may have to eliminate restrictions on campaign financing—not impose new limits.

Campaigning for the House

When state and local parties were strong, candidates could count on their parties to finance and manage their campaigns. House candidates were on the "party ticket," and precinct workers who brought out the vote for local candidates would also help them. Today all that has changed.

Nominating campaigns. In recent years as many as two-thirds of the nominations have been won either by self-recruited candidates or by candidates who have been encouraged to run by local community groups, PACs, or national party organizations. The contenders put together their own new politics organizations and field staffs. The primary vote is generally low—usually between 10 and 50 percent of the registered party voters cast ballots, which makes the electorate somewhat unrepresentative.[32] In a multicandidate contest, each candidate will rely on core supporters (for example, minorities, women, college students, union members, or ethnic or religious groups) to win the primary.[33]

Election campaigns. Congressional elections are oriented toward the techniques of media politics. By 1978 more than one-third of the campaigns no longer relied on field organizers or precinct canvassing, and fewer than one fifth of voters are now contacted directly by party workers in House races. By 1980 most House contests used some media campaigning, and more than two-thirds of campaign expenditures now go to some form of advertising.[34] Today, the typical campaign has five full-time staffers, who are oriented toward the media rather than toward precincts.

Republican candidates rely on media politics because most run in districts in which Democrats outnumber Republicans. To win, they must appeal to independents and get voters to cross party lines. Television, radio, and direct mailings help them do this.[35] Democratic candidates have lagged in this regard, many being more comfortable with traditional grass-roots precinct canvassing.

ASSISTANCE FROM THE NATIONAL PARTY. Congressional races are not as lucrative for media consultants as statewide contests, and these consultants are abandoning the field to PACs and the parties. If the party provides services, the campaigns tend to focus on national party themes—especially economic issues—and this gives them some coherence. If ideological and single-issue PACs dominate the campaigns, the party is splintered and there is a different focus in each contest.

The Republicans are way ahead of the Democrats in unifying House campaigns and giving them a common focus. The RNC pinpoints fifty or so vulnerable Democratic seats and recruits challengers, backing them in primaries if

A Republican Party commercial attacked Democratic House Speaker Tip O'Neill in the 1982 congressional campaign. (*Photo by Barry S. Surman from "The Spot: The Rise of Political Advertising on Television," M.I.T. Press.*)

necessary. Its political education seminars and its one-week Campaign Management College, run by its Political Education Department, help campaign managers develop strategies, conduct public opinion polls, prepare commercials, and set up phone canvass banks and direct-mail operations. They can hook up local campaigns to the Republican Information Network, a computerized system which carries news of committee and floor activity in the House, presidential activities, and the position of the Republican Party on the issues, thus providing the campaign with up-to-the minute information. The NRCC will prepare advertisements and do the time buying on local media, for much less money than campaign advertising firms charge. In 1984 it used videotapes of House proceedings to make campaign commercials. (Under House rules, incumbents could not use the tapes, but Republican challengers could, and they excerpted speeches of their Democratic opponents.) To conduct these activities the NRCC has a staff of eighty-four and a budget of more than $37 million.

The DCCC has a budget of only $6 million and a staff of thirty-two. It has a national media center that makes audiotapes and videotapes, which it can broadcast via satellite to local television and radio stations. It runs a news information service that puts out press releases attacking Republican candidates. It provides computerized research on the financial reports, voting records, and positions of Republican incumbents. It runs a school for candidates, provides direct-mail services to challengers in close races, and commissions and pays for national polls in off-year elections. The DCCC spends $2 million or more on national media campaigns to counter the Republicans' commercials.

INTEREST GROUPS. Because party organizations are weak, interest groups provide volunteers, who do phone and precinct canvassing in House elections. Depending on the district, civil rights groups, women's rights organizations, labor unions, or nuclear freeze activists, for example, will take over much of the field organization of a Democratic candidate's campaign for the House, while Republican candidates benefit from the volunteer work done by corporate executives and by groups opposing gun control and abortion.[36] Environmentalists are the most bipartisan of the grass-roots groups: the Sierra Club, Friends of the Earth, and the League of Conservation Voters gave millions of dollars in assistance to candidates from both parties.

Voting for the House

After all the campaigning, it is the voters who have the last word. The outcome of an election depends not so much on which candidate has the best organization or the most funds (provided the organization and the funds are adequate) as on the size of the turnout, party identification in the district, whether one candidate was an incumbent, the candidates' personalities, and the issues.

How voters decide. House contests are less important than presidential elections and Senate races, and voters usually have less information about the candidates and fewer clues as to what would constitute a rational decision. Incumbents go to considerable lengths to take stands on issues. They introduce bills (even bills that have no chance of passage) on issues that the folks back home care about. They mail voters excerpts from their floor speeches. They vote on nonbinding resolutions and on election-year bills to put the other party on the spot.[37] They pass laws providing more benefits in election

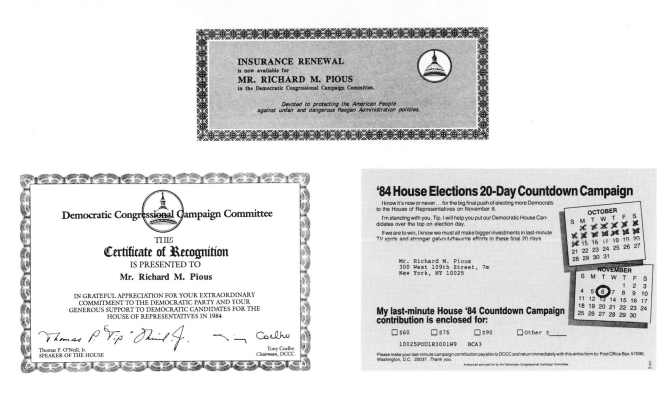

Some of the fund-raising literature mailed to the author during the 1984 congressional elections.

years (such as larger social security payments) and defer new costs (such as additional social security taxes) until after the elections.

In spite of these *position-taking* activities, some studies have shown that three-fifths of the electorate cannot distinguish between the two candidates' positions on what the voters believe to be the most important issue of a campaign.[38] Fewer than one-fifth of voters can specify accurately how their representatives voted on issues.[39] With little information to go on, voters are receptive to anything which might simplify their choice.

REPUBLICAN VERSUS DEMOCRAT. One clue is party identification: voters who are Democrats can rationally support a Democrat, even if they have no other knowledge of the candidate (and Republicans can rationally support a Republican). If voters are influenced by party identification, the Democrats are favored, because there are usually more registered Democrats than Republicans in most districts. Between 1952 and 1964, when loyalty to parties was high, 9 out of 10 strongly partisan voters voted for their party's candidate, as Figure 7-7 shows.

But party ties have weakened, and the proportion of independent voters has increased; by 1980 only 6 out of 10 voters chose to vote for their party's candidate for the House simply on the basis of party identification (many did so for other reasons). This trend favors the Republicans.

LIBERAL VERSUS CONSERVATIVE. While voters do not follow most issues, they can identify themselves as liberal or conservative, and often they choose a candidate whose stance is closest to their own. The more liberal voters are, the more likely they are to vote for Democrats in House elections; the more conservative voters are, the more likely it is that they will vote for Republicans. This tendency is a rational response to the programs offered by House members of the two parties.[40] But at times liberal voters may vote for a conservative who takes a position on programs which they favor, and a significant percentage of conservative voters may help elect a liberal who supports such programs as

221

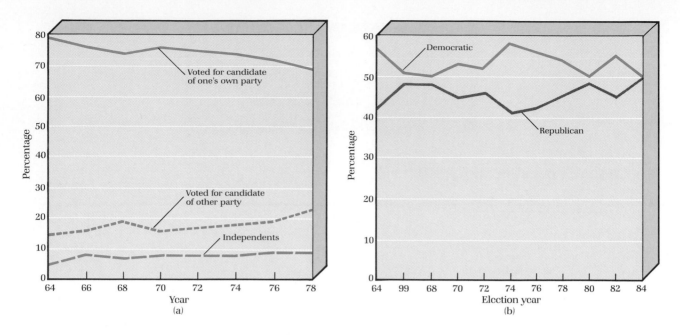

Year
(a)

Election year
(b)

social security and Medicare. In House elections, voters are influenced more by a candidate's position on specific programs than by party ideology.

MALE VERSUS FEMALE. There are significant differences between male and female voters in some congressional elections. In 1984, for example, while a majority of both men and women voted for the Republican candidate for president, in some House and Senate races they split, with a small majority of women voting for the Democrat and a small majority of men voting for the Republican. In a number of House and Senate races this split enabled Democratic candidates to win, even against the Reagan landslide, and some analysts believe that this helped Democrats—almost all of them male—who emphasized women's issues.

INCUMBENT VERSUS CHALLENGER. Most people who defect from the party with which they are identified support incumbents of the opposition party. In 1980, 55 percent of the Democrats who defected voted for Republican incumbents in their districts, and 35 percent of the Republicans who defected voted for Democratic incumbents.[41] About three-fourths of those who defect vote for incumbents, and only one-fourth cross party lines to vote for a challenger against an incumbent.[42] This favors the Democrats.

National and local influences. "All politics are local," claims Tip O'Neill, the Speaker of the House. Most House elections are won or lost on the basis of local factors: party identification within the district and the way district lines are drawn; the skill that an incumbent demonstrates in serving his or her district and in promoting defections from the other party; the ability of challengers to raise cash and mount media campaigns; and the effect of such image making on voters.

The importance of local factors like these has increased in recent years.[43] In elections held in the 1970s, attitudes toward the candidates, incumbency, and party identification in the district could explain all but 2 percent of the vote.[44]

But national factors can still be important; even a shift of 2 percent of the vote, if based on national issues, might be enough to change the results in dozens of close races. In the 1980s, the activities of PACs and advertising by the

222

Figure 7-7. Opposite page: Party voting in House elections. (a) Although most voters remain likely to vote for House candidates of their own party, the percentage who vote for candidates of the other party has increased and now accounts for more than one fifth of voters. The percentage of independent voters has also increased, weakening further the impact of party identification on congressional elections. (Source: Thomas Mann and Raymond Wolfinger, "Candidates and Parties in Congressional Elections," *American Political Science Review*, September 1980, vol. 24, no. 3, table 2, p. 620. (b) In 1984, Republican candidates for the House of Representatives won as many votes as the Democrats, a change from the normal pattern. Owing to the way Democratic-controlled state legislatures drew district lines, however, their party retained control of the House by a 252–183 margin. Some Republican analysts argued that the party could never win control of the House until it won enough state legislatures to redraw district lines favorably after the 1990 census. The Republican National Congressional Committee planned in the interim a special $5 million effort to unseat thirty of the most vulnerable Democrats in the 1986 midterm elections. (Sources: 1964–1978, *Historical Abstract of the United States: Colonial Times to 1970*, part 2, Bureau of the Census, Washington, D.C., 1975, p. 1084; 1972–1982, *Statistical Abstract of the United States*; 1984, *Congressional Quarterly Weekly Reports*, Nov. 10, 1984, pp. 2923–2930.)

national parties have tied House races more closely to presidential politics, with its media campaigns. Using national issues is a strategy that can help Republican challengers overcome their disadvantages when running against Democratic incumbents.

SUPPORT FOR THE PRESIDENT. Basing congressional elections on national issues helps the party that wins the White House in a presidential election year, but it almost always hurts that party in the succeeding off-year election. In the past, independents who have opposed the president have outnumbered those who have supported him in midterm elections. Members of the president's party who have been unhappy with his performance and have defected to the opposition have outnumbered members of the opposition party who have liked the president and have defected to support House candidates of his party.[45] To the extent that midterm congressional elections have become a referendum on the president's performance, the flow of votes has been away from his party, because protestors are more easily mobilized in midterm elections than supporters.

Most voters do not tie their decisions directly to the popularity or unpopularity of a president. The president's popularity or unpopularity had some impact in 1970 and 1974, but in other elections, such as that in 1978, polls detected none.[46] In 1982, polls indicated that most voters liked Reagan and appreciated the job he was doing; yet his party still suffered a larger-than-normal defeat in the off-year election.

THE PRESIDENT'S MANAGEMENT OF THE ECONOMY. In most congressional elections the economy is the biggest issue. The 1978 and 1982 elections were fought on that issue, both through national media campaigns and in most local contests. Democrats defeated twenty-six Republican incumbents who were identified as strong supporters of "Reaganomics." Most polls taken of people as they leave voting booths show a strong correlation between voters' attitudes toward the president's management of the economy and their party voting in House elections. A New York Times/CBS poll asked who was more to blame for economic problems—Reagan or previous Democratic policies? Of those who blamed Reagan, 87 percent voted Democratic, compared with 9 percent who voted Republican; of those who blamed the problems on the Democrats, 69 percent voted Republican and only 26 percent voted Democratic in 1982.[47]

There is a clear association between the president's popularity and per capita income figures and the percentage of the House vote that the president's party wins in midterm elections. Every decline of 10 percent in the president's popularity during the first two years costs the president's congressional party 1.3 percent of the vote. And every drop of $100 in real per capita income (due to recession or inflation) costs the president's party 3.5 percent of the vote.[48]

While acknowledging this association, political scientists have not yet found any direct connection between decisions of individual voters and economic performance. But it is not necessary for most voters to have economic concerns on their minds. Even if most people vote on the basis of party, incumbency, and local factors, a very small group of voters who decide on the basis of the economy can cause significant shifts of seats in the House.

The economy can also induce good candidates to make a race or deter them from entering it. When the economy is weak, strong challengers appear in the

Table 7-4. Split-result districts, 1964 to 1980

Year	Percent of House districts with split results[a]
1964	33.3
1968	32.0
1972	44.1
1976	28.5
1980	32.8
1984	44.0

a. Districts carried by a presidential candidate of one party and a House candidate of another party.

Source: John F. Bibby, Thomas E. Mann, and Norman Ornstein, *Vital Statistics on Congress, 1980*, American Enterprise Institute, Washington, D.C., 1981, table 1-13, p. 19.

opposition party, while some shaky incumbents from the president's party may decide to retire before being defeated. When economic conditions are good and the president is popular, the president's party gets the good challengers and candidates for open seats, while the opposition party cannot get its best people to make the race and is likely to win fewer seats.[49]

THE PRESIDENT'S COATTAILS. At one time a strong presidential candidate at the top of the ticket could help other party candidates who were running for lower offices. This was due partly to the *party ticket:* before 1890 there were no government ballots listing all candidates, and a person cast a vote by taking a ticket (provided by a party worker) that listed all the candidates of one party and putting it in the ballot box. If a voter took the ticket showing the name of the Republican presidential candidate, this naturally helped all the other Republican candidates, and the same was true when a voter took the Democratic ticket. When voting machines were first introduced, the ***party-column ballot*** listed all candidates of the party in one column and allowed a person to make a straight-ticket vote by marking off the party box at the top. Strong party identification was more apt to lead to a straight-ticket than to a split-ticket vote.

With the weakening of party identification and the replacement of the party-column ballot in most states by the ***office-column ballot*** (in which candidates are grouped by office rather than by party and which provides no way to vote a straight ticket with a single mark), the overall rate of ticket splitting increased from 13 percent in 1952 to 25 percent by 1976.[50] The ***coattail effect*** has just about vanished.[51] As a result, the number of congressional districts which support the candidate for president from one party but also elect a representative from the other party—*split-result* districts—has increased in recent elections, as Table 7-4 shows.

Presidents rarely help most congressional candidates. In both the 1972 and the 1984 elections, popular Republican presidents won overwhelming personal victories, and yet in each case their party lost two Senate seats and won only a dozen or so seats in the House. Voters clearly differentiate between support of the president and support of the president's party: it is as if we had two distinct national electoral systems.

If presidents are unpopular (especially because of their management of the economy or as a result of a military adventure), they can do a great deal of damage to their own party. Presidents may remain out of some districts (Johnson in 1966, Nixon in 1974, Carter in 1978, and Reagan in 1982) at the request of House candidates. In 1982 many Republicans in the House focused on their incumbency and on local issues. "I know people appreciate that I'm in touch with the voters," Congressman Ed Weber observed; "I don't want people to think I've sold my soul to Ronald Reagan." "I do not support Reagan economics," said Congressman Jim Dunn; "I support Michigan economics."[52]

But in 100 districts where Reagan was popular, he appeared with Republican incumbents in commercials in which the House member was seen "briefing" him. As one party leader put it, "On a 30-second commercial, if you've got the guy briefing the President for 18 seconds, it looks like he lives over here."[53] And in 1984 the president made joint commercials with many challengers—though to little effect.

HOUSE COATTAILS. Far from being grateful for the help they supposedly get from the president's coattails, most members of the House argue that they are the ones with the coattails and that the presidential candidate of their party benefited from their strength. In 1976 Carter won the White House with slightly more than 50 percent of the vote, while 208 Democratic congressional candidates won their districts with more than 60 percent of the vote. Carter received a total of 40,828,587 votes, but Democratic candidates for the House received more—41,749,411 in all. It was more likely that Carter benefited from the popularity of Democrats in Congress than vice versa.

In 1980 Reagan won the presidency, and 192 Republicans were elected to the House. Most owed little to Reagan, even though the White House claimed that his presence on the ballot was worth 2 points. In ninety-four districts the winning Republican received more votes than Reagan and John Anderson, the third-party candidate, combined; in 134 districts the winning Republican received more votes than Reagan; and in 149 districts he or she had a larger percentage of the two-party vote. Votes for the 192 winning Republicans totaled 24,928,623, compared with 22,607,238 cast for Reagan from these districts. The coattails belonged to the Republican candidates for the House, not to Reagan. In 1984 the president's coattails may have worked in fewer than a dozen races, since most Republicans won with a greater margin than the president, even though his victory was a landslide.

RUNNING FOR THE SENATE

Senate and House elections differ. The entire House runs for reelection every two years, while only one-third of the Senate does so. House terms are for two years, and members think constantly about reelection; senators serve for six years and therefore can take a longer view. House members run from districts (except those from states with only one member), while senators must represent an entire state. The typical House member is a virtual unknown, while the typical senator is known in the state and may even be a national celebrity. A Senate seat is considered a valuable prize by members of the House, while in modern times only a few ex-senators have subsequently run for the House.

Incumbents and challengers

While most House members have safe seats and will win landslide reelections, the prospects for senators are precarious: they have competitive primaries, they are more likely to run in close elections and to win with less than 60 percent of the two-party vote, and they are more likely to be defeated (though this was not the case in 1982 or 1984). They *feel* more vulnerable than members of the House. (See Table 7-5.)

Table 7-5. Turnover in Senate elections, 1966 to 1986

Year	Incumbents in election	Defeated in primary	Defeated in election	Percent reelected
1966	32	3	1	88
1968	28	4	4	71.4
1972	27	2	5	77.1
1974	27	2	2	85
1976	25	0	9	64
1978	25	3	7	60
1980	29	4	9	55.2
1982	30	0	2	93.2
1984	29	0	3	89.7
1986	28	0	7	75

Source: John F. Bibby, Thomas E. Mann, and Norman Ornstein, *Vital Statistics on Congress, 1980*, American Enterprise Institute, Washington, D.C., 1980, table 1-8; and author's calculations.

Senators cannot personally know a large percentage of their electorate or assist many of their constituents with casework. There are no districts to be gerrymandered to favor an incumbent. Senators, unlike House members, are covered by national news networks, weekly news magazines, and major newspapers, whose reporting is tougher than that of the local media and leaves voters more critical of them.[54]

Incumbent senators do what they can to erase negative images: in 1982 they sent 245 million pieces of mail to their constituents. Republicans (organized as the Senate Republican Conference) have set up a communications division with ten staffers whose job is to prepare press releases, packaged radio and television tapes, and columns and op-ed pieces which can be distributed to the media under the names of senators.

Most challengers are self-recruited. They tend to be statewide officeholders (sometimes governors who cannot succeed themselves according to the state constitution) or members of Congress. Occasionally, people who are not involved in politics at all—wealthy businesspeople (Frank Lautenberg of New Jersey), heirs to fortunes (John Heinz of Pennsylvania), movie stars (George Murphy of California), husband of movie stars (John Warner of Virginia, at the time married to Elizabeth Taylor), astronauts (John Glenn of Ohio and Harrison Schmidt of New Mexico), and athletes (Bill Bradley of New Jersey)—may decide to run. Presidents sometimes encourage and recruit challengers, and they may induce a weak incumbent to retire (by offering an ambassadorship or other position) in an effort to save the seat for their party.

Senate contests revolve around personalities, issues, and other statewide gubernatorial and presidential races. Party voting is relatively unimportant: one measure is the sharp rise, from fourteen in 1959 to twenty-three in 1985, in the number of states which have senators from both parties. Because many of the candidates are popular politicians or celebrities or have the money to run media campaigns, they become as well known to voters as the incumbents.[55]

One of the most effective spots ever produced propelled an Ivy-Leaguer, Malcolm Wallop, to the Senate by casting him as a hard-riding cowboy. (*Photo by Barry S. Surman from "The Spot: The Rise of Political Advertising on Television," M.I.T. Press.*)

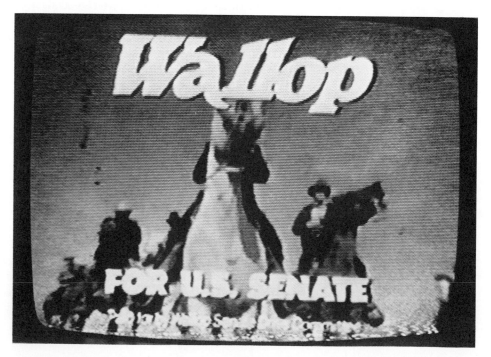

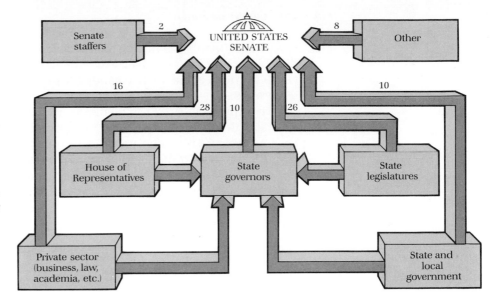

Figure 7-8. Career paths to the Senate, 1981–1982. Most senators have had previous public careers. Slightly more than one-fourth enter directly from the House. One-tenth were elected from state legislatures or governorships. Most others served in state and local government. (Source: *Congressional Directory*, 98th Congress, U.S. Government Printing Office, 1983.)

Senate candidates

Occupations. About two-thirds of the senators in 1985 listed their profession as lawyer, although only half had ever practiced. Businesspeople accounted for another fifth. About one-tenth had taught, most at the college level. A handful had been publishers, insurance brokers, journalists, farmers, bankers, or realtors.

Social characteristics. Ninety-eight senators were male in 1985. Women get nominations against strong incumbents, and a few get open-seat nominations. In 1984 a record number (twelve ran, but almost all against unbeatable men, and many got the nominations because other men and women declined, as in Oregon, Nebraska, and Rhode Island. A loosely knit group of women known as "Emily" (it stands for "*early money is like yeast*") encourage women in the House to run for the Senate by offering them financial backing, but as yet most of the strong potential candidates have declined to run. There were only two women in the Senate after the 1984 elections, both Republicans.

Since Reconstruction only one black has won election to the Senate (the Republican Edward Brooke of Massachusetts). No other black politician has been able to appeal successfully to a statewide electorate, and few have tried. Several Hispanic senators from New Mexico have been elected, and Arizona and California are likely to have Hispanic senators in the future. Asian Americans have been represented by S. I. Hayakawa, a former college president, who won a California seat, and by several senators from Hawaii.

Political experience. Most senators are professional politicians, and a majority start near the bottom of the ladder. In 1985, more than one-third had served in state legislatures, and one-third had served in the House of Representatives. Another third had come from state, county, or local government, and one-tenth had served as governors (Figure 7-8).

Financing Senate campaigns

In Senate elections three things are crucial: money, money, and more money. Senate elections cost more than House contests because challengers are more likely to be well financed. In 1974 only $28.4 million was raised by all the candidates, and only seven more than $1 million; in 1980 all the candidates spent more than $76.9 million, and ten spent more than $2 million. The median spent by winners in 1982 was $1,746,230; in 1984 it was over $2 million. In North Carolina alone the two candidates spent more than $22 million in 1984 (Figure 7-9).

Heavy spending is clearly related to victory. In 1982, 27 of the 33 winners outspent their opponents. But it does not always work: in Minnesota, Mark Dayton spent $6.9 million (most of it from a fortune that he inherited) and managed to lose to the incumbent, David Durenberger, who spent half that amount. But the successful campaigns of millionaires such as Frank Lautenberg (New Jersey), Howard Metzenbaum (Ohio), John Heinz (Pennsylvania), and John Denforth (Missouri) also show that sometimes throwing money at the voters in a media campaign works.

Raising money. Some candidates provide nearly all their own campaign funds, while others contribute almost nothing: typically the contender provides one-tenth. Another tenth may come from state and national party committees, especially in the case of Republican candidates; these committees may contribute up to $17,500 to a candidate for the Senate and provide coordinated funding for services such as direct mailings or polling, paying up to 2 cents per voting-age person in the state. Another fifth come from PACs. The biggest proportion comes from individual contributions: one-fifth of all funds consist of gifts over $500, but two-fifths involve smaller amounts.[56] Republicans get more than Democrats from the national and state parties; Democrats rely more than Republicans on large individual donors.

The parties and financing. The Republicans outraise and outspend the Democrats. The National Republican Senatorial Committee (NRSC), with a staff of eighty-four, raised more than $50 million in the 1982 elections and provided more than $10 million to candidates and $2 million to a national advertising campaign. In 1984 the Republicans raised more than $80 million. The Democratic Senatorial Campaign Committee, with a staff of only six, raised only $6

Figure 7-9. Campaign expenditures in Senate elections, 1972–1982. Incumbents from both parties had a financial advantage against challengers. In open-seat contests the contenders were closely matched. Excluding Jesse Helms's expenditures, the mean for Republican incumbents in 1978 is $1,526,145. [Source: Data for 1974–1980 from Norman J. Ornstein et al., *Vital Statistics on Congress, 1984–1985 Edition*, American Enterprise Institute, Washington, D.C., 1984, table 3-4, pp. 69–70. Data for 1982 from U.S. Federal Elections Commission, *Reports on Financial Activity, 1981–1982, Final Report* (*U.S. Senate and House Campaigns*), December 1983.]

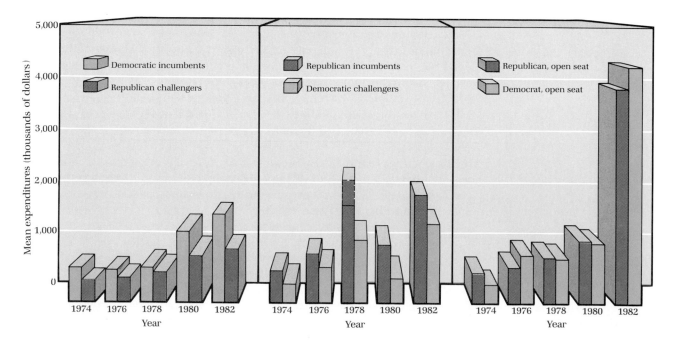

One campaign strategy is to associate an opponent with an unpopular politician. Jesse Helms of North Carolina was reelected to his Senate seat in 1984 after his opponent, Governor Jim Hunt, was tied to Mondale's losing presidential campaign. (*Sian Evans.*)

million and provided hardly any funding to its candidates in 1982, and in 1984 it did little better. Both parties could channel contributions of $20,000 made by individuals to party committees into campaigns of specified candidates. In return for large contributions, the NRSC maintained five staffers whose job it was to help contributors get access to senators or members of the administration if they had any problems. Senate rules allow members to use leftover funds for office expenses, and so the NRSC, taking advantage of this loophole, gets friendly PACs to contribute to campaigns; afterward, senators divert the money to office accounts and spend it on newsletters to solidify their support in the next election.

PACs and negative campaigns. PACs may contribute $10,000 to any Senate candidate for the primary and the general election. PACs also play an important role in fund-raising by soliciting contributions to a campaign and then sending them along as if they were made directly to the candidate. Such *bundling* of money enables a campaign to defray the costs of fund-raising by letting PACs do it.

Liberal and conservative PACs provide some money to candidates, but their most important function is to run negative campaigns against incumbents they oppose. In 1978 and 1980 conservative PACs targeted liberal Democrats for defeat. The Fund for a Conservative Majority, Citizens for the Republic, the Committee for the Survival of a Free Congress, and the National Conservative PAC (NCPAC) spent millions on so-called uncoordinated campaigns. They cast doubt on the honesty, the integrity, and even the patriotism of incumbent senators, sometimes years before an election and before a challenger had even been nominated. These campaigns eliminated six Democratic liberals from the Senate and replaced them with conservative Republicans.

In 1982 liberal PACs counterattacked. The National Committee for an Effective Congress, Democrats for the '80s, Americans for Democratic Action, and Progressive PAC sent direct mailings to liberals all over the nation, inviting them to send money to defend liberal senators and defeat conservatives. The result: PACs fought to a standoff. Senator Paul Sarbanes of Maryland, the chief target of a $1 million NCPAC negative campaign in 1982, created Marylanders for Fair and Honest Elections, a group which had on its governing board Milton Eisenhower (the brother of President Eisenhower and a former president of Johns Hopkins University in Maryland), Reverend David Leighton (an Epis-

HOW TO BUILD A CONGRESSIONAL OBSTACLE:

In North Carolina's hard-fought 1984 senatorial election, PROPAC (Progressive Political Action Committee) got in its digs at Senator Helms on behalf of Governor Hunt. (*AP Laserphoto.*)

copal bishop of Maryland), and Brooks Robinson (a former third baseman for the Baltimore Orioles). Sarbanes used the committee to deflect NCPAC's campaign and win reelection.

Republican Party leaders are not particularly happy about the negative campaigns of PACs. For one thing, PACs are their competitors in recruiting, financing, and staffing. PACs claim credit for electing conservatives—the same credit which is claimed by the party. Negative campaigns jeopardize potential Republican victories because Democrats raise them as an issue. In some states candidates now pledge not to take PAC money, and in 1984 Massachusetts became the first state to hold a primary (Republican) in which all the candidates took such a pledge.

Campaigning for the Senate

Campaign organization. Because Senate contests are statewide elections, the state parties have traditionally played important roles. But in the age of new politics these organizations have lost their control of nominations. Senate candidates now create their own organizations for both the nomination and the election—high on media, low on fieldwork, and only loosely coordinated with the state and local parties.

Media exposure. The media campaign becomes the centerpiece of the senatorial campaign. Unlike House contests, which media consultants find neither very profitable nor very interesting, a Senate race is both, and it attracts the best operators of new politics. The result is an increasing divergence between House campaigns, which are now largely in the hands of party-oriented campaign managers, and Senate contests. This may partly explain why Republican members of the House are likely to be "team players" who follow the national party line, while Republican senators are increasingly independent of the White House and the national party.

Voting for the Senate

How voters decide. In Senate contests neither party identification nor incumbency counts for much. The most important factor is the media campaign and how it presents personality and issues. In most states, elections are local rather than national affairs. In 1982, the national economy was the issue in House elections, as the parties tried to make them a "referendum" on Reaganomics; in Senate races the issue involved claims by incumbents that they had created jobs in their states or claims by challengers that they could bring new jobs into a state. Because there are fewer senators and because they serve for longer terms, each has more of a chance to make a record, and elections are fought partly on that record and partly on the character and accomplishments of the challenger and the incumbent.

Coattails. In the past, the president's coattails have been effective in some elections. But often the coattails work in reverse. In 1976, 20 of the 21 winning Democratic senators had greater margins of victory than Carter, and in all they won almost 1 million more votes than Carter. In 1980, eight Republican senators received more votes than Reagan, and his total vote in these senators' states just barely exceeded theirs. In 1984, 11 of the 18 winning Republican senators received more votes than Reagan in their states, and a number of Republican challengers were defeated in states in which Reagan ran well, in part a result of split-ticket voting among women.

Ticket-splitting. Surveys show a close connection between weakening party identification and ticket-splitting in Senate contests. Independents are most likely to vote for one party's candidate for president and for the other's candidate for senator; the voters who are least likely to do so are those with a strong party identification. Overall, between 1952 and 1976 the rate of ticket-splitting doubled, from 12 to 24 percent.[57] This too has weakened the effect of the president's coattails and leads most senators to believe—correctly—that they are stronger in their states than their party's presidential candidate.

ISSUE AND DEBATE

REFORM OF CONGRESSIONAL ELECTIONS. Some political scientists want to change the way we elect representatives and senators. Some reforms are designed to make it easy for presidents to lead Congress, while others would preserve congressional autonomy.

The background. Most reforms which would strengthen presidential leadership of Congress require drastic constitutional changes. One proposal is to have four-year terms for senators and representatives, with elections to be held in the presidential election year. To some extent this would focus congressional elections on national issues. All members of Congress would know that their next election would be in a presidential election year (under the present system those who are elected in a presidential election year have their next election in an off year). It would increase the impact of the president's coattails and would tie the fortunes of legislators more closely to presidential success or failure.

Another proposal is to put a limit of twelve years on service in the House and Senate. This would strengthen the presidency at the expense of Congress, since the most experienced and powerful legislators would run up against the provision for forced retirement.

Another proposal for change would automatically give the party that won the White House enough "bonus" seats in Congress to give it control. No longer could one party win the presidency and the other win the legislature, nor could the Senate be controlled by one party and the House by the other.

The case for reforms. Proponents argue that these measures would end congressional obstruction and the delay of presidential programs. They believe that Congress is too often dominated by incumbents who are out of touch with public opinion, too concerned with their own districts to recognize the national interest, and more interested in their own power than in the public interest. They believe that newly elected presidents better represent the will of the people than most legislators from safe seats.

The case against reforms. Opponents say that these changes would erode or eliminate the system of checks and balances and would go against the fundamental principles of the Constitution. Four-year terms tied to presidential elections would weaken the diversity inherent in localized campaigns. Legislators might be elected or defeated simply on the basis of a nationwide media campaign rather than on the basis of character, competence, and representation of district or state interests. The twelve-year limit, they argue, is fundamentally unconstitutional: it restricts the choice of voters, weakens the incentives of the best people to run for Congress, and converts the best legislators (that is, those who have been elected time and time again) into "lame ducks" after a decade. If the public wants "new blood," it can elect new members whenever it likes. If it wants to keep experienced incumbents, why should the Constitution be amended to prevent this?

A system of bonus seats in Congress for the party that wins the White House would just about end the system of checks and balances. Presidents, according to critics, could always get their way with the legislature, and that is not what the framers of the Constitution had in mind. Far better to require the president to persuade autonomous legislators than to provide an automatic majority.

Public opinion. Gallup public opinion polls show that by as much as a 2 to 1 margin, people favor four-year terms for representatives and senators and a twelve-year limit on service in Congress. (There have been no polls on the idea of bonus seats.)

The prospects. It is very doubtful that these reforms will be adopted. Senators do not want to lop two years off their terms. No member of Congress wants to limit service to twelve years, and so it is doubtful that such an amendment will be adopted (although an amendment did limit presidents to two terms). Finally, there is no desire among the members of Congress to add 100 or so new members to the House just so that the president can dominate congressional proceedings. Any change in Senate representation is limited by the provision of the Constitution that bars changing the arrangement by which each state is represented by two senators—the one part of the Constitution that cannot be amended.

IN CONCLUSION

How members of Congress climb up Capitol Hill has a lot to do with what happens once they get there. Representatives have an easier time getting reelected than senators but consider themselves just as vulnerable, and both representatives and senators organize their activities around reelection efforts. They finance their campaigns with their own funds and with PAC and party contributions (though in races for both the House and the Senate the major source of funds remains individual contributions from supporters), and therefore they are highly responsive to interest groups once they are in office. Increasingly, national party committees are helping in House elections, especially in terms of developing media campaigns, while Senate contests remain in the hands of independent campaign consultants.

The congressional election system maximizes the role of PACs and provides for some influence by the national parties, but it does not as yet give the parties control over legislators. The coattail effect is a factor, but the evidence seems strong that the president benefits from legislators' coattails, not the reverse, which minimizes presidential influence in Congress. Most members of Congress who are in the president's party view the president as a potential liability who may cost them the next election, rather than as an asset who can help them win.

James Madison wanted a constitutional system of checks and balances, one in which "ambition must counteract ambition." Our congressional election system has succeeded in that regard. It ensures that the fundamental constitutional understandings which create competition for power between different branches remain in place. Neither the president nor the leaders of the president's party control nominations, financing, or campaigning for Congress, and therefore they do not control legislators once they have arrived on Capitol Hill. All aspects of national government are affected by that fact.

NOTES

1. Letters sent by the Republican National Committee, Oct. 20, 1982, and by the Democratic Congressional Campaign Committee, Sept. 30, 1982.

2. Diane E. Kincaid, "Over His Dead Body: A Positive Perspective on Widows in the United States Congress," *Western Political Quarterly*, vol. 31, no. 1, March 1978, pp. 97–99.

3. Gary Jacobson, *The Politics of Congressional Elections*, Little, Brown, Boston, 1983, p. 19.

4. David Mayhew, "Congressional Elections: The Case of the Vanishing Marginals," *Polity*, vol. 6, no. 1, spring 1974, p. 305.

5. Richard F. Fenno, Jr., "If, as Ralph Nader Says, Congress Is 'the Broken Branch,' How Come We Love Our Congressmen So Much?" in Norman Ornstein (ed.), *Congress in Change: Evolution and Reform*, Praeger, New York, 1975, pp. 277–278.

6. Quoted in Gary Jacobson, *Money in Congressional Elections*, Yale University Press, New Haven, Conn., 1980, p. 113.

7. Diane E. Yiannakis, "The Grateful Electorate. Casework and Congressional Elections," *American Journal of Political Science*, vol. 25, no. 3, August 1981, p. 113.

8. Albert D. Cover, "Contacting Congressional Constituents," *American Journal of Political Science*, vol. 24, no. 1, February 1980, p. 125.

9. Michael Robinson, "Three Faces of Congressional Media," in Thomas Mann and Norman Ornstein (eds.), *The New Congress*, American Enterprise Institute, Washington, D.C., 1981, pp. 55–94.

10. Thomas Mann and Raymond Wolfinger, "Candidates and Parties in Congressional Elections," *American Political Science Review*, vol. 74, no. 3, September 1980, p. 622.

11. Roger Davidson and Walter Oleszek, *Congress and Its Members*, Congressional Quarterly Press, Washington, D.C., 1981, table 3.4, p. 86.

12. Morris Fiorina, "The Case of the Vanishing Marginals: The Bureaucracy Did It," *American Political Science Review*, vol. 71, no. 1, March 1977, pp. 177–181.

13. Warren Miller et al., *American National Election Studies Data Sourcebook*, Harvard University Press, Cambridge, Mass., 1980, table 4.20.

14. Albert D. Cover and David R. Mayhew, "Congressional Dynamics and the Decline of Competitive Congressional Elections," in Lawrence Dodd and Bruce Oppenheimer (eds.), *Congress Reconsidered*, 2d ed., Congressional Quarterly Press, Washington, D.C., 1981, p. 70.

15. Robert Erikkson, "The Advantages of Incumbency in Congressional Elections," *Polity*, vol. 3, no. 1, spring 1971, pp. 395–405; and "Is There Such a Thing as a Safe Seat?" *Polity*, vol. 8, no. 2, summer 1976, pp. 623–633.

16. Richard Fenno, *Home Style: House Members in Their Districts*, Little Brown, Boston, 1978; see also Jacobson, *The Politics of Congressional Elections*, pp. 44–45.

17. John Peters and Susan Welch, "The Effects of Charges of Corruption on Voting Behavior in Congressional Elections," *American Political Science Review*, vol. 74, no. 3, September 1980, pp. 697–708.

18. *Wesberry v. Sanders*, 376 U.S. 1 (1964).

19. Charles S. Bullock III, "The Inexact Science of Congressional Redistricting," *P.S.*, summer 1982. On the expected Republican gains and how they failed to happen, see Richard E.Cohen, "Despite the Map Maker's Best Efforts, Redistricting Won't Help Either Party," *The National Journal*, vol. 14, no. 18, May 1, 1982.

20. Davidson and Oleszek, op. cit., p. 63.

21. *The National Journal*, Apr. 6, 1982, vol. 14, no. 14, p. 1887.

22. Stephen Frantzich, "Opting Out: Retirement from the House of Representatives, 1966–1974," *American Politics Quarterly*, vol. 6, no. 3, 1978, pp. 251–273.

23. Joseph Cooper and William West, "The Congressional Career in the 1970s," in Dodd and Oppenheimer, op. cit., pp. 83–106.

24. David Rhode, "Risk-Bearing and Progressive Ambition," *American Journal of Political Science*, vol. 23, no. 1, Feburary 1979, pp. 1–26.

25. Harvey L. Schlantz, "Contested and Uncontested Primaries for the U.S. House," *Legislative Studies Quarterly*, vol. 5, no. 4, 1980, p. 550.

26. Edie N. Goldenberg and Michael W. Traugott, *Campaigning for Congress*, Congressional Quarterly Press, Washington, D.C., 1984, p. 21.
27. Jimmy Breslin, *How the Good Guys Finally Won*, Ballantine Books, New York, 1975, p. 14.
28. *The New York Times*, July 26, 1982.
29. *The New York Times*, Nov. 5, 1982.
30. Goldenberg and Traugott, op. cit., p. 71.
31. Jacobson, *Money in Congressional Elections*, Yale University Press, New Haven, Conn., 1980, p. xvii.
32. Bruce W. Robeck, "The Representativeness of Congressional Primary Voters," *Congress and the Presidency*, vol. 11, no. 1, spring 1984, pp. 59–67.
33. L. Sandy Maisel, *From Obscurity to Oblivion: Congressional Primary Elections in 1978*, University of Tennessee Press, Knoxville, 1983.
34. Larry Sabato, *The Rise of Political Consultants*, Basic Books, New York, 1980, pp. 116, 197.
35. Majorie Hershey, *The Making of Campaign Strategy*, Lexington Books, Lexington, Ky., 1974, p. 91.
36. Goldenberg and Traugott, op. cit, pp. 30–31.
37. David Mayhew, *Congress: The Electoral Connection*, Yale University Press, New Haven, Conn., 1974.
38. Barbara Hinckley, *Congressional Elections*, Congressional Quarterly Press, Washington, D.C., 1981, p. 104.
39. Patricia Hurley and K. Hill, "The Prospects for Issue-Voting in Contemporary Elections," *American Politics Quarterly*, vol. 8, no. 4, October 1980, pp. 425–448.
40. Paul Abramson et al., *Change and Continuity in the 1980 Elections*, Congressional Quarterly Press, Washington, D.C., 1981, p. 214.
41. Ibid., p. 218.
42. Cover and Mayhew, op. cit., p. 75.
43. Thomas Mann, *Unsafe at Any Margin*, American Enterprise Institute, Washington, D.C., 1978.
44. Hinckley, op. cit., p. 86.
45. Samuel Kernell, "Presidential Popularity and Negative Voting," *American Political Review*, vol. 71, no. 1, March 1977, pp. 44–66.
46. Lynn Ragsdale, "The Fiction of Congressional Elections as Presidential Events," *American Politics Quarterly*, vol. 8, no. 4, October 1980, p. 394.
47. *The New York Times*, Nov. 11, 1982.
48. Edward Tufte, *Political Control of the Economy*, Princeton University Press, Princeton, N.J., 1978.
49. Gary Jacobson and Samuel Kernell, *Strategy and Choice in Congressional Elections*, Yale University Press, New Haven, Conn., 1982.
50. Miller et al., op. cit., table 6.4.
51. George C. Edwards, "The Impact of Presidential Coattails on Outcomes of Congressional Elections," *American Politics Quarterly*, vol. 7, no. 1, January 1979, pp. 94–108.
52. *The New York Times*, Oct. 28, 1982.
53. *Newsweek*, Oct. 18, 1982, p. 36.
54. Robinson, op. cit., p. 58.
55. Davidson and Oleszek, op. cit., p. 86.
56. Michael Malbin (ed.), *Parties, Interest Groups and Campaign Finance Laws*, American Enterprise Institute, Washington, D.C., 1980, pp. 154–155.
57. Miller et al., op. cit., table 6.67.

FURTHER READING

Crotty, William: *American Parties in Decline*, 2d ed., Little, Brown, Boston, 1984. A treatise on the connections between party structure, voting behavior, and congressional elections, emphasizing the decline in party strength.

Drew, Elizabeth: *Politics and Money*, Macmillan, New York, 1983. An account of the way in which politicians circumvent campaign finance regulations in congressional elections.

Evans, Susan: *Covering Campaigns: Journalism in Congressional Elections*, Stanford University Press, Stanford, Calif., 1983. An account of news coverage of House candidates.

Fenno, Richard: *Home Style*, Little, Brown, Boston, 1978. A study of the advantages of incumbency.

Goldenberg, Edie N., and Michael W. Traugott: *Campaigning for Congress*, Congressional Quarterly Press, Washington, D.C, 1984. Surveys of campaign managers and how they run their operations.

Hinckley, Barbara: *Congressional Elections*, Congressional Quarterly Press, Washington, D.C., 1981. An account of how voters make their decisions.

Jacobson, Gary: *Money in Congressional Elections*, Yale University Press, New Haven, Conn., 1980. A book dealing with campaign finance regulations and the impact of money on campaigns.

———— : *The Politics of Congressional Elections*, Little, Brown, Boston, 1983. A comprehensive and up-to-date account of congressional elections.

———— : and Samuel Kernell: *Strategy and Choice in Congressional Elections*, Yale University Press, New Haven, Conn., 1982. A study of how the recruitment of candidates affects party competition.

Mayhew, David: *Congress: The Electoral Connection*, Yale University Press, New Haven, Conn., 1974. A discussion of how the prospect of reelection conditions almost every aspect of a House member's career.

Sabato, Larry J.: *PAC Power: Inside the World of Political Action Committees*, Norton, New York, 1984. A study of PACs and how they help in congressional campaigns.

Tufte, Edward: *Political Control of the Economy*, Princeton University Press, Princeton, N.J., 1978. A book arguing that changes in the president's popularity and the gross national product have a measurable impact on party competition in the House.

THE STUDY BREAK

Caro, Robert: *The Years of Lyndon Johnson*, vol. 1, Knopf, New York, 1983. A fascinating and detailed account of Johnson's first congressional campaign in Texas.

Clancy, Paul, and Shirley Elder: *TIP*, Macmillin, New York, 1980. A study of machine politics in O'Neill's Boston district.

USEFUL SOURCES

Barone, Michael, et al.: *The Almanac of American Politics*, National Journal, Washington, D.C., annually. Information on House and Senate elections.

Congressional Quarterly Weekly Reports, A publication that follows the campaigns and reports on election results.

Grotton, Martha V. (ed.): *Congressional Districts in the 1980s*, Congressional Quarterly Press, Washington, D.C., 1983. A source of information on district lines and relevant demographic and political data.

Martis, Kenneth C., and Ruth Anderson Rowles: *The Historical Atlas of United States Congressional Districts, 1789–1983*, Free Press, New York, 1982. A source of information on district lines.

ORGANIZATIONS

Democratic Congressional Campaign Committee. 400 North Capitol Street, N.W., Washington, D.C. 20001. For more information phone 202-789-2920.

Democratic Senatorial Campaign Committee. 400 North Capitol Street, N.W., Washington, D.C. 20001. For more information phone 202-224-2446.

National Republican Congressional Committee. 320 First Street, S.E., Washington, D.C. 20003. For more information phone 202-479-7000.

National Republican Senatorial Committee. 404 C Street, N.E., Washington, D.C. 20002. For more information phone 202-224-2351.

CHAPTER 8

PRESIDENTIAL NOMINATIONS: PRIMARIES, CAUCUSES, AND CONVENTIONS

National conventions conduct political business but today are primarily media events. Above: The Republicans nominated Benjamin Harrison at Chicago in 1888. Below: The Democrats in San Francisco in 1984. (*Brown Brothers; Eli Reed: Magnum Photos.*)

Alexander Hamilton wrote in 1788, "The time will assuredly come when every vital question of state will be merged in the question, 'Who shall be the next President?'"[1] The answer to that question depends on how the two major parties nominate their presidential candidates. The people who make up the field of contenders, how the field runs in primaries and caucuses, and what happens at the nominating conventions affect not only the general election but also the way in which our national government works.

"The system itself is becoming increasingly irrational, self-defeating and destructive," charges Walter Mondale.[2] Critics claim that nominations add little to the public's understanding of issues and shed no light on the competence and character of candidates and their associates or on the kind of administration they would form. "All told, the primary system is a disaster," says the political scientist Michael Robinson." It costs too much; it takes too long; it makes pseudo-enemies out of true political allies; and it makes pseudo-winners out of true losers. And, more importantly, the primary system has made the process of becoming President so dispiriting, so distasteful, that those would become, shouldn't."[3]

But others see things differently. "What Americans have constructed, mostly by accident," Stephen Hess argues, "is a partial stimulation of the presidency," which enables voters to see how potential presidents act under the kind of pressure they would face in the White House.[4] "Primaries are the most effective of the existing means of involving the populace in the nominating process," Thomas Cronin says, adding: "If, as the critics have remarked, primaries are democracy gone mad, the response can only be to paraphrase Shakespeare: Ah, but there is some method in this madness."[5]

This chapter will examine the method in the madness. We will consider how the field of contenders is chosen and how contenders campaign for money and votes during the primary and caucus season, and we will discuss the activities of nominating conventions. The chapter concludes with an assessment of some proposals for reform in the light of the key issues of legitimacy, authority, and the power to govern.

WHO RUNS FOR PRESIDENT?

The field of contenders for the major-party nominations is determined by constitutional, legal, social, and political factors.

Constitutional provisions

Article II, section 4, of the Constitution restricts eligibility for the presidency to natural-born citizens (those born within United States territory and presumably those born abroad of American parents) who are at least 35 years old (upon entering office) and who have spent at least fourteen years in the United States. The Constitution bars any religious tests.

Social and political factors

Social acceptability. The Constitution puts up no barriers to eligibility based on race, ethnicity, or gender. Major-party nominees must be acceptable to

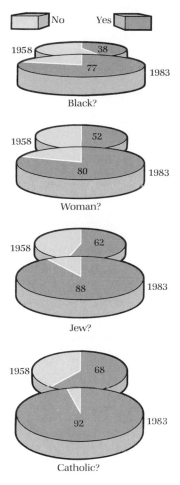

Figure 8-1. Social acceptability for presidents. In the past quarter-century the percentage of voters who say they would not vote for a woman, black, Jew, or Catholic has decreased greatly. The survey question ("Would you consider voting for a ——— for president?") may not, however, be an accurate measure of the remaining prejudice against candidates from these groups. (Source: Gallup polls.)

most of the voters. Until recently this ruled out divorced men, women, non-whites, and non-Christians, and the field was composed almost exclusively of white Protestant males of English, Scottish-Irish, or German descent. But times have changed. Two Roman Catholics—Al Smith in 1928 and John Kennedy in 1960—were nominated, and others have competed strongly (Robert Kennedy, Ted Kennedy, Edmund Muskie, and Jerry Brown). The post-Civil War bias against southerners was broken by Lyndon Johnson in 1964 and by Jimmy Carter in 1976. Ronald Reagan, though he had been divorced and had remarried, won the presidency in 1980 and 1984. Nonwhites, non-Christians, and women still have not won a major-party nomination. Residual voter prejudices would make it difficult for such persons to head the ticket, but in the near future such prejudices will, it is hoped, continue to diminish (Figure 8-1)

Political experience. Most contenders for major-party nominations have been senators, governors, vice presidents, or Cabinet members. A recent trend is for former officials to run. Richard Nixon, Jimmy Carter, Ronald Reagan, and Walter Mondale all ran as private citizens. Howard Baker retired as majority leader of the Senate and as senator in 1984 to make his bid in 1988.

When state and local bosses dominated the national conventions, governors had the best chance, and members of Congress were rarely considered.[6] After the Second World War senators were the preferred choices, and some analysts theorized that the importance of national security issues and senators' media exposure in Washington would give them permanent advantages over governors.[7] Just as these generalizations were taking hold, former governors Carter and Reagan won the White House!

Nine of the sixteen major-party vice presidential nominees between 1952 and 1984 later ran for the presidency or were considered potential presidential nominees. Of the nineteen vice presidents elected since 1901, fifteen were involved in the presidential sweepstakes in later elections. And vice presidents who succeed to the presidency, such as Truman, Johnson and Ford, are likely to win the next presidential nomination.

Party leadership. Presidents usually win renomination, even if it comes down to the wire, as it did in 1976 (when Reagan challenged Ford) and in 1980 (when Kennedy challenged Carter). Since the Twenty-Second Amendment bars a reelected president from running for a third term, usually strong potential contenders prefer to wait rather than challenge an incumbent.

The party of a president who is not running for renomination has no recognized "leader," and the same holds true for the opposition party. The defeated nominee in the prior election has no formal party position, and no function, as a European or Canadian opposition leader would. A defeated nominee who wishes to compete for the next nomination must do so as a member of the field, with no special advantage and with the disadvantage of being labeled a "loser" by opponents. For this reason, with only a few exceptions, the loser of a presidential contest usually does not get another chance. Often, however, defeated vice presidential contenders or nominees later win their party's presidential nomination: John Kennedy, Richard Nixon, and Walter Mondale, for example.

A comparative perspective: Apprentices versus entrepreneurs. In parlia-

The careers of three contemporary western European leaders illustrate different routes to top governmental positions. Helmut Kohl, chancellor of the Federal Republic of Germany since 1982, rose through the ranks in his home-state legislature, eventually becoming a state governor and federal senator. As leader of the Christian Democratic Union, he became chancellor when his party came to power. (*Regis Bossu: Sygma.*)

Francois Mitterand won the French presidency in 1981 on his third try in sixteen years. A Socialist, he ended more than two decades of Gaullist-conservative dominance. In the postwar years he had been a deputy in the National Assembly and a cabinet minister in coalition governments. (*Jean Gaumy: Magnum.*)

mentary systems leaders serve long apprenticeships before heading the government. Members of the British Parliament, like Margaret Thatcher, start in the "back benches" and demonstrate their talents on minor assignments. They become junior ministers, assisting veteran members in running a department and defending its policies in debates. Later they become ministers and eventually might be chosen as parliamentary leaders. They spend many years rising to the top of their party by gaining the respect and friendship of their colleagues. By the time such a person takes over as prime minister, he or she knows all the ins and outs of government.

In the early 1800s, presidential nominations were made by congressional parties, but since that time we have had no similar system. In the era of the boss-dominated conventions, party leaders chose novices who were easy to manipulate, like General Ulysses S. Grant, or mediocrities, like Senator Warren Harding. Today the field consists of any senator, governor, House member, or other figure who wants to run. Candidates are self-recruited entrepreneurs who can raise the money and organize primary campaigns. The intraparty contests become bloodbaths, in which competitors find it difficult afterward to unite for the general election (Muskie and McGovern in 1972, Reagan and Ford in 1976, and Carter and Kennedy in 1980).

There is no orderly line of succession, no "shadow cabinet" in the opposition waiting to form a government if elected. Given the anti-Washington mood of voters, outsiders who know little about the ways of the capital, such as Eisenhower, Carter, and Reagan, stand a good chance of winning the nomination.

Joining the field

The exploratory committee. If you were a major-party officeholder (or former officeholder) and decided to join the field, after discussing the idea with your family and friends, you would form an ***exploratory committee,*** such as Jack Kemp's Kemp Associates or Lew Lehrman's Citizens for America. You would be able to spend up to $50,000 of your own money as well as money contributed by PACs ($5000 each) and individuals ($1000 each) to pay your expenses while you traveled around the country speaking to audiences and meeting with party leaders. The committee would be able to commission public opinion polls and pay for your speaking engagements. Later you would be able to organize your own PAC, which could make contributions (up to $5000) to candidates in congressional elections; in 1984 Jack Kemp gave 100 Republican House candidates $220,000 from his organization, the Campaign for Prosperity.

Polishing the image. You might commission a ghostwriter to provide you with a campaign autobiography or publish a book of your ideas or speeches. You would visit Ireland, Italy, and Israel (the "three I's" of ethnic politics) and arrange interviews with leaders of other nations. You would shape up and get a new wardrobe. Ray Strother (Gary Hart's media adviser in 1984) takes candidates to a video studio for rehearsals. "In that studio," he says, "we teach the candidate how to stand, how to address the camera, how to address a reporter's question."[8]

Margaret Thatcher, prime minister of Great Britain since 1979, was elected leader of the Conservative Party in 1975 after sixteen years in the House of Commons. She had served in subcabinet and minor cabinet posts in education, science, and social welfare. Her apprenticeship was unusual for a British prime minister in that it included no major cabinet portfolios. (*Stuart Franklin: Sygma.*)

If you were a Democrat, you would show up at your party's midterm convention; if you were a Republican, you would attend the annual Tidewater Conference to meet party leaders. You would go to various state conventions in the year before the nomination—nicknamed the "cattle shows"—so that county leaders could have a look at you.

The screening committee. David Broder, a columnist for the *Washington Post*, once argued that an inner club of newspaper editorialists and columnists acted as a kind of screening committee for the field. In fact, columnists such as James Reston, Tom Wicker, Jack Germond, and Broder himself were the talent scouts who sought out and identified presidential possibilities who might otherwise have been overlooked by party professionals.

Contenders will court columnists and broadcasters, hoping that what Russell Baker calls the "great mentioner" will mention them. You would know that you had hit the jackpot when you got a full-length feature story in *The New York Times Magazine*; made the cover of *Time*, *Newsweek*, or *U.S. News and World Report*; or were a guest on one of the Sunday morning network talk shows: *Issue and Answers*, *Face the Nation*, or *Meet the Press*.

MODERN NOMINATING POLITICS: PRECONVENTION CAMPAIGNS

Candidates simultaneously conduct four campaigns: for money, for supporters, for media recognition, and for votes. Doing well in one helps them in the others. These four campaigns are run in two different periods: the preelection years constitute phase 1; the three months in which primaries and caucuses are held constitute phase 2.

Phase 1: Politics in the preelection years

The first phase lasts from the preceding presidential election to January of the presidential election year.

The campaign for cash. What separates serious contenders from those who drop out early is money. The campaign must raise about $30 to $40 million for the nomination. Before 1974 candidates financed the early stages of their campaigns from the deep pockets of wealthy contributors, who made legal (or illegal corporate) contributions of hundreds of thousands of dollars. Since 1974 candidates have been able to contribute only $50,000 of their own money, and their backers are limited to $1000. "Prenomination Campaign Regulations" describes the various ceilings on contributions and expenditures.

Wealthy people are still important, but more for *whom* they know (other people who can contribute $1000) than for what they can give personally. A lawyer-lobbyist, a PAC manager, a corporate executive, a business entrepreneur, and a union leader can each hold a fund-raising party, and the small contributions add up to amounts that are donated by clearly identified constituencies interests in particular issues. Often partners in large law firms or lobbyists in trade associations will "bundle" many small checks from their friends and business associates and present them to campaign managers—who will remember later where the money came from and be responsive to those who raised it.

Candidates' PACs use initial funds to develop their direct-mail campaigns. Specialists such as Morris Dees raised $20 million from 700,000 donors in 1972 for the McGovern campaign. The Reagan-Bush '84 Committee raised $24 mil-

---

PRENOMINATION CAMPAIGN REGULATIONS

- Contenders for president and vice president may contribute up to $50,000 to their own campaigns.
- Individuals may contribute up to $1000 each year to each candidate for president or vice president (and up to $25,000 to all candidates running for federal office).
- PACs may contribute up to $5000 to each presidential contender; there is no limit on the number of such contributions.
- Contenders are eligible for matching funds from the Treasury. To qualify, a contender must obtain, in each of twenty states, $5000 in contributions (in amounts of $250 or less). The Treasury then matches, on a dollar-for-dollar basis, all contributions of $250 or less.
- The overall spending limit for a contender who accepts matching funds from the Treasury is $10 million, plus $2 million in expenses and a cost-of-living adjustment (COLA). The adjusted limit in 1984 was $24.24 million. There are ceilings on expenditures for each state based on its population.
- An amount equivalent to 20 percent of the adjusted limit may be spent on fund-raising and is not counted toward the adjusted limit.
- The national parties receive $3 million plus a COLA in public funds for the nominating conventions; in 1984 this amounted to $6.06 million.

---

lion (the maximum permitted by law) for the preconvention period in six months by using direct mailings and concentrating on small contributors, thus saving its big contributors for party-building and congressional campaign efforts. The Mondale campaign hired marketing firms with demographic data on 80 million Americans and integrated this information with its phone-bank operations so that only those people who expressed some support for Mondale would be solicited for contributions or volunteer work.

Campaign organization. Campaigns must be organized two years in advance of a primary season. Field operations in key primary and caucus states start as much as a year before an election; staffers hire organizers who have worked the state in previous campaigns and who know the local politicians. Sometimes a candidate benefits from an organization that is already in place. Jesse Jackson's victory in the Louisiana primary in 1984, for example, was due in large measure to an existing computerized network, set up in New Orleans by black politicians, which could reach 125,000 black voters by telephone or direct mail. Tape-recorded phone messages from black leaders were used in a "get out the vote" drive.

The exploratory committee begins direct-mail fund-raising. It may, like Walter Mondale's Committee for the Future of America, send out a "national issues survey" and invite contributors to join its "new agenda network." When it is announced that the contender is now a candidate, the exploratory committee is transformed into a presidential campaign committee, and contributions to it qualify for federal matching funds.

Peddling the scenario. Candidates provide media commentators with a scenario: a game plan which indicates where the candidates think they stand, what they intend to do, and how they intend to win. Walter Mondale's 1983 scenario specified that he would win a quick knockout in the first few primaries and caucuses. Gary Hart saw himself as a long shot who would get to the "front tier" in Iowa; come in second in New Hampshire; go one-on-one with Mondale, whom he referred to as "mush"; and win a long, drawn-out campaign.

Phase 2: Primaries and caucuses

By the beginning of the nomination year the candidates have created their national organizations and fund-raising apparatuses. They have met with media columnists and with state and local party leaders at the cattle shows. The wire services poll county leaders, and the pollsters query voters, to see which contender has the most support. A front-runner emerges, followed by a first tier and a second tier of candidates, and the field then enters the primary and caucus season, which takes place from March to June.

Primaries: The party-in-the-electorate. In the 1970s media politics delegitimized boss-dominated politics: if the candidate-centered campaign organizations could appeal directly to voters in state and congressional races, why could they not do so in presidential nominating contests? Journalists and television broadcasters discovered that primaries make interesting news and best-selling books. They set up the primary period as a kind of pennant race— an elimination bout preceding the World Series of the general election. At the same time many party organizations asked their state legislatures to replace caucuses and conventions with primaries. They wanted to keep antiwar activists, civil rights groups, party reformers, women's liberationists, environmentalists, and others as far away from them as possible. Caucuses and conventions would only attract these people into local party politics; instituting direct primaries seemed a way of segregating local and state party matters from the national politics that concerned these groups. For the same reason most states decided not to hold their local and statewide elections in a presidential election year, and many held presidential and congressional primaries on different dates. Thus presidential nominating contests were *disaggregated* from state and local politics, and in many states the parties remained neutral and let candidate-centered organizations battle it out.

Most states adopted primaries in the 1970s, as Figure 8-2 shows. Votes for a candidate translated (directly or indirectly) into votes for delegates to the national convention.

Contenders run in most or all of these primaries. The days when a contender could compete in four primaries and win the nomination, as Jack Kennedy did in 1960, are long gone. In 1976, Jimmy Carter proved that the winning candidate must compete in all the states.

PRIMARIES AS PLEBISCITES. Primaries are plebiscites: registered voters get the chance to express their preferences in *closed primaries;* registered party voters and independents participate in *open primaries.* In the former, candidates can demonstrate their appeal to the party faithfuls; in the latter, they can appeal to a wider electorate.

The nominating convention has been transformed from a representative assembly of state parties convened to bargain with potential candidates into something quite different—a device to register the preferences of the party-in-the-electorate. The winner of each convention since 1972 (with the exception of the 1976 Republican convention) has been the candidate with the largest share of primary notes.

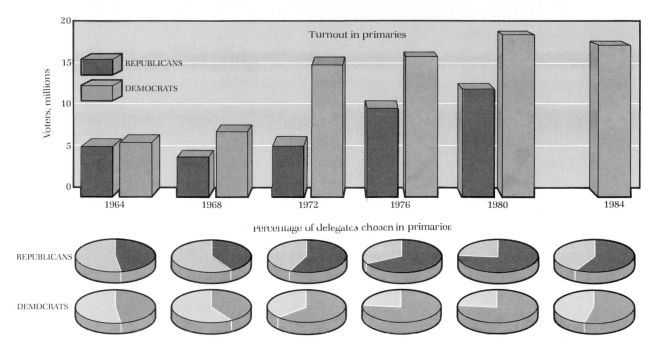

Figure 8-2. Growth of presidential primaries. In the past two decades, the number of primaries has increased and the numbers of voters who participate has tripled. The high point for primaries may have been 1980; since then their number has diminished. (Note: Reagan was virtually unopposed for the Republican nomination of 1984. Source: Congressional Quarterly, *Presidential Elections since 1789*, 3d ed., Washington D.C., 1983.)

PRIMARIES: THE END OF PEER REVIEW? Primaries involve an implicit contract between the electorate and the candidates. Neither voters nor the media will tolerate a return to either the congressional caucus or the boss-dominated convention. But minimizing the role of members of Congress or state party leaders ends peer review: there is no way for voters to take the measure of contenders in person and separate the ones with character and ability from the media hypesters. At most recent conventions, especially Democratic Party conventions, national politicians have been conspicuously absent, as Figure 8-3 shows.

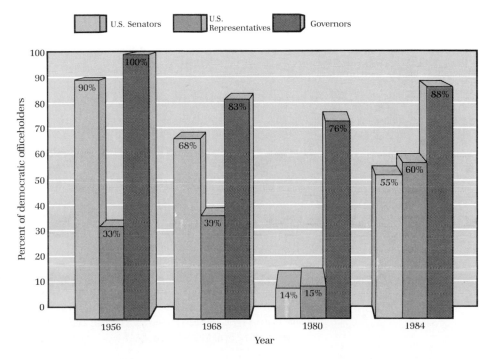

Figure 8-3. Elected officials at Democratic national conventions. Participation of governors, senators, and representatives greatly increased in 1984 as a result of new party rules giving a greater role to the party-in-government. (Source: Democratic National Committee.)

In 1984 the Democrats brought back some element of peer review. They created 566 superdelegates—14 percent of the convention—chosen from among House members (164), senators (27), state elected officials, and party leaders. It was originally thought that most superdelegates would remain uncommitted and, in a close contest, would be in a position to swing the nomination. But the candidates lobbied intensively with the superdelegates for their support. After the last primary there was a steady flow toward Mondale, who amassed the support of 85 percent of them before the convention. The superdelegates helped clinch Mondale's victory.

Critics of the primary system believe that incompetent candidates can use the media to fool voters. They point to the many impressive candidates whom professional party leaders have given the public in the twentieth century. Defenders claim that the media can expose phonies, and they point out that peer review in the nineteenth century led to mediocre nominees with whom politicians were comfortable, while only the advent of primaries has induced party bosses to back better candidates.

Critics argue that the bargaining between bosses and managers at conventions served a useful purpose: it constrained nominees by reminding them that they needed the party. But if candidates can win the nomination by going directly to the voters, they may think that they owe nothing to party leaders or workers—who may later decide that they owe nothing to them either. Nominees sever links with their own party. Primaries promote an individualistic rather than a collegial approach to politics and lead to charges of an "imperial president" who ignores the party and rides roughshod over its interests.[9]

Defenders say that the constraints which bosses placed on presidents hardly served the public interest and that we are better off without the horse-trading over cabinet posts and contracts. Presidents are constrained, but in different ways: they no longer can ignore the interests of the party rank and file, since they will have to run the primary gauntlet for renomination.

The vulnerability of an unpopular incumbent president may be the most significant problem with primaries. Do we really want a president, like Ford in 1976 or Carter in 1980, to be distracted for a whole year by nomination politics? Are the values of intraparty democracy so important that we are prepared to see presidents devote most of their time to fending off opponents within their own party? To defenders, the answers to both these questions is yes: presidents must compete in primaries to preserve accountable government. If they are unpopular, it might be a good thing to keep them vulnerable, or even to deny them renomination.

Caucuses: The resurgence of party politics. The party caucuses, which were an integral part of the boss-dominated conventions, have been modernized. Since 1972 they have been open to any registered party member who wishes to participate. From clubby meetings of party officials going routinely through the motions of sending delegates to state *nominating conventions,* caucuses have been transformed into contests between candidates' organizations. Unlike a primary (a party election, held in one of the usual polling places and involving a secret ballot), a caucus is a meeting, held in a special meeting hall (for example, a high school gym), at which people must vote openly, often by going to a designated part of the hall where their presence is counted as a vote for a candidate. This first tier of *precinct caucuses* is usually followed by

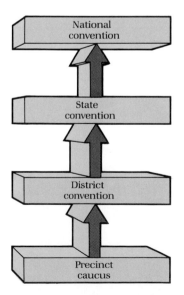

Figure 8-4. Caucus-convention system.

a second tier in which delegates attend *district conventions* (congressional, state, legislative, or county), all of which culminates in a **statewide convention** that elects delegates to the national convention. (See Figure 8-4.)

Caucuses, with their complex procedures, give local party professionals advantages over outsiders. Nevertheless, in recent years candidates have fashioned their own organizations to compete for convention delegates at every tier of the process. They do so by "flooding" the caucuses with their followers. The only way they can do this, however, is by relying on the support of unions, ethnic groups, professional associations, and others who can bring their members out to the precinct caucuses. Thus caucuses force candidates to obtain the support of interest groups and fashion effective field organizations.

Many states which adopted primaries in the 1970s abandoned them in the 1980s because of the additional expense or because their party organizations once again tried to send uncommitted delegates to the national convention. In 1984, twenty-seven states used caucuses, at which about 31 percent of the delegates (some of whom remained uncommitted until the end of the primary season) were chosen. The resurgence of state and local parties has led many to revive caucuses; some still hold preference primaries (in which no delegates are selected), but the party organizations dominate delegate selection through separate caucuses. A candidate might win the primary but lose the caucus badly—as Gary Hart did on several occasions—and therefore win few convention delegates.

CLOSE-UP

JESSE JACKSON RUNS FOR PRESIDENT. "Run, Jesse, run," the crowds roared through the winter and spring of 1984; "run, run, run." And Jesse Jackson ran with their cadenced chants.

"When you run, your enemies can't write you off and your friends can't take you for granted," he argued.

"If you run, you may lose," he told the crowds, "but if you don't run, you're guaranteed to lose. And if you run," he concluded, "you might win."

Jackson was off and running for the Democratic nomination for president, the first black candidate ever to be taken seriously, by blacks and whites alike, for the highest office. "From freedom to equality, from charity to parity," was the message he brought to the Democratic Party. "From aid to trade, from welfare to our share, from slave ship to championship—our time has come."

Reverend Jesse Jackson was the first black candidate to amass substantial delegates at a major-party convention in his 1984 run for the presidency. (*K. Hawkins: Sygma.*)

Jesse Jackson is not a career politician. Born poor, he pushed himself to academic and athletic achievements in high school and college and then went to divinity school. He became a Baptist minister, participated with the Reverend Martin Luther King, Jr., in the civil rights struggles in the 1960s, and was the leader of PUSH (People United to Save Humanity), a Chicago-based organization which organized boycotts and negotiated with large corporations to make more jobs available to minorities.

Jackson knew that he stood no chance of winning the nomination. His purpose was to send his party a message, to galvanize the minorities who constituted the most loyal of the Democratic supporters, to increase their participation, and to win them new power in party councils. It was to be a "rainbow coalition" that would bring together as many of the minorities as possible, but its effect would be to solidify a black power base in the party.

From the beginning the campaign was strong on rhetoric, issues, and ideas and weak on strategy and tactics. The idea of a rainbow coalition ignored the great differences between blacks, Hispanics, and Asians. In spite of a few publicized endorsements, most women's organizations did not join in. Jackson alienated Jews by referring to New York City as "Hymietown," and the phalanx of Black Muslim bodyguards who surrounded him and the pending indictment of his campaign manager, Arnold Pinckney, in a corruption case in Cleveland gave many other voters a negative impression. The campaign never did create a rainbow coalition—most of its support came from blacks.

Hundreds of thousands of blacks, and then more than a million, registered to vote in the primaries for him. In state after state where black voters were numerous—in the north and the south—Jackson won 10, then 20, and then 30 percent of the votes, and he won several primaries. His delegate totals mounted into the hundreds. He outlasted many of the other contenders and, along with Hart and Mondale, remained one of the three finalists. In the televised debates, he got his chance to bring his issues to the voters.

At the convention itself the Hart and Mondale delegates united to prevent Jackson from gaining enough support to bring his four platform planks to the floor of the convention: no first use of nuclear weapons, cutting the Pentagon budget, no runoff primaries (which he claimed discriminated against black candidates), and numerical quotas to end discrimination. The Mondale camp did allow a platform amendment that called for "verifiable measurements" to end discrimination, and it agreed on a "fairness commission" to study nominating rules for the next convention, so that Jackson could at least win something and would be willing to campaign for the ticket.

Jackson gave a brilliant hour-long televised address to the convention, the party, and the nation. He was once again the preacher, using his ministry for a public dialogue, rich in biblical imagery and rhyme, as when he called on the nation to join him in his mission to help "the desperate, the damned, the disinherited, the disrespected and the despised." He called for reconciliation and made his own apology: "If in my low moments, in word, deed or attitude, through some error of temper, taste or tone, I have caused anyone discomfort, created pain or revived someone's fears," he said, "that was not my truest self. . . . As I develop and serve, be patient. God is not finished with me yet." And for millions of Americans, black and white, that speech was indeed Jackson's "joy bell," ringing with the affirmation that American politics would never be the same.

Campaigning in the primaries and caucuses. PRIMARIES AND CAUCUSES AS ENDURANCE TESTS.

The patchwork quilt of primaries and caucuses requires contenders to travel all over the country, in the space of fifteen weeks. Senator Bob Packwood argues that "the present system is more of a test for the Olympics than for the presidency," adding that "The test now is, can you fly from New Hampshire to California to Illinois in a day and make three intelligent speeches? This is no way to select a president."

Symptomatic of this approach is the "live shot for the locals," which is campaign jargon for a brief airport stop timed to coincide with the local evening news. Armed with minicams and microwave transmitters, a news crew can conduct a live interview with a candidate and feed it back to the local television station, and from there to the news audience. Interviews last five minutes, and so a candidate can appear on all the local stations that day.

Scurrying around the country gives candidates little time to think, to read, to reflect on the issues, or to work closely with people they might want in their administration. Staffers and media advisers with little experience in government peddle their own policies. The campaign functions in its own little universe, which negates much of the value of campaigning.

PRIMARIES AND CAUCUSES AS A STEEPLECHASE. Candidates want to avoid a poor showing and quick elimination; each wants to become the only contender from one of the wings of the party by eliminating rivals. They want to win some of the big-state primaries and accumulate enough delegates in other states to take the lead. It is not necessary to have a majority; in modern times any front-runner who has 41 percent or more of the delegates by the end of the season has won the nomination.[10]

Contenders may use a defensive strategy, trying to defeat others within the same party wing in order to remain survivors of the winnowing that occurs in the first primaries. Using an offensive strategy, candidates try to break out of the pack and distinguish themselves from the rest of the field.[11] By getting many more votes than expected in the early primaries, they hope to get good media coverage, move up in the polls, and get more PAC and direct-mail contributions, since winners get a major boost in the subsequent polls.[12]

The key primaries and caucuses are the preliminary rounds, which give extensive media coverage to the winners; the core contests, in which many delegates from the large states are chosen; and the watershed primaries, which are "do or die" for one or more contenders.

THE PRELIMINARY ROUNDS: IOWA AND NEW HAMPSHIRE. Since 1976 these two states have held a unique place in the nominating game. Iowa goes first with its caucus and convention. The contenders must organize in the state as much as a year in advance. Union members, farmers, and teachers play a major role in bringing out the vote. Jimmy Carter in 1976 and 1980 had the backing of the National Education Association and rewarded it by establishing the Department of Education after his election. Turnouts in Iowa approach 10 percent of the registered party voters, which gives the caucuses the flavor of a primary. A win, or even a strong second-place finish, propels a candidate into the front rank of contenders. (For the Democrats, this is somewhat ironic, since Iowa almost always votes Republican in the general election.) In 1984 Gary Hart took second place, and George McGovern took third (the difference between them was fewer than 1500 caucus voters), and yet Hart received an enormous amount of publicity for his showing, while McGovern was ignored.

Senator Gary Hart of Colorado hit the bulls-eye with an ax at both a New Hampshire county fair and its Democratic primary in 1984. (*Ira Wynam: Sygma.*)

New Hampshire runs the first of the direct primaries. Because of the enormous media exposure it generates for the winner, it is also one of the most important primaries. Consider Jimmy Carter's experience after his first-place finish in 1976:

> Carter's face appeared on the covers of *Time* and *Newsweek*. On the inside, he got 2,630 lines. The second place finisher, Udall, got only 96 lines; in fact, all of Carter's opponents together received only 300 lines. That week, Carter got three times the television evening news coverage as his typical major candidate rival. He also got four times as much front-page newspaper coverage and over three times as much inside space.[13]

In 1984 Gary Hart's surprise victory gave him the same media boost, resulting in a huge jump in support in the polls, from about 4 to 40 percent in two weeks. Surveys of voters conducted just before and just after the network evening news for several days after the New Hampshire primary showed a surge in support for Hart following each evening's coverage. By early March he was the only Democratic contender to lead President Reagan in the "trial heats" of the pollsters.

The preliminary contests give unknowns like Carter and Hart publicity and name recognition across the country, and this boosts them in the polls and gets them funds. Rivals who do poorly begin to drop out of the race. Voters in other states reassess their tentative decisions about which candidate to support. They move from second-tier candidates who have no chance to the front-runners, and they move toward a "comer," like Carter or Hart, who seems to have momentum. In the six weeks after the new Hampshire primary in 1984, 8 percent of Democrats who supported second-tier candidates switched to Mondale and 14 percent switched to Hart, and 14 percent switched from Mondale to Hart.

CORE AND WATERSHED CONTESTS. As the primary season progresses, most contenders drop out. The core primaries and caucuses give the remaining two or three a chance to win large numbers of delegates. In some states delegates are apportioned solely on the basis of the percentage of votes a candidate received, but in others there are "bonus" allocations or winner-take-all delegate contests (based on results in districts within the state), and these give a candidate who narrowly wins the popular vote a huge lead in delegates.

Those who do poorly in these states get unfavorable media coverage, and their expenses outrun new contributions. The watershed contests eliminate them if they fail to meet media expectations; conversely, a good finish can restore a sagging campaign, as it did for Ronald Reagan in several southern primaries in 1976.

The role of the media in primaries and caucuses. Broadcast and print journalists bring the public campaign news (where the candidates went and what they did and said—known in the trade as "here they come, there they go" stories), analysis of strategy and tactics, evaluations of candidates, and discussion of the issues. They pay too little attention to issues and too much attention to daily events and to the horse race. Dan Rather, the CBS anchor, says, "We have no apologies for covering the horserace aspect of this. They want to know who lost, who won, and why. I don't think they want a lengthy discussion of the issues."[14]

But critics fault the media for their pervasive inability even to get the horse-race aspects right. The media commission polls, which they report before and after each round of primaries; these are designed to explain how people voted and why. The media also make forecasts of how campaigns will do. Most of these forecasts are incorrect. In 1968 media gurus insisted that an incumbent president could not be denied renomination, but Eugene McCarthy's near tie with Lyndon Johnson in the New Hampshire primary led to the president's decision to withdraw from the race. In 1972 the media thought that the front-runner, Edmund Muskie, had the Democratic nomination locked up and that George McGovern was a fringe candidate with no chance—several months later Muskie was gone and McGovern was the nominee. In 1976 the conventional wisdom had it that no contender could obtain a majority of delegates in a lengthy primary season, and Jimmy Carter was considered an obscure regional contender whose real goal was the vice presidency. On the Republican side, Gerald Ford was thought to have an easy run for nomination. Yet he barely held off Ronald Reagan, and eventually he lost to Carter in the general election. Going into the winter of 1980, commentators thought that Ted Kennedy could wrest the nomination from Carter; by late spring they were sure that Carter was unbeatable, and by early summer they did not know which way to bet. Few gave Reagan a chance before the 1980 primary season; by the following January he was president. A New York Times poll—conducted with technical advice from political scientists—pronounced, just before the 1984 New Hampshire primary, that Walter Mondale enjoyed the largest lead ever recorded by a Democratic presidential hopeful in the party. Yet Gary Hart proceeded to win the primary, and subsequent polls showed him advancing 30 points within two weeks.

The polls are mush, almost completely unreliable: the samples are not always valid, and voters change their opinions up to the time they step into the booths. But the savvy candidate can take advantage of the media's addiction for prediction. By peddling a scenario which downplays strength in the early caucuses and primaries and by releasing or publicizing unfavorable polls, a candidate can keep media expectations low. Then a good performance will be taken as evidence of a surge of support, and the media will report favorably on the surprise showing. Candidates who do better than expected will win the "media primary" even though they lost the actual one. "The elimination of candidates occurs," David Broder argues, "not because of the actual votes they receive, but because they get discouraged; volunteers and contributors desert them and the press sours on them when the returns are disappointing. What happens, and what is written and broadcast, the day after the primary is more important than what happens at the polls."[15] Even winners who do worse than expected—like Lyndon Johnson in 1968 and Edmund Muskie in 1972 in New Hampshire—can "lose" the media primary even though they won the real one.

WOLFPACK JOURNALISM. A campaign can be derailed if the candidate commits a *gaffe:* makes a slip of the tongue, tells an ethnic joke, has an outburst of temper, or blows up at reporters. Consider what happened to Jesse Jackson's campaign in 1984 after he referred to New York City as "Hymietown" and to Jews as "Hymies." His remarks were reported in the *Washington Post* by Milton Coleman, a black reporter. Jackson first claimed that he did not remember making them, and then he appeared before a Jewish congregation in New Hamsphire to apologize; meanwhile, his campaign lost weeks of momentum. Later he had to disassociate himself from anti-Semitic remarks made by one of his supporters, the Black Muslim leader Louis Farrakhan (who also threatened Coleman's life). Although Jackson was successful in mobilizing black voters in the primaries, the media concentrated on these gaffes, not on the issues that Jackson wanted to discuss—which was a major reason he was running in the first place.

Other candidates have had their problems: Hart's change of name (from Hartpence) and the fact that he said that he was one year younger than he really was also dogged him for weeks, while he tried vainly to interest the media in his "new ideas" theme. And he lost the New Jersey primary in large measure because of a slip: while in California, he jokingly told a crowd of supporters that his wife was lucky to be campaigning there, while he had to go back to New Jersey and campaign at toxic-waste dumps.

CONTROLLED MEDIA: POSITIONING THE CAMPAIGN. As candidates move from one state to another, they usually concentrate on national and local themes. Gary Hart talked about new ideas to the nation, but about toxic-waste dumps to people in New Jersey and about nuclear power plants to California residents. Walter Mondale talked about experience to the nation, but about gun control to New Yorkers and about the Chrysler loan program to people in the industrial midwest. Jesse Jackson talked about the rainbow coalition to the nation, but said "our time has come" to black inner-city audiences. Candidates use direct mailings, radio and television advertisements on local stations, and local news coverage to deliver these specialized messages.

Candidates use the techniques of new politics to project their personalities. Robert Goodman, the media adviser to George Bush in 1980, used exciting theme music, actors impersonating secret service agents, and youthful crowds. Bush was featured pledging that he would move the nation "into a position of strength. We're gonna be strong, we're gonna lead, and we're gonna win." The 1976 advertisements for Gerald Ford looked like soft-drink pitches, with a bouncy "we're feelin' good about America" theme.[16]

Dan Wasserman, Los Angeles Times Syndicate; reprinted by permission.

Primary campaigns can take a negative turn. Consider one of Carter's successful advertisements in 1980:

MAN: I don't think Kennedy's qualified to be President.
WOMAN: I don't think he has any credibility. . . .
MAN: I don't trust him.
WOMAN: You're taking a chance with Kennedy.
MAN: Between Kennedy and Carter, I would definitely go with Carter myself.
    I trust him.[17]

Candidates can use commercials to position themselves on the issues. They can take an extreme or a centrist position within their party, or they can position themselves closest to the overall electorate. They can also choose direction as well as position: moving toward the center from one of the extremes or sharpening differences with the rest of the field by moving away from the center.[18]

In *closed* primaries or caucuses, candidates go either with mainstream attitudes in their party or with a faction. In *open* primaries or caucuses, they have more flexibility because they can also do well by appealing to independents. Walter Mondale, who emphasized traditional liberalism, did well in closed contests; Gary Hart, who was skeptical about interest groups and government welfare programs and who opposed gun control, did better in open primaries.

Voters in primaries often do not know or misperceive a candidate's stance on issues. Eugene McCarthy was the antiwar candidate in New Hampshire in 1968, and yet almost half of his primary supporters voted for him even though they were hawkish on the war, and some thought that he was a hawk as well. Many of the white blue-collar voters who supported Robert Kennedy in the

Trendy graphics characterized Gary Hart's primary commercials. (*Photo by Barry S. Surman from "The Spot: The Rise of Political Advertising on Television," M.I.T. Press.*)

1968 primaries later voted for George Wallace (a third-party candidate) in the general election; Wallace was opposed to most of the issues that Kennedy stood for, but nevertheless he could tap the same vein of protest against Washington that had been a theme of the Kennedy campaign.

PRIMARY DEBATES. Contenders may be invited by networks, civic groups, or universities to participate in debates. In 1984 the Democrats held six candidate forums, which had a major impact on the primary contests. Many voters, knowing that debates would be held, remained uncommitted or tentative, preferring to obtain more information about the candidates in the course of one evening's debate. The low-keyed John Glenn did poorly, while Jesse Jackson and Gary Hart picked up strength. Walter Mondale regained the offensive

The eight starters in the 1984 race for the Democratic nomination began the winnowing-out process with their first debate at Dartmouth College in Hanover, New Hampshire. (*John Ficara: Woodfin Camp.*)

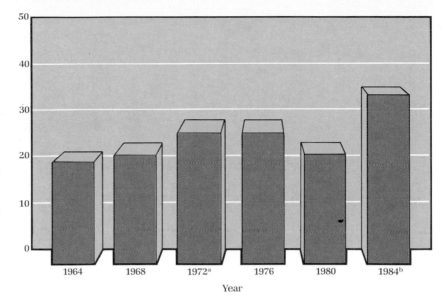

Figure 8-5. Primary turnouts, 1964–1984. Turnouts rose in the 1970s but declined in the 1980 nominating contests, even with highly competitive races in both parties. In 1984 President Reagan had almost no opposition in Republican primaries and the percentages refer only to Democratic contests. (Sources: Austin Ranney, *Participation in American Presidential Nominations*, Washington, American Enterprise Institute, 1976, and author's calculations.)

a. Nixon renominated with little serious opposition; Republican turnouts included.

b. Reagan renominated with no opposition. Republican turnouts excluded; figures are only for Democratic primaries.

against Hart, and Jackson finally reached a national audience with his ideas.

Front-runners prefer not to debate because the risks are considerable. This can backfire. In 1980 Ronald Reagan refused to debate in Iowa and lost a state he should have won. In New Hampshire the front-runner, George Bush, refused to debate in a large field, demanding to go one-on-one with Reagan; the latter made an issue of it and put Bush on the defensive. Jimmy Carter, who was ahead in the polls in the 1980 primary season, refused to debate Ted Kennedy, but this time the strategy worked.

Primaries and caucuses: How democratic are they? Are primaries and caucuses the most democratic way to choose a party nominee for president? Or are they unrepresentative charades, dominated by media manipulators and likely to produce nominees who are unrepresentative of the will of the party-in-the-electorate?

PARTICIPATION. Primaries are now mass-participation events (Figure 8-5). The average turnout in caucuses was only 2.6 percent in 1984, and that was higher than usual. Compare this with the 35 percent turnout in the Democratic primaries in 1984 and the 23 to 28 percent turnouts in preceding Republican and Democratic contests. Only 11 million people participated in primaries in 1968; by 1980 (when both parties had serious contests) that number had tripled to more than 33 million. In states which hold closed primaries, usually between 40 and 60 percent of the eligible registered voters participate. The highest rates of participation occur in states in which primaries are held before anyone sews up the nomination; in which contenders' names are on the ballot; which are closed to registered party voters; and in which primaries have been held in the past and voters have become used to them.[19]

REPRESENTATIVENESS OF THE PRIMARY VOTE. Some people argue that primaries draw a disproportionate number of voters from higher socioeconomic

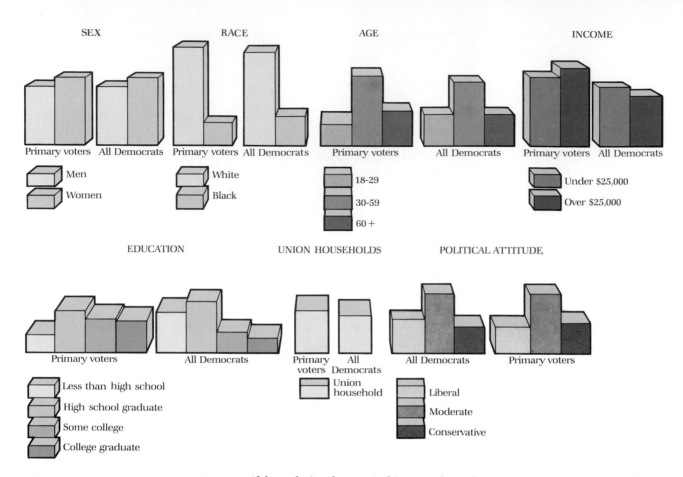

Figure 8-6. Democrats in general versus Democratic primary voters, 1984. Primary voters were more likely to be white, older, liberal, well-educated, and with higher incomes than all Democrats. But most of these differences were small, and some might be accounted for by the margin of error in the poll samples. (Source: *The New York Times*, based on polls conducted in twenty-four primary states by NYT/CBS, CBS News, NBC News, and ABC News.)

groups. Although in the past this may have been true, recent surveys have shown similarities between voters in primaries and voters in general elections. The Democrats who voted in the 1984 primaries were quite similar to all rank-and-file Democrats, as Figure 8-6 makes clear, although they were better educated, older, more affluent, and slightly more liberal (in 1980 voters in primaries were ideologically similar to voters in the general election).[20] Small differences remain, but it is not true that voters in primaries are quite different from the party rank and file or that there is a marked upper-class bias in primary systems. The large turnouts of minority voters in 1984 (up 82 percent in Alabama, 43 percent in Florida, 103 percent in New York, and 38 percent in Pennsylvania from 1980) have made the system much more representative. However, those who participate in caucuses do not mirror the overall party-in-the-electorate, but overrepresent particular interest groups, extreme ideological voters, religious fundamentalists (in Republican states), and more affluent voters.

LEGITIMACY OF THE PRIMARY SYSTEM. Primaries are supposed to give the nomination to the choice of the party rank and file. Do they? In almost all cases the winner of the primary season also becomes the first choice of the party voters; this has been true in 25 of the past 26 contests (the only exception was Barry Goldwater in 1964). By virtue of the struggle itself, the winner is transformed into the party's choice.[21] In 1984, for example, by the end of the primary season Walter Mondale was the choice of 53 percent of black Democrats, and Jesse Jackson was the choice of 31 percent, event though the majority had voted for Jackson in the primaries.[22] (See Figure 8-7.)

But the legitimacy of a nomination may be called into question because of the way delegates are allotted. Consider the 1984 contest (Figure 8-8). Gary Hart won sixteen primaries to Walter Mondale's eleven, and he claimed to be the popular choice. However, because Mondale received 38.6 percent of the votes, (compared with 36.2 percent won by Hart), because he led in preference polls

Figure 8-7. Jackson's popular vote in primaries and share of delegates.

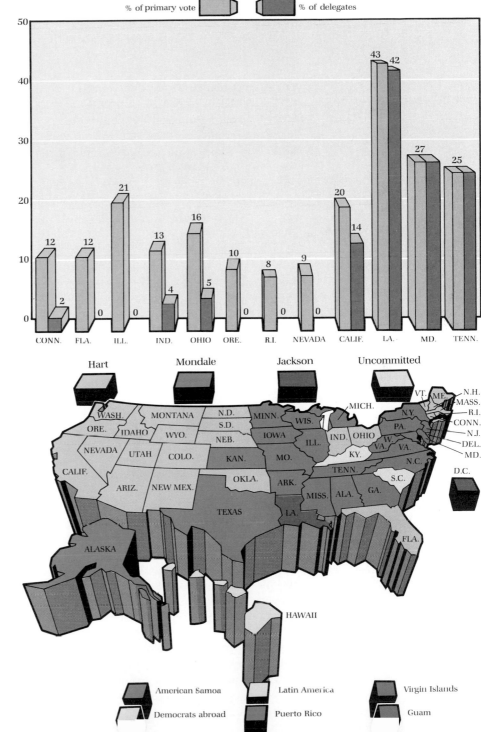

Figure 8-8. Mondale's strength was concentrated in the industrial northeast and midwest and the south, traditional areas of Democratic strength. Hart's base was the plains and western states and New England, all regions which vote Republican in most presidential elections. Many of Hart's supporters did vote for Reagan against Mondale in the general election.

of party identifiers, and because he did better than Hart in trial heats against President Reagan, Hart's claims could be dismissed. But suppose that Hart had received a larger percentage of the popular vote and had done better in the polls of party identifiers and the trial heats? Mondale still would have won the majority of delegates, but perhaps some of the uncommitted delegates and superdelegates would have gone with Hart. And the party itself would have been divided, with some claiming that Hart should have received the nomination because of the popular vote and with others claiming that Mondale should have won because he came out ahead in delegate contests.

THE NOMINATING CONVENTION

"The convention does not decide and it does not debate," concludes Senator Pat Moynihan of New York; "the rise of the primaries has made it inevitable that the nomination is settled before the convention begins."[23] Approximately 4000 Democratic and 2000 Republican convention delegates must, in a four-day period, approve the party rules and settle challenges to delegates' credentials, agree on the platform, nominate a presidential candidate, and nominate a vice presidential candidate. They must accomplish all this in such a way as to win rather than lose the support of a nationwide television audience, which they do by promoting an image of a united party rather than a divided one. The coalition that controls the convention must convert its intraparty enemies into willing allies in the general election. If it fails to do so, the other party often wins the White House, as happened to the Democrats in 1968, 1972, and 1980 and to the Republicans in 1976. An intraparty bloodbath weakens the authority even of a candidate who can win the presidency.

Managing the convention: Nominating the president

Front-runners try to hold onto their delegates, and in some cases (Carter in 1976 and Mondale in 1984) they must obtain more support for a majority. They lobby the superdelegates and convince uncommitted delegates (who are likely to come from caucus states) to join the bandwagon. Trailing candidates attempt to break up the coalition. There are only three ways to stop front-runners: challenge the credentials of rival delegates on the first day, provoke a platform fight that divides their followers on the issues on the second day, or raise a procedural issue that causes defections before the presidential nomination on the third day.

In the boss-dominated conventions these tactics worked because some bosses, nominally in one coalition, were prepared to double-cross their partners and accept a better deal from another coalition. Votes on credentials or party rules became tests to see whether a coalition could control the convention.

In most conventions front-runners have maintained control against challengers. Delegates come to the convention to nominate the candidate to whom they pledged themselves in the primaries. The front-runner's organization keeps in constant contact with delegates through an elaborate "whip" system. Instructions can be relayed from the campaign headquarters (a hotel suite in the convention city) to the communications trailer located off the convention floor, and from there by walkie-talkie to aids who can signal the front-runner's supporters. If the front-runner manages things well, delegates are not diverted by extraneous issues, nor are they interested in deal and defections.

Managing the convention for the media

Since the networks dropped gavel-to-gavel convention coverage in 1984, opting instead to broadcast only the highlights, the leading contender have had to organize the convention business into segments, each of which shows the party favorably. The Republicans in 1984 produced an eighteen-minute film introducing Ronald Reagan (at a cost of $425,000), which they showed to the delegates. The national committee and the platform and rules committees control these segments to ensure that everything will proceed according to plan.

Nevertheless, a well-managed convention, to the extent that it becomes a floor show rather than a political contest, may defeat its purpose. During the Republican convention in 1984 a Marx Brothers movie swept the television ratings in several cities. In New York City the Mets and Yankees won over the Democratic convention. All the networks got a combined share of 13 percent of all homes. Only 19 million Americans watched each convention at any one time. Usually the networks get 42 percent of the television audience in July—during the conventions their coverage got only 21 percent. As the ratings have dropped, so has the coverage: from 142 hours in 1976, to 110 in 1980, and to only 76 in 1984.

Rules and credentials

Opponents propose changes in party rules and challenge delegates' credentials to break up the front-runner's coalition. The strategy goes all the way back to Martin Van Buren, who in 1832 proposed that a two-thirds majority be required to nominate the Democratic candidate for vice president—a proposal made solely to keep the incumbent, John Calhoun, from winning renomination. Van Buren later attacked the two-thirds rule as applied to presidential nominations in his own failed attempt in 1844 (yet the rule lasted until 1936).

Front-runners use rules changes to solidify their position. George McGovern, whose party commission proposed rules changes for the Democratic convention of 1972, capitalized on the new rules to win the Democratic nomination. At the convention itself, McGovern's forces voted to seat the California delegation—chosen by a winner-take-all procedure which in principle he had opposed—because he had won the California primary. Meanwhile, party oppo-

Nancy Reagan waves to husband, Ron, watching her perform before a nationwide television audience as she delivers a short speech to delegates at the Dallas convention. (*Sygma.*)

nents, who in the past had supported the winner-take-all procedure, argued for proportional representation of the delegation because that would have reduced McGovern's proportion from 100 to 44 percent.

Consider the **pledge rule,** which binds delegates to vote at the convention for the contender to whom they pledged support in the primaries, a rule used by the Republicans in 1976 and by the Democrats in 1980 and then discarded by both. The front-runners (Ford and Carter) referred to it as the "justice" rule, arguing that it is only right that the convention enforce the primary results. Their opponents (Reagan and Kennedy) referred to it as the "robot" rule and argued instead for a "conscience" rule, which would permit delegates to vote for whomever they chose, regardless of the primary results, thus creating an "open" convention. Such a proposal is derided by front-runners, who say that it would negate the democratic principle on which the primary rests and return control to the party organization. In any event, both rules challenges failed.

Nevertheless, there is a serious argument to be made against the pledge rule. It prevents a convention from making an assessment, on the basis of new information or changed circumstances, about the merits of the contenders. And it removes the last vestiges of the representative function from conventions, converting them into registering devices, pure and simple. For these reasons, both parties have discarded the rule.

Platform politics

A party's platform specifies its principles and proposed programs. While it does not bind a candidate once in office, a majority of platform pledges are implemented.[24] Several months before the nomination the party's national committee appoints a temporary platform committee and staff members. The state parties also appoint temporary members, who, after the primaries and caucuses, are replaced by elected delegates who represent the candidates. The platform committee then holds public hearings around the country or in Washington. It then meets a few weeks before the convention for final hearings. Then it drafts the platform and any minority reports. On the second day the convention considers and adopts the platform and accepts or rejects any minority reports. In recent years party rules have prevented any amendments from the floor; this keeps things running smoothly and gives everyone an incentive to work things out in committee.

The worst thing that can happen to a nominee is to have key parts of the platform written by delegates who support other contenders. In 1976 the Republicans approved a foreign policy plank which repudiated the policies of President Ford and Secretary of State Kissinger and endorsed the approach taken by Ronald Reagan. In 1980, rather than try to win a divisive fight against Ted Kennedy's forces, President Carter compromised, and key parts of the Democratic platform incorporated Kennedy's positions. In both cases incumbent presidents demonstrated weakness that presaged trouble in the fall elections.

Republican convention delegates divide into a large conservative majority and a smaller "progressive" wing. Even conservative Republican nominees sometimes try to keep their delegates from putting strong conservative positions into their platform, since this might cost them the election, and they are likely to ignore the provisions that they do not want to run on. After the "hard right" had won most of its platform fights with the moderates, Richard

Viguerie, the direct-mail specialist for right-wing causes, cautioned his supporters, saying, "I would not advise you to bet the farm that they are going to keep the promises in this platform any better than they did in the last platform."[25]

The Democrats fragment into various "issues caucuses" that meet during the first two days of the convention. Delegates who are committed to causes—ranging from the environment to a nuclear freeze and from putting a woman on the ticket to guaranteeing full employment—meet to draft their own statements on issues, culminating several months of preconvention organizing. These caucuses often pressure the platform committee, which meets several weeks before the convention in Washington, to adopt their causes. In theory, the candidate and the candidate's deputies control all the committees which meet and can adopt their own provisions by majority vote over proposals of other nominees. But in fact, much of the content of the platform is dictated by the pragmatic compromises that the candidate has to make with these caucuses.

Nominating the vice president

On the fourth day the convention nominates a vice president. The delegates have by then ratified the choice of their presidential candidate, usually announced days or weeks before the convention meets. The purpose behind the choice for vice president, as Barry Goldwater succinctly put it, "is to get more votes."

The nominee for vice president usually balances the ticket by region and sometimes by religion: in 1960 John Kennedy, a Catholic from the north, ran with Lyndon Johnson, a Protestant from the south, and in 1964, 1968, 1972, and 1984 Catholic candidates ran for the vice presidency. In 1984 the Democrats produced the first gender-balanced ticket by nominating Geraldine Ferraro. Occasionally a liberal will choose a conservative, or vice versa, but contrary to popular belief, such balancing is rare. In most cases presidential nominees choose people whose beliefs are compatible with their own: Kennedy and Johnson, Goldwater and Miller, Carter and Mondale, Reagan and Bush, and Mondale and Ferraro, for example. Often a governor or former governor who is running for president chooses a Washington insider (usually someone who has served in Congress), though senators rarely reciprocate, usually picking someone else with experience in Washington rather than a governor. In the boss-dominated conventions the vice presidency was either a consolation prize given to a defeated coalition to unify the party or bait to build the winning coalition—tactics used to nominate Woodrow Wilson and Franklin Roosevelt for president. But coalition-building deals produced mediocre men for the vice presidency: in the nineteenth century six were not even renominated, none of the four vice presidents who succeeded to the presidency on the death of the incumbent won the nomination on their own, and only Martin Van Buren parlayed the vice presidency into a subsequent presidential nomination and election.

Since World War II the quality of nominees has improved. Men like Harry Truman, Lyndon Johnson, Walter Mondale, and George Bush all had impressive credentials when they joined the presidential ticket. In fact, between 1952 and 1984, eleven vice presidential nominees were more experienced in civilian politics than the presidential nominee. Republican presidential nominees averaged 12.25 years in public office, compared with 11.125 for their running mates; corresponding figures for the Democrats are 12 years for the presidential nominee and 15.5 years for the vice presidential nominee (though 1984 was an exception).[26]

In the past, the major problem with the selection process has been that it has come at the end of the convention, when the candidate and his advisers were exhausted and when they may not have devoted sufficient time to their choice.

A hurried decision resulted in the selection of Tom Eagleton, a distinguished liberal Democratic senator from Missouri whose past history of shock treatments surfaced after his nomination, forcing his withdrawal from the ticket and damaging George McGovern's chances. Yet it is not at all clear that unhurried consideration, lengthy interviewing of contenders, or extensive consultation within the party produces a better nominee than the rush jobs. Last-minute nominees include Lyndon Johnson, Edmund Muskie, Robert Dole, and George Bush, all of whom were well qualified for the presidency. More leisurely consideration gave us Spiro Agnew, a mediocre and corrupt political hack who ultimately resigned from the vice presidency in disgrace after pleading no contest to charges of corruption involving his conduct as county executive and governor in Maryland and as vice president. Although Walter Mondale used a lengthy interviewing process, his staff failed to uncover any of the irregularities involving the financial dealings of Geraldine Ferraro's husband, matters which hurt her campaign.

FOCUS

A WOMAN ON THE TICKET. The memo to Walter Mondale from his campaign field director, Mike Ford, was blunt. Mondale always seemed to play it safe—always running the ball and never daring to pass. It looked at though he might do that again when choosing a vice president for his ticket. "A run is another white male," Ford wrote. "We are behind. A pass should be considered. A black, Hispanic, or woman."

Mondale called his choice for vice president "the most important decision I will make as the Democratic nominee." His list narrowed to four: Henry Cisneros, the Hispanic mayor of San Antonio; Tom Bradley, the black mayor of Los Angeles; Diane Feinstein, the mayor of San Francisco; and Geraldine Ferraro, the third-term representative of the "Archie Bunker" district in Queens, New York.

Bradley, 66, and Cisneros, 37, were dropped because of their age. A staff memo warned that choosing Cisneros might cause hard feelings among blacks. Feinstein, the mayor of a liberal city with a large gay population (to whom she had been politically responsive), might not present the right image to middle America. Ferraro could appeal to the Catholic voters of the northeast, to the descendants of southern and eastern European immigrants, and to the liberal and feminist wings of the Democratic Party.

So it was to be Ferraro.

Like anything else that happens in presidental nominating campaigns, Mondale's decision involved behind-the-scenes organization, a media campaign, political maneuvering and pressure, and a dash of luck. He picked a woman (rather than a male governor from a southern or border state or his rival, Gary Hart) because he was pushed in that direction by the women in the Democratic Party and by women's political organizations.

In the weeks before the convention the National Organization of Women (NOW)

New York Representative Geraldine Ferraro chaired the 1984 platform hearings and went on to receive the vice-presidential nomination. (*UPI; Bettmann Archive.*)

made it clear that the price for support from the women's movement would be a woman on the ticket. If Mondale chose a man, warned Judy Goldsmith, the president of NOW, "one strong possibility is a nomination from the floor," and NOW's national meeting passed a resolution to that effect. NOW's Democratic Task Force started to organize woman delegates and line up votes on the convention floor by conducting a telephone survey and generating a computerized list of delegates who would support a floor fight. The Gender Gap Action Campaign put pressure on Mondale through press conferences and advertisements in newspapers. Kathy Wilson, the president of the National Women's Political Caucus, argued that the 33 million unregistered women in the country would come out for a woman vice president. The caucus would have 400 members as delegates to the convention, and it released a poll late in June of a sample of all Democratic delegates indicating that 74 percent though that "a well-qualified woman would be a real help in defeating Ronald Reagan," while only 10 percent thought that a woman would hurt the ticket. Several state delegations and state parties—including those from New York, Louisiana, Idaho, Washington, Vermont, and Wisconsin—passed resolutions calling for a woman on the ticket. And fifteen leading Democratic women met privately with Mondale to lobby with him. Many male Democratic politicians agreed. "The real challenge is for the men of the Democratic Party to share power with the women who have done so much to make the party the progressive force it is today," argued Anthony Earl, the governor of Wisconsin, while another governor, Richard Celeste of Ohio, thought that nominating a woman would "generate fresh excitement coming out of the convention."

Geraldine Ferraro played her cards perfectly. "I don't know whether a woman would help the ticket," she confessed to one women's organization. "Quite frankly, whether I would do it would [depend] on whether it was the strongest ticket." After a meeting with Mondale, she said that she would not let her name be placed in nomination in a floor fight against Mondale's choice, and she helped organize other women in the party against an attempt to dictate to Mondale. On the other hand, she made it clear after a three-hour meeting with Mondale in North Oaks that she wanted to be on the ticket and thought that she would help the campaign. The Speaker of the House, Tip O'Neill, endorsed her candidacy;

with his backing she had become the secretary of the Democratic Caucus (the meeting of all House Democrats), a member of the House Budget Committee, and chair of the platform committee of the national convention. "Tip's comfortable with Gerry carrying on the traditional values of the party in the language of a new generation," explained Ann Lewis, the political director of the Democratic National Committee.

So were the convention delegates. Polls showed that Ferraro had the support of 23.1 percent of the woman delegates, compared with 21.7 percent who supported Hart, and was the first choice of Mondale delegates, with the backing of 21.8 percent, compared with 17.6 percent for Hart. Rank-and-file Democrats, however, were not nearly as enthusiastic. A New York Times/CBS poll showed that Hart was well ahead of Ferraro as their choice for vice president: 23 percent favored Hart, 9 percent favored Jackson, 3 percent favored Feinstein, and 2 percent favored Ferraro.

The nomination of a woman would not by itself change many votes: a New York Times/CBS poll of registered voters (taken on July 12, 1984) indicated that 6 percent of the voters were more likely, and 8 percent were less likely, to vote for the Democratic ticket, while more than 80 percent said that having a woman on the ticket would make no difference in their vote.

The delegates

Who are the ***convention delegates,*** and how representative can they be of the party rank and file? These are important questions: if the delegates do not reflect the preferences of party identifiers, the party may be in serious trouble when it tries to win the support of these identifiers in the fall elections.

How representative are the convention delegates? DEMOGRAPHICS. In the era of the boss-dominated conventions, all the delegates were white male local

Figure 8-9: Characteristics of convention delegates, 1968–1984. Democrats have significantly increased the percentage of blacks and women as a result of party reform rules. Jews and Catholics are overrepresented according to their proportion of the population, owing to their historic support for the Democratic coalition. Republicans have significantly increased their proportion of women but remain a forum for white, predominantly Protestant delegates. (Sources: Public Opinion, October-November 1980; Democratic National Committee; and *The New York Times,* reporting on 1984 CBS News and New York Times/CBS News polls.)

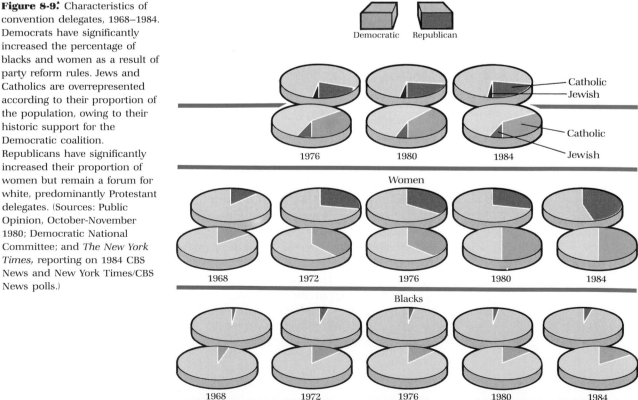

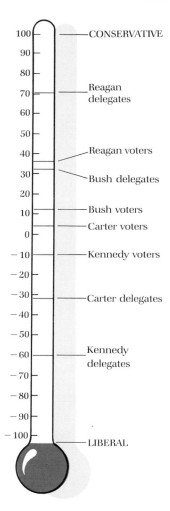

Figure 8-10. Ideological orientation of primary voters and convention delegates, 1980. Samples of voters and convention delegates were asked to place themselves on a "thermometer" with readings from 0 (coldest) to 100 (warmest). Voters were asked how they felt about liberals and conservatives: the former score would be subtracted from the latter, giving each a possible net score, or placement, between −100 (most liberal) to +100 (most conservative). The general electorate places close to 0, with equal feelings towards liberals and conservatives. There is only a loose correspondence between the placement of voters who favored a particular candidate in the primaries and the delegates pledged to that candidate. Carter voters in 1980 were on average slightly conservative, while his delegates were moderately liberal. Reagan voters were moderately conservative while his delegates were extremely conservative. (Source: Barbara Farah, "The Representativeness of Direct Primaries," fig. 1.C, "Ideological Orientation of Primary State Convention Delegates and Their Partisan Identifiers, 1980.")

party politicians. Since 1968 the Democrats have reformed their procedures to make convention delegates more demographically representative. In 1972 there were quotas for minorities and younger delegates; in 1976 these were dropped in favor of affirmative action goals. Since 1980 the rules have required that half the delegates be male and that half be female. In 1984, 50 percent of the delegates were women, 17.5 percent were black, 6.4 percent were Hispanic, 1.9 percent were Asian American, and 0.9 percent were American Indian. The Republicans have shied away from formal rules about demographic diversity; since 1976 the proportion of woman Republican delegates has increased to 44 percent, but there are few minority delegates. Figure 8-9 shows the differences between the two parties; these differences are understandable in light of the electoral support that different groups give to the parties.

SOCIOECONOMICS. Delegates from both parties are better educated and more affluent than the general population, as one would expect of any group of politicians. More than two-thirds have finished college; almost one-fifth of the Republican delegates have law degrees (slightly more than the Democratic delegates), and one-fifth of the Democratic delegates have masters and doctorates (slightly more than the Republican delegates). The Republican delegates in 1984 had higher incomes than the Democratic delegates: 57 percent of the Republicans and 42 percent of the Democrats had incomes over $50,000. More Democratic delegates are teachers and union leaders and members, while more Republican delegates are businesspeople, professionals, white-collar workers, and farmers.[27]

IDEOLOGY. Delegates are not very representative of registered party voters in terms of issues and ideology (Figure 8-10). While some come from pragmatic county and local party organizations, many are recruited as delegates by a candidate's own campaign organization, which selects people from the single-issue groups that work with the candidate in the primaries. In 1980 the National Education Association had 279 tightly organized and disciplined national convention delegates supporting Jimmy Carter at the convention; also present in large numbers were environmentalists and members of the National Women's Political Caucus, the National Organization of Women, and civil rights organizations. Although delegates will vote for the candidate, they remain free to express their own views when drafting the party platform, passing on rules changes, and acquiescing or objecting to the choice of a vice presidential nominee. The result is that Democratic convention delegates are more likely to be liberal and to be identified with particular issues or causes than Democratic party identifiers. In 1984 the ***Equal Rights Amendment*** (ERA) was supported by 9 out of 10 Democratic delegates and by 6 out of 10 Democratic

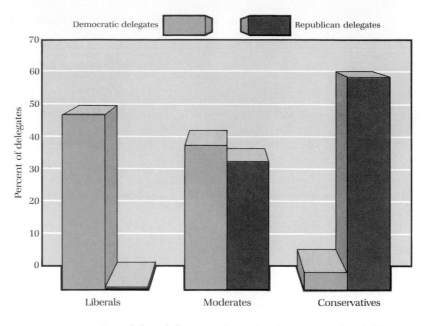

Democratic delegates　　Republican delegates

Figure 8-11. Ideology of convention delegates, 1984. Most Democratic convention delegates are liberals or moderates. A majority of Republican delegates are conservative. Approximately the same results were obtained for the 1980 conventions. (Source: CBS News delegate survey.)

voters; a majority of the delegates thought that taxes should be raised, while fewer than 20 percent of the rank and file agreed; the delegates opposed the draft, while a majority of the Democratic voters favored it; and the delegates opposed military intervention against the spread of communism, while almost two-thirds of the Democratic voters favored it. Republican delegates are more conservative and more likely to be identified with conservative causes (against abortion, gun control, and the ERA) than Republican identifiers.

In 1972 the Democratic delegates, especially those who supported McGovern, were far more liberal than the Democratic voters—so much so that the Republican *delegates* were closer to the Democratic *voters!* Some have argued that this accounted for McGovern's overwhelming defeat: the convention activists who nominated him were out of touch with their own constituencies. But since then Democratic delegates have moved closer to the center; in 1984 half described themselves as liberals, 42 percent as moderates, and only 5 percent as conservatives—and they are still able to lose massively. In contrast, Republican delegates have moved further from the center, and in 1980 and 1984 they were skewed to the right: 1 percent said that they were liberals, 35 percent said that they were moderates, and 60 percent said that they were conservatives. (See Figure 8-11.) Yet in both years the Republicans won a massive victory, proving that conventions need not mirror either the electorate as a whole or even the party identifiers to win—provided that candidates do not let the ideology of their delegates determine their campaign stance in the general election.

Delegates' orientation: partisans, personalists, purists. In the days of the boss-dominated conventions, delegates were ***partisans*** attuned to the needs of state parties. Today, delegates are oriented toward candidates first and party second.

Approximately two-thirds of convention delegates have been active in some state or local party politics and have held public or party office. Some are partisans; their first loyalties remain with their home organizations. But others, the ***personalists,*** are committed to candidates rather than to their party organizations at the convention. Some delegates, the ***purists,*** are oriented toward issues. They back the contender as a way to advance their causes. They will be more independent on convention business, especially on the platform. Moderates—such as Ford, Carter, and Mondale—are likely to attract party professionals and personalists; ideological candidates, like McGovern and Reagan, attract more purists.[28]

Old-style versus new-style conventions

Convention delegates differ significantly from the party rank and file, but this was so in the era of the old-style conventions as well.[29] At least the modern conventions no longer shut out women, minorities, or youthful voters. In any event, today the national conventions are accountable to voters in primary and caucus states because they accurately reflect their preferences—or at least the choice of a plurality of voters. And the very process of going through primaries seems to give the winner the support from the registered party voters that is necessary to legitimize the system.

What, then, is a modern convention good for? If it is merely a ratifying device for the party-in-the-electorate, should it not be abolished? The answer is no. A convention is useful for morale building among party activists. It sets a mood, tone, and direction for the party in the general election. "Our activists and leaders still need to meet with each other," says Newt Gingrich, a conservative representative, about Republican conventions, "to talk about what is really going on in this country, about their beliefs and about the future."[30]

And a convention sets the stage for the next nomination. It gives party leaders across the nation a chance to see potential candidates in action: holding receptions and giving interviews, making convention addresses, conducting news briefings, and participating in platform fights. The early betting line can even be established on front-runners when the media poll the convention delegates about their choices for the next contest.

THE REFORM AGENDA

NOMINATIONS. The choices boil down to three: do we want to maximize the power of the party-in-the-electorate, the party organization, or the party-in-government? Those in favor of the first alternative believe that it will increase voter participation and lessen apathy and alienation, that it will make nominees more accountable to the party, and that it will encourage contenders who have stamina and leadership qualities. Those in favor of a larger role for party politicians believe that they are more likely to bring out the vote if they have played the major role at a convention, that their relationships with the candidate are what keeps contenders responsive to the needs of the party and accountable to its members, and that professionals are most likely to recognize presidential leadership qualities. Those who want a larger role for the party-in-government point to the apprenticeship and peer review of parliamentary systems, claiming that these can produce another "Virginia line" of Washingtons, Jeffersons, and Madisons.

The public is not likely to accept a return to the congressional caucus, nor will it allow party bosses to dominate conventions. Party reforms that create open caucuses and mass-participation primaries are here to stay, although the mix between caucus and primary states varies from one election to the next.

New ideas, new leadership. Lengthening the primary season would give underdogs a better chance. Proportional representation of delegates, rather than winner-take-all votes at the district level, benefits underdogs, not front-runners. Outlawing "bonus" delegates for those who win the state or districts also favors them. Providing free media time for all contenders and designing debate formats that would include the entire field would slow down front-runners. Contests could start with the smaller states (which would make less expensive personal campaigning possible) and build up to the larger, media-oriented states at the end, giving long shots more time to get the money to compete and build their organizations. The problem with this reform is that it would prolong the fragmentation of the parties and might result in brokered conventions and weak compromise candidates whose authority and legitimacy would be eroded by charges that they were tools of special interests.

Party unification. Some argue that short and intense campaigns would maximize party unity in preparation for the fall elections: either the front-runner would demonstrate strength and wrap the whole thing up early, or else another contender would make a successful challenge and win early. Reforms include statewide winner-take-all allocation of delegates; holding primaries in the large, media-oriented states first; and reducing matching public funds and raising the qualifying amounts. Another change would be to hold a national primary (or to hold all state primaries on the same day), which would require huge media expenditures and previous name recognition.

Peer review. To create an open convention in which the delegates could evaluate the field and choose the strongest candidate for the election, party officials or public officeholders could be made ex officio delegates (that is, delegates by virtue of their other offices). The Democrats allow states to fill 8 percent of their delegations committed to candidates with party officials, and they provide an additional 14 percent of elected and party officials (the superdelegates) who are officially uncommitted. To maximize peer review, half the delegates could be made into superdelegates. This reform, of course, would not mean that the convention would elect a winner. Party professionals on the Democratic side gave the nation Adlai Stevenson (twice) and Hubert Humphrey, and they overwhelmingly supported Walter Mondale; thus their judgment about winners may not be any better than that of voters in primaries. Likewise, Republican professionals were more likely to back Ford than Reagan.

A national primary. The role of the party-in-the-electorate would be maximized by a national primary, which would replace the existing state primaries and the nominating covention and would give all power to the party-in-the-electorate. The vast majority of Americans favor such a system: 72 percent in 1952 and 67 percent in 1984.[31] But the national primary would favor front-runners. It would end all peer review, leaving the way open for new politics contenders, who could successfully manipulate voters in a one-shot event. Unlike the present system, which provides a sequence of events and a chance for the nation to see how candidates react to a series of challenges, it would force a single decision on a single day. It would also provide an opportunity for voters in small states to make judgments about candidates who campaign personally among them.

The mechanisms of a national primary would also create problems. In a crowded field, no one might win a majority. Either a candidate could win with a plurality, opening the way for an extremist, or a runoff contest would be required between the top two contenders. Runoffs, as it turns out, do not necessarily produce the first choice of party voters, or even their "compromise choice," but can result in a nominee who is unrepresentative both ways.[32] Holding runoffs means yet another contest, with the attendant expense and commitment of time. It would probably reduce rather than increase turnouts. It would intensify the fragmentation of the parties, as each of their different ideological, racial, ethnic, and economic constituencies fought it out.

IN CONCLUSION

The road to the White House leads first to the primaries and open caucuses in the states and then to a national convention. The system has been transformed: power has been transferred from the party-in-government and its congressional caucus, to the party organization and its boss-dominated convention, to the party-in-the-electorate and its open caucuses and primaries. In each case technological change and the ambitions of politicians have intersected to delegitimize the existing methods and spur the adoption of new ones. Better transportation led to the national convention and increased the power of state party leaders, and advances in communication have allowed candidates to communicate to voters in primaries without using party organizations; this has resulted in the modern-day mass primaries. Telephone canvassing and direct mailings have changed the way candidates organize and fund their campaigns and have also limited the importance of state and local parties and increased the importance of obtaining the support of PACs, single-issue groups, and professional and trade organizations and unions.

The present nominating system is open and fluid: almost anything can happen if an incumbent is not running. There is no apprenticeship and no formal party leader, and so the field is wide open, though in practice it narrows down to politicians who have the money to put together a large organization to compete for delegates in the states. There is no system of peer review, and relative unknowns (such as Carter) or outsiders (such as Reagan) can obtain the nomination even though they are by no means the choice of the congressional party-in-government with whom they will later have to work. The nominating system divides presidents from their parties and leaves them with bitter intraparty enemies, thus weakening their authority.

Voters in primaries are nearly representative of all party voters, but the delegates selected are not, in terms of either personal or political characteristics. Delegates are more ideological and issue-oriented and are more committed to candidates than to party than the rank and file is. They nominate the voters' choice, but they may adopt a platform that is not fully in tune with the opinions of the majority of party followers. Candidates tend to ignore the platform during the election, though they are likely to implement a majority of its provisions once they are in office. Delegates today are no less representative of their constituents than the delegates to the boss-dominated conventions were.

The Democrats are more likely to make extensive reforms than the Republicans, but in recent years Republican nominees have won the presidency, leading some Democrats to wonder whether their efforts are not misplaced. The idea, after all, is to win the White House: even the most representative nominating procedure should be a means to an end, not an end in itself.

NOTES

1. *The Federalist*, number 68.
2. Walter Mondale, *The Accountability of Power*, McKay, New York, 1975, p. 30.
3. Michael Robinson, "An Idea Whose Time Has Come—Again," *The Congressional Record*, June 19, 1975, p. E 3336.
4. Stephen Hess, *The Presidential Campaign*, Brookings, Washington, D.C., 1974, p. 42.
5. Thomas Cronin, *The State of the Presidency*, 2d ed., Little, Brown, Boston, 1980, p. 39.
6. Moseii Ostragorski, *Democracy and the Organization of Political Parties*, vol. 2 (1902), Anchor Books ed., Garden City, New York, 1964, pp. 133–144.
7. Louis Harris, "Why the Odds Are against a Governor's Becoming President," *Public Opinion Quarterly*, fall 1959; Robert L. Peabody and Eve Lubalin, "The Making of

Presidential Candidates," in Charles Dunn (ed.), *American Democracy Debated*, General Learning Press, 1975, p. 27.

8. *The New York Times*, Mar. 26, 1984.
9. Donald R Matthews (ed.), *Perspectives on Presidential Selection*, Brookings, Washington, D.C., 1973, p. 46.
10. Steven J. Brams, *The Presidential Election Game*, Yale University Press, New Haven, Conn., 1978, p. 69.
11. John H. Aldrich, *Before the Convention*, University of Chicago Press, Chicago, 1980, p. 161.
12. James Beniger, "Winning the Presidential Nomination: National Polls and State Primary Elections," *Public Opinion Quarterly*, vol. 10, no. 1, spring 1976, pp. 22–39; see also Harvey Zeidenstein, "Presidential Primaries—Reflections of the 'The People's Choice,'" *Journal of Politics*, vol. 32, no. 4, November 1970, pp. 856–874.
13. Stephen J. Wayne, *The Road to the White House*, 1st ed., St. Martin's, New York, 1981, p. 101.
14. *The New York Times*, Apr. 14, 1984.
15. Cronin, op. cit., p. 37.
16. David Broder et al., *The Pursuit of the Presidency, 1980*, Berkeley Books, New York, 1980, p. 33.
17. Broder, op. cit., pp. 115–116.
18. Benjamin Page, *Choices Not Echoes*, University of Chicago Press, Chicago, 1980.
19. Richard Rubin, "Presidential Primaries: Continuities, Dimensions of Change, and Politicial Implications," in William Crotty (ed.), *The Party Symbol*, Freeman, San Francisco, 1981.
20. *ISR Newsletter*, winter 1981, p. 1.
21. William H. Lucy, "Polls, Primaries and Presidential Nominations," *Journal of Politics*, vol. 35, no. 4, November 1973, p. 837.
22. New York Times/CBS poll, June 23–28, 1984.
23. *The New York Times*, July 20, 1984.
24. Gerald Pomper, *Elections In America*, Harper and Row, New York, 1973, pp. 181–189.
25. *The New York Times*, Aug. 19, 1984
26. Joel K. Goldstein, *The Modern American Vice Presidency*, Princeton University Press, Princeton, N.J., 1982, p. 85.
27. Warren J. Mitofsky and Martin Plissner, "The Making of the Delegates, 1968–1980," *Public Opinion*, vol. 3, no. 5, October–November 1980, pp. 37–43.
28. *Washington Post*, Aug. 17, 1976.
29. Barbara Farah, "The Representativeness of Direct Primaries: Linkage between Partisan Voters and Convention Delegates, 1972, 1976, 1980," University of Michigan, Survey Research Center, Ann Arbor, 1982.
30. Newt Gingrich, "Transition Shaped by an Elite," *The New York Times*, Aug. 19, 1984.
31. Gallup poll, June 22–25, 1984.
32. Steven J. Brams and Peter Fishburn, *Approval Voting*, Birkhauser, Boston, 1983.

FURTHER READING

Aldrich, John H.: *Before the Convention*, University of Chicago Press, Chicago, 1980. A study of the strategies and choices open to contenders, with interesting mathematical applications.

Brams, Steven J.: *The Presidential Election Game*, Yale University Press, New Haven, Conn., 1978. A discussion of mathematical models and game theory used to explore primary strategies in multicandidate races.

———— and Peter Fishburn: *Approval Voting*, Birkhauser, Boston, 1983. An account of how multicandidate primaries distort the preferences of voters and what can be done about it.

Broder, David, et al.: *The Pursuit of the Presidency, 1980*, Berkeley Books, New York, 1980. An in-depth look at new politics contenders by *Washington Post* reporters.

Bryce, James: *The American Commonwealth*, Macmillan, London, 1888. A classic nineteenth-century critique of the boss-dominated conventions and the candidates they produced.

Ceasar, James: *Presidential Selection*, Princeton University Press, Princeton, N.J., 1979. A book by political theorist dealing with power, authority, and legitimacy in nominating systems past and present.

Chase, James S.: *Emergence of the Presidential Nominating Convention, 1789–1832*, University of Illinois Press, Urbana, 1973. A treatment of the nominating process from congressional caucuses to the convention.

Davis, James W.: *National Conventions in Age of Party Reform*, Greenwood Press, Westport, Conn., 1983. A history of nominating conventions.

Kirkpatrick, Jean: *The New Presidential Elite*, Russell Sage Foundation and Twentieth Century Fund, New York, 1976. Attitudes and behavior of delegates in the 1970s.

Rubin, Richard: *Party Dynamics*, Oxford University Press, New York, 1976. How party factions are influenced by nominating politics.

Shafer, Byron E.: *Quiet Revolution*, Russell Sage, New York, 1984. A comprehensive account of the reform of Democratic Party nominating rules from 1968 to 1972.

Wayne, Stephen J.: *The Road to the White House*, 2d ed., St. Martin's, 1984. A comprehensive account of primary campaigns and convention politics.

White, Theodore: *The Making of the President, 1960*, Atheneum, New York, 1961. The first of White's narratives of the primary seasons, including a discussion of what primaries could and could not do at the end of the era of boss-dominated coventions.

THE STUDY BREAK

Crouse, Timothy: *The Boys on the Bus*, Ballantine Books, New York, 1973. An irreverent account of journalists on the campaign trail.

Kozinski, Jerzy: *Being There* (1979). How to get nominated for vice president, the easy way; starring Peter Sellers.

The Manchurian Candidate (1962). A movie, based on Richard Condon's novel, about a plot by the Soviets to put one of their agents in the White House.

Thompson, Hunter: *Fear and Loathing on the Campaign Trail '72*. Warner Books, New York, 1983. A spacy and spicy account of campaigns.

SOURCES

Bain, Richard C., and Judith H. Parris: *Convention Decisions and Voting Records*, 2d ed., Brookings, Washington, D.C., 1973. Votes on rules, nominations, and party platforms.

Congressional Quarterly Weekly Reports. A weekly publication containing information on primaries and caucuses, including rules, political lineups, and results.

Johnson, Donald Bruce: *National Party PLatforms*, rev. ed., University of Illinois Press, Urbana, 1978, 2 vols. The texts of each party's platform, including the platforms of minor parties (supplements available for 1980 and 1984).

National Party Conventions: 1831–1980, Congressional Quarterly Press, Washington, D.C., 1983. Descriptions of each convention and its results.

1984 Presidential Campaign Summary Reports, Federal Elections Commission, Washington, D.C., 1985. A computerized index and data file on the financial activities of all presidental contenders, based on reports filed by their campaigns, including summary totals of contributions and expenditures, by category.

Presidential Elections since 1789, 3d ed., Congressional Quarterly Press, Washington, D.C., 1983. Gives complete primary and caucus results, by state.

ORGANIZATIONS

Democratic National Committee. 1625 Massachusetts Avenue, N.W., Washington, D.C. 20036. For more information phone 202-797-5900.

Federal Election Commission. 1325 K Street, N.W., Washington, D.C. 20436. For more information phone 800-424-9530.

Republican National Committee. 310 First Street, S.W., Washington, D.C. 20003. For more information phone 202-484-6764.

CHAPTER 9

PRESIDENTIAL ELECTIONS: CAMPAIGNING, VOTING, AND THE PARTY SYSTEM

The first presidential inauguration, in 1789, took place at Federal Hall in New York; the most recent, in 1985 in Washington. (*New-York Historical Society; Sygma.*)

$\mathbf{T}$he humorist Russell Baker once proposed a constitutional amendment that would provide for "separation of state and race." Pointing out that "skill at running for President has little relationship to the job of being President," he suggested that winning candidates be barred from office—they would merely run on behalf of politicians who, "because of low charisma, bad teeth and distaste for looking foolish, couldn't run successfully for a bus"—let alone for the White House.[1]

Baker's proposal points up the loose relationship between running for, and serving as, president. Elections shape presidential priorities, influence the president's relationships with Congress, and affect the programs of the bureaucracies. But do campaigns tell voters about a candidate's character and competence? Do they give them real policy alternatives? Do they tell them anything about what a candidate would do in office? Can voters be relied upon to choose what is in their best interests, or are they manipulated by slick media campaigns?

This chapter will consider these issues by describing the environment in which presidential elections are waged: the three-month campaign for electoral college votes. We will look in depth at the campaigns for money, organization, image, and popular votes. The chapter concludes by analyzing some trends and assessing proposed reforms. The overall focus remains on the issues of legitimacy, authority, and power: our free democratic elections maintain the legitimacy of our government, but do they provide the president with the authority and the power necessary to govern?

THE ELECTORAL ENVIRONMENT

Presidential elections are frantic affairs: there are just three months (August, September, and October) in which to finance, organize, and campaign. On the first Tuesday after the first Monday in November, voters choose the electors whose votes determine the winner, and so it is with the electoral college that we must begin.

How the electoral college works

Everyone knows that the president and the vice president are the only two officials who are elected by all the American people—but everyone is wrong. They are the only elected officials in the American government who are *not* chosen directly by the people. The Constitution provides for their selection by an electoral college. Each state chooses its electors (equal to its Senate and House representation) by any method that its state legislature prescribes. The Constitution does not require a popular vote. In the early 1800s many state legislatures chose the electors; all the states but South Carolina had switched to the popular vote by 1832, and it changed over in 1856.

The electors chosen by the voters in each state (and the District of Columbia) meet in their state capitals on the first Monday after the second Wednesday in December (the electoral college never meets as a body) and cast secret ballots for president and vice president. These ballots are sent to the capital, where

---

THE ROAD TO THE WHITE HOUSE: SOME ALTERNATIVE ROUTES

On the death of a president, the vice president takes the oath of office and succeeds to the presidency, filling out the remainder of the predecessor's term, under the provisions of Article II, Section 1. The same provision applies if a president resigns.

If a president is disabled, the Twenty-Fifth Amendment provides that the vice president acts as president (but does not assume the office of president) until the incumbent can resume the office. The president can declare disability and invite the vice president to act as president. Or the vice president, together with a majority of the Cabinet, can find the president to be disabled, in which case the vice president can act as president. In either case the president determines when to resume the duties of the office. If the vice president (acting for the president) and the Cabinet disagree with the president, the final determination is made by Congress. A two-third vote by each house of Congress is required to permit the vice president to continue in office as acting president.

The Constitution, under the terms of the Twenty-Fifth Admendment, provides for a vacancy in the vice-presidency. In such a case, the president can nominate a vice president, who takes office upon confirmation by a majority vote of both houses of Congress.

If there is a double vacancy, a law passed by Congress in 1947 provides for a line of succession. The Speaker of the House is next in line for the presidency, followed in turn by the president pro tem of the Senate and the Cabinet Secretaries, in the order in which their departments were founded, starting with the secretary of state.

---

they are opened early in January by the incumbent (and possibly outgoing) vice president in the presence of the *newly elected* Congress. (In 1960 this meant that outgoing vice president Nixon announced that John Kennedy had defeated him for the presidency; in 1968 outgoing vice president Humphrey announced that Nixon had beaten him.)

Contingency elections. If the electoral college does not produce a majority for president—270 of the 538 votes—the newly elected House chooses from among the three candidates who received the most electoral votes. Each state's House delegation casts one vote (determined by its majority), and a majority of states elects the president (the District of Columbia has no vote). If there is no electoral college majority for vice president, that election goes to the Senate, which chooses from between the two candidates who received the most electoral votes. Each senator casts one vote, and a majority elects. If no president is elected by the House, the vice president serves as acting president until the House decides—even if it is necessary to serve the full term. Such elections are known as ***contingency elections.***

Candidates, parties, and the electoral college. Electors have always been the agents of candidates running for office. Slates of electors are put up in each state under the name of the candidate. The popular vote is cast for the presidential and vice presidential ticket, and a plurality of the popular vote in each state elects a pledged slate. The electoral college is a registering device which records the preferences of each state's voters. Only a handful of electors have violated their pledges and voted for someone else, and none has ever influenced the outcome of an election.

Sometimes the electoral college works badly. The elections of 1800 and 1824 were settled by contingency elections in the House of Representatives, amid charges of corruption and deals. The election of 1876 required a special commission to determine which set of electors in several southern states should be counted. Sometimes the college narrowly avoids a deadlock, as it did in 1960, 1968, and 1976—in 1976 a shift of fewer than 12,000 votes in Delaware and Ohio would have produced a 269 to 269 tie vote.

In several elections the candidate with the most popular votes has been defeated: in 1824, when John Quincy Adams was elected by the House, although Andrew Jackson had a plurality of popular votes; in 1876, when Rutherford B. Hayes defeated the more popular Samuel J. Tilden; and in 1888, when Benjamin Harrison defeated Grover Cleveland. In 1960, contrary to popular opinion, John Kennedy did not win more popular votes when he beat Richard Nixon—Kennedy's totals included votes in Alabama (where he was not even on the ballot) cast for uncommitted Democratic electors. If Kennedy had not had these popular votes, Nixon would have had the edge.[2] Mathematicians claim that a disrepancy between the popular majority and the electoral majority should occur in 1 out of every 3 elections in which the vote margin is less than 300,000 and in 1 out of every 4 elections in which the margin is less than 1 million; thus a problem in the future is likely.[3]

How the electoral college affects campaigns

Winner-take-all and campaign strategy. All states except Maine give all their electoral votes to the candidate with a plurality of the statewide popular vote. The other candidates get no electoral votes. In effect, the winner is rewarded with the electoral votes which the loser would have received under a system of proportional representation. Nothing in the Constitution requires this system of *winner-take-all elections.* The states can apportion electors as they wish, and some have done so by holding contests in each congressional district: South Carolina until 1856, Michigan in 1892, and Maine since 1972. But the states prefer the winner-take-all method because it makes winning a state more important to a candidate.[4]

The winner-take-all system determines campaign strategy. The general election devolves into fifty separate state contests (and one in the District of Columbia). Obviously:

- It makes sense to concentrate on states with many electoral votes.
- It is better to win more states by small margins than fewer states by large margins.
- It is more important to campaign in states which are close than in states in which the candidate will definitely win or definitely lose.

Candidates spend their time on the campaign trail according to the ³⁄₂ *rule:* take the square root of a state's electoral college vote and then cube that number. Thus in comparing New Jersey, which has sixteen votes, with Montana, which has four, the ³⁄₂ rule gives New Jersey a factor of 64 and Montana a factor of 8—which means that candidates are likely to spend 8 times as much time and effort in New Jersey as in Montana, even though it has only 4 times as many electoral college votes. (Try this out with a state that has forty-seven electoral college votes.[5]) Candidates concentrate their campaigns on the "big twelve": the eleven largest states (plus any one of three in twelfth place), which themselves provide an electoral college majority (Figure 9-1).

Geopolitical strategy. Candidates must come up with a strategy to win an

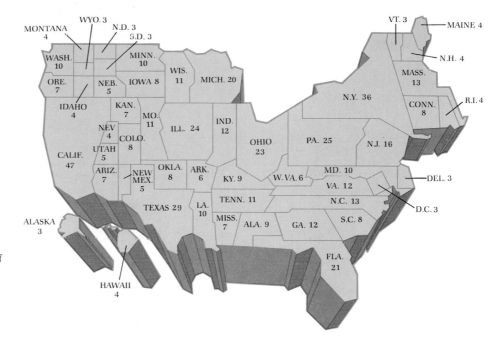

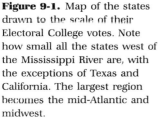

Figure 9-1. Map of the states drawn to the scale of their Electoral College votes. Note how small all the states west of the Mississippi River are, with the exceptions of Texas and California. The largest region becomes the mid-Atlantic and midwest.

electoral college majority. Between 1932 and 1944 (Figure 9-2a), Democrats won all four national elections handily by relying on their strength in the "solid south" (which after the Civil War became a one-party Democratic region) and on votes in the industrial north, which was suffering from the depression. In the post-New Deal period, 1948 to 1960 (Figure 9-2b), competition for electoral votes was more balanced. The Democrats' strength in the south and west splintered, and it eroded in the New England, upper midwest, Great Plains, and Rocky Mountain states. In the past twenty years (Figure 9-2c) the Republicans have consolidated their strength west of the Mississippi and have made the south highly competitive—in most recent elections they have trounced the Democrats everywhere but in the northeast quadrant.[6]

The Democrats win presidential elections when they hold onto a majority of southern and border states and win a majority of the large, competitive northern states, such as New York, Ohio, Pennsylvania, Michigan, and Massachusetts. They have not won a national election since 1948 without a border or southern politician on the ticket. The Republicans can win by combining the west with big states (Illinois, Michigan, Texas, Florida, and Virginia), by combining the west with the south in a sun belt strategy, or by winning a landslide in all regions (Figures 9-3 and 9-4, pages 278–279).

THE CAMPAIGN FOR FUNDS

The costs of presidential elections have skyrocketed, largely as a result of media expenditures, as Table 9-1 (page 280) shows. In spite of recent reforms, campaigners devote much of their time to raising funds and trying to outspend one another.

Past practices

The financing of general elections followed the same pattern as that for nomination campaigns until 1976. Candidates relied on their own funds, on contributions from the heirs to great family fortunes (Astors, du Ponts, Fords, Harrimans, Lehmans, Loebs, Mellons, Pews, Rockefellers, Schiffs, Scaifes, Watsons, Whitneys, and the like), and on funds from corporate executives, lawyer-lobbyists, trade association representatives, and union leaders.[7]

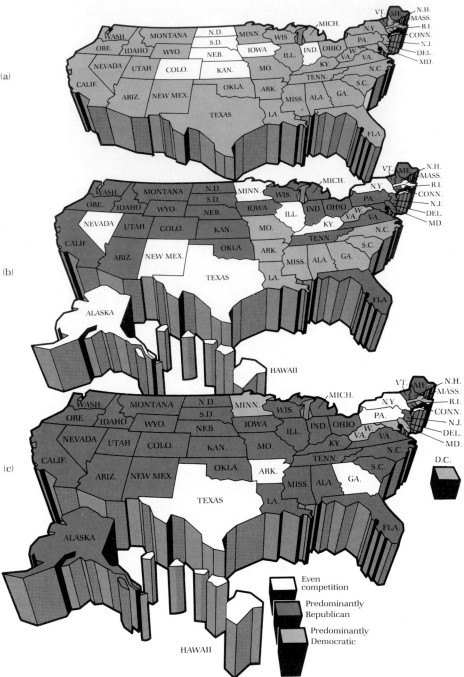

Figure 9-2. Electoral college competition since 1932. (*a*) When Republicans won the presidency in the nineteenth century they coined the phrase "As Maine goes, so goes the nation." Democrats in the New Deal period (1932–1944) responded "As Maine goes, so goes Vermont," since those two New England states were the only ones to vote solidly Republican in this period. Most states voted Democratic three or four times, including the southern and western states past the Great Plains. (*b*) In the post-New Deal period (1948–1960) the Democratic "solid south" broke up as Republican candidates made inroads in Texas, Florida, Virginia, and Tennessee. Republicans dominated the west and most of the midwest. States in red voted Democratic less than twice; states in blue voted Republican less than twice. (*c*) Between 1964 and 1984 Republicans solidified their southern and western regional bases. Not a single region of the nation could be considered solidly Democratic. The map is almost the reverse of the New Deal electoral map.

Donations were made to influence policies, gain access to the next administration, obtain lenient regulatory treatment by government agencies or favorable treatment in the tax code, or get government business. Ambassadorships to European countries were given to some contributors. Dr. Ruth Farkas, for example, contributed $250,000 to Nixon's 1972 campaign and, when offered the embassy in Costa Rica, replied, "I am interested in Europe, I think; isn't $250,000 an awful lot for Costa Rica?" For $50,000 more she got Luxembourg.[8]

Corporations and nationally chartered banks (since 1907) and unions (since

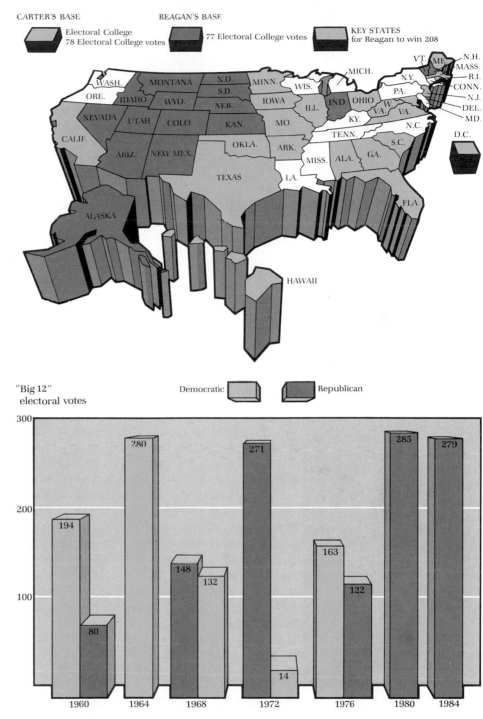

Figure 9-3. The Reagan strategists' first calculations in planning the general election campaign of 1980. Their strategy was based on taking several "key states," including California, Texas, Florida, Virginia, Ohio, and Illinois. (Source: Richard B. Wirthlin, "The Republican Strategy," in S. M. Lipset, ed., *Party Coalitions in the 1980s*, San Francisco, Institute for Contemporary Studies, 1981.)

Figure 9-4. In every election the candidate who wins a majority of the "big twelve" wins the White House. (The number of electoral votes in "big twelve" states shifts each decade owing to reapportionment of seats in the House of Representatives.)

1947) cannot contribute to federal election campaigns. But corporations have made "loans" to campaigns and then written them off. They have underbilled for their services or delayed billing, in effect giving candidates interest-free loans. Unions have let their workers help out while keeping them on the payroll. By means of pay raises, bonuses, or padded expense accounts for their employees, corporations and trade associations have laundered funds to campaigns, making them look like individual contributions. George Steinbrenner, the principal owner of the New York Yankees, used this method to get funds

Table 9-1. Presidential election costs, 1952 to 1984

Year	Total costs[a]		Radio and television costs	
	Republicans	**Democrats**	**Republicans**	**Democrats**
1952	$ 6,608,623	$ 5,032,926	$ 2,046,000	$ 1,500,000
1956	$ 7,778,702	$ 5,106,651	$ 2,886,000	$ 1,763,000
1960	$10,128,000	$ 9,797,000	$ 1,865,000	$ 1,142,000
1964	$16,026,000	$ 8,757,000	$ 6,370,000	$ 4,674,000
1968	$25,402,000	$11,594,000	$12,598,000	$ 6,143,000
1972	$61,400,000	$30,000,000	$ 4,300,000	$ 9,081,321
1976	$21,786,641	$21,800,000	$ 7,875,000	$ 9,081,321
1980	$29,188,888	$29,352,768	$14,600,000	$19,500,000
1984	$42,563,759	$41,828,811	n.a.	n.a.

a. Since 1976 total costs have been limited by law for any campaign
   that chooses to use public funds.
Source: Herbert Alexander, *Financing Politics*, Congressional Quarterly
   Press, Washington, D.C., 1980, pp. 5, 8, 10.

from his American Shipbuilding Company to the Nixon campaign—and then had his employees cover up before a grand jury (he eventually pleaded guilty in a federal court to charges of violating campaign law). Corporations and unions have allowed law, advertising, accounting, engineering, architectural, shipping, food service, and travel firms to overbill them—with the understanding that these firms would make contributions to certain campaigns.[9]

In 1972 Nixon's fund-raisers went through the files of regulatory agencies and the Justice Department, looking for matters involving large corporations. They then met with corporate executives, brought up these cases, and set specific figures which they expected to be contributed—usually on the basis of the net worth of the top leaders of the company. A list of more than 2000 such contributors, dubbed "Rosemary's baby," was kept by Nixon's secretary, Rosemary Woods.[10] Executives of many of these corporations pleaded guilty in federal courts to charges of contributing corporate funds; most of them were fined, and their companies later rewarded them for their trouble with bonuses, salary increases, or retirement settlements.

Reforms in campaign financing

The 1974 amendments to the Federal Election Campaign Act created the Presidential Election Campaign Fund, to which individuals can allocate $1 of their taxes each year. (Almost one-third of taxpayers do so, providing about $36 million annually.[11]) Major-party candidates for president can choose to finance their campaigns entirely from this fund, in which case they receive $20 million plus a cost-of-living adjustment (COLA) ($40.4 million in 1984). The law also provides that national committees may raise funds from private sources for an election campaign, but it limits each party to spending $3.4 million plus a COLA ($6.9 million in 1984). A candidate may forgo federal funds and raise money privately (in which case there is no limitation on spending), but none has ever done so.

Minor-party candidates (defined as those whose parties received between 5 and 25 percent of the popular vote in the preceding presidential election) are eligible for a proportional share of federal funds. New parties and independent candidates must raise funds privately, but they are eligible for reimbursement by the Treasury if they receive 5 percent or more of the popular vote.

Campaign financing today

The failure of the reforms. The reforms have not ended the influence of large contributors or of corporate and union money. Congress left loopholes in the 1974 and 1979 laws.

STATE PARTY BUILDING. State parties may spend unlimited amounts on party building and voter registration in presidential election years. These efforts can be privately funded, and there are no limits on contributions. In twenty-eight states corporations may make direct contributions, and in forty-one states unions may do so. Expenditures are not charged off against the limits on spending for presidential campaigns.[12]

The national parties have set up *soft-money accounts* for their state parties; supposedly they collect funds from private donors and then give them to the state parties, but actually they determine how the money will be spent as part of the national presidential campaign. The Republicans raised approximately $15 million in 1980 and twice that amount in 1984.[13] The Democrats received $1.3 million in 1980, most of it from unions, and they raised more than $10 million in 1984. Candidates may also decide to convert their nomination PACs into a nonfederal account which can receive contributions destined for state parties.

NATIONAL PARTY SUPPORT. Private donors may give $20,000 every two years to a national party. They may also give funds to tax-exempt foundations (which gives them a tax deduction) set up by the parties; these foundations pay for the mortgages and upkeep of national headquarters or provide educational materials and training for party workers.

"NONPARTISAN" VOTER REGISTRATION. Party professionals may establish "nonpartisan" organizations to raise money from private donors for voter registration activities. Leaders of the Reagan-Bush Finance Committee set up a supposedly nonpartisan group, Leadership '84, to raise $2 million for voter registration (also tax-deductible). Most of the contributions were made by Republican Eagles and contributors to the annual Republican House-Senate dinner. This money in turn was given to Americans for Responsible Government, a conservative organization, which then funneled it to grass-roots conservative organizations that intended to register nonvoters as Republicans.[14]

NONCOORDINATED CAMPAIGNS. Individuals and PACs may spend unlimited amounts to support a candidate, provided they do not coordinate their expenditures with those of the candidate's own committee. In 1980 conservative PACs spent more than $12 million for Reagan; in contrast, campaigns for Carter totaled only $46,000. Such *noncoordinated campaigns* in the past have favored the Republicans by bringing out conservative voters. The Supreme Court has ruled that these campaigns are protected by the First Amendment—to limit them, the Court decided, would infringe on freedom of speech.[15]

Campaigning for funds: The Republicans' advantage. Because federal funding for campaigns gives each major party exactly the same amount, many people have the impression that neither party has an advantage in terms of funding for presidential elections. But loopholes in the law give the Republicans an advantage: they raise more than $4 million a month in a presidential election year—most of it from small contributors who are contacted by mail. In 1984 they kicked off their campaign by raising $10.6 million (as of August) that could go for national and state party activities; this enabled them to run big advertising campaigns even during the Democratic primary season and the convention. Meanwhile, the Democrats were burdened with debts: their national committee owed $7 million for its new party headquarters and media center and for services that it had contracted for. Its contenders for the nomination owed $13.3 million![16] After the convention, the Democratic candidate must campaign furiously for funds to pay off nomination debts, to build up state and county parties, and to raise funds for the national party so that the Republicans' advantage can be neutralized.

CLOSE-UP

RICHARD M. NIXON AND WATERGATE. The Watergate crisis involved an attempt by President Nixon to interfere with the integrity of a presidential election—through burglary, wiretapping, intimidation, and dirty tricks—and then to cover up evidence of federal crimes when he was investigated by the FBI, congressional committees, and a federal grand jury. Ultimately, it culminated in an impeachment inquiry by the House of Representatives and in the president's resignation.

Richard Nixon entered Congress in 1946 as a Republican after defeating a Democratic incumbent with a dirty-tricks campaign. In 1950 he was elected to the United States Senate after a smear campaign against Helen Gahagan Douglas (which earned him the nickname "Tricky Dickie"). In 1952 he was elected vice president. After surviving a campaign scandal (it was revealed that he had accepted funds from some wealthy businesspeople) by means of a televised speech that won him popular support, Nixon went on to serve two terms as vice president. In 1960 he lost the presidential election to John F. Kennedy, amid charges of vote fraud by Democrats in Texas and Illinois, and in 1962 he lost the gubernatorial election in California.

Nixon seemed to have learned three lessons from his campaigns: never hesitate to use dirty tricks (his campaigns to get into the House and the Senate), never let them steal one from you (1960), and never take anything for granted (a 15-point lead dwindled to 1 in his 1968 presidential victory). Early in 1972, as the Democrats headed into their primary season, it appeared that they might nominate Edmund Muskie, a centrist candidate from Maine with a good chance of winning. The White House decided to derail Muskie and the other Democrats during the pri-

President Nixon and well-wishers on the campaign trail. (*Raymond Depardon: Magnum.*)

mary season. Dirty-tricks artists disrupted the Muskie campaign. The headquarters of the Democratic National Committee were burglarized, and phones were tapped.

On June 17, 1972, five Cubans were caught burglarizing the DNC headquarters at the Watergate complex. They named Gordon Liddy, counsel to the Committee to Reelect the President, as an accomplice. Nixon met with his two top aides, H. R. Haldeman and John D. Erlichman, and they decided to get the Central Intelligence Agency to impede the pending FBI investigation of the break-in by having the CIA claim that it was a national security matter. For a while the strategy worked, and Nixon won a landslide reelection victory.

But the break-in could not be contained. The Watergate burglars were sentenced to long prison terms by John Sirica, a federal judge, who hoped to prod them into talking. Nixon and his aides decided on a fallback strategy: if the probe pointed to higher-ups, they would blame Attorney General John Mitchell. John Dean, the White House counsel, realized that he was being set up as another fall guy for the break-in and cover-up, and he went to the Justice Department with his lawyer to confess his role in the matter and implicate other aides. On April 30, 1973, Nixon accepted the resignation of Haldeman and Erlichman, as the investigation spread to them.

The Senate Select Committee on Watergate, chaired by Sam Ervin, a senator from North Carolina, opened televised hearings. Dean's testimony implicated the president, but could not be corroborated. After Haldeman's aide, Alexander Butterfield, admitted that the White House had a taping system, the Justice Department's special prosecutor, Archibald Cox, demanded that Nixon turn over any recorded conversations about Watergate. Nixon turned over some of the evidence and then told Cox (as a Justice Department employee) not to press for the remaining tapes. Cox refused to back down, and on October 20, 1973, Nixon ordered his attorney general, Elliot Richardson, to fire Cox. Richardson resigned in protest, and Deputy Attorney General William Ruckelshaus also refused and was himself fired; finally another Justice Department official was found who would carry out Nixon's order. This "Saturday night massacre" unleashed a fire storm of protest. Shortly thereafter the House Judiciary Committee opened an impeachment investigation.

The House Committee deliberated until July 24, 1974, at which time it voted on three articles of impeachment. One involved obstruction of justice (the cover-up of White House involvement in the Watergate burglary), another involved abuse of power (misuse of the CIA, the FBI, and the Internal Revenue Service to harass opponents in the administration), and the third cited Nixon's refusal to answer committee subpoenas for evidence. Meanwhile the Supreme Court, in *U.S. v. Nixon,* ordered the president to turn his tapes and other evidence over to the federal district court judge who was trying the Watergate cases. (One of the tapes released later did, in fact, show that Nixon had conspired with his closest aides to cover up White House involvement in the Watergate crimes, in itself a crime and an impeachable offense.)

Shortly thereafter a delegation of senior Republicans in Congress, led by Barry Goldwater, a conservative, advised Nixon that the Senate would probably convict him if an impeachment trial were held. Nixon resigned from office on August 9, 1974. He was later pardoned for all Watergate-related crimes by his successor, Gerald Ford.[17]

ORGANIZING THE CAMPAIGN

Within the space of a few months, a candidate must transform the nomination organization—essentially a media operation and field unit which goes into a few states at a time—into an operation capable of waging fifty state contests simultaneously. To do so, the candidate must mesh the state and county party organizations with campaign aides, volunteer field organizations, and allied interest groups. This is easier said than done.

The inner circles

A candidate retains top advisers from the nominating campaign, but adds to them the party leaders and a few of the campaign operatives from rival camps. This results in overlapping circles, diffuse rather than clear lines of authority, a proliferation of titles ("campaign chairperson," "campaign director," "campaign manager," and so on), and general confusion. There are tensions between "the plane" (that is, wherever the candidate is and whomever the candidate is with) and "headquarters" and between both these units and the party's national committee.[18]

The party national committee

The presidential nominee takes control of the party's national committee, which conducts the state party-building and fund-raising operation and voter registration drives, encourages religious and ethnic groups to become allied with the party, and runs some of the polling efforts. By custom the nominee may name a new chairperson, although Walter Mondale's attempts to do so in 1984 met with such resistance at the convention that he backed down (he designated Bert Lance, a former official in the Carter administration who was forced to leave office after charges of improprieties in his dealings as a private banker). Usually, either candidates choose to mesh the committee with their own campaign—in which case they appoint the director and deputy director of the campaign's political operations or put their own staff aides in charge of these operations—or else they ignore the committee and run everything from their own campaign headquarters. The Republicans have gone toward complete integration of campaign efforts; the Democrats have vacillated between ignoring the committee and seeking to dominate it.

Walter Mondale chose Jimmy Carter's former budget director, Bert Lance, as Democratic National Chairman and then withdrew the nomination a few days later to avoid a party split. This was the first of many mishaps in his campaign. (*Larry Downing: Woodfin Camp.*)

The state and county parties

The state and county parties play an important role in a presidential election. If they are headed by chairpersons who are enthusiastic, they can be the focal point for the statewide contest. They can conduct effective voter registration and field canvassing operations and can deliver the state for the candidate. But often these parties favor another contender, have misgivings about the candidate, and believe that the ticket will lose. They may sit on their hands or concentrate on local elections. Candidates usually try to rally these parties by fund-raising and campaigning for local candidates, modifying their positions or taking stances that are regionally popular. But sometimes, as Goldwater, Humphrey, McGovern, Carter, and Mondale all discovered, nothing works. Failure to get state and local parties actively involved in a campaign is a good sign that the candidacy is doomed.

The Democratic Party is a bottom-up party in an election; the state and county parties concentrate on winning local elections and then give what resources and aid they can to the national ticket. They assume that a presidential nominee cannot help them, but can only snatch defeat from the jaws of their impending victories. The Republican Party is a top-down party; the Republicans rely on national funding and advertising and on the popularity of a presidential nominee to help them win state and local contests. They expect a presidential nominee to help them, although they are often quite disappointed when a state goes presidentially Republican but locally Democratic.

CAMPAIGN THEMES AND IMAGES

A candidate must develop a campaign theme and, through television, project a favorable image to more than 85 million households. Each campaign in 1984 spent more than $25 million on national advertising; the Mondale campaign estimated that it made more than 3 billion "gross impressions" on voters, with each household seeing an average of twenty commercials during the campaign. The Reagan campaign put more than forty top advertising executives in its "Tuesday group," including some who worked on the spectacular Michael Jackson advertisements for Pepsi-Cola. Marketing a presidential candidate is not dissimilar to marketing a product.

The overall theme

An incumbent president wants to run on peace, prosperity, and "you never had it so good." Consider the soft sell used in Reagan's 1984 commercials: "Life is better. . . ." "America's back. . . ." "People have a sense of pride they never thought they'd feel again." An incumbent president whose party is united can contrast this with what is happening in the opposition party. As James Lake, the director of communications for the Reagan-Bush campaign, put it, Republican advertisements during the primary season were designed to show "a positive presidency, an alternative to the trashing going on on the other side." A challenger tries to capitalize on the public's dissatisfaction with the party in power and to generate a protest vote, or a mandate for change. "If you're thinking of voting for Ronald Reagan in 1984," Mondale's campaign warned in one advertisement, "think of what will happen—in 1985." The themes and images must be unified, coherent, and fairly easy to understand. Complex arguments that are constantly shifting do more to confuse than enlighten voters. The campaigns that project the best image integrate the paid advertisements with the news coverage of the campaign: if the networks show the president dealing with foreign leaders, the advertisements also project the

One of the earliest television commercials—1952. Ike answers viewers' queries. (*These photos by Barry S. Surman from "The Spot: The Rise of Political Advertising on Television," M.I.T. Press.*)

One of the dirtiest commercials—1964. When the little girl finishes "counting down" from ten to zero as she picks petals off the daisy, an atomic bomb explodes. This anti-Goldwater ad was removed from the air by the Democrats after Republican protests.

One of the best commercials. Tanya, a Russian girl who died during the seige of Leningrad in World War II, is eulogized by President Nixon in this 1972 spot in which he promises to "work toward a more peaceful world."

One of the most boring commercials. Jimmy Carter introduces himself to the voters in 1976.

"leader" image. The operative slogan of a media campaign can be expressed in the acronym KISS ("Keep it simple, stupid.").

The political scientist James David Barber argues that the theme a campaign uses is likely to assume one of three forms: *partisan conflict* between the parties; a *crusade of conscience*, in which a hero is pitted against a villain; or a *campaign of reconciliation*, which offers the nation a chance for compromise, moderation, and the healing of wounds. The 1984 campaign was won with a campaign of reconciliation by the Republicans, who called on voters to endorse an "opportunity society" for all Americans. Barber believes that these themes run in a cycle, one following predictably after the other; even if this is not the case, his typology is useful in highlighting some of the themes candidates use.[19]

"REACH OUT":
A THEME COMMERCIAL FROM THE 1968 NIXON CAMPAIGN

Video	*Audio*
1. Opening network disclaimer: "A political announcement."	
2. Fade-up on zoom into the crowd. Nixon is surrounded by people.	Music up full.
3. Nixon moves through the crowd: various shots from different perspectives.	Nixon: "What has to be done, has to be done by the president and people together; or it won't be done at all. I am asking not that you give something *to* your country, but that you do something *with* your country; I am asking not for your gifts, but for your hands."
4. MCUs of the above sequence.	
5. WS Nixon and crowd separated by roof of a car. Zoom in to hands, as they reach toward each other.	
6. Montage of reaching hands and smiling faces—Nixon and people, increasing tempo.	Music up full.
7. Pull back from clasped hands of Nixon and people. Tilt from people in window to "Nixon for President" sign. Pan to CU of Nixon.	Music under. Nixon: "Together we can hardly fail, for there is no force on earth to match the will and spirit of the people of America."
8. Zoom out from CUI word "Nixon" to reveal sign "Nixon's the one" above Nixon cavalcade surrounded by cheering throngs. Hold. Fade-out.	Music up full. Music out.
9. Fade-up title: "This time vote like your whole world depended on it."	
10. Dissolve to title word, "Nixon." Zoom into CU. Hold. Fade-out.	(Source: Joe McGinnis, *The Selling of the President*, 1968, Simon and Schuster, New York, 1969, p. 250.)

Whatever else they do, candidates must offer meaningful reasons to support them—an overall theme with some excitement and drama. Examine "A Theme Commercial from the 1968 Nixon Campaign." Does this commercial really say anything? Hardly; yet with music and dramatic visual effects, it came alive on television and provided a dramatic theme.[20]

Media formats

The media formats available to candidates make it possible for them to project their themes and images in different ways.

Candidate-controlled formats. Television and radio commercials, billboards and posters, and newspaper and magazine advertising all give candidates maximum control. The message is produced solely by the campaign. The images emphasize traits which voters believe that presidents should have: strength, experience, competence, knowledge, character, and empathy.[21] Campaign commercials include "voter-in-the-street" endorsements; "feeling good" imitations of soft-drink ads; "introductions" to candidates and their families, "scare ads" claiming that opponents are warmongers or against social security; "issues" which position candidates; "looking at the record," or attacking past performance; and "experience" ads, about candidates' careers. Incumbent presidents use "Rose Garden" commercials that show them signing legislation or dealing with national problems and meeting with foreign leaders.

Images are the key to a campaign. The producer of Nixon's campaign commercials admitted:

> Let's face it, a lot of people think Nixon is dull. Think he's a bore, a pain in the ass. They look at him as the kind of kid who always carried a bookbag. Who was forty-two years old the day he was born. They figure other kids got footballs for Christmas, Nixon got a briefcase and he loved it. He'd always have his homework done and he'd never let you copy."[22]

According to the speech writer Ray Price: "It's not the man we have to change, but rather the received impression. And this impression often depends more on the medium and its uses than it does on the candidate himself."[23] A media blitz converted Nixon from a partisan street fighter into a mature, experienced statesman.

Candidate-dominated formats. Rallies, staged news events, and news releases all offer a candidate opportunities to emphasize themes or issues. Yet they provide no opportunity for the press to question or confront the candidate. Nixon capitalized on a closed media strategy in 1968 and 1972. He re-

Before jet travel, candidates rented trains and embarked on "whistle-stop" campaigns, as Franklin D. Roosevelt and John N. Garner did. Here they are photographed at a stop in Topeka, Kansas, in their 1932 campaign. (*Bettman Archive.*)

The Illinois-born Californian Ronald Reagan and the Connecticut reared ex-Texas Congressman George Bush get a warm welcome in Texas in 1984. (*Bill Fitzpatrick: White House.*)

fused to debate his opponents and stayed away from press conferences. He would travel to a city, stage some sort of dramatic pictorial event (in time for the evening news), and deliver a speech in an auditorium. His campaign provided the media with only one event each day, and therefore he controlled the daily campaign theme. Instead of holding real press conferences (he held only seven the year he ran for reelection), Nixon made commercials in which he was "interviewed" by a celebrity—his favorite was the football coach Bud Wilkinson—and he barred reporter from the set. Jules Witcover, a reporter, after trying to question Nixon one day, recalls, "No soap. Couldn't get to him. They hustled him off. Just the idea of your going up there and confronting the candidate—the guys around him were startled, they couldn't believe their eyes that you were doing this. And they learned, very quickly, and it didn't happen much after that."[24] "Without television Richard Nixon would not have a chance," admitted Frank Shakespeare, a campaign adviser. "He would not have a prayer of being elected because the press would not let him get through to the people. But because he is so good he will get through despite the press. The press doesn't matter anymore."[25]

Ronald Reagan used a similar strategy in 1984. "Our goal is to have one set of pictures and one story a day out of the White House," according to his press secretary.[26] A July tour of the polluted Chesapeake Bay, for example, allowed the president to demonstrate his concern for the environment. When reporters tried to question him about some controversial appointments to an environmental advisory committee, worsening conditions in the bay, and condemnation of his record by environmental organizations, staffers hustled them away, turned off the lights (so that the television cameras could not function), and put their hands over the camera lenses. Reagan held no news conferences all summer or fall.

Reporter-dominated formats. Interviews, press conferences, public affairs panel programs, and other formats in which candidates and their key staffers respond to reporters' questions are dangerous for candidates. A reporter can edit responses, determine the emphasis on each point, and slant the story. Some candidates, including losers (like Humphrey and McGovern) and winners (like Kennedy and Carter), believed that there was more mileage to be gained by being open and accessible. Their staffs helped rather than blocked the press. The result? Stories about staff disagreements, candidates' temper tantrums, conflicts over strategy and tactics, and even attempts to stroke the media. An open campaign may even given the impression that it is trying to manipulate voters because reporters get access to the media politics practitioners. Reporters have a field day covering an open campaign critically, while doing little to uncover what goes on in a totally controlled operation.

Media-controlled formats. Documentaries, investigative and analytical reports on issues and strategy, discussion of polling data, stories on campgin financing, and voter-in-the-street interviews—these can provide a picture of a campaign that is completely at variance with the one projected by the candidate.

Most media-controlled stories fall into one of several categories. The majority of stories involve the candidate's travels and speeches, what the news producer Av Westin refers to as "here he comes, there he goes" reporting; this is the traditional "wire service" style of objective, neutral reporting. Related are the "horse-race" stories: who is in the lead and who has the momentum.[27] Some reporters make their living as tipsters, giving us the latest gossip about campaign friction, while others are "assistant district attorneys" who report on campaign financing, potential conflict of interest, and the medical histories of the candidates and their staffers. Still others, breaking away from objective reporting, act as "assistant campaign managers" and offer candidates advice or even help out with campaign tasks (for example, the columnist George Will helped prepare Reagan for the 1980 debates)—roles which other journalists believe are inappropriate.[28]

Beginning in 1980 a constructive new format was introduced. Television networks were stung by the charges of the investigative reporter Brit Hume that the media report "what one candidate said, then they go and report what the other candidate said with equal credibility. They never get around to finding out if the guy is telling the truth. They just pass the speeches along without trying to confirm the substances of what the candidates are saying. What they pass off as objectivity is just a mindless kind of neutrality."[29] Reporters now often produce analytic pieces which demonstrate candidates' inconsistencies, exaggerations, or outright falsehoods.

Note: The media as sources of campaign information. Two-thirds of voters rely primarily on television for campaign information, compared with one-third who rely primarily on newspapers. Those who read the papers are much better informed, since the typical television story is the equivalent of no more than one or two paragraphs in a newspaper. Since most stories, whether in the print or the broadcast media, involve the horse race rather than the issues, it is not surprising that the media provide less information about issues than the candidates' own campaign advertisements do. The political scientists Thomas

Patterson and Robert McClure, in their analysis of election coverage, concluded that "television news adds little to the average voter's understanding of election issues. Network news may be fascinating. It may be highly entertaining. But it is simply not informative."[30] In 1972 during the last six weeks of the campaign, ABC, CBS, and NBC devoted a total of thirty-five, forty-six, and twenty-six *minutes*, respectively, to the issues.[31]

Polls

Using and misusing the independent polls. Horse-race coverage relies on public opinion polls.[32] These polls are conducted by independent concerns such as Gallup, Harris, and Roper; by people who work for candidates, such as David Garth Associates and Peter Hart Associates; by firms that work for the media (ABC/Harris, NBC/Associated Press, CBS/New York Times, and Time/Yankelovich); and by organizations which conduct statewide polls (Eagleton in New Jersey and Field in California, for example), either by themselves or under contract to local newspapers.

Different pollsters get different results.[33] There was a 14-point spread between the support for Reagan in the first week of July 1984 recorded by NBC and ABC polls. Some pollsters present the opinions of the adult population. Others question only registered voters (Harris, Roper, and CBS/New York Times) but differ by as much as 10 percent on the proportion of Republicans in their samples. Others use a sample of "likely voters" (Gallup and Time/Yankelovich). Sometimes, as is true of the NBC/Associated Press poll, only the opinions of voters who are registered and have made up their minds are recorded. Most of the published polls match up candidates and ask voters for their preferences or voting choices. Results differ depending on the wording of the questions. Some ask for feelings about candidates (evaluation of another). Others ask whether the respondent supports or intends to vote for the candidate (self-evaluation). Results are reported as if a candidate were ahead or behind in a race. But an election is not a race; it is a single, discrete event, held on a single day. In one sense, the only poll result that really counts is the vote on election day. But the results of published polls can affect campaign contributors, workers, and even voters.[34]

Candidates who are ahead in the polls play them up. Those who are behind try to ignore them. They claim that voters have not really made up their minds and that the campaign will catch on once all its themes have been presented. They emphasize the statistical margin of error (the usual claim is that there is a 95 percent probability that the poll results are accurate to within 3 percentage points) if the results are close. They point to inconsistencies among different polls. They note the large number of undecided voters and claim that those who support their opponents are "mushy" and can be won away. They concentrate on gaining ground and momentum rather than on standings.[35] They point to the incorrect calls made by pollsters (Gallup missed in 1976, and Harris called 1968 wrong), ignoring the fact that in most elections the final Gallup and Harris polls are within 1 or 2 points of the actual results.

Candidates' polls. Presidential candidates run much more sophisticated polling operations than do news services. The Republican Party, in 1980 and 1984, used PINs (Political Information Systems), which consisted of a data bank with information on the 3041 counties: census data, economic information from the Bureau of Labor Statistics, demographic and market research data,

---

WORLD SERIES WINNER KEY TO PRESIDENCY?

Jon Margolis, a Washington correspondent for *The Chicago Tribune*, claims that if in a presidential election year the National League wins the World Series, the Democrats will win the election. Since 1903 there have been twenty-one presidential elections, and the theory has held up fifteen times.

Newton's law (not Isaac, but Wayne W.) holds that in a good vintage year for the Bordeaux wines of France, a Democrat wins the presidency.

The party that is rated ahead in the October Gallup poll on the ability to handle the nation's most important problem has won every presidential election since 1964.

The *Weekly Reader's* poll of 100,000 elementary school and high school students has picked every winner since 1956. In 1984 Reagan scored higher than Mondale in this poll, 64 to 33 percent.

---

voter registration data, voting records from past elections, spending patterns in congressional races from the Federal Elections Commission, polling data sponsored by state parties and PACs, and nightly tracking polls sponsored by the RNC. It also used a market research technique, TRACE, which allowed members of a test audience who viewed commercials or the debates to record positive or negative feelings about them on hand-held calculators; the calculators had five buttons that allowed viewers to record their reactions (ranging from most positive to most negative), and the data were fed into a computer.

This information was used to simulate the effects of any change in Republican (or Democratic) strategy, tactics, or campaign rhetoric on each county's projected vote. Should Reagan play up environmental issues, or should he play them down? Should he move to the center on social issues, or should he take a conservative position? The computerized system could forecast the effect of any move.[36]

Presidential debates

The centerpiece of recent presidential elections has been the debate between the major-party candidates. In the first three—1960 1976, and 1980—the party that controlled the White House lost the election. Mondale won a narrow victory in the 1984 debates, but changed few votes, a reversal of the previous pattern. Still, debates may be the great equalizer, offsetting advantages of incumbency, funding, and organization.

The stakes. Debates attract a huge audience: 107 million adults in 1960 and 122 million in 1976 viewed at least one in the series, while more than 100 million saw the debates in 1980 and 1984. Debates raise voters' interest and provide information. In close contests many voters wait for the debates before making their decision. Strong Democrats and Republicans are likely to watch selectively (that is, they think that the candidate of their party has won the debates), and they are least likely to reconsider their choice. Weaker identifiers, independents, and voters with doubts about their party's nominee are likely to use the debates to help them decide. Those who watch debates tend to vote on the basis of the issues, while those who do not watch are more likely to vote on the basis of personality.[37]

Debates may change votes. They can soften up viewers by dispelling negative impressions. Roper polls showed that 6 percent of the public—4 million voters—based their votes in 1960 on the debates, and of these, Kennedy won 72 percent. We cannot tell whether he would have won these votes otherwise,

Nixon and Kennedy in their fourth presidential debate in 1960. (*AP: Wide World.*)

Reagan and Mondale in 1984 continued the modern tradition of presidential debates. (*Larry Downing: Woodfin Camp.*)

but the election was close and his good performance must have helped. In 1980 polls shows that Reagan picked up ground among undecided voters and independents.[38] In 1984 after the first debate, Reagan lost a few points among undecided voters, but later he won them back.

To debate or not. The public overwhelmingly favors debates, but after 1960 none were held in 1964, 1968, or 1972, when at least one of the candidates refused to debate because he had nothing to gain. Ford challenged Carter to debate in 1976, violating the "rule" that an incumbent president does not give the challenger equal standing. But Ford was in no position to ignore his opponent. He had entered the White House via the Twenty-Fifth Amendment rather than popular election, was nominated by a badly split convention, ran as the candidate of the minority party, and was tarnished by his pardon of Nixon for Watergate-related crimes. He began campaigning 30 points behind in the polls. Why, then, did Carter agree to debate? Because his lead was slipping as a result of an interview he had given to *Playboy* in which he discussed the "lust" he sometimes felt for women and in which he used swear words.

In 1980 Carter was behind in the polls and eager to debate. He wanted to portray Reagan as an extremist. At first Reagan ducked, but then when his campaign coverage turned sour, he changed his mind. He was also worried that Carter might pull a presidential "October surprise" (like negotiating an end to the Iranian hostage crisis). Anyway, how could a former actor like Reagan resist performing on the biggest stage, and before the largest audience, of his career?

Rehearsal and performance. Candidates prepare for debates by rehearsing in studio mock-ups. Their top campaign officials prepare briefing books which provide background, as well as script segments which lay out issues, defend their record, and attack their opponents. They are coached on posture, mannerisms, and diction.

Candidates do best when they give long answers which directly address the concerns of the audience. They do worst when they try to rebut what their opponent has said or try to contradict the opponent's arguments. Scoring debating points is less important than presenting ideas and themes to a national audience. Candidates must keep on their own strongest ground, define the terms in which the issues are framed, and use vivid examples—even parables and metaphors to illustrate their point. They learn how to slide away from questions put to them by a panel of reporters or by the other candidate and to get back to a planned segment.[39] They can calculate a show of emotion. Reagan's exasperated gibe at Carter—"There you go again"—was an eloquent retort to what Reagan claimed was Carter's distortion of Reagan's positions. (Of course, Reagan was aided in the 1980 debate because his campaign had obtained access to Carter's briefing books, and therefore Reagan knew exactly what Carter would say.) In 1984, when Reagan used that line again, Mondale was prepared, and he effectively counterattacked with a direct question ("Remember when you last used that line, Mr President?") that disconcerted Reagan.

Debates give candidates a chance to neutralize an issue. Consider the second sentence of Reagan's opening remarks in the 1980 debate: "And I'm only here to tell you that I believe with all my heart that our first priority must be world peace. . . ." Later he added, "I have seen four wars in my lifetime. I'm a father of sons; I have a grandson. I don't ever want to see another generation of young Americans bleed their lives into the sandy beachheads of the Pacific . . ." and so on.[40]

Candidates aim their comments at specific groups: independents, voters who often switch back and forth, potential defects from the opposition, and members of their party who have doubts. In 1984 Mondale, according to his pollster, Peter Hart, aimed his appeals primarily at blue-collar workers and Catholics, whom Hart described as "shaky as a bowl of Jell-O."

Media verdicts. The media not only report the debates but also announce the winner and the loser. This results in a *sleeper effect:* the cumulative impact which media coverage, subsequent analysis, and verdicts can have on viewers. Consider what happened in 1976. Ford did well in the first debate; then in the second debate he startled knowledgeable people with the misstatement that the people of eastern Europe do not live under Soviet domination. Initially most viewers were unaffected by this slip. But Ford took more than a week to admit that he had made a mistake, and the error and his refusal to concede it became a major media issue. ("Is Ford too dumb to run the country?" "Is he too stubborn to admit that he made a mistake?") Ford's campaign manager, Don Chaney, argued later that "it was not a significant item until after it received extensive comment and coverage in the press."[41]

In 1984 the first New York Times/CBS survey of voters, take just after the debate, showed that Mondale won a narrow victory over Reagan—43 to 34. After a week of media coverage, polls showed that Mondale was the winner— 66 to 17. It is not always how the candidates did, but how the media say they did, that determines who won or lost a debate.

The winner of a debate can expect an infusion of cash. After Mondale's success the Democratic Victory Fund swelled with checks dated that evening. The 19,800 fund-raising parties held during the debate raised more than $4.5 million. More people had favorable views of Mondale after his victory: his favorable ratings went up in the Washington Post/ABC polls from 41 to 57 percent in the following week.[42]

But winners cannot always expect to get votes on the basis of their performance in a debate. Most voters believed that in the first debate, Reagan simply had an "off night." By defusing fears that he would cut social security and by lightly poking fun at the age issue ("I will not make an issue of my opponent's youth and inexperience"), Reagan gained more than he lost. As a result of the debates Reagan gained ground on two issues: controlling nuclear arms and keeping the nation out of war. Mondale picked up at most 3 points in the first debate and none in the second, according to Peter Hart—and thereafter began his steady slide to defeat.

ISSUE AND DEBATE

THE FUTURE OF PRESIDENTIAL DEBATES. *The background.* Debates were held in 1960 and have been held in every presidential election year since 1976 under the auspices of the League of Women Voters. A panel of reporters (acceptable to both candidates) questions the candidates, and they are given time to rebut their opponent's statements. Debates have not yet become a routine feature of presidential elections. One or both candidates may refuse to debate (as happened in 1964, 1968, and 1972). The ground rules are negotiated by their staffers and change from one election to the next. Minor candidates, such as John Anderson in 1980, may participate in a separate debate but not be invited to the main event, but there are no criteria for inclusion or exclusion.

The Proposals for reform. Some reforms would take control over the debates away from the candidates and the League of Women Voters and have them organized by a presidential debate commission. One idea is to have former presidential and vice presidential candidates from both major parties serve. A proposal to strengthen the two-party system would allow the Republican and the Democratic national committees to sponsor party-oriented debates which would include Cabinet members, governors, and congressional leaders.

Newton Minow, the former chairman of the Federal Communications Commission, has proposed a series of such party-controlled national debates which would not be confined to the election season. He has also proposed that the national committee of the opposition party have the right of reply to any presidential radio or television address made during the ten months preceding a presidential election or the ninety days preceding a midterm congressional election. During the election season the candidates on the presidential ticket would receive six half-hour prime-time slots (minor-party candidates would receive proportional allocations).

Other proposed reforms take aim at the panels which question candidates. Some reporters ask frivolous questions or seem poorly informed. Few challenge candidates when they make errors or falsify facts. Perhaps candidates should not be able to "veto" panelists. The pool could be broadened to include presidential scholars and former officials. The television networks have proposed that distinguished public figures chair the debates and serve on the panels, but candidates have held out for newscasters. The networks have also suggested that candidates hold real debates, in which each would directly address the other and ask direct questions, with no holds barred. Candidates have refused to engage in such real debates; they prefer panels of reporters and the familiar "news conference" format.

Another idea is for candidates to participate in "town meetings" so that a cross section of the public could question them; the format would be similar to that of William Buckley's *Firing Line* or public television's *MacNeil, Lehrer Newshour*.

The pros.   Those who favor these proposals argue that the existing format allows a front-runner either to get away without really debating or to insist on rules that minimize the effect of a debate. Candidates can get by using their basic stump speeches. Debates do not test their knowledge or their ability to react under pressure. What is needed, the proponents of reform claim, is a lengthy series of debates on the issues, organized by the parties, that would focus not merely on presidential candidates but also on the entire spectrum of party leadership so that the public could make the most informed choice.

The cons.   Those who oppose reform argue that the League of Women Voters has done an excellent job of mediating between candidates and fashioning debates that take into account the particular conditions of each campaign. They believe that a new commission at best would duplicate the league's work and at worst would lock debates into an inflexible format. They believe that reporters do ask the candidates tough questions and that their questioning is more likely to keep the candidates focused on the issues than a straight debate would. They do not believe that the public would be interested in a series of party-sponsored debates on the issues, and they claim that the audience would be small and would not include the least informed voters, who need debates the most.

The outlook.   It is not likely that Congress will legislate ground rules for presidential debates, though it has been suggested that any candidate or party that accepts public funding be obligated to participate in forums devised by a national commission. In 1985 the two major parties announced an agreement to sponsor the 1988 presidential debates.

HOW VOTERS DECIDE

To understand how candidates appeal to different kinds of voters, we must discuss the way voters think about parties, candidates, and campaigns.

The American voter

Surveys conducted in the 1952, 1956, and 1960 elections showed that most voters were only mildly interested in politics, took little interest in campaigns, and did not participate in politics. Most did not think much or know much about issues. They were inconsistent, taking liberal or conservative positions on different issues, and they changed their positions from one year to the next.[43]

Party identification—the standing decision to favor one party over the other—was strong in these years and remained fixed from one election to the next. Like religious or ethnic identity, it was usually transmitted from one generation to the next within a family.[44] Straight-ticket voting was high, and even when voters defected (as many Democrats did to vote for Eisenhower), they retained their original party identification.

Although issues and candidates were more important factors in voting choice than party identification, feelings about parties conditioned how people felt about candidates and issues. Moreover, although issues and candidates might change from one election to the next, party identifications remained the same: knowing the party identifications of voters was the best way to predict voting choice.

The changing American voter. Since Goldwater's campaign in 1964, presidential politics has become more ideological and issue-oriented. Moderates and conservatives fought pitched nomination battles in the Republican Party in 1964, 1976, and 1980, and liberals and moderates have fought it out in the Democratic Party in every contest since 1968. Voters have become more ideological and issue-oriented as well. They care more and know more about issues. They have begun to array issues, candidates, and themselves along liberal-conservative dimensions. They are less likely to identify themselves as moderates. They have become more consistent in taking liberal or conservative stands on related issues, and they are less likely to change their views from one year to the next.[45]

Party identifications have become less significant in influencing voters' positions on candidates and issues, and voters rely less on party identification in deciding for whom to vote. Both parties have lost ground to independents, largely as a result of young voters' decision not to affiliate with either party; about half of young voters had become unaffiliated by 1976. Between 10 and 20 percent of voters have switched parties or have become independents between each election. They have fewer positive feelings about parties and think that the parties are not responsive on issues.[46] By 1972 almost half the voters had become ticket switchers, up from one-fourth in the 1950s. Many southern Democrats have become *presidential Republicans*—they have maintained their Democratic affiliation but vote regularly for Republican candidates in presidential elections. In the north some moderate and liberal Republicans have become more independent. (See Table 9-2.)

Since the 1964 elections, issues have become more significant for voters, and party identification has become less important, as Figure 9-5 indicates. In 1980, three-fifths of the voters surveyed could place themselves and the two major-party candidates on the issues. More than half perceived important differences

Table 9-2. Defection rates of party identifiers

	Democratic victories: 1960, 1964, 1976	Republican victories: 1968, 1972, 1980
	Percent of voters who defected from their parties	
Strong Democrats	7.7	15.3
Weak Democrats	23.7	43.7
Independent Democrats	16.7	45.3
Independent Republicans	17.3	15.3
Weak Republicans	26.0	8.7
Strong Republicans	5.0	3.7

Source: Arthur H. Miller and Warren E. Miller, "Partisanship and Performance: Rational Choice in the 1976 Presidential Elections," APSA paper, 1977; Paul Abramson et al., *Change and Continuity in the 1980 Elections*, Congressional Quarterly Press, Washington, D.C., 1982, table 8.4, p. 167.

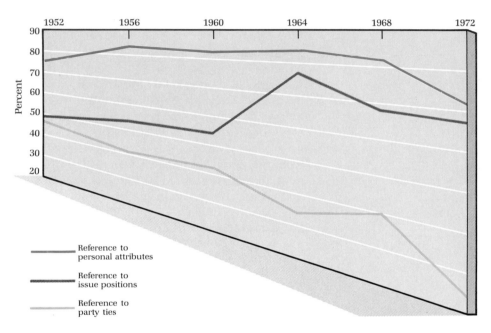

Figure 9-5. Beginning with the 1964 election, voters evaluated candidates increasingly in terms of their positions on the issues, while their party identification played less of a role. This helps account for Nixon's reelection and Reagan's two victories in a period in which the majority of voters retained their Democratic affiliations. (Source: Norman H. Nie, Sidney Verba, and John R. Petrocik, *The Changing American Voter*, A Twentieth Century Fund Study, 1976, Twentieth Century Fund, New York, fig. 10.6, p. 167.)

between Carter and Reagan; of this group, four-fifths perceived these differences correctly, and 70 percent cast their ballots for the candidate who was closer to their own position (though not necessarily because of that positioning).[47]

Voters have come to link their ideology with their party identification. In the 1980 elections, of those voters who supported a major-party candidate for president, 70 percent of the liberals voted for Carter and 30 percent voted for Reagan, while 72 percent of the conservatives voted for Reagan and 28 percent voted for Carter. These figures are associated with party identification: most Republicans backed Reagan (and most identified themselves as conservative), and many conservative Democrats also supported him; Democrats who voted for Carter were more likely to be liberal than those who defected to vote for Reagan. The ideological lineup was due in part to party identification, just as party identification was due in part to the different positions of the parties and the candidates. By the 1980s, for many voters party identification had become a *conscious* decision, based on issues and ideology, rather than simply a *standing* decision, based on habit, family ties, or social affiliation.[48]

The normal vote. The Republicans have some advantages when they begin a campaign: access to more money, better discipline within their party structure, and more effective image-making and polling apparatuses. But the Democrats also have an advantage: a majority of party identifiers, as Figure 9-6 shows.

The significance of this imbalance is best explained by using the concept of the ***normal vote:*** the calculation as to how the election would be decided if there were no candidates and no campaigning—only party identification. (The calculation also takes into account expected turnout rates.[49]) The normal vote is therefore not a prediction of the actual vote. (In this sense, *normal* is a misnomer.) It is simply a way of handicapping the contest. Since the Democrats have more identifiers, in the absence of a campaign they should win every election.

The normal-vote concept affects the strategies of the two parties. Democratic candidates emphasize party identification and party loyalty, while Republican candidates sometimes do not even mention their party affiliation.

Stable factors in voting. Party identification remains fairly stable over time. So do turnout rates (which have declined only a few percentage points from one election to the next). The tendency for different kinds of people to support one party or another often remains stable from one election to the next. Changes may occur, but they are usually minor variations. Party identification, group support of a party, and turnout rates are the ***stable factors.*** They tell us which party has the advantage going into a campaign.

Although historically the Republicans have had higher turnout rates, the Democrats have had the advantage in terms of group support: in most elections between 1932 and 1980 this included blacks, Hispanics, Jews, Catholics, eastern and southern Europeans, union members and their families, and southerners. Combined with their advantage in party identification, the Democrats have had an impressive edge in the stable factors.

But the Democrats often lose presidential elections. Between 1948 and 1980, even with their advantages, they received 291.6 million presidential votes, com-

Figure 9-6. While Democratic and Republican party identifications have declined gradually since 1936, independent identifications have increased sharply. In the wake of President Reagan's reelection many polls showed the Republicans closing the gap with the Democrats. If this holds through the 1986 midterm elections, it may signal a fundamental realignment in party identification. (Source: 1920–1944 data reconstructed by Kristi Andersen from Norman H. Nie, Sidney Verba, and John R. Petrocik, *The Changing American Voter,* A Twentieth Century Fund Study, 1976, Twentieth Century Fund, New York, fig. 5.1, p. 83. Later data from SRC, Institute for Social Research, National Election Studies.)

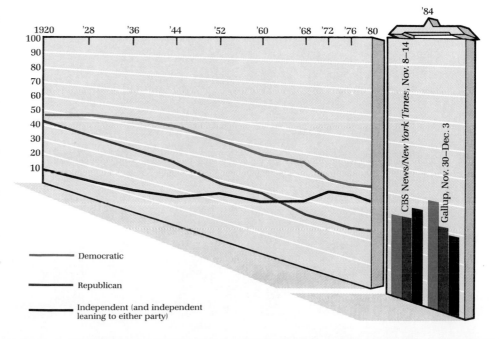

pared with 314.8 million received by the Republicans. They averaged 43 percent of the vote between 1968 and 1980, compared with 51 percent for the Republicans, and in 1984 they were crushed 60 to 40 by Reagan. Clearly, the normal vote and the stable factors cannot explain actual election results.

Dynamic factors in voting.   Personality, issues and ideology, and specific events (such as the impact of Watergate in 1976, the Iranian hostage crisis in 1980, and the selection of a woman vice presidential nominee in 1984) are the ***dynamic factors*** in any campaign because they change from one election to the next. The stable factors *structure* a race (for example, the Democrats always have the advantage in terms of party identification), but the dynamic factors *decide it*, allowing the Republicans to overcome the initial edge of the Democrats.

In recent elections the dynamic factors have become more significant than the stable factors. There are more independents and voters whose attachments to parties are weak. Members of ethnic, religious, and economic groups are less likely to follow leadership endorsements or even to take their group affiliation into account when deciding on a candidate. Turnout rates are no longer quite so predictable. The so-called normal vote is harder to calculate and is of less value. The impact of convention coverage, campaign commercials, and presidential debates—all dynamic factors—has increased.

Retrospective voting.   Voters also look at the record. They think retrospectively about how candidates and parties have acted in the past in order to make a judgment about who should govern in the future. The simplest kind of ***retrospective voting*** involves meting out rough justice to incumbents.[50] Voters can reward good performance and punish bad performance (in 18 of the last 22 elections through 1984, either a president or a vice president was running). There is a high correlation between a favorable evaluation of a president and a subsequent vote for reelection.[51] In a New York Times/CBS poll taken in August 1984, 72 percent of the voters who thought that the United States was better off than it had been four years earlier were planning to vote for Reagan; only 15 percent said that they would vote for Mondale. Of those who thought that the

Reprinted by permission:
Tribune Media Series, Inc.

country was worse off, 58 percent planned to vote for Mondale, and only 20 percent planned to vote for Reagan.

Voters can also make *projective comparisons:* they look at the past record of the candidates and their parties in terms of missed opportunities—what would have happened if the party out of power had been in the White House for the past four years. Would things have been better or worse? Ironically, hard times might actually reinforce support for an incumbent: when unemployment goes up during a Democratic administration, most Democrats think that things would have been even worse if the Republicans had been in office; when inflation goes up during a Republican administration, most Republicans think that the Democrats would have done even worse.

Candidates ask unsophisticated voters for a protest vote, as Reagan did when, as part of his closing remarks during the debate with Carter in 1980, he asked, "Are you better off than you were four years ago?" Mondale's attempt to raise the same question in 1984 backfired: polls showed that a majority of Americans (especially younger white males, who were crucial to the Democrats' success) believed that they were better off, gave the Republicans the credit for it, and intended to vote for Reagan.

Swaying voters: Campaign strategy and tactics

The Democrats' campaign strategy and tactics are designed to reinforce existing party identifications and group allegiances; the Republicans' campaign strategy and tactics arc designed to break them up and create new alignments.

Party coalitions. Parties have concentrated on different regions and on different racial, ethnic, religious, and occupational groups. This does not mean that all members of a group vote for one party or that all Republicans are members of some groups and that all Democrats are members of others. It does mean that there is a greater *probability* that some kinds of people will identify with a party and vote for its candidate than can be accounted for by chance (Figure 9-7).

ETHNIC, RACIAL, AND RELIGIOUS GROUPS. The Republicans do well among white Protestants in the north who are of English, Scottish, Welsh, Scotish-Irish, or German descent; among the wealthy and well educated; among farmers in the north and the midwest; and among male voters between the ages of 18 and 24. A majority of white Protestants have voted for Republican candidates in every presidential election since 1944 (with the single exception of

Figure 9-7. Each pie chart shows how voters from various groups split between the Democratic and Republican presidential candidates in the six presidential elections through 1980. White indicates votes for third-party candidates. (Source: *Gallup Opinion Index,* December 1980, pp. 6–7.)

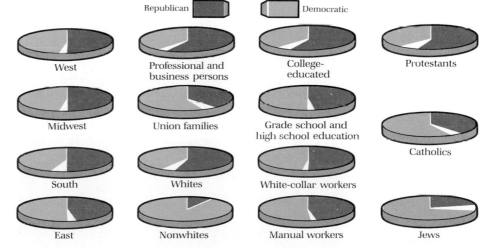

that held in 1964). In 1980 Reagan received 61 percent of this vote, and in 1984 he received close to 70 percent.

Blacks are almost exclusively Democratic identifiers and voters. Since 1964 they have given at least 85 percent of their vote to Democratic candidates. Hispanics give a large margin to Democrats (except for Cuban Americans in Florida, who register 60 percent Republican). Together, these minorities account for one-fifth of the Democratic vote. The Democrats count on union members and their families, who provide between one-third and one-fourth of their votes. Jews since 1944 have been the most heavily Democratic of all religious groups: the Democrats won a majority from them in every election between 1944 and 1980 (when Carter won only a plurality), and in 1984 they won two-thirds of their vote. Because of their small numbers (5.7 million, a declining proportion of the total electorate), they are not as influential as other groups: in the past three elections they have provided only 1 vote in 20 received by Democrats. Nevertheless, because of the large numbers of Jewish voters in the big states (New York, California, Pennsylvania, Florida, and New Jersey), a swing in their vote can have significant consequences in the electoral college. Solid majorities of Catholics voted Democratic in 6 of the 7 elections between 1944 and 1968, but in 1972 and 1980 the Republicans won a majority of their vote, and in 1984 they won 58 percent. Upper-income and Polish and Irish Catholics are most likely to shift toward the Republicans.

GENDER. Women have become increasingly more Democratic in their party orientation. Today women constitute 60 percent of Democratic identifiers and 40 percent of Republican identifiers; for men, the figures are reversed. The gender gap (that is, differentials in voting between men and women) can favor either party. In 1980 Reagan won a far greater margin of votes from men than from women in defeating Carter. In the 1982 congressional elections, there was a wide gender gap going the other way: the Democrats won the women's vote (62 to 38), while barely winning the male vote (52 to 48). But in the 1984 presidential election, contrary to the hopes of Democratic strategists, party identification and the nomination of a woman vice presidential candidate did not keep women in the Democratic column. Only 3 percentage points separated men and women in their support for Reagan, and he won majorities from both.

While the Democrats argue that the Republicans have a "female problem," the Republicans make a more compelling case that the Democrats have a "male problem." Only 30 percent of white males now vote Democratic in presidential elections, and a sharply declining percentage of them identify with the Democratic Party. The Democrats never quite figured out how to play the gender gap in 1984. In the debates both Mondale and Ferraro tried to show how "tough" they could be on the Russians, in an unsuccessful attempt to "out-macho" the Republicans and win back the defecting white males.

INSTABILITY OF GROUP ALIGNMENTS. Unlike the situation in the New Deal period (1932–1948), today the level of *polarization* is low: in most cases the groups are split, with only a small margin between the parties; in only a few cases (for example, blacks and Jews) are groups overwhelmingly aligned with one party. Members of most groups have only weak party attachments, and so in any given election just about any group can split or provide a decisive margin to the candidate of either major party. Reagan won a majority or plurality in 1980 from several groups that traditionally support Democrats. In 1964 Johnson won large majorities from several groups that usually vote Republi-

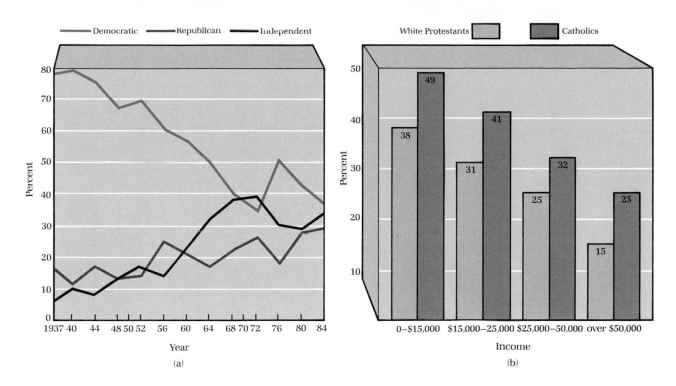

Democratic   Republican   Independent   White Protestants   Catholics

(a)

(b)

Figure 9-8. The key groups in presidential politics are upper-income Catholics in the north and upper-income white Protestants in the south. When these groups defect from the Democratic Party, its presidential candidates lose. Similarly, if Democrats can induce defections from white working-class Protestants in the north, they have a good chance of winning the industrial states. (a) Republicans have made small but steady gains in party identification among southern whites while Democrats have suffered large losses since 1936. Most of those defecting from the Democrats became independents and voted either for Republican or third-party candidates (in 1948 and 1968). The Democrats have reversed the tide only once since 1952, when a Georgian, Jimmy Carter, headed their ticket. (Source: Gallup polls.) (b) The 1980 data for percent of vote received by Carter show Carter's failure to hold the votes of Catholic Democratic identifiers, even those in lower-income groups. (Source: SRC National Election Studies.)

can. The Republicans won the south in 1972, the Democrats retook it in 1976 and then lost it again in 1980, and so on.

Breaking up coalitions. The Democrats win presidential elections by minimizing defections from their existing coalition and by making inroads among lower-income white Protestant voters in the north by emphasizing unemployment and other economic issues. The Republicans win by adding to their existing base: they go after white southerners, conservative Democrats in all regions, and upper-income Catholic and Jewish voters. The Republicans win by keeping white Protestants together, regardless of class differences, while splitting Catholic voters on class lines. The Democrats win by keeping Catholic voters with them, while splitting Protestant voters along class lines. (See Figure 9-8.)

THE SOUTH. The Republican Party promotes itself as the party of states' rights, decentralization, local control, neighborhood schools, and new federalism. The new breed of Republican "populists" attack the Democrats for high interest rates and inflation, which hurt working-class people as well as the wealthy. They paint the Democratic Party as the party of big government trampling on states' rights, beholden to minorities, and willing to weaken the country's defenses. Their appeal to white voters in the south has increased. The south no longer votes Democratic in presidential elections, as it did (with few exceptions) for a century after the Civil War.

THE NORTH. The Republicans have broken up the New Deal coalition of union members, Catholics, and Jews. They portray the Democratic Party as a "permissive" party when it comes to abortion, gay rights, prayer in schools, drugs, crime, busing, and other social and family issues. The Republicans favor aid to parochial and private schools, an issue which unites Protestant fundamentalists and Catholics. They no longer emphasize issues such as prohibition of gambling or the sale of alcoholic beverages—issues which once divided

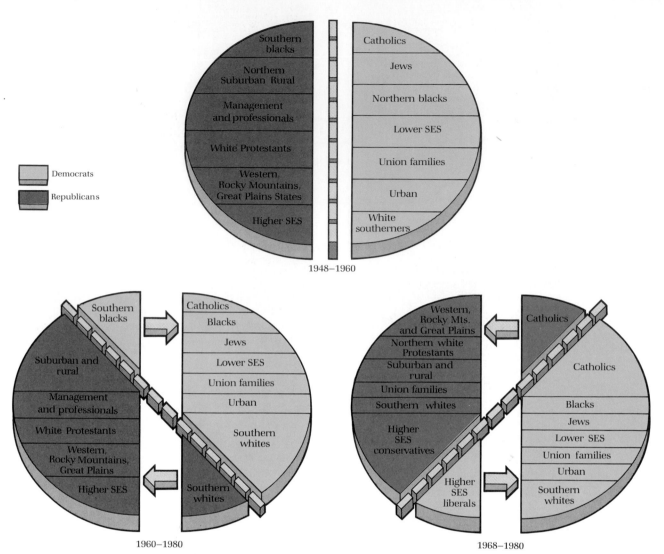

Figure 9-9. The majority New Deal coalition put together by the Democratic party pitted unions against management, and religious and racial minorities and working-class voters against wealthier white Protestants in the North; and it took advantage of the "solid south" heritage of the Civil War. After 1964 Republicans broke up this coalition. First they emphasized their opposition to busing and used a "southern strategy" to become competitive in the south. As southern whites joined the Republican party, southern blacks left and became Democrats: on balance the Republicans gained. Later, Republicans emphasized the "social issues" to bring northern Catholics and southern fundamentalists to their party. In response to their conservative stance, some moderate Republicans in the north defected; but once again on balance the Republicans gained many more voters than they lost, especially in presidential elections.

Protestants and Catholics. Instead, they unite these groups with calls for a war on drugs and pornography. Issues of race (for example, busing, quotas, and affirmative action) and morality displace issues of class, on which the Democrats often have greater appeal. "We are for life and against abortion," Reagan told parishioners at St. Ann's church in Newark during the 1984 campaign. "We are for prayer in the schools, we are for tuition tax credits and, in Central America, we are rather more inclined to listen to the testimony of his holiness the Pope than the claims of the Communist Sandinistas."[52]

CROSSCUTTING ISSUES. The Republicans have found issues which cut across existing divisions, break up the New Deal coalition, unite their followers, and divide the Democrats. Their stand on racial issues may alienate the small number of liberal Republicans, but meanwhile the Democrats are bitterly divided: blacks debate Jews on quotas and affirmative action; southern conservatives who are opposed to busing fight black activists in the courts; and many Democrats switch to the Republican Party. On family and social issues the Republicans have lost the liberal wing, but they have gained support from southern Protestant fundamentalists and northern Catholics (Figure 9-9).

REFERENCE GROUPS. Campaigns also try to get voters to think of themselves as members of groups which the party has helped. People have many group affiliations; they may be veterans, union members, suburbanites, or churchgoers, for example. Usually they identify with a party and support a candidate on the basis of a few of these identifications. The campaign gets voters to make other self-identifications: union members who expect to vote Democratic may start thinking of themselves as suburbanites concerned about inflation and interest rates—which may induce them to vote Republican.

The Democrats campaign by reaffirming traditional party identifications and reassuring voters that their party is still better for the unions, Jews, blacks, the south, and so forth. Rather than try to convince voters otherwise, the Republicans have created a set of reference groups with which voters can identify—for example, middle Americans, forgotten Americans, and the new American majority. Their campaign advertising is geared toward convincing people (such as family-oriented middle- and working-class taxpayers) that they are members of these groups and that their interests are best served by the Republicans. In addition, their rhetoric creates reference groups with which a majority of people do not identify—welfare cheats, career criminals, liberal elitists, secular humanists, drug abusers, and women's liberationists—suggesting that the Democratic Party is the party of these and similar groups.

TRENDS: ELECTION RESULTS AND THEIR MEANING

Election results tell us much more than which candidate will occupy the White House for the next four years. The voting returns are connected to governance: how a candidate campaigns and how voters make up their minds have much to do with how the country will be governed.

Types of presidential elections

We can classify elections according to their impact on the stable factors: party identification, party coalitions, and turnout rates. In some elections the campaigns make no impact on these factors, while in others there are dramatic changes.[53] Each type of election has a different impact on presidential power, the prospects for presidential leadership of Congress, and the policies that the White House might pursue.

The maintaining election. An election in which there is little or no measurable change in the stable factors and in which the party with the normal-vote advantage wins is a *maintaining election.*

The reinforcing election. An election that is won by the party with the normal-vote advantage, which gives it even greater strength in terms of the stable factors, is a *reinforcing election.* It gives the president great influence with the party; not only has the president won, but the victory also helps other candidates on the ticket and attracts new party supporters.

The critical election. Conversely, consider an election which is won by the party with the normal-vote advantage but in which the advantage in terms of the stable factors decreases. Voters defect from the party, one or more groups leave the party coalition, and turnout among supporters is down. Even though the party won, the new president may be in trouble: the president may have lost some partisans in Congress, will have trailed the ticket in many areas, and will be subject to criticism for having conducted a poor campaign. This is a *critical election.*

Alternatively, there is the election in which even though a party wins a great victory, a particular group has shifted its party identification. Although Herbert Hoover a Republican, won a landslide victory in 1928, his election can be considered critical rather than reinforcing because northern urban Catholics supported a Catholic Democratic candidate and began a massive shift to the Democratic party.[54]

The deviating election. An election that is won by a popular candidate of the minority party who appeals to voters on issues or whose candidacy is a protest is a *deviating election.* The candidate takes advantage of the dynamic factors and wins a personal victory, but there is no change in party identification or underlying group allegiance to the majority party. Voters defected to the candidate, but still do not identify with the minority party. This is a deviation from the normal vote. The newly elected president may be confronted with a hostile Congress controlled by the opposition. Members of the president's own party remain somewhat dissatisfied because the personal victory did not help them. The Republicans won deviating elections in 1952, 1956, 1968, 1972, and 1980.

The reinstating election. After one or two deviating elections the party with the normal-vote advantage eventually regains the White House in a *reinstating election.* A newly elected president comes into conflict with leading members of the winning party in Congress, who see the reinstating election as their opportunity to implement their own priorities. Kennedy and Carter both had problems with their own party after such elections.

The realigning election. In a *realigning election,* the minority party uses crosscutting issues and reference groups to break up the majority coalition. It gets large numbers of people in critical groups not only to defect in their vote but also to switch their party identification—either in that presidential election or the subsequent one. The minority party, by virtue of these defections, becomes the majority party. Such elections involve drastic changes in the stable factors: the advantage in terms of party identification shifts, groups swing decisively from one party to the other, regional political competition changes, and turnout rates may suddenly move up or down by as much as 20 percentage points. After such a political earthquake there is usually a thirty- to sixty-year period in which most factors remain fairly stable—until there is another realigning election. The Republicans won a realigning election in 1896, when they won over many white working-class factory employees and immi-

President-elect Jimmy Carter
savors the newspaper headlines
in 1976. (*Sygma.*)

grants. The Republican Party remained the dominant party in Congress and at
the state level for almost forty years. The Democrats realigned the party system
in the elections of 1932 and 1936, creating the New Deal coalition. Since then,
they have lost deviating elections (1952, 1956, 1968, 1972, and 1980), won reinstating elections (1960 and 1976), and once, in 1964, managed to win a reinforcing election. In 1984 Republicans almost pulled even with Democrats in party
identification within the electorate, leading some Republicans to argue that
the 1980 and 1984 elections had produced a realignment of two-party competition.

Obviously, the minority party would much rather win a realigning election
than a deviating election. For one thing, it is then less likely to lose the subsequent election and more likely to run off a string of victories. Winning a realigning election also gives other party candidates the normal-vote advantage, making their races easier. It gives the president partisans in Congress and the state
legislatures, which helps the president implement programs (though there is
usually a lag of four to eight years before a realignment at the national level is
fully reflected in state politics).

**Election results and
governance**

While elections have some impact on policy, it would be grossly misleading to
state that they are the major determinant. Nevertheless, history allows us to
make some tentative generalizations. Reinforcing and realigning elections are
associated with policy breakthroughs. A party wins big because voters are
attracted to a presidential candidate's vision of the future. Once in office, the
president can capitalize on public opinion, at least in the first year, to get
proposals through. Franklin Roosevelt's New Deal and Lyndon Johnson's
"great society" involved regulation of the economy or redistribution of resources and were implemented after the incumbent went to the country and
made appeals on the basis of his election mandate.

Maintaining, critical, and reinstating elections are associated with more er-
ratic presidential performance. Truman, Kennedy, and Carter all found it hard

to get along with Congress—including members of their own parties. There were few great policy breakthroughs; more often, there were incremental changes in existing programs. Presidents who have won in such elections have found it hard to lead the public and hard to claim a mandate or implement one.

Deviating elections usually lead to centrist accommodations with an opposition congressional majority (the Eisenhower pattern), to intense confrontations between the two branches (the Nixon pattern), or to an attempt to replicate the election success by going to the country and putting the pressure of public opinion on Congress (the Reagan pattern).

But these generalizations do not always hold true, especially as the memory of the election results fades and as the parties look toward the next set of congressional and presidential contests. The winner of a deviating election is not always weaker than the winner of a realigning or a reinforcing election. Woodrow Wilson and Ronald Reagan both implemented most of their far-reaching domestic programs in their first terms.

Although it seems logical that a president who wins a reinforcing election will be a strong leader, it does not always work out that way. Franklin Roosevelt's 1936 election was followed by open revolt within his party and paralysis of much of his program by 1938. Lyndon Johnson's reinforcing election of 1964 was followed in 1966 by defections in Congress over issues of foreign policy, a result of the unpopularity of the Vietnamese war.

Dealignment theory

The preceding discussion assumes that the stable factors really are stable. This is debatable. The coalition that elected Franklin Roosevelt in 1932 was somewhat different from the one that elected John Kennedy in 1960, and that coalition was quite different from the one that elected Jimmy Carter in 1976. The demographic characteristics of voters, their turnout rates, and their group affiliations changed somewhat. The above discussion also assumes that the stable factors are critically important and can still structure party competition. This too is debatable in the era of weakening party identification and media manipulation through the techniques of media politics.

The long-awaited realignment predicted by the election typology still has not occurred. Analysts thought that Nixon's reelection in 1972 would be the breakthrough, but Nixon was unable to win congressional majorities, and by 1976 his party not only had lost the White House but also had been thumped in congressional and state elections, leaving what some analysts referred to as a "one-and-a-half" party system. In 1980 Reagan won the White House, and the Republicans won the Senate, but during Reagan's first term the Republicans barely made a dent in the Democrats' advantage in terms of party identification. They did poorly in the 1982 midterm congressional elections, and their modest gains in governorships and state legislative seats were rolled back. In 1984, even Reagan's landslide could not make up for those losses. However, the Republicans did make some gains in southern state legislative seats, which indicated that realignment might be taking place.

The joke on economic forecasters is that they have predicted five of the last two recessions. So, too, realignment theorists have predicted four Republican realignments (1952, 1972, 1980, and 1984), but none has yet occurred. When a theory, no matter how elegant, has little predictive value, it may be time to consider a new one.[55]

Third-party and independent candidacies can play a significant role. Governor George Wallace of Alabama created the American Independent Party for his 1968 run for the presidency; John Anderson ran as an independent in 1980. (*Constantine Manos: Magnum; Susan McElhinney: Woodfin Camp.*)

Voters are becoming unmoored from party and group orientations. Most are weak or independent party identifiers or pure independents. Voters have become ticket splitters and habitual defectors in presidential elections. In 1968 and 1980 many people voted for third-party candidates as a stopover on their way to switching parties. Voters decide on the basis of issues, ideologies, and retrospective evaluations, not party identification or group affiliations. Politics has become nationalized as a result of the impact of the news media and campaign advertisements: no longer is it class against class, region against region, or religion against religion, in predictable patterns. Like unsecured cargo on a ship, most groups can swing from one side to another, depending on the political weather.

The stable factors are not very stable. Normal-vote patterns no longer exist. The dynamic factors are the key to the vote, and therefore to any meaning which an analyst can find in it.

The party system may be involved in voter dealignment rather than realignment; if the trends discussed above continue to dominate electoral choice.

THE REFORM AGENDA

ELECTING THE PRESIDENT. During the past two centuries our electoral process has been transformed; we have gone from limited suffrage to mass suffrage, from congressional caucuses to open nominations decided by the voters, from a one-party system to a two-party system (including five different party alignments), and from canvassing by local party workers to new politics advertising. There is no reason to assume that our political institutions and practices will not change in the future.

The electoral college. Why keep the electoral college—an archaic system with a great potential for disaster? There are several reasons. First, it discourages minor parties and independent candidates unless they can win states outright—they get nothing for winning less than a purality. Second, the smaller states get more representation than they would be entitled to on a pure arithmetic basis: Alaska, for example, has three electors who represent 140,000 persons each, while California has forty-seven electors, each of whom represents more than 500,000 people. Third, the influence of voters in the large states is maximized because of the winner-take-all system. (Suppose that in an election voters in Alaska and California were tied and that you could cast a vote in either state to break the tie. Which state would you choose to vote in? You would pick California, because your vote would determine forty-seven electoral college votes.)

Those who are opposed to the electoral college system argue that it breaks down and that it can give an election to the less popular candidate. Opponents have proposed several changes. The simplest would be to abolish the position of elector and count votes automatically. The most drastic change would be to eliminate the electoral college and hold direct popular elections.[56] The winner would have to receive 40 percent of the vote, or else there would be a runoff between the top two contenders. (Another variation would provide for a runoff between the top three contenders, with Congress deciding if no one received 40 percent of the vote on the second round.)

Critics of direct popular elections argue that they might result in a proliferation of minor-party candidates. The 40 percent rule might lead to presidents elected by plurality rather than majority vote. Major-party candidates would probably make deals with small parties that represented ideologies, single-issue groups, or racial and ethnic constituencies, thus fragmenting the parties and increasing public disillusionment. Runoff elections would probably result in lower turnouts and less interest on the part of voters, since they would become saturated with campaigning.

Two proposals would retain the electoral college while solving some of its problems. First, the electoral college vote could be apportioned within each state according to the popular vote. This would ensure that the popular and electoral winners were the same and would deemphasize the importance of the large states and swing voters within them. But it would encourage minor-party candidacies, with all their attendant problems. Second, we could use congressional district lines to select 435 electors and use state contests to select 103 electors from the states and from the District of Columbia. The Republicans favor this plan; if it had been in operation in 1960, Nixon would have won the election because Republicans often "win" more congressional districts in presidential voting than Democrats. This proposal would inhibit many minor-party candidates but would encourage those with regional support or support from minority racial and ethnic groups. Third-party or minority-group electors might hold the balance of power in the electoral college, which would lead to bargaining or even to a House contingency election.

Another proposal, this one put forth by the Twentieth Century Fund's Commission on Presidential Selection, would give a bonus of 102 electoral votes to the person who won a plurality of the popular vote. This would keep all the advantages of the present system, while ensuring that the winner of the popular vote also won a majority in the electoral college.

Campaign financing. The public is unhappy with the existing system of campaign financing. An Associated Press poll conducted in July 1984 indicated that 86 percent of the public think that candidates spend too much and that 82 percent favor more restrictions on campaign financing. The national party committees, rather than the candidates, could be given public funds, which would tie a candidate more closely to the party organization. Limits could be placed on contributions for state party building, and unions, corporations, and banks could be prohibited from contributing to state party accounts that spend money directly or indirectly on presidential campaigns. A candidate who was attacked by an independent committee could be given extra federal funds as an equalizer or free media time to respond. But the prospects for reform are poor: the Republicans do not want their soft-money state accounts touched, and the Democrats do not want reforms to inhibit union support for their candidates. Limits on contributions to parties are likely to be raised, but serious limits on spending are not likely to be enforced.

Election-night coverage. Proposed federal legislation would bar network projections of the winner (based on exit polls or actual precinct tallies) until the last state voted; this would prevent any possibility that voters in western states might choose not to go to the polls if a projected winner had already been announced. Other proposals include voluntary agreement by the networks to forestall such a law and a synchronized set of voting hours so that the forty-eight continental states could complete their voting at exactly the same time. The networks claim (and some empirical studies back them up) that very few people decide not to vote on the basis of network projections and that in almost no congressional or presidential contests have such decisions made any difference in the outcomes.

Responsible parties. In addition to these piecemeal proposals for reform, some political scientists have suggested comprehensive reforms that simultaneously strengthen the party structures (by providing that all financing go through them), link *presidential parties* and *congressional parties* (by providing for simultaneous four-year terms for House members, senators, and the president), and give the president a working majority in Congress, which would end the possibility of a deviating election (by giving the party that wins the White House a "bonus" of 100 or so seats in the House). These reforms would create a system of presidential government quite at odds with our original constitutional understandings. If we amend the Constitution we can have such a system, but we should be clear about what we are doing: trading the safeguards of separate institutions that compete for power for the possibility that presidential government will be effective enough to solve national problems. Instituting such reforms would be quite a constitutional gamble, and as yet there is no indication that the nation is prepared to take so drastic a step.

IN CONCLUSION

Presidential campaigns, unlike primary contests, are short, intense affairs which involve campaigns for money, organization, image, and finally votes. The Republicans do better at funding and organization, and they have pioneered in media politics, which offset the Democrats' advantages in terms of party identification and group affiliation. Even though the Democrats have the normal-vote advantage, the Republicans have won more than half the elections since 1952. The Republicans Party has not, however, been able to convert itself into the majority party. We seem stuck in a pattern of deviating and reinstating elections, which leaves presidents of both parties weakened in dealing with Congress and their state parties. The system may now be so unmoored from its traditional bearings that no fundamental realignment is possible, and most trends seem to point to a party system that is more ideological, functioning in a nominating system that is more fluid and open to change. The consequences are that candidates, their coalitions, and their ideas can change drastically from one election to the next. There is a lengthy agenda of reforms, but most of them are unlikely to be adopted, especially proposals for a responsible party system.

NOTES

1. Russell Baker, "Observer," *The New York Times*, Apr. 12, 1980.
2. Lawrence Longley and Alan Braun, *The Politics of Electoral College Reform*, Yale University Press, New Haven, Conn., 1972, p. 3.
3. Ibid.
4. Lucius Wilmerding, *The Electoral College*, Rutgers University Press, New Brunswick, N.J., 1953, pp. 47–61.
5. Raymond Tatelovich, "Electoral Votes and Presidential Campaign Trails: 1932–1976," *American Politics Quarterly*, vol. 7, no. 4, October 1971, pp. 489–497; Steven J. Brams and Morton D. Davis, "The ⅜'s Rule in Presidential Campaigning," *American Political Science Review*, vol. 68, no. 1, March 1974, pp. 113–134.
6. Michael Goldstein, *A Handbook for Presidential Campaigns*, Public Affairs and Communications, Washington, D.C., 1984.
7. Herbert Alexander, *Financing Politics*, Congressional Quarterly Press, Washington, D.C., 1980, p. 10.
8. *Final Report of the Senate Select Committee on Presidential Campaign Activities*, 93d Cong., 2d Sess., 1974, p. 904.
9. Herbert Alexander, *Financing the 1968 Elections*, Heath, Boston, 1971, chap. 10.
10. The list was printed in *The New York Times*, Mar. 20, 1974.
11. Alexander, *Financing Politics*, op. cit., p. 159.
12. Elizabeth Drew, "Politics and Money," *The New Yorker*, Dec. 11, 1982, p. 64.
13. *The Wall Street Journal*, July 5, 1984, p. 1.
14. Ibid.

15. *Federal Elections Commission v. National Conservative Political Action Committee et al.*, 53 Law Week, 4293, March 19, 1985.

16. Brooks Jackson, "Democrats Must Stump for Dollars," *The Wall Street Journal*, July 3, 1984.

17. Researched by Arthur Larkin, Columbia College.

18. John Kessel, *Presidential Campaign Politics*, 2d ed., Dorsey, Homewood, Ill., 1984.

19. James David Barber, *The Pulse of Politics*, Norton, New York, 1980, pp. 3–4.

20. Richard Jensen, "Armies, Admen and Crusaders: Strategies to Win Elections," *Public Opinion*, vol. 3, no. 5, October–November 1980, pp. 44–53.

21. Benjamin Page, *Choices and Echoes in Presidential Elections*, University of Chicago Press, Chicago, 1978, pp. 232–265.

22. Joe McGinnis, *The Selling of the President, 1968*, Pocket Books, New York, 1969, p. 54.

23. Ibid., p. 31.

24. Timothy Crouse, *The Boys on the Bus*, Ballantine Books, New York, 1973, p. 303.

25. McGinnis, op.cit., p. 54.

26. *The New York Times*, July 16, 1984.

27. Av Westin, *Newswatch*, Simon and Schuster, New York, 1982, p. 93.

28. David S. Broder, "Political Reporters in Presidential Politics," in James I. Lengle and Byron E. Shafer (eds.), *Presidential Politics*, St. Martin's, New York, 1980, p. 497.

29. Crouse, op. cit, p. 323.

30. Thomas Patterson and Robert McClure, *The Unseeing Eye*, Putnam, New York, 1976, p. 58.

31. Ibid.

32. Irving Crespi, "Polls as Journalism," *Public Opinion Quarterly*, vol. 44, no. 4, winter 1980, pp. 516–517; C. Anthony Broh, "Horse-Race Journalism," *Public Opinion Quarterly*, vol. 44, no. 4, winter 1980, pp. 516–517.

33. Seymour Martin Lipset, "Different Polls, Different Results in 1980 Politics," *Public Opinion*, vol. 3, no. 4, August–September 1980, pp. 19–20; Barry Sussman, "Reagan vs. Mondale: Who's on First and Who's on Second," *Washington Post National Weekly Edition*, Aug. 6, 1984, p. 37.

34. Michael Wheeler, "Reining in Horserace Journalism," *Public Opinion*, vol. 3, no. 1a, February–March 1980, pp. 41–45; Burns W. Roper, "The Media and the Polls," *Public Opinion*, vol. 3, no. 1a, February–March 1980, pp. 46–49.

35. Roper reports, August–September 4, 1976.

36. Elizabeth Drew, "A Political Journal," *The New Yorker*, Sept. 10, 1984, pp. 102–106; Oct. 8, 1984, pp. 118–120.

37. Evron Kirkpatrick, "What Can We Learn from 1960?" in Austin Ranney (ed.), *The Past, Present and Future of Presidential Debates*, American Enterprise Institute, Washington, D.C., 1979, pp. 26–29; Steven H. Chaffee and Jack Dennis, "Wisconsin Panel Survey," as reported in Chaffee and Dennis, "Presidential Debates: An Empirical Assessment," in Ranney, op. cit., pp. 90–94.

38. *The New York Times*, Oct. 30, 1980, p. A-1; Paul Abramson et al., *Change and Continuity in the 1980 Elections*, Congressional Quarterly Press, Washington, D.C., 1982, pp. 129–134.

39. Marilyn Jackson-Beeck and Robert G. Meadow, "The Triple Agenda of Presidential Debates," *Public Opinion Quarterly*, vol. 43, no. 2, summer 1979, pp. 173–180.

40. Washington Post, *The Pursuit of the Presidency, 1980*, Berkely Books, New York, 1980, p. 361.

41. Richard Chaney, "The 1976 Debates: A Republican Perspective," in Ranney, op. cit., p. 128.

42. Barry Sussman, "How T.V.'s Power Has Again Transformed Public Opinion," *Washington Post National Weekly Edition*, Oct. 15, 1984, p. 37.

43. Norman Nie, Sidney Verba, and John Petrocik, *The Changing American Voter*, Harvard University Press, Cambridge, Mass., 1979, pp. 21, 26–27, 33.

44. Ibid., p. 29.
45. Ibid., pp. 97–99, 105–109, 113, 133, 143–150, 199–205.
46. Ibid., pp. 57, 105.
47. Abramson et al., loc. cit.
48. Morris Fiorina, *Retrospective Voting in American National Elections*, Yale University Press, New Haven, Conn., 1981, chap. 5.
49. Angus Campbell et al., *Elections and the Political Order*, Wiley, New York, 1966, chap. 1.
50. V. O. Key, *Politics, Parties and Pressure Groups*, 5th ed., Thomas Y. Crowell, New York, 1964, p. 588.
51. Fiorina, op. cit., p. 85–89, 102, 185.
52. *The New York Times*, July 27, 1984.
53. Walter Dean Burnham, *Critical Elections and the Mainsprings of American Politics*, Norton, New York, 1970, pp. 135–195.
54. V. O. Key, Jr., "A Theory of Critical Elections," *Journal of Politics*, vol. 17, no. 1, 1955, pp. 3–18.
55. On elections and party systems, see Seymour Martin Lipset (ed.), *Party Coalitions in the 1980s*, Institute for Contemporary Studies, Berkeley, Calif., 1980.
56. Stephen J. Wayne, *The Road to the White House*, St. Martin's, New York, 1980, pp. 15–22.

FURTHER READING

Alexander, Herbert: *Financing Politics*, 2d ed., Congressional Quarterly Press, Washington, D.C., 1981. A comprehensive and critical discussion of present-day campaign financing.

Altshuler, Bruce E.: *Keeping a Finger on the Public Pulse*, Greenwood Press, Westport, Conn., 1982. An account of the role of private pollsters in presidential elections.

Barber James David: *The Pulse of Politics*, Norton, New York, 1980. A treatment of campaign rhetoric.

Drew, Elizbeth: *Portrait of an Election*, Simon and Schuster, New York, 1981. A journalistic account, including a shrewd discussion of strategy, tactics, and personalities.

Fiorina, Morris: *Retrospective Voting in American National Elections*, Yale University Press, New Haven, Conn., 1981. A study of the way people's thoughts about the past and the future influence their vote.

Heard, Alexander: *The Costs of Democracy*, University of North Carolina Press, Chapel Hill, 1960. A classic study of traditional campaign financing.

Jamieson, Kathleen H.: *Packaging the Presidency: A History and Criticism of Presidential Campaign Advertising*, Oxford University Press, New York, 1984. A study of the development of new politics in presidential campaigns.

Kessel, John: *Presidential Campaign Politics*, 2d ed., Dorsey, Homewood, Ill., 1984. A study of the way campaigns are organized.

Lengle, James I., and Byron E. Shafer (eds.): *Presidential Politics*, 2d ed., St. Martin's, New York, 1983. Articles on election politics, focusing on the rules of the game.

Linsky, Martin (ed.): *Television and the Presidential Elections*, Lexington Books, Lexington, Mass., 1983. Proceedings of a conference held at the Institute of Politics, Kennedy School of Government, Harvard University.

Nie, Norman H., Sidney Verba, and John R. Petrocik: *The Changing American Voter*, Harvard University Press, Cambridge, Mass., 1976. A treatise on voting behavior and how it has evolved in the past thirty years.

Page, Benjamin: *Choices and Echoes in Presidential Elections*, University of Chicago Press, Chicago, 1978. A study of how candidates position themselves on the issues.

Patterson, Thomas: *The Mass Media Election*, Praeger, New York, 1980. An analysis of the 1976 elections.

Ranney, Austin (ed.): *The Past, Present and Future of Presidential Debates*, American Enterprise Institute, Washington, D.C., 1979. A collection of essays on presidential debates.

Robinson, Michael, and Margaret Sheehan: *Over the Wire and on T.V.: CBS and UPI in Campaign '80*, Russell Sage, New York, 1980. A discussion of how networks and wire services cover campaigns.

Rosenstone, Steven: *Forecasting Presidential Elections*, Yale University Press, New Haven, Conn., 1983. A discussion of the techniques used by political scientists.

Rubin, Richard: *Press, Party and Presidency*, Norton, New York, 1981. A book that traces the changing relationships between the media and presidential campaign politics and develops implications for government.

Schramm, Martin: *Running for President, 1976*, Stein and Day, New York, 1977. A journalist's account of the Carter campaign, containing strategy memorandums from both camps.

Twentieth Century Fund Task Force: *With the Nation Watching*, Lexington Books, Lexington, Mass., 1979. A report on presidential debates.

Wayne, Stephen J.: *The Road to the White House*, 2d ed., St. Martin's, New York, 1984. An overview of presidential election politics.

THE STUDY BREAK

Crouse, Timothy: *The Boys on the Bus*, Ballantine Books, New York, 1973. A book about how the media covered the 1972 campaign.

McGinnis, Joe: *The Selling of the President, 1968*, Pocket Books, New York, 1969. An account of Nixon's media campaign, including some hilarious stories about the candidate.

USEFUL SOURCES

Roseboom, Eugene: *A History of Presidential Elections, from George Washington to Jimmy Carter*, 4th ed., Macmillan, New York, 1979. Short histories of presidential campaigns from Washington's time to 1976.

Scammon, Richard (ed.): *America Votes, 1984*, vol. 16, Congressional Quarterly Press, Washington, D.C., 1985. Voting statistics on the 1984 presidential election. A new volume is published the year after each presidential election.

Schlesinger, Arthur M., Jr. (ed.): *The Coming to Power: Critical Presidential Elections in American History*, Chelsea House, New York, 1981. Important campaigns, as described by distinguished historians.

Abraham Lincoln near the front at Antietam
and Ronald Reagan at the DMZ between
North and South Korea illustrate the
president's responsibilities as commander in
chief. (*Culver Pictures; Bill Fitzpatrick: White
House*.)

CHAPTER 10

PRESIDENTIAL POWER: CONSTITUTIONAL PREROGATIVES AND POLITICAL LEADERSHIP

PREROGATIVE POWERS

Using prerogative powers
Legitimizing prerogative powers
Risks of using prerogative powers
Criteria for use of prerogative powers

POWER AND LEADERSHIP

The power problem
Limits to power politics
Principles and power

IN CONCLUSION

President Nixon conferring with former president Lyndon Johnson in 1970. Both men's use of their powers as commander in chief contributed to what some political scientists call the *imperial presidency.* (*Elliott Erwitt: Magnum.*)

The presidency, Theodore Roosevelt once said, is a "bully good pulpit." It is the keystone of our government. The president is chief of state, representing our sovereignty; chief diplomat, communicating with other nations; commander in chief, presiding over the armed forces in peace and war; chief executive, overseeing the departments; chief legislator, presenting new programs and the federal budget to Congress; chief economist, proposing new taxing and spending policies; and, finally, chief of a political party. The president can be a catalyst for social change or a consolidator; a defender of existing economic interests or a proponent of new ones. At times the presidency functions, in the words of James MacGregor Burns, as "a weapon that has served Americans well in the long struggle for freedom and equality at home and in the search for stable and democratic politics abroad."[1] At other times it has been an ***imperial presidency***, riding roughshod over civil liberties, the constitutional powers of the other two branches, and even international law.

If we have a president who is strong enough to govern, is that, as Alexander Hamilton asked, "inconsistent with the genius of republican government?"[2] Do we have, as former president Gerald Ford suggests, an *imperiled* rather than an *imperial* presidency? Or has Ronald Reagan, as Arthur Schlesinger argues, "dispelled doubts about the ability of a President to govern and revived national confidence in the workability of the system?"[3]

CHIEF SCAPEGOAT: EVALUATING PRESIDENTS

"Before you get to be President you think you can do anything," Lyndon Johnson told Richard Nixon, as he left the White House, "but when you get in that tall chair, as you're gonna find out, Mr. President, you can't count on people. You'll find your hands tied and people cussin' you. The office is kind a like the little country boy found the hoochie-koochie show at the carnival, once he'd paid his dime and got inside the tent: 'It ain't exactly as it was advertised.' "[4] Johnson's disappointment in the office matches the disappointment that the American people often have in those who occupy it; presidents are the chief scapegoats in American politics. Their performance almost always falls short of our expectations.

We are ambivalent about presidents and their powers. We want the occupant of the Oval Office to take charge, and yet we are fearful and suspicious of presidential powers. We want a strong president, but one who works with Congress within the system of checks and balances. We believe in checks and balances and in separation of powers, but we give high marks to presidents who lead and to Congresses which follow.[5] We want the president to have the aristocratic bearing of Franklin Roosevelt and the common touch of Harry Truman, to project the father image of Dwight Eisenhower and the youthful energy of John Kennedy, to possess the political instincts of Lyndon Johnson and the moral bearing of Jimmy Carter, and to display the combativeness of Teddy Roosevelt and the geniality of Ronald Reagan.[6]

We compare presidents' accomplishments with those of their predecessors:

George Washington and the founding of the union, Abraham Lincoln and its preservation, and Theodore Roosevelt and Franklin Roosevelt and the emergence of the United States as a world power. We consider the great ones, as the former White House counselor Ed Meese observed, to be "leaders who put the stamp of their own personality on the office and the nation—men who swashbuckled their way through great events, who delighted in battle, despised the status quo, and never shied away from the use of the personal pronoun. Men, in short, who centralized authority and personified change."[7] The greatest of them created new political movements or parties or led the nation to military victories; yet while in office, even they were not perceived as great.

When asked to choose, the public prefers moral qualities such as courage, honesty, and convictions to political skills in its presidents. We want someone who acts for the good of the nation rather than for personal power or for narrow party interests—a leader rather than a politician.[8] We prefer people with convictions even if they do not always follow public opinion.

The impression that most people have about the presidency is that if only good people who knew how to govern were chosen for the office, the problems facing the nation could be solved. This belief is based on an underlying set of assumptions:

- Presidents head the government.
- Congress and the bureaucracy work under them.
- By virtue of their election they receive a mandate.
- Their own party should support them.
- Congress should pass their programs.

These assumptions are wrong. The best of presidents—with all the requisite political skills and moral qualities and the expertise of advisers—cannot lead Congress or their party on most issues most of the time.

PRESIDENTIAL POWERS

The constitutional principles that make the president the chief executive in theory hinder exercise of power in fact, because the Constitution itself assumes that power should not be concentrated in a single institution, but is to be divided, checked, and balanced in separate institutions. The politicians who run for office in these institutions are to share in, and compete for, the power to govern. Presidents must come to grips with this constitutional legacy.

The Constitution is not a blueprint which defines powers with precision: it is undefined, underdefined, ambiguous, incomplete, or silent on some important points. Nothing in the Constitution gives the president full responsibility to conduct foreign affairs, manage the economy, solve social problems, or even supervise government agencies. But nothing in the Constitution prevents the president from trying to do these things. "We elect a king for four years," Secretary of State William Seward observed during the Civil War, "and give him vast powers, which after all he can interpret for himself."

Constitutional powers

The executive power. Article II of the Constitution invests the president with the *executive power* of the United States. This power permits the president to make policy and to command subordinates, and it is constitutionally exercised solely by the president. Although for a period of about twenty years in the early 1800s presidents governed through Cabinet consensus, most later incumbents have followed Lincoln's approach: once, when his entire Cabinet disagreed with a decision he was about to make, he announced the results of the deliberations by saying, "Six nays and one aye, and the ayes have it."

Running the government. Presidents have few explicit powers over government agencies. Their nominations to office must be consented to by the Senate. Their right to fire subordinates is not explicitly mentioned in the Constitution, although the courts have accepted it since the 1920s. They may require department secretaries to give their opinion in writing on any matter. Congress can also issue instructions to officials through laws, and the courts do the same in their decisions, and if presidential orders conflict with these, the courts may nullify them.

Commander in chief. The president is commander in chief of the armed forces and of the state militias (that is, the National Guard) when called into federal service. But the Constitution does not list any express powers which presidents might exercise. Can they command troops, direct military officers, or make war policy? Can they commence or end hostilities? Can they do these things without obtaining the approval of Congress? May Congress restrict presidents when they exercise their powers, by using the necessary and proper clause? Congress itself has many war powers which potentially conflict with the president's: it declares war, punishes offenses against international law, raises and supports the armed forces and issues regulations concerning them, and raises and organizes the state militias, and the Senate consents to or rejects presidential commissions for the officer corps.

Diplomatic powers. The president receives foreign ambassadors and, by and with the advice and consent of the Senate, nominates our ambassadors. Does this entail the power to grant or refuse recognition to other nations? The Constitution does not say. The president, by and with the advice and consent of the Senate, makes treaties with other nations. Does this mean that the president decides to ratify them (that is, put them in force) after Senate approval? Or must the president also obtain the consent of the Senate to put a treaty in force? What if conditions change or if the other side refuses to abide by the terms of a treaty? Can the president abrogate the agreement unilaterally or only with the consent of the Senate? The Constitution is silent on these points, though in all such cases presidents have successfully expanded their powers.

Economic management. The president has no explicit constitutional power to manage the economy, in contrast to Congress, which has the power to tax and spend, to regulate the currency and coinage, to regulate commerce between the states and foreign commerce, to manage the national debt, and to exercise all "necessary and proper" powers. Yet presidents take the responsibility for proposing economic policies, including tax programs, the budget, and regulatory policies.

Interpreting constitutional powers: Four strategies. Presidents cannot confine themselves to the literal Constitution of 1787. Instead, they must interpret their powers expansively by invoking the *living Constitution*, which has the adaptability to give them enough powers to meet national needs.[9] "The President is at liberty, both in law and in conscience," Woodrow Wilson argued, "to be as big a man as he can. Only his capacity will set the limit."[10] Presidents expand the Constitution, not as a matter of abstract legal reasoning, but to give themselves *legitimacy* when they make important decisions. They look at the Constitution as a power base, useful to them insofar as it permits them to act decisively. No matter if a provision has been interpreted in the past by the courts or Congress as a limitation or boundary that restricts their power: presidents often are willing and even eager to break new ground and cut through parchment barriers.

CLAIMING THE SILENCES. Presidents argue that any function not mentioned in the Constitution should be assigned to them by virtue of the oath of office, the executive power, and clauses naming the president commander in chief. This was the argument that George Washington used in 1792 when he declared neutrality in a war between Britain and France—even though the Constitution does not mention such a power.

EXPLOITING AMBIGUITIES. Incumbents argue that *the executive power* is a general term, which gives them all the powers that any executive would have unless specifically excluded by the Constitution. Thus they claim that they have the power to set policies and to fire officials, give them orders, and supervise their work.

PYRAMIDING RESPONSIBILITIES. Presidents can point to specific duties and then claim all related responsibilities. They argue that their duty to receive foreign ambassadors and to nominate ours makes them the "sole voice" in communicating with other nations. They then argue that the president is responsible for the entire field of foreign affairs, with only such exceptions as the Constitution provides for Congress—and that these are to be construed narrowly.

COMBINING POWERS. Presidents combine several constitutional provisions to create powers. They fuse the executive power, the oath of office, and the commander-in-chief clauses, claiming the general responsibility to do all that is not specifically forbidden by the Constitution, even if that involves exercising powers not mentioned in the Constitution or exercising powers given to Congress. The idea is that presidents are allowed to do anything that the Constitution does not forbid them to do.

Delegated powers

Most of the powers that presidents exercise, including some war and emergency powers, are delegated by Congress, using the necessary and proper clause. In a national emergency, the president uses delegated power to confine persons who are considered threats to national security, restrict travel in and out of the country, require persons to register with the government, control employment in the public and private sectors, deny jobs to persons who are considered security risks, stockpile strategic raw materials, impose rationing, institute import and export restrictions, allocate materials and personnel for defense, require companies to give priority to government contracts, seize plants, fix wages and prices, set standards for working conditions, and regulate communications. Congress makes a *conditional delegation*: the president must declare that a national emergency exists and report to Congress periodically. Congress may at any time end the state of emergency by passing a joint resolution (subject to presidential veto).

Congress is of two minds about presidential power: it wants to defend its own prerogatives, but public opinion usually favors legislators who cooperate with the administration. Often Congress passes the buck to the White House, delegating responsibilities that it wants to avoid because of the potential political fallout such as setting tariffs for imports and pay scales for federal employees.

Congress often grants presidents responsibility but circumscribes them with detailed rules and regulations in subsequent laws. Often the president acts as a *clerk* for the bureaucracy, members of Congress, or state and local officials and takes action, but according to *their* priorities and for *their* interests.[11] While Congress often delegates conditionally or restrictively, presidents assume that when Congress gives them powers, these should be interpreted permissively. They exploit any ambiguities and omissions in the laws as well as in the Constitution. President Carter did this, for example, when he interpreted a law dealing with foreign trade in a way that enabled him to conclude an agreement with Iran that traded Iranian assets frozen in the United States in return for American diplomats held hostage. To do so, Carter had to infringe on the rights of American individuals and companies to sue Iran in American courts for damages claimed to their interests—yet the Supreme Court, in reading the provisions of the law, interpreted them almost out of recognition in order to uphold presidential diplomatic authority in this crisis.

PRESIDENTS AS POPULAR LEADERS

Presidents engage in a kind of high-wire balancing act as they interpret the Constitution and the laws which delegate them power: their safety net becomes public support. "Public sentiment is everything," Lincoln said as he expanded the powers of the presidency during the Civil War; "with public sentiment nothing can fail; without it nothing can succeed." Woodrow Wilson, writing about Theodore Roosevelt's presidency, concluded that the presi-

President John F. Kennedy calling on the public to support his "new frontier" program. (*Cornell Capa: Magnum.*)

dent's power is based on public opinion: "Let him once win the admiration and confidence of the country, and no other single force can withstand him; no combination of forces can easily overpower him." Walter Mondale thought that Jimmy Carter had spent too much time sweating the small stuff and not enough time leading the public. "I'd rather give up the veto than the bully pulpit," he concluded.[12] Presidents need not obtain public approval for all, or even most, of their policies. But no president can sustain important policies for very long in the face of severe public disapproval.

But just as the Constitution does not give presidents all the powers they need to govern, neither does the public or the party give them sufficient political support. Just as they interpret the Constitution in such a way as to obtain the powers they need, so too they must work to maintain their legitimacy and authority. Presidents like Franklin Roosevelt, Dwight Eisenhower, and Ronald Reagan use their successes as popular leaders to expand their powers, pass much of their legislative programs, and win reelection landslides. Presidents who fail to retain their authority or to defend the legitimacy of their actions may be characterized as "imperial presidents" (Lyndon Johnson and Richard Nixon), find their legislative programs stalled (Harry Truman and Gerald Ford), decide not to seek renomination (Harry Truman and Lyndon Johnson), or be defeated in the next election (Gerald Ford and Jimmy Carter).

Presidential approval scores

Slightly more than half of those who are eligible to vote in presidential elections do so, and of these, slightly more than half vote for the winner: most presidents enter office with the expressed support of little more than one-fourth of the adult population. Initially they start with a much larger base, as a result of the ***honeymoon effect***: the tendency of most Americans to wish a new president well and to rally together after a divisive political campaign. Figure 10-1 compares the percentage of the voting-age population which supported several presidents with their approval ratings in early public opinion polls.

The honeymoon does not last long. Presidential approval ratings (Figure 10-2), traditionally start fairly high, then fall during the term, and finally rise

Figure 10-1. The initial approval score for each president has been much higher than his percentage of the popular vote. (Source: Gallup polls.)

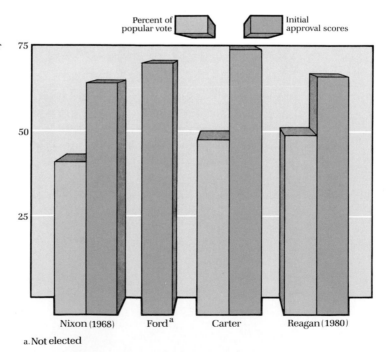

a. Not elected

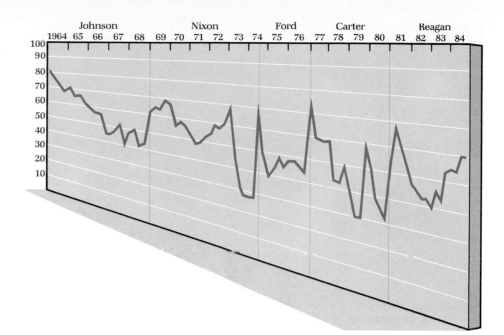

Figure 10-2. Presidential approval ratings, 1964–1984. (Source: *Gallup Opinion Index*.)

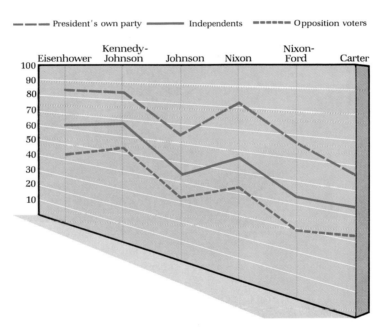

- - - - President's own party ———— Independents ------ Opposition voters

Figure 10-3. Approval scores for presidents, by party. Presidents receive their greatest support from members of their own party, followed by independents and opposition party identifiers. (Source: Gallup polls.)

near the end, though not to the initial levels. Party identifiers continue to support the president long after opposition identifiers and some independents have begun to fall away (Figure 10-3). The declines in public support tend to be quite sharp, to occur fairly early in the term, and to leave the president for much of the term in office with fairly low approval ratings (Ronald Reagan's rise in popularity during his third and fourth years in office is an exceptional case). The ratings are volatile: within a few months a president can rise or sink dramatically. One reason is the *rally-round-the-flag effect*: the rise in support when the president faces a major international crisis, even if it is not handled particularly well.

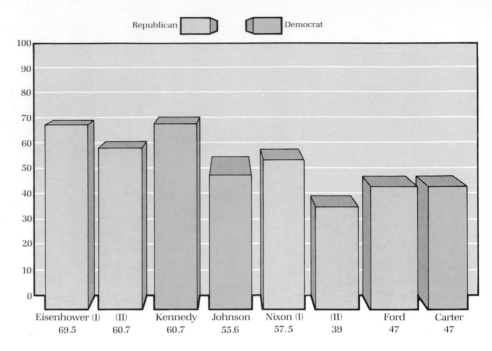

Republican ▭   ▭ Democrat

	Eisenhower (I)	(II)	Kennedy	Johnson	Nixon (I)	(II)	Ford	Carter
	69.5	60.7	60.7	55.6	57.5	39	47	47

Figure 10-4. Mean presidential approval scores, 1953–1980. In recent years presidents have had lower approval scores than their predecessors. Through the first two years of Reagan's second term, his popularity matched Eisenhower's. (Source: *Gallup Opinion Index.*)

The overall level of public support for presidents is lower today than it was in the 1950s and 1960s (Figure 10-4). Moreover, each president since Eisenhower has begun office with lower ratings than the last president of his own party. According to some political scientists, this is in some measure the result of greater cynicism, skepticism, or apathy on the part of the public due to government policies and to the legitimacy crises brought about by Watergate and the Vietnamese war. Others correlate the high rates of inflation and the lower growth rates of the late 1960s and early 1970s with lessened popularity.[13] Approval of presidents has declined along with support for most other governmental and social institutions. A related explanation focuses on changes in campaigns: the public's inflated expectations, which are due to the hype of media politics campaign commercials, are followed by disillusionment when presidents' performance fails to match their promises and when the media harp on the administration's in-fighting and friction with Congress. The lower percentage of partisan voters and the increase in the proportion of independents are one explanation for the volatility in the approval scores. Finally, the decline in support scores may occur because presidents cannot keep their promises to all the groups that initially support them. It is only natural that during the course of a term the president will retain the support of those who are satisfied and will lose the support of those who are disappointed.[14]

Reagan: The Teflon presidency

Ronald Reagan has confounded most of these political orthodoxies. True, he began with high approval ratings and then suffered a sharp decline, but during his third and fourth years in office his ratings rose sharply, into the high 50s and 60s. "Such a strong upward trend on the part of an incumbent president seeking reelection is without precedent in Gallup's 50 years of polling experience," George Gallup noted.[15] Reagan's popularity increased even though voters disapproved of some of his specific policies—in Lebanon, in Central America, and regarding the environment. "He walks away from more political car crashes than anyone," says his longtime adviser, John Sears.[16] Representative Patricia Schroeder, a Democrat from Colorado, charged in a speech to the

House that Reagan was "perfecting the Teflon-coated presidency." Nothing stuck to him, and voters refused to hold him personally responsible for his policies. One possible explanation: "When Reagan talks, the government is never 'we'; it's always 'them,'" according to the pollster Peter Hart. "Things never become his problem; they're always the government's problem."[17]

But another explanation is more satisfying to Republicans. A Washington Post/ABC survey taken early in 1984 indicated that most voters could distinguish between Reagan and his policies. Those who liked Reagan *and* his policies voted for him, but most of those who liked him and *not* his policies were prepared to vote against him.[18] By the time of the election Reagan's landslide could be explained, in terms not of Teflon but of policy: the public agreed with many of his policies and supported them. Polls taken throughout the election year showed that his economic program (tax cuts and lowered inflation) and foreign policy (the promise of new negotiations with the Soviets, the withdrawal of American troops from Lebanon, and the invasion of Grenada) commanded wide support, a reversal of the normal pattern, in which support for presidential policies erodes.

CLOSE-UP

PRESIDENT DWIGHT DAVID EISENHOWER. President Eisenhower was overwhelmingly elected to two terms (1953 to 1961), and had it not been for the Twenty-Second Amendment, he could easily have been elected to a third. During his administration the Korean war ended, involvement in Vietnam was averted, and the nation remained at peace. Inflation was low and the standard of living surged, in spite of two severe recessions. Yet two decades ago most historians and political scientists viewed Eisenhower as a political amateur who reigned too much and ruled too little, as an intellectual lightweight, and as a passive non-leader. "This man neither liked the game he was engaged in nor had gained much understanding of its rules," argued Richard Neustadt in 1960.[19] Was this true? Hardly.

Dwight D. Eisenhower.
(*Bettmann Archive.*)

For one thing, Eisenhower was highly political while serving in the Army. He was a deputy to the assistant secretary; he was chief aide to General Douglas MacArthur (a highly political officer) in the Philippines, where he worked closely with its civilian government as chief of staff of the Third Army; he served in the Planning Division of the War Department after Pearl Harbor; and in 1942 President Roosevelt appointed him commanding general of the European theater of operations. In his last post he had to smooth over disputes between Allied officers and negotiate with French officials in the Vichy government over the landings in north Africa, and eventually he worked closely with Roosevelt, Churchill, de Gaulle, Stalin, and other world leaders as the Allied armies moved toward victory.

Fred Greenstein, a political scientist at Princeton, analyzed Eisenhower's military career and found that while in the military, he developed a leadership style with five important characteristics that later served him well in the White House:

- *Hidden-hand leadership.* Eisenhower was a skilled political operator who chose not to let others realize that fact. He camouflaged his participation in politics by relying on others to conduct his political business and concealing his own role.
- *Use of language.* Eisenhower often used language that was deliberately ambiguous or spoke in an evasive, noncommittal, or seemingly confused way in order to make his adversaries (or the press) underestimate him or to get himself off the hook in a controversy. His use of jumbled syntax at press conferences was a deliberate ploy that allowed him to avoid making a comment when he did not wish to.
- *Avoiding personal comments.* Eisenhower tried never to attack anyone else's motives or to make personal comments about his political rivals or convert them into enemies. He could mask his own negative feelings about those with whom he had to work (such as his own congressional leaders).
- *Personality analysis.* Eisenhower could step into other people's shoes, understand how they viewed a situation and how they were likely to respond, and then shape his own strategy and tactics accordingly. He could figure out how to use the strengths of his subordinates and get around their weaknesses.
- *Selective delegation.* Eisenhower delegated responsibility, but never to the extent that he lost control of policy. He supervised Secretary of State Dulles closely (because he personally knew most of the world leaders) and in effect ran his own Defense Department. He would share credit for the successes of subordinates, but even more important, he would diffuse blame for failures, preserving his image as head of state while allowing others to take the heat for partisan politics or failing policies.[20]

Eisenhower's admirers believe that his hidden-hand style of leadership was effective. He managed to defuse the destructive attempts of Joe McCarthy, a Republican senator from Wisconsin, to meddle in military and diplomatic matters while on a supposed hunt for communist spies in government. He forged a bipartisan consensus in foreign policy that kept us at peace, while allowing intelligence agencies to influence foreign governments and even help replace several unfriendly regimes (in Iran and Guatemala, for example). On the domestic front he presided over the consolidation of the New Deal social programs and even expanded them, in the process creating the Department of Health, Education and Welfare—again by working with leaders of both parties in Congress.

While conceding these points, Eisenhower's critics remind us that the hidden hand often was so well hidden that no one could detect Eisenhower's leadership.

True, he preserved his own reputation and popularity, but he never transferred these to his party, which suffered disastrous defeats in state and congressional elections in 1958 and then lost the presidency in 1960. He exerted no moral leadership on one of the key domestic issues of the time: racial desegregation of public schools. And his economic policies resulted in slow rates of growth and two severe recessions. He never groomed anyone to succeed him, and he left his party in considerable disarray, with no prospect of a realignment.

Why do we care whether Eisenhower was an effective politician or an amateur? It is an important consideration because it raises the question of the leadership styles of other presidents. Many political scientists and journalists now say the same things about Reagan that used to be said about Eisenhower; perhaps in twenty years, Reagan's presidency will be similarly reassessed.

PARTY LEADERSHIP

While presidents retain the support of their party rank and file, they cannot translate that support into long-term leadership of their party-in-government. More damage is done to presidents by their own congressional leaders than by the opposition. "Party loyalty or responsibility means damn little," President Kennedy observed; "they've got to take care of themselves first."[21] "It doesn't matter what kind of majority you came in with, you've got just one year when they treat you right, before they start worrying about themselves," Lyndon Johnson said. "They'll come along and they'll give you almost everything you want for awhile, and then they'll turn on you. They always do. They'll lay in waiting, waiting for you to make a slip and you will. They'll give you almost everything and then they'll make you pay for it."[22]

Party competition

Thomas Jefferson early in his first term, Andrew Jackson with his bank veto, Franklin Roosevelt with his 100 days, and Ronald Reagan with his supply-side economics—all capitalized on the momentum of election landslides, and their major legislative accomplishments all came early rather than late in their terms. Under what circumstances are presidents effective party leaders? Most often when they represent political and economic interests that seize the public's imagination, capitalize on crises, and replace worn-out ideas and practices with something new.

Such periods of energetic presidential leadership often coincide with, and are intimately related to, party competition. When the dominant party, because of its approach to public policy, loses its authority, the result is a party realignment. Coincidental with realignment is effective presidential party leadership. Later, when the party has run out of new ideas and is merely marking time, deviating, critical, and reinstating elections are likely; in such circumstances presidents of neither party do very well. The dominant party may reinvigorate itself, as the Democrats did under Lyndon Johnson and his "great society" program, but eventually a new realignment occurs, the opposition assumes power, and the cycle begins again.[23] But unless we have a president who founds a party (such as Jefferson) or leads one to realignment or a reinforcing election, the prospects for sustained party leadership in the White House are poor.

The legislative party

Thomas Jefferson got on so badly with his House majority leader that he attempted to engineer his defeat in the next congressional election. Abraham

Lincoln fought with congressional leaders over the conduct of the Civil War. Woodrow Wilson could not obtain the support of several congressional leaders for his policy that led the United States to enter World War I. Members of Franklin Roosevelt's own party stopped his efforts to "pack" the Supreme Court, and their alliance with Republicans stalled the New Deal economic program after 1937. Dwight Eisenhower was openly contemptuous of his congressional leaders, and at one point he threatened to create a new political party if they did not give his programs more support. The major opposition to John Kennedy's civil rights initiatives and Lyndon Johnson's Vietnamese war policies came from Democratic committee leaders..The pressure of Republican Senate leaders finally convinced Richard Nixon to resign from office rather than fight impeachment charges.

Jimmy Carter's programs were modified beyond recognition by committees controlled by his own party. He had no strong supporters among the leadership. When a reporter asked Jim Wright, the majority leader, whether the president was "big enough" for the job, Wright replied, "No one is big enough for the job, so we have to settle for what we've got."[24] Ronald Reagan, after initial successes with his economic program, found that his party leaders were insistent on modifying his tax program, reforming the Environmental Protection Agency, changing his posture at arms talks with the Soviets, ending the mining of the harbors of Nicaragua, and stalling his proposals for constitutional amendments concerning prayer in schools, abortion, busing, and a balanced budget. At the start of his second term, Reagan's new majority leader, Robert Dole, announced that Senate Republicans would substitute their own deficit-reduction plan for the budget that even then was being prepared by the president.

The original constitutional arrangements are at the root of all presidents' friction with their own party. As James Madison explained in *Federalist* 51, it is necessary for each branch to "have a will of its own." This could be achieved by "giving to those who administer each department the necessary constitutional means and personal motives to resist the encroachments of the others. . . ." Under this arrangement, "Ambition must be made to counteract ambition. The interests of the man must be connected with the constitutional rights of the place." Today this means that the ambition of the president to lead Congress collides with the ambitions of party leaders to develop their own programs, extend their own powers, and advance their own careers. Every president comes to agree with Kennedy's assessment that "the Congress looks more powerful sitting here that it did when I was there. . . . But that's because when you're in Congress you're one of a hundred in the Senate, or one of 435 in the House, so that your—the power is divided. But from here I look at a Congress and I look at the collective power of the Congress, particularly to block action, and it's substantial power."[25] As one of Reagan's advisers explained, "You can push Congress only so long. Eventually they get tired of the pressure, tired of the complaints back home about some program that's being cut, and they get mad."[26]

Constitutional arrangements for elections mean that after a presidential election every member of Congress next runs in a midterm election, in which no presidential coattails can help. Members of the president's party will *distance* themselves from unpopular presidential policies. Survey research indicates that in midterm congressional elections people who oppose the president are somewhat more likely to vote than supporters. Party identifiers who dislike the president's performance are 3 times more likely to vote for a congressional candidate of the other party than members of the other party who like it are to vote for a congressional candidate of the president's party.[27] Members of the president's party have always realized that he could not help them with a good effort but could hurt them badly with a poor one, and have therefore been his strongest critics. The president controls none of the important elements in a successful congressional career: nominations, campaign financing, advertising, polling, and local party organizations. What the Constitution separates, the president's policies cannot reunite.

The president as titular party leader

The president is chief of the party, but that does not entail much power over the party organization. Some presidents become fierce partisans, like Franklin Roosevelt, Jack Kennedy, and Ronald Reagan, helping build up state organizations and win their support; others disdain party leaders, ignore party committees, and govern in a more personal way—Lyndon Johnson, Richard Nixon, and Jimmy Carter, for example. But whether they are attracted to, or repelled by, party affairs, most presidents find themselves performing chores for their parties—fund-raising, campaigning, and appointing party members to office and getting very little in return.[28]

The president can get supporters elected as chairs and deputy chairs of the national party committee. A Republican president can also dominate the House and Senate congressional campaign committees, which are tied in closely with the Republican National Committee (RNC); a Democratic president has no such influence over the party's congressional campaign committees, which have traditions of complete independence from the White House. But even on the Republican side, the party committees have little influence on legislators. Rich Bond, the deputy chair of the RNC, told Republicans to vote for Reagan's tax program in 1981, warning them that he would "nail them to the wall" on campaign funding if they voted against the administration. But after a congressional uproar Richard Richards, the chairman of the RNC, apologized, saying, "It has never been, and never will become, the policy of the RNC to put pressure on members of Congress."[29]

ISSUE AND DEBATE

CABINET GOVERNMENT? *The background.* Should we abandon separation of powers and the system of checks and balances and adopt cabinet government? This question has been asked for more than a century.

Henry C. Lockwood, in his book *The Abolition of the Presidency* (1884), proposed to abolish the presidency by constitutional amendment: Congress would appoint department officers to an executive council, chaired by the secretary of state; the members would sit in Congress, initiate legislation, and participate in debates. They could be removed by Congress. Even earlier, Woodrow Wilson's article in *The International Review*, written when he was a senior at Princeton, proposed that the president select members of the Cabinet from Congress. They would retain seats in Congress and have the power to initiate legislation. They would resign if Congress rejected their programs; thus the majority party would determine the president's Cabinet.

Others have called for joint councils of legislators and Cabinet secretaries to coordinate government policies. For example, in 1946 Thomas Finletter proposed a "joint cabinet of Congress" consisting of eighteen congressional committee chairs; nine of these chairs and nine Cabinet secretaries would constitute a "joint executive-legislative cabinet." In 1979 Representative Henry Reuss proposed a constitutional amendment that would permit up to fifty legislators to serve in high executive offices while remaining in Congress.

Other proposals would allow Congress to vote "no confidence" in presidents and call for new presidential elections, and allow presidents to dissolve Congress and require new congressional elections if it refused to pass their programs. Each would require a constitutional amendment.

The pros. Proponents of cabinet government argue that it would reduce friction and increase coordination between the executive and legislative branches. It would lessen congressional resistance to a president's program and would allow electoral mandates to be translated into policy sooner. It would centralize the powers of government in the executive branch, but would make the executive branch accountable to congressional majorities and would reduce the possibility of an imperial presidency. Party discipline would increase, since the majority party would have to support the administration to keep it in power. Since the cabinet would enjoy the confidence of a majority of Congress (or else it would resign), there would be no need to rely on presidential prerogatives to push through policies; like the prerogatives of the crown in England, these powers would become mere formalities, and all that needed doing could be accomplished by legislation and by delegation of power from Congress to the president.

The cons. Opponents argue that the friction between the executive and legislative branches is useful; for example, it clipped the wings of an imperial presidency in the 1970s. Coordination, they believe is only a euphemism for presidential control of the government, even when it appears that Congress will control the Cabinet: in the British system, Parliament has become a rubber stamp for the prime minister as leader of the majority party. Opponents believe that the two legislative parties have just as much of an electoral mandate as the president, and they favor retaining midterm elections because they permit voters to renew or modify their mandate every two years.

Opponents argue that centralizing power eliminates the beneficial effects of redundancy and load sharing. Voters can use the two branches to exercise a double control on the bureaucracy: the president holds appointees responsible for implementing policies and may dismiss them if the public demands it; and an independent Congress can also influence the bureaucracy by means of laws, appropriations, and investigations to win public support, thus allowing voters to choose which branch to support when the branches come into conflict over their attempts to control the departments.

The outlook. At present none of the proposals for cabinet government are likely to pass Congress as constitutional amendments. Even at the height of the furor over the imperial presidency, proposals for the "vote of no confidence" went nowhere. Legislators want to make their own proposals and criticize the president without being part of a supercabinet that might inhibit their freedom of action or force them to share accountability for presidential decisions.

THE INSTITUTIONALIZED PRESIDENCY

No one person can meet all the demands of the presidency. The president needs help, and gets it from a number of agencies which constitute the *presidency*. These give the office some permanence, a routine, and a "memory" of how things are done; thus we say that we have an ***institutionalized presidency.*** The presidency consists of more than a dozen agencies and thousands of officials. They help the president communicate with the public and the media, develop new programs, and formulate a budget. But these agencies, while sometimes a great help to the president, also can create as many problems as they solve.

Presidential institutions

The White House Office. The president's personal and political aides are located in the White House Office (Figure 10-5). These staffers give the president advice on political matters; maintain liaison with congressional leaders,

Figure 10-5. Organization of the White House Office, 1981: the formal table of organization for the White House Office in President Reagan's first term. In 1985 the new chief of staff, Donald Regan, scrapped this structure and replaced it with an entirely new system in which all officials reported through him to the president. (Source: Presidency Research Group Newsletter, vol. 3, no. 2, April 1981.)

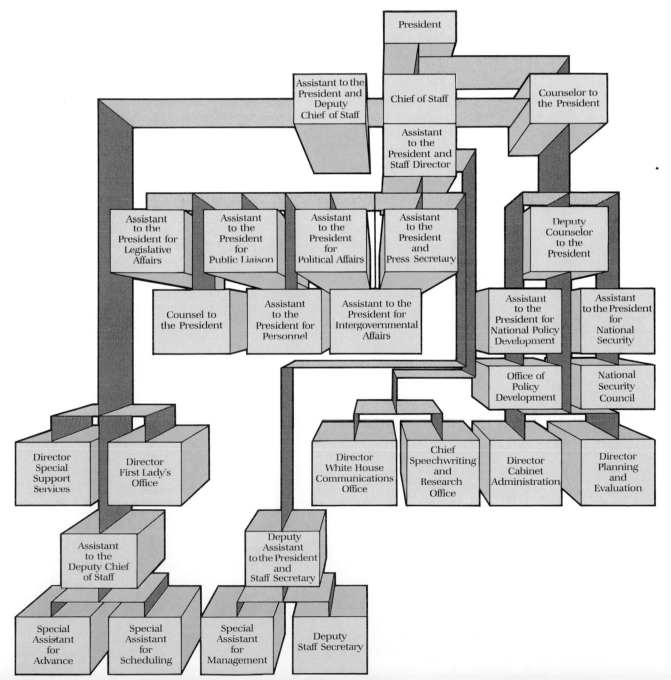

governors, mayors, and interest groups; supervise the department secretaries on matters of presidential concern; prepare messages and documents; draft presidential speeches; and give advice and counsel on the constitutionality and legality of proposed presidential actions. Support staff members run the White House and its grounds, assist the First Lady (they will someday assist the First Husband) and the First Family, and do the advance work for presidential trips. The way the Reagan White House was organized is shown in Figure 10-5.

The staff has grown enormously since it was created in 1939. Today it works out of two White House wings and the basement, and it overflows into the Executive Office Building next door. The staff consists of four groups: an inner circle of five to seven senior aides who consult regularly with the president; a second tier of top-level aides, each of whom is responsible for a particular function and runs his or her own "shop" with several assistants (but reports to someone in the inner circle rather than directly to the president); the remaining professional employees who report to a top-level aide; and, finally, the several hundred clerical and administrative workers who provide support. In addition to White House staffers, department personnel may be *detailed* to work in the White House; this expands the staff without enlarging the White House payroll. Figure 10-6 shows the great increase in staffing.

The Executive Office of the President. The president is also assisted by several agencies, known collectively as the ***Executive Office of the President*** (Figure 10-7). Unlike the White House staff, these agencies are concerned more with policies and processes than with communication and image—both are concerned with politics, but approach it from different angles. The Office of Management and Budget prepares the president's budget proposals to Congress, promotes more effective management of the bureaucracy, reviews proposed legislation from the departments and can recommend them to Congress as part of the president's program, and advises the president on whether to sign or veto bills passed by Congress. The Council of Economic Advisors

Figure 10-6. Growth of the White House Office, from Roosevelt to Ford. The White House staff and employees detailed from the departments have increased enormously since creation of the White House Office in 1939. About half the employees are clerical or support and half are professional and political. (Source: Hugh Heclo, *Studying the Presidency: A Report to the Ford Foundation*, New York, 1977, pp. 36–37.)

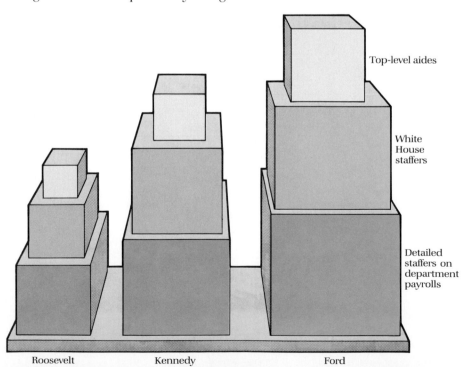

Top-level aides

White House staffers

Detailed staffers on department payrolls

Roosevelt   Kennedy   Ford

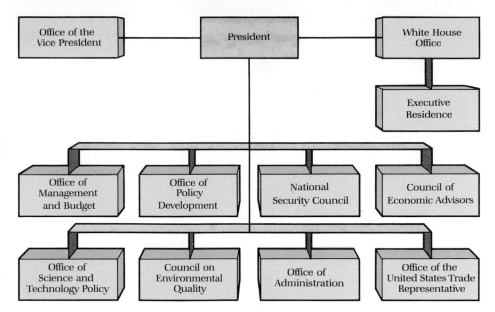

Figure 10-7. The Executive Office of the President comprises several agencies. (Their addresses and telephone numbers are given at the end of the chapter.)

prepares the president's economic report and advises on economic policy. The National Security Council deals with important military and diplomatic issues. These and other presidential agencies formulate programs to be submitted to Congress, coordinate activities that cross departmental boundaries, resolve conflicts between departments, impose presidential priorities on lower-level officials, implement important presidential orders, and help defend the White House program before Congress and in the media.

The presidential advisory system. To make decisions, presidents need advice and information. They can draw on a wide variety of sources:

- *The Cabinet*, which in some administrations meets frequently, but in others meets hardly at all. Usually the Cabinet is convened to give the president political advice, to serve as a sounding board for the president's ideas, or to make sure that top officials understand and speak for the president's policies.
- *Cabinet councils*, consisting of several Cabinet secretaries who work together on problems cutting across departmental boundaries.
- *Interagency task forces*, consisting of lower-level officials who work together on problems. In recent years these have included task forces on famine relief for African nations, child abuse, and immigration.
- *National commissions*, consisting of leaders from business, labor, and government, which advise the president on major national problems, such as juvenile delinquency, the environment, and the social security system. Experts are hired by the commission, and expert witnesses testify and propose new policies. Eventually the commission issues a report to the president.
- *"The wise men,"* usually former government officials who have served at the highest levels or former presidents, whom the president consults. They may also be asked to take on assignments, such as delivering messages to foreign leaders. They are often asked to serve as members of special study groups or national commissions.
- *"On-line" computer conferences*, such as the one held by the White House for 200 top business executives who made recommendations to a White House conference on productivity in 1983.

President Reagan confers with Vice President Bush in the White House oval office. (*Michael Evans: White House.*)

- *The vice president*, whose only function used to be to inquire after the health of the president. Today all that has changed. A "new vice presidency" has emerged as a result of the efforts of Nelson Rockefeller, Walter Mondale, and George Bush. While vice presidents still stand in for the president at apple-blossom festivals and homecomings, they also stand in at Cabinet meetings and represent the president on diplomatic visits abroad. They play a key role in midterm campaigns, are lobbyists for the president with Congress and governors, and serve as top presidential advisers. They have offices in the west wing, close to the president; large staffs which parallel the presidential agencies (Bush has about seventy aides); and even a mansion for entertaining. Provided they are team players, give the president all the credit for success and shoulder some of the blame, and do not leak stories to the press about their frustrations, vice presidents can play an important role in formulating policy.[30]

The advisory system allows presidents to make two claims: (1) that they have obtained the best advice available and (2) that by virtue of being the only nationally elected officials (other than vice presidents), their perspective and therefore their programs best represent the national interest.[31]

But these are only claims, designed to legitimize a program that may be quite political and partisan. The presidential counsels and councils, experts and advisers, have usually not been able to give the president proposals which were so persuasive on their merits that he could, simply by making them public, convince Congress and the nation to embrace them. The theories may be unproven, the proposed methods controversial. Critics cry doom even before the results are in, especially those who work for Congress, interest groups, and the media.

Problems with the institutionalized presidency

Sometimes the institutionalized presidency hurts presidents more than it helps them. For one thing, there are too many aides. They trip over one another trying to maintain their access to the president. They undercut one another, and their feuds are picked up by the media, which present the image of an administration in disarray. Even without the office politics, the White House Office would still be a hotbed of conflict: aides, by the nature of their job, have problems with Cabinet secretaries who resent their attempts to transmit orders in the name of the president, especially relatively junior aides who give orders to their seniors. The White House staff tries to insulate the president from the demands of Cabinet secretaries and may keep a secretary away from the Oval Office for months. The secretaries of state, defense, and the Treasury always square off against staffers whom they accuse of meddling. Meanwhile, presidential agencies become embroiled in a three-way tug-of-war with White House aides and Cabinet secretaries over who will make policy.

In actuality, all administrations are organized not according to formal tables of organization, but rather according to the way in which confidence flows down from the president to subordinates. Those whose power is increasing are those to whom the president listens and gives assignments; the others, no matter what their title or job description, are of less weight. Since there is no way to measure one's "confidence level" with the president accurately, aides are insecure, somewhat paranoid, and rather compulsive about serving their boss. "You don't understand," Henry Kissinger once chided a reporter, who was complaining about the way he hovered around Nixon; "when I'm not talking to the president, someone else is."

All this maneuvering around the president involves *court politics*. George Reedy, who served as press secretary in Lyndon Johnson's White House, described it as "a mass of intrigue, posturing, strutting, and cringing"; he considered this kind of politics to be nothing more than a conspiracy of "the untalented, the unpassionate, and the insincere. . . ."[32] Presidents may be surrounded by sycophants who are adept at telling them what they want to hear rather than what they ought to hear; and this may happen because, with dozens of aides to pick and choose from, presidents want it that way.

Presidents are faced with a no-win situation in staffing the White House. If they delegate great responsibility to staffers or presidential agencies, the media charge them with overdelegating and characterize them as lazy, inattentive, ignorant, and stupid. Eisenhower, Ford, and Reagan faced such charges. But if presidents immerse themselves in the details of most issues, keep their aides on a tight string, and closely guard all the important decisions, they are likely to become exhausted by the sheer mass of government business they must face. Then the media portray them as "grinds" who are too immersed in the details to understand the big picture or inspire the public—the charge made against Carter.

Organizational strategies

Presidents organize their staffs and presidential agencies differently, but the best of them recognize that the most important problem is not administrative efficiency but political efficacy. Some, like Dwight Eisenhower and Ronald Reagan, create highly formalized systems in which all issues move up a "ladder" for full consultation and briefings (Reagan even has a computerized system for tracking the progress of issues through the advisory system). Others, like Franklin Roosevelt, John Kennedy, and Lyndon Johnson, organize their operations more informally, making specific assignments to staffers who report back to them.

Those who prefer the staff-and-briefing system argue that it ensures that problems arrive at the president's desk after all options have been examined, all affected interests have been consulted, and all agencies have had their say. Critics claim that such a system is cumbersome, cautious, and slow and that it makes the president a captive of the staff. Presidents' options may be narrowed down by staffers; and presidents may be faced with a staff consensus that they have had no part in shaping. The informal system, however, sometimes loses track of important issues, especially if aides don't tell presidents about all the options or issues.

Presidents can sometimes take action to keep their staffers and agencies in line. Franklin Roosevelt fostered *competition*: he gave aides and even Cabinet officials overlapping assignments or jurisdictions and then waited for the fireworks. All officials found that others were interfering with or duplicating their functions, and each went to the president with negative information about a rival. Roosevelt obtained all the information and proposals he needed from the rivals, and therefore he knew more about every situation than any single aide.[33] The drawback with the competition approach, of course, is the sheer amount of time and energy that a president must invest to make it work.

A second approach is to allow one agency to carry out an assignment, but if it fails to produce, is criticized by the media, or acts contrary to presidential wishes, allow another agency to take over. *Redundancy* has been used by presidents as diverse as Nixon, Ford, Carter, and Reagan, who alternated between officials in the State Department, the National Security Council, the Defense Department, and the CIA in carrying out sensitive national security policies.

Multiple advocacy involves organizing the advisory system in such a way that the ideas of all those with different viewpoints and options are debated in the hearing of the president. This approach complements the staffing system but gives presidents a personal role; they can ask questions, uncover biases, and prevent officials from compromising over differences and presenting a consensus that forecloses the president's own options.[34]

PRESIDENTIAL LEADERSHIP: THE POWER TO PERSUADE

Presidents rarely have the constitutional powers or political support to do what they want to do, what the public expects them to do, and what they think they must do. The idealized version of presidential government, in which staffers and department secretaries work together smoothly, under the direction of the White House, does not exist. As Richard Chaney, the former chief of staff in the Ford administration, put it, "While you're here trying to do things, you are far more aware of the constraints than you are of the power. You spend most of your time trying to overcome obstacles getting what the President wants done."[35]

But some presidents succeed. Like Theodore Roosevelt and Richard Nixon, they conduct new diplomatic initiatives. Like Woodrow Wilson, Franklin Roosevelt, and Lyndon Johnson, they get major legislation through Congress. Like Ronald Reagan, they completely reverse the course of a generation of politicians before them. How do they do it?

Negotiating, compromising, and bargaining

To get what they want, presidents must bargain, even with members of their own party. American politicians are used to negotiation. It is the essence of the American political style. Listen to Ronald Reagan on the subject:

My belief is that in this democratic process which entails compromise, you seek what you think should be done and if you only get half of it, three-quarters of it, and politically it's impossible to get beyond that, I don't think it makes any sense to dig in your heels and say, then "I won't play." No, you take what you can get and tuck it away in your mind that you'll wait and come back another time and try to get the next bite. . . . And suppose even at the very end you've only gotten 70 or 75 percent of the goal. Well, that's a lot better than being back where you started.[36]

The president can provide things that other politicians want: patronage appointments for their supporters, contracts and programs for their constituents, and help for their projects. The president's powers can be used for their purposes. Sometimes the president trades powers for their help on other matters as a quid pro quo—a specific exchange of favor for favor. White House aides may organize a large package deal that offers tangible benefits to many legislators: they can point out the exact number of job-training slots allotted to a congressional district, the amount of money that each urban area will get as a result of a new housing bill, or the number of jobs that a construction measure will bring to each state.

The president has *vantage points*: formal powers which can block things that other politicians want. Presidents can threaten to veto pork-barrel bills and then lift their veto in return for promises to support bills they want. Franklin Roosevelt reportedly asked his aides occasionally to "give me something I can veto," just so that he could remind Congress that he had the power. Presidential vetoes are rarely overturned. (Vetoes of recent presidents are noted in Table 10-1.) The threat of a veto often results in compromises between the president and Congress, and so its influence is important, even though it may not actually be used.

Presidents do not always trade in specific favors. For one thing, if they trade with people who initially oppose their programs, the word gets out that the best way to get something from the White House is to announce opposition to the president's program. For another, people who support the president and get nothing in return will feel that they were taken for granted.

Table 10-1. Presidential vetoes, 1961 to 1985

John Kennedy	21
Lyndon Johnson	30
Richard Nixon	43
Gerald Ford	66
Jimmy Carter	31
Ronald Reagan (first term)	39

President Harry Truman's veto of the 1947 Taft-Hartley Act limiting the power of labor unions was overridden by a Republican-controlled Congress. (*Culver Pictures, Inc.*)

So presidents trade in **favor** rather than in *favors*: a relationship in which the people involved expect to help one another and therefore benefit from mutual support.[37] Presidents bestow their favor on legislators who support them most of the time, and they withdraw favor from those who desert them on crucial issues. They minimize the number of specific deals they enter into with the rule that they will reward an overall pattern of support rather than specific votes. (Sometime, of course, they have to abandon this rule when they are dealing with a particularly important party or committee leader or with someone who can cast a key vote at a crucial stage.) Sometimes presidents will not deal because they have neither the time nor the energy, because they cannot deliver, or because they are unwilling to offer what a legislator wants. They must then use other methods.

Persuasion

Presidential power largely consists in the ability to persuade people to do what the president wants them to do and to convince them that it is in their best interests to do it. "A leader is a man who has the ability to get other people to do what they don't want to do, and like it," Harry Truman said.[38] A president who can get people to take action of their own volition has converted them from trading partners into willing allies.

Lyndon Johnson used "the treatment." He brought his prey into the Oval Office, where he would argue, cajole, buttonhole, plea, browbeat, and wear down his opponent with every psychological ploy he could think of. The opposite approach is to "stroke" legislators, by offering them seats in the presidential boxes at Kennedy Center and inviting them to lunches, dinners, and diplomatic receptions, all in an effort to "break the ice" and trade friendship for support. Eisenhower's late-night poker games with congressional leaders of the opposition party did him more good than any lobbying ever could have.

Each president has persuaded by pointing out to others that what he wants them to do is what their own appraisal of their political position should impel them to do in their own interest. A president can point out not only the objective merit of a proposal, but also its political merits, and why in the long run it may help others, even though in the short run it may cost them some support. Or a president may offer people *compensation* if they take political heat: funding and campaign speeches in the next election and even a job with the administration if they lose.

There is the *grass-roots* strategy: the White House can pressure a legislator by appealing to influential constituents. Members of Congress may hear from defense contractors who want them to support the president's military budget, from business executives who want them to vote for a tax program, or from bankers who want them to vote for a new mortgage program for housing.

Finally, there is always *persuasion on the merits*. If a difficult policy issue offers no rewards and may present a danger to the public if it is not dealt with—such as toxic-waste disposal, acid rain, air and water pollution, or the soundness of the social security system—presidents may offer Congress a way out. They can appoint national commissions on a bipartisan basis which deal with the problem primarily in terms of expertise and the public interest and allow each party to share the credit and the blame for the proposal equally.

Presidential reputation and the power to persuade

No president can find the time to persuade or bargain with hundreds of legislators and top administration officials, let alone fifty governors, thousands of majors, and all the lobbyists in Washington.[39] Presidents must therefore find a way to cut down on face-to-face and telephone communications. The other people, in turn, must find a way to take the measure of a president, even without direct communication. Both sides solve their problem by considering the president's *reputation*.[40]

Reputation and anticipated reactions. Politicians make calculations about what the president might do under certain circumstances and then modify their own behavior accordingly. They do so because of the law of *anticipated reactions*: what you do in any situation is based in part on your assumptions about how other people will respond to your action. Politicians take reputation into account as they calculate the president's probable response to anything they might do—even though the president may not be talking directly with them or even know who they are.

All presidents come to Washington with a reputation, based on their conduct during the campaign and the transition period and on their previous record in public life. Those who have to work with the president have questions: Is the president a lightweight, a deep thinker, or a person of action? A compromiser and bargainer, or a tenacious fighter for all goals? Can the president see others' points of view and be sympathetic to their concerns—or, on the other hand, is the president self-centered? Does the president reward friends and punish enemies, or forget friends and buy off enemies? Is the president's word to be trusted?

Guarding reputation. By what they do, the presidents can influence answers to these and other questions. Suppose that a presidential aide is accused in the newspapers of corruption. You might think that the president should suspend that official, pending the outcome of an investigation. But consider the issue in terms of reputation. If the staffer is suspended, all the other officials will feel vulnerable and will assume that the president will abandon them at the first sign of trouble. Opponents will calculate that they can neutralize other assistants by threatening to make similar accusations. Presidents are better off sticking by their aides and striking back hard at those who make charges. By doing so, they send a message: an attack on an aide will be treated as an attack on the president. Morale in the administration is protected, and opponents come to understand that they had better be justified in making charges and that making them should be worth incurring presidential wrath.

Suppose that a president submits a highly controversial bill to Congress and stitches together a coalition of supporters by bargaining and persuasion. Now along come the president's economic advisers, who want to abandon the bill because of its expense. The president must, once again, consider reputation. A coalition of supporters who are risking their political careers has been created. What kind of reputation will the president have with them if they find themselves suddenly deserted? Are they likely to join another such coalition in the future? If the president decides to retreat, it must be done in a way that protects supporters.

Presidents who fail to guard their reputations will be viewed by others as ignorant, irresolute, and indecisive. Officials will assume that such presidents cannot help them and must fail in what they attempt. It is better to distance oneself from presidents like this than to work with them. And the president's problems will multiply.

NATIONAL AGENDA POLITICS

How national agenda politics works

Presidents who find themselves losing a political struggle in one arena may move it to another in which they have an advantage. If presidents cannot get what they want by using bargaining and persuasion with Washington insiders, they might try to appeal to the public using a strategy of **national agenda politics**. The president might follow the advice of Carter's pollster, Pat Cadell, who argued that "governing with public approval requires a continuing political campaign."[41] Increasingly, presidents have "gone public." They have increased their prime-time televised addresses, and there has been a fivefold increase in minor presidential speeches and public appearances in the past two decades.[42]

National agenda issues. Consider two examples of national agenda issues. First, when Richard Nixon was president, some Democrats called for comprehensive health insurance that would cost upward of $20 billion. In a bold move, Nixon gained control of the health care issue by redefining it. He argued that the way to improve health care was not to provide more aid to those who were already ill, but rather to do more basic research and conquer dreaded diseases. Focusing on cancer, Nixon announced the creation of a National Cancer Institute and a "war on cancer." By redefining the issue, Nixon avoided a major budget commitment; he spent only a few hundred million dollars on the cancer center, and even that money was transferred from other programs.

Second, the Democrats made "excellence in education" a major theme of

President Woodrow Wilson on a nationwide speaking tour to win public support for the League of Nations, at the San Francisco City Hall. (*Culver Pictures.*)

The constitutionally mandated state of the union message was usually sent to Congress in the nineteenth century. Today presidents deliver it in person to a national television audience. (*Wally McNamee: Woodfin Camp.*)

the 1984 presidential campaign. Reagan was able to redefine and take control of the issue. Instead of agreeing that major new funding was needed, the president proposed "merit pay" for excellent teachers, more local control of schools, and a "back to basics" approach—none of which would cost any federal money.

Presidents use national agenda politics to push their programs through Congress. Franklin Roosevelt's 100 days of recovery legislation in the midst of the depression included radio addresses that explained what Congress was doing; this maintained his authority, enhanced his reputation, and gave Congress the confidence to continue. Lyndon Johnson's "great society" programs were passed amid a blitz of television, radio, newspaper, and magazine publicity for his proposals, especially those dealing with antipoverty efforts. Ronald Reagan used a national agenda strategy to get Congress to pass his supply-side tax and spending cuts.

The January messages. Each year the president has the first shot at the national agenda, delivering several *January messages* to Congress. These include the state of the union address, usually delivered in person to a joint session of Congress; the economic message, which accompanies the *Report of the Council of Economic Advisors*; and the budget message, which accompanies the *Budget of the United States*. At times the president may make an address to the nation about an economic program or budget shortly after submitting it to Congress. These messages and speeches form the core of the president's program. The White House press officials highlight the most important parts for the media in briefings just before their release. Interviews are arranged with the president, Cabinet secretaries, and other top officials to further the administration's viewpoint. These messages and reports always give the president the political initiative: politicians from both parties must react to the president's agenda.

It takes several months (in the case of the budget, almost a year) to prepare the January messages. The White House asks the Cabinet secretaries and career bureaucrats for their ideas. Outside experts are consulted. The presidential agencies consider these proposals and make their own recommendations. Differences are thrashed out in Cabinet councils. Eventually the president and a small group of senior aides determine the priorities. The president then calls in speech writers and outlines proposals. Competing drafts for speeches become a battlefield on which aides and Cabinet secretaries can make their arguments.

The January messages, speeches, and reports are prepared through **action-forcing cycles**: they require the administration to (1) canvass departments and the advisory system to develop new programs; (2) debate the priorities and policies of the government; (3) make decisions and resolve disputes; and (4) present a program to Congress by a specific date. Then the process starts all over again in a new annual cycle. It therefore becomes convenient for all those involved to organize their work around the four cycles in a presidential term. Because of the length of time involved, the president can allow aides to float trial balloons: leaks to reporters about possible programs. Thus public reaction can be gauged before it is decided whether to put them in the messages.

Presidential television. Presidents make other televised addresses to the nation. They may address a joint session of Congress, either during a crisis or when they introduce a major piece of legislation. They may speak to the public directly from the White House by obtaining free time from the major networks. Some observers believe that presidents can overwhelm the opposition using television, and proposals have been made to give the other party a formal right of reply and to provide for regular "national debates" between the two parties.[43] The opposition does receive free time from the networks to reply to the State of the Union address and some other speeches, but the time slots are less favorable, and not all networks carry them. The White House cues in the media before, during, and after the presidential address, highlighting the argument

Public persuasion is an important presidential resource. President Kennedy consults with his speechwriter, Theodore Sorensen (far right). (*Jacques Lowe: Woodfin Camp.*)

President Reagan dramatizes his "back to basics" theme by sitting in on a high school English class. (*Michael Evans: White House.*)

and giving reporters summaries of the speech and the key points. Important columnists may get interviews with the president. But media coverage of presidential speeches is often skeptical and sometimes hostile. Attempts by the White House to spoon-feed reporters and influence coverage become an issue that is critically reported.

Televised presidential addresses have not unbalanced American politics. Occasionally, a White House request for network time will be denied if it seems partisan. More often, the networks negotiate on timing so as not to disrupt their schedules. Presidents themselves are reluctant to bump popular programs off the air (they even postpone the inaugural ceremony if it conflicts with the NFL Superbowl game) and they find that taking to the airwaves too often results in lower ratings and lessened impact. Presidents' use of television is self-regulating: too much exposure to the Oval Office jades the audience, and so the White House limits it.

Pseudo events. Presidents rely on *pseudo events* in their use of television. Carter's "town meetings" and Reagan's visits to schoolhouses, where he read Shakespeare to students, are examples. Presidents leave Washington and campaign for their programs because it is fun to be on the road and because it permits them to bypass the critical Washington press corps and gain coverage from a local press, which is more likely to be favorable.[44] Even some of the summit conferences, such as the annual economic summit for the heads of major noncommunist industrial powers, are primarily public relations showcases. (The Reagan White House put on an election-year road show in 1984, including trips in the spring to Korea, Japan, China, and Ireland, capped by a London economic summit.) One event a day is planned, held early so that it will make the evening news. It is packaged to provide good "visuals," and ample "photo opportunities" are arranged each day by the White House Photo Office—but no opportunity for reporters to question the president.

The president's relations with the media are sometimes cooperative, sometimes antagonistic, but usually difficult and uncertain. Presidents seldom get an opportunity to show their frustration with the media. Addressing the 1983 White House press photographers' dinner, President Reagan felt free to poke fun at his hosts, believing that the event was off the record. It wasn't. (*Gerald Martineau: Washington Post.*)

News conferences. News conferences, which were started by Woodrow Wilson, were first used extensively by Franklin Roosevelt, who had twenty or so White House reporters crowd into the Oval Office periodically for interviews. This informal approach was transformed by Dwight Eisenhower into a staged conference, held in a larger room and filmed and shown on television. John Kennedy moved his news conferences into an auditorium and permitted live television coverage. Presidents use news conferences to address the nation directly. "I would rather have 60 million people watch President Reagan than have 30 million people seeing him interpreted by Sam Donaldson on the evening news," says Michael Deaver, a former Reagan aide.[45] The president makes a brief opening statement, which is followed by reporters' questions: first from AP and UPI wire service reporters, and then from correspondents for the three national networks, and then from other reporters.

The president prepares for news conferences during briefings conducted by the staff and important Cabinet officials. The purpose of these sessions is to rehearse positions on existing policy, and they may also be used as action-forcing processes to spur the development of new policies in anticipation of a question. The president can use a news conference to signal policy changes to members of Congress and to foreign governments.

Presidents need not hold news conferences when they are on the defensive, since the conferences are scheduled solely at the president's discretion.[46] Some presidents are more accessible than others. Roosevelt and Kennedy held frequent conferences; Johnson held many early in his term, when things were going well, and then he tapered off; and Nixon held few, especially during his second term. Carter held fifty-nine, but Reagan held only twenty-seven during his first term. The average for all presidents is around one conference a month.

Recently the White House has decided to bypass the national media and work more closely with local reporters. A White House wire and computer service feeds documents, speeches, and press releases directly to local news desks. In 1985 the White House television studio began to set up teleconferences so that local reporters could interview Washington officials; the videotapes were sent by satellite to local stations for rebroadcast.

Public liaison. Presidents communicate with leaders of labor, business, scientific, cultural, religious, and ethnic groups. Presidential aides give these people briefings and information and invite them to lunches and meetings with the president and Cabinet leaders. The president bestows favor for their support, and they have access to the president when they want the government to do something for them. The president hopes that in return, they will influence Congress.

Sometimes the White House simulates support. It may orchestrate a series of phone calls, letters, and telegrams, supposedly from people supporting the president after a speech, but actually coming from political operatives and local party workers in each state. The White House may channel leftover campaign funds to its supporters so that they can take out newspaper advertisements praising the administration's decisions.[47]

Pollsters. The same pollsters who help presidents during the campaign are hired by the party to conduct polls during their administrations. Polls help the president shape not only national agenda politics but also a whole program.

President Reagan relies on Richard Wirthlin, who does nightly "tracking" polls to detect shifts in attitudes. He also does monthly "eagles," which are in-depth polls for the White House and the RNC. His firm, Decision Making Information, receives close to $1 million annually from the RNC.[48] Wirthlin meets with White House aides regularly and with Reagan once a month to discuss political strategy.

Limits to national agenda politics

Presidential shortcomings. National agenda politics is not a cure for a president's weakness. For one thing, most presidents (Reagan aside) have been poor media performers. Theodore Sorensen, a speech writer for President Kennedy, noted a "longterm decline over several administrations in the quality of English spoken at the White House."[49] Presidents Johnson, Nixon, Ford, and Carter were ineffective in front of cameras and microphones.

Most presidential speeches that try to sway public opinion are unsuccessful. President Ford's speech unveiling his economic program, complete with its WIN button (standing for "whip inflation now"), became a national joke. The more President Carter appealed for support for his energy program, the lower his approval ratings fell. After delivering five speeches, he canceled a sixth one at the last minute because he knew that it would just make things worse. Only one-third of the public believed that the energy crisis was real and approved of his handling of it.[50] One study by political scientists of fifty-six public issues between the early 1930s and the early 1970s showed that on only a few did a president sway public opinion, and then only when he was popular; otherwise, his efforts often made things worse.[51]

Presidents may lose control of the timing of national agenda politics, as Kennedy did when he had to advance his own schedule for the introduction of civil rights legislation after massive demonstrations by civil rights marchers in the south. Presidents may also lose control of the definition of an issue, as Nixon did when a combination of Harvard medical researchers and members of Congress discovered that people were hungry in the United States; the result was a massive expansion of the food stamp program. Moreover, presidents may not communicate their own sense of urgency; this happened to Reagan in dealing with El Salvador and Nicaragua. Finally, a president may even lose the debate on an issue, as Truman found out when the American Medical Association convinced the public that his plan for health insurance was a form of "socialized medicine."

The media and the national agenda. The national news media may have more influence on the national agenda than the president. Commentators can raise issues, and news departments can cover events, provide their own context and explanations, and challenge the administration's version. Some network news programs cover the president using the *diary* format: what the president did that day. Others use the *tipster* approach, offering the "inside story" as to why the president did something. The White House becomes most upset, however, if a network takes the *populist* approach, focusing on the impact of a presidential decision by suggesting that ordinary people are going to suffer because the president is favoring the "interests" of the wealthy. According to a study conducted for *TV Guide*, over a two-week period in 1983 the networks differed significantly in their reporting of news about the president. While NBC and ABC concentrated on the diary and analysis approaches, CBS took the populist approach. It presented more stories about the White House, and most of them, by a 7-to-1 margin, were negative.[52] The CBS anchor, Dan Rather, has complained strongly about White House pressure on his network superiors to change the tone of his coverage.

The White House complains most bitterly about lengthy documentaries which seek to influence the national agenda. In 1982 CBS produced a documentary entitled *People Like Us*, which depicted three families and a church program, all of which were affected by Reagan's cutbacks of social programs. The network denied the administration's request to reply. As one White House official put it, "This was a powerful emotional documentary, to which we had no way of responding. It was like being hit with a two-by-four."[53]

The media can publicize other national agenda challenges to the president. It is always a story when someone who is invited to the White House attacks a presidential policy. Consider a 17-year-old high school student, Ariela Gross, who was to receive an award as a "presidential scholar." She decided to present Reagan with a petition urging his support for a congressional nuclear freeze resolution. After the story hit the papers, the White House invited her to a twenty-minute meeting in the Oval Office. Ms. Gross had her meeting with Reagan, and then she gave interviews on the White House lawn, concluding: "He said here today that we should be proud of a country that wants to remain strong. And I say that I am ashamed of the leaders of this country who can vote for nuclear freeze and then turn around and vote for the most dangerous and expensive missile system that this country has ever suggested."[54] All in all, it was quite a good day for Ms. Gross, and a bad one for the president.

Runaway national commissions and task forces can also embarrass the president. The White House Conference on Civil Rights in 1966 had an agenda that went considerably further than President Johnson's, and his attempts to manipulate the delegates were uncovered by the media, to his embarrassment. The Kerner Commission, which blamed urban unrest on "white racism," was disavowed by Johnson, who feared white backlash against these charges. Rich-

Presidents can use Air Force 1 to crisscross the nation, making brief airport speeches in support of their programs. (*Max Winter: Picture Group.*)

ard Nixon repudiated the findings of the Eisenhower Commission on Campus Unrest because it did not pin the blame on student demonstrators, whom Nixon called "bums." When Ronald Reagan's Private Sector Survey on Cost Control issued a report detailing a plan that it believed could save the government $54 billion, Reagan found the proposals to be so politically controversial that he distanced the White House from them. Instead of allowing Peter Grace, the chairman, to present his report in person at the White House, Reagan arranged for a briefing to be held in a Commerce Department auditorium, and he did not attend. One White House official, asked about the site, responded that the briefing should have been held in Siberia.[55]

Presidents often resort to overblown rhetoric and hyperbole. They declare "war" on poverty, cancer, and crime. They proclaim that a summit meeting with the Chinese is the most important event of the twentieth century or that a treaty between Egypt and Israel is the diplomatic triumph of the decade. They appoint a "czar" to coordinate government efforts to solve one crisis after another. This rhetorical excess leaves the public with inflated expectations, and when the euphoria wears off, the burden of proof is on the president. The White House tries to lead, but many people do not have the energy or the interest to follow.[56] Instead of sounding good, the president appears to be sounding off.

The public these days is therefore more likely to trust media sources than the White House. Summing up the problem, the political scientist George Edwards concluded that "presidents cannot depend upon leading the public any more than they can rely on understanding public opinion."[57] Or, as put more elegantly by John Travolta, "I can do all that Reagan does. I do it all the time and have a bigger audience."[58]

PREROGATIVE POWERS

Presidential ***prerogative powers*** are those powers granted to the president by the Constitution. They include ***express powers,*** which are explicitly mentioned, such as the veto and appointment powers; **implied powers,** which presidents say they need in order to accomplish what is expressly permitted; and **inherent powers** (that is, all executive functions) which the president claims because of separation of powers.

The **Lockean prerogative,** named after the English philosopher John Locke, is the power to act without reference to the law, and sometimes even against it, in a crisis when the existence of the nation is at stake.[59] Presidents never forget that to protect the people, they may have to go beyond the confines of the Constitution or temporarily suspend the execution of the laws, even though they will be acting illegally or unconstitutionally (though no president admits to that). In some nations emergency power is provided in the constitution itself, which provides for martial law or for a state of emergency or a state of siege. Our Constitution makes no mention of such powers or of the Lockean prerogative. Presidents fashion their own such powers, although they claim that they are not violating the Constitution when they do so. Richard Nixon even argued, after he resigned from office, that a president cannot violate the Constitution or laws because "if the President does it, it is legal."[60] The Supreme Court has ruled that presidents may not be sued for their acts committed while in office, no matter how damaging (which goes a long way toward ratifying Nixon's idea), although aides may be sued and the president remains liable for criminal prosecution and impeachment.[61]

·**Using prerogative powers**

Presidents have used prerogative powers when they could not get what they wanted by persuading Congress. George Washington declared neutrality in the wars between Britain and France on his own authority because he knew that Congress would not do so. Thomas Jefferson purchased the Louisiana Territory from Napoleon without law or appropriation. James Polk, on his own authority, maneuvered American forces in disputed territories to begin the Mexican-American war. Abraham Lincoln used emergency powers to raise military forces, provide weapons to union loyalists in West Virginia, suspend the writ of habeas corpus, and arrest suspected Confederate sympathizers; then he called Congress into session to retroactively ratify these and other actions taken at the outset of the Civil War. Theodore Roosevelt mediated a war between Russia and Japan and won a Nobel peace prize for his efforts, even though no such responsibility is mentioned in the Constitution. Woodrow Wilson invaded Mexico and the Soviet Union without congressional sanction. Franklin Roosevelt ordered the Navy into a shooting war with Axis ships in the north Atlantic before the United States entered World War II. On their own authority, Harry Truman, Lyndon Johnson, and Richard Nixon sent American forces to fight undeclared wars in Korea, Vietnam, and Cambodia. Jimmy Carter abrogated a mutual security treaty with Taiwan to cement a diplomatic relationship with China.

The exercise of prerogative powers follows a characteristic pattern. Presidents make decisions with the help of a circle of close and trusted advisers, often keeping their intentions secret not only from Congress but also from career officials. They issue orders to their subordinates, who are expected to carry them out without regard to their legality. In a crisis, the president may bypass many layers of bureaucracy and establish a direct chain of command with officials at the scene. The policies are implemented suddenly, as *faits accomplis* (accomplished facts), and then presented to Congress and the nation, often in a televised presidential address.

Departments and agencies rarely participate in deliberations, as in national agenda politics. There is no bargaining with, or persuasion of, subordinates and members of Congress before action is taken, as there is in routine negotiating politics. In fact, legislative leaders are just as much in the dark about what the White House is up to as is the American public.

Legitimizing prerogative powers

The use of prerogative powers leaves presidents open to charges that they are abusing their own powers, usurping those of Congress, and instituting an imperial presidency. They must therefore legitimize their actions with the public. Voters want strong, decisive leadership, but they trust congressional decision making more than presidential decision making in foreign affairs as well as domestic issues, and they are reluctant to grant prerogative powers to presidents.[62] Close to three-fifths of the people want Congress and the president to share responsibility, while fewer than one-tenth want the president to make decisions unilaterally.[63] Presidential approval ratings rise when both branches work together, and they fall when the branches confront each other.

Party conflict. The White House tries to unify the president's party and split the opposition. It briefs legislators and prepares speeches which they can deliver on the floor of Congress. It gives classified information to them so that they can discredit charges by critics. But usually the president's own party splits badly, while the opposition unites. This was the case in 1808, when Jefferson's foreign policy was repudiated by Congress; in 1832, when Jackson's vetoes and his firing of a Treasury secretary led many Democrats to leave his party and unite with the new Whig Party; and in 1968, when the fiercest opposition to the Vietnamese war came not from Republicans but from a Democrat, William Fulbright, the chair of the Senate Foreign Relations Committee.

Public support. Presidents often lose the battle for public support. After Truman seized the steel mills in 1950 to keep production going during a labor dispute in the midst of the Korean war, the mill owners fought back with charges that he was paying off a political debt to the unions. Public opinion swung against the president. Eventually the Supreme Court found the seizure unconstitutional, which was a major blow to presidential war powers. Truman, Johnson, and Nixon all lost home-front battles for public support of the wars in Korea and Indochina as casualties mounted; ultimately this resulted in settlements that were less advantageous than might otherwise have been obtained. In the post-Vietnam era, Reagan felt so constrained by public opinion that he could not keep marines in Lebanon after 250 had been killed in a suicide bombing, and he could not continue mining the harbors of Nicaragua after the role of the CIA was disclosed by the media.

The case for the president. In their attempts to legitimize the use of prerogative powers, presidents are assisted by the legal counsel in the White House, who runs a seven-person "law firm for the president," and by the attorney general and the assistant attorney general in charge of the Office of Legal Counsel, who prepare briefs defending the presidential exercise of power. These officials see their main function as defending and expanding the powers of the presidency in the face of attacks by critics. (The attorney general may submit a formal *opinion* in advance of an important presidential order, as Robert Jackson did when Franklin Roosevelt transferred destroyers to Great

Britain during World War II, in spite of congressional laws which seemed to forbid that action.) Counsel for the Defense Department and the State Department prepare legal briefs which set forth the gravity of a situation and justify presidential powers. They emphasize administration intelligence which cannot be revealed. Spokespersons for presidents claim that they are acting in the national interest and that opponents lack the information and expertise necessary for correct decisions. They cite the presidential oath of office and responsibility to protect the nation.

Assessing presidential claims. We need not accept all these presidential claims at face value. Presidents do not restrict their use of prerogative powers to crises. They use secrecy, commands, vetoes, appointments and removals, withholding of funds, and suspension of the execution of laws as vantage points, creating bargaining opportunities in routine politics. And presidents use emergency powers in situations that are not really emergencies, as the Supreme Court found when it chastised Truman for seizing the steel mills when other ways to settle the dispute were available.

Presidents claim that they have more information and expertise than their critics, but this is not always true. Nixon, for example, invoked **executive privilege** and claimed that Watergate involved "national security matters," which justified his refusal to testify before Congress and to provide evidence to the courts. But this claim was merely a ploy to get the FBI to stop investigating the burglary of the Democratic National Committee headquarters. Even when wars or covert intelligence operations are involved, the main issue between the president and the critics is the wisdom of the policy, and it is rare that any particular bit of secret information that the president has would be decisive in discrediting the arguments of critics.

Checking prerogative powers. Congress can exercise the impeachment power, but it will not do so when the president invokes prerogative powers for diplomatic or military purposes, however controversial. And the process itself may be stalled or nullified by presidents who keep their actions secret, classify vital information, or invoke executive privilege against Congress and the courts. A president may even be able to stave off inquiries into impeachable offenses. Presidents can also use their pardon prerogative for the benefit of people caught breaking the law on their behalf (although they may not pardon anyone in an impeachment proceeding); this might induce people to withhold testimony or to lie for the president during an inquiry.

It is true that the ultimate check remains: retribution by the voters at the polls. But even this can be threatened by prerogative powers if they are used for surveillance of opponents to obtain political intelligence; for blackmail, intimidation, or dirty tricks to harass and disrupt the opposition; or for secrecy to keep such sordid operations from the public.

Risks of using prerogative powers

Using prerogative powers is risky. It can result in the *frontlash* effect: the president resolves a crisis successfully and, by doing so, establishes a consensus in the parties and in Congress that the exercise of the powers involved is legitimate. Examples include George Washington's diplomacy and proclamation of neutrality in the 1790s, Franklin Roosevelt's diplomatic and war powers during the Second World War, and Jimmy Carter's observance of SALT II limitations in

The first and only president to resign the office, Richard Nixon departs for California on August 10, 1974. (*Holland Freeman: Magnum Photos.*)

the absence of a treaty with the Soviet Union. But there is also a possibility of a *backlash*: the president controls the situation, but the president's own party splits on the issue, and there is considerable opposition in Congress, which may pass laws that curb powers or regulate presidential powers; and the Supreme Court or lower federal courts may declare the exercise of power unconstitutional. The president may retire or be defeated at the polls. Examples include controversies surrounding Andrew Jackson's use of the veto and removal power, Harry Truman's seizure of the steel mills and entry into the Korean war, Lyndon Johnson's involvement in the Vietnamese war, and Richard Nixon's refusal to spend funds appropriated by Congress.

There is the *overshoot and collapse* effect: to members of Congress and to much of the public, the exercise of prerogative powers seems to involve a serious abuse of power. The actions seem illegitimate, and congressional leaders hold hearings in order to force the removal of lower-level officials and repudiate a policy or even begin proceedings to censure (Andrew Jackson and John Tyler) or impeach (Andrew Johnson and Richard Nixon) the president.

No president has ever been convicted and removed from office as a result of impeachment proceedings. Only Andrew Johnson was actually impeached and tried, and Richard Nixon resigned before the House took any action; in both cases, however, efforts to impeach were accompanied by a resurgence of congressional power and a major reshaping of the presidency. Johnson survived impeachment, but only by giving up several claims to power and agreeing to follow Congress on most issues. During the months leading up to Nixon's resignation, Congress passed laws regulating presidential war powers and preventing the president from withholding funds appropriated by Congress; and the Supreme Court indicated that the judiciary, not the White House, would determine the president's proper use of the executive privilege and would examine any evidence in the president's possession.

Criteria for use of prerogative powers

We can make a distinction between an *imperial presidency* and a *crisis presidency*: the former undermines the system of checks and balances to institute unrestrained presidential government. While Congress and the courts remain, they have no independent power; in ancient Rome, this happened to the senate after the assumption of almost total power by the Caesars. The crisis presidency, however, is instituted to *preserve* the fundamental values of a democratic and constitutional government when the very life of the nation may be at stake.[64] To distinguish between the abuse of power and its vigorous use in crises, the following standards may be helpful:

- Emergency powers should not be used for personal or party advantage.
- There should be no interference with the next elections.
- Controversial prerogative powers should be exercised only when a crisis is extreme, when a delay might prove fatal, and when the regular constitutional procedures would involve such a delay.
- These powers should be exercised only when no laws provide viable alternatives and when nothing in the Constitution expressly prohibits the action.
- The use of these powers should be preceded by the widest possible advance consultation among top officials and, if possible, congressional leaders.
- The president should make available to Congress and the judiciary (when court cases are involved) the full record of actions in the crisis. The courts should make the final determination if the president wants to withhold information and claims executive privilege.
- After the emergency, Congress should legislate and put presidential powers and actions under law, retroactively if necessary.
- Congress by law should be able to override presidential actions.
- The impeachment powers should function throughout the emergency.[65]

President Lincoln, whose statesmanship in preserving the union created the standard by which we still evaluate the performance of presidents in crises today. (*Culver Pictures.*)

If presidents act as Lincoln did during the Civil War—if they hold elections, respect the system of checks and balances, and confine the use of prerogative powers to an emergency—then these powers, even those which seem to disregard the Constitution, can be accommodated by our political system. Even so, it is always useful to remember the warning given by the Supreme Court, at the end of the Civil War, when it observed that "wicked men, ambitious of power, with a hatred of liberty and contempt of law, may fill the place once occupied by Washington and Lincoln."[66]

POWER AND LEADERSHIP

Leadership is at the core of presidential power. Presidents must have a sense of timing and pace, and they must know how to bluff, how to compromise, how to persuade, and how to bargain. They have to know the pros and cons of negotiating, setting the national agenda, and using prerogative powers—and they must know how to combine these tactics into an overall strategy suitable for each issue. They need to have the personal skills necessary to inspire their supporters, and they must be able to build different coalitions on different issues, converting adversaries on one issue into backers on another. They have to know when to press their advantage and when to stop, so that adversaries will not become enemies. They must know how to advance, but just as important, they have to know how to retreat and cut their losses. And above all, presidents must understand power.

The power problem

"What Presidents do every day," according to Richard Neustadt, a political scientist and former White House aide, "is to make decisions that are mostly thrust upon them, the deadlines all too often outside their control, on options mostly framed by others, about issues crammed with technical complexities and uncertain outcomes."[67] Or, as Ronald Reagan put it, "Sometimes I have to read the papers to find out what I did yesterday." Under these circumstances presidents may become "clerks" whose powers are exercised as often for the benefit of others as for themselves, unless they extricate themselves from the pressures converging on them and find some room to maneuver.

At the heart of an effective presidency is the incumbent's search for *personal influence*. Presidents get advice from aides and experts, but only they can understand their own stakes and guard their own reputation. Presidents must want power and feel comfortable exercising it. Presidents must influence the calculations and behavior of people who make and carry out policy. Presidents must use their resources for their own purposes. No one with whom they deal, whether legislators, department secretaries, or interest-group lobbyists, has their responsibilities or their viewpoint. Presidents must come to their own decisions in terms of stakes and political risks—but they must also recognize the stakes and risks of others and extend their authority by communicating their reasoning effectively to others.

Much of the public believes that effective presidents first figure out their goals, in terms of the national interest, and then develop political strategy and tactics. This view is dead wrong. Principles do not precede political strategy, and the *ends* do not determine the *means*. Instead, the *means* often determine the *ends*. The power stakes of presidents often determine what they decide they want to do. As presidents examine issues, they think about their own reputations, their own authority, and even their own legitimacy. They consider how any decision made about an issue today will boost or diminish their chances for winning another contest tomorrow. They consider how a particular issue will help them unify a coalition of supporters and split the opposition party; how they can develop a reputation as a winner; how they can time decisions so that unpopular sacrifices come early in the term and benefits to voters come in the third and fourth years, in time for renomination and reelection.

Those who believe that presidents should consider power stakes and use them to determine goals argue that there is no such thing as the "national interest" which can be considered apart from presidential power. Richard Neustadt argues that "the things a President must think about if he would build his influence are not unlike those bearing on the viability of public policy. The correspondence may be inexact, but it is close. And because the President's own frame of reference is at once so all-encompassing and so political, what he sees as a balance for himself is likely to be close to what is viable in terms of public policy."[68] As Neustadt concludes, "In a relative but real sense one can say of a President what Eisenhower's first Secretary of Defense once said of General Motors: What is good for the country is good for the President and vice versa."[69]

Limits to power politics

The power politics approach to the presidency has left many people dissatisfied.[70] For one thing, in the post-Watergate era, it is difficult to sustain the proposition that what is good for the president is always good for the country. A president like Nixon who condones and covers up a violation of the Constitution and the laws is a danger to the country, and when such a president guards power stakes, it is not in the public interest. For another, it is not always clear how a president goes about guarding power stakes. As Neustadt admits, "The insights power offers into policy diverge, pointing many ways at once, thus limiting their usefulness as guides to viability."[71] To tell presidents that "insights diverge" may leave them muttering about consulting the stars or tea leaves, if that is the best their advisers can do. Presidents must remember that power is not the only value to be considered: the legitimacy of presidential action is also at issue (as Neustadt recognizes), and it is as important to keep within the bounds of law and propriety as it is to exercise maximum influence.

Perhaps most important of all, a presidency that is based on bargaining, persuasion, manipulation of public opinion, and prerogative actions may ultimately leave the American people without ideals, without principles, and without faith in the government or its leaders. Moving the nation may involve more than instrumental use of political techniques, for as James MacGregor Burns asks, "In protecting themselves—their reputations, choices, resources— what are chief executives guarding? If they constantly protect themselves, to what extent are they also guarding the *purpose* they are supposedly ultimately to be serving? How do they draw the line between preserving power for themselves and expending it for broader goals?"[72]

Principles and power

Ultimately presidents can lead the nation only if they inspire it through an appeal to principle. They must have a vision, not merely of their own power stakes but also of a better future, and they must communicate that vision to the people in a way that enhances their authority.

Most of our great presidents exercised what James MacGregor Burns has called ***transformational leadership***: they went beyond the existing divisions and deals of the politics of their time and summoned politicians and the people to enter new and uncharted territory. They possessed a deep-felt sense of where they wanted to take the country. They transformed the nature of the debates, the terms of reference, and even the style of politics. They created new constitutional arrangements, as George Washington did with the formation of the union, as Abraham Lincoln did with its preservation, and as Franklin Roosevelt did with the country's assumption of vast new powers in economic matters. They transformed the party system by shaping new electoral coalitions. They were able to simplify issues down to the bare essentials so that everyone would be emotionally as well as intellectually affected by their arguments. They provided a sense of common and overriding national purpose rather than a set of bargains. Presidents who exercise transformational leadership may be rare, but they accomplish more in one or two terms than a generation of other presidents do through politics as usual.

An appeal to principle may well turn out to be the way to reverse the declining fortunes of the modern presidency. A reputation for statesmanship and principled leadership may yet turn out to be the best presidential politics.

IN CONCLUSION

The powers of the president are not clearly defined by the Constitution, which remains silent, ambiguous, and underdefined on some important points. Except in periods of realignment or reinforcement of the party system, presidents control neither the party as organization nor the legislative party, which means that they do not lead disciplined party majorities as in a parliamentary system. To exert effective leadership, presidents must create coalitions: they do so by bargaining, and if that fails they go to the people by dominating the national agenda. In recent years presidents have relied increasingly on use of the media, at a time when presidential popularity has declined. Presidents may also use prerogative powers unilaterally to resolve issues when they believe that they cannot get support from Congress. The exercise of such powers may lead to a frontlash effect, which expands our conception of the presidency; to a backlash effect, which diminishes the powers of the office; or, in rare cases, to a collapse in the authority and legitimacy of an administration. The most effective presidents know how to guard their reputations, recognize their power stakes, and understand that means and ends are inextricably linked. But the truly great ones are also transformational leaders, who move the nation more by force of argument and vision than by the maneuvers they make and the prerogative powers they must exercise.

NOTES

1. James MacGregor Burns, *Presidential Government*, Avon, New York, 1965, p. 351.
2. *The Federalist*, number 70.
3. *Time*, Nov. 10, 1980, p. 30; "Making Reagan Accountable," *The Wall Street Journal*, Apr. 20, 1984.
4. Bobby Baker, *Wheeling and Dealing*, Norton, New York, 1971, p. 265.
5. Michael Nelson, "Evaluating the Presidency," in Michael Nelson (ed.), *The Presidency and the Political System*, Congressional Quarterly Press, Washington, D.C., 1984, pp. 5–28.
6. Thomas Cronin, *The State of the Presidency*, 2d ed., Little, Brown, Boston, 1980, p. 5.
7. Edwin Meese, "The Institutional Presidency: A View from the White House," *Presidential Studies Quarterly*, vol. 13, no. 2, spring 1983, p. 191.
8. George Edwards III, *The Public Presidency: The Pursuit of Popular Support*, St. Martin's, New York, 1983, pp. 187–210; Eric B. Herzik and Mary L. Dodson, "The President and Public Expectations: A Research Note," *Presidential Studies Quarterly*, vol. 12, no. 2, spring 1982, pp. 168–173.
9. Jeffrey Tulis, "The Two Constitutional Presidencies," in Nelson, op. cit., pp. 59–86.
10. Woodrow Wilson, *The Principles of Constitutional Government*, Columbia University Press, New York, 1908, p. 30.
11. On the concept of clerkship, see Richard Neustadt, *Presidential Power: The Politics of Leadership from FDR to Carter*, Wiley, New York, 1980, p. 6.
12. Quoted in Jack Valenti, *A Very Human President*, Norton, New York, 1975, p. 261; Wilson, op. cit., p. 30; *The National Journal*, Oct. 16, 1984, p. 1870.
13. James Stimson, "Public Support for American Presidents: A Cyclical Model," *Public Opinion Quarterly*, vol. 40, no. 1, spring 1976, pp. 1–21; Henry Kenski, "The Impact of Economic Conditions on Presidential Popularity," *Journal of Politics*, vol. 39, no. 3, August 1977, pp. 764–773; Samuel Kernell, "Expanding Presidential Popularity," *American Political Science Review*, vol. 72, no. 3, June 1978, pp. 506–522.
14. Stephen J. Wayne, "Great Expectations: Contemporary Views of the President," in Thomas Cronin (ed.), *Rethinking the Presidency*, Little, Brown, Boston, 1982.

15. Lou Cannon, "They Don't Call Reagan the Teflon President for Nothing," *Washington Post National Weekly Edition*, Apr. 30, 1984.
16. *The Wall Street Journal*, Apr. 20, 1984.
17. Cannon, op. cit.
18. Barry Sussman, "Reagan's Policies Are the Key—Not His Personality," *Washington Post National Weekly Edition*, Feb. 13, 1984, p. 37.
19. Richard Neustadt, *Presidential Power*, Wiley, New York, 1960, p. 121.
20. Fred Greenstein, *The Hidden-Hand Presidency*, Basic Books, New York, 1982.
21. Theodore Sorensen, *Kennedy*, Bantam, New York, 1966, p 387.
22. Godfrey Hodgson, *All Things to All Men*, Simon and Schuster, New York, 1980, p. 31; David Halberstam, *The Best and the Brightest*, Random House, New York, 1969, p. 516.
23. Steven Skowrenek, "The Presidency and Political Time," in Nelson, op. cit., pp. 87–133.
24. *The New York Times*, Mar. 7, 1979.
25. PBS transcript, Apr. 26, 1973, p. 3.
26. Elizabeth Drew, "Reporter at Large," *The New Yorker*, June 8, 1981, p. 138.
27. Samuel Kernell, "Presidential Popularity and Negative Voting," *American Political Science Review*, vol. 71, no. 1, March 1977, pp. 44–66.
28. Roger G. Brown and David M. Welborn, "Presidents and Their Parties," *Presidential Studies Quarterly*, vol. 12, no. 3, summer 1982, pp. 302–315.
29. *The Wall Street Journal*, Aug. 19, 1982.
30. Paul Light, *Vice-Presidential Power*, Johns Hopkins Press, Baltimore, 1984.
31. Thomas Cronin, "The Textbook Presidency and Political Science," paper delivered at the American Political Science Association Convention, 1969.
32. George Reedy, *The Twilight of the Presidency*, New American Library, New York, 1970, p. xiv.
33. Arthur Schlesinger, *The Coming of the New Deal*, Houghton Mifflin, Boston, 1958, sec. 8, pp. 511–588.
34. Alexander George, *Presidential Decisionmaking and Foreign Policy*, Praeger, New York, 1982, pp. 191–208.
35. Cited in Stephen J. Wayne, "Working in the White House: Psychological Dimensions of the Job," paper presented at the annual meeting of the Southern Political Science Association, New Orleans, 1977, p. 10.
36. *Newsweek*, Feb. 16, 1984, p. 12.
37. John Manley, "Presidential Power and White House Lobbying," *Political Science Quarterly*, vol. 93, no. 2, summer 1978, pp. 255–275.
38. Meese, op. cit., p. 192.
39. Peter W. Sperlich, "Bargaining and Overload: An Essay on Presidential Power," in Aaron Wildvasky (ed.), pp. 168–192.
40. On reputation, see Neustadt, *Presidential Power: The Politics of Leadership from FDR to Carter*, pp. 46–49.
41. Cited in Richard A. Watson and Norman Thomas, *The Politics of the Presidency*, Wiley, New York, 1983, p. 165.
42. Samuel Kernell, "The Presidency and the People," in Nelson, op. cit., pp. 233–263.
43. See the proposals made in Newton Minow et al., *Presidential Television*, Basic Books, New York, 1973, pp. 159–166.
44. On the use of the local strategy, see Robert Locander, "Modern Presidential In-Office communication," *Presidential Studies Quarterly*, vol. 13, no. 2, spring 1983, pp. 242-254.
45. *The New York Times*, Feb. 16, 1982.
46. William Lammers, "Presidential Press Conference Schedules: Who Hides and When?" *Political Science Quarterly*, vol. 96, no. 2, summer 1981, pp. 261–267.
47. Edwards, op. cit., p. 77.
48. *The New York Times*, Nov. 16, 1981; Barry Sussman, "Why the GOP Pays Richard Wirthlin $1 Million a Year," *Washington Post National Weekly Edition*, Dec. 26, 1983, p. 35.

49. Theodore Sorensen, "Presidents and the King's English," *The New York Times*, Aug. 19, 1979.

50. New York Times/CBS poll, July 18, 1979.

51. Benjamin Page and Robert Shapiro, *Presidents as Opinion Leaders: Some New Evidence*, National Opinion Research Center, Chicago, June 1983.

52. John Weisman, "Who's Toughest on the White House—and Why," *TV Guide*, Aug. 27–Sept. 2, 1983.

53. *The New York Times*, Apr. 23, 1982.

54. *The New York Times*, June 17, 1982.

55. *The New York Times*, Apr. 6, 1983.

56. James Ceasar et al., "The Rise of the Rhetorical Presidency," *Presidential Studies Quarterly*, vol. 11, no. 2, spring 1981, pp. 159–160.

57. Edwards, op. cit., p. 4.

58. *California Magazine*, May 1982.

59. John Locke, *Two Treatises of Government*, Cambridge University Press, Cambridge, 1960, p. 422.

60. Nixon is quoted in Christopher Pyle and Richard Pious, *Presidents, Congress and the Constitution*, Free Press, New York, 1984, p. 74.

61. *Nixon v. Fitzgerald*, 457 U.S. 731 (1982).

62. Hazel Erskine, "The Polls: Presidential Power," *Public Opinion Quarterly*, vol. 37, no. 3, fall 1973, pp. 488–503.

63. Robert E. DiClerico, *The American President*, Prentice-Hall, Englewood Cliffs, N.J., 1983, table 5–3, p. 156.

64. Clinton Rossiter, *Constitutional Dictatorship*, Princeton University Press, Princeton, N.J., 1948.

65. Similar lists compiled by Rossiter and Schlesinger appear in Pyle and Pious, op. cit., pp. 140–143.

66. *Ex Parte Milligan*, 71 U.S. 125 (1866).

67. Neustadt, *Presidential Power: The Politics of Leadership from FDR to Carter*, p. 185

68. Ibid, p. 135.

69. Ibid., p. 136.

70. Useful critiques of this approach include Thomas E. Cronin and Rexford G. Tugwell (eds.), *The Presidency Reappraised*, Praeger, New York, 1974; and Sperlich, op. cit, pp. 168–192.

71. Neustadt, *Presidential Power; The Politics of Leadership from FDR to Carter*, p. 189.

72. James MacGregor Burns, *Leadership*, Harper and Row, New York, 1978, p. 396.

FURTHER READING

Barber, James David: *The Presidential Character*, Prentice-Hall, Englewood Cliffs, N.J., 1972. An analysis of the character of several presidents, including predictive theory of how presidents behave in office.

Bessette, Joseph M. and Jeffrey Tulis (eds.): *The Presidency in the Constitutional Order*, Louisiana State University Press, Baton Rouge, 1981. Articles on presidential powers.

Burns, James MacGregor: *Roosevelt: The Lion and the Fox*, Harcourt, Brace and World, New York, 1956. A biography of Franklin Roosevelt, emphasizing his political skills.

Cronin, Thomas: *The State of the Presidency*, rev. ed., Little, Brown, Boston, 1980. A textbook based on original research on the workings of the presidential agencies and advisory system.

Edwards, George C. III: *The Public Presidency: The Pursuit of Popular Support*, St. Martin's, New York, 1983. A study of national agenda politics and presidential successes and failures.

————and Stephen J. Wayne: *Presidential Leadership*, St. Martin's, New York, 1985. A textbook that emphasizes empirical data about the performance of presidents as leaders of their party, Congress, and public opinion.

Fisher, Louis: *Constitutional Conflicts between Congress and the President*, Princeton University Press, Princeton, N.J., 1985. An up-to-date analysis of conflicts between the two branches over important administrative and foreign affairs powers.

Glad, Betty: *Jimmy Carter: In Search of the Great White House*, Norton, New York, 1980. A book about Carter's quest for the presidency and his performance in office.

Greenstein, Fred I.: *The Hidden-Hand Presidency*, Basic Books, New York, 1982. An account of political strategy and tactics used by Eisenhower, revealing him to have been a thoughtful and savvy politician.

Grossman, Michael, and Martha Kumar: *Portraying the President: The White House and the News Media*, Johns Hopkins, Baltimore, 1981. An account of the way the White House and the news media interact.

Kearns, Doris: *Lyndon Johnson and the American Dream*, Harper and Row, New York, 1976. A biography of Johnson by a political scientist who served in the White House.

Koenig, Louis: *The Chief Executive*, 4th ed., Harcourt Brace Jovanovich, New York, 1981. A leading textbook emphasizing the benefits of vigorous presidential leadership.

Leuchtenberg, William: *In the Shadow of FDR*, rev. ed., Cornell University Press, Ithaca, 1985. An account of the impact of Franklin Roosevelt's activist administration on later presidents.

Light, Paul C.: *The President's Agenda*, Johns Hopkins, Baltimore, 1984. A discussion of how issues reach presidents and how presidents set their priorities.

Lowi, Theodore J.: *The Personal President*, Cornell University Press, Ithaca, 1985. A study of the plebiscitary presidency.

Nelson, Michael (ed.): *The Presidency and the Political System*, Congressional Quarterly Press, Washington, D.C., 1984. Articles by scholars assessing the modern presidency.

Neustadt, Richard: *Presidential Power: The Politics of Leadership from FDR to Carter*, Wiley, New York, 1980. A classic study of presidential power as influence.

Pious, Richard M.: *The American Presidency*, Basic Books, New York, 1979. A treatment of presidential power as prerogatives.

Pyle, Christopher, and Richard Pious: *Presidents, Congress and the Constitution*, Free Press, New York, 1984. Cases and materials on presidential powers and congressional and judicial responses.

Rockman, Bert A.: *The Leadership Question: The Presidency and the American System*, Praeger, New York, 1984. A book that puts the presidency in the context of the American political culture, discusses its relationship to three time cycles of politics, and provides a comparative perspective with leadership positions in other nations.

Rubin, Richard: *Press, Party and Presidency*, Norton, New York, 1981. A theoretical and empirical analysis of the influence of the mass media on presidential powers.

Schlesinger, Arthur M., Jr.: *The Imperial Presidency*, Houghton Mifflin, Boston, 1973. A study of the growth of presidential powers and the dangers inherent in an unbalanced presidency.

————: *A Thousand Days*, Houghton Mifflin, Boston, 1965. An account of John Kennedy's presidency written by a historian who served in his administration.

Watson, Richard, and Norman Thomas: *The Politics of the Presidency*, Wiley, New York, 1983. A comprehensive and up-to-date text.

Wayne, Stephen J.: *The Legislative Presidency*, Harper and Row, New York, 1978. A book about the way administrations develop legislation and win support for it in Congress.

THE STUDY BREAK

Eleanor and Franklin: The White House Years. An award-winning television movie, produced in 1977 and starring Jane Alexander, adapted from Joesph Lash's Pulitzer prizewinning biography, *Eleanor and Franklin*.

John F. Kennedy: Years of Lightning, Day of Drums. A movie commissioned in 1966 by the United States Information Agency for foreign distribution. A classic, it is now shown on television in this country.

The Man. A 1971 movie about a black vice president who is suddenly elevated to the Oval Office, starring James Earl Jones and Burgess Meredith and adapted by Rod Serling from a book by Irving Wallace.

The President's Analyst. A satiric movie, released in 1967, about what happens to the president's analyst (played by James Coburn) when he quits his job. A brilliant parody of Washington politics.

USEFUL SOURCES

Dennis A. Burton, et. al. (eds.), *A Guide to Manuscripts In the Presidential Libraries*, Research Materials Corp., College Park, Maryland, 1985. Indexed descriptions of manuscripts, microfilms, and oral histories in seven presidential libraries.

Byrne, Pamela R. (ed.): *The American Presidency: A Historical Bibliography*, ABC-CLIO, Santa Barbara, Calif., 1984.

Congressional Quarterly Weekly Reports. Reports on the presidential program and Congressional responses.

Edwards, George III, and Stephen J. Wayne: *Studying the Presidency*, University of Tennessee Press, Nashville, 1983. A book containing several articles on how to use sources and how to work in presidential libraries.

William M. Goldsmith, *The Growth of Presidential Power: A Documentary History*, Vols I–III, Chelsea House, New York, 1974. Key speeches, executive orders, legal opinions and court cases involving presidential powers.

The Journal of Law and Politics. A journal devoted to presidential and congressional powers.

The National Journal. A weekly journal on politics in the executive branch.

Presidential Studies Quarterly. A journal containing articles on the institutionalized presidency.

Presidents and Congress. A journal covering relations between the president and Congress.

Public Papers of the Presidents of the United States, GPO, Washington, D.C., issued in several volumes for each president, annually as their terms progress. Bound volumes containing some significant presidential documents, though not the classified or limited-distribution documents.

Weekly Compilation of Presidential Documents, GPO, Washington, D.C. Speeches, transcripts of news conferences, and executive orders and proclamations issued each week by the White House. (Much of this material can be accessed by commercial computer services, which since 1985 have been supplied with these documents by the White House.)

ORGANIZATIONS

Center for the Study of the Presidency. 208 East 75th Street, New York, N.Y. 10021. For more information phone 212-249-1200.

The Executive Office of the President (see also Figure 10-7) comprises the following:

Council of Economic Advisors. Old Executive Office Building, Washington, D.C. 20500. For more information phone 202-395-5042.

Council on Environmental Quality. 722 Jackson Place, N.W., Washington, D.C. 20006. For more information phone 202-395-5080.

National Security Council. Old Executive Office Building, Washington, D.C. 20506. For more information phone 202-456-2255.

Office of Administration. Old Executive Office Building, Washington, D.C. 20500. For more information phone 202-456-7052.

Office of Management and Budget. Old Executive Office Building, Washington, D.C. 20503. For more information phone 202-395-3000.

Office of Policy Development. Old Executive Office Building, Washington, D.C. 20500. For more information phone 202-456-6515.

Office of Science and Technology Policy. Old Executive Office Building, Washington, D.C. 20506. For more information phone 202-456-7116.

Office of the United States Trade Representative. Winder Building, 600 Seventeenth Street, N.W., Washington, D.C. 20506. For more information phone 202-395-3204.

Office of the Vice President. Old Executive Office Building, Washington, D.C. 20501. For more information phone 202-456-2326.

The White House Office. 1600 Pennsylvania Avenue, N.W., Washington, D.C. 20500. For more information phone 202-456-1414 (executive residence, 202-456-2957).

CHAPTER 11

CONGRESSIONAL POWER: REPRESENTATION AND LEGISLATION

The creation of a new national capital with impressive national monuments was part of the agenda of the young republic. The view toward Capitol Hill was already such a sight in 1837. Today the Hill is crowded with office buildings housing congressional staffers and agencies. (*Granger Collection; Owen Franken: Sygma.*)

How does Congress work? How do bills become law? A good way to start to understand the legislative process is to see it through the eyes of Eric Redman, who in 1971 was 22 years old and just out of college (but still writing his senior essay so that he could get his degree from Princeton). Redman had just gotten a job with Senator Warren Magnuson, a Democrat from Washington, who had been put in charge of a bill to create a national health service corps—the pet project of a pediatrician who was a friend of the senator.[1]

Redman tried to get officials in the Nixon administration to support the bill, but when he could not get their help with a big program, he decided to press for a small "demonstration" project that would put a few dozen doctors from the Public Health Service (PHS) into several communities. Following the advice of some seasoned staffers, Redman explored the possibility of putting such a pilot program into operation without any new legislation by getting the PHS to agree to reallocate some of its funds for the project. However, the Senate's legislative counsel told him that a new law would be needed.

Redman realized that he would have to run the entire legislative gantlet with his little project; this lowered the odds, since only 1 in 20 bills introduced ever passes Congress. Fortunately, Senator Ralph Yarborough, chair of the Education and Labor Committee, agreed to hold hearings because he was incensed that Nixon had threatened to kill the entire PHS as part of a proposed health care reorganization plan: this bill would be a way of signaling Nixon to back down. Unfortunately, however, the Republicans were boycotting the committee because they did not want it to report some other, completely unrelated measure; their boycott meant that no bills would be reported from the committee.

Eventually the boycott ended when Yarborough made a deal with the Republicans on another bill. Redman's measure got through the committee and went to the Senate floor. But when it came up for a vote, both Magnuson and Yarborough were out of town, and there was no senator to act as floor manager for it—to explain its provisions to members in the Senate debate. Magnuson's staff rounded up Senator Peter Dominick, a conservative Republican, who agreed to shepherd it through as a favor to Magnuson. The bill passed, even though most senators had never heard of it before: no one wanted to vote against it and incur Magnuson's wrath, since he chaired the appropriations subcommittee that funded health care and hospitals.

Meanwhile, time was running out; the congressional session was nearly over, and the House committee had yet to hold hearings or report the bill to the full House. Luckily, Paul Rogers, who ran the subcommittee in the House that would consider the measure, needed Magnuson's help on a different bill and was willing to cooperate. The chair of the parent committee, Harley Staggers, was being pressured by medical school students and faculty members in West Virginia to support the bill, and so he too agreed to help. The subcommittee and the committee approved the bill.

Next it went to the House Rules Committee, which had to provide a rule that set the procedures for debate. Not all bills get rules near the end of the session, but for some reason Nixon pressured the committee to report all its pending measures (so that he could get some of his bills out of committee), and the PHS measure was swept through as well. The next hurdle was the end-of-session traffic jam on the floor. After another long delay the House approved the bill, but in a form slightly different from the Senate's version.

This presented a problem, since all laws must be passed by both chambers with exactly the same wording. With time running out, there was no way to reconcile the two bills, and so Yarborough's Senate committee agreed to accept the House bill, and it was taken directly from the House to the Senate floor and was repassed by the Senate. Congress finally had passed the bill into law.

The bill went to President Nixon within ten days of the scheduled adjournment of Congress; and in that time period, the Constitution permits the president to "pocket veto" a measure. But Nixon had recently used the pocket veto on the Family Practice Act, another health measure, and had touched off a storm of protest. (It seems that he used it while Congress was on vacation, which might have been unconstitutional, since Congress had recessed rather than adjourned.) With members of Congress threatening a lawsuit over presidential power (a case which Senator Edward Kennedy eventually took to the Supreme Court and won), Nixon's political advisers recommended that he not veto another health bill, and so he signed it.

Redman later wrote a book, called *The Dance of Legislation*, about his experiences working on this bill. The "dance" he refers to is the informal whirl of personal motives and friendships, favors given and received, accidents, and luck—all going on in the hectic atmosphere of a congressional office. How Congress actually works is far different from the way the smooth flowcharts in most textbooks describe the "legislative process." In the case of Redman's bill, much depended on personalities, favors, and luck. Had Redman not been on the Senate floor when the bill was suddenly called up (which made it possible for him to get Dominick to act as floor manager), it would have died then and there. Favors and influence (in this case, Dominick's friendship with Magnuson and Roger's need to deal with Magnuson's committee) are at least as important as party and ideology. Bills going through Congress are like canoes shooting the rapids.

CONGRESS: THE FIRST BRANCH?

The Constitution makes Congress the "first branch" of government, and so did the architects of the District of Columbia: Congress meets atop Capitol Hill, which looms over the White House and the executive departments on the mall. From the vantage point of the president and foreign leaders, Congress shares the power to govern: it can check and balance, and every president knows that confrontations with the legislature can weaken or even destroy an administration.

But some observers consider Congress the worst branch. It is "the greatest menace in our country to the successful operation of the democratic process," according to Joseph Clark, a former senator. "It is gutless beyond my power to describe it to you," said one representative.[2] Howard Baker, a former Republican Senate majority leader, proposed that members of Congress get out of town for six months every year to find out what was going on in the country.

A congressman, Les Aspin, at work in Washington. (*Sepp Seitz: Woodfin Camp.*)

And one Cub Scout in Oklahoma, asked by Representative Mike Synar to explain the difference between Congress and the Cub Scouts, replied, "We have adult supervision."[3]

The case against Congress is that it is not responsive enough to the national interest, too responsive to special interests, lazy (it operates on a Tuesday-to-Thursday schedule), slow, and inefficient. It does not operate according to laws it passes: it exempts itself from the Civil Rights Acts, the Equal Pay Act, the National Labor Relations Act, the Fair Labor Standards Act, the Occupational Safety and Health Act, the Social Security Act, the Privacy Act, and the Age Discrimination Act.[4] A majority of the public believes that legislators would take bribes and rates Congress low on lists of important institutions.[5]

Yet most members of Congress are honest, hardworking men and women whose twelve-hour working days leave them little time for a private life. They are on a Capitol Hill treadmill, running from one committee meeting to another, meeting and serving constituents (and traveling back and forth from their home states or districts just about every weekend), supervising their staffs, and responding like Pavlov's dogs to the sound of the bell calling for their presence on the House or Senate floor for a vote. While public approval of Congress declined from 60 percent in 1964 to 20 percent in 1980, most voters rate their own members highly and elect them again and again.[6]

"The Senate and the Congress as a whole is choking on its own processes," says Sam Nunn,[7] a senator from Georgia. Why is Congress—so frustrating and seemingly unworkable to those on the inside—so formidable to presidents and heads of foreign governments? Why is it so slow and cumbersome, and yet also so innovative when it tackles big issues? Why does the public rate it so low as a collective body, and yet think so highly of its individual members? We will consider these questions by focusing on the members and leaders of Congress and on their formal and informal powers. Our concern will be the problem of congressional power: how can legislators—who represent separate geographic jurisdictions and competing interests, are organized into two separate chambers, and are divided into two parties—make Congress work?

ON CAPITOL HILL

There are 535 voting members of Congress. They come to their jobs with different talents, temperaments, and goals. Reconciling their individual goals to fashion lawmaking majorities is what legislative politics is all about.

What legislators want

As soon as legislators are elected, they start to worry about being reelected. House members know that sooner or later one-third of them will be defeated, and so they are understandably nervous. Senators serve for six years, but they are more likely to lose in their next election, and so they also run scared. "The President does not have to run for reelection anymore," Bob Dole, the Senate majority leader, explained to reporters who wanted to know why he announced his intention to oppose much of Reagan's budget plan in 1985, "but a lot of the rest of us do."[8] Legislators look for soft landings if they lose: jobs in the executive branch or as lobbyists or registered agents for foreign governments, positions held by 250 former representatives. For example, Paul Rogers, a former congressman from Florida, monitors bills involving savings and loan institutions; former congressman James Corman represents the Tobacco Institute; and former congressman Jack McDonald lobbies for the American Express Company.[9]

Legislators are hospitable to constituents and important fund-raisers and to PACs who can help them stay in Congress or help them when they leave. They build up hundreds of thousands of dollars in campaign warchests out of contributions from interest groups; members who were elected before 1980 may transfer these funds to their own bank accounts after they retire or fail to win reelection. They are sensitive to ideological groups and single-issue organizations which "scorecard" them and publicize their votes on controversial issues.

Legislative roles

Members must decide what roles they will play in Congress. Some have become **legislative party leaders** (for example, Jim Wright of Texas became the House Democratic *majority leader*, and Bob Michaels of Illinois became the House Republican *minority leader*). They communicate with different factions and leaders, make deals to unite disparate interests, unify their parties, and smoothe out intraparty friction. Others have become **committee leaders,** whose

Senator Henry "Scoop" Jackson, who was one of the most powerful men in Congress in foreign affairs, advises president-elect Reagan during the transition in 1980. (*AP Laserphoto.*)

influence comes from their policy expertise and committee jurisdictions (for example, Russell Long, a Democratic senator from Louisiana; and Orrin Hatch, a Republican senator from Utah, both became committee leaders). Other members (for example, Daniel Moynihan of New York, Sam Nunn of Georgia, and Bill Cohen of Maine) have become *policy experts;* they are looked to by others for guidance on policy.

Democratic legislators like Edward Kennedy of Massachusetts and Gary Hart of Colorado and Republicans like Jack Kemp of New York and Robert Dole of Kansas are *presidential hopefuls;* they use Congress as a stage to reach a national audience. *Factional leaders,* like Jesse Helms of North Carolina and Paul Sarbanes of Maryland, seek to move their party to the right or the left. *Gadflies,* such as Lowell Weicker of Connecticut and William Proxmire of Wisconsin, are mavericks who treasure their independence and can raise new issues for the public.

Representative roles

Area representation. Congress represents the "scuffle of local interests," as the journalist Henry Jones Ford put it at the turn of the century, and surveys have shown that almost half the House members would put their local interests ahead of the national interest.[10] "I'm here to represent my district," said one, "What is good for the majority of my district is good for the country. What snarls up the system is those so-called statesmen-congressmen who vote for what they think is the country's best interest." "I've got many, many families in my district who make a living on tobacco," said another, who was about to cast a vote for tobacco subsidies, because "If you don't you aren't going to be around here very long."[11] Yet over half the members weigh national factors, and on the most important issues almost all can rise above their districts.

Functional representation. On issues which are public and on which voters have strong views, some legislators are **delegates;** they simply determine the wishes of some group in their district or in the nation and then vote accordingly. But on many issues they find that their constituents have no views, care little, or are uninformed. Then they may become **trustees** for their constituents: they protect their interests. "Your representative owes you, not his industry only, but his judgment," wrote the British parliamentarian Edmund Burke to his constituents 200 years ago, "and he betrays, instead of serving you, if he sacrifices it to your opinion."[12] Senator Robert Byrd of West Virginia used almost the identical words when he explained to voters in his state why he had defied their wishes and voted for the Panama Canal treaty.

Some legislators are wheeler-dealers, willing to bargain and trade their votes on one issue if this will help their careers and their constituents on another. These **politicos** will "vote the district" on issues that affect their chances for reelection, "vote the conscience" on issues of national security, and trade votes on everything else. Representatives from Texas helped New York City get loan guarantees in the 1970s. "We were very interested in the problems of Brooklyn and the Bronx," recalls Congressman Charles Wilson of Texas, "but we also expected they'd remember." The New York delegation reciprocated on defense and agriculture bills which helped Texas.

Personal representation. Legislators bring their experiences and interests to their work. Cecil Heftel, a representative from Hawaii who was severely injured in a car crash, later became the sponsor of automobile safety legislation. Paula Hawkins, a senator from Florida, suffered sexual abuse as a child and has fought for laws against child abuse. Senator Edward Kennedy, whose two brothers were assassinated, has sponsored legislation banning handguns. Senator Robert Dole, who was badly wounded and permanently disabled in World War II, fights for aid for the handicapped and veterans.

Interest-group representation. Most legislators have received direct PAC funds, "bundled" funds, or individual contributions stimulated by PAC direct-mail campaigns. Once winners arrive in Washington, however, they are greeted by PACs and by lobbyists who represent labor, corporations, trade associations, and professional groups—close to 20,000 of them. They want access to members of Congress so that they can press for new legislation or block measures that would be harmful to the groups they represent. They can be extremely helpful to members: they do research, draft proposed bills and supporting speeches, make introductions and help new members get the committee assignments they want, and even help new members and their families get oriented to Washington. They invite members on all-expenses-paid trips and give them honorariums (that is, fees) for speaking engagements.

PACs expect members of Congress to represent their interests in committees and to vote for their bills on the floor. The American Medical Association and the American Dental Association gave more than $3 million in campaign contributions to House members just before a vote that would exempt doctors and dentists from certain federal regulations. Used-car dealers gave more than $1 million to overturn a Federal Trade Commission ruling requiring that certain information about used cars be disclosed to potential buyers. Three dairy PACs gave more than $1 million to prevent Congress from removing dairy price supports.[13]

PAC lobbyists argue that they do not trade money for votes, but simply give to members who would be likely to support them anyway. Political scientists have examined these claims, and some have determined that PAC contributions measurably increase the probability that members will vote the way the PAC wishes and that such votes substantially increase the amount of later contributions that PACs make to these members.[14]

Getting along on the Hill

In the past, new members went along with the traditional ways in which their chamber conducted its business; otherwise, they earned reputations as mavericks and outsiders and were frozen out by the leadership. Senior members judged junior members: some were considered thoughtful, hardworking "comers" who would gain powerful mentors; and others were dismissed as lightweights, publicity hounds, or just plain bad news—they would be expected to lose out on good committee assignments, have their pet projects stalled, and be denied advancement. "There are two kinds of congressmen," Carl Hayden was told when he arrived in Washington, "show horses and workhorses. If you want to get your name in the paper, be a showhorse. If you want to gain the respect of your colleagues, keep quiet and be a workhorse."

Today these traditions and norms are less important. New members speak up more and expect to do more early in their first term: they have to, in order to get the media publicity and the PAC contributions they need to be reelected.

There is no longer any real apprenticeship or mentorship on the Hill, and that makes it more difficult than ever for Congress to work effectively.

Specialization. Members of the House are expected to specialize in a few areas, while senators are more likely to be generalists. New representatives are expected to work hard on their committees, provide "language" for bills initially only on minor matters, and master the complicated parliamentary rules according to which the House does its business. They are asked by party leaders to remember Speaker Sam Rayburn's advice: "To get along, go along." Members are supposed to make some sacrifices to help their party pass its programs. "To serve his constituents at home," Rayburn said, a member of Congress "must also serve his colleagues here in the House."[15]

Deference. In the past, senators were expected to wait a year or more before making a "maiden" speech. "You just *had* to talk, didn't you," hissed a colleague to Senator Carl Hayden after his first Senate speech. "Keep your mouth shut for a while," was Senator Hubert Humphrey's advice to Joseph Clark, a newcomer.[16] Today senators arrive on the Hill with their mouths still open from nonstop media campaigning. They get subcommittee chairs within two years (all Republican senators have such assignments) and are assigned important committee responsibilities in their first term. They can become floor managers for important bills. "The point is to get things done," concluded Senator Bill Bradley—no senator wants to remain on the bench while others carry the ball.[17]

At one time, House members were also expected to know their place. "When you pass a committee chairman in the hall, bow low from the waist," John McCormack, the Speaker of the House, told incoming freshmen in the 1960s. But today newcomers bow to no one. Most come from marginal districts and need to make a name for themselves and accomplish something for their districts to solidify their base. They can hire experienced staffers (whose former bosses resigned or were defeated) to get them off to a fast start. They band together with other freshmen to force party leaders to give them decent committee assignments.[18]

Reciprocity. Every member can help a colleague, knowing that sooner or later the favor will be returned. The Republican House leader, Bob Michel, trades favors on scheduling and debate with the Democratic House leader, Jim Wright. Southern tobacco and cotton growers deal on issues of farm benefits with the wheat growers of the midwest and then get urban legislators from northern cities to join with them in return for support on a mass-transit bill. "Milt, I would just like you to tell me how to vote about wheat and sugar beets and things like that," said Senator Sam Ervin of North Carolina to Senator Milton Young of North Dakota one day, "if you just help me out on tobacco and things like that."[19] Senator Gaylord Nelson of Wisconsin, on arriving late to a meeting of the Senate Finance Committee, requested Russell Long, the chairman, to accept an amendment to a bill to give some tax breaks to ferry operators in his state. "I'll be happy to give you that one," Long replied, "but I expect you in exchange to vote for this next tax credit we're about to discuss."[20]

These alliances cross party and ideological lines. Henry Waxman, a liberal House Democrat, and Orrin Hatch, a conservative Republican senator, are

Congress relies on its own staff for technical expertise. Alice Rivlin, then the Congressional budget director, testifies before the Senate Finance Committee. (*UPI; Bettmann Archive.*)

THE UNELECTED CONGRESS: STAFFERS ON THE HILL

There are close to 20,000 legislative and committee staffers: they are the unelected "representatives," and they have a great impact on Congress.[a]

Each representative receives a "clerk-hire" allowance of more than $400,000 annually and has fifteen or so workers. Senate allowances are based on state population and range from $600,000 to more than $2 million; the number of employees averages thirty-one. Each committee has approximately thirty staffers, most of whom work for subcommittees. The majority party hires two-thirds of them, and the minority party hires one-third.

Most staffers are under 45, two-thirds are men, and a few are minorities. Half have undergraduate college degrees, one-fifth have M.A.s, and one-tenth have Ph.D.s; half of the staffers in the Senate, and one-fourth of those in the House, are lawyers.

Staffers answer the 40 million letters sent to House members and the 29 million letters sent to senators each year. They do casework for constituents. They prepare newsletters, press releases, and videotapes and audiotapes of their bosses at work. They research and draft bills, negotiate with lobbyists, prepare for hearings, suggest changes in language when bills are revised in committee, and write speeches and drafts of committee reports.

Most legislators rely heavily on their staffers. A 1977 study showed that three-fifths of the House members had staffers give them briefings on their committee work or cue them about how to vote on bills from other committees. Half relied on staffers to brief them on important national issues.[b]

The *neutral professionals* are expert technicians who facilitate the goals of their bosses. The *policy entrepreneurs* have their own agendas. "We see it as part of our job to present alternatives to the senator," said one, "to lay out things before him that he might want to do."[c] "This committee spends most of its time arguing with its own staff," said Senator Robert Griffin, "summing up the negative side of working with ambitious staffers."[d] But staffers have strengthened laws dealing with automobile safety, health, education, consumer protection, and nuclear energy. The neutral professionals, on the other hand, have been closely connected with taxing, appropriations, revenue sharing, and agriculture—matters on which members have clear priorities but need technical expertise. Staffers may be delegated responsibility by a lazy or indifferent legislator, sit in on committees, negotiate and trade for votes, and go off on tangents with their own pet projects. Legislators may become clerks for their own staffers. An informal network of staffers, lobbyists, and officials at the sub-Cabinet level may negotiate their own deals, and sometimes the results are different from what would have been obtained had their bosses been involved. Alternatively, personality conflicts lead to situations in which deals fail because staffers cannot agree, even though their bosses might have come to an understanding. The influence of the unelected representatives is strong, and the problems they pose are serious. But Congress would get far less done without them.[e]

a. Harrison W. Fox and Susan W. Hammond, *Congressional Staffs*, Free Press, New York, 1977, p. 171; Roger Davidson and Walter Oleszek, *Congress and Its Members*, Congressional Quarterly Press, Washington, D.C., 1981, p. 238.
b. David Vogler, *The Politics of Congress*, 4th ed., Allyn and Bacon, Boston, 1983, p. 131.
c. David E. Price, "Professionals and Entrepreneurs: Staff Orientations and Policy Making on Three Senate Committees," *Journal of Politics*, vol. 33, no. 2, May 1971, p. 324.
d. Norris Cotton, *In the Senate*, Dodd, Mead, New York, 1978, p. 67.
e. Michael Malbin, *Unelected Representatives*, Basic Books, New York, 1980.

---

called "the odd couple" because of their alliance in pushing for health care legislation. Waxman helped Hatch get aid for Utah residents who claimed that their leukemia had been caused by atom bomb tests in the 1950s; Hatch

---

THE CONGRESSIONAL AGENCIES

Congressional Budget Office (CBO). This agency was established in 1974 to give Congress information about tax receipts, department expenditures, and the impact of pending legislation on the federal budget. The CBO also studies and evaluates presidential budget requests and provides alternatives for Congress.

Congressional Research Service (CRS). This agency is part of the Library of Congress. Formerly the Legislative Reference Service, it has been in existence since 1946. Its 400 researchers draft bills for members and work on more than 450,000 questions that they assign annually, preparing over 50,000 studies or briefs.

General Accounting Office (GAO). This agency was created in 1921 as an independent agency accountable to Congress. Its comptroller general is appointed by the president and confirmed by the Senate for a fifteen-year term. The GAO is a watchdog over government expenditures. It conducts field audits of agencies' accounts, suggests improvements in agencies' accounting and auditing procedures, and rules on the legality of government expenditures.

Office of Technology Assessment (OTA). This agency was created in 1972 and assists members of Congress in understanding scientific and technical matters. It drafts bills and conducts policy evaluations at the request of committees. It helps legislators obtain the best scientific advice from outside experts, and it contracts with universities and think tanks for some of its research studies.

---

helped Waxman with a bill that would encourage manufacturers to develop certain new drugs that were not likely to be profitable.

Respect. Most members, especially those who become party leaders, learn to respect their political opponents and stop attacking their motives or their sincerity. "The reality is that there are responsible and often persuasive arguments on both sides of an issue," says Steven Solarz, a representative from Brooklyn, "and that no one has a monopoly on truth and wisdom."[21] Opposing committee and party leaders must work with one another to schedule their business. Sometimes this leads to friendships: Tip O'Neill, the Democratic Speaker of the House, is a golfing companion of Bob Michel, the Republican minority leader; Senator Gary Hart, a Democrat, wrote a detective novel in collaboration with Senator Bill Cohen, a Republican. The web of friendships makes it possible for bipartisan majorities to form.

THE CONGRESSIONAL POWER STRUCTURE

Constitutional leaders

Article I, Section 2, of the Constitution provides that the vice president of the United States is also the president of the Senate—the presiding officer with the power to vote in case of a tie. The president of the Senate may also issue rulings on Senate procedure which can be important in controlling debate. In the absence of the president of the Senate, the chief constitutional officer is the *president pro tem,* who presides over the Senate. Since 1910 the president pro tem has been the most senior member of the majority party (usually turning over the job of presiding to the most junior senators). The president pro tem signs bills sent to the president and appoints senators to serve on conference committees that negotiate the final drafts of bills with the House. The *Speaker of the House* is the constitutional leader of the House. The Speaker almost always presides (and rarely votes)—the reverse of the role of the president pro tem of the Senate. The Speaker also signs bills sent to the president and appoints the House members of conference committees.

Congressional leaders enjoy high status at the White House. Bob Michel, the House minority leader, speaks to the press on a compromise worked out with the White House staff on the MX missile. (*UPI; Bettmann Archive.*)

Party leaders

Party leaders include the Speaker of the House, the House majority and minority leaders, and the majority and minority leaders of the Senate. They are chosen by, and remain responsible to, the legislative parties of Congress: House and Senate Republicans and House and Senate Democrats. "When I'm talking about my party," says Speaker Tip O'Neill, "I'm talking about the House [party]."[22] They remain independent of the White House and national party leaders; at the beginning of President Reagan's second term, for example, a moderate group of Republicans took over the party leadership posts in the Senate, and none were beholden to the White House.

Party leaders schedule the business of their chamber and control floor proceedings. They assign bills to committees and try to coordinate the committees' work. They attempt to instill party spirit and loyalty and to round up votes for the party position. They are spokespersons on the nightly news and the talk shows. They serve as intermediaries between the White House and their legislative parties. Some are potential presidential candidates who will try to position themselves for the next nominating season. But they do not control their legislative parties. "You have a hunting license to persuade," according to Jim Wright, the House majority leader; "that's about all you have."[23]

House caucuses and party leaders. The Democrats organize as the House Democratic Caucus, and the Republicans organize as the House Republican Conference—but each party's meeting is known as its *caucus* (Figure 11-1). Membership is open to those elected on the party line and to independents (if any). Members must vote with the party at the beginning of each session, when the House elects the Speaker and the committee chairs and assigns committee members. Otherwise, they are free to vote as they wish.

The leader of the majority caucus becomes the Speaker of the House. In modern times he has always been a senior member, averaging more than twenty years in Congress before his election and serving for an average of six years thereafter. The majority caucus also elects a majority leader (a post created in 1899), who leads the party in floor debates, while the Speaker presides. The minority caucus elects its own minority leader (referred to by the Republicans as the *Republican leader* rather than the *minority leader*).

Each caucus elects a chief whip and various deputy and assistant whips (posts created by the Republicans in 1897 and by the Democrats in 1900); their function is to find out how members intend to vote.

Figure 11-1. Party leaders in the House: (a) Democrats; (b) Republicans. All party committees and leaders are formally chosen by the caucus or conference.

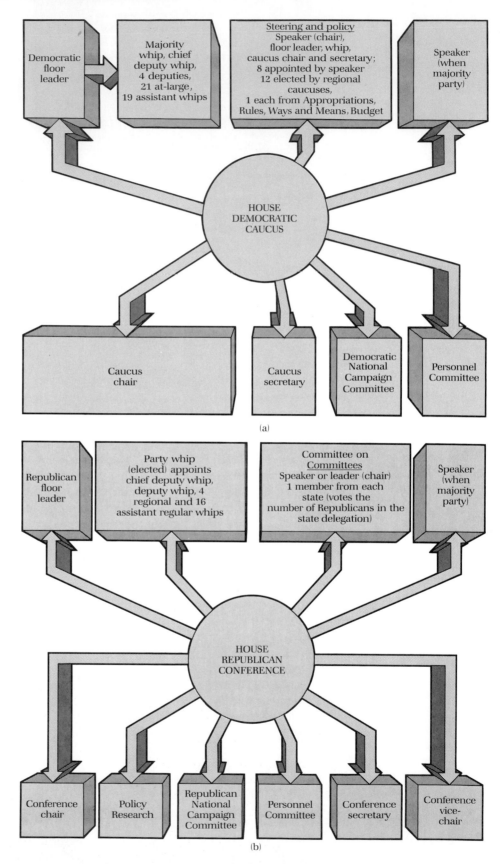

Democratic floor leader

Majority whip, chief deputy whip, 4 deputies, 21 at-large, 19 assistant whips

Steering and policy
Speaker (chair), floor leader, whip, caucus chair and secretary; 8 appointed by speaker 12 elected by regional caucuses, 1 each from Appropriations, Rules, Ways and Means, Budget

Speaker (when majority party)

HOUSE DEMOCRATIC CAUCUS

Caucus chair

Caucus secretary

Democratic National Campaign Committee

Personnel Committee

(a)

Republican floor leader

Party whip (elected) appoints chief deputy whip, deputy whip, 4 regional and 16 assistant regular whips

Committee on Committees
Speaker or leader (chair) 1 member from each state (votes the number of Republicans in the state delegation)

Speaker (when majority party)

HOUSE REPUBLICAN CONFERENCE

Conference chair

Policy Research

Republican National Campaign Committee

Personnel Committee

Conference secretary

Conference vice-chair

(b)

The Democratic caucus has a Steering and Policy Committee; the members are elected by regional caucuses, selected by the Speaker, or sit by virtue of other party office. This committee makes Democratic assignments to legislative committees. House Republicans use a Committee on Committees to make their legislative committee assignments, and they have separate policy and research committees to set their agenda.

FOCUS

SPEAKERS REED AND CANNON Almost a century ago the House engaged in a twenty-year-long experiment in strong party government. Its failure sheds some light on the difficulties that presidents and party leaders have today in getting the House to act according to a party program.

The Speaker—Thomas "Boss" Reed, elected in 1889—changed House rules so that he could control floor debates and end minority-party obstruction of the Republican program. He packed two important committees (Ways and Means and Appropriations) with his allies and controlled the flow of tax and spending favors to the members. He chaired the Rules Committee, which determined procedures for each bill on the floor, and when he came up with an unfair rule, he cheerily informed the Democratic minority: "Gentlemen, we have decided to perpetrate the following outrage." He made all appointments to committees and could remove members if they defied him. His successor, Joe ("Uncle Joe") Cannon, instituted a binding rule in the Republican caucus so that members would vote in committee and on the floor in accordance with caucus instructions. Speaker Cannon also saw that some important bills in a session were passed before making committee assignments, thus forcing members to demonstrate their loyalty.

Both Reed and Cannon acted according to the doctrine of party responsibility. The only function of the minority party was to oppose, and the majority party would not permit it to obstruct the working of the House. The function of the majority party was to govern—to pass laws and make policy and to take the responsibility for the consequences in the next elections. As early as 1891, Albert Hart, a professor at Harvard, commented on this situation, saying that "the Speaker is likely to become, and perhaps is already, more powerful, both for good

Thomas Reed. (*Bettmann Archive.*)   Joe Cannon. (*Bettmann Archive.*)

and for evil, than the President of the United States.[24] In 1896, Mary P. Follett, a political scientist, referred to Reed in her definitive study of the role of the Speaker as the "Speaker-Premier" of government—a clear reference to the power of the British prime minister.[25] Woodrow Wilson, then president of Princeton University, wrote in 1908 that "when matters of legislation are under discussion the country is apt to think of the Speaker as the chief figure in Washington rather than the President."[26]

Eventually public opinion, newspaper editorialists, and many members of Congress turned against "Czar" Cannon. In 1910 a combination of Democrats and disgruntled Republicans staged a revolt and changed some of the House rules to minimize his powers. They also removed him from the Rules Committee. In the subsequent elections, the Democrats became the majority; committed to a weak Speaker system, they gave the power to make committee assignments to their members on the Ways and Means (that is, taxation) Committee. They also made its chairman their floor leader, weakening the Speaker even more, and in 1919 they created a separate majority leader, further diffusing power.[27] Since the 1910 revolt, neither Democrats nor Republicans have tried to institute centralized control or party government in the House.

Senate caucuses and party leaders. Senate Democrats meet as the Democratic Conference (Figure 11-2a). They elect a leader, who chairs the conference, as well as the Policy Committee (made up of nine senators who plot legislative strategy) and the Steering Committee (which consists of twenty-two members who make committee assignments). The conference elects a party whip, but the chief deputy whip and the deputy whips are chosen by the leader.

The Republicans use collective leadership (Figure 11-2b): their conference elects a leader, but he or she does not chair any other committees. Instead, the conference elects a chair, who chooses a seventeen-member Committee on Committees (with its own chair), which makes legislative committee assignments. A Policy Committee (with its own chair), develops legislative strategy.

Power and influence of party leaders. Leaders do not have formal powers which enable them to dominate the legislative parties. They do not control committee assignments or choose committee or subcommittee chairs. The party caucuses cannot bind members to vote the "party line" on pending bills. Both parties used such rules only briefly—the Republicans between 1890 and 1910, and the Democrats between 1911 and 1915. Leaders can influence their party Committee on Committees when they make assignments. They can make newcomers their protégés, as Senator Robert Kerr did with Lyndon Johnson and as Speaker Tip O'Neill did with Geraldine Ferraro. They can make a member's priority their own and bring it to the caucus. They can intercede with the White House and get someone a favor. They can introduce members to important lobbyists and PAC managers who might fund their future campaigns. And, like the president, they can offer *favor*—they can reward those who work with them.

Party leaders rely mostly on influence rather than pressure. "You can't do those things by arm-twisting. I don't believe in that. You have to reason with them," says Tip O'Neill.[28] And so he reasons group by group, though he admits

Figure 11-2. Party leaders in the Senate: (*a*) Democrats; (*b*) Republicans. The Republican conference chooses all the party leaders. The Democratic conference chooses the majority or minority leader, who then select most other party leaders.

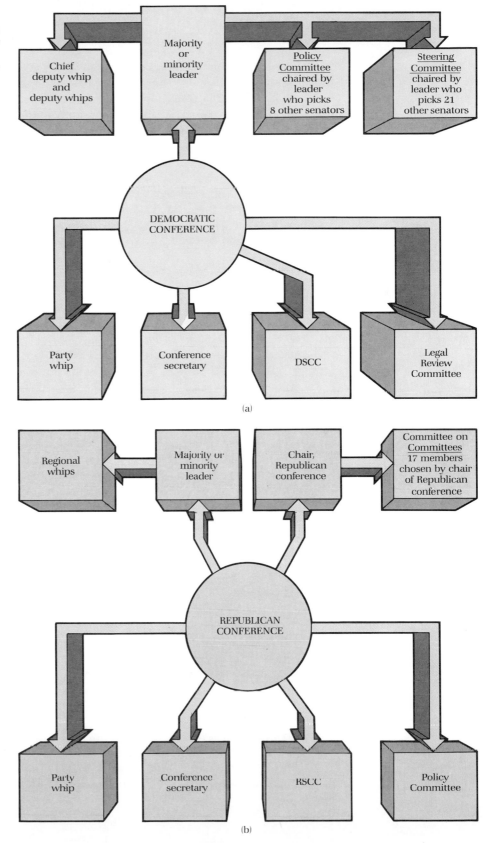

that "in any other country in the world, the Democrats would be five different parties." "I've never even once threatened to punish a member," says Ted Stevens, a former Senate Republican whip. "We probably don't even have the power to do so if we wanted to."[29] Influence comes more through force of personality than through formal powers. Lyndon Johnson was a master of persuasion. He knew everybody's weaknesses and strengths. "The treatment," which was administered in the Senate cloakroom, on the Senate floor, or in his office, was "an almost hypnotic experience and rendered the target stunned and helpless," according to reporters who observed its effects.[30] Johnson was a tireless negotiator and a shrewd compromiser. Yet even he could not control his colleagues: he was a protégé of a small clique of senior senators who had chosen him to handle their exhausting chores. Often it was their public backing for a bill that convinced hesitant colleagues to go along.

Although Johnson was successful, he was no better—as measured by the percentage of senators who supported the party and by the percentage of bills passed—than his low-key successor, Mike Mansfield, who relied on mild persuasion.[31] The success of Howard Baker (another mild-mannered leader on the Republican side) in the 1980s shows that more than one style of party leadership can work.

Committees and their leaders

"It is not far from the truth," Woodrow Wilson wrote a century ago, "to say that Congress in session in its Committee rooms is Congress at work."[32] All the 10,000 to 20,000 bills introduced in Congress are immediately referred to one of the House and one of the Senate standing committees, which can take the following actions:

- Conduct *hearings* so that officials in the executive branch, interest-group lobbyists, and academic experts can offer opinions or suggest amendments.
- Hold *markup* sessions, at which time (by majority vote) committee members can rewrite a bill or even substitute a completely new version.
- Write and submit to Congress a *report* discussing a proposal, complete with minority and dissenting views.

Committee members lead the floor debate, for or against a measure, when it is considered by the entire chamber. They work with party leaders to round up votes for their position, briefing members who are unfamiliar with the issues. Some serve on the Conference Committee, which reconciles the versions passed by each chamber and reports back a single version to be repassed in identical language before being sent to the president.

There are twenty-two standing committees in the House and sixteen in the Senate. In addition, there are three Senate and four House select committees, which may study issues and report to Congress but which do not handle legislation. (There are also four joint committees, two of which study economic and tax issues, and two of which handle the Government Printing Office and the Library of Congress.)

The committees are composed of subcommittees: 103 in the Senate and 144 in the House, as of 1985. They do the preliminary work on measures referred to full committees; increasingly, they hold the hearings and draft the report, and the full committee modifies their initiatives. Representatives serve on an average of 1.7 committees and 4 subcommittees, while senators serve on an av-

HOUSE AND SENATE COMMITTEES

House committees

Rules: Gives each bill reported to the floor a "rule" specifying the procedures for debate. It is an arm of the majority caucus and leadership.

Five major committees

Ways and Means: Handles all revenue measures and funding for many important programs which do not require appropriations.

Appropriations: Handles all appropriations bills, which fund about half of all government agencies.

Budget: Reports resolutions which set taxing and spending targets for the federal budget.

Armed Services: Handles all bills involving the military, including base construction and weapons procurement.

Foreign Affairs: Handles the foreign aid program, the State Department, and international agreements.

Other important committees

Education and Labor
Science and Technology
Judiciary
Agriculture
Banking, Finance, and Urban Affairs
Energy and Commerce
Merchant Marine and Fisheries
Public Works and Transportation
Interior and Insular Affairs

Minor committees

Veterans Affairs
Small Business
Government Operations
Post Office and Civil Service
District of Columbia
Standards of Official Conduct
House Administration

Select committees

On Aging
On Children, Youth and Families
On Intelligence
On Narcotics Abuse and Control

Senate committees

Five major committees

Finance: Handles revenue measures and funding for programs that do not require appropriations.

Appropriations: Funds about half of all government agencies through appropriations bills.

Budget: Reports resolutions which set taxing and spending targets for the federal budget.

Armed Services: Legislates on the military services.

Foreign Relations: Has jurisdiction over treaties, nomination of ambassadors and important national security officials, foreign aid programs, and the State Department.

Other important committees

Labor and Human Resources
Commerce, Science and Transportation
Judiciary
Agriculture
Banking, Housing and Urban Affairs
Energy and Natural Resources
Environment and Public Works

Special committee

On Aging

Minor committees

Small Business
Governmental Affairs
Rules and Administration
Veterans Affairs

Select committees

On Ethics
On Indian Affairs
On Intelligence

erage of 2.3 committees and 8.1 subcommittees. Because they have fewer as-signments, House members are better able to specialize.

Party control of committees. Since the 1830s all committees have been con-trolled by the majority party in the chamber—even if the other party has controlled the White House—and the majority party determines how many seats are allocated to each party. The ratio of Republican to Democratic com-mittee members follows the party ratio in the chamber: if there are sixty Re-publicans and forty Democrats in the Senate, Republicans will constitute 60 percent of most committees. On important committees the majority party sometimes increases the ratio to ensure its control even if one or two of its members defect. The majority party also gives itself a disproportionate number of subcommittee seats, and it chairs every subcommittee.

Committee assignments. Once the ratios have been determined, each legis-lative party makes its own committee assignments, which are rubber-stamped by Congress. The White House and the national party committees have no influence. Moreover, committee members are almost never dropped or reas-signed from one committee to another without their consent (this has not happened since 1853 in the Senate and since 1870 in the House), which means that neither the president nor any party leader can discipline members by threatening to take away their committee seats.[33]

To get on a committee (or to be reassigned to a better one), a member puts in a request to the legislative party's Committee on Committees, just before the new Congress convenes. In making assignments, the Committee on Commit-tees heavily weighs ***chamber seniority***—years of uninterrupted service in the House or Senate. The committee also tries to accommodate party leaders, who want members (preferably from safe seats) who will vote with the party. Com-mittee chairs also have their favorites. Lobbyists push for members who are sympathetic to their causes. They remind the committee how useful their PACs have been in previous elections. Seats are denominated by geographic *zones* so that no more than two members from the same zone may serve on a committee in the House. About two-fifths of the seats on committees are infor-mally reserved for particular states by past custom: for example, New York always gets a seat on the taxing and spending committees, while members from western states always get assignments to committees dealing with water and public lands.

The "freshman class" always pressures the committee for good assignments. When control of the Senate shifts from one part to the other, freshmen from the new majority party get better assignments than at other times.[34] Otherwise they take whatever they can get. In 1979 James Shannon of Massachusetts, a freshman, got on the Ways and Means Committee, a plum assignment, in part because he had written his master's thesis in political science on Tip O'Neill, the Speaker of the House. Another freshman—Robert Mrazek, a Democrat from New York—went in to see the Speaker in 1983 to ask about getting on the Appropriations Committee. O'Neill told him that the committee would never assign a freshman, but then asked whom he had defeated to get to the House. Mrazek replied, "LeBoutillier," a Republican who had once compared Tip O'Neill to the federal budget, saying that they were both "fat, bloated, and out of control." Later, according to a member of the Committee on Committees,

O'Neill kept saying, "He beat LeBoutillier, he beat LeBoutillier"—and the freshman got his committee assignment!

Committee lineups. Party lineups mean less than the ideologies of the members or the interests they represent. Some committees, such as the House Education and Labor Committee and the House Foreign Affairs Committee, are dominated by liberals. Others, such as the House Appropriations Committee and the House Ways and Means Committee, are dominated by conservatives and moderates. Republicans control both the Senate Foreign Relations Committee and the Senate Armed Services Committee, but the former is run by moderates and liberals, and the latter is run by conservatives, which means that the two committees often square off against each other.

Members of committees dealing with agriculture, public works, water projects, and natural resources usually work closely with interest groups and career bureaucrats to get projects and services for their constituents and contracts or changes in the laws for their local companies—and their interests usually cross party and ideological lines. Some committees work in a very

---

COMMITTEE ASSIGNMENTS IN CONGRESS

House Democrats. Requests for assignments and reassignments go to the Steering and Policy Committee, which is chaired by the Speaker. Every member must receive at least one good committee assignment. The list of proposed assignments is accepted or rejected by the entire Democratic caucus at the beginning of the congressional session.

Committee chairs and the subcommittee chairs of the Appropriations Committee are nominated by the Steering and Policy Committee, almost always on the basis of seniority. Nominations are voted on by the Democratic caucus.

Other subcommittee chairs are elected by the Democrats on the parent committee. No member may chair more than one subcommittee on each committee.

The Speaker selects the Democratic members and the chair of the Rules Committee.

House Republicans. Requests for assignments and reassignments go to the Committee on Committees, which is chaired by the Republican leader. Its Executive Committee makes nominations, which are approved by the committee and then by the Republican House Policy Committee.

Ranking minority members of committees and subcommittees (or chairs) are chosen on the basis of seniority. The House Republican Conference approves the nominations by secret ballot.

Senate Democrats. Requests for assignments and reassignments go to the Steering Committee. Each Democrat must receive one good committee assignment before any senator receives a second good committee assignment. The Democratic Conference approves all nominations.

The ranking Democrat (or chair) is selected according to the rule of seniority, subject to approval by the conference if one-fifth of the members request a vote.

Senate Republicans. Requests for assignments and reassignments go to the Committee on Committees, whose members are appointed by the chair of the Republican Conference. Members receive preference according to seniority. No member may serve on more than one of the "big four" (Appropriations, Armed Services, Finance, and Foreign Relations) until all others who have applied are accommodated.

The chairs (or ranking minority members) are chosen on the basis of seniority. Nominations are subject to vote by committee Republicans.

Table 11-1. Seniority in the House, 1881 to 1963

Congressional sessions	Percentage of positions as chair in which seniority rule was not followed
1881–1889	60.4
1891–1899	49.4
1901–1909	19
1911–1919	30
1921–1929	26
1931–1939	23
1941–1949	14
1951–1963	0.7

Source: Data reworked from Nelson Polsby et al., "The Growth of the Seniority System in the U.S. House of Representatives", *American Political Science Review*, vol. 53, no. 3, September 1969, table 1, p. 792.

partisan fashion (usually liberal Democrats confront conservative Republicans), while others have always worked in a bipartisan spirit (usually moderate Republicans and Democrats hold the balance of power). And when it comes to getting "goodies" from the government, conservative legislators like Barry Goldwater and Jesse Helms are just as likely as liberals to feed at the federal trough. In fact, in 1985 Helms refused to accept the position of chair of the Senate Foreign Relations Committee (where he could have advanced his principles) so that he could remain chairman of the Senate Agriculture Committee (where he could advance the interests of the tobacco industry in his home state).

Committee leadership. Committees are always chaired by a member of the majority party. Other leaders include the ranking majority member (next in line to be chair) and the ranking minority member (who would become chair if his or her party controlled the chamber). If you examine a committee roster, you will notice that all Democrats are ranked on one side and that all Republicans are ranked on the other, according to *committee seniority:* years of uninterrupted service on the committee. *Chamber* seniority gets people on a committee, but only *committee* seniority gets them ahead within the committee. Someone with twenty years of chamber seniority starts at the bottom when going on a new committee.

Usually the position of chair is assigned according to strict committee seniority, a practice known as ***seniority rule*** (Table 11-1). In most cases, subcommittee chairs are also assigned on the basis of seniority, with high-ranking members most likely to be chosen by other committee members or by the party caucus.[35] Since 1921 the Senate has used the seniority rule for assigning most chairs (before that time, chairs were appointed by the president of the Senate, by the president pro tem, by the entire Senate, or on the basis of chamber seniority). In the House, the rule gradually took hold between 1880 and 1950.

ISSUE AND DEBATE

THE SENIORITY SYSTEM. *The background.* The seniority system favors legislators from states or districts that do not have a competitive two-party system, because they can be elected time and time again and accumulate more and more chamber and committee seniority. "We pick 'em young, we pick 'em honest, and we send 'em back," is how Speaker Sam Rayburn described the way so many Texans became chairs from the 1930s through the 1960s, when Texas was a one-party state. Up until the 1970s, southern Democrats had far more than their proportional share of positions as chairs, which gave Congress a conservative cast. But these things change: by the 1980s western Republicans were having their turn in the Senate, and northern liberals and minorities in the House were benefiting from their seniority (William Gray, a black representative, became chairman of the powerful House Budget Committee, for example), while the proportion of chairs controlled by the south plummeted as a result of the emergence of a two-party system and the retirement and death of many elderly southern members.

The cons. The seniority system may be ideologically unrepresentative. Conservatives from the south had a disproportionate amount of influence in the 1950s; in the 1980s, a minority of moderate Republican senators have had much more influence than a majority of their more conservative (but junior in terms of seniority) colleagues. When the country shifts direction, Congress is likely to lag.

The seniority system retards political change. The most powerful leaders in Congress now come from the least competitive districts. They won their first elections one or two decades ago, and they represent the political currents of the past. The freshmen, who are more attuned to changes in the electorate and are more likely to have won in competitive districts by being responsive to new ideas, are relegated to the bottom of the congressional power structure. When women and people from religious, racial, and ethnic minorities gain more representation in Congress, their legislators also start at the bottom. Nader's Raiders (a group affiliated with Ralph Nader, a consumer activist) referred to the seniority system as the "senility system" because it keeps elderly members in important positions long after they are past their prime. "It is tired, it is old, it is insane," was how John Rhodes, the House Republican leader, characterized it.[36]

The pros. The seniority rule helps preserve the cohesion and autonomy of the legislative party. It dispenses formal leadership positions on committees in a clockwork, automatic fashion. There are no contests or jockeying for position by committee rivals when the rule is fully in effect. Moreover, the selection of leaders is no longer bound up with the election of the Speaker or of Senate party leaders, as was the case in the nineteenth century. Congress is no longer torn apart at the beginning of each session by ambitious members struggling to become chairs. Most important, presidents have no influence in the selection of committee leaders. They must work with whomever the rule generates as leaders in the next congressional session. The combination of chamber and committee seniority rules gives the president almost no influence in distributing the coveted prizes to legislators, and this preserves their autonomy in the face of pressure from the White House.

The 1970s reforms in the seniority rule. Rules changes in the 1970s made seniority leaders more responsive to the party caucuses. Since 1975, committee and subcommittee chairs have been voted on by the party caucuses (or by party members of the committee involved). "Chairmen are not serving by divine right," the reformer Jack Bingham observed after the rules change, "but as representatives of the caucus."[37] They now follow the caucus priorities and policies and are not likely to obstruct the party leaders. While most assignments are still made on the basis of the seniority rule, in 1975 House Democrats removed three chairs from their posts because they had abused their power, violated committee procedures, or were out of touch with their members.[38] Later, two others who were involved in sex scandals resigned because of pressure from party leaders. Several subcommittee chairs were removed from their posts in 1977 and 1983 for conduct unbecoming a member, and in 1985 Melvin Price, the elderly chair of the House Armed Services Committee, was replaced by the caucus with seventh-ranked Les Aspin, a strong critic of waste in the Pentagon.

Power of committee chairs. Until recently, chairs reigned supreme. "You can go to hell," the chairman of the Rules Committee once told his colleagues; "it makes no difference what a majority of you decide; if it meets with my disapproval, it shall not be done. I am the committee."[39] Chairs set meeting times, convened or adjourned committees at will, controlled the workload and the agenda, set priorities, and determined which bills would be taken up. They appointed the entire staff, created subcommittees, defined their jurisdiction, and appointed their members.[40]

Chairs used their power to exchange favors and keep junior members in line. They could bargain with the president for favors, since they controlled a "choke point" through which the president's program had to pass. They dominated Cabinet departments in the same way, with jurisdiction over their authority and their funds. "Uncle Carl" Vinson, who served for half a century in the House as chairman of the Armed Services Committee, used to ask generals, "Boy, what did you say your name was?" when they testified before him. "I'd rather run the Pentagon from up here," was the way he put it when declining offers to serve as secretary of defense.[41] NASA even had to allow Jake Garn, a Republican senator from Utah, to fly in the space shuttle simply because he headed the subcommittee which had jurisdiction over NASA's budget.

Committee leaders controlled (and could deliver) their committees, and the committees in turn could usually deliver the votes in the chamber to pass a bill. The president had to deal with only a few party and committee leaders. All this has changed. Committee chairs are now responsive to their committee members and to party caucuses, who can replace them if they are abusive or obstructive. Committee majorities now make the rules, set the agenda, and determine priorities. Chairs cannot keep junior members in line; they must bargain with them and trade for favors. Chairs no longer can automatically deliver their committees. It does presidents no good to bargain just with a chair; they must obtain the backing of a majority of the committee.

Subcommittee government. The number of subcommittees has increased. They have their own budgets, jurisdiction, and staff. In 1973 the House Democrats wrote a Subcommittee Bill of Rights, which guarantees their right to receive bills from committees and requires committees to take up their reports. Since 1971 subcommittee chairs have had the right to manage bills on the floor of the House, and they are now the floor leaders on two-thirds of the bills reported out of the full committee.[42] The subcommittee chairs and ranking minority members are no longer selected by the committee leaders, but instead are chosen either by the legislative caucus (through its Committee on Committees) or by party members on the parent committee. They cannot be removed by the committee chair (although they can be replaced by committee members or the party caucus). Committee chairs no longer control the subcommittees. Often a subcommittee obtains a majority for its own proposal and gets it to the floor against the wishes of the committee chair.

Subcommittees make it difficult for the White House to influence the legislative agenda. Work is conducted by 250 subcommittees, each of which jealously guards its independence. "We're becoming a mobocracy," is how John LoFalce, a Democrat from New York, put it; "the leadership has . . . said to its members, do your own thing."[43] The committee government of the past has become today's subcommittee government, which is free-lance government, as individual legislators go whichever way their spirit and their staff aides move them.[44] A subcommittee chair becomes a soapbox for junior members—a way for them to conduct hearings and get a twenty-second spot on the network news or a local station.

POWERS OF CONGRESS

This section considers what Congress does—that is, its formal and informal powers.

Legislative powers

Article I of the Constitution grants Congress substantial powers—"all legislative powers herein granted"—and Section 8 of that article enumerates seventeen specific powers. The eighteenth clause gives Congress the power "to make all laws which shall be necessary and proper for carrying into execution the foregoing Powers, and all other Powers vested by this Constitution in the Government of the United States, or any Department or Officer thereof."

This so-called elastic clause allows Congress to make laws that are necessary and proper to execute *its own powers.* But it also lets Congress pass laws that are necessary and proper for *the other two branches*—the presidency and the judiciary—to operate. It establishes the lower court system. It establishes and funds the Executive Office of the President. It delegates authority to the executive branch. It creates and funds the departments of government.

Policy innovation

Congress can pass the president's program intact, make major changes, or reject parts of it. Although the administration does not have formal control over the congressional calendar, its important measures are always considered by committees, and party leaders usually see that they are taken up within a reasonable time. Yet only during the initial "honeymoon" phase of the presidency or in a national emergency do bills go through Congress without substantial change. Usually bills are thoroughly "marked up" by committees and are further amended on the floor.

Congress must reauthorize existing programs, and that in turn usually means substantial amendment. Even in the case of programs that are initially proposed by the president, such as the "war on poverty" of 1964 and the Voting Rights Act of 1965, two decades of congressional action are likely to convert them into laws which mirror congressional priorities. Presidents and Cabinet secretaries often use national agenda politics to obtain a national consensus for a new program, but long after the media and the public have lost interest, legislators reshape the laws for their own purposes.

Congress may also pass its own measures. Many important bills—such as the National Labor Relations Act, the Taft-Hartley labor law, national pensions legislation, and environmental protection and consumer safety measures—originated in Congress. Sometimes Congress has "incubated" an idea for a substantial time, holding hearings without taking action, until a new president picked it up and made it part of his program. Much of John Kennedy's "new frontier," including the Peace Corps, had been developed by congressional Democrats in the four years preceding his term. Similarly, Reagan's 1981 supply-side tax cuts and his proposals for a flat tax in 1985 were originated by House Republicans.

Informal checks

Congress can use the threat of legislation to get executive officials to respond to its wishes. It can threaten to hold controversial hearings to get them to delay or modify decisions. It can hold hearings which become media events and influence the national agenda. Committees can conduct full-scale investigations (on the basis of the necessary and proper clause) which can put the president on the defensive; they can force resignations (the Senate Select Committee on Campaign Activities that investigated Watergate-related crimes forced the resignation of four top Nixon staffers, for example) or policy shifts (such as the 1983 housecleaning in the Environmental Protection Agency); and they can provide a legislator with a springboard for a future presidential race (for example, Jack Kennedy's investigation of labor unions and Lyndon John-

Senators Sam Ervin (D.-N. C.) and Howard Baker (R.-Tenn) examine a letter from the Nixon White House as other senators and staffers look on, during the Judiciary Committee's investigation of Watergate crimes. (*J. P. Laffont: Sygma.*)

son's hearings on defense preparedness were useful in their 1960 presidential nomination bids).

Congressional headline hunters can abuse their power. In the 1950s Senator Joe McCarthy, a Republican from Wisconsin, charged that communists had infiltrated the State Department and the Army. His Permanent Investigations Subcommittee smeared the reputation of many loyal Foreign Service and Army officers without uncovering any evidence of communist subversion. Senators who spoke out against his lie and smear tactics (which made the word *McCarthyism* part of the American political vocabulary) were defeated for reelection after he campaigned against them in 1952. An intimidated President Eisenhower allowed McCarthy to control the personnel policies of the State Department, leading to the resignations of some of the most able career diplomats. Eventually McCarthy attacked the secretary of the Army in televised hearings, and public opinion turned against him when he failed to produce any evidence. The Senate ultimately censured McCarthy for "conduct unbecoming to the Senate," and he died a few years later, a broken and powerless outcast.

Censure and impeachment: Checks and checkmate

Either chamber may vote a resolution of ***censure*** against the president or any other official, although there is no mention of this power in the Constitution. President Jackson was censured by the Senate after removing Treasury Secretary Duane from office. After Jackson left office, his supporters got the Senate to expunge the resolution. His censure played a major part in the formation of the pro-Jackson Democratic Party and the anti-Jackson Whig Party. A House committee censured President Tyler for vetoing several bills. President Buchanan was censured by the House for alleged bribery involving a federal appointment. In each case the opposition used the censure to score political points, and the president argued that censure was unconstitutional and challenged Congress to impeach him.

The process. Although no president has ever been removed from office, impeachment has been used successfully against several federal judges. First, a resolution of impeachment is introduced by a member of the House and is referred to the House Judiciary Committee. The House must approve committee hearings. The committee then drafts and votes articles of impeachment, laying out its charge. It sends them, together with a report, to the House, which debates the charges and by majority vote can adopt one or more of them. Andrew Johnson was the only president ever to be impeached; Richard Nixon would have been the second, had he not resigned.

Once the House has voted to impeach, it appoints five managers (that is, prosecutors) who read the articles to the Senate, which then conducts a trial; the members of the Senate serve as the "jury," and if the case is against the president the chief justice of the Supreme Court presides as the "judge." The House managers and the counsel for the official who is being impeached can submit legal briefs, call witnesses and cross-examine them, and enter evidence. After the trial, each article is voted on separately. If two-thirds of the senators present vote for any of them, the official is convicted and removed from office. (In the trial of a president, the vice president of the United States would then be brought immediately into the chamber after the voting to take the presidential oath.)

Grounds for impeachment. Both Andrew Johnson and Richard Nixon argued that grounds for impeachment must be limited to serious federal crimes. The Republicans and the Democrats reversed their positions in the two proceedings: in the Johnson case, the Republicans argued that *abuse of power* (which might not involve a criminal violation) could be grounds for impeach-

The Senate has been called the "most exclusive club in the world." Like a club, it is mostly self-policing. Senator Joseph McCarthy (left) was eventually censured for intemperate conduct during his anti-Communist hearings in the 1950s. (*UPI; Bettmann Archive.*)

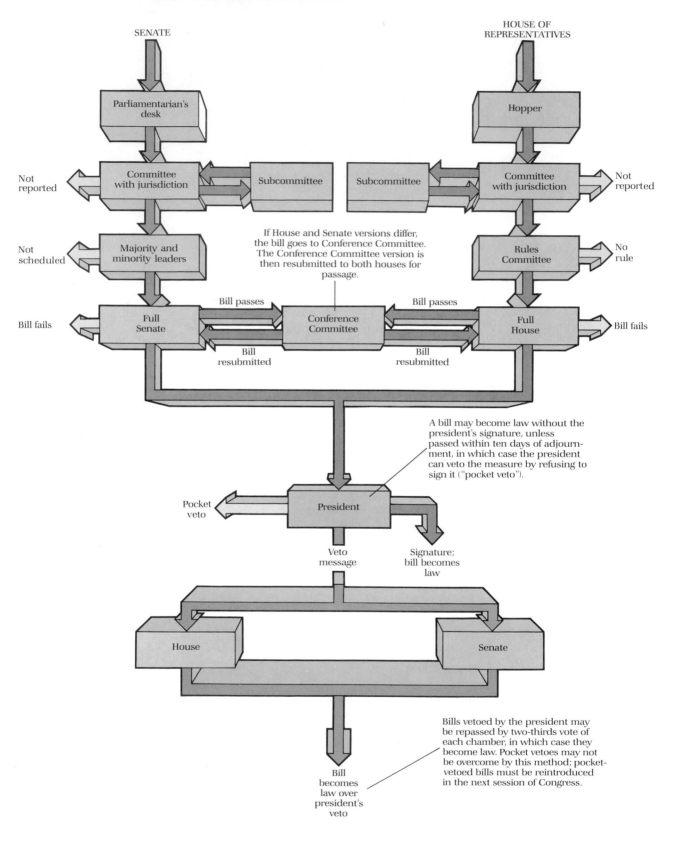

After the House had exercised its power to impeach a president for the first and only time, in 1868, President Andrew Johnson was summoned to trial by the Senate, where conviction failed by one vote. (*Granger Collection.*)

ment; later, when Nixon was involved, they reversed themselves. The Democrats, who defended Johnson by demanding evidence of a crime, later argued that Nixon could be impeached without having violated federal law. *Abuse of power* is a vague term. A congressional majority could remove a president whose policies it disagreed with. But thus far, Congress has acted responsibly.

THE LEGISLATIVE STRUGGLE

Now that we know something about life on the Hill, the power structure, and the formal powers of Congress, we can consider the legislative process: the sequence of events from the introduction of a bill to its final passage (Figure 11-3).

The process

Figure 11-3. Opposite: How a bill becomes a law. How bills are introduced, dealt with by committees and party leaders, considered by each chamber and sent to conference, and finally sent to the president for signature or veto. The actual progress of any particular bill is likely to diverge significantly from this chart, and most bills never make it all the way to final passage.

Referral to committee. Bills are drafted by members (or by their aides, with the assistance of congressional agencies or the House or Senate legislative counsel). They are dropped into the House hopper, a mahogany box at one end of the Speaker's desk, or are put on the desk of the Senate parliamentarian (the Senate employee who advises the presiding officer during debate). Party leaders then refer bills to the committee with jurisdiction. In some cases the choice may be crucial; in 1964, for example, civil rights measures were sent to the Judiciary Committee in the House but to the Commerce Committee in the Senate because the Senate Judiciary Committee would have killed them. In 1978 energy legislation went to several House committees for preliminary work and were then referred to a select committee dominated by House Democratic leaders, who put together a comprehensive package.

Subcommittees conduct hearings and report back to the full committee, usually taking a leading role in revising the language of the bill in the committee, when it marks up the bill line by line and makes revisions, by majority vote. The bill is then reported to the chamber, accompanied by a printed report expressing majority and minority views.

Scheduling in the House and Senate. In the House, bills reported by committees must go to the Rules Committee, which since 1961 has been an arm of the majority party leadership and whose members are appointed by the Speaker, where they are given a special rule governing debate. An ***open rule*** allows members to amend the measure on the House floor; a ***closed rule*** restricts amendments to members of the committee with jurisdiction. Most rules provide for no more than two hours of debate. The Speaker of the House then schedules debate (in consultation with the minority leader) and the vote for final passage. In the Senate the majority leader schedules legislation by working out ***unanimous-consent*** agreements with the minority leader; these suspend the formal Senate rules (which usually provide for unlimited debate) and replace them with ad hoc rules that move the bill along much faster.

Senate filibusters. In theory, senators have the right of unlimited speech, though in practice they usually abide by unanimous-consent agreements and limit their remarks. Occasionally one or more senators who strongly oppose a measure will ***filibuster:*** they require the Senate to abide by its rule that a senator who has the floor need not relinquish it, and they make extended speeches, hoping to force the leadership to drop consideration of a measure. A filibuster can be ended only if three-fifths of the senators vote for ***cloture*** (an end to debate). Cloture was first used in 1919 in a filibuster against the Treaty of Versailles and was later employed in the 1950s and 1960s when southerners filibustered against civil rights bills. In the past two decades liberals such as Howard Metzenbaum have filibustered to protest energy and environmental legislation favoring business. Gary Hart filibustered against the MX missile to boost his presidential chances. There were thirty votes to impose cloture between 1981 and 1985, cast so that the Senate could continue to function.

Each senator's privilege of almost unlimited speaking time—the filibuster—can make for long nights in the Senate when an issue is hotly contested. (*George Tames: New York Times.*)

Debate and amendment. Congressional debate sometimes strongly influences the final version of a bill. Often provisions are poorly drafted or are ambiguous. The sponsors and the floor managers can discuss the language and explain what is means or how the bill might apply in specific circumstances. These discussions become part of the *legislative history* of a bill: along with hearings and the reports, they are used by judges and administrators to determine how the law should be applied.

Usually the committee supports *friendly amendments* which clarify the language of a bill, strengthen its provisions, or add to its roster of supporters. *Christmas tree amendments* are put on measures to give legislators and their constituents presents (such as tax loopholes), and this ensures the necessary votes for passage. *Unfriendly amendments* are put on if opponents try to gut a measure, limit its scope or duration, or make it unworkable. Some amendments are designed to split the majority by introducing extraneous issues. Opponents of a bill vote with one group of its supporters to tack on an amendment that another group opposes strongly; then they join with the second group to kill the whole measure. In 1919, for example, the Senate killed the Treaty of Versailles and kept the United States out of the League of Nations. Opponents of the treaty combined with a group that favored it and put some reservations into the treaty draft; an infuriated President Wilson then asked his supporters to vote against the whole treaty with its unacceptable amendments, and this group, combined with the antitreaty group, killed the entire bill.

Final motions. The final maneuvering comes after a bill has been amended. First, opponents make a motion to recommit the bill to its original committee. This is actually a vote to kill the bill, even though it looks like a mere procedural vote. If the motion fails, the next vote is for final passage. This twofold system allows people who tried to kill a popular measure to get on the bandwagon and vote for final passage. Thus members can have it both ways: first they get a chance to defeat a bill on a procedural vote, which most voters will never know about; but if that fails, they can support a popular bill.

Conference. Since the House and Senate usually pass different versions of the same bill, they must reconcile the differences. Sometimes a bill passed by one chamber is voted on by the other chamber (even without full committee consideration) if the session is ending. Otherwise, each chamber appoints members to a **conference committee:** an ad hoc group which meets to iron out the differences and come up with a single version. The committee need not limit itself to reconciling the language of the two versions. It can write new provisions which had not previously been considered by either chamber—a practice used extensively in 1981 and 1982 in connection with tax and spending measures. The committee can modify, compromise on, or even remove language which both chambers had previously agreed to. At this stage the president has a last chance to threaten to use the veto, which is sometimes effective in getting the conference committee to modify a bill to meet the president's objections.

The conference report. The conference committee produces a single bill—known as the **conference report**—which is sent back to each chamber to be voted up or down (but which cannot be amended). If both chambers approve the conference report, the bill is signed by the Speaker of the House and the president pro tem of the Senate and is sent to the White House.

Politics of the legislative process

The above description of the sequence of events is not an accurate picture of what really goes on in Congress. During every session, between 10,000 and 20,000 bills are introduced, and fewer than 1000 are enacted into law. Many bills are introduced without any expectation that they will be passed. The most important function of Congress is to bury proposed legislation, and the committees are the graveyards. Important administration measures are considered, but the pet projects of individual legislators are dealt with on a reciprocal basis. A subcommittee may take up a measure in return for a member's vote on a completely unrelated matter. It takes time and effort to schedule hearings, and the legislative agenda is crowded; one "buys" time from colleagues only in exchange for something of equal value—favor for favor.

Even so, more bills get out of committee than Congress can deal with. Party and committee leaders bargain with one another for floor time. Some bills must be moved back to the end of the session or are bumped from the calendar entirely. Bills are bottled up, delayed, amended, gutted, and killed. They can be defeated by any obstructive majority in a subcommittee, in a committee, or on the floor in either house. The process favors those who want to derail a measure, and sometimes it seems a miracle, given all the confusion and obstacles, that any bills are passed at all. Near the end of a session, however, discipline breaks down. Appropriations bills, debt extension measures, and continuing resolutions to allow the government to spend (until appropriations have passed)—all become vehicles onto which riders, amendments, and even whole bills can be attached, making them resemble a freight train lumbering down the tracks.

Coalition building. How does Congress get anything done? It accomplishes its work by building coalitions through compromise and negotiation, which it

Members of Congress introduce many bills just for home consumption, such as H. R. 7349, which needless to say was never enacted into law.

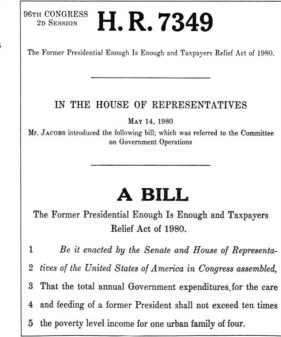

96TH CONGRESS
2D SESSION

H. R. 7349

The Former Presidential Enough Is Enough and Taxpayers Relief Act of 1980.

———————

IN THE HOUSE OF REPRESENTATIVES

MAY 14, 1980

Mr. JACOBS introduced the following bill; which was referred to the Committee on Government Operations

———————

A BILL

The Former Presidential Enough Is Enough and Taxpayers Relief Act of 1980.

1   *Be it enacted by the Senate and House of Representa-*
2   *tives of the United States of America in Congress assembled,*
3   That the total annual Government expenditures for the care
4   and feeding of a former President shall not exceed ten times
5   the poverty level income for one urban family of four.

does by drafting and revising bills so that they will appeal to a majority coalition and by means of presidential and leadership lobbying of the rank and file. This is known as ***coalition building.*** Even before bills are introduced, legislators modify their bills to attract potential supporters on the important subcommittees and committees. One good strategy is to give things to committee members; in the case of a 1983 jobs bill, for example, Bob Mrazek explained that "all members of the subcommittee worked together to select worthwhile projects," adding: "Needless to say, for most of us these projects were in our districts."[45] Members engage in the classic *logroll:* they include pet projects for many different committee members so that each one finds something to vote for in a large bill. On measures involving public works, rivers and harbors, job training, housing, and transportation, it is common to provide members with computer printouts showing exactly how much money will go to each state and each congressional district so that all those involved can see what they will get if they vote for the measures. In the case of a *time logroll*, one group will gain from a bill and therefore solicits the support of other committee members, promising them that in a later bill their help will be reciprocated. If northern Democrats vote today for a farm bill and rural public works and water projects, for example, later in the session southern and western Democrats will vote for housing and mass-transit bills.

The reverse of the logroll is the ***package deal:*** the logroll is organized from the "bottom up" by members who want their pet projects included, while the package deal is organized from the "top down" by the White House. It offers a comprehensive solution to a set of hard problems, incorporated into one single measure. The president tells Congress to take it or leave it, threatening to use the veto if anything in the package is changed and appealing to the public "over the heads of Congress," as Reagan did successfully with his economic program. The inducement for supporting the deal is that it takes care of the problem with a single vote, and if enough people agree to support it, the risk of voting for an unpopular measure is shared by both parties. In fact, the legislators can even gain a measure of credit for their political courage.

To get support, it is sometimes necessary for party leaders or the White House to offer favors which have nothing to do with a bill under consideration; these are known as ***side payments.*** Party and committee leaders may offer to schedule hearings on someone's pet project or to consider a coveted assignment to a committee. Lobbyists may offer campaign contributions from their PACs. The president may offer help in getting a federal appointment or contract for a legislator's friend.

Conflict resolution. Sometimes the sponsor of a bill can make modifications to split the opposition coalition. Some measures lend themselves to *compromise:* each side moves to the center from an extreme position. Bills with "more or less" provisions—like the amount of funding—are ideally suited for compromises. But not all issues have such provisions: social issues like prayer in schools, busing for racial integration, handgun control, and abortion are "either or" issues by their nature, and it is hard to find room to compromise on such issues of morality. Consequently, the legislators of the new right who are concerned with them have a reputation for being uncompromising and rigid.

On some issues it is possible to *horse-trade:* each side gives up something it wants if the other side does likewise. Trades can be negotiated when a bill contains many small but discrete items (or when a policy can be broken up into discrete components), such as coverage and contingencies. An example is minimum wage legislation: it is a *compromise* if those who want the minimum wage to be $6 and those who want it to be $3 agree on $5—it is a *horse trade* if they agree that agricultural and laundry workers will receive the minimum wage, but not people under the age of 16 or immigrant workers.

Sometimes sponsors make important provisions *ambiguous* so that all those in their coalition can read into a bill what they wish. Later the judges and administrators can sort things out, after the bill has passed. Support can be obtained by adding *loopholes* (so that people can avoid the impact of the law), *exemptions* (for certain categories of people or business), or *contingency provisions* (so that the law takes effect only under certain circumstances). *Timetables* for implementation can be extended to ease the impact of a measure and provide for a transition.

All these techniques are used in regulatory bills, such as those dealing with air and water quality, as environmental groups push for stricter standards and speedy timetables and as industry groups fight for weaker provisions.

Party politics

To win anything from Congress, the president or party leaders must put together transitory coalitions, which form for each bill and then dissolve. One month, a Dole-Bradley energy bill amendment brings together a Republican senator and a Democratic senator who are trying to forge a bipartisan coalition; a short time later, Dole leads the charge against Bradley's amendment to tax windfall profits of oil companies. There are no permanent friends or enemies in Congress.

The majority of roll-call votes in the House and Senate are **bipartisan:** majorities of both parties support, and minorities of both parties oppose, close to 7 out of every 10 bills. But *partisan voting*—in which a majority of one party opposes a majority of the other—is high on the important bills of the president's program, especially those involving the budget and controversial defense and foreign policy measures.

With all the problems that party leaders have in dealing with committees and rank-and-file members, legislators can be counted on to vote with a majority of the members of their party about 70 percent of the time. Moreover, the influence of party membership is stronger than the influence of constituency.[46] Rural Democrats, for example, are more likely to support big-city legislation than urban Republicans.[47] Logrolls and side payments organized by party leaders, reciprocity, and the desire to join the party majority—all these can counterbalance conflicting pressures from constituencies.

Coalition splitting and ideological wings. Often members break away from their party, usually on ideological grounds. A ***conservative coalition*** forms when southern Democrats (organized since 1980 in the House as the Conservative Democratic Forum and before that time known informally as the "Dixiecrats") join with Republicans (the most conservative of whom have organized the Conservative Opportunity Society). Republican presidents and party leaders usually do well when they can engineer such a coalition. It forms on approximately one-fifth to one-sixth of the votes (more when a Democrat is in the White House), it wins three-fifths to nine-tenths of the time, and its chances improve about 20 percent when a Republican president can give some help by lobbying and offering side payments.[48] The conservative coalition usually allies with a Republican president, supporting the administration's bills 75 percent of the time and opposing them only 25 percent of the time; it supports fewer than 10 percent of a Democratic administration's bills. (Of course if a moderate Democrat like Lyndon Johnson wins a huge victory and the Democrats enlarge their majority in the House, the conservative coalition, when it appears, is likely to be on the losing side more than half the time, as it was in 1965 and 1966.)

A majority of Democrats belong to the Democratic Study Group (DSG), which consists of approximately 180 liberal to moderate members, almost none from the south. They try to avoid an open split with the Conservative Democratic Forum by giving them leadership positions and promoting enough reciprocal deals to keep them from defecting to the Republicans. They promote geographic splits, trying to pick up support from Republicans in New England and in the mid-Atlantic states and the midwest. They try to get votes from the thirty or so moderate, urban-oriented northern Republicans (known as the "Gypsy Moths" in the House) and from the "Gang of Six" Republican liberals in the Senate.

Nonparty coalition building.   Thirty groups with staffing and funding provided by Congress—such as the Congressional Black Caucus, the Hispanic Caucus, and the Women's Caucus—as well as hundreds of informal groups serve as the focal point for PACs and lobbyists trying to gain access to Congress and trade campaign contributions for support of their bills. They provide a network that can lobby with other members on various committees to push bills. If members exert pressure, they can trade their votes with the leadership in return for favorable floor scheduling. The legislative party then becomes the sponsor of interest-group rather than party legislation. Often both parties join in a bipartisan coalition organized by a caucus and share the credit and future campaign contributions.

Far from being monolithic, Congress consists of many political groups. Mondale seeks the support of the Congressional Black Caucus during the presidential campaign in 1984. (*Larry Downing; Woodfin Group.*)

Table 11-2. Support for the president's program, by party, 1954 to 1984

President	House		Senate	
	Presidential party	Opposition party	Presidential party	Opposition party
Eisenhower	68	54	80	52
Kennedy	83	41	75	47
Johnson	81	49	71	56
Nixon	73	53	73	50
Ford	65	41	72	48
Carter	69	42	74	52
Reagan (1981)	68	42	80	49
Reagan (1982)	64	39	74	43
Reagan (1983)	70	28	73	42
Reagan (1984)	60	34	76	41

Sources: Randall Ripley, *Congress: Process and Policy*, 3d ed., Norton, New York, 1983, table 9.2, p. 360. The data on Reagan are from *Congressional Quarterly Weekly Reports*, Jan. 15, 1983, p. 96; Dec. 15, 1984.

The White House and floating coalitions. Presidents run a substantial lobbying operation from the White House; an Office of Congressional Liaison and about twenty staffers cover the House and Senate. Presidents also use their Cabinet secretaries and sub-Cabinet officials and their contacts in business and labor to lobby on the Hill.

One might think that an incumbent who is a master at lobbying and has previous experience in Congress, like Lyndon Johnson, would do better than a newcomer without such experience, like Jimmy Carter. As it turns out, the impact of these lobbying activities is less important in getting votes than presidential popularity ratings: Carter did as well as Johnson in getting congressional support, probably because neither of them remained popular very long.[49] Presidents do best, of course, when their popularity is high and climbing. They always get more support from their own party than from the opposition (Table 11-2), but they must contend with the possibility of defectors, which means that they must usually get votes from the other party. To do this, they use one or more *floating coalition* strategies:

- Keeping most of their own party and obtaining a majority with the help of a splinter opposition group, by offering either compromises or side payments
- Obtaining a bipartisan majority by forgoing political advantage and sharing credit or blame, often by creating a bipartisan study commission
- Holding a minority of their own party but gaining a majority of the opposition (a rare gambit)

Presidents get more support from their own party when the economy is doing well, when they are riding high in the popularity polls, and when it is likely that their party is headed for victory in the next elections. They do worst either when Congress is controlled by the opposition or when their own party splits over a presidential action involving war or another foreign policy crisis.

IN CONCLUSION

ASSESSING CONGRESSIONAL POWER. There are two sources of influence on Congress. Pressures from the top down come from the White House, national party leaders, and ideological PACs, all trying to organize broad-based coalitions to deal comprehensively with important national problems. Pressures from the bottom up come from a "scuffle of local interests," including constituency groups, state delegations, and narrowly focused legislative caucuses and affiliated interest groups. In the absence of a strong national party organization or presidential control over the legislative party, the balance tilts toward the interest groups and toward the concerns of constituencies—unless the president can dominate the national agenda and build a temporary coalition to address national problems.

If left to its own devices, Congress usually delays, obstructs, or waters down measures. It delegates its powers and policy-making responsibilities to the bureaucracy, or else it ties the bureaucracy in knots with petty restrictions. It distributes goods and services in "shotgun" fashion, by logrolling so that everyone gets a piece of the action. It creates many small programs with overlapping and competing jurisdictions in fields such as job training and vocational education, programs which are explainable only in terms of subcommittee and committee turf. Congress is oriented toward pressures from organized interest groups and is less responsive to the unorganized and politically unsophisticated. It decentralizes power by giving states, counties, and cities a large role in administering federal programs. Because of logrolling and reciprocity, it honors so many claims and gives in to so many special interests that the overall scope of government activity increases—even when action by the federal government cannot solve local problems.

Congress is prone to making false starts. Subcommittee chairs posture and introduce measures or hold hearings when their proposals have no chance of passage. There is a great deal of media smoke and not much legislative fire. The system is clogged with pet projects in a topsy-turvey Hill: energy and attention are focused on the small stuff rather than on national issues. "We have diffused power to such an extent that there is no power anywhere," argues Senator Don Quayle, Republican from Indiana.[50]

But sometimes the top-down system transforms Congress. It debates key issues. Committees conduct important hearings on the president's program or on misconduct in office. Parties line up against each other (most notably on budgets, taxes, and deficits). The American people witness a real debate on alternatives, and public opinion, as transmitted to the White House and Congress via the polls, has a significant effect on policy.

So there are really two Congresses. One is a parochial, pluralistic, inward-looking, and inefficient legislature, deadlocking American democracy with its inaction and its irresponsibility. The other is a powerful branch of government, collaborating with the administration or checking its excesses and legislating seriously and comprehensively on important issues.

The current fragmentation of Congress reinforces its twofold character. The more it is democratized, the more it lets relatively junior members in on the action, and the less likely it is to work effectively except in a crisis. The decentralization of congressional power has resulted in legislative impotence and the resurgence of the post-Watergate presidency.[51] Paradoxically, in order for there to be a resurgence of congressional power, legislators may have to sacrifice some of their autonomy, modify the seniority system and the committee structure, and be willing to get into the party harness. The balance between representational and legislative functions may require a new shift.

NOTES

1. This account is taken from Eric Redman, *The Dance of Legislation*, Simon and Schuster, New York, 1973.

2. Joseph Clark, *Congress: The Sapless Branch*, Harper and Row, New York, 1964, p. 23; *Washington Post*, Oct. 16, 1978, p. A-6; Richard Fenno, *Homestyle: House Members in Their Districts*, Little Brown, Boston, 1978, p. 97.

3. Gregg Easterbrook, "What's Wrong with Congress?" *The Atlantic*, December 1984, p. 57.

4. Martin Tolchin, "Some Rules to Live by, for Everyone Else Only," *The New York Times*, Mar. 1, 1983.

5. CBS/New York Times survey, February 1980.

6. David J. Vogler, *The Politics of Congress*, 4th ed., Allyn and Bacon, Boston; 1983, p. 7.

7. *The New York Times*, Nov. 30, 1984.

8. *The New York Times*, Jan. 9, 1985.

9. Dom Bonafede, "Life after Congress—Former Members Stay in Town as Political Insiders," *The National Journal*, vol. 14, no. 36, Sept. 4, 1982, pp. 1507–1511.

10. Roger H. Davidson, *The Role of the Congressman*, Bobbs-Merrill, Indianapolis, 1969, pp. 117–122.

11. Lewis A. Dexter, "The Representative in His District," in Robert Peabody and Nelson Polsby (eds.), *New Perspectives on the House of Representatives*, Rand McNally, Chicago, 1969, p. 6.; John Kingdon, *Congressmen's Voting Decisions*, 2d ed., Harper and Row, New York, 1980, p. 37.

12. *The Works of the Right Honorable Edmund Burke*, John Nimmo, London, 1899, vol. 2, "Speech to the Electors of Bristol."

13. John B. Oakes, "The PAC-MAN Game: Eating Legislators," *The New York Times*, Sept. 6, 1984.

14. See W. P. Welch, "Campaign Contributions and Legislative Voting: Milk Money and Dairy Price Supports," *Western Political Quarterly*, vol. 35, no. 4, December 1982, pp. 478–495; Henry W. Chappell, "Campaign Contributions and Congressional Voting," *The Review of Economics and Statistics*, vol. 64, no. 1, February 1982, pp. 77–83; Kirk F. Brown, "Campaign Contributions and Congressional Voting," paper presented at the annual meeting of the American Political Science Association, Chicago, Sept. 1–3, 1983.

15. Roger Davidson and Walter J. Oleszek, *Congress and Its Members*, Congressional Quarterly Press, Washington, D.C., 1981, p. 10.

16. Clark, op. cit., p. 2; Ross K. Baker, "Upstart Senate Frosh," *The New York Times*, Nov. 13, 1979.

17. Martin Tolchin, "Senate Freshman Class Doesn't Defer to Anyone," *The New York Times*, Dec. 11, 1979, p. B-20.

18. Herbert Asher, "The Changing Status of the Freshman Representative," in Norman Ornstein (ed.), *Congress in Change*, Praeger, New York, 1975, pp. 216–239.

19. Randall P. Ripley, *Congress: Process and Policy*, 3d ed., Norton, New York, 1983, p. 129.

20. Ibid., p. 183.

21. *The New York Times*, Aug. 7, 1984.

22. *The New York Times*, Mar. 27, 1977.

23. Vogler, op. cit., p. 125.

24. Albert B. Hart, *Practical Essays on American Government*, Longmans, London, 1894, p. 19.

25. Mary P. Follett, *The Speaker and the House of Representatives*, Longmans, London, 1896, p. 274.

26. Woodrow Wilson, *Constitutional Government in the United States*, Columbia University Press, New York, 1908, p. 107.

27. Charles Beard and C. R. Atkinson, "The Syndication of the Speakership," *Political*

Science Quarterly, vol. 26, no. 3, September 1911, pp. 381–414; George R. Brown, *The Leadership of Congress*, Bobbs-Merrill, Indianapolis, 1963.

28. *Congressional Quarterly Weekly Reports*, Sept. 13, 1980, p. 2696.
27. Ibid., p. 2698.
30. Rowland Evans and Robert Novak, *Lyndon B. Johnson: The Exercise of Power*, New American Library, New York, 1966, p. 104; Ralph K. Huitt, "Democratic Party Leadership in the Senate," *American Political Science Review*, vol. 55, no. 2, June 1961, pp. 333–344.
31. John G. Stewart, "Central Party Organs in Congress," in Harvey C. Mansfield, Sr. (ed.), *Congress against the President*, Academy of Political Science, New York, 1975, pp. 20–33.
32. Woodrow Wilson, *Congressional Government*, Houghton Mifflin, Boston, 1886, p. 69.
33. There have been occasional purges. Thirteen Republicans were stripped of their committee posts for supporting the Progressive presidential candidate in 1924. Democrats purged two members from Mississippi who did not support the national ticket in 1964. But in 1948, 1956, and 1980 Democrats who backed other candidates went unpunished.
34. Richard A. Champagne, "Realignment in the Senate," *Legislative Studies Quarterly*, vol. 8, no. 2, May 1983, p. 233.
35. Barbara Hinckley, *Stability and Change in Congress*, Harper and Row, New York, 1983, p. 163.
36. John Rhodes, *The Futile System*, EMS Publications, Garden City, N.Y., 1976, p. 72; Mark Green, *Who Runs Congress?* 3d ed., Viking, New York, 1979, pp. 64–66.
37. *The New York Times*, Jan. 24, 1975.
38. Glenn R. Parker, "The Selection of Committee Leaders in the House of Representatives," *American Politics Quarterly*, vol. 7, no. 1, January 1979, pp. 71–93.
39. Richard Bolling, *House out of Order*, Dutton, New York, 1966, pp. 17–42.
40. Donald R. Matthews, *U.S. Senators and Their World*, Random House, New York, 1960, pp. 147–165.
41. Bolling, op. cit., p. 88.
42. Christopher J. Deering, "Subcommittee Government in the U.S. House: An Analysis of Bill Management," *Legislative Studies Quarterly*, vol. 7, no. 4, November 1982, p. 537.
43. *The New York Times*, Oct. 25, 1979.
44. Lawrence C. Dodd and Bruce I. Oppenhemier, "The House in Transition: Change and Consolidation," in Lawrence C. Dodd and Bruce I. Oppenheimer (eds.), *Congress Reconsidered*, 2d ed., Congressional Quarterly Press, Washington, D.C., 1981, pp. 31–61.
45. *The New York Times*, Mar. 2, 1983.
46. Ripley, op. cit., p. 319.
47. Demetrios Caraley, "Congressional Politics and Urban Aid," *Political Science Quarterly*, vol. 91, no. 1, spring 1976, p. 26.
48. Mark C. Shelley II, "Presidents and the Conservative Coalition in the U.S. Congress," *Legislative Studies Quarterly*, vol. 85, no. 1, February 1983, p. 81.
49. "Presidential Support Scores," *Congressional Quarterly Weekly Reports*, vol. 42, Oct. 27, 1984, p. 2802.
50. *The New York Times*, Nov. 25, 1984.
51. Lawrence Dodd, "Congress, the Constitution and the Crisis of Legitimation," in Dodd and Oppenheimer, op. cit., p. 415.

FURTHER READING

Baker, Bobby: *Wheeling and Dealing*, Norton, New York, 1978. A book about the wheeling and dealing done by senators Robert Kerr and Lyndon Johnson, written by their former staffers.

Baker, John (ed.): *Member of the House*, Scribner, New York, 1962. Letters to constituents by Clem Miller, describing the House in its prereform era.

Davidson, Roger H., and Walter J. Oleszek: *Congress and Its Members*, Congressional Quarterly Press, Washington, D.C., 1981. An excellent description of how Congress works.

Dodd, Lawrence C., and Bruce I. Oppenheimer (eds.): *Congress Reconsidered*, 2d ed., Congressional Quarterly Press, Washington, D.C., 1981. Essays describing Congress in transition.

Harris, Fred R.: *Potomac Fever*, Norton, New York, 1972. An account of the experiences of a Democratic senator from a plains state.

Hinckley, Barbara: *Stability and Change in Congress*, 3d ed., Harper and Row, New York, 1983. A study of Congress, emphasizing what has changed and what has not changed in the recent reform period.

Jones, Charles O.: *The United States Congress: People, Place and Policy*, Dorsey, Homewood, Ill., 1982. A study of Congress in the postreform era.

Redman, Eric: *The Dance of Legislation*, Simon and Schuster, New York, 1973. An account of young Senate aide's efforts to get his pet project passed into law.

Ripley, Randall: *Congress: Process and Policy*, 3d. ed., Norton, New York, 1983. A book linking the structure of power in Congress to the policies it adopts.

Rovere, Richard: *Senator Joe McCarthy*, Vintage Books, New York, 1960. A study of the damage that McCarthy inflicted on American institutions chronicled by a reporter.

Vogler, David: *The Politics of Congress*, 4th ed., Allyn and Bacon, Boston, 1983. A short but comprehensive treatment of how Congress works.

THE STUDY BREAK

Mr. Smith Goes to Washington. A late-night movie, made in 1939, about how the Washington establishment tries to corrupt innocents from Main Street, U.S.A.

The Seduction of Joe Tynan. A 1979 movie, starring Alan Alda and Meryl Streep, about a senator's moral dilemmas.

Tail Gunner Joe. A movie made in 1977 starring Peter Boyle as Senator Joe McCarthy, chronicling his rise and fall.

Washington-Merry-Go-Round. A 1932 movie about an idealistic young member of Congress who gets into trouble when he opposes a key appropriations bill.

USEFUL SOURCES

Barone, Michael, and Grant Ujifusa: *The Almanac of American Politics*, The National Journal, Washington, D.C.; annually. A compendium of the political careers of every member of the House and Senate, complete with their past electoral records and their present-day interests.

CIS Microfiche Library, Congressional Information Service, Washington, D.C. The complete texts of congressional hearings, reports, and documents, filmed and distributed monthly to subscribing libraries.

C-Span. Cable television coverage of Congress.

Congress and the Nation, Congressional Quarterly Press, Washington, D.C., vols 1–6. Massive volumes which record congressional actions over a four-year period, arranged topically for easy reference.

Congressional Committee Prints Index and *Congressional Committee Hearings Index*, Congressional Information Service, Washington, D.C. A monthly, quarterly, and annual index of all hearings, reports, and committee prints published during each session of Congress, listed by subject matter and committee.

Congressional Directory, 99th Congress, Publications Office of the Joint Committee on Printing, Washington, D.C., 1985. A source listing members of Congress, committee assignments, office addresses, and telephone numbers.

Congressional Monitor. A daily report on committee and floor actions, complete with advance hearing schedules and a weekly update on the status of all pending legislation.

Congressional Quarterly Weekly Reports. A weekly guide to congressional activities, including the status of legislation, committee actions, and voting records.

The Congressional Record, GPO, Washington, D.C. A transcript of the proceedings on the floor of the House and Senate, published and distributed daily.

Congressional Staff Directory Advance Locator for Capitol Hill, 1984, Congressional Staff Directory, Mount Vernon, N.Y., 1984. A who's who of congressional staffers, with offices and phone numbers.

Digest of Public General Bills and Resolutions, GPO, Washington, D.C. Descriptions of all bills and resolutions introduced into Congress, in five annual issues.

Elliot, Jeffrey M., and Sheikh R. Ali: *The Presidential-Congressional Political Dictionary*, ABC-CLIO, Santa Barbara, Calif., 1984.

Goehlert, Robert: *Congress and Law-Making: Researching the Legislative Process*, ABC-CLIO, Santa Barbara, Calif., 1979. A guide for beginners, telling how to trace the progress of legislation from the introduction of a bill through final passage.

———— and John Sayre: *The United States Congress: A Bibliography*, Free Press, New York, 1982. A guide to books and articles on Congress.

Guide to Congress, 3d ed., Congressional Quarterly Press, Washington, D.C., 1982. A massive compendium of information on congressional structure and process.

United States Code, GPO, Washington, D.C. A codification of the laws passed by Congress, published every six years (with interim updates).

U.S. Code Congressional and Administrative News, West, Saint Paul, Minn., monthly. Committee reports on selected bills and the text of all laws passed by Congress.

ORGANIZATIONS

LEGI-SLATE. 111 Massachusetts Avenue, N.W., Washington, D.C. 20001. A computer-based service containing all votes from the start of the Ninety-sixth Congress (1979), together with programs to create customized voting analyses. For more information phone 202-898-2300.

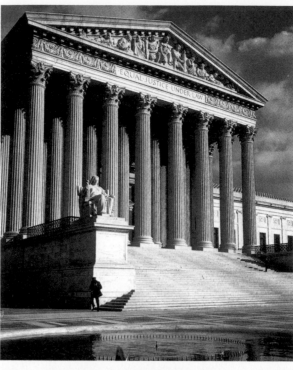

JUDICIAL POWER: THE LEAST DANGEROUS BRANCH

Opposite page, above: The Supreme Court meets in this white marble building, located just behind the Capitol. (*Alex Webb: Magnum.*) Below: Ira Brown, a federal district judge, presiding over lawsuits involving asbestos-related diseases. So many suits were filed that the case was heard in Nourse Auditorium in San Francisco. (*Eli Reed: Magnum.*)

Alexis de Tocqueville, the greatest foreign commentator on American society, once said, "Scarcely any political question arises in the United States that is not resolved, sooner or later, into a judicial question."[1] Our judicial issues are political because our Constitution is the highest law of the land and because judges hold the actions of government to constitutional and statutory standards. And court decisions are political because they impose costs and confer benefits; they help determine who gets what, when, and how.

In *The Federalist*, Alexander Hamilton called the Supreme Court the "least dangerous branch," lacking both sword and purse and therefore needing the cooperation of the other two branches and public support.[2] Robert Dahl, a political scientist at Yale, has argued that "the policy views dominant on the Court are never for long out of line with the policy views dominant among the lawmaking majorities of the United States."[3] But throughout American history the judiciary has been involved in controversy. President Thomas Jefferson had Congress impeach Justice Samuel Chase (he was acquitted), impeach and convict a lower court judge, pass a law preventing the Supreme Court from sitting for a year, and revoke a law establishing new federal judgeships—all in a vain attempt to bring the Court into line with the policies of his party. Populists in the 1890s made the Supreme Court into an election issue, attacking it for decisions favoring Wall Street over Main Street and calling for popular election of judges. President Franklin Roosevelt in the 1930s unsuccessfully tried to "pack" the Court by proposing a law that would have let him add new members in order to overturn decisions invalidating part of his New Deal. In the 1980s the new right has tried to strip the federal courts of jurisdiction in cases concerning abortion, prayer in schools, and busing.

The danger that such controversies create for the courts was understood by Hamilton, who argued that the judiciary "is in continual jeopardy of being overpowered, awed, or influenced by its co-ordinate branches."[4] That is the power problem for the judiciary, and this chapter will consider how the courts try to solve it.

JUDICIAL POWERS

What the federal courts do

Article III of the Constitution provides that "the Judicial Power of the United States" is vested in the Supreme Court and such other courts as Congress may establish by law. The federal courts decide cases involving national or state laws, administrative regulations, and actions of the executive branch, provided they contain a constitutional issue or legal issue involving a "substantial federal question."

Statutory interpretation. In most cases the courts determine the meaning of existing laws or administrative rulings and apply them to the facts at hand; this is ***statutory interpretation.*** "A federal statute finally means what the Court says it means," said Chief Justice Charles Evans Hughes.[5] The federal courts have to "fill in the blanks" after Congress passes laws. When college faculty

Former president Jimmy Carter welcoming back the first of the American diplomats and servicemen freed from Iran, at a military base in Wiesbaden, Germany. His executive agreement with Iran which led to the release of the hostages, signed on his last day in office, was later tested in the federal courts by American companies which objected to the provision for an international claims tribunal. The Supreme Court interpreted federal laws expansively in order to uphold the agreement. (*Sigma*.)

members organize a union and the board of trustees refuses to recognize it, claiming that the faculty members are not "workers" covered by federal labor laws, for example, it is up to the courts to interpret the laws and decide whether the faculty members are covered. The courts have interpreted federal copyright laws to permit home videotaping of movies, something that Congress could not have foreseen when it passed the original copyright laws.

Sometimes Congress passes laws which are unclear in order to keep a coalition intact. It assumes that the courts can deal with the problems created by the ambiguous language.[6] If Congress does not like the way the courts interpret a law, it can always amend its original law to overturn the courts' decision. Any judicial decision which interprets a federal law or an administrative ruling is *provisional:* it can always be changed by Congress. In 1978 the Supreme Court, in *Zurcher v. Stanford Daily*, ruled that police officers armed with a warrant could make an unannounced search of a campus newspaper office to obtain evidence involving a criminal case, even though the paper was merely reporting the crime and had no involvement in it.[7] The paper argued that the police should have obtained a court subpoena, rather than make an intrusive search and disrupt the newsroom. Congress then passed a law which prohibits federal, state, and local police officers from searching or seizing the "work products" of news organizations, including notes, photographs, and other documents, unless a reporter is suspected of having committed a crime or the materials are needed immediately to prevent a death or injury. The large majority of laws overruling court decisions involve commerce, labor-management disputes, and environmental issues.

Table 12-1. Judicial review and the Supreme Court, 1800 to 1983

Period	Number of laws of Congress overturned	Number of state laws overturned
1800–1859	2	35
1860–1919	35	297
1920–1983	88	700 +

Source: Congressional Research Service.

Judicial review. The state and federal courts have the power to declare actions of the national government and the state governments unconstitutional (Table 12-1). The power of **judicial review** encompasses every action of government: laws, treaties, interstate compacts, executive agreements, administrative regulations, rulings by independent commissions, provisions of state constitutions, initiatives and referendums, and actions or decisions of state courts. Only the Constitution or its amendments cannot be overturned. The Supreme Court has increasingly made use of this power, making it a "continuous Constitutional Convention," in the words of Justice Robert Jackson.[8]

Judicial actions. The parties involved in a federal court case hope to obtain specific court orders. Even before the trial they may seek a *restraining order*, which prevents someone from taking action until a hearing can be held, and a *temporary injunction*, granted after the hearing, which prevents action from being taken until a trial is held. After trial, the court issues a *decision* in favor of one of the parties and issues one or more *orders*, which include:

- *Permanent injunction*, which requires a party to refrain from taking action
- *Mandatory injunction*, which requires a party to do something and specifies how it must be done
- *Writ of mandamus*, which directs a government official to perform certain duties
- *Declaratory judgment*, which gives the opinion of the court on a legal question but does not require that anything be done (used to guide lower courts)

The higher federal courts supervise both the lower federal courts and the state courts: they may *affirm* a lower court decision, *modify* it in crucial ways, or *overturn* it, in which case they will *vacate* the orders of the lower court and substitute their own. They may also *stay* the execution of a lower court order (similar to the temporary restraining order). They may *remand* a case to a lower court for retrial on a new issue so that the lower court can issue final decrees which follow the instructions of the higher court.

Class action suits. Some cases are ***class actions:*** the decision of the court affects not only the party which brought the case but also "all members of the class similarly situated." When the National Coalition of Independent College and University Students asked a federal court to prohibit collection of fees by the College Entrance Examination Board and the American College Testing Program, claiming that this violated a 1980 law prohibiting charging low-income students such fees, more than 500,000 students were in a class affected by the ruling. Class action suits are often brought in cases involving civil rights, price-fixing, product liability, consumer rights, and environmental issues.

Judicial powers in the context of government

Shared powers. Statutory interpretation gives the courts a share in legislative power: their decisions flesh out the bare bones of statutes and provide explicit guidance to cover contingencies, as the tax courts do with the internal revenue laws, for example. Because of their powers to issue injunctions, writs of mandamus, and other judicial orders, the courts also share in the executive power. For example, a federal judge, by issuing a stream of orders in a single case, can to all intents and purposes take over the responsibility for health care in a hospital, the busing of children to desegregate a school system, or the recruitment and promotion policies of a police or fire department. While such ***judicial administration*** is rare, it can be quite sweeping: in the 1970s a federal judge in Alabama controlled the state police, prisons, and mental hospitals.

Judicial enforcement. Judicial orders are delivered to the parties by federal marshals assigned to each district court. Anyone who refuses to obey these orders is in ***contempt of court:*** civil contempt involves refusal to obey an order granted to one of the parties in a case; and criminal contempt involves acts which disrupt the courts or the administration of justice or which show disrespect for the courts' enforcement powers. Civil contempt is usually followed by a fine and imprisonment until the individual agrees to obey the court. Criminal contempt involves fines and a jury trial if the jail term imposed exceeds six months.

The courts' enforcement powers rest not with a few marshals in each district, but with the full power of the national government. Presidents have the constitutional duty to maintain the supremacy of the Constitution. They may place state National Guard troops in national service to enforce an order, as President Eisenhower did in 1957 when mobs tried to prevent the desegregation of Little Rock Central High School. They may send in armed marshals and even federal troops, as President Kennedy did in 1961 in upholding court orders desegregating the universities of Mississippi and Alabama. Such instances are rare; usually the mere presence of a federal marshal ensures compliance with a court order.

FOCUS

THE SUPREME COURT EXPANDS ITS POWERS. The judicial branch checks and balances the other two branches with judicial review: the power to declare laws and official acts unconstitutional. This power itself is nowhere explicitly assigned to the federal courts by the Constitution. The Supreme Court gained it in *Marbury v. Madison,* a case which it decided.

When the Supreme Court started hearing cases in 1790, it had no power of judicial review. The power was not unknown, however; in England it had been asserted more than 100 years earlier to strike down laws of Parliament, although it had not been used much thereafter. State courts had used it at least eight times against state legislatures before the Constitutional Convention, and thereafter ten state courts gained the power.

The supremacy clause of the Constitution gives the federal courts the power to review and, if necessary, overturn decisions of the state courts involving interpretations of federal law, a power which Congress recognized in passing the Judiciary Act of 1789. But did the Constitution also allow the Supreme Court and the lower federal courts to use judicial review against Congress and the president and against executive officials?

Debates during the Constitutional Convention shed little light on the issue.

Gouverneur Morris argued that the courts could not "be bound to say that a direct violation of the Constitution was law."[9] But John Mercer of Delaware argued against "the doctrine that the judges as expositors of the Constitution should have the authority to declare a law void."[10] Charles G. Haines, the leading historian on judicial review, has concluded that the convention delegates in favor of granting judges such authority—including Washington, Madison, Morris, and Hamilton—decided "to allow the definite assertion of the right of judicial review to come through interpretation . . . rather than arouse controversy and suspicion by incorporating a direct grant to the judiciary."[11]

The issue became bound up in the politics of the first party system. The Federalist Party favored judicial review. As Alexander Hamilton put it, "Whenever a particular statute contravenes the Constitution, it will be the duty of the judicial tribunals to adhere to the latter and disregard the former."[12] But the Republicans, faced with Federalist judges when they took control of the White House and Congress in 1801, opposed giving judges this power, since they might declare laws of the new Congress unconstitutional.

Before surrendering power, the outgoing Federalist Congress passed a judiciary act that increased the number of federal judges. President John Adams nominated, and the outgoing Senate confirmed, loyal Federalists for these positions. When the Republicans took office, seventeen of the commissions had not yet been delivered. The incoming Republican secretary of state, James Madison, literally tossed his predecessor, John Marshall, out of the office and then kept the commissions under lock and key, refusing to deliver them to the Federalist appointees and arguing that the final decision to give out the commissions was a political act to be taken at the discretion of the new administration. Then Congress passed a law which revoked the judgeships and provided that the Supreme Court was not to meet for more than a year; it also impeached and convicted a federal district judge, as a clear warning to the judiciary not to oppose the Republican program.

William Marbury went to the Supreme Court when it reconvened and asked it to rule that Madison had acted illegally and unconstitutionally by withholding his commission. The Supreme Court, dominated by Federalists and headed by none other than John Marshall (who had been named chief justice by the outgoing Federalists in 1800), now had a golden opportunity. It could declare Madison's actions unconstitutional and exercise the power of judicial review against the executive. It could order President Jefferson and Secretary of State Madison to deliver the commissions, establishing the principle that executive officials must obey the Constitution as interpreted by the Court.

Or could it? Suppose that Marshall had ordered Madison to release the commissions. Madison would not have obeyed. "Judicial supremacy may be made to bow before the strong arm of Legislative authority," warned Caesar Rodney, one of Jefferson's followers, a week before the decision.[13] The Republicans were looking for an opportunity to weaken the Supreme Court and, in Rodney's words, to show the nation who was "master of the ship." John Marshall recognized the power problem: he had to prevent the Republicans from disobeying a Supreme Court order. But how could the Court extricate itself without admitting defeat? If Marshall had ruled in favor of the Republicans, he would have sanctioned Madison's illegal withholding of the commissions and rendered a personally humiliating judgment, since he was the person who had surrendered the commissions to Madison in the first place! The White House would have intimidated the Court—hardly a way to protect its power.

John Marshall, chief justice of the United States. (*New York Public Library.*)

But Marshall's choices were not limited to a humiliating run or a suicidal fight. He conceived a plan which let the Republicans gain the political victory but which allowed the Federalists to establish the principle of judicial review—and which could not be disobeyed. Before considering the merits of cases, courts first take up procedural issues. Among them is the question of *jurisdiction:* Marbury took his case directly to the Supreme Court, bypassing the lower federal courts. He acted according to Section 13 of the Judiciary Act of 1789, which allowed the Supreme Court to issue writs of mandamus to compel national officials to perform their duties—in this case, to give Marbury his commission. Marshall seized upon a jurisdictional question: Was Marbury entitled to bring his case directly to the Supreme Court?

To answer that question, the Supreme Court had to look at what the Constitution says about its jurisdiction. In Article III the Constitution sets forth the cases in which the Supreme Court has original jurisdiction. But nowhere in the Constitution are writs of mandamus mentioned; such original jurisdiction came solely from the Judiciary Act of 1789. Now Marshall asked the key question: Could an act of Congress add to the original jurisdiction of the Court? Marshall compared the grant of original jurisdiction in Article III with the provisions of Section 13 of the law passed by Congress and found the two provisions to be inconsistent—the law added jurisdiction that was not contemplated by the Constitution. Marshall concluded that "a law repugnant to the Constitution is void."[14] And because Section 13 was unconstitutional, the Supreme Court did not have original jurisdiction over the case and could not issue the writ of mandamus against Madison. Marbury would have to go to the lower courts first. The Court exercised the power of judicial review by striking down a provision of a law passed by Congress. The decision was implemented by the Court itself, which refused to give Marbury the writ. Thus the Court established its power of judicial review without confronting Congress or the president. It could make the decision stick without the cooperation of the Republican president or of Congress. In fact, the Republicans had no way of disobeying the decision. They could still argue that the courts could not overturn a law passed by Congress, but Marshall had already done so.

Marbury v. Madison illustrates some of the principles of judicial power. Marshall considered the power problem of the Court: the need to protect the judiciary from elected politicians ready to disobey it or strike out against it. He had to protect the Court's authority and legitimacy against the stronger branches. Thus he would not make a decision that could not be enforced. Marshall gained additional authority for the Court, even though he had to give up some power to do it. The Supreme Court not only let Madison keep the commissions but also gave up the power to issue writs of mandamus against federal officials as part of its original jurisdiction. This was realistic: Marshall gave up commissions that he could never hope to obtain physically and a power to issue writs which he knew would never be obeyed—in reality he gave up nothing that the Court might reasonably have ever possessed. An awareness of power stakes, an understanding of the limits of judicial power, an emphasis on procedure, and a desire to minimize political confrontations with the other two branches—these are the things that distinguish the successful exercise of judicial powers.

THE JUDICIARY AND GROUP CONFLICT

The federal courts often decide controversies between interest groups and between these groups and the government. Parties bring cases to the federal courts to win victories that have eluded them in Congress, government agencies, and state government.

Which groups litigate?

Interest groups view litigation as one political strategy which complements others. Trade associations, unions, and professional associations may litigate against one another or against state and federal officials. Just as interest groups create PACs for electoral politics, so too they create or support litigating organizations, such as the probusiness Capital Legal Foundation, the Washington Legal Foundation, the Pacific Legal Foundation, and the Mountain States Legal Foundation, which oppose environmental and consumer groups, such as Consumer's Union (product safety), the Sierra Club (the environment), and Common Cause (campaign financing laws).

What interest groups do

An interest group may exercise complete control over a case by having someone test a law or challenge an administrative ruling. This enables it to set up the facts of the case in a favorable way; groups that challenged government funding of religious activities, for example, preferred to choose plaintiffs who were themselves religious, were pillars of their communities, but favored separation of church and state. Interest groups conduct research and prepare legal briefs, as the National Consumer's League did in defending state wage and hour laws against a hostile federal judiciary in the early 1900s and as the National Association for the Advancement of Colored People did in arguing the landmark 1954 case that ended racial segregation in public schools. A group picks the lawyers, develops the legal strategy, and pays the hundreds of thousands of dollars necessary to carry a case all the way to the Supreme Court. A more limited way to participate is by filing an amicus curiae (literally, "friend of the court") brief in a case started by other parties.

Groups may bring cases even when they do not expect to win. Their use of the courts may be a delaying strategy: an environmentalists group, for example, can bring a case which ties up the construction of a power plant or a transportation system for years; then, as costs mount and as plans become outdated, the delay itself may result in the project's being dropped or modified to meet the group's objections.

The increase in group-sponsored litigation

Group-sponsored litigation has increased in the federal courts in the past sixty years. Supreme Court cases in which such groups filed amicus curiae briefs increased from fewer than 2 percent between 1928 and 1940 to more than 53 percent between 1970 and 1980. Interest groups litigate most cases of race or sex discrimination and most civil liberties cases; they are involved in slightly more than one-third of criminal cases and cases involving commercial matters. Between 1951 and 1971, sixty-seven church-state cases were decided by the Supreme Court; three groups that were opposed to government funding of religious institutions—the American Civil Liberties Union, the American Jewish Congress, and Americans United for Separation of Church and State (a Protestant group)—were involved in fifty-one of them.[15] Group-sponsored litigation activity has increased because more public interest groups have organized and see the judiciary as a favorable forum; because these groups have a stake in interpreting hundreds of new federal laws providing rights, benefits, or entitlements to goods and services to their members; and because the Supreme Court is more likely to accept their appeals than those from individuals.

THE FEDERAL COURTS

Constitutional courts and legislative courts

Figure 12-1. The American judicial system consists of fifty state court systems (and federal courts for the District of Columbia and American territories), as well as federal constitutional and statutory courts created by Congress with jurisdiction over federal law and federal questions throughout the union. (In recent years Chief Justice Warren Burger has proposed still another federal court, one that would handle the thirty or so cases each year that involve conflicting rulings by different federal courts of appeals.)

Congress has established **constitutional courts,** which deal with all matters of constitutional law and most matters of statutory law, and **legislative courts,** which deal with specific statutes (Figure 12-1).

Constitutional courts. The states and territories of the United States are divided into ninety-five judicial districts, each with jurisdiction over federal cases within its area. None of the districts crosses state lines, and the 515 or so federal judges must by law reside in their districts. The judges, who are appointed for life, preside over cases involving federal civil and criminal law, diversity cases between citizens of different states (involving amounts over $10,000), cases involving a "substantial federal question" (where federal law or the Constitution is involved), rulings of administrative agencies, and admiralty and maritime cases.

The losing party in any federal case may challenge the decision in one of thirteen circuit courts of appeals. Eleven circuits cover the states, one covers the District of Columbia (it handles a majority of cases involving federal agencies), and one handles customs and patent cases; these courts are staffed by 144 or so judges, who are also appointed for life.

Legislative courts. The military courts and the Court of Military Appeals handle cases involving the armed forces (including courts-martial). Customs and tariffs issues go to the Court of Trade. The tax laws are considered by the United States Tax Court. Suits against the federal government are handled by the United States Court of Claims. Requests from the FBI or the CIA for judicial warrants to conduct surveillance for foreign intelligence are considered by the

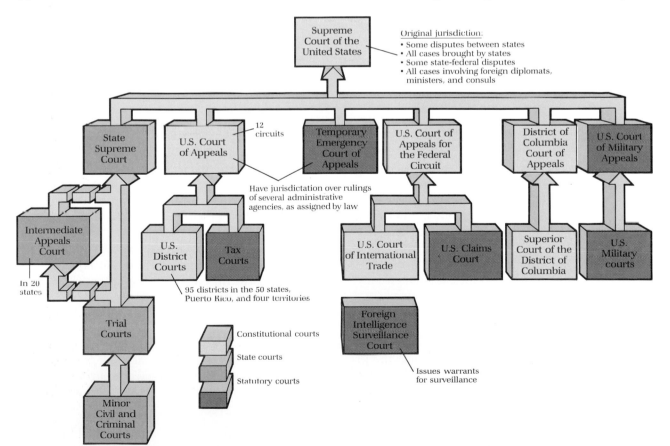

FISA Court, which is a closed-door panel of seven federal district judges appointed by the chief justice of the United States to administer the Foreign Intelligence and Surveillance Act of 1978. Judges on these courts are appointed for fixed terms.

Relationship between state and federal courts

Each state has its own court system, including lower trial courts, intermediate appeals courts, and a court of last appeal. All told, there are 17,000 state courts which hand down millions of decisions each year—about 95 percent of all cases decided.[16] They have exclusive jurisdiction when cases involve purely state matters and concurrent jurisdiction with the federal courts over other matters, such as corporate cases and bank robberies. The state courts have powers of judicial review and statutory interpretation, and they construe the United States Constitution and federal laws and regulations as well as their state constitutions and laws.

The Supreme Court reviews state court rulings which hold federal laws unconstitutional or which uphold state laws or constitutions against claims that they violate the United States Constitution, treaties, or interstate compacts.

Cases in which one of the parties claims that federal law is in conflict with state law may involve a "substantial federal question," and when they have worked their way through the state court of last appeal, they may be appealed in the Supreme Court, which is limited to reviewing the federal questions presented by these cases. It decides such questions and then sends the cases back to the state courts, which render final decisions "not inconsistent" with the decisions of the Supreme Court.

Cases in federal courts

The courts' caseloads. THE LOWER COURTS. Each year the federal district courts decide approximately a quarter of a million civil cases and 35,000 or so criminal cases. The courts of appeals handle approximately 30,000 cases annually. The civil caseload of the federal courts has increased greatly in the past twenty-five years; in 1960 federal judges decided an average of 242 cases per year; in 1981 the figure had increased to 350 per judge. The number of cases in the courts of appeals more than doubled between 1975 and 1985, with each judge handling more than 200 cases each year.[17]

Why the huge increase? Congress has passed more laws of greater complexity, requiring more statutory interpretation. More lawyers (350,000 in 1970 and 700,000 in 1986) mean more cases, and more cases mean more appeals.

THE SUPREME COURT. On the average, the Supreme Court handles more than 5000 cases each year. It decides most of them summarily (without legal briefs or oral argument, but simply on the basis of the petitions for review). It decides about 125 cases with written briefs, but without hearing oral argument from the lawyers. It hears about 175 cases with full argument. Of these, 150 or so are decided with signed, written opinions of the justices, and another 25 are decided per curiam (by the entire Court, without written opinions).[18]

In recent years, justices have complained about the number of cases on their dockets, which increased from 1000 a year in the 1930s to 2000 in the 1950s and is now heading toward 6000. "Supreme Court justices must now work beyond any sound maximum limits," warns Chief Justice Warren Burger, adding that "the precious time for reflection so necessary to a court that decides cases with far-reaching consequences has been reduced to, and possibly below, an absolute minimum."[19] As a consequence, more cases are decided

A camera operator for WPBT-TV records *Florida v. Zamora*, a case in which Florida allowed local stations to televise trials without the consent of the participants. The Supreme Court later ruled that televising the trial did not violate the defendant's constitutional rights. (*Public Broadcasting System.*)

HOW THE SUPREME COURT REVIEWS CASES: APPEALS AND CERTIORARI

Cases reaching the Court by appeal (10 percent)
From the state court of last appeal:

1. When it has declared a federal law or treaty (or a provision) unconstitutional
2. When a state court has upheld a state law or a provision of the state constitution against the challenge that it conflicts with the Constitution, treaties, or laws of the United States

From the federal constitutional courts:

1. When a state law or a provision of a state constitution has been struck down because of a conflict with the Constitution, treaties, or laws of the United States
2. When a federal law has been held unconstitutional and the United States is a party to the suit
3. When the United states is a party to a suit involving interstate commerce, communication, or antitrust laws
4. When a district court has granted or denied an injunction in a suit brought to restrain enforcement of federal or state statutes or orders of state administrative agencies

From other courts of the United States (such as a court of claims or a court of customs and patent appeals):

1. When a federal law has been declared unconstitutional, provided that the United States is a party to the case

Cases reaching the Court by writ of certiorari (90 percent)
From the state court of last appeal
From the United States Court of Appeals and other courts of the United States:

1. When a case involves the application or interpretation of the Constitution, treaties, or laws of the United States
2. When the court has upheld a state law or a provision of a state constitution against the challenge that it conflicts with the Constitution, treaties, or laws of the United States

The conference room of the justices, being prepared for consideration of petitions for certeriori and appeals. (*Supreme Court Historical Society.*)

summarily (which usually means that the claim of the government is upheld against that of someone who is complaining about official actions) or are decided without adequate attention to the issues.

How the Supreme Court controls its agenda. The huge caseload of the federal and state courts gives the Supreme Court an opportunity to pick and choose the cases involving the most important issues. "How the Supreme Court Reviews Cases" describes the way cases are filed.

CERTIORARI. The most common method involves the petition of *certiorari* (from the Latin, meaning "to be informed"). These petitions may be no more than thirty pages long; accompanied by a $200 fee, they set forth the reasons why the losing party believes that there is a constitutional question of interest to the Supreme Court which has been decided improperly by the lower courts. (Convicted criminals may file in forma pauperis, which requires no fee.)

APPEAL. In theory, certain cases must be heard by the Supreme Court on appeal, especially those involving state laws or constitutional provisions. Even so, the Supreme Court does not always give such cases full consideration. Most are decided summarily, simply by affirming the decision of the lower federal court without a full hearing or even a written opinion. Even if the decision of the appeals court is reversed, the Supreme Court may simply issue a *per curiam* opinion: one which expresses the opinion of the Court without identifying the author and without even hearing argument by the parties. Only in a few appeals will the Court permit full consideration: argument by opposing counsel, full discussion in conference, and lengthy signed opinions.

How the Supreme Court decides what cases to hear. Each of the nine Supreme Court justices has four law clerks (recent law school graduates) who

416

THE COURT CALENDAR

The term. The term lasts from the first Monday in October to the end of June or the first week of July. The term is designated by the year in which it begins.

The month. Each term is split into *sittings*, which last two weeks, and *recesses*, which also last two weeks. The Court hears cases and holds conferences during its sittings (some conferences are held during recesses). Opinions are written during recesses. The Court sits through the entire months of May and June.

The week. During sittings the Court holds *open sessions* on Mondays, Tuesdays, and Wednesdays for two weeks. It holds two conferences during each week that it is sitting: Wednesdays and Fridays.

The day. Open sessions are held from 10 A.M. until noon and from 1 P.M. to 3 P.M. The Court hears two cases in the morning and two in the afternoon. One hour for argument is allotted to each case, with each side receiving thirty minutes.

---

review the petitions and appeals. They recommend the most significant cases (fewer than one-fourth of those filed). The chief justice then puts these cases on a "discussion list" for consideration in conference. To "grant cert," four justices must agree to hear a case; if three feel strongly enough about it, another justice may "lend" a vote. Only 5 percent of the petitions for cert, fewer than 1 percent of the in forma pauperis filings, and fewer than one-third of the appeals will go to argument and decision.

The Supreme Court chooses cases that interest it, including those which develop new doctrines of constitutional law, especially cases involving separation of powers, civil rights and liberties, and federalism. It also resolves conflicts between different circuit courts in order to ensure uniformity in federal case law. Yet about 90 percent of conflicting lower court decisions do not even reach the Supreme Court because it does not consider the issues important enough to resolve.

The Court accepts approximately two-thirds of the cases brought by the government itself, represented by the solicitor general, who is the third-ranking official in the Justice Department. It also gives preference to cases brought by private parties if they are accompanied by a brief from the Justice Department asking the Court to take them. (In contrast, the Court accepts fewer than 3 percent of petitions submitted by private parties without such a brief.) The Court is more likely to consider government cases because the solicitor general has already screened them and weeded out those of lesser importance.[20]

Federal judges and Supreme Court justices

Most men and women who become judges have the backing of their party organizations, senators, and professional bar associations. They are hardly a cross section of the American public, or even of the legal profession.

Lower court nominations. There are no constitutional requirements to be a federal judge, since the Constitution makes no mention of federal judges. Congress by law has provided that the president nominates federal judges and appoints them with the advice and consent of the Senate. Each year the president nominates from forty to fifty judges for district and circuit courts and specialized legislative courts. These nominations are made after the White House consults with the attorney general and with members of the president's party in Congress.

Since 1840, senators of the president's party from states in which there are vacancies have been able to block a Senate vote on a nomination. Each senator extends to every other senator this **senatorial courtesy,** which is in effect a "veto" over the nomination of federal judges in his or her state. Thus the president must discuss proposed nominations with the affected senators in advance. In consultation with local party leaders, senators make suggestions for filling vacancies, and the president and the attorney general may exercise a veto over *their* choice. (When one senator is from the opposition party, he or she is usually given 25 percent of the nominations.) Since 1978 about half the senators have established their own "screening panels" to ensure that their choices are professionally qualified.

Nominations for the courts of appeals are usually made by the president, after consulting with members of the Senate for a "clearance" but without conceding them a veto power. Since the circuits comprise several states, no senator can dictate nominations. The White House itself has its own screening committee.

PROFESSIONAL STANDARDS. Nominees are subjected to intensive scrutiny. The FBI runs a background check. The Standing Committee on the Federal Judiciary of the American Bar Association (ABA) rates all nominees— exceptionally qualified, highly qualified, qualified, or not qualified (Table 12-2). Between 1953 and 1977 it was consulted by all attorneys general, who referred lists of prospective nominees to it.[21] Some presidents have even given the committee a virtual veto on nominations or have withdrawn the names of those whom the committee found unqualified. Presidents rarely nominate someone who is unqualified, although John Kennedy got eight such persons through the Senate, Gerald Ford got one, and Jimmy Carter got three.[22]

PARTY AFFILIATION. Presidents nominate members of their own party at better than a 90 percent rate. Party affiliation has a direct bearing on how federal judges decide cases. Democratic judges are more likely to favor defendants in criminal prosecutions, regulatory agencies in conflict with corporations, consumer and environmentalist groups suing corporations, minorities and women in affirmative action cases, and individuals in civil liberties cases against the government. Republican judges are more likely to favor the government in criminal and civil liberties cases and corporations in suits brought against them by environmentalists, labor, consumer, and minority groups.

Table 12-2. ABA ratings of lower court nominees

	Exceptionally well qualified	Well qualified	Qualified	Unqualified
Eisenhower	17.1	44.6	32.6	5.7
Kennedy	16.6	45.6	31.5	6.3
Johnson	12.2	43.3	41.7	2.8
Nixon	6.3	42.8	50.9	0
Ford	3.0	47.0	48.5	1.5
Carter	6.1	49.6	43.1	1.1
Reagan (first term)	9.6	40.7	49.7	0

Sources: The statistics on Eisenhower, Kennedy, and Johnson are adapted from Harold W. Chase, *Federal Judges: The Appointing Process*, 1972. The statistics on Ford are from a study by Sheldon Goldman of the University of Massachusetts at Amherst. The statistics on Carter, Nixon, and Reagan were compiled by Congressional Quarterly from data of the American Bar Association. This table is reprinted from *Congressional Quarterly Weekly Reports*, Dec. 8, 1984, p. 3074.

Table 12-3. Women and minorities in federal judgeships

	United States courts of appeals				United States district courts		
	Women	Blacks	Hispanics		Women	Blacks	Hispanics
Democrats:				Democrats:			
Johnson	2.5	5.0	n.a.	Johnson	1.6	3.3	2.5
Carter	19.6	16.1	3.6	Carter	14.1	14.1	6.8
Republicans:				Republicans:			
Nixon	0	0	n.a.	Nixon	0.6	2.8	1.1
Ford	0	0	n.a.	Ford	1.9	5.8	1.9
Reagan	9.1	3.0	3.0	Reagan (first term)	9.2	0.8	5.4

Sources: The statistics on Johnson, Nixon, and Ford are from a study by Sheldon Goldman of the University of Massachusetts at Amherst. The statistics on Carter and Reagan were compiled by Congressional Quarterly on the basis of figures from the Justice Department and the Senate Judiciary Committee. This table is reprinted from *Congressional Quarterly Weekly Reports*, Dec. 8, 1984, p. 3075.

OCCUPATION. About two-fifths of judges are lawyers with close ties to sponsoring senators and party organizations. Another one-fourth come directly from state courts, and two-thirds have had some previous judicial experience or have been prosecuting attorneys. About 5 percent are state legislators, and 5 percent are state or federal officials. Only a sprinkling have been law school professors or businesspersons. In the past thirty years hardly any have come from Congress.

Nominees to the circuit courts are likely to be lawyers in private practice (one-third) who are well connected to the White House or important senators. About one-fifth come from state or federal courts, and one-eighth are former national officials. One-tenth are from state legislatures or executive agencies. There are considerably more former law professors than at the district court level. Again, almost none come from Congress.

SOCIAL CHARACTERISTICS. The majority of federal judges are white male Protestants from affluent families. Democratic presidents are much more likely to nominate women, blacks, Hispanics, Catholics, and Jews, reflecting their electoral coalitions, as Table 12-3 indicates.

As of 1982, 47 women were federal judges (7.6 percent), compared with 619 men. (In contrast, 17 percent of state judges were women.) Considering that women constitute more than 15 percent of all lawyers and 35 percent of all law students, it is clear that they have not achieved representation proportional to their numbers in the legal profession.

POLICY ORIENTATIONS. Presidents try to appoint judges who agree with them on the issues. The Reagan administration appointed judges to the circuit and legislative courts whose judicial philosophy was consistent with the 1980 Republican Party platform, which called for judges who believed in "the decentralization of the federal government and efforts to return decision-making power to state and local elected officials." Reagan appointed conservatives to the traditionally liberal Court of Appeals of the District of Columbia, and by 1985 it had a 6–6 balance of liberal and conservative judges. During Reagan's second term most of the other circuit courts have had conservative majorities as a result of his appointments.

To find nominees, Reagan relied on the Justice Department's Office of Legal Policy, which solicited names from interest groups allied to conservative and right-wing Republican PACs and legislators. Names were sent to White House aides, who sent prospective nominees to the president after an FBI field check and consultation with ABA's Standing Committee on the Federal Judiciary and with sponsoring senators. Democratic presidents consult with liberal law professors and think tanks and with litigating organizations for the poor, minorities, women, and environmentalist groups, as well as with party organizations.

Supreme Court nominations. Presidents appoint an average of two Supreme Court justices a term, which in theory means that even during two terms they cannot appoint a majority. But averages are deceiving: in four years Carter appointed none, Nixon appointed four, and Reagan appointed one. No other appointments that a president makes have a longer-term impact on government. A president like William Taft or Franklin Roosevelt can appoint six justices, thus creating a majority that controls the Court for several decades. In a period of eight years, Richard Nixon and Gerald Ford made 5 out of 9 Supreme Court appointments. The quality of appointees to the Supreme Court is a measure of presidential performance, and for that reason alone no incumbent cedes this prerogative to senators or to the Justice Department.

Although no senatorial courtesy is involved in Supreme Court nominations, pressure is exerted on presidents by leading members of their party. Justices themselves may influence presidential nominations. On at least sixty-six occasions they have made suggestions for filling vacancies.[23] Warren Burger recommended Harry Blackmun, his colleague from Minnesota, to Nixon, and William Rehnquist lobbied Reagan on behalf of Sandra Day O'Connor, one of his classmates at Stanford Law School.

PROFESSIONAL QUALIFICATIONS. The Constitution includes no requirements for Supreme Court justices—not even a law degree, though all have been lawyers. Some have served as distinguished private counsels in corporations or have been partners in firms which represent corporations. Occasionally a president chooses a lawyer who has represented labor, the poor, or minorities (Woodrow Wilson's choice of Louis Brandeis or Lyndon Johnson's choice of Thurgood Marshall, for example). The majority have been judges (three-fifths), but only a little more than two-fifths have served five years or more on another court. Some come from high state courts (William Brennan and Sandra Day O'Connor, for example), while others (such as Warren Burger, Harry Blackmun, and John Stevens) have come from the federal circuit courts. Eight chief justices, including Earl Warren, had no prior judicial experience.

Of the 102 justices who had served through 1985, one had been president. Thirty-one had served in the executive branch (twenty-one of them in the Cabinet), and of these, twenty-two went directly from the executive branch to the Court. Eight attorneys general (none recently) and nine other Justice Department officials have been appointed. Twenty-eight had served in Congress: only five senators and seven representatives in the twentieth century.

Republican presidents are likely to choose former state or federal judges or leading corporate lawyers (they have done so in 26 out of their 29 nominations). Democratic presidents lean toward politicians, who have served in high executive positions. Since the 1860s they have made 17 out of their 29 appointments from outside the judiciary.[24]

Democratic presidents sometimes pick their political buddies: Harry Truman nominated a Republican, Harold Burton, who had served with him on the

The justices of the Supreme Court as of 1985. Left to right: Blackmun, Marshall, Brennan, Burger (then chief justice), O'Connor, White, Powell, Rehnquist, and Stevens. In 1986, Rehnquist became chief justice after Burger's resignation, and Antonin Scalia was appointed associate justice. (*Bill Fitz-Patrick: White House.*)

"Truman committee" during World War II, investigating abuses in defense industries. He also elevated Sherman Minton, a senator who had a desk adjoining Truman's. John Kennedy picked his touch-football buddy, Byron White, and Lyndon Johnson chose Abe Fortas, a close adviser who handled some of his legal matters.

ABA's Standing Committee on the Federal Judiciary rates nominees as exceptionally qualified, highly qualified, qualified or not qualified. It has *never* rated a nominee, no matter how poorly qualified, as not qualified. Some presidents have sought the ABA's approval before publicly announcing their nominations. Nixon followed Eisenhower's practice of consulting with bar leaders in advance, but after several leaks to the press he ended such consultations. Ford allowed the ABA to screen a list of potential nominees before he made his final choice, but neither Carter nor Reagan did so.

PARTISANSHIP. Republican presidents have nominated only 9 Democrats out of their 30 appointments, and Democratic presidents have nominated only 3 Republicans out of their 29 appointments (since 1860). Dwight Eisenhower chose William Brennan to win support among northern Catholics, while Richard Nixon nominated a Virginia Democrat, Lewis Powell (and nominated two other southerners who were not confirmed by the senate), as part of his southern strategy.

SOCIAL CHARACTERISTICS. Like their counterparts in the lower courts, the justices have been almost exclusively white males (only one woman and one black have ever served). Most have been over 50 and have come from middle-class or upper-middle-class professional backgrounds. Most have served in the military (six on the present Court served in World War II). Ninety-one have been Protestants, six have been Catholics, and five have been Jewish. There has been a "Catholic seat" since 1898 (there were Catholic justices even earlier), and between 1916 and 1969 there was a "Jewish seat" as well. Nixon dropped the Jewish seat on the Court in 1969 when he revived the notion of a "southern seat" with two unsuccessful nominations and the subsequent appointment of Justice Powell.

Justices do not represent their race, class, gender, or religion on the bench. A Court consisting almost entirely of wealthy white males has rendered many decisions favorable to women, minorities, and the poor. Nevertheless, such a Court is likely to move slowly on most issues involving social change: it took almost a century for the Court to move decisively on issues of racial segregation, and its approach to issues of gender has been cautious.

POLICY ORIENTATIONS. Presidents consider carefully the policy orientations of potential justices. "I should hold myself as guilty of an irreparable wrong to the nation if I should put any man on who was not absolutely sane and sound on the great national policies for which we stand in public life," said Theodore Roosevelt. In justifying his nomination of a Democrat, Horace Lurton, he pointed out that although Lurton was from the other party, "he is right on the Negro question; he is right on the power of the federal government; he is right on the insular business; he is right about corporations; and he is right about labor."[25]

Presidents who choose lower court judges for the Supreme Court are least likely to be disappointed, since these justices usually continue along the same path they followed in the lower courts.[26] Sandra Day O'Connor, for example, wrote an article for a law review the summer before her nomination in which she argued that state judges should be given more leeway and be subjected to less oversight by the federal courts. On the Supreme Court she figured in several major decisions in which the Court agreed to do just that.

Yet justices often disappoint presidents. Chief Justice Salmon Chase (who had been Treasury secretary during the Civil War) was put on the Supreme Court to uphold the government's wartime currency; yet he wrote the Court opinion holding the system unconstitutional. Harry Truman, when asked about the biggest mistake he ever made as president, said that it was his appointment of Justice Tom Clark. When asked why, he responded, "He was no damn good as Attorney General, and on the Supreme Court . . . it doesn't seem possible, but he's even worse. He hasn't made one right decision that I can think of."[27] Truman later observed that "whenever you put a man on the Supreme Court he ceases to be your friend."[28] After Chief Justice Earl Warren marshaled the Court for the decision overturning racial segregation in public schools, President Eisenhower is said to have remarked that appointing Warren was "the biggest damnfool mistake I ever made."[29]

"When one puts on the robe," says Justice Rehnquist, "one enters a world of public scrutiny and professional criticism which sets great store by individual performance and much less store upon the virtue of being a 'team player.'"[30] The justices wish to demonstrate their independence from the White House; no justice wants a reputation as a presidential flunky.

SENATE CONSENT. The Constitution requires Senate consent for Supreme Court nominations. There have been 140 nominations (some of the 102 justices received a second nomination for chief justice), and of these, 113 have been approved, 11 have been rejected, and 16 have been withdrawn or permitted to lapse. Since 1894, only 5 out of 53 nominations have been rejected or withdrawn: Robert Parker (1932), Abe Fortas for chief justice and Homer Thornberry

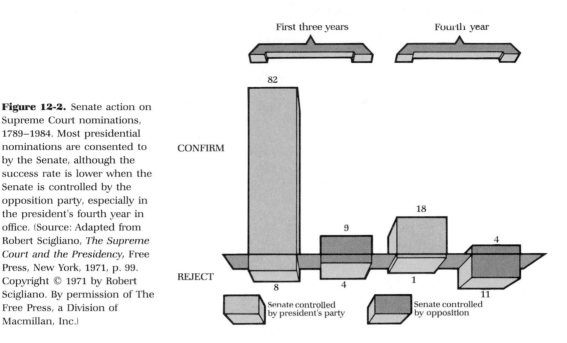

Figure 12-2. Senate action on Supreme Court nominations, 1789–1984. Most presidential nominations are consented to by the Senate, although the success rate is lower when the Senate is controlled by the opposition party, especially in the president's fourth year in office. (Source: Adapted from Robert Scigliano, *The Supreme Court and the Presidency*, Free Press, New York, 1971, p. 99. Copyright © 1971 by Robert Scigliano. By permission of The Free Press, a Division of Macmillan, Inc.)

First three years

Fourth year

CONFIRM

82

18

9

4

REJECT

8

4

1

11

Senate controlled by president's party

Senate controlled by opposition

for his post as associate justice (1968), Clement Haynsworth (1969), and Robert Carswell (1970).

Although Senate consent is no certainty, the odds favor the president. When the president's party controls the Senate, better than 90 percent of the nominations are approved; when the opposition controls the Senate, the approval rate drops to 48 percent. Presidential nominees are also more vulnerable in an election year (in such years the opposition party has refused 11 out of 15 nominations, hoping that it would win the White House) and in the lame-duck period before a change of party in the White House.[31] (See Figure 12-2.)

The Senate considers the integrity, judicial competence, and issue orientation of nominees. Parker was turned down because of antilabor decisions in a lower court; Haynsworth, because of his segregationist views; and Carswell, because of mediocrity—many of his decisions had been reversed by higher federal courts. Abe Fortas, who was already an associate justice, was defeated by the Senate because of conflicts of interest (he received payments from a foundation while on the bench), and later he resigned from the Supreme Court to avoid being impeached.

CLOSE-UP

ASSOCIATE JUSTICE SANDRA DAY O'CONNOR. Sandra Day O'Connor is the first woman to serve on the Supreme Court. In 1952 she graduated from Stanford Law School, where she was an editor of its law review and ranked among the top ten students in her class. Despite her brilliant record, she could not get a job in a law firm. When she applied to the firm in which William French Smith (an attorney general in the Reagan administration) was a partner, she was offered a job as a legal secretary.

O'Connor served as a deputy county attorney in San Mateo, California, and then as an assistant attorney general in Arizona, where she became active in Republican Party politics. She became a state senator in Arizona and eventually Senate majority leader (the first woman in the nation ever to hold such a state legislative position). She was then elected county judge, a position that she held for five

Associate Justice Sandra Day O'Connor. (*Supreme Court Historical Soiety.*)

years. Governor Bruce Babbit then appointed her to Arizona's highest court of appeals, where she served between 1979 and 1981.

When Justice Potter Stewart announced his resignation from the Supreme Court, President Ronald Reagan chose O'Connor to replace him, fulfilling a 1980 campaign pledge that "one of the first Supreme Court vacancies in my administration will be filled by the most qualified woman I can find." O'Connor was a woman, a westerner, a conservative, and a state court judge—all this was in her favor, as was the enthusiastic backing of Senator Barry Goldwater of Arizona, dean of the Republican conservatives. Also working for her was Associate Justice William Rehnquist, a classmate at Stanford (and also among the top ten students in the class).

Liberals such as Representative Morris Udall and Senator Edward Kennedy and women's groups such as the National Organization of Woman praised the nomination. But right-wing groups charged that O'Connor favored abortion and ratification of the Equal Rights Amendment, then pending in state legislatures. Jerry Falwell, the head of the Moral Majority, said that her nomination was a disaster. But the American Bar Association's Standing Committee on the Federal Judiciary found her "qualified" for the Supreme Court.

O'Connor breezed through the nomination hearings conducted by the Senate. Most members congratulated her in advance of her testimony. In her testimony O'Connor argued that "the personal views and philosophies . . . of a Supreme Court Justice and indeed any judge should be set aside insofar as it is possible to do that in resolving matters that come before the Court." She said that she personally was opposed to abortion and mentioned her "own abhorrence of abortion as a remedy." But she also said, as most nominees do in such hearings, that she could not promise anyone what she would do in future cases, could not comment on pending cases, and would not comment on previous cases. She also said that she felt it would be inappropriate for a Supreme Court justice to speak out on behalf of the Equal Rights Amendment. She was confirmed by the Senate Judiciary Committee by a 17–0 vote and by the entire Senate by a 99–0 vote.

In her few years on the Court, O'Connor has made a large impact. She has voted consistently with conservative justices on most issues, creating a cohesive 6–3 bloc that upholds most exercise of executive and legislative power at the national level, and she has broadened the powers of the state and local police. Her opinions are noted for their sharp and acerbic flavor, and she is part of the combative judicial tradition, more likely to polarize than to conciliate her colleagues. A Republican president might well consider her for the next "first"—chief justice of the United States.

Deciding cases

Each branch of government has its own power problem: for the president, it is the problem of reconciling prerogative and persuasion; for Congress, it is the difficulty of reconciling representational and legislative functions; and for the judiciary, especially the Supreme Court, it is the problem of reconciling its legal function with its political environment. The judiciary must uphold the rule of law, while at the same time remaining responsive to public opinion and deferential to the power of the other two branches.

The judicial vantage point: Access to the courts. By opening or closing access to the courts on procedural grounds, as in *Marbury v. Madison*, the courts can determine—without seeming to do so—important political and constitutional issues.

STANDING. A court may decide that a party bringing a case has no right to sue. The federal courts do not usually grant *standing* to taxpayers alleging that the government would be spending their money unconstitutionally or illegally. Consumers are limited in suing corporations under federal antitrust laws. In most instances states may not sue the national government on behalf of their citizens. But if the courts wish, they may reverse these rules: in some instances taxpayers, consumers, and states have obtained standing to sue.

CASE OR CONTROVERSY. A court does not issue advisory opinions, but requires a real case. It can sidestep requests by government officials for "advance approval" and maintain its freedom to use judicial review to strike down their actions.

RIPENESS. A court may decide that an issue presented by a case is not ready for decision; sometimes this is done to avoid taking sides in a controversy between the president and Congress.[32] In 1979, for example, President Carter abrogated the defense treaty with Taiwan, a condition insisted on by the People's Republic of China before it would exchange ambassadors with the United States. Several senators challenged Carter's action, arguing that the Constitution did not give him such power. They claimed that since the Senate had consented to the treaty in the first place, it had to approve any subsequent abrogation. The district court ruled that Congress had to share in the power to abrogate; the appeals court reversed this decision and ruled that the president did have the constitutional power to act alone. The Supreme Court dismissed the case; many of the justices felt that it was not ripe, arguing that Congress as a whole had not challenged the president by law or resolution (only a few members of Congress had gone to court on their own initiative). The Court let Carter's decision stand, but it did so without legitimizing his action.[33]

MOOTNESS. A court will not decide a case in which, because of changing circumstances, its opinion no longer can have any effect. This rule favors the executive branch, which can take unilateral actions to resolve an issue or negotiate and reach a settlement before the court has had a chance to rule on the constitutional issues.

EXHAUSTION OF REMEDIES. Usually a higher court will not hear a case until the issues have been fully considered by officials in the executive branch and the lower courts. Only when all administrative appeals for redress have been exhausted and when the trial courts have issued a decision can the case be appealed. This principle favors the government at the expense of private parties, since it is time-consuming, expensive, and emotionally draining to pursue remedies.

The courts may disregard this principle when they want to decide certain kinds of cases. The Supreme Court has ruled that certain civil rights matters based on the Civil Rights Act of 1871 may be taken to a federal district court before state administrative remedies are exhausted.

POLITICAL QUESTIONS. A court may identify certain controversies as *nonjusticiable:* not subject to a judicial remedy. It turns these cases back to the president and Congress or to the state government. Such cases include those in which there is a need for the government to speak with a single voice (some diplomatic or national security issues); in which the Constitution clearly confides resolution of the issue to the political branches; and in which the courts are not competent to create a manageable standard of judgment. These are vague criteria. How can one tell whether a case is or is not justiciable? Critics of the doctrine of *political questions* claim that the courts use it as a cop-out for any set of cases which are too controversial for them to decide, such as those involving presidential war powers.[24]

Judicial restraint versus judicial activism. Judges must decide whether to give the other two branches maximum scope in policy-making and pay deference to their interpretations of the Constitution and the laws or whether to play a policy-making role—whether to practice *judicial restraint* or *judicial activism.* "In a constitutional democracy the moral content of the law must be given by the morality of the framer or the legislator, never by the morality of the judge," argues Robert Bork, a judge on the Court of Appeals.[35] In contrast is the approach taken by Chief Justice Earl Warren, who at times would cut through the complicated legal arguments of his colleagues to pose the question, "But is it just?" and if Warren thought that something was unjust, he and other judicial activists were prepared to strike it down, using broad constitutional principles rather than narrow, technical interpretations of the laws if necessary.

THE BURDEN OF PROOF. Judicial restraint emphasizes presumptive governmental rationality: the courts must assume that the elected officials know what they are doing. Justice Frankfurter cautioned his colleagues that "the Constitution has not authorized the justices to sit in judgment on the wisdom of what Congress and the executive branch do. . . ."[36] The burden of proof is on the complainants to demonstrate beyond a reasonable doubt that the government has acted irrationally, unconstitutionally, or illegally—the benefit of the doubt goes to the government.

Judicial activism relies on the principle of suspect governmental action: the courts must protect the people against intrusions on their rights and liberties. In certain kinds of cases (civil liberties cases, for example), the courts must be especially vigilant: the government must show that any action it took was constitutional and legal and that it had no alternative except to act as it did. In the areas of economic and social policy, judicial activism can sometimes give way to policy activism, in which judges may deliberately or inadvertently substitute their own notions of what would be best public policy for those of the legislature.

STARE DECISIS: PRECEDENTS. A court decides cases in part by examining the precedents—previously decided cases (even those decided 200 years ago). These are brought to the attention of the court in the legal briefs filed by the parties. The judges can *rely* on these precedents (that is, rule the same way) or *distinguish* the present case from them and determine that they do not apply. A court may also *overrule* a precedent by issuing a decision that establishes new rules to decide the present case and those to follow.

Consider the strength of precedent in the cases involving major-league baseball. In 1922, in the Federal League case, Justice Oliver Wendell Holmes decided that organized baseball was not subject to the Sherman Anti-Trust Act, a decision which benefited owners at the expense of players. This precedent was reaffirmed in *Toolson v. New York Yankees* in 1953. In 1957, however, the Supreme Court, in *Radovich v. NFL*, decided that organized football was subject to the Sherman act. In 1971, the baseball star Curt Flood sued organized baseball, hoping that the Supreme Court would follow the Radovich case. In-

Curt Flood, a star ballplayer for the St. Louis Cardinals, sued major league baseball for restraint of trade. (*St. Louis Cardinals.*)

stead, Justice Blackmun based his decision on the precedents set in the two earlier cases involving baseball, ruling that the exemption for baseball remained "a confirmed aberration" in antitrust law which the Court would not overturn. Sometimes, as justices are apt to say, "it is more important that the law be settled than that it be settled right."

The courts often decide on the basis of **stare decisis:** to stand by that which has been previously decided. A court which gives great weight to this principle will not interfere with legal doctrines decided in the past and will uphold them even though, in their absence, it might have decided a present case differently. Judges who believe in judicial restraint rely heavily on this doctrine; they uphold precedent where they can, and instead of overruling, they prefer to distinguish a present case. Judicial activists, on the other hand, seek opportunities to transform existing legal doctrines and overrule outmoded precedents. In their view, predictability and certainty are far less important than making the law rational and equitable. Justice William Douglas argued that the good judge "remembers above all else that it is the Constitution which he swore to support and defend, not the gloss which his predecessors may have put on it."[37]

Between 1810 and 1956 the Supreme Court overruled its previous decisions only ninety times, but recently it has overturned an average of four of its own decisions each year.[38] But this understates matters: large numbers of other decisions are simply disregarded by the courts and lose their precedential value.

REACHING CONSTITUTIONAL ISSUES. An activist judge always wants to reach the heart of the matter in any case: the crucial statutory or constitutional issues. But the order in which the courts must consider issues is weighted toward judicial restraint. The courts fully consider procedural issues, and often there are grounds for disposing of a case without consideration. Even when substantive issues are reached, the courts are required, by their own

rules, to consider statutory grounds on which a decision might be based before reaching constitutional issues.[39] Judicial review may be used only when
no other approach to a case can settle the issues.

LANDMARK VERSUS INCREMENTAL DECISIONS. The greatest difference between
judicial activists and those who favor restraint involves the kind of decision
they prefer. Activists prefer **landmark decisions,** in which broad principles of
law are announced, new private rights and liberties are recognized, new definitions of governmental powers are established, or controversies between the
president and Congress over the scope of their powers are settled. Supreme
Court decisions such as those in *Gideon v. Wainright* (which established the
right of defendants to have lawyers in state criminal trials) and *Roe v. Wade*
(which guaranteed the right of women to have an abortion in the first trimester
of pregnancy) are landmark decisions. In each, the Court overturned scores of
state laws, administrative regulations, and previous cases.

Those who favor judicial restraint craft decisions to minimize their impact.
Their opinions may limit a decision to the particular issues at hand rather
than fashion general principles. And they prefer a series of small steps—each
one seemingly inconsequential, but adding up to a significant transformation.
Thus the Supreme Court has extended the rights of women in the workplace
over the past two decades, but it would be difficult to think of any one landmark ruling.

Litigating strategies.
At the appeals stage, a lawyer must make some deci-
sions about his or her brief: a document which sets forth arguments about the
facts and the law. It is an old legal maxim that you argue the facts when you do
not have good law on your side and that you argue the law when you do not
have good facts. Arguing the facts, in the context of a federal case, means using
economic, sociological, psychological, and other evidence provided by experts
to present the facts of a situation (air pollution, for example). The purpose
often is to show that the policy of the government is not rational. Such a factual
argument can shake judges' confidence that they can rely on judicial restraint
and presumptive governmental rationality. It invites them to distinguish precedents or take a policy-making role or to look for new constitutional doctrines
that might apply. Briefs based on factual arguments are sometimes called
Brandeis briefs, after Louis D. Brandeis, an attorney (and later a Supreme
Court justice) who won several cases before the Court by marshaling a tremendous amount of evidence about industrial conditions in the early 1900s.

THE AMICUS CURIAE BRIEF. The courts permit briefs to be filed by groups
which are not parties to, but are interested in the outcome of, a case; these are
amicus curiae briefs. Supposedly, the function of these briefs is to bring to the
attention of a court information which it might otherwise not obtain. The real
purpose of filing such briefs is to lobby the court, much as Congress is lobbied
when organizations submit written statements for committee hearings. There
may be amicus curiae briefs on both sides of an important case, which gives
the court some indication of group concerns. In addition, the solicitor general
may direct the Justice Department to submit its own brief outlining the position of the government.

INFLUENCING JUDICIAL OPINION. Judges are not cloistered monks and nuns,
oblivious to what goes on around them. They are affected by the intellectual
and political currents of their day. The "hot" issues are usually treated in

Louis D. Brandeis as a young
litigator. His "Brandeis briefs"
changed the way cases involving
economic issues were argued in
federal courts. He later became
the first Jewish justice
appointed to the Supreme
Court. (*Supreme Court Historical
Society.*)

articles in law reviews (published by law schools and containing notes by student editors and articles by professors, judges, and practitioners), even as the courts are dealing with them. Often the purpose of such an article is not to describe doctrines that are already shaped but rather to influence the federal courts in considering current cases. Litigating organizations may assist in the preparation of these articles; reciprocally, the authors may help prepare briefs or even argue cases. Articles in law reviews are cited in briefs and sometimes in judicial decisions.

The justices decide. After argument by the attorneys, the justices meet in the conference room to argue and decide the cases they have heard. This small-group environment has an effect on how the justices decide.

THE RULES OF THE GAME. The justices consider cases at their all-day Friday conference and on other afternoons in their conference room, behind locked doors. No one but the justices may enter the room, and the deliberations remain secret. The chief justice presides at a large rectangular table. The chief justice's own views are presented first, followed by those of the other justices in order of seniority. Voting follows reverse seniority, with the most junior members going first. The Supreme Court decides cases by majority vote (a tie vote upholds the decision of the lower court). If chief justices join the majority, they assign the decisions; if they do not, the most senior justice on the majority has that prerogative. Drafts are written and circulated for review and discussion by all the justices, sometimes several times before a final vote is taken.

THE INFLUENCE OF CHIEF JUSTICES. Chief justices are only first among equals, but they often can move the Court in their own direction. They may get the vote of a wavering justice by assigning an opinion to that justice. They may take an opinion themselves in order to make the concessions necessary to build a larger majority. Charles Evans Hughs admitted that if he needed the vote of a justice, he would put that justice's argument into the opinion, even if it conflicted with his own, and "let the legal commentators sort it all out." Chief justices may hold additional conferences and schedule more discussion in order to keep or enlarge their majority. In the most significant cases, the pressure to "marshal the Court" and obtain a unanimous opinion may lead chief justices to withhold final voting and announcement of a decision until they have gained as many votes as they can, as Chief Justice Earl Warren did in the 1954 decision to desegregate public schools.

JUDICIAL STRATEGIES. No matter how brilliant or eloquent a jurist is, the key to gaining judicial power is to get the support of at least four colleagues. This puts a premium on knowing how to win friends and influence justices.[40] A talent for negotiation is helpful, since conceding on certain points or incorporating arguments of other justices helps create a coalition. Justice Stone once wrote to his colleague Frankfurter proposing such an arrangement: "If you wish to write [the opinion] placing the case on the ground which I think tenable or desirable, I shall cheerfully join you. If not, I will add a few observations for myself."[41] Between the first and final votes there are shifts in three-fifths of Supreme Court cases, indicating that persuasion and bargaining are pervasive.[42] In these instances justices in the minority gave in and supported the majority. In fact, in 14 percent of the cases a skillful justice converted a minority opinion into the majority decision.[43]

LOSING INFLUENCE. Justices who antagonize their colleagues may have reputations as brilliant jurists outside the Court but little influence within it. A supercilious justice who picks fights and tries to embarrass colleagues by showing them up in written decisions is likely to lose support. A justice who refuses to compromise may author brilliant dissents (which are studied in the law schools as models of legal reasoning), but they are dissents nonetheless.

THE LEAST DANGEROUS BRANCH

To many Americans the judiciary seems to be stronger than the other two branches of government because of judicial review. Nothing could be further from the truth. The size, jurisdiction, structure, and powers of the judicial branch are subject to presidential and congressional control, and the federal courts remain subject to political forces which greatly influence how and what they decide.

The scope of judicial power

Judicial supremacy. The doctrine of *judicial supremacy* rests on three principles: (1) the Supreme Court's power of judicial review provides a definitive interpretation of the Constitution; (2) this interpretation must be accepted by the other two branches; and (3) these branches must obey and enforce the Court's decisions and not evade or overturn them. This doctrine was used by Chief Justice John Marshall, who not only declared an act of Congress null and void in *Marbury v. Madison* but also voided an executive order issued by President John Adams on the grounds that it conflicted with an act of Congress, thus establishing judicial review over the presidency as well.[44]

Legislative supremacy. The doctrine of *legislative supremacy* assigns a very different role to the federal courts. Laws passed by Congress may be interpreted by the courts, but the courts must begin with the premise that all acts passed by Congress are constitutional. This doctrine was advanced by Jefferson's followers in Congress, by the Whig Party, by Populists at the turn of the century, and by New Dealers in the 1930s. Although the Supreme Court opposes this doctrine, it is by no means a crackpot approach to judicial powers. There is no power of judicial review of the acts of Parliament in Britain or in most other democracies.

Coordinate powers. Most presidents argue that each branch must interpret the Constitution for itself. Judicial review may be used only for a particular case, and decisions are not to be taken as general principles in guiding or limiting Congress or the president in future matters.[45] Although the Supreme Court ruled that Congress could create a national bank, for example, President Jackson later vetoed a bill rechartering it on the grounds that he believed a national bank to be unconstitutional. In his message to Congress he argued that "the opinions of the judges have no more authority over Congress than the opinion of Congress has over the judges, and on that point the President is independent of both."[46]

The reality: Concurrent review. The reality is more complex than any doctrine: the Constitution and laws are interpreted every day by all units of government. When the courts exercise judicial review, they are exercising not an exclusive function, but one that is shared throughout the government. Judicial review is followed by political review in which the public, the parties, and the politicians either accept the judicial decision or create the conditions under which it can be modified, evaded, or overturned.

The judiciary as referee among the branches

Richard Neustadt argues that "the Constitutional Convention is supposed to have created a government of 'separated powers.' It did nothing of the sort. Rather, it created a government of separated institutions sharing powers."[47] And, one might add, it created a government of separated institutions that compete fiercely for these powers. The federal courts are often called upon to settle the legitimacy of claims to power.

The courts and presidential power. DEFENDING PRESIDENTIAL PREROGATIVE POWERS. After presidents use a controversial prerogative power, they legitimize their action by claiming:

- That their power to act came from the express or implied provisions of the Constitution
- That they acted according to laws passed by Congress
- That Congress has not protested and therefore has acquiesced or has taken other actions that advance and "ratify" the policy
- That in an emergency or when national security is involved, the courts should construe the president's legal and constitutional authority broadly
- That the courts should show maximum deference to the president and recognize the limits of their own competence to judge complex national security matters
- That boundary disputes between the president and Congress are "political questions" and are beyond the competence of the courts to decide

Let us consider how these claims intersect with judicial powers by looking at the cases decided by the federal courts during the Vietnamese war. Some draftees argued that the war was unconstitutional because it had not been declared by Congress. They claimed that it was unconstitutional and illegal for the president and the secretary of defense to send them to Vietnam to fight. Officials in the Johnson and Nixon administrations argued that the power to wage war was a sovereign power of the nation which could be exercised *either* by Congress through a declaration of war *or* by the president as commander in chief. They argued that the president could send draftees anywhere, since this was a power of the commander in chief and was not shared with Congress or subject to review by the courts. Then they argued that Congress had acquiesced and collaborated in the war effort: that it had renewed the draft and provided budgeting authority. Administration officials said that the war was a collaborative effort, not a presidential usurpation of power. Finally, they claimed that arguments over war powers are political questions—that it is up to Congress, if it believes that its powers have been usurped, to act against the president. By and large, the federal courts in the forty or so cases brought before them agreed with these arguments.

CHECKING PRESIDENTIAL POWER. The Federal courts rarely use judicial review to nullify actions of the president or the executive branch. Between 1789 and 1956 the Supreme Court declared sixteen presidential orders unconstitutional, and only eight more between then and 1975.[48] Most involved cases in which the president made a national security claim in matters involving partisan, domestic politics and in which Congress and at least one of the political parties strongly opposed the president; in which the president had made a sweeping claim of power and had denied the power of the courts to interfere; and in which the courts believed that the integrity of the constitutional system had been undermined by a presidential action.

The courts sometimes check the president indirectly. A case may involve a presidential policy and a claim of presidential power, but it is decided as if a subordinate were acting without reference to presidential orders.[49] President Nixon argued that he had the constitutional power to refuse to spend funds appropriated by Congress and that he had been given legislative authority to do so under certain economic stabilization laws. The federal courts narrowed down the issue to the simple question of whether Congress had directed that the money be spent. Finding that it had, they ordered officials to comply with the law; the courts never directly confronted the president.[50]

Occasionally the Supreme Court overturns a presidential policy. In *Ex Parte Milligan* the Supreme Court lectured President Lincoln about the impropriety of using courts-martial to try civilians in states in which the regular courts remained open during the Civil War. But this case was not quite a great confrontation between judicial civil power and presidential military power: the war had already ended and Lincoln himself was dead.[51]

In modern times, the most celebrated case involving judicial review of a president's actions had to do with the steel strike of 1952. Steelworkers went on strike, and compromises proposed by the government were rejected by the steel companies. Truman decided to bring pressure on them to settle by seizing the mills and ordering a resumption of production with a pay raise for the workers. He justified his action with the claim that the Defense Department needed steel to fight the Korean war.

The steel companies went to federal court, arguing that nowhere in the Constitution or laws was Truman given the authority to seize the mills. A majority of the Supreme Court agreed. Brushing aside the claims of national emergency, the majority decided that Truman had disregarded a procedure established by Congress to settle strikes and had seized the mills without any power to do so. In a concurring opinion, Associate Justice Robert Jackson (a noted supporter of expanded presidential powers) set out a threefold test for the federal courts to apply in evaluating presidential actions: (1) When the president acts pursuant to law, presidential authority is at a maximum; (2) when the president acts without congressional authorization, the courts should scrutinize the action carefully, but "there is a zone of twilight in which he and Congress may have concurrent authority, or in which its distribution is uncertain," and therefore the courts might well uphold the action; and (3) when the president acts in ways that are incompatible with the expressed or implied will of Congress, "his power is at its lowest ebb, for then he can rely only upon his own constitutional power minus any constitutional powers of Congress over the matter."[52]

The strategy for presidents is clear enough: any claim of power should be placed in the first category, by arguing that Congress has explicitly or implicitly collaborated in its exercise, or in the second category, by arguing that Congress has acquiesced in the matter or even invited the president to act. If possible, presidents should avoid the third situation, in which they act against the express or implied will of Congress.

The courts and congressional power. The courts rarely overturn acts passed by Congress. After *Marbury v. Madison*, it was more than fifty years before another provision of Congress was declared unconstitutional. But occasionally the courts have decisively confronted Congress. Consider what happened in the 1930s when six conservative justices squared off against Franklin Roosevelt, the Democratic Congress, and the New Deal program for economic recovery.

STRIKING DOWN NEW DEAL LAWS. Roosevelt recommended, and Congress enacted, measures to stabilize prices against decline by regulating the supply of goods provided on the market. Instead of having a free market and fluctuating prices, prices were set by government-industry committees. Although these programs were supported by many business groups (and many were initiated by such groups) and were favored by a majority of the public, the federal courts struck them down, arguing that Congress could not delegate such vast powers to administrative agencies. In 1935, in *Schechter v. United States*, the Supreme Court invalidated the entire industrial recovery program; in the same year, in *Carter v. Carter Coal Co.*, it struck down a federal tax on coal producers who had not accepted the coal association's production code; and in 1936, in *United States v. Butler*, it struck down the Agricultural Adjustment Act, which involved a processing tax used to pay subsidies to farmers who accepted acreage controls or production quotas set jointly by farmers' associations and the Department of Agriculture.[53] All told, between 1935 and 1937 the Supreme Court struck down seventy-six laws passed by Congress, almost all of them regulating the economy.

THE SWITCH IN TIME SAVES NINE. But in 1937, after Roosevelt's reelection, the Court reversed itself and accepted the constitutionality of revised New Deal laws. Why did it back down? It was threatened by a presidential court-packing scheme which would have added an additional justice for each one who had reached the age of 70. Had Congress passed the measure, Roosevelt could have nominated six new justices and gained a majority on the Court. Faced with this threat, Chief Justice Hughes and Justice Roberts began to vote with three pro-New Deal justices to create a 5–4 majority that would uphold congressional measures. The upshot was a series of cases signaling the withdrawal of the federal courts from judicial review of economic legislation. In 1937, the Court upheld the National Labor Relations Act in *NLRB v. Jones and Laughlin* and the unemployment insurance and social security programs in *Seward Machine Co. v. Davis* and *Helvering v. Davis*. In 1941, in *United States v. Darby*, the Fair Labor Standards Act, which regulated wages and hours and prohibited child labor, was upheld.[54] As the Court backtracked, Congress refused to support the president's plan.

Since 1937 the federal courts have not struck down any important laws regulating the economy, and instead have turned to issues of state economic legislation and civil rights and liberties, rather than continue constitutional confrontations with the president and congress over economic powers.

Protecting judicial power. The Supreme Court uses judicial review to protect its powers against challenges by the executive and legislative branches, as in *United States v. Nixon*. The constitutional issue boiled down to whether President Nixon could use executive privilege to withhold information about

Watergate-related crimes committed by him and his associates from the grand jury of a federal district court. It is a maxim in American law that a jury is entitled to hear evidence from everyone involved. There is no Fifth Amendment right to remain silent in a grand jury proceeding, although testimony that incriminates a witness may not be used in a subsequent trial unless the witness "waived immunity" when testifying before the grand jury. But Nixon claimed that he alone would determine what evidence to turn over to the grand jury. The Watergate special prosecutor, taking Nixon to court over the issue, argued that in matters involving criminal offenses, executive privilege must yield to the right of the grand jury to have evidence.

The Supreme Court acted to uphold judicial prerogative powers. It made it clear in its decision that in ordinary criminal cases, the grand jury was to have evidence from the president. And in any kind of case, the Court went on, it,

The scope of executive privilege in judicial proceedings was argued before the Supreme Court by James St. Clair, White House counsel, and Leon Jaworski, the Justice Department's special prosecutor. In *United States v. Nixon*, the Court decided that the president could not withhold from the federal courts evidence involving a crime. (*James St. Clair—A. Grace: Sygma. Leon Jaworski—J. P. Laffont: Sygma.*)

not the president, would be the federal trial judge, and it would determine what evidence would be made public, what would be revealed to a grand jury in secret, and what would be withheld from a grand jury. The president and the president's lawyers could never withhold evidence from judicial scrutiny.[55]

Checks and balances and judicial power

The courts treat presidents and Congress with deference. They legitimize most presidential actions or stay out of presidents' way in cases involving national security, diplomacy, and war powers. They immunize presidents from civil lawsuits and make it difficult for their subordinates to be sued.[56] They accept claims of executive privilege in national security matters. Only when presidents flagrantly violate the Constitution on domestic issues or defy the courts will they try to check the White House. Even then they wait until they have public and congressional support. At the same time, presidents have shown increasing deference to the courts. Nineteenth-century attacks on the legitimacy of judicial review, threats to impeach federal judges, evasion or defiance of court orders, and other forms of coercion have given way to presidents' acceptance of decisions directed against them: Truman turned the steel mills back to the companies, and Nixon turned the evidence over to the Watergate special prosecutor. Presidents enforce court decisions with which they strongly disagree, as Eisenhower did when he used the military to desegregate public schools.

The question remains: Why should the courts defer to presidents and Congress? To understand why they do, we must examine the potential and actual application of checks and balances against the judiciary.

Jurisdiction. The federal courts can lose power if Congress exercises its constitutional power to regulate the appellate jurisdiction of the Supreme Court and the original jurisdiction of the lower federal courts. In 1868 Congress passed a law providing that the Supreme Court could not review circuit court decisions involving petitions for habeas corpus, and in 1914 it passed the Clayton Act, which established the Federal Trade Commission and removed certain cases from the federal courts. In order to prevent federal judges from issuing injunctions in peaceful labor disputes, Congress has also restricted their power to hold people in contempt of court.

Attempts to strip the Supreme Court of jurisdiction may influence its subsequent decisions. In 1957, after the Court began protecting the civil liberties of communists, Senator Jenner introduced a bill to strip the Court of jurisdiction in matters involving contempt of Congress, the hiring and firing of federal employees on national security grounds, and the admission of communists to state bars. Although Congress did not pass this bill, the Court backtracked in several other civil liberties cases, and its rejection of such claims soared from one-fourth in 1957 to one-half in 1958.

New right politicians—upset with Supreme Court decisions outlawing voluntary prayer and Bible reading in public schools, requiring busing to overcome racial imbalance, and allowing abortions—have sponsored legislation to curb the jurisdiction of the courts. These forty or so bills do one or more of the following: (1) remove certain cases from court consideration, (2) require the courts to make certain findings or apply certain legal rules, and (3) limit the kind of orders which the courts may issue. The Senate passed one measure, the Neighborhood Schools Act, which bars the federal courts from ordering children who live more than 5 miles or 15 minutes away from their schools to be bused to overcome racial imbalance. Another bill would establish that at conception a fetus is a person within the meaning of the Fourteenth Amendment and would prevent the federal courts from striking down any national or state laws regulating or prohibiting abortions.

Liberal and conservative opponents, including the dean of congressional conservatives, Barry Goldwater, have argued that such measures are inconsistent with the Constitution and are at odds with the intentions of the framers. Robert Bork, a former solicitor general and acting attorney general in the Nixon administration, argued that it "would not be in keeping with the spirit of the Constitution, nor would it be in keeping with its structure."[57] Six former Justice Department officials, spanning four administrations, agreed. The American Bar Association's House of Delegates passed a resolution opposing court stripping in 1981.

The Reagan administration has not supported these measures. In part this may reflect the desire of Justice Department lawyers not to antagonize federal judges before whom they try their cases. And President Reagan and William French Smith, the former attorney general, have indicated that they would rather use constitutional amendments than court-stripping.

It is not even clear that Congress has the constitutional power to strip the courts of whole categories of its jurisdiction. Some lawyers argue that the Constitution provides federal courts with their jurisdiction and that Congress may legislate only to create the court system and assign different kinds of cases to different federal courts—it cannot simply remove whole categories of cases from the federal courts. The Supreme Court itself ultimately can determine whether such legislation is constitutional. In several cases already decided, the Court has hinted that it would not acquiesce in the wholesale elimination of categories of cases. Whenever it has upheld congressional legislation involving its jurisdiction, it has been careful to observe that there were still ways for the cases to reach the federal courts. The Supreme Court has indicated that Congress can regulate the jurisdiction of the courts only in a manner that is consistent with judicial independence. It may not change the Supreme Court's jurisdiction as a way of affecting policy indirectly—as a means to a legislative end.

Amending the Constitution. Decisions based on judicial review may be overturned by a constitutional amendment. The Eleventh Amendment was adopted in 1795 in response to a Supreme Court decision permitting a state to be sued by a citizen of another state. This amendment was itself held constitutional in 1798 by the Supreme Court, which recognized that any amendment to the Constitution, by definition, was not subject to judicial review.[58] In 1895 the Court ruled that an income tax law passed by Congress was unconstitutional.[59] The Sixteenth Amendment, ratified in 1913, overturned that ruling. In 1970 the Supreme Court ruled that Congress could not reduce the voting age in state elections to 18; the following year the Twenty-Sixth Amendment was ratified, giving Congress that power.[60]

The main impetus to amend the Constitution to overturn court decisions

Jerry Falwell, the leader of Moral Majority, and Senator Jesse Helms (R.-N.C.) confer at the White House after hearing President Reagan endorse a school-prayer amendment to the Constitution in May 1982. (*Shepard Sherbell: Picture Group.*)

today comes from conservative, right-wing, and "profamily" groups concerned with **social issues.** "The purpose of the constitutional amendment is to circumvent the Supreme Court and put it out of their reach," says Jerry Falwell, the head of the Moral Majority.[61] He was referring to an amendment proposed by President Reagan that would permit voluntary prayer and Bible reading in schools. Another proposed amendment, the Human Life Federalism Amendment, would give both the states and Congress the power to outlaw abortions.

Supporters argue that adopting these amendments would be a legitimate way to settle political issues. They view the amending process as a way for the people to overturn federal court decisions which depart from the will of the majority (as they count noses).

Opponents argue that it is unwise to resolve policy disputes by amending the Constitution. The adoption and later repeal of the Prohibition amendment is cited as evidence that policies should be settled in the political branches, where transitory majorities can pass, amend, and even repeal laws to their hearts' content. They say that the Constitution should remain the fundamental law, a higher law that concentrates on procedures rather than substance and on means rather than ends; to use the Constitution to embody opinions on divisive social issues will, in the long run, diminish respect for it and weaken its authority.

IN CONCLUSION

The federal court system consists of constitutional and legislative courts, each of whose appellate jurisdiction and structure are determined by Congress. Judges and justices are nominated by the president and appointed with the advice and consent of the Senate; in practice, senatorial courtesy and senatorial clearance give Congress a strong voice in the selection of lower court judges. Most judges have had extensive government or judicial experience and have been rated as qualified or as highly qualified by professional associations. The vast majority are white male Protestants, although Democratic presidents have increased the representation of racial and religious minorities and of women.

The federal courts use access to the judicial system as a means of gaining influence over the other two branches, as demonstrated in *Marbury v. Madison*, which established the power of judicial review. Individual members of the Supreme Court choose whether to be activists or to embrace the principles of judicial restraint. They also gain more or less influence with their colleagues depending on their willingness or unwillingness to bargain and compromise when they write decisions.

The courts remain subject to the checks and balances of the other two branches, vindicating Hamilton's observation that they suffer from strategic weakness. Because of threats to their jurisdiction and powers, the overturning of their decisions by new statutes and constitutional amendments, and changes in their personnel, the courts do not remain long apart from the national consensus on issues. The judiciary usually does not engage in direct confrontations with the president, and it overturns far more state statutes than congressional statutes. It remains the weakest of the three branches.

NOTES

1. Alexis de Tocqueville, *Democracy in America*, Knopf, New York, 1945, vol. 1, p. 280.
2. *The Federalist*, number 78.
3. Robert Dahl, "Decision-Making in a Democracy: The Supreme Court as National Policy-Maker," *Journal of Politics*, vol. 6, no. 2, 1958, pp. 279–295.
4. *The Federalist*, number 78.
5. Charles Evan Hughes, *The Supreme Court of the United States*, Columbia University Press, New York, 1927, p. 230.
6. Arthur S. Miller, "Statutory Language and the Purposive Use of Ambiguity," *Virginia Law Review*, vol. 42, no. 1, January 1956, pp. 23–39.
7. *Zurcher v. The Stanford Daily*, 436 U.S. 547 (1978).
8. Robert Jackson, *The Struggle for Judicial Supremacy*, Knopf, New York, 1941, pp. x–xi.
9. James Madison, *Notes of the Debates in the Federal Convention*, Ohio State University Press, Columbus, 1966, p. 463.
10. Ibid., p. 462.
11. Charles G. Haines, *The American Doctrine of Judicial Supremacy*, 2d ed., Russell and Russell, New York, 1959, p. 134.
12. *The Federalist*, number 78.
13. Charles Warren, *The Supreme Court in United States History*, Little, Brown, Boston, 1923, vol. 1, p. 229.
14. *Marbury v. Madison*, 1 Cranch 137 (1803).
15. Frank Sorauf, "Winning in the Courts: Interest Groups and Constitutional Change," *The Constitution*, vol. 1, fall 1984, pp. 12–14.
16. Henry Glick, *Courts, Politics, and Justice*, McGraw-Hill, New York, 1983, p. 33.
17. Administrative Office of the United States Courts, 1985.
18. *Annual Report of the Administrative Office of the United States Courts*, GPO, Washington, D.C., 1985, table A-1.
19. *The New York Times*, Dec. 30, 1984.
20. Robert Scigliano, "The President and the Judiciary," in Michael Nelson (ed.), *The

Presidency and the Political System, Congressional Quarterly Press, Washington, D.C., 1984, p. 400.

21. Joel Grossman, *Lawyer and Judges: The ABA and the Politics of Judicial Selection*, Wiley, New York, 1965.

22. Robert G. Scigliano, *The Supreme Court and the Presidency*, Free Press, New York, 1971, pp. 109–123.

23. Henry J. Abraham and Bruce A. Murphy, "The Influence of Sitting and Retired Justices on Presidential Supreme Court Nominations," *Hastings Law Quarterly*, vol. 3, no. 1, winter 1976, pp. 37–63.

24. Scigliano, op. cit., p. 115.

25. Ibid., p. 196.

26. David W. Rohde and Harold J. Spaeth, *Supreme Court Decision-Making*, Freeman, San Francisco, 1976, pp. 107–109.

27. Merle Miller, *Plain Speaking*, Berkley Publishing, New York, 1974, p. 226.

28. Henry J. Abraham, *Justices and Presidents: A Political History of Appointments to the Supreme Court*, Oxford University Press, New York, 1974, p. 62.

29. Steve Neal, *The Eisenhowers: Reluctant Dynasty*, rev. ed., University Press of Kansas, Wichita, 1984, p. 382.

30. *The New York Times*, Oct. 20, 1984.

31. Baum, p. 45.

32. See Felix Frankfurter's opinion in *Maryland V. Baltimore Radio Show, Inc.* 338 U.S. 912 (1950).

33. *Goldwater v. Carter*, 444 U.S. 996 (1979).

34. Philippa Strum, *The Supreme Court and "Political Questions": A Study in Judicial Evasion*, University of Alabama Press, 1974.

35. *The New York Times*, Jan. 4, 1985.

36. *Trop v. Dulles*, 356 U.S. 86 (1958).

37. Alan Westin (ed.), *The Supreme Court: Views from the Inside*, Norton, New York, 1961, p. 123.

38. Albert P. Blaustein and Andrew H. Field, "Overruling Opinions in the Supreme Court," *Michigan Law Review*, vol. 57, no. 4, December 1958, pp. 151–194.

39. See Justice Brandeis's opinion in *Ashwander v. T.V.A.*, 297 U.S. 288 (1936).

40. Walter Murphy, *Elements of Judicial Strategy*, University of Chicago Press, Chicago, 1964, pp. 37–91.

41. Alpheus T. Mason, *Harlan Fiske Stone: Pillar of the Law*, Viking, New York, 1956, p. 501.

42. Glick, op. cit., p. 265.

43. Ibid.

44. *Little v. Bareme*, 2 Cranch 170 (1804).

45. Quoted in Walter Murphy, *Congress and the Court*, University of Chicago Press, Chicago, 1962, p. 25.

46. Andrew Jackson, "Bank Veto Message," in Richardson (ed.), *Messages and Papers of the Presidents*, Bureau of National Literature and Art, Washington, D.C., 1900, vol. 2, pp. 576–591.

47. Richard Neustadt, *Presidential Power: The Politics of Leadership from FDR to Carter*, Wiley, New York, 1980, p. 26.

48. Scigliano, op. cit., p. 408.

49. Ibid., pp. 406–410.

50. *Train v. City of New York*, 420 U.S. 35 (1974).

51. *Ex Parte Milligan*, 71 U.S. 2 (1866).

52. *Youngstown Sheet and Tube Co. v. Sawyer*, 343 U.S. 579 (1952).

53. *Schechter v. United States*, 295 U.S. 495 (1935); *Carter v. Carter Coal Co.*, 298 U.S. 238 (1936); *United States v. Butler*, 297 U.S. 1 (1936).

54. *NLRB v. Jones and Laughlin*, 301 U.S. 1 (1937); *Seward Machine Co. v. Davis*, 301 U.S.

548 (1937); *Helvering v. Davis*, 301 U.S. 619 (1937); *United States v. Darby*, 312 U.S. 100 (1941).

55. *United States v. Nixon*, 418 U.S. 683 (1974).
56. *Nixon v. Fitzgerald*, 457 U.S. 731 (1982).
57. *Congressional Quarterly*, May 30, 1981, p. 948.
58. *Hollingsworth v. Va.*, 3 Dallas 378 (1798).
59. *Pollock v. Farmers Loan and Trust Co.*, 157 U.S. 429 (1895).
60. *Oregon v. Mitchell*, 400 U.S. 112 (1970).
61. *The New York Times*, May 7, 1982.

FURTHER READING

Abraham, Henry J.: *Justices and Presidents: A Political History of Appointments to the Supreme Court*, Oxford University Press, New York, 1974. A discussion of the politics of presidential nominations.

Bickel, Alexander: *The Least Dangerous Branch*, Bobbs-Merrill, Indianapolis, 1962. A study of the political context in which the Supreme Court operates.

Cardozo, Benjamin: *The Nature of the Judicial Process*, Yale University Press, New Haven, Conn., 1921. An introduction to what judges do and how law is made.

Hughes, Charles Evans: *The Supreme Court of the United States*, Columbia University Press, New York, 1928. Lectures by the chief justice on the functions of the Supreme Court.

Glick, Henry: *Courts, Politics, and Justice*, McGraw-Hill, New York, 1983. An introduction to the state and federal courts.

Jackson, Robert H.: *The Supreme Court in the American System of Government*, Harvard University Press, Cambridge, Mass., 1955. A discussion, by an associate justice, of the role of the Supreme Court.

Murphy, Walter F.: *Congress and the Court*, University of Chicago Press, Chicago, 1962. An account of controversies between the Warren Court and congressional conservatives.

Scigliano, Robert G.: *The Supreme Court and the Presidency*, Free Press, New York, 1971. A book about confrontations between presidents and the judiciary.

THE STUDY BREAK

The First Monday in October. A movie, made in 1981, about the collision between the first woman Supreme Court justice (played by Jill Clayburgh) and her brethren, especially a crusty conservative, played by Walter Matthau.

The Magnificent Yankee. A 1950 movie about the life of Justice Oliver Wendell Holmes.

Twelve Angry Men. A movie made in 1957, with a brilliant cast, about the attempts of one man (played by Henry Fonda) to convince his fellow jurors of the innocence of a boy on trial for murder.

Woodward, Robert, and Scott Armstrong: *The Brethren,* Simon and Schuster, New York, 1979. An inside account by some law clerks of how the Supreme Court operates.

USEFUL SOURCES

Biographical Directory of the Federal Judiciary, Gale Research Company, Detroit, 1976. Data on the lower federal courts.

Congressional Quarterly's Guide to the U.S. Supreme Court, Congressional Quarterly Press, Washington, D.C., 1979. A thorough description of the Court and its justices.

Fein, Bruce E.: *Significant Decisions of the Supreme Court,* American Enterprise Institute, Washington, D.C. An annual review of the work of the Supreme Court.

Freund, Paul A. (ed.): *History of the Supreme Court of the United States,* Macmillan, New York, 1969–1974. A multivolume definitive history of the courts.

Friedman, Leon, and Fred L. Israel (eds.): *The Justices of the United States Supreme Court, 1789–1971,* Bowker, New York, 1978, 5 vols. Biographical information on the justices and their most important opinions.

Kurland, Philip, and Gerhard Casper (eds.): *Landmark Briefs and Arguments of the Supreme Court of the United States: Constitutional Law,* University Publications of America, Washington, D.C., 1975. Briefs, oral arguments, and decisions between 1793 and 1973.

United States Law Week, Bureau of National Affairs, Washington, D.C. A weekly compendium of the work of the Supreme Court.

United States Reports, GPO, Washington, D.C. Daily "slip opinions" and annual bound volumes of the decisions and proceedings of the Supreme Court.

ORGANIZATIONS

Supreme Court of the United States. U.S. Supreme Court Building, 1 First Street, N.E., Washington, D.C. 20543. For more information telephone 202-252-3000.

Administrative Office of the United States Courts. Washington, D.C. 20544. Handles personnel, budget and administrative matters for all federal courts (except the Supreme Court) and publishes an annual report on judicial performance. For more information telephone 202-633-6097.

Federal Judicial Center. Dolley Madison House, 1520 H Street, N.W. Washington, D.C. 20005. Conducts research on the operations of the federal judiciary. For more information telephone 202-633-6011.

The original cabinet consisted of Henry Knox, secretary of war; Thomas Jefferson, secretary of state; Edmund Randolph, attorney general; and Alexander Hamilton, secretary of the treasury. The modern cabinet is three times as large, but less influential. (*Granger Collection; Sebastiao Selgado, Jr.: Magnum.*)

CHAPTER 13

BUREAUCRATIC POLITICS: IRON TRIANGLES AND ISSUE NETWORKS

The bureaucracy is the "fourth branch" of government; it is deeply involved in politics and highly responsive to the other three branches. Officials must respond to pressures from clienteles and interest groups that have a stake in their operations, and their activities can become a national agenda issue. Governmental effectiveness is primarily a political rather than a managerial problem.

Critics charge that bureaucrats are too rigid—that they drown the nation in paperwork and red tape and do things "by the book," disregarding the human consequences. But they also charge that bureaucrats are too political: prone to favoritism and special exceptions. Surveys have shown that the public rates the federal bureaucracy last among the major institutions in terms of ability to get things done.[1] Yet the public strongly supports most domestic programs and wants greater federal involvement in the areas of pollution control, consumer protection, toxic-waste disposal, and disaster relief. Presidents come into office pledging to cut the size of "big government," freeze hiring, and reduce the size of the federal work force. Yet each president adds to the government's activities.

This chapter will examine the political setting of the bureaucracy. It will consider how presidents, Congress, and the judiciary try to cope with this fourth branch; how officials forge alliances with congressional committees and interest groups; and whether big government is really the crucial problem or whether there are more important issues involved in making government more efficient and accountable.

WHAT IS BUREAUCRACY?

Bureaucratic organization

A bureaucracy is an organization which functions according to set procedures, usually embodied in formal rules and regulations and in informal "norms" of acceptable employee conduct. The activities of an organization are assigned to units, and the power to command is given only to officials who run them.[2] Employees are trained to perform complex tasks. They are appointed on the basis of assessments of their merit, rather than because of their family ties or social connections, as would happen in a tribal or feudal system.[3] Their career advancement depends largely on their performance.

What bureaucracies do

Making goals operational. Officials take general goals (for example, ending hunger in the United States or improving the quality of our air) and turn them into specific targets with measurable indicators.[4] To end hunger, they can identify everyone whose caloric intake is 20 percent lower than the minimum recommended level and then devise a program to raise these people's intake to that level. To clean the air, they can measure particulates (dust and smoke) and then attempt to reduce the particulate levels. Operationalizing a goal helps define it more clearly, allows for gradual improvement, and enables officials to measure progress and quantify performance.

HUD officials at the New England regional office review disaster-relief claims processed by field workers. (*Department of Housing and Urban Development.*)

Developing programs. Bureaucracies devise programs: sequences of activities, such as forecasting the weather or mailing social security checks. Each program can be subdivided into routines which require a repertoire of skills or techniques that employees acquire through training or on the job. A weather forecast, for example, involves field measurement and reporting, computer-assisted data analysis at headquarters, preparation of maps and tables, and transmission of information to the media and to subscribers to special services. Division of labor enables an organization to perform complex tasks.

Evaluating programs. Programs must be monitored to see whether they are meeting performance standards or implementation timetables and are remaining within their budgets. Sometimes agencies do their own evaluations, but often they contract out to management consultants, academic think tanks, or even interest groups. Officials are evaluated by presidential and congressional staff agencies and by public interest groups. Poor performance may become a national agenda issue and lead to shake ups and firings.

The federal bureaucracy

The federal bureaucracy consists of thirteen departments and other nondepartmental agencies within the executive branch, agencies outside the executive branch, a few dozen independent regulatory agencies, and government corporations.[5] Each of these organizations divides itself into smaller units (known as *offices*, *services*, *bureaus*, or *divisions*) which run programs; examples are the Passport Office and the Bureau of Labor Statistics (Figure 13-1).

Government agencies are established and funded by Congress, which also sets general rules of procedure and defines and limits the duties of all officials. They operate according to internal agency rules based on these statutes.

445

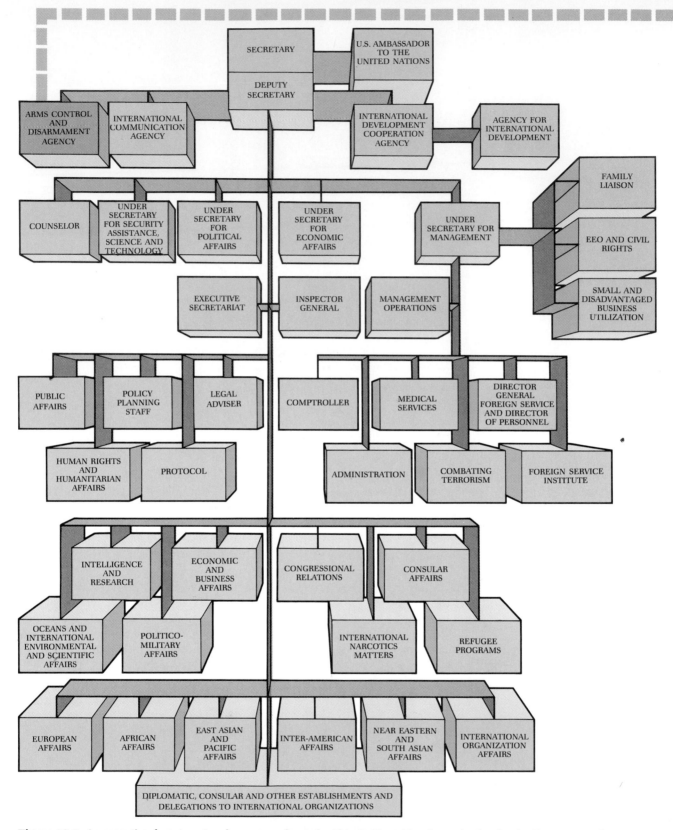

Figure 13-1. An executive department and an agency located within it. The table of organization for the Department of State (above) and for one of its affiliated agencies, the Arms Control and Disarmament Agency (opposite). Each of the other agencies located within the Department of State has its own table of organization. (Source: *U.S. Government Organization Manual*, 1984.)

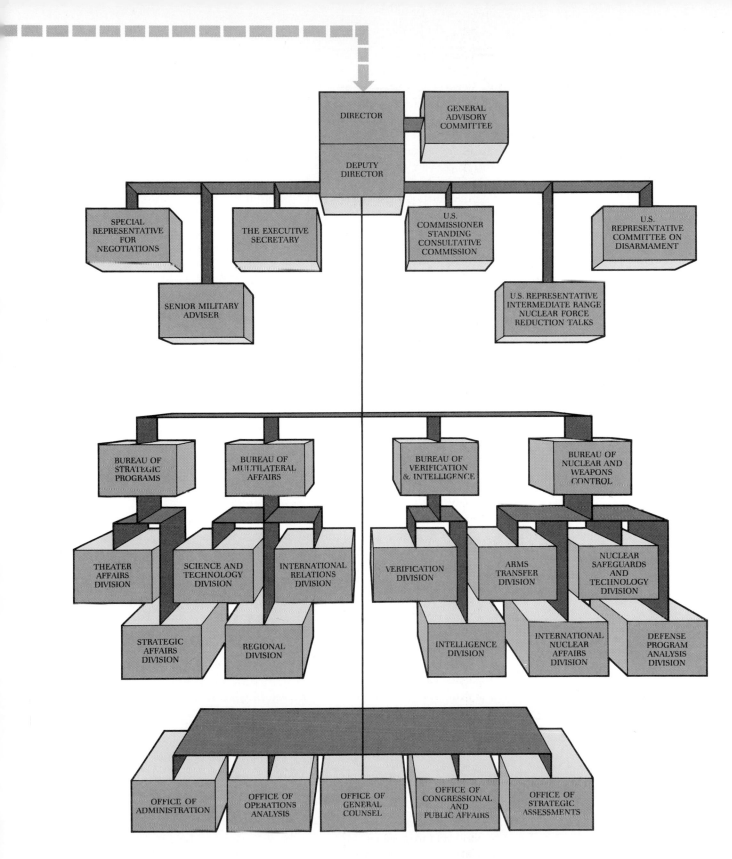

Politics versus administration. Both national and state agencies were organized in the nineteenth century as repositories for party patronage and people with good social connections.[6] They were not expected to act impartially: the operative rule was, "To the victor belong the spoils." Their regulations and procedures for awarding contracts or making payments benefited friends of the party in power. Almost a century ago reformers and some political scientists argued that administration could be separated from politics. Congress and the president could be confined to giving policy direction to officials, who would then impartially apply the law and rules to specific cases with all the demeanor and honesty that one associates with federal judges.[7] In practice, bureaucrats have always cultivated good relations with those close to the president, with congressional committee leaders, and with interest-group lobbyists—and the way to get on with these people is to bend, and sometimes even to break, the rules in their favor. Bureaucrats are as much politicians as they are managers.

Agency missions. Officials of an agency use their positions to form policy, even as they execute it, by defining the mission of the agency and by operationalizing its goals. All its programs, and indeed its mission itself, are subject to challenge by those wanting it to adopt a different mission, operationalize its goals differently, or create new programs. This is the reason for the conflicts within the Interior Department between probusiness officials, who see its mission as involving "multiple use" of land for recreation and business, and conservationists, who believe that certain areas should remain completely protected wilderness.

Empire building. "No one with a day's experience in government fails to realize that in all bureaucracies there are three implacable spirits," warned Herbert Hoover, a former president and the head of two national commissions on bureaucratic reform: "self-perpetuation, expansion, and an incessant demand for more power".[8] Officials want higher salaries; more assistants; better benefits, offices, and facilities; and funds for training and retraining, for conferences and travel, and for research and evaluation. "Gradually a hierarchy of administrative officers, executive officers, budget officers, congressional liaison officers, and public relations officers grows up, almost the sole purpose of which is fund-wheedling," says one.[9]

Bureaucrats are ambitious: programs want to become bureaus, bureaus want to absorb other bureaus with related functions and become a large agency within a department; and the very largest agencies may eventually want to become full-fledged departments with Cabinet status. Alternatively, they try to become independent executive agencies or public corporations, legally insulated from White House control.

Direct and indirect services. Some federal agencies, such as the FBI, the Selective Service, the Internal Revenue Service, and the Immigration and Naturalization Service, deal directly with the public. But most have an indirect relationship: government and private organizations at the state and local levels receive contracts to perform services or provide goods. The Job Training Partnership Act provides an example. The Labor Department distributed $3.5 billion to state personnel offices, which in turn contracted with private companies and vocational schools for actual job training. Planning for the program was conducted in 500 "service delivery areas," where industry councils composed of the heads of leading local corporations determined the kind of training most suitable for the local economy. Many bureaucracies use partnerships to deliver services; once the private groups are involved, they become constituencies which put pressure on Congress and the president to expand these programs.

Administrative pluralism. Congress often requires bureaus to work closely with state and local agencies or private groups. It may give the governor or local agencies the option of participating in, or staying out of, programs, such as those involving social services. It may give them a veto over the activities of federal agencies (such as legal services for the poor.) It may route funding through state offices and require them to coordinate their plans with a state planning agency concerned with transportation or the environment, for example. Local community planning boards may have a veto over federally assisted construction (housing and urban renewal programs). Congress allows private interest groups to help administer and evaluate federal programs, conduct research and development for them, and even provide direct services (such as job training). Often the federal officials who work in regional or district offices are there because their state congressional delegations recommended them (or had an informal veto over their appointment). If such federal officials antagonize the governor or the mayor, they may find themselves transferred.

Sometimes a federal agency is really a hollow shell that provides funds, statistical information, or technical assistance to private groups. Scientists receive most of their funding for basic research from the federal government: federal agencies delegate the funding decisions to outside review panels—consisting of scientists.[10]

FOCUS

TECHNOLOGY AND TURF WARS. In January 1984 West German officials seized a Digital Equipment Company VAX 11-782 minicomputer just minutes before it was to be sent to the Soviet Union. The VAX could have helped the Russians with their air defense system in Europe. The United States Customs Service and the Treasury Department held a new conference, with the computer on display, and Treasury Secretary Donald Regan called the incident an "espionage coup" for the United States. But was it? "Dozens of VAXs are missing," said Richard Perle, an assistant secretary of defense, "and we presume the Soviets have them."[11]

The Soviet Union seeks American technology involving supercomputers and minicomputers, metallurgy, semiconductor design and manufacture, telemetry, radar, lasers, telecommunications, and biotechnology. The Soviets try to bring manufactured products incorporating advanced technology into their country, in spite of American export regulations which prohibit the export of items on the Pentagon's "militarily critical technologies list." In 1979 Congress passed the Export Administration Control Act, which authorizes the Commerce Department's Office of Export Administration to make regulations involving these manufactured goods. Customs agents do not allow these goods to leave the United States without licenses issued by the Commerce Department. There are more than 300,000 items which require special permission to export. But the Soviets get around the law by setting up, or working with, trading corporations in other nations, which order goods from an American company or its foreign distributor or subsidiary.

More than 750 high-tech corporations export over $20 billion annually in manu-

Customs agents control the movement of goods and people at the entry points to the United States. (*Department of the Treasury.*)

factured goods. They have a vital stake in the regulations, as do the states in which they operate. Governors, company lobbyists, and trade association representatives come to Washington and meet with bureaucrats and presidential aides whenever new regulations are proposed, claiming that tough laws would add to their costs, cause delays in shipping that would lose them sales to legitimate distributors, and do nothing to prevent the Soviets from obtaining the technologies. They also call for the Commerce Department to appoint industry representatives to a technical advisory committee, as authorized by law, to give officials advice and play a role in the administration of the law. In 1985 they got the Commerce Department to agree to new regulations emphasizing industry self-regulation: companies must institute their own control programs and screen the companies to which they export.[12]

The export control issue has sparked a turf war in the Washington bureaucracy. We need the cooperation of our allies, especially the fifteen advanced industrial nations who are members of a coordinating committee dealing with such trade (COCOM). But who in the American government should represent the United States at COCOM? The State Department and its Bureau of East-West Trade? The deputy assistant secretary of defense, who prepares the critical technologies list? The White House Office of Special Trade Representative? And who should chair the working group of senior officials from different departments who must make policy? The secretary of commerce? The secretary of the treasury, who chairs the Senior Interagency Group on International Economic Policy? And, finally, which government agency should administer the export control program? The Strategic Investigations Division of the United States Customs Service (which lets goods in and out of the country) or the Commerce Department's Office of Export Administration (which grants the licenses)?

Answers to these questions affect policy. The Commerce Department works closely with high-tech corporations and wants to export as much as possible. The Custom Department scornfully refers to the Commerce Department's proposals as the "KGB relief bill," arguing that they will make the efforts of the Soviet intelligence agencies that much easier. At the Pentagon, Richard Perle, who favors the toughest possible restrictions, calls the Commerce Department's export control office "hopelessly parochial and turf conscious." At the Commerce Department, Assistant Secretary William Archey says that the Pentagon should keep out of the matter, since "all they seem to do is sit around contemplating their navels, while companies lose sales."[13]

Eventually Congress must decide. The Export Control Act lapsed in 1984, and since then the authority to restrict exports rests on a presidential executive order. In 1985 the House and Senate were deadlocked on the bureaucratic issues: the House favored the Commerce Department, and the Senate favored the Customs Service. While the two branches fought it out, the Senate Investigations Subcommittee warned in its own report that the continuation of the turf war "can only mean less effective enforcement and the continued loss of important technology to potential adversaries."

RUNNING THE BUREAUCRACY

The officials who run the federal bureaucracy include the 1000 or so political executives appointed by the presidents, 3500 top-level officials who are in positions which by law may be offered to career officials or political appointees, 3500 other top career officials in the Senior Executive Service, middle managers in the civil service, and lower-level employees and temporary workers who implement the programs—the "line" workers.

Most political executives are appointed by the president with the advice and consent of the Senate. The most important are the thirteen department secretaries and the dozen or so agency directors (such as the director of the Central Intelligence Agency). They propose new programs and defend agency budgets in testimony before congressional committees, supervise the bureaus and coordinate their work with the work of other agencies and of state and local governments, and maintain good relations with interest groups. They are spokespersons for the administration, especially during a campaign season.[14]

The inner and outer circles. The top officials can be divided into two groups: the inner circle, which consults regularly with the president, and the outer circle, which rarely gets access. The inner circle includes the secretaries of defense, state, and the Treasury; the director of the CIA; and the national security adviser. Sometimes other officials, such as the attorney general, may be included. The president sees them individually on a weekly or even a daily basis or in small, informal group settings.

The outer circle consists of the "clientele departments" (Education, Commerce, Labor, and Agriculture), whose secretaries have close ties with interest groups affected by agency operations. They may have been appointed to satisfy these groups during an election campaign. Some owe as much allegiance to their constituencies as to the president. Their advice on issues other than those directly affecting their programs is not valued or sought by the president or the president's advisers. The White House staff usually protects the president from their requests for meetings, and they are confined to ceremonial occasions and rare formal Cabinet meetings. They see the president when the president finds fault with them or has to deny their budget requests. The president wants them to hew to the White House line, run their agencies without public controversy, and prevent lower-level officials from getting to Congress with requests for more money.

These secretaries usually mediate between the White House and their departments. Margaret Heckler, former secretary of health and human services in the Reagan administration, for example, was a moderate Republican congresswoman who once declared that she was "not a Reagan clone." Heckler's aides passed the word that her first allegiance was to her department. She tripled funding for research into the cause of AIDS, in spite of White House objections. She ended a crackdown on recipients of social security disability assistance which had been ordered by the White House. At the same time, she strongly stumped for Reagan in his reelection campaign and defended his program against the Democrats' charges of unfairness, thus temporarily retaining her political value to the administration.[15]

Sub-Cabinet officials. Below the secretaries are the 1000 or so deputy secretaries, under secretaries, assistant secretaries, and deputy assistant secretaries who staff the departments. They are appointed by the president with the consent of the Senate. Many of them are appointed on the recommendation of members of Congress or interest groups. In the past, these "nominations" have enabled the president to win political support but have made it more difficult

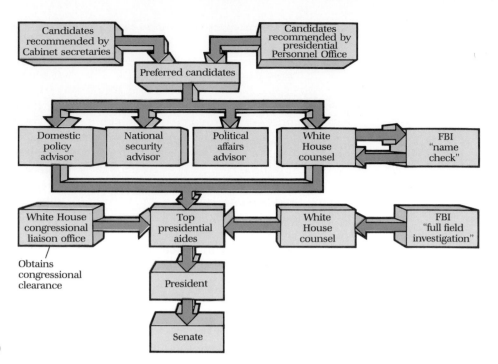

Figure 13-2. Appointments clearance process in the Reagan administration, July 1981. This flowchart shows the steps, from top to bottom, which were taken to make appointments in the first year of the Reagan administration. (Source: G. Calvin Mackenzie, "Cabinet and Subcabinet Personnel Selection in Reagan's First Year: New Variations on Some Not-So-Old Themes," APSA Annual Meeting, New York, City, September 1981.)

Within the figure:
- Candidates recommended by Cabinet secretaries
- Candidates recommended by presidential Personnel Office
- Preferred candidates
- Domestic policy advisor
- National security advisor
- Political affairs advisor
- White House counsel
- FBI "name check"
- White House congressional liaison office
- Obtains congressional clearance
- Top presidential aides
- White House counsel
- FBI "full field investigation"
- President
- Senate

for him to run the executive branch, since these officials have been "his" in name only. Figure 13-2 shows the appointment process during Reagan's first term.

The number two person is the deputy secretary. Most deputy secretaries come from large corporations, law firms, or financial institutions, rather than from public service. Below them are one or two under secretaries, who take charge of policy formulation, department administration, or some important matter given to them by the secretary or the president.

Below these officials are the assistant and deputy assistant secretaries in charge of the bureaus. They are responsible for implementing the presidential and departmental programs. In a sense they are caught in the middle: they must represent the president's program to the career officials and the interests of the bureaus to the White House. If they are too "presidential," the lower bureaucrats may circumvent or ignore them, leak their mistakes to the media, or isolate them. But if they champion the interests of the bureaucracy, the White House assumes that they have been "captured" by the bureaucracy or have "gone native," and it ignores or replaces them.

Most of these appointees come from business, finance, and the law; a few are from academia, labor, and nonprofit organizations. Often the president appoints people from agribusiness to the Agriculture Department, people from Wall Street to the Treasury Department, people from large corporations to the Commerce Department, people from unions to the Labor Department, and people involved in ranching, mining, or logging to the Interior Department. As is true of the judiciary, Democratic presidents are much more likely than Republican presidents to appoint minorities and women (though Reagan has appointed more women to Cabinet-level positions than any Democrat): 21 percent of Carter's appointees were from minority groups, and 22 percent were women; 7.6 percent of Reagan's appointees were from minority groups, and 14.3 percent were women.[16] These figures reflect each party's electoral coalition.

The typical department secretary keeps the job for two or three years, while assistant secretaries remain on average eighteen months. Many of these positions remain vacant for months at a time; in 1983 five departments lacked deputy secretaries and in 1985 many important slots for assistant secretary were not filled. The reason? Appointees have to move to Washington, where the costs of housing and education are high, and usually they take a substantial salary cut if they have come from business. Many would be precluded from returning to their old jobs if their government position involved distributing contracts. They must sell investments which might involve a conflict of interest and then take up the confirmation gauntlet in the United States Senate. It is not easy to get potential appointees—especially those at the peak of their careers—to come to Washington or stay under these circumstances.[17] Many political executives hardly have time to learn their jobs before they move on, which makes it more difficult for them to translate administration policy into bureaucratic performance. Lower-level officials simply outlast them.

Layering. Half a century ago presidents got along with few officials. There were ten Cabinet secretaries and forty to fifty assistant secretaries. They handled congressional relations and political matters (such as getting spoils for some local party leaders). Since then, departments have added layer upon layer of officials with new staff functions (budgeting, accounting, and auditing personnel; inspectors general to stop corruption; legal advisers; personnel managers; training and program evaluators; policy planners; public affairs personnel; and congressional liaisons, for example) and have expanded their programs. Figure 13-3 shows what has happened in the Labor Department.

A GOVERNMENT OF STRANGERS. Presidents cannot possibly know more than a few of these officials. They preside, according to Hugh Heclo, over a "government of strangers."[18] In fact, they may not even know their own secretaries; President Reagan, at a meeting of the U.S. Conference of Governors, said, "Hello, Mr. Mayor" to his own secretary of housing and urban development, Samuel Pierce, seeming not to recognize him until he had been briefed by his aides. The secretaries do not know the president, other members of the Cabinet, or their own subordinates very well. "A secretary rarely gets to pick his own deputy, and so the two men are often at the disadvantage of being absolute strangers before they begin working together," according to Robert Wood, a former deputy secretary.[19]

Most political executives have never held elective office or worked in party politics. They are corporate executives, lawyers, investment bankers, academics, trade association lobbyists, or state or local officials. They usually have little knowledge of, or patience with, the ins and outs of legislative politics.

CENTRALIZING WHITE HOUSE CONTROLS. Because they have no public following, political executives are not able to challenge increasing centralization by the White House. "The typical cabinet officer's immediate superior is one or more members of the White House staff," says Joseph Barlett, a former undersecretary of commerce.[20] They must carry out presidential policies and the orders of White House aides and directors of presidential agencies. In recent years the influence of the White House has increased, in part because of a computerized executive data link system, which connects several hundred top officials with one another and with the White House. Speeches, congressional testimony, and policy proposals can all be monitored by presidential aides.

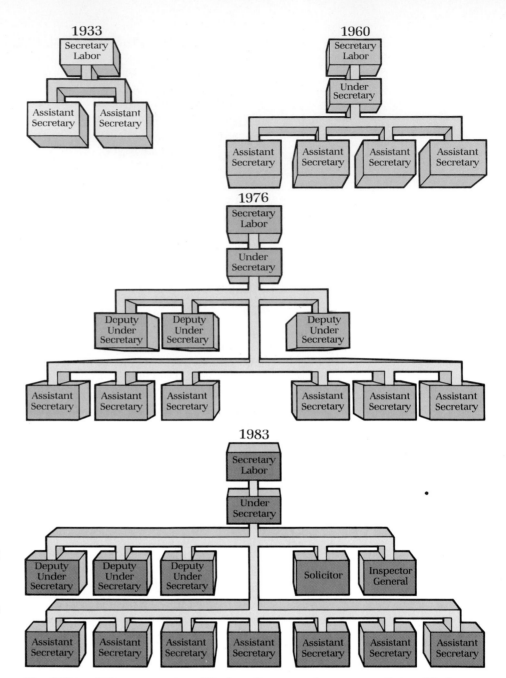

Figure 13-3. Political executives in the Labor Department. Between 1933 and 1983, the number of assistant secretaries increased from two to seven, and two supervisory layers were added between the secretary and the assistant secretaries. (Source: *U.S. Government Organization Manual,* 1984.)

The Office of Management and Budget, for example, can negotiate with departments on budgets, spending totals, and proposed congressional testimony, taking half an hour to communicate by electronic mail; this used to take days and require formal meetings. The assistant secretaries for management, congressional liaison, and budgeting are all plugged into the new network.[21] If differences with presidential aides are irreconcilable, officials resign. They do so quietly and with little fanfare, citing personal reasons, to keep their reputations for being discreet, to avoid being labeled troublemakers, and to stay in line for other assignments in the future.[22]

The Senior Executive Service

Below the political executives are the 7000 officials in the *Senior Executive Service* (SES) and the 1500 top-ranking officials in the State Department and its related agencies. Most are career civil servants, though by law 10 percent of the SES positions (and all the top foreign affairs slots) may be filled with political appointees.[23] The SES was created in 1978 to make top-level civil servants more responsive to the administration; members are given greater responsibility and can get pay increases and bonuses on the basis of superior performance. But they give up some of the protection of the civil service system: it is easier for their superiors to transfer them or put them in less important positions, to demote them back to the civil service, or even to fire them. Reagan has filled 850 SES posts with his own political executives: political appointees now operate at lower levels in the bureaucracy than ever before. Meanwhile, the Office of Personnel Management began awarding pay raises on the basis of performance appraisals in the other services in order to make lower-level officials more responsive to the White House.

Critics of the SES contend that it fosters favoritism, politics, and slavish adherence to the administration by civil servants angling for more pay. Supporters say that it gives the president more flexibility, creates a more responsive bureaucracy, and makes for better relations between political executives and senior civil servants.

The civil service and other services

More than 99.8 percent of all government employees are in the government services: the Postal Service employs almost half a million people; the technical and professional services (such as the Foreign Service, the Public Health Service, and the Forest Service) have about 100,000 workers; and there are 1.2 million employees of the General Service (GS), which staffs most federal departments and agencies. The total civilian federal work force numbered about 2.6 million in 1985, down 75,000 since 1981.

Grade levels. Civil servants are nonpartisan employees who get their jobs on the basis of competitive entrance examinations and personal interviews. Skilled positions are competitive: there are more than twenty applications for each high-level administrative and professional job and more than thirty applications for middle-management positions for every available opening. Employees are given grades on the basis of education, experience, and responsibilities.

Emergency relief is directed to victims of flooding in Kentucky. (*Department of Housing and Urban Development.*)

There are eighteen grades: GS 1 to GS 5 (clerical and office workers), GS 6 to GS 11 (more skilled office workers and newly hired managers), GS 12 to GS 15 (experienced managers and technical and scientific employees), and GS 16 to GS 18 (the very top officials covered by civil service protections, most of whom have left to join the SES, with its higher pay and larger bonuses).

Merit systems. The premise of the *civil service* and other services is that recruitment, promotion, assignment, and pay are to be based on merit, not partisan politics. The Hatch Acts, passed by Congress, provide that officials may not contribute to political campaigns or work in them (these laws, originally designed to protect workers from pressure by political executives, have been weakened by the courts as workers have insisted on their right to participate in political campaigns). Officials cannot run for office and remain federal employees.

Their tenure in office is protected by an elaborate system of disciplinary hearings, agency appeals procedures, and finally systemwide hearings and appeals. Although civil service tenure was originally designed to protect officials against wholesale firing after a change of party in the White House, today its critics charge that it protects incompetent officials from being disciplined, demoted, or fired and that it lowers morale among good employees.

Size of the work force. In absolute numbers, the federal work force has expanded from 2.3 million employees in 1955 to 2.6 million in 1985 (Figure 13-4). But federal workers accounted for 37 percent of all government workers in 1955 and for just 16 percent in 1985 (state and local workers accounted for the rest), and as a proportion of the total civilian work force, they declined from a high of 3.8 percent in 1968 to 2.5 percent in 1985.

What accounts for the notion that big government is getting bigger? The pay scales and perquisites of federal employees have improved dramatically in the past two decades. Congress requires "pay comparability" with the private sector in order to attract a qualified work force. This provision has been interpreted generously, by comparing government pay scales with those of corporations paying the highest salaries. Although the federal work force has not expanded greatly because many programs are implemented by state and local governments or by organizations in the private sector, the number of state and

Figure 13-4. Growth of federal civilian employees, 1789–1986. The large upsurge in employment is accounted for by the Second World War. Since the end of the Korean War, federal employment has leveled off to the equivalent of about 2.1 million full-time workers. (Source: Office of Personnel Management.)

1789	350
1883	60,000
1945	3,400,000
1986	2,684,000

Not all federal office workers are paper-shufflers. Many, like this park ranger, work directly with the public. (*Richard Frear: National Park Service.*)

local government workers has increased greatly in recent years, and there are close to 6 million people in the private sector whose activities are funded by the national government. As the government takes on more functions and issues more regulations, the visibility of officials increases, and so we think that there must be more of them.

Unions and the civil service. Labor unions have been recognized for collective bargaining since President Kennedy signed an executive order in 1962. In 1978 Congress gave civil service workers (other than FBI, CIA, and military personnel) a statutory right to organize. Today more than ninety unions represent almost 60 percent of all federal workers. The biggest include the Postal Workers, the American Federation of Government Employees, the National Association of Government Employees, the Metal Trades and Machinists, and the National Treasury Employees Union. The Federal Labor Relations Authority conducts union elections and decides which bargaining units to recognize. A union may not organize a union shop (in which everyone must belong to the union in order to work), and so many people work under union contracts but

Federal employees have the right to organize and bargain collectively, but no right to strike. (*John Ficara: Woodfin Camp.*)

are not union members—only about 35 percent of workers covered under union contacts actually *belong* to the unions that represent them. Unions sometimes get involved in policy-making. They have brought court cases against officials in the Nixon and Reagan administrations who tried to cut funding for agencies below levels set by Congress or even to dismantle them when Congress had authorized them to keep operating.[24]

Managers and policy-making. Civil servants usually begin and end their careers in government, working for only one or two agencies. Top managers average twenty years of service by the time they are put in charge of programs of bureaus. They identify strongly with the goals and missions of their units. They fight to maintain programs that their superiors want to modify or eliminate. They put their bureaucratic and career interests ahead of the interests of the current administration. They tend to discount the priorities of the "two-year wonders" who show up as assistant secretaries through what seems to be a revolving door. They do not take kindly to directives instructing them that, for the good of a president who may serve for only four years, they should sacrifice programs for which they have worked all their lives.

So in dealing with political executives, civil servants engage in "education from below." Instead of stating flatly that they will not carry out orders, they present their superiors with unpleasant alternatives; for example, if budget cuts are instituted, essential services must be cut, or if procedures are changed, constituencies will be inconvenienced. Most activities have been created by statute, and career civil servants may inform their superior that, much as they would like to institute the administration's policies, it would be illegal to do so. They force their superiors to confront reality: bureaucracies usually provide services which Congress has mandated and which the public wants, and one cannot simply modify or cut services without incurring political costs.

These tactics do not always work. When William B. Reynolds took over as head of the Justice Department's Civil Rights Division, he instructed it to oppose busing for desegregation of public schools and also to oppose affirmative action to end job discrimination, and he started to negotiate with, rather than litigate against, mental hospitals and prisons that were accused of violating civil rights. The staff lawyers opposed his new policies but were unable to slow him down or change his approach; instead, sixteen of the eighteen staff lawyers resigned.

The line employees

The line workers who implement programs and deal with the public also can affect policy. Their operations are at a level where supervision is minimal and their discretion is high. Their own values, priorities, and ways of working may determine what actually gets done (or what does not get done, as the case may be). At some airports flight controllers follow all safety rules, while at others they bend the rules so that more flights can be scheduled. Agricultural extension agents choose which farmers to assist in their communities; often they work with the more prosperous ones and let the others continue to use obsolete methods until eventually they leave their land. Lawyers for the poor can concentrate on individual cases (which are the least controversial) and build up local connections before leaving government service for private practice, or they can adopt more militant tactics in representing the poor. During the Vietnamese war some local draft boards made it hard for conscientious objectors, while others gave them deferments or exemptions.

Employees who disagree with the policies of their superiors can become *whistle-blowers:* they can photostat documents and leak them to the press or to congressional committee staffers. When corruption, cutbacks, or poor performance is at issue, the result may be a congressional investigation. Whistle-blowers have forced the resignation of many top officials, and Congress does what it can to shield them against reprisals by agency officials in order to protect its sources of information in the future. Lower-level officials in the Environmental Protection Agency, for example, circulated memos in 1983 detailing attempts by Reagan appointees to undercut full enforcement of laws concerning toxic-waste disposal; in the resulting furor, top officials had to resign, the agency was completely revamped, and the White House appointed a "Mr. Clean" to undo the damage.

CONTROLLING THE BUREAUCRACY

Most people believe that all national departments and agencies are part of the executive branch and that the president supervises them through a chain of command, as shown in Figure 13-5 (page 460).

The reality is quite different. To begin with, the Constitution makes no mention of an executive branch. When it mentions the "executive power" of the United States, it refers only to the president as a political officer with certain express and implied constitutional powers—some of which involve the departments. The Constitution does not prevent Congress or the judiciary from supervising national officials.

It is more accurate to think of a "fourth branch"—a separate bureaucratic establishment which is supervised by the other three branches. Thus presidents who enter office expecting to overhaul the work of the departments or to cut back on their functions find themselves checked and balanced by the courts and stalemated by Congress. The only way for the president and Congress to gain control of the bureaucracy over the long term is to cooperate. And that is easier said than done because of the decentralized nature of the parties, the diffusion of power, and the systems of checks and balances.

Congressional control

Historically, Congress has had the most influence on the departments. In fact, during most of the nineteenth century, the secretaries worked closely with the committee chairs. Most secretaries were politicians (and many had served in Congress), and so they knew how important it was to cultivate good congressional relations. Many had presidential ambitions and believed that the best way to advance was to get support from Congress. Woodrow Wilson made his academic reputation as a political scientist with *Congressional Government*, published in 1885, in which he showed how Cabinet secretaries were influenced by congressional leaders.[25] The president then was little more than a clerk, lacking control of the departments' budgets and legislative requests to Congress and with little power to make policies involving the departments. Figure 13-6 outlines this post-Civil War system of congressional government.

Today, Congress no longer dominates the departments, but it still has considerable powers.

Creation and reorganization. By laws, Congress creates and abolishes all departments, agencies, bureaus, and programs and specifies their exact organization. By joint resolution, it approves or vetoes plans for reorganization submitted by the president. It creates, defines, and limits all offices, and it

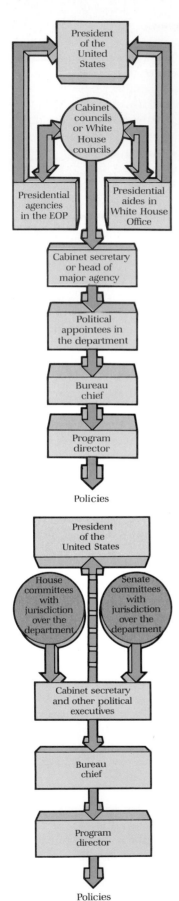

Figure 13-5. Left, above: The illusion of presidential government. Presidents and their advisors issue orders to cabinet secretaries, who transmit them to political executives, down through the chain of command to bureaucrats who implement them. In reality presidents transmit few direct orders this way, and there is no "chain of command" that can ensure that a president's orders or suggestions will always be carried out in a timely and responsive manner.

Figure 13-6. Left, below: Congressional government. In the nineteenth century Congress directed department business through laws and appropriations. Department secretaries reported to the president, who sent their budget and legislative requests directly to Congress. The main executive function of the president was to see that the laws were faithfully executed and to provide the patronage demanded by the party leaders.

specifies job qualifications. It determines grades and salaries and may set ceilings on how many officials can be hired and at what levels. It determines which positions are filled by political executives, SES officials, or lower-level civil service workers. It can determine travel allowances, expense accounts, office facilities and furnishings, and other "perks."

Appointment to office. The Senate must advise on and consent to presidential appointments of political executives. It may not directly attach conditions to its assent, nor can it require a nominee to promise to take certain actions. But informally it may gain reassurances from a nominee who is worried about rounding up a majority on the committee considering the nomination.

Senators "nominate" officials for positions affecting their states; these include regional and district personnel and federal judges, attorneys, and marshals. At times senators are given a veto by the administration. Senatorial courtesy enables the senator of a state affected by any nomination subject to Senate confirmation to declare that a prospective nominee is "personally obnoxious," in which case the Senate will hold up the nomination indefinitely.

Senate committees can put nominations on hold until the president or the president's nominee provides assurances on policy. They can cast a negative vote and refuse to send the nomination to the full Senate. The Senate can pass a resolution requesting the president to withdraw a nomination, or if necessary it can defeat the nomination on the floor.

The Senate usually does not block presidential appointments. Most investigations involve conflict of interest, divestiture of stocks and other investments before entering government service, or allegations against the character of a nominee. Many investigations are superficial, even when there is some evidence that a nominee has had unsavory business connections or links to organized crime. The Senate usually takes the position that presidents are entitled to have whomever they want in their administrations.

But there are some exceptions. A nominee whose background involves racial discrimination is in for rough sledding. Nominees who lack the background and skills necessary for the position may withdraw rather than face criticism, although some, especially those who are nominated for foreign affairs posts, promise the Senate that they will be "quick learners" if confirmed (one potential ambassador to Ceylon could not tell the Senate Foreign Affairs Committee the name of its capital, for example). A nominee who in a previous government position was abusive to senators may face defeat; for just such a reason Senator Clinton Anderson of New Mexico managed to clobber the Eisenhower administration when it nominated Lewis Strauss to be secretary of commerce. The word gets around that officials should be responsive and honest in dealing with legislators if they plan on serving in higher positions.

Most high federal positions require confirmation by the Senate. Theodore Sorensen (center), nominated by President Carter in 1977 to be director of the CIA, withdrew in the face of strong opposition, one of the few nominees for high office who failed to win quick backing from the Senate. (*AP/Wide World.*)

The Senate occasionally blocks a series of nominations to prevent the president from gaining control of an independent agency—especially if it believes that the president would use such control to dismember it. President Reagan made twenty-five nominations at various times for the Legal Services Corporation's eleven-member board of directors and was unable to get a single appointment past the Senate in his first term.

Nevertheless the president can sometimes evade senatorial checks by filling posts with temporary appointees when the Senate is in recess. Reagan used this strategy to make changes in the operation of the Legal Services Corporation. He made eleven appointments to its board while the Senate was in recess, filling the vacancies with people whom the Senate had previously refused to confirm!

Authorizations. Congress gives agency officials all their powers through various *statutory authorizations.* These are granted for one year, or several years, or they may be permanent. Usually they are accompanied by informal understandings between members of committees and agency officials as to how the agency will operate after it has been given its grant of power. Congress often places restrictions on these powers, specifying in detail what an agency may not do (for example, use federal funds for abortions or for school busing). It gives *conditional* authority: the president may reorganize agencies during wartime, for example, but these emergency powers end once the war is over. Congress also gives *contingent authority;* thus it may provide for extension of unemployment payments to jobless workers, but only if the unemployment rate in a state exceeds a specified percentage. It can give *standby authority,* which may later be triggered by a presidential certification or by a congressional resolution (standby wage and price controls in case of runaway inflation are an example). It provides for *concurrences:* agencies cannot act until they receive approval from a state or local government or from interest groups.

These authorizations may be delegated to the president, who in turn

Officials in regulatory agencies are particularly vulnerable to charges of conflicts of interest. Anne Burford stepped down as head of the Environmental Protection Administration because of such a controversy. (*Sebastian: Sygma.*)

subdelegates them to departments and agencies; this gives the president the most power to direct the bureaucracy. Alternatively, Congress may delegate power directly to lower-level officials, specifying what they are to do and how they are to do it—a sign that the president is not expected to interfere. A president who does interfere may be checked by the courts.

Oversight. Congress can examine how agencies are implementing the laws through ***legislative oversight.*** It may hold investigations and public hearings, which can turn the spotlight on corruption, conflicts of interest, and lack of enforcement. It can force the resignation of high-ranking officials and changes in agency procedures, and it can recommend new laws to restrict an agency. The General Accounting Office audits agencies and can disallow unlawful expenditures.

Members' inquiries. Representatives or senators can ask agencies to help their constituents. In addition, they pressure agencies to institute special programs, often going through the White House and presidential agencies. Senator Al D'Amato, a Republican from New York, earned a reputation for being "tough on crime" by getting the Reagan administration to assign thirty-eight agents from the Drug Enforcement Administration to New York and its "operation pressure point" program, aimed at ridding the Lower East Side of drug pushers.

The legislative veto. Until 1983 Congress could also impose a legislative veto: one or both chambers of Congress, or even one of its committees, could by law "veto" a proposed decision of an agency. For example, Congress could pass a law allowing the secretary of defense to close down military bases—unless his decision was "vetoed" by the Armed Services Committee. Such vetoes could be used in connection with sales of arms and nuclear reactors to foreign nations, the construction of atomic reactors, presidential states of emergency, impoundments of funds, presidential requests for reorganization, and about 200 other matters. The Supreme Court in 1983 ruled these legislative vetoes to be unconstitutional violations of the separation of powers because they allowed Congress to interfere in administrative actions. Moreover, the Court argued that these vetoes constituted "acts of Congress," which under the Constitution should have been taken by both chambers and sent to the *president* for approval or veto.[26] Congress now uses a *joint* resolution when it vetoes an agency action, which is then sent to the president for approval or veto, thus attempting to meet the objections of the Court.

Sunshine and secrecy. Congress regulates disclosure of information. It can provide criminal penalties for disclosure and transmission, as it does with military and atomic secrets. Its "sunshine laws" may require agencies to conduct open meetings, give greater access to government files (the Freedom of Information Act), and regulate the government's computer files. Loopholes allow agencies to protect information about "ongoing operations" or "pending decisions." Critics charge that these acts have been ineffective because government agencies are reluctant to comply with them. Defenders argue that many of the requests would damage government operations or result in the disclosure of valuable private trade secrets.

Presidential control

Early in our history, presidents presided as figureheads over the departments, compiling their reports and budget requests and transmitting them to Congress for action. But in the twentieth century presidents have become chief executives whose aides and agencies attempt, often with success, to supervise the bureaucracy.

Nominations. Presidents nominate all political executives in departments, in executive agencies, and even in the independent agencies and corporations. Each year one-fourth of these positions open up (closer to half of sub-Cabinet positions in executive agencies), and so presidents have regular opportunities to make policy through appointments.

Removals. Presidents have the power to remove executive agency appointees. Most of the time they need not resort to this power: they can usually arrange a "negotiated departure" instead of firing someone. They may even request undated letters of resignation as a condition of an initial appointment, or they may request such letters later (as Lincoln did during the Civil War with his entire Cabinet). Presidents' aides can leak stories to the press that the White House would like an official to resign. By law, presidents, their Office of Personnel Management, and their appointees may promote, transfer, demote,

Policies on civil rights changed dramatically after President Reagan appointed Clarence M. Pendleton, Jr., to chair the Civil Rights Commission in 1981. (*U.S. Commission on Civil Rights.*)

THE PRESIDENTIAL REMOVAL POWER

The presidential removal power is not directly specified by the Constitution. Presidents have claimed it on the basis of the executive power, their oath of office, and their duty to see that the laws are faithfully executed. James Madison, while serving in the first Congress, argued that separation of powers required the president to be able to remove officials; otherwise, the president's responsibility for executing the laws according to the Constitution could not be fixed. Madison believed that a president who had this power would be more, not less, accountable to Congress.

During the nineteenth century Congress claimed the power as its own. After Andrew Jackson fired William Duane, the secretary of the Treasury, the reaction against "King Andrew" was so strong that it led to the formation of the opposition Whig Party and a motion of censure against the president. After the Civil War, Congress passed tenure-of-office acts that prevented the president from removing top officials until the Senate had consented to their successors—in effect giving the Senate the final say on removals. The House voted to impeach Andrew Johnson after he removed Edwin Stanton, the secretary of war, in violation of this law.

The issue between presidents and Congress simmered for another sixty years. Congress eventually modified and later repealed the tenure-of-office laws for high-level officials, but kept some protections for lower-level civil servants, who went to court to get damages when removed by presidents. The issue was finally settled by the Supreme Court in two key decisions. In 1926, in *Myers v. United States*, Chief Justice (and former president) William Taft ruled for the majority that Congress could not by law restrict the president's power to remove officials whom the president had appointed. This sweeping decision was modified in 1935, in *Humphrey's Executor v. United States*, in which the Court ruled that the president's power to remove officials could be limited by Congress in the case of "administrative agencies" which issued "quasi-legislative" rules or made "quasi-judicial" decisions in cases involving administrative law. These agencies include all the independent regulatory commissions; other agencies, such as the Federal Reserve Board; and most independent government corporations.

---

or even fire officials in the Senior Executive Service. By the end of their first year in office, presidents can have senior officials working for them who are responsive to their wishes.

Policy direction. Presidents construe the executive power of the United States and their duty to see that the laws are faithfully executed to mean that department offficials are their subordinates who must obey their orders. As President Franklin Roosevelt put it in a 1939 report on administrative reform, "The Presidency was established as a single strong Chief Executive Office in which was vested the entire executive power of the National Government."[27] Congress argues that officials must obey the laws of the United States and therefore are also subordinate to Congress. The federal courts, refereeing this conflict, distinguish between routine *ministerial duties*, which involve no discretion, and *executive duties*, which involve discretion and political judgments. The courts agree that Congress may by law direct officials to perform ministerial duties, and they will enforce these laws even if the president has issued orders to the contrary. But the president may issue orders involving executive duties. The upshot is that both Congress and the president may direct officials, but in different ways, and the boundary lines remain unclear and subject to judicial resolution on a case-by-case basis.

Presidential agencies. Presidents cannot take the time to supervise officials personally; they must rely on White House aides, presidential agencies, department executives, and SES officials, layers which stand between them and the bureaucrats and which make it difficult for them to understand what the bureaucrats want, and vice versa.

What presidents cannot do personally their agencies may do for them. Aides in the White House Office may take on functions which involve them in the work of departments, as when they negotiate directly with a foreign government or a governor. Or they may act as "fire fighters," resolving an issue that has generated bad publicity. They may also be coordinators, heading off impasses between departments, smoothing personal relations, and suggesting compromises.

The Office of Management and Budget (OMB), whose director is also a presidential assistant, helps supervise the bureaucracy. All department legislative proposals since the 1940s and all agency regulations since 1981 have had to be submitted to the OMB for clearance: the president then decides whether they are to be part of the program, can stand on their own, or are to be shelved. All budget requests similarly go to the OMB. Bills passed by Congress go to the OMB (which recommends signature or veto) for review before being sent to the president.

The OMB's Management Division tries to get agencies to introduce new management and budgeting methods. These attempts are not usually effective, since departments often resist innovations. A special unit, the Management Reform Task Force, is in charge of instituting "Reform 88," a special effort to upgrade the way departments manage themselves. The OMB is more successful with spending controls: its Budget Division can order reprogramming of funds within an agency or even a transfer of money from one activity to another, crossing agency lines. Usually these transfers receive informal approval or veto from congressional committees with jurisdiction. Proposed executive agency regulations are sent to the OMB's Division of Information and Regulatory Affairs for cost-benefit analysis and for confirmation that they conform to the presidential program of regulatory reform. During Reagan's first three years in office, the administration's special Task Force on Regulatory Relief, chaired by Vice President Bush, reviewed 6700 existing regulations and got agencies to withdraw 3 percent of them, claiming savings for consumers and companies of more than $150 billion in the next ten years. The OMB's Division of Federal Procurement Policy recommends ways of cutting procurement costs, which are far higher than procurement costs in the private sector.

The Office of Personnel Management (OPM) recommends changes in pay and benefits (increases or decreases) and supervises agency recruitment, training, promotion, and other personnel practices. It prods agencies into meeting presidential targets for reductions in the federal work force.

Presidential policy agencies and councils—such as the National Security Council, the Council of Economic Advisors, the Council on Environmental Quality, and the various Cabinet councils—are also involved with departmental operations. They are supposed to set overall policy and to coordinate agency activities and media relations. They try to control sub-Cabinet appointments to agencies, putting their loyalists in control, and they also try to influence transfers and promotions in the SES and to establish "clearance" procedures to dominate departmental legislative and budget requests. Needless to say, they come into conflict with department secretaries.

For the White House, the resulting friction (and even the chaos) is useful: it allows presidents to make choices. They can side either with a department secretary or with the head of a presidential agency or council. Thus presidents do nothing to prevent, and often they encourage, these conflicts, and some have become Washington institutions: the secretary of the treasury versus the chair of the Council of Economic Advisors; the secretary of state versus the presidential assistant for national security affairs; the president's science adviser versus NASA; and the White House Domestic Council versus the secretary of health and human resources and the secretary of education.

Rewarding and punishing agencies. Formal powers are used by presidents and White House officials to reward or punish agencies. An agency which the president wants to boost is reorganized into a larger unit and is given more responsibilities (the new Department of Education in the Carter administration, for example). The president encourages new proposals and larger budget requests for the agency; it becomes the lead agency in interdepartmental councils and task forces, and with White House backing it coordinates other agencies. The White House may tie its own political fortunes to the agency's programs, in which case the presidential aides will handle public relations for the agency.

An agency that is marked for retrenchment, extinction, or scapegoating for the failure of a preceding administration is given different treatment—the Occupational Safety and Health Administration in the Reagan administration is an example. The president appointed officials who were hostile to the agency's mission, and they assigned SES managers who cut back on its activities and powers of enforcement; the number of inspectors was reduced, and voluntary compliance programs were instituted instead of legal actions. The results: In 1982 there were only eighteen fines of more than $10,000 whereas in 1980 there had been ninety-eight, and the number of fines over $5000 dropped from 600 to fewer than 25. Vulnerable agencies also find that their budget requests are slashed, that their quarterly allotments are reduced by the OMB, and that their personnel ceilings are lowered by the OPM. An agency may even be ordered to shut down its operations in anticipation of a presidential request to Congress—although until Congress acts, the courts will require that the agency remain open.

Bureau autonomy and professional standards

Bureaus may win autonomy by claiming that professional standards must control their activities. These may involve formal arrangements which include:

- The requirement that top officials have certain professional qualifications or experience
- A fixed term for an agency or program director
- A professional service, like the Foreign Service, the Forest Service, or the Public Health Service, with its own code of ethics and professional standards

Some of these arrangements make a professional association or interest group, such as the American Bar Association (ABA) or the American Medical Assocation (AMA), the arbiter of what constitutes professional conduct in the bureaucracy. This enables career officials to balance presidential or congressional directives with the claim that to obey would compromise them professionally. Thus antipoverty lawyers argue that to prevent them from representing the poor in cases involving divorce or abortion would violate the ABA Canons of Professional Ethics, since the poor are entitled to be represented in all legal matters. The AMA argues that its codes of professional conduct should take precedence over federal regulations aimed at limiting the kind of medical care that Medicare or Medicaid patients may receive.

CLOSE-UP

J. EDGAR HOOVER AND THE FBI. "In politics you do not attack Santa Claus and you do not attack God," one senator said, by way of explaining how J. Edgar Hoover escaped congressional criticism for his administration of the Federal Bureau of Investigation. For forty-eight years Hoover was its director, and he kept it virtually immune from effective control by the White House or Congress. Dean Rusk, secretary of state during the Kennedy and Johnson administrations, observed that "he had created a kind of kingdom . . . almost unparalleled in the administration branch of our Government, a combination of professional performance on the job, some element of fear, very astute relations with Congress, and very effective public relations."[28]

Hoover was the consummate bureau chief, concerned with professional performance rather than partisan politics, and he took the directorship in 1924 only after informing Attorney General Harlan Stone that all appointments within his agency would be based on merit. During the 1930s the FBI concentrated on arresting gangsters, such as John Dillinger and "Machine Gun" Kelly. During World War II it was responsible for counterespionage. It has always done effective work in investigating bank robberies, automobile theft, and kidnappings. Critics point out, however, that the FBI was slow to develop effective techniques against organized crime, had a poor record in civil rights enforcement, and violated the civil liberties of many individuals and organizations through programs of domestic surveillance and mail interception.

Hoover's power rested partly on fear. Few people dared to speak out against FBI abuses; because of Hoover's information networks, his informers, and his powers of surveillance, he had information about the private lives of too many people in Washington. But he also cultivated members of Congress, especially those in the conservative wing. Criticism of the FBI would lead them to counterattack. Finally, Hoover was a master of public relations. Public opinion polls gave him and the FBI overwhelming support: in 1971 a Gallup poll showed that 80 percent of the public rated his work as good or excellent. Hoover's personal popularity helped the bu-

J. Edgar Hoover (seated).
(*Bettmann Archive.*)

reau. The House Appropriations Committee always gave him all the money he asked for and sometimes more, while the Senate Appropriations Committee approved these requests without even asking him to testify.

When Robert Kennedy, Hoover's nominal superior as attorney general, showed up one day at the Justice Department building without a pass, the guard refused to let him in, remarking, "I don't care if you're J. Edgar Hoover himself, you don't get in." That gives some indication of how Hoover was regarded in Washington. When he reached the mandatory retirement age of 70, President Johnson waived it, telling him, "The nation cannot afford to lose you." Nixon also asked Hoover to remain in office. Only the Kennedy administration tried to bring the director under control. Robert Kennedy insisted on approving Hoover's public speeches, communicated directly with FBI field offices without going through the director, and forced the agency to protect civil rights demonstrators. But the problems Hoover had with the Kennedys were unusual. For the most part, Hoover was untouchable—the most powerful bureau chief that Washington has ever known.[29]

Judicial control

The federal courts can also control officials. They provide access to government employees unions, interest groups, state and local governments, and other interested parties who seek to have agencies comply with the Constitution and the laws. The courts can declare an agency's actions to be unconstitutional or illegal, and they can also interpret the laws to define their powers. They also ensure that agencies operate according to due process of law.

Adhering to procedures. The courts make agency officials act in conformity to procedures already established by the agency itself; thus bureaucrats cannot change their own rules in midstream simply because the rules are inconvenient. In 1984, for example, the Interior Department settled a lawsuit brought by environmentalists charging that it was disregarding its own rules by failing to enforce regulations requiring strip-mining companies to restore land to its original contours. The courts also require officials to follow procedures mandated by Congress. After Congress passed a law requiring the Department of Transportation to consider safety data in making a decision about whether to require air bags in cars, the department used a different approach: it weighed the costs of the bags against the total number of lives which might be saved and concluded that requiring air bags would cost too much. An insurance company sued the department, arguing that Congress wanted not a cost-benefit analysis, but only a safety-risk analysis; the Supreme Court required the department to reverse its decision.[30]

Upholding the laws. The judiciary requires agencies to conform to laws. When Congress directs or prohibits something, it must be obeyed. What Congress appropriates must be spent. Thus federal district judges in 1984 required the Legal Services Corporation to spend money which its board of directors had attempted to withhold. Sometimes Congress gives people **entitlements:** the rights to receive something from the government, such as welfare or unemployment checks, medical care, access to transportation for the disabled, and bilingual education for linguistic minorities. Such people can go into the federal courts if their entitlements are reduced or taken away. The Labor Department spent only $25 million of $123 million in job-training funds which Congress appropriated for workers who had been laid off because of foreign competition; the United Auto Workers sued the department, and a federal judge ordered that the full amount be spent. In another case, a federal judge described the Department of Health and Human Services as "a heartless and indifferent bureaucratic monster destroying the lives of disabled citizens" in a decision ordering the department to end procedures denying certain disabled people social security benefits mandated by Congress. In the 30,000 or so disability cases heard in the federal courts in Reagan's first term, the reversal rate against the department was 49 percent.[31]

BUREAUCRACIES AND THEIR ALLIES

Bureaucrats deal with the political branches by playing them off against one another and by looking for allies among the groups and clienteles they serve; these activities have consequences for policy-making and policy implementation.

The iron triangle

The classic description of bureaucratic alliance building is the **iron triangle,** also known as the *subgovernment* or the *triple alliance* in political science literature (Figure 13-7): it refers to the relationships between top-level agency officials, lobbyists for a group that the agency serves, and congressional committee leaders with jurisdiction. The triangle may exist at the departmental, bureau, or program level.[32]

Agency officials consult with lobbyists on new legislation, budget submissions, reorganization plans, personnel matters, and proposed regulations. Such consultation is often formalized in group membership on an agency advisory committee. Often industry representatives are named by the president to administer an agency or are put in sub-Cabinet positions in the departments. In return, the bureau expects the interest group to endorse its work in congressional testimony and in the media.[33]

Bureaucrats and lobbyists work closely with congressional committees and subcommittees. They provide services for constituents, assist staffers in preparing for hearings (even going so far as to tell them the questions that legislators will ask), and offer amendments to bills which a committee may adopt. In return for being so solicitous of the committee's interests, they hope that the committee will champion their budgets and authorizations before the entire Congress and protect them from White House cuts.

The iron triangles maintain themselves because of the close professional relationships of the participants: lobbyists and top bureaucrats may work together for twenty years or more. By helping reelect allies in Congress and by getting sympathetic newcomers on committees, the PACs behind the lobbyists also reinforce the system. PACs also try to influence committee and party leaders to appoint sympathetic newcomers so that the triangle will perpetuate itself.

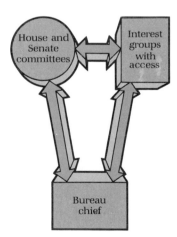

Figure 13-7. The iron triangle. The iron triangle or "subgovernment" consists of a bureau chief or program director who works closely with House and Senate committee leaders and their key staffers, as well as with the Washington lobbyists for interest groups affected by their operations. There are hundreds of such subgovernments in Washington.

Examples of iron triangles. The Department of Agriculture was established because of farm organizations, which permeate its bureaus and work closely with subcommittees of the two agriculture committees. The Interior Department works with ranchers, farmers who need irrigation on dry western lands, and forestry and mining companies. The Nuclear Regulatory Commission maintains close ties with nuclear plant operators, especially on matters of plant shutdowns. The Public Health Service, the maritime unions, and the House Merchant Marine and Fisheries Committee protect hospitals that benefit members of the merchant marine. The United Mine Workers, the Labor Department, and the House Education and Labor Committee protect the black-lung program from proposed cuts by the OMB.

Iron triangles and policy formulation. Iron triangles provide continuity in policy-making. They have expertise and technical skills that political appointees can rarely match. They give groups access to government decision making and implementation, a load-sharing device which takes some of the burden off presidents in times of crises, especially when they are preoccupied with foreign affairs or the economy. During the Civil War, for example, while Lincoln dealt with the secession, the iron triangles revamped banking and the currency, land use, and the agricultural policies of the nation; one result was the creation of the land-grant colleges, which are now the great southern and midwestern state universities.

But iron triangles have their disadvantages. Continuity is not always good. Sometimes the people vote for innovation and new policies. Then the president will be frustrated by these alliances, and presidential rhetoric will not be matched by accomplishment, which further erodes public support of the government. Iron triangles lead to corruption and conflicts of interest. Many political appointees, members of the SES, and top civil servants intend to leave government service and go into the private sector. They may decide to arrange a "soft landing" by taking actions favorable to the industries they are supposed to regulate. They may give contracts for research to the "beltway bandits" (the research firms that line the beltway surrounding the capital) and then join these same outfits later.

Iron triangles are created either to get things from the government or to get the government out of their business. Lax regulation enables interest groups to cut their costs in such areas as environmental protection and health and safety regulations. Iron triangles reinforce private-sector dependence on government largesse, which in turn prevents the free market from disciplining inefficient businesses or superfluous nonprofit organizations. They substitute political influence for market competition in allocating resources. They wheedle contracts for goods and services, research and development, and capital construction, which the government may not need. They obtain subsidies, guaranteed and below-market-rate loans, and tax expenditures. They get regulations which freeze out competitors and just about guarantee them a profit. They substitute connections and influence for the impartial administration of the law.[34] And as one group or industry establishes such an arrangement and distorts the operation of market forces, others must also do so in order to survive.

Finally, iron triangles guarantee some groups access and preferences at the expense of others. Wealthier family farmers and agribusiness dominate the Department of Agriculture, while poorer farmers—tenants and sharecroppers—have less access to services and are forced off the land. Environmentalists get frozen out of policy-making in the Interior Department, which favor companies doing business on public lands under the theory of multiple use. The iron-triangle system penalizes groups that are unorganized (the poor), have organized late (consumers and environmentalists), have innovative ways of doing business, or are more concerned with broader public policy than with their own immediate economic interests. It benefits members of groups, especially corporate and trade associations, which establish PACs and make campaign contributions; which hire the best public relations, lobbying, and law firms; and which know the ins and outs of Washington politics.

Issue networks

Sometimes iron triangles are superseded by *issue networks:* more complex but somewhat looser networks of relationships between bureaucrats, journalists, academics, foundation officers, White House and congressional staffers, lobbyists, and others who represent interest groups.[35] They think about issues in a broader context and are interested in rational problem solving, efficient allocation of resources, and the use of new decision-making techniques. They are professionals who get satisfaction from influencing policy, exercising power, and enjoying the respect of their peers, and they are less interested in bureaucratic empire building, lobbying for the benefit of a particular industry, or their own personal economic gain. They concentrate on innovative policies or major redistributions of wealth rather than on narrow regulatory or distributive outcomes. A distinction made in Chapter 6 about party professionals applies here: participants in iron triangles live *off* politics (in the sense that they are involved for the purpose of making an economic gain, establishing bureaucratic careers, or winning reelection), while participants in issue networks live *for* politics (because they measure their success in terms of policy influence).

Examples of issue networks. The difference between iron triangles and issue networks is best explained by an example. Agricultural policy has traditionally been dominated by iron triangles consisting of bureaus in the Agriculture Department, subcommittees organized around particular crops in the Agriculture Committee, and the national farmers' organizations. Their goals have been to dominate decision making in the department, obtain funds for their organizations, and get higher income for farmers. Contrast this alliance with the issue network devoted to feeding malnourished Americans: foundations have awarded several "think tank" grants to groups such as the Food Research and Action Center to find out how many people in this country are going hungry and why; the Senate Select Committee on Nutrition was created after a national agenda campaign to make hunger a major issue; and Congress is pressured by Bread for the World and the Child Nutrition Forum (two citizens' lobbies) to stop cuts in food programs for the poor. Various antipoverty agencies, legal services lawyers, local community groups, and others involved in the National Anti-Hunger Coalition have gone into the federal courts to obtain orders making it easier for people to obtain food stamps and other government assistance.

Usually issue networks must contend with entrenched iron triangles. This is the case when defense analysts attack procurement decisions that benefit specific companies, when environmentalists concerned about acid rain are opposed by congressional spokespersons for "smokestack industries," and when transportation safety experts and insurance companies square off against automobile manufacturers over the issue of air bags and seat belts.

The work of the issue network involves policy analysis, national agenda politics, and the formation of broad citizen coalitions to pressure Congress; in

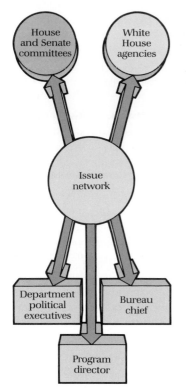

Figure 13-8. The issue network and executive agencies. Members of an issue network may join together in a coalition to influence government policy at the program, bureau, or department level; or they may bypass the bureaucracy and try to influence congressional committees or the White House.

contrast, the iron triangles have fewer participants, eschew publicity, and focus on economic benefits for the producers and campaign contributions to sympathetic members of Congress (Figure 13-8).

Network activism. Networks form when some of the people concerned about an issue realize that they have similar points of view and use similar methods of analysis. They may have communicated at academic conferences or in national commissions or task forces, or they may have read one another's books and articles. They may even be linked together by computer networks formed to study and exchange views on issues. Eventually they may try to influence policy. Their strategy is threefold: to convince the White House and Congress that their analysis is correct; to get the president to name a key member of the network to a high position, who in turn can bring others into sensitive posts; and to win over the presidential advisory system and obtain a mandate from the president to control the resolution of the issue.

USING THE MEDIA. Issue networks gain much of their strength through their effective use of the media. They try to isolate, discredit, and eventually remove their opponents from the administration. They may leak government documents and information about agency plans to favored reporters, who in effect become publicists for them. Well-timed and well-publicized op-ed articles in newspapers, research reports, articles, books, interviews on the Sunday television talk shows, and congressional testimony can discredit their opponents.

GOVERNMENTS IN EXILE. Think tanks and private research institutes—such as the conservative American Enterprise Institute, Heritage Foundation, and Hoover Institution; the centrist Brookings Institution; and the radical Institute for Policy Studies—have resident scholars who follow and analyze public policy. Many are former officials who left office after a change of control in the White House. Loose networks of these former officials and others in law firms or universities constitute a kind of "government in exile" whose members are available for high government positions after a change of party control of the White House. Often presidents make policy by deciding on the "crowd" they intend to tap for their administrations.

RATIONAL DECISION MAKING. Issue networks emphasize rational decision making based on all the relevant data. Consider the 1984 decision by the Department of Transportation to speed up the passage of rules banning lead from gasoline. Traditional iron-triangle politics would have involved delays, exemptions, and loopholes favoring the refiners of leaded gasoline. Yet even within the Reagan administration, dedicated to deregulation, the evidence that leaded gasoline was causing irreparable damage to children (especially inner-city youngsters) proved compelling, and that evidence was gathered and evaluated through an issue network devoted to the relationship between the environment and transportation policy.

PRESIDENTIAL OPTIONS. While iron triangles tend to frustrate presidents, limit their options, and slow down change, the issue networks have the reverse effect. All presidents find themselves caught in the middle of conflicts between different networks: supply-siders versus fiscal conservatives in economic policy; hawks versus doves on arms control; and advocates of nuclear energy versus advocates of coal and oil in energy policy. Often the media coverage, fueled by the leaks of sensitive documents from competing issue networks, gives the impression of an administration in disarray. But in fact the competition between different issue networks is good for the president. It brings more participants and a wider range of views before the public and the administration. It provides a constant launching of trial balloons, enabling the president to gauge public opinion. It allows participants to "get out in front" of the White House, bring the public and Congress around, and then get the president to "sign on" and support their plans. It enables groups which are weak politically to win arguments through the force of their ideas. It serves as an antidote for entrenched bureaucratic interests, secrecy, and political privilege.

Presidents encourage conflict between issue networks because it gives them information and options. It makes each network dependent on the White House for a final resolution. Presidents often organize their staffs and agencies in such a way as to encourage the networks to have it out with one another. One may control the Council of Economic Advisors, but it will be balanced by another which dominates the Treasury. One may control the disarmament agency, but another will be in charge at the State Department. Presidents act as magistrates: they listen to the arguments, gauge public opinion, canvass Congress and their advisers, and then make a final decision on policy.

PROBLEMS WITH THE BUREAUCRACY

There are two important problems with the federal bureaucracy: erosion of authority and lack of accountability.

Authority

Officials in government agencies do not always know what they are doing. They usually work with incomplete, inaccurate, and out-of-date information. Their planning and budgeting systems are poorly designed and often yield ludicrous results which even the bureaucrats ignore as useless. Sometimes they operate on the basis of controversial and unproven theories: in the 1960s this was the case with the liberal antipoverty programs, and in the 1980s it has been true of the conservative programs aimed at stopping crime, drug use, and pregnancy among teenagers. The program evaluations of officials in government agencies are often self-serving.

Most government agencies do not handle routine management functions well. Their financial control systems (accounting, bookkeeping, and auditing) are antiquated. Their computer systems have not been state-of-the-art since the late 1960s. Their recruitment, training, classification, and merit systems do not match up to those in the private sector. They are overstaffed. Their procurement costs are enormous, compared with those of private organizations.

The federal government structure is inefficient. Agencies often duplicate one another's work, have overlapping jurisdictions, or leave crucial matters unattended to; in the 1980s, for example, there has been no government agency with jurisdiction over the release of new genetic material into the environment, even though such release could have catastrophic consequences. Agencies cover up mistakes and mishaps (such as the Three Mile Island nuclear reactor shutdown), hide behind loopholes in the Freedom of Information Act, and stonewall when confronted with evidence of incompetence. They punish whistle-blowers rather than reward them.

The bureaucracies are inflexible where they should be flexible (in providing people with services), and they are freewheeling and highly politicized where they should not be (in dealing with interest groups and organized constituents). They bend or break the rules for the powerful, while adhering to them with a vengeance against everyone else.

The end result is a crisis of authority. Everyone running for office attacks big government, and yet no one does anything about it because it is not the problem. The size of government cannot be reduced substantially because the public wants fairer and more efficient administration of programs, not their elimination. Thus the politics of baiting the bureaucracy misses the point, however better it makes voters feel.

Accountability

In theory, the fourth branch is supervised by the other three branches. In practice, the decentralization of congressional power, the autonomy of the legislative parties, and the competition for power within the institutionalized presidency all limit that supervision. It remains extremely difficult for the White House to impose a chain of command on most bureaus and to control the workings of most programs. Congressional oversight remains intermittent and works best in controlling distributions or tempering regulations for the benefit of the iron triangles. Supervision by the judiciary is intermittent, and its legitimacy is denied by an increasing number of conservative judges who have been appointed in the past few years.

The question of to whom the bureaucracy should be accountable has never been resolved.[36] The president and Congress contend for control, and the courts referee their dispute. Meanwhile, the alliance of professional associations, interest groups, and bureaucrats works for agency autonomy, insisting that professionalism rather than partisan politics should be the standard for agency operations. In turn, a looser issue network tries to use national agenda politics to assert a public interest, often at the expense of the political branches and the career bureaucrats.

The public usually remains confused by this conflict, especially since there are good arguments to be made on all sides. Agencies should be responsive to their clienteles, but they also should maintain professional standards. They should be responsive to the president, but they should also follow the laws laid down by Congress. If issue networks have better ideas, perhaps the existing iron triangles should be overturned.

How do we ensure that bureaucracies are accountable to the public interest? There are no easy answers. Iron triangles form in response to pressures on bureaucrats which are unlikely to fade away. But the White House, through the kind of appointments it makes, can bring in more policy experts from the issue networks. The presidential agencies can foster *multiple advocacy* so that the issue networks will compete with one another and the president can choose from among many options. The resulting interactions between presidential agencies, departments, and issue networks would involve a good deal of competition and redundancy, and different combinations of presidential agencies and bureaus would be ready to implement proposals, once the president approved them. It would be a messy system; but the more councils, boards, and presidential agencies there are, the more flexible the top levels of the administration are and the more options the president and Congress have. That might increase the accountability of the fourth branch to the other three.

IN CONCLUSION

Bureaucratic organization, which involves a chain of command, formal procedures, division of labor, and specialization, is the predominant way of organizing public and private activities. The national government is organized bureaucratically: there are thirteen major departments, as well as other executive and nonexecutive agencies and independent commissions. These are run by political executives appointed by the president to make policy; a Senior Executive Service, responsive to the president to oversee implementation; a career civil service to administer departments; and line personnel to carry out orders and see to implementation. There is no separation of politics from administration: each level of officialdom has its own ideas, priorities, and political interests.

The fourth branch is supervised by the other three branches. Presidential agencies use the appointment and removal power, budget and legislative clearances, and centralized management to impose a chain of command on executive agencies. Congress uses its power to consent to presidential appointments, its power of authorization and appropriation, and legislative oversight to influence what departments do. The judiciary referees the struggle between the executive and the legislative branches, sometimes making officials follow presidential or departmental orders, but enforcing laws where they conflict with these orders.

The bureaucracies try to gain autonomy by emphasizing professional standards rather than political supervision and by joining in the iron triangles with interest groups and congressional committees. In turn, these triangles may be challenged by issue networks, which use national agenda politics or persuasion based on research and policy analysis to propose policies that are in the public interest.

While most reforms would strengthen presidential control or congressional oversight of the bureaucracy, few are likely to be adopted, and most miss the point—which is to make officials more accountable to the public and less likely to betray the public's trust and promote narrow interests. The increasing strength of issue networks will have a greater effect on the way government works than any proposed reforms.

NOTES

1. Seymour Martin Lipset and William Schneider, *The Confidence Gap*, Free Press, New York, 1983, pp. 48–49.
2. H. H. Gerth and C. Wright Mills, *From Max Weber: Essays in Sociology*, Oxford University Press, New York, 1958, pp. 196–198.
3. Max Weber, *The Theory of Social and Economic Organization*, A. M. Henderson, (trans.) and Talcott Parsons (trans.), Free Press, New York, 1947, "The Essentials of Bureaucratic Organization: An Ideal Type Construction," pp. 329–347.
4. Alice Rivlin, *Systematic Thinking for Social Action*, Brookings, Washington, D.C., 1971.
5. *U.S. Government Organization Manual, 1985*, Government Printing Office, Washington, D.C., 1985.
6. Leonard White, *The Jacksonians and the Republicans*, Macmillan, New York, 1955.
7. Woodrow Wilson, "The Study of Administration," *Political Science Quarterly*, vol. 2, no. 2, June 1887, pp. 197–222.
8. Herbert Hoover, *The Challenge to Liberty*, Herbert Hoover Presidential Library Association, Rockford, Ill., 1971, p. 114.
9. Charles Peters, *How Washington Really Works*, 2d ed., Addition-Wesley, Reading, Mass., 1983, p. 38.
10. Donald K. Price, *Government and Science*, Galaxy Books, New York, 1962, pp. 66–78.
11. *The New York Times*, Jan. 1, 1985, p. 38.
12. "High Tech Firms Push for New Export Controls," *High Technology*, vol. 4, no. 12, December 1984, p. 83.
13. *The New York Times*, Jan. 1, 1985, p. 38.
14. Richard Fenno, *The President's Cabinet*, Vintage Books, New York, 1959, chap. 6.
15. Linda Demkovich, "Margaret Heckler Shows Fighting Style," *The National Journal*, vol. 16, no. 19, May 19, 1984, pp. 977–981.

16. U.S. Commission on Civil Rights, *Equal Opportunity in Presidential Appointments*, GPO, Washington, D.C., 1984.

17. Calvin McKenzie, John W. Macy, et al., *America's Un-elected Government*, Ballinger, Cambridge, Mass., 1984.

18. Hugh Heclo, *A Government of Stangers: Executive Politics in Washington*, Brookings, Washington, D.C., 1977.

19. *The New York Times*, July 21, 1983.

20. Joseph Barlett and Douglas Jones, "Managing a Cabinet Agency," *Public Administration Review*, vol. 34, no. 1, January 1974, pp. 62–70.

21. David Burnham, "White House Link: Computer in Ohio," *The New York Times*, July 15, 1983.

22. Thomas M. Franck and Edward Weisband, *Resignation in Protest*, Viking, New York, 1976, p. 59.

23. U.S. Senate Government Operations Committee, *U.S. Government Policy and Support Positions*, GPO, Washington, D.C., 1985.

24. *Local 2677, The American Federation of Government Employees v. Phillips*, 356 F. Supp. 60 D.D.C (1973).

25. Woodrow Wilson, *Congressional Government*, Houghton Mifflin, Boston, 1885.

26. *Chadha v. INS*, 77 L. Ed. 2d 317 (1983).

27. President's Committee on Administrative Management, *Report with Special Studies*, GPO, Washington, D.C., 1937, p. v.

28. Arthur Schlesinger, Jr., *Robert Kennedy and His Times*, Houghton Mifflin, Boston, 1978, p. 250.

29. This biography was prepared with the assistance of Jeff Adler of Columbia College.

30. *Motor Vehicle Manufacturers Association v. State Farm Insurance Co.*, 103 S. Ct. 2856 (1983).

31. *The New York Times*, June 8, 1984

32. J. Lieper Freeman, *The Political Process*, Random House, New York, 1965.

33. Grant McConnell, *Private Power and American Democracy*, Knopf, New York, 1966.

34. Theodore Lowi, *The End of Liberalism*, Norton, New York, 1969.

35. Hugh Heclo, "Issue Networks and the Executive Establishment," in Anthony King (ed.), *The New American Political System*, American Enterprise Institute, Washington, D.C., 1978, pp. 87–124.

36. Frederick Mosher, *Democracy and the Public Service*, Oxford University Press, New York, 1968.

FURTHER READING

Cater, Douglas: *Power in Washington*, Vintage, Books, New York, 1964. A journalistic account of how iron triangles work.

Downs, Anthony: *Inside Bureaucracy*, Little Brown, Boston, 1967. A classic account of the principles of bureaucratic organization.

Heclo, Hugh: *A Government of Strangers: Executive Politics in Washington*, Brookings, Washington, D.C., 1977. An account of the way top executives are recruited into the administration and why they cannot work as a team.

Lowi, Theodore J.: *The End of Liberalism*, Norton, New York, 1969. An argument for a return to statutory standards and less delegation of power from Congress to officials, including a description of the performance of programs in the 1960s.

Lynn, Laurence E., Jr.: *Managing the Public's Business*, Basic Books, New York, 1981. Suggestions by a former staffer in three departments and the National Security Council about how officials could improve their performance.

McConnell, Grant: *Private Power and American Democracy*, Knopf, New York, 1966. A study of the way government policies are shaped by private groups which share in the administration of programs.

Nathan, Richard: *The Administrative Presidency*, Wiley, New York, 1983. An account of the strategies used by Nixon and Reagan in dealing with the bureaucracy.

Peters, Charles: *How Washington Really Works*, 2d ed., Addison-Wesley, Reading, Mass., 1983. A journalist's look at the foibles of bureaucrats.

Pressman, Jeffrey, and Aaron Wildavsky: *Implementation*, University of California Press, Berkeley, 1973. An account of how federal programs are actually run at the local level, including a theory as to why they diverge from the intent of national policymakers.

Seidman, Harold: *Politics, Position and Power*, 2d ed., Oxford University Press, New York, 1975. Shrewd observations by a former Budget Bureau official about the games that federal bureaucrats play.

THE STUDY BREAK

Parkinson, C. Northcote: *Parkinson's Law*, Houghton Mifflin, Boston, 1962. Just as the British Empire was breaking up after World War II, the British Colonial Office was expanding its personnel and budget. The author tried to discover why, and in the process developed some very funny laws about bureaucratic empire building.

The Right Stuff. A 1984 movie, based on a novel by Tom Wolfe, about the space program and the clash between the worlds of bureaucrats and test pilots.

USEFUL SOURCES

Adzigian, Denise A. (ed.): *Encyclopedia of Governmental Advisory Organizations*, 4th ed., Gale Research Company, Detroit, 1983. A directory of advisory groups attached to bureaucracies.

Budget of the United States Government, GPO, Washington, D.C. Annual budgetary data for the bureaucracy.

Encyclopedia of Associations, Gale Research Company, Detriot, 1983. A directory of interest groups.

Federal Yellow Book, The Washington Monitor, Washington D.C., 1985. Names and phone numbers of 29,000 top officials in the White House, presidential agencies, and federal departments and agencies.

The Federal Register, GPO, Washington D.C. A daily compendium of proposed and adopted agency rules.

The National Journal. A weekly journalistic account of the activities of important government agencies.

Public Administration Review. A quarterly journal devoted to improvement in public administration.

U.S. Government Organization Manual, GPO, Washington, D.C. An annual compendium of all government agencies and the top officials in each, including addresses and phone numbers and the table organization of each department and agency.

The Washington Monthly. A magazine with many articles detailing the empire-building tendencies of bureaucrats.

ORGANIZATIONS

General Accounting Office. General Accounting Office Building, 441 G Street, Washington, D.C., 20548. Conducts audits and policy analyses of the bureaucracy for Congress. For more information telephone 202-275-2812.

Committee on Post Office and Civil Service. U.S. House of Representatives, suite 309, Cannon House Office Building, Washington, D.C. 20515. Issues reports on the personnel practices of the bureaucracy. For more information telephone 202-225-4054.

Office of Management and Budget. Executive Office Building, Washington, D.C. 20503. Management units monitor agency compliance with presidential priorities and attempt to strengthen presidential controls. For more information telephone 202-395-3080.

Office of Personnel Management. 1900 E Street, N.W., Washington, D.C. 20415. Administers the appointment, promotion, and other personnel policies for the President. For more information telephone 202-632-5491.

Committee on Government Operations. U.S. House of Representatives, suite B-377, Rayburn House Office Building, Washington, D.C., 20515.

Committee on Governmental Affairs. U.S. Senate, suite 342, SDOB, Washington, D.C., 20510. Both the Committee on Government Affairs and the Committee on Government Operations study the overall effectiveness of the departments and issue reports and studies. For more information telephone 202-225-4407 (House) and 202-242-4751.

Budget planning involves close cooperation between executive and legislative leaders. The federal budget affects, and is affected by, the entire economy, including the New York Stock Exchange. (*Michael Evans: White House; Sepp Seitz.*)

CHAPTER 14

BUDGET POLITICS: CONTROLLING UNCONTROLLABLES

To budget is to govern. To control what goes into a budget answers the key political question, "Who gets what, when, and how?" "There are no money questions of any moment which are not also policy questions," says a high-ranking budget official. Robert Michel, the House Republican leader, observed that in budgeting, "The issue is not one of figures, but philosophy; it spells out who we are and where we are going."[1]

"To find out how anything really works," according to a House member, "you have to look at the budget."[2] This chapter begins with a discussion of the functions of a budget; then we will see how presidents put their budgets together, and we will look at the congressional budget process. The chapter concludes by examining presidential budget strategies; thus it is also a case study of presidential-congressional relations.

WHAT A BUDGET DOES

First let us consider what a budget does and how the *Budget of the United States Government* is organized.

A budget—whether for a household, a corporation, a university, or a government—does several things:

- It plans activities for the coming year.
- It specifies priorities and timing for these activities. It decides among alternatives and among claimants for scarce resources.
- It determines what agencies can do during the year.
- It is a source of prizes and payments, which those who control it can use to reward others who cooperate with them.

The government budgets according to a fiscal rather than a calendar year. The *fiscal year,* FY, begins October 1 and ends September 30, taking its number from the year in which it ends. FY 1986 begins October 1, 1985, and ends September 30, 1986.

The national budget not only determines what goes on inside the government but also influences the allocation of national wealth. It can redistribute income, by taxing those who earn and providing payments and services to nonworkers or low-paid workers, or it can be neutral, providing services to people that cost about the same as they paid in taxes.

The budget can affect the size, composition, and performance of organizations in the private sector. Agencies can be funded to compete with private companies, as in the field of telecommunications satellites. The government can subsidize corporate research and development, as it did with the space shuttle. The budget determines which sectors of the economy get subsidies, loans, loan guarantees, contracts, and insurance.

The budget is a claim on national wealth. It shows not only the activities of the government but also the proportion of the gross national product (GNP) that its activities consume. Both the government's expenditures and its share of the GNP have increased in recent years. Spending has gone from $728.4

Senior citizens protest Reagan's budget cuts. Congress is traditionally protective of popular programs and usually rejects attempts to cut them. (*John Ficara: Woodfin Camp.*)

billion in FY 1982 to more than $1 trillion in FY 1986, while its proportion of the GNP has gone from 20.4 percent in FY 1972 to 24.4 percent in FY 1985. Liberals who believe that the government should make decisions about the investment and consumption of national wealth look favorably on these developments; their goal is to emulate the mixed economies of western Europe, in which governments typically allocate from 30 to 50 percent of the GNP. Conservatives argue that there should be a gradual movement downward, perhaps to 15 percent of the GNP, with the government concentrating only on national security and essential domestic activities. Both are likely to be disappointed: the most liberal and the most conservative American administrations will probably not move out of the 20 to 25 percent range. (See Figure 14-1.)

Budgets also allow politicians to make promises about the future, to take

Figure 14-1. In recent years the largest increases in government expenditures have involved military spending and direct payments to individuals. Note the increase in interest payments on the national debt and the sharp decrease in other programs. The figures are in 1972 dollars adjusted for inflation. In current (1985) dollars the expenditures are close to $1 trillion. (Source: Office of Management and Budget.)

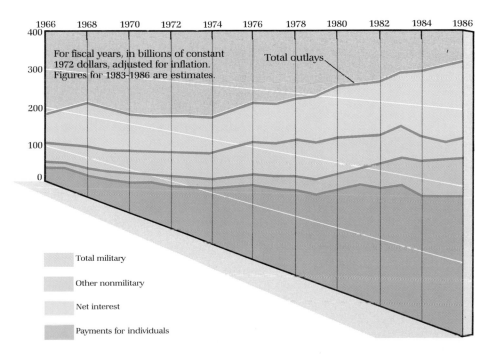

positions on issues, to reassure constituents, and to campaign for votes. Both the Democrats and the Republicans gear much of their national television advertising toward taxing and spending issues. But there is more to budgeting than just campaign rhetoric. Budgets are highly sensitive to changes in party control of government: it makes a difference who wins an election. Overall spending and levels for particular programs shift greatly when a different party takes power, just as they do in other democratic nations.[3] The White House and legislative parties circle warily around the budget, trying to develop strategies for the next elections. Should the president promise more programs or become "curtailer in chief" and promise to curb big government? Should the president's party in Congress support the president, or should members distance themselves from unpopular proposals? Should the opposition cooperate with or confront the president?

Each party plays it differently. The Democrats are good at winning votes by promising more programs. But their "spend, spend, elect, elect" approach to coalition building makes it difficult for them to restrain spending without alienating core supporters, and they have little credibility when they shift gears and pose as budget cutters. The Republicans have credibility as budget cutters (at least for domestic programs), but that is as much a liability as a benefit. Senator Mark Hatfield, a Republican, observed that his party was viewed by many Americans as an instrument to transfer wealth "from the needy to the greedy," because of cuts in programs for the poor.[4] The Republicans have their own electoral constituencies, which simultaneously want smaller budgets and greater spending on domestic programs that benefit them.

THE FEDERAL BUDGET: A CLOSER LOOK

Income and expenditures

By FY 1986 the income and outlays of the federal government each added up to around $1 trillion, organized in the following overall aggregates:

- *Total receipts.* These include the total income that the government expects to receive. The money comes from borrowing by the Treasury (20 percent), personal income taxes (36 percent), social security and unemployment insurance taxes (29 percent), corporate taxes (8 percent), excise taxes (on gasoline and tobacco, for example, 4 percent), and estate taxes, gift taxes, customs fees, and taxes on the sale of property and other income (3 percent). In good times receipts soar, while during recessions they drop. Usually there is much greater fluctuation in receipts than in spending, which accounts for most of the changes in the deficit. Revenues (other than borrowings) totaled over $800 billion in FY 1986.
- *Total outlays.* These are the total expenditures for the fiscal year. They include direct payments to individuals (42 percent); defense spending (29 percent); interest on the national debt (13 percent); grants to states, counties, and cities (1 percent); and all other federal operations (5 percent). They totaled over $990 billion in FY 1986.
- *Deficit or surplus.* The difference between receipts and outlays yields the deficit or surplus for the fiscal year. In almost every year a deficit is recorded. In FY 1983 it was $195 billion, and in FY 1984 it was $175 billion—figures far greater than in any other peacetime year.
- *National debt.* Not to be confused with the *deficit* for a single fiscal year, the national debt includes money owed from previous years (from the sale of Treasury savings bonds, bills, and notes). It also includes new borrow-

ing for the deficit in the fiscal year, as well as the interest on the debt. In recent years, because of high interest rates and the soaring size of the debt, interest payments have accounted for as much as 15 percent of the budget. The total national debt now approaches $2 trillion, a figure which represents 22 percent of all public (national, state, and local) and private debt.

Government expenditures

Types of spending. TAX EXPENDITURES. The government spends money in different ways. There are *tax expenditures:* income which the Treasury forgoes through loopholes in the tax laws designed to encourage people to do certain things. For example, if an industry cannot get the government to spend money to clean up toxic wastes, it might get tax breaks if it installs nonpolluting equipment. Disadvantaged youths age 16 and 17 who are employed during the summer provide tax breaks of 85 percent of their salaries, up to $2555 per worker, to employers. By 1985 there were 104 such tax expenditure programs, equaling 25 percent of actual government outlays (more than $250 billion), and therefore they constitute a major part of government "spending."

The biggest break, more than $40 billion, goes to homeowners and other property owners, who can deduct interest on their mortgages and more than $15 billion in property taxes. Taxpayers who itemize deductions on their federal returns can take charitable contributions as deductions from income. Future retirees benefit from more than $40 billion that is exempt from taxes until their retirement benefits are paid; taxpayers with IRA and Keogh plans benefit similarly. Deductions for state and local income taxes amount to more than $40 billion for individuals who itemize. In 1987 some deductions were being phased out as part of tax reform, including contributions to IRA plans, interest on loans, state and local sales taxes, and exemption of scholarship and fellowship income.

OUTLAYS. Next come actual government payments to individuals, corporations, nonprofit organizations, and state and local governments. When Congress approves presidential budget requests, it means that agencies can incur *obligations:* they can hire employers, rent office space, buy goods and services, and so forth. *Total obligational authority* (TOA) is the amount that the government can commit in the current fiscal year and future fiscal years. TOA in turn can be divided into *previous year authority* (money allocated in previous years but not yet spent) and *new obligational authority* (NOA), which is money requested for the current fiscal year. These figures in the budget indicate how much the government is permitted to spend, but *not* the actual amounts it pays out. These are *outlays;* payments made in the fiscal year in the form of checks, cash, bonds or debentures, and accrual of interest on agency debts in order to liquidate obligations. As Figure 14-2 shows, annual outlays are a mixture of previous and new obligational authority. Figure 14-3 shows the relationship between obligational authority, obligations incurred, and outlays.

Often yearly outlays exceed new obligational authority (because of spending based on previous authority)—there is no close relationship between either TOA or NOA and annual spending. This means that when the administration and Congress try to control spending by limiting budget TOA or NOA, actual outlays may remain quite high; this often happens with military spending. Alternatively, some programs may be given large budget authority, but actual

Figure 14-2. The mix of government spending. Government agencies are permitted to spend money based on prior years and new obligational authority (laws passed by Congress). This budget authority provides for spending in the current fiscal year as well as in future fiscal years. Thus Congress cannot simply pass new laws which immediately reduce spending in the current fiscal year by large amounts; the impact of its decisions is usually spread over several years.

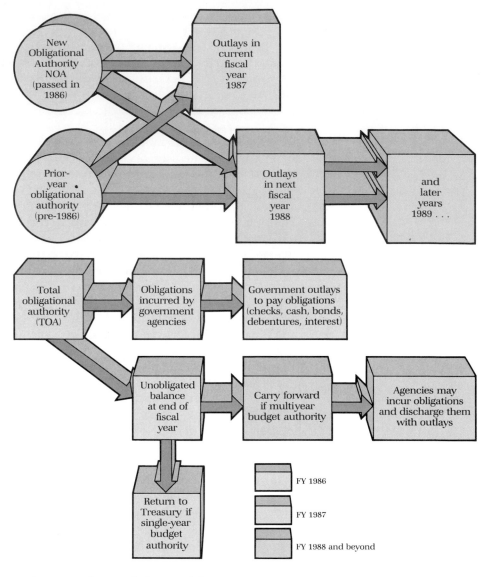

Figure 14-3. Obligations, outlays, and budget authority. After Congress provides agencies with their budget authority (TOA), they may incur obligations and pay for them with checks drawn on the United States Treasury. The TOA which is not obligated by agencies at the end of the fiscal year is returned to the Treasury or carried forward into future fiscal years if Congress has provided for multiyear authority.

outlays may be much lower if the program runs for several years, if there are delays, or if the administration decides not to spend all the money.

Spending authority: Budget authority versus legislative authority. Congress grants two kinds of spending authority: legislative authority and budget authority. *Legislative authority* gives an agency permission to do something and may set a ceiling on the amount that can be spent. Permission is not the same as funding, however; the actual money comes from **budget authority,** which requires one or more of the following from Congress:

- *Appropriation:* a bill reported by the appropriations committees for annual, multiyear, or permanent funding of a government agency, specifying the amounts (and staying within the limit of the legislative authorization). An example is military procurement. Two-fifths of all government expenditures come from appropriations.

- *Contract authority:* a bill reported by any standing committee which allows an agency to contract for goods or services with public or private agencies. Congress pledges its full faith and credit: it will provide appropriations when needed to meet the contractual obligations. Certain farm programs involve contracts between the government and growers, for example.
- *Loan or credit authority:* a bill which allows an agency to make a loan or extend credit to individuals, corporations, cooperatives, and state, local, and foreign governments. The government may also buy loans made by financial institutions to individuals, making more credit available for new loans; the student loan program is an example.
- *Loan guarantee authority:* a bill which allows an agency to guarantee bonds issued by, or a loan made to, a local government or corporation. The guarantee provides funds to near-bankrupt operations (such as Chrysler, Lockheed, and New York City in the 1970s) or allows them to obtain funds at below-market rates.
- *Borrowing authority:* a bill which allows an agency to borrow money from the Treasury or the private bond markets to finance its operations, with interest and principal to be repaid by fees collected. Certain government corporations, such as the Tennessee Valley Authority and COMSAT (space communications), finance their capital construction this way.

Agencies must obtain both *legislative* authority, which gives them permission to do certain things; and *budget* authority, which directs the Treasury to fund these activities or allows the agencies access to private money markets. Congress usually forbids agencies to ask for budget authority until their legislative authority has been granted. In most instances, legislative authority establishes a ceiling beyond which budget authority does not go. "Never lose sight of the fact that the Appropriations Committees are the saucers that cool the legislative tea. Just because you have an authorization doesn't mean a thing to us . . . ," Representative John Rooney once told a State Department official who reminded him that the department had received large legislative authorizations.[5]

Congress maintains the twofold system of legislative and budget authority as its own internal check: the system fragments congressional power and sets the legislative committees (which like to increase funding for their pet projects) off against the appropriations committees. When the latter get too niggardly with their funding, other committees can often get changes in congressional rules which allow them to provide loan, contract, or borrowing authority to agencies; this is known as *backdoor funding.* In recent years federal credit and guaranteed loans from government agencies and government-sponsored corporations have increased from less than $275 billion in FY 1971 to more than $1 trillion in FY 1985, as Figure 14-4 (page 486) shows.

Controllable and uncontrollable expenditures. Expenditures can also be categorized as relatively controllable or as uncontrollable. Uncontrollable expenditures involve government provision of goods and services to people who can legally make a claim to them. They include social security, Medicare, Medicaid, and welfare payments to individuals; pensions for military personnel and civilian workers; interest on the national debt; and payments for long-term

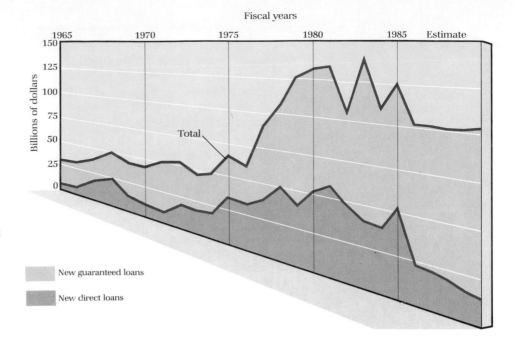

Figure 14-4. The large increases in federal loans and guaranteed loans (made by financial institutions) triggered an effort by the Reagan administration to cut back on these politically popular programs in 1986. (Source: *Budget of the United States Government, FY 1984*, Special Analysis F, p. f-7.)

capital construction contracts. Such expenditures are uncontrollable in the sense that it is politically difficult to change the laws that guarantee the payments; but occasionally when the deficits loom too large, it is possible to make cuts in these programs (though not in interest payments).

Personnel costs, such as salaries and benefits, are also relatively uncontrollable. By law, these payments must be competitive with the payments in the private sector. By 1984 the government's own pay commission estimated that increases averaging 20 percent would be needed to compete with pay in the private sector.

What is left is *discretionary* or *controllable* spending: spending for military and civil programs that are not locked into long-term contracts and are not part of the entitlement system. *Only 20 percent of the entire budget fits into this category.* For example, only 4 percent of the expenditures of the Department of Health and Human Services do not involve personnel costs or entitlement programs. Thus it is impossible to make meaningful spending cuts without going after these entitlement programs. It is easier to cut new obligational authority in discretionary programs, but not much money is saved by doing so. If really big amounts are involved, either all the controllable programs must be eliminated, or the government must make cuts in the uncontrollable programs. Either way, those who would limit government expenditures face excruciatingly difficult choices.

Expenditure equivalents. Sometimes legislative authority has an impact equivalent to that of budget authority, and the government can propose expenditure equivalents as a substitute for new spending. When Congress passes regulations, it imposes costs. Regulatory relief, as implemented by the Reagan administration, either for a company or for industry, may be just as useful as federal funding. Regulatory changes and lax enforcement of existing laws can lower the cost of toxic-waste disposal and mine-tailing cleanups, for example, which for the affected companies is the equivalent of federal funding. If state and local governments cannot obtain enough money to build ramps and other means of access for the handicapped, they will propose weakening existing regulations that require them to provide such access. If Congress cuts Medicaid funding, it will soften the blow to state governments by changing eligibility requirements and reducing services. Imposing tariffs or quotas on foreign goods may be just as useful to companies that are threatened by foreign competition as giving them tax expenditures (in the form of investment tax credits) or subsidizing their research costs. Expenditure equivalents may reduce interest-group pressure for government funds.

FOCUS

BACKDOOR BUDGETING. Many government agencies are not funded by appropriations, but instead have backdoor access to the Treasury. Some are not even listed in the *Budget of the United States Government.* Most of these make loans, borrow money, or charge fees; they include the Federal Reserve Board, the Strategic Petroleum Reserve, the Postal Service, the United States Railway Association, the United States Synfuel Corporation, and the Federal Financing Bank (FFB).

The largest off-budget entity is the FFB, which made more than $14 billion in loans to other government agencies in FY 1984 and has a total of more than $110 billion in loans outstanding. It is the second largest "bank" in the United States. It makes loans to other government agencies—known as *sponsored borrowing*—such as the Student Loan Marketing Association (Sallie Mae). Here is how the system works: Banks make loans to students so that they can attend college. These loans are then sold to Sallie Mae, which provides the banks with more money for more student loans. In turn, Sallie Mae markets the loans to the FFB, which gives it money so that it can buy more loans from the banks. Where does the FFB get the money to buy the loans from Sallie Mae? It raises money from the Treasury, which lends it funds (using the original student loans as collatoral).

Why go through this tortuous process of raising money? For one thing, the FFB makes loans to Sallie Mae at below-market rates, which ultimately means that the banks can lend students money at low rates. For another, if many government agencies raised money by borrowing, the money markets would be flooded with strange bonds; the existing process eliminates most agency financings, leaving it up to the Treasury to market its well-known bonds and bills in private money markets. Finally, the process operates as a revolving door with no limits, something that sponsors of student loans, farmers' housing, and other programs like. Loans to farmers soared from $4 billion in 1974 to more than $16 billion in 1980, with more than $40 billion outstanding; this would have been impossible if the program had been subject to annual appropriations.

THE BUDGET PROCESS

Budgeting as an action-forcing process

Budgeting is like preparing the state of the union message: it is an action-forcing process, requiring advance preparation to meet deadlines. Fourteen days after the Monday on which Congress convenes each January, the president sends the budget to Congress. To meet the deadline, the budget must be at the printer's in early January. That requires the president, along with the *Office of Management and Budget* (OMB), to finish work on the budget in late December. In turn, the OMB and the executive departments must complete their work early in the fall, which means that agency officials must start sometime in the preceding spring. Most planning for new programs, drafting bills for Congress to consider, and evaluating existing activities, is tied to budget deadlines and is part of the budget process.

Budgeting takes a long time. Consider the budget enacted for FY 1986. It was developed by agencies and departments in the winter and spring of 1984 and was then submitted in the summer to the OMB, which prepared its draft budget for the White House in the fall. In January 1985, the president sent the budget to Congress, which considered and modified it for nine months. It went into effect on October 1, 1985, and remained in effect until September 30, 1986. Departments had to plan a budget in 1984 that would determine their spending through most of 1986 (and in 1984 they were spending money they had planned for in 1982).

The length and the complexity of the process tend to slow down innovation. Abolishing or reducing the size of programs also takes a long time—often until the legislative and budgetary authority expires, which may be several years. It helps to take a long perspective when you budget.

Budgeting is a bit like driving a huge truck, loaded with lumber, down an icy mountain road. Decisions that you made 100 yards back about whether to use the brakes or downshift affect what you can do now to control the truck. The way you handle it now will limit your options 100 yards down the road. It is snowing, visibility is low, and a competitor is ready to take over your job as soon as your truck overturns.

Steps in the budget process

The budget process can be divided into the time before the fiscal year when the budget is prepared; the fiscal year itself, when outlays are expended from previous and current budget authority; and subsequent fiscal years, when some of the funds authorized will be spent.

The budget call. The OMB requires departments to submit their budgets two years before the president's version is sent to Congress. Its budget call instructs them to plan on the expansion or contraction of their programs, on the basis of economic forecasts.

Agency budgeting. Agencies within each department estimate what it would cost to maintain programs at their existing levels in the next fiscal year (taking inflation into account); this becomes their *current services budget*, also known as their *base.* Next, they ask for what they consider to be their *fair share* of any increases in federal spending. Most agencies expect to make only minor changes in activities in any single year. Thus they budget incrementally, rarely asking for more than 10 or 15 percent in additional funds.[6]

Department budgeting. Department officials review agencies' requests. Most departments make nonincremental changes; they add to some programs and cut others, even though overall department budgets do not change very much from year to year.[7] In the past, agencies that "thought big" and asked for major increases were likely to get them; the size of the request, especially if it was backed up with good arguments, not the existing base, seemed to be the key to additional funding.[8] More recently, departments have been asked by the White House to "freeze" many of their operations, and agency officials who ask for large increases and who aggressively lobby for them may be reprimanded by higher-ups.

Some department budget officials use program budgets: they compare the fit between an agency's goals and line-item requests, and they may reject parts of the budget if it does not have immediate relevance to the agency's goal. Others use cost-benefit analysis to rank projects in terms of costs versus projected benefits, rejecting those with the lowest ratios. Sometimes programs from different agencies are put into the "pit" against each other, and the ones with the lowest cost-to-benefit ratio are cut back or ended. Some departments even experiment with *zero-base budgeting:* no agency has a guaranteed base, and all must justify the next year's expenditures starting from zero.

OMB budget guidance. The OMB guides departmental review of agency budget submissions. In relatively flush years the word goes out to prepare new programs and accept agencies' incremental requests. In leaner years the OMB requires departments to use restrictive definitions of the base—small inflation adjustments (or none at all) or exclusion of low-priority programs. It may instruct agencies to make across-the-board percentage cutbacks, to make cuts in functions (like regulatory enforcement), to freeze all new programs and hiring, or to ban or limit activities such as nonessential travel or publications.

OMB budget review. Departments submit their proposed budgets to the OMB for review. These include *language sheets*, which estimate spending authority, and *green sheets*, which estimate outlays. They are reviewed by the OMB's Budget Review Division; its examiners make recommendations for every agency and program in the department. These in turn go to the OMB program associate directors, political appointees who make sure that the recommendations follow the administration's policies. Finally, the budget director holds "review sessions" with top White House staffers, during which department secretaries can plead their cases before the director briefs the president.

Presidential budget review. Presidents consider spending proposals in the context of their overall economic program. They meet with political advisers and with officials from presidential advisory agencies before changing the OMB's recommendations. Sometimes department secretaries get one last chance to appeal directly to the president. Truman, Ford, and Carter listened to such appeals carefully, acting like judges deciding cases. Other presidents, such as Nixon and Reagan, have had an intermediate "appellate level" consisting of the OMB director and several White House aides to screen appeals. Few presidents ever reverse the decisions of their budget directors; to do so would simply invite more appeals and weaken their authority. In some administrations (Kennedy's and Reagan's, for example) the OMB must appeal against Pentagon budget requests, rather than the other way around.

Figure 14-5 (page 490) shows in more detail all the formal steps involved in the formulation of the budget; but the actual sequence can be far messier and more out of step than these neat flowcharts indicate.

The budget game

Imagine a game in which the players come on or off the field at will; in which the rules change from one season to the next; in which the object of the game may be to put more points on the board—or fewer; in which a new team forms on every play, only to dissolve before the next play; in which no one, even

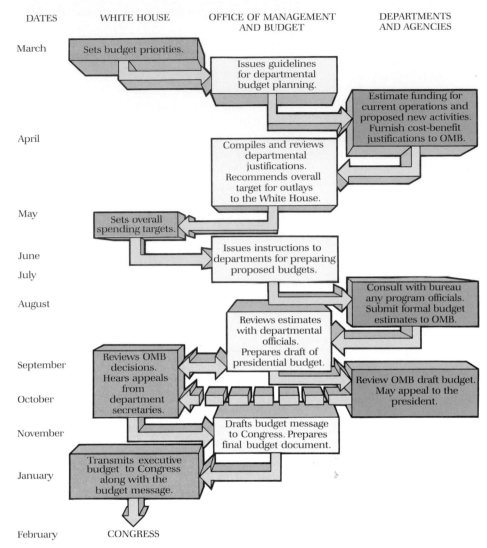

Figure 14-5. Preparation of the executive budget. The Office of Management and Budget (OMB) takes primary responsibility for translating general presidential priorities into specific instructions which guide departments and agencies when they submit their budget requests. The OMB eventually prepares the budget of the United States for submission by the president to Congress, a process which takes almost a year to complete.

those on the same team, gives anyone correct information; and in which the scoreboard always exaggerates. If you can imagine such a game, you are ready to play executive budget politics.

The agencies. The submissions that agencies make to their departments are not exactly what they need, or even what they want. Instead, they are padded, in anticipation of departmental and OMB cuts. If agencies think that the president will increase their funds, the president gets their support. Otherwise, they plan end runs around the OMB to the more sympathetic Congress. They find interest groups to serve, as the Department of Agriculture has done with farmers, as the Pentagon has done with contractors and subcontractors of weapons systems, and as the Department of Health and Human Services has done with doctors and hospital administrators. Officials include programs and services for important committee leaders so that they can build a coalition that will make their higher-ups think twice before suggesting cuts. They may even use federal funds to organize their constituents into interest groups; this technique was pioneered by the Agriculture Department with farmers and then was used by antipoverty agencies in the 1960s. Federal money can even be used to lobby Congress for more funding, something that Pentagon contractors specialize in.

To protect themselves against cuts, agencies can mount their own national agenda campaigns. Some advertise their mission, like the National Guard with its television commercials and the Forest Service with Smokey the Bear. The military cites Soviet arms buildups just before its budget requests are reviewed by the White House. The United States Geological Survey makes widely publicized predictions about earthquakes when its budget is in danger, and the Weather Service mounts new hurricane, tornado, and flood watches.

Agencies that are pressured to make cuts may announce that the cuts will be made in popular programs. The Coast Guard claims that it will not be able to stop illegal immigrants from entering the country. The Postal Service says that it will have to stop Saturday mail delivery. The Park Service says that it will have to restrict visiting hours at the Washington Monument and reduce the number of rangers in the national parks. The Securities and Exchange Commission says that it will have to close the office that handles investors' complaints. The idea is to get interest groups and voting constituencies to pressure the administration not to make the cuts.

The departments. Sometimes the departments play games with the agencies. They may impose restrictive new budgeting methods in order to change an agency's priorities. Top Defense Department officials use the budget to discipline the military services and force them to coordinate their missions and programs. When heavy cuts are required, sometimes a department secretary engages in an elaborate hoax with the OMB: instead of letting the secretary be the villain, the OMB does the heavy cutting—even making cuts which the department itself secretly proposed. When departments want more money, of course, they try to build a coalition that includes the leading members of the legislative and appropriations committees so that they will be able to stand up to the OMB and the White House.

John Block, then secretary of agriculture, prepares the USDA budget. (*United States Department of Agriculture.*)

The OMB. The OMB has its own games to play. Often it tries to cut department submissions. Its examiners look for padding and duplication in agency and department submissions. It requires departments to use restrictive budget techniques and penalizes them if their submissions do not comply. It may force departments to plan for lower outlays than its obligational authority would indicate. It has the power to make quarterly allotments of funds, and it can provide less money than Congress gave. But sometimes the OMB tries to moderate demands for severe budget cuts. Then it takes an optimistic view of the economy, forecasting major increases in tax revenues and shortfalls in projected outlays—all in an effort to reduce projected deficits and therefore lessen the pressure on the president to make more spending cuts. Its forecasts in turn may be challenged by the Treasury (which is likely to be more pessimistic) or the Council of Economic Advisors.

The OMB may even disavow the president's budget if it cannot get its own way, as it did in 1984, when in congressional testimony David Stockman, the budget director, called on Congress to enact spending cuts (especially in defense) and tax increases that were not even mentioned in the presidential budget.

The White House. Presidents must decide how deeply involved in budget politics they want to become. Some lobby heavily with Congress to get their budgets enacted, as Reagan did in 1981 and 1985; others walk away from their own budget submissions, refuse to defend the figures, and distance themselves, as Eisenhower did in 1958 and as Reagan did in 1983.

Some presidents, such as Kennedy and Johnson, are fortunate enough to budget in periods of economic expansion. During their administrations, tax receipts soared along with the GNP, and there was money for new domestic programs. Between 1961 and 1964 domestic spending increased 35 percent, and it increased another 24 percent between 1964 and 1968. Budget choices for the White House in such times are simply choices between what to do first and what to delay. The OMB becomes a programming agency; its examiners organize task forces to plan new government activities, and then they take the lead in getting these programs through Congress and seeing that they are implemented.

Other presidents—including Nixon, Ford, and Carter—have had to budget

President Reagan discusses the growing federal deficit in a speech at the White House, April 29, 1982. (*J. T. Atlan: Sygma.*)

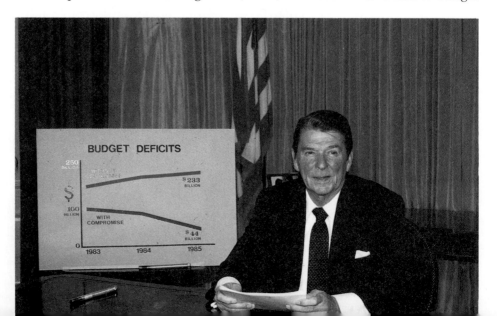

Courtesy of Gamble,
Florida Times-Union.

in periods of recession or **stagflation** (high inflation and low economic growth). They had to become "curtailers in chief." But spending during these presidents' administrations continued to rise (25 percent between 1969 and 1972 and 31 percent between 1973 and 1976), even though receipts did not keep pace. The result was growing pressure to "do something" about the deficit. The budget game changed significantly in 1978, when Carter proclaimed that retrenchment was the order of the day. As one OMB official, W. Bowman Cutter (!), observed about Carter, "He was puzzled and irritated by the fact that the choices were so brutal. He grew to hate the budget process."[9] Reagan managed a 5 percent cutback in domestic spending between 1981 and 1984, halted cutbacks for the 1984 elections, and then proposed sweeping and drastic new cuts in 1985. Yet overall outlays still rose.

When the media cover the presidential budget, they focus on the overall size and on the projected deficits. Presidents do what they can to minimize the damage. After a change of party in the White House, entering presidents submit a budget designed to embarrass their predecessors (claiming that they underestimated the problems), and they exaggerate the gravity of the situation. On leaving office, most presidents submit a final budget document that overestimates income and underestimates expenditures, showing a plan for a balanced budget in one or two years. These are fairy-tale figures, cooked up to make the outgoing president look good and the incoming president look bad; they are revised in mid-March, when the new president claims to have inherited an unbelievable mess.

Most presidents forecast balanced budgets several years in the near future, no matter what the present deficit is, reminding one of the queen in *Through the Looking Glass* who promised jam yesterday and jam tomorrow, but never jam today. Reagan used this trick in his 1981 budget submissions and in the 1984 elections, when he argued that the huge deficits would be reduced by the end of his second term. Other presidents use accounting tricks to avoid passing crucial milestones; Johnson even postponed some expenditures for a year to avoid spending $100 billion in 1964, and Reagan did the same thing two decades later, when the deficit approached the $1 trillion mark. Candidates who are running for office decry huge deficits; once in office, they tend to minimize the problem and focus on other economic data. If the economy is doing poorly, they argue that deficit spending will stimulate it to recovery; if the economy is booming, they argue that the deficit will soon come down and that the nation can afford it anyway.

CLOSE-UP

DAVID STOCKMAN. David Stockman spearheaded the 1981 and 1985 drives of the Reagan administration to slash domestic spending. He was a liberal antiwar activist in the 1960s at the University of Michigan, and then at Harvard he became a neoconservative under the influence of two political scientists, Daniel Moynihan (now a senator from New York) and James Q. Wilson. Stockman worked as a congressional aide for John Anderson, and in 1976 he was elected as a representative from Michigan. In Congress he was a hardworking and principled conservative: he was the only legislator from his state, the automobile capital of the nation, to vote against the Chrysler bailout.

After the 1980 elections, Reagan made Stockman director of the OMB. Shortly before the inauguration, he and Representative Jack Kemp teamed up on a memo to Reagan which proposed tax reform and reductions, spending cuts, deregulation of business, and decontrol of oil prices. In January he began to implement his own spending recommendations, making a proposal for a first round of cuts totaling $40 billion. Many of the programs involved were political sacred cows that had previously been immune to cuts. Stockman argued that cuts should be made regardless of who would be hurt: "We are interested in cutting weak claims rather than weak clients; . . . we have to show that we are willing to attack powerful clients with weak claims."[10] But the largest cuts were made in social service agencies with politically weak clienteles; defense contractors, large corporations, farmers, the elderly, and other organized interests were affected far less.

Stockman played an important role in getting Congress to go along. He consulted closely with legislators from both parties, making compromises when necessary. When Howard Baker, the Senate majority leader, insisted on funding the Clinch River nuclear reactor in Tennessee, Stockman backed off. "It just wasn't worth fighting," he said. "The package will go nowhere without Baker and Clinch River is just life or death to Baker."[11] Stockman was unable to dominate the administration's revenue program. He favored a flat tax with only minor reductions in revenue, and he did not believe the supply-siders' argument that large cuts would stimulate the economy and result in increased revenues. "I was a budget cutter before I was a tax cutter," he said.[12] To make the system fairer and produce more revenue, he tried to increase user fees for government services and elimi-

As director of the OMB, David Stockman had final responsibility for presenting the administration's budget proposals to Congress. (*Shephard Sherbell: Picture Group.*)

nate some tax loopholes, deductions, and exemptions. President Reagan turned down some of these proposals and Congress rejected others. The bill as passed reduced revenues by $750 billion over the period 1981–1986.

At the end of his first year in office, Stockman faced another setback. In November 1981 William Greider, a Washington reporter, published an article in *The Atlantic* based on extensive personal interviews with him. In the article Stockman conceded that the main purpose of the tax cuts was to reduce the rate for the rich. He admitted that neither he nor anyone else had confidence in many of the budget numbers which had been used and that the computer models had been changed on the basis of some optimistic assumptions and unproven theories. The Democrats pounced on these admissions and took some of them out of context, charging that Stockman was dishonest, incompetent, and duplicitous. Tip O'Neill, the Speaker of the House, said that Stockman "knew firsthand the fundamental weaknesses in the Reagan program and chose to cover them up."[13] Many Republicans urged him to resign. After a well-publicized lunch with President Reagan, Stockman came out and informed reporters that the meeting was "in the nature of a visit to the woodshed after supper."[14] His offer of resignation had not been accepted.

Stockman recovered from this political blow but never regained his former authority with his colleagues or with Congress. In part this may account for the fact that Reagan's 1982, 1983, and 1984 budgets were virtually ignored by members of Congress, including Republicans in the Senate, and for the fact that his 1985 proposals were under attack by his own party in Congress even before he submitted them.[15] Stockman resigned his post in 1985.

CONGRESSIONAL ACTION ON THE PRESIDENTIAL BUDGET

The president submits the *Budget of the United States Government* to Congress in January (Figure 14-6). It is an accurate description of current budget authority and past outlays—but it is only a set of recommendations for the next fiscal year. Most of the figures are agreed to by the OMB and the White House, although Congress, by law, has required that the budget contain the recommendations of several agencies (the Consumer Product Safety Commission, the Federal Elections Commission, the Interstate Commerce Commission, and the Federal Energy Regulatory Commission), along with the final OMB figures.[16]

Congress, by law, requires the president to propose a budget, but the Constitution, in Article I, Section 9, provides that it is Congress that disposes of the budget, through the provision that "no Money shall be drawn from the Treasury but in Consequence of Appropriations made by law." As James Madison once said, "The legislative department alone has access to the pockets of the people."[17] The president's requests are converted by Congress into budget authority. Officials in the executive branch know that the figures in the presidential budget are not written in cement— these officials have one more chance to get what they want from Congress.

The budget committees

The House and Senate budget committees report resolutions in March and September before the beginning of the fiscal year; this enables Congress to set total tax and spending levels as well as targets for thirteen or so large categories of spending—defense and agriculture, for example. (See Figure 14-7.) "Per-

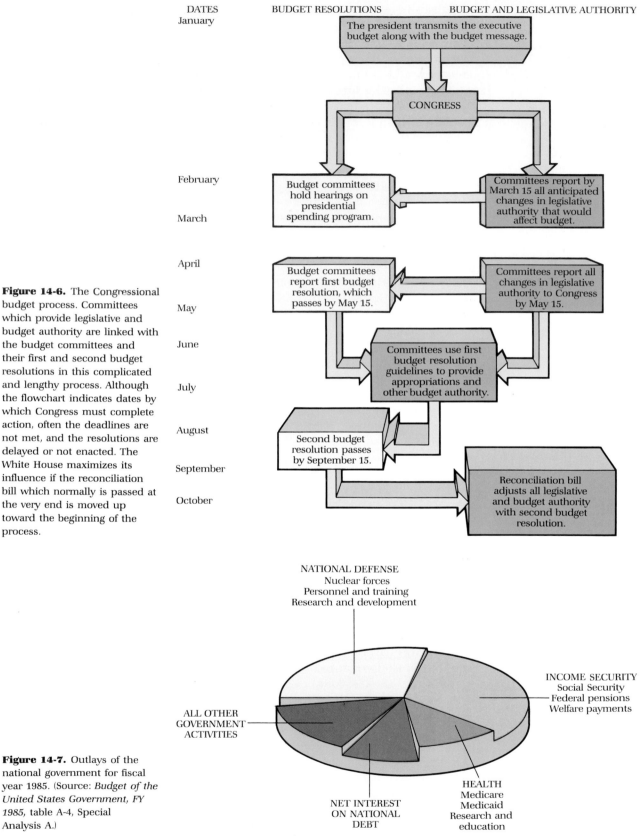

Figure 14-6. The Congressional budget process. Committees which provide legislative and budget authority are linked with the budget committees and their first and second budget resolutions in this complicated and lengthy process. Although the flowchart indicates dates by which Congress must complete action, often the deadlines are not met, and the resolutions are delayed or not enacted. The White House maximizes its influence if the reconciliation bill which normally is passed at the very end is moved up toward the beginning of the process.

DATES   BUDGET RESOLUTIONS   BUDGET AND LEGISLATIVE AUTHORITY

January

The president transmits the executive budget along with the budget message.

CONGRESS

February

March

Budget committees hold hearings on presidential spending program.

Committees report by March 15 all anticipated changes in legislative authority that would affect budget.

April

May

Budget committees report first budget resolution, which passes by May 15.

Committees report all changes in legislative authority to Congress by May 15.

June

July

Committees use first budget resolution guidelines to provide appropriations and other budget authority.

August

September

Second budget resolution passes by September 15.

October

Reconciliation bill adjusts all legislative and budget authority with second budget resolution.

NATIONAL DEFENSE
Nuclear forces
Personnel and training
Research and development

INCOME SECURITY
Social Security
Federal pensions
Welfare payments

ALL OTHER
GOVERNMENT
ACTIVITIES

NET INTEREST
ON NATIONAL
DEBT

HEALTH
Medicare
Medicaid
Research and
education

Figure 14-7. Outlays of the national government for fiscal year 1985. (Source: *Budget of the United States Government, FY 1985*, table A-4, Special Analysis A.)

haps the most important aspect of the resolution," according to Brock Adams, a former House chairman, "is the fact that it contains the budget of Congress and not that of the President."[18]

The House Budget Committee has thirty-one members, five of whom come from the Appropriations Committee and five from the Ways and Means Committee. The House party leaders also choose several, and the House legislative caucuses choose the remainder. The Democrats, who control the House, give themselves a large majority ratio. The House Budget Committee is highly partisan, with liberal Democrats confronting conservative Republicans. The Democrats write their own budget resolution and ignore the Republicans. Yet the members are more pragmatic than their ideological stances would suggest. "One thing that happens, regardless of philosophical stripe," says Jim Jones, a former chairman, "is that once they sit on the Budget Committee they become pragmatic. They become driven by the numbers."[19] House members can serve on the committee for only four years in any decade, and so they do not gain much expertise, nor do they have much incentive to build up the committee's power at the expense of other House committees. They are usually inclined to compromise with the Appropriations Committee and the Ways and Means Committee.

The Senate Budget Committee consists of twenty members. They too are pragmatic. Unlike their counterparts in the House, they usually form a centrist bipartisan coalition, freezing out extremists.[20] The members can serve for as long as they wish, which gives them an incentive to expand their power at the expense of other committees. They have had many battles with the Appropriations Committee, the Finance Committee, and the Armed Services Committee because their budget recommendations often attempt to predetermine policies to be considered later by these committees.

The appropriations committees

The two appropriations committees report out thirteen bills (and several supplemental bills) which provide about two-fifths of the total budget authority. At one time members prided themselves on their role as "guardians of the Treasury." Members were strongly conservative, and Republicans combined with southern and border-state Democrats to fashion a bipartisan majority. According to one representative, "No subcommittee of which I have ever been a member has ever reported out a bill without a cut in the budget."[21] Between 1947 and 1959 the House Appropriations Committee cut estimates more than three-fourths of the time in thirty-seven agencies.[22] (This did not mean that agencies took cuts below their base; most of the time the committee simply cut a part of the *increase* proposed in the president's budget.) In the 1970s the committee changed. Republican presidents began suggesting absolute cuts or small increases, and the committee Democrats championed these programs.

There are thirteen subcommittees—one for each appropriations bill. They see the budget as a storehouse of goodies. The unit with jurisdiction over the Interior Department, for example, received requests from 260 members to include their pet projects in the appropriations bill in 1984. As the former director of the OMB David Stockman observed, "There is no such thing as a fiscal conservative when it comes to his district or his subcommittee."[23] Funding defense contracts, military bases, highways, hospitals, airports, and harbors helps committee members get reelected, and they also can use job-training, education, and health programs as a form of "human resources" pork barrel,

Urban representatives are especially sensitive to cuts in expenditures for bridges, tunnels, and mass transit. (*Gerard Rancinan: Sygma.*)

creating their own political machines with the aid of officials who receive federal grants. Members of Congress get on subcommittees that have jurisdiction over programs which benefit their districts or states. New committee assignments and transfers bring on people who want to increase funding and expand programs.[24]

The Senate Appropriations Committee has always counterbalanced the House Appropriations Committee. In the 1950s and 1960s, when the House cut presidential requests, the senators acted as a "court of appeal" for executive agencies: they could testify before the Senate committee and try to get it to recommend more money than its counterpart in the House. Senate rules reinforced the tendency of the committee to up the ante; subcommittee meetings are open to senators who are not on the full committee but who express an interest in programs being considered by the committee—and mostly they come to boost these programs. Since the Republicans took control of the Senate in 1981, the committee has served as a buffer between right-wing Republican senators intent on making very large cuts (even larger than those proposed by the president) and moderate to liberal House Democrats intent on preventing all cuts proposed by the OMB.

The congressional budget process

The president's budget is referred simultaneously to the budget committees, which consider overall tax and spending policies, and to the appropriations committees and other committees which have jurisdiction over spending. The committees that deal with legislative authority report out new authorizations no later than May 15. On the same date Congress passes the ***first budget resolution,*** setting overall spending limits and providing targets for specific categories. As the appropriations committees begin their work, they are caught between authorizing committees that want Congress to approve new activities and budget committees that call for cutbacks.

Granting budget authority. The committees that report bills granting budget authority (the most important of which are the appropriations committees) have several options. They have the ***current services estimate*** in the presidential budget, which tells them what it would cost simply to continue funding an agency at existing levels. They have the president's request. At hearings they can find out what an agency or department originally asked for. They have alternatives prepared by the Congressional Budget Office. And they have target figures from the budget resolutions.

Officials in agencies in the executive branch testify before the subcommittees, sometimes daring to ask for more money than the president requested. "Mr. Chairman, you would not think that it would be proper for me to be in charge of this work and not be enthusiastic about it and not think that I ought to have a lot more money, would you?" asked an assistant chief of the Forest Service.[25] Such witnesses are followed by lobbyists for interest groups, who ask for even more money.

Members of the subcommittees have so many programs to consider and so many numbers to deal with that they must adopt a strategy to simplify their calculations. They cannot go through every line in the budget or consider every program in detail. Instead, they assume that most programs should be funded at past levels (adjusting for inflation), matching the incremental approach of the agencies whose budgets they are considering. In the case of certain sacred cows, such as the Federal Bureau of Investigation, they always follow or even exceed the president's requests. A program is reviewed carefully if the president proposes major changes, if committee members strongly like or dislike it, or if the program can help members get reelected. Subcommittee members specialize and defer on minor matters to others with expertise. Specialization and reciprocal deference help members cope but mean that they take a fragmented view: they see small parts of the budget, not the whole picture.

The committees *mark up* the president's budget and substitute their own figures. They may keep the current level of funding, make across-the-board increases or cuts, or develop their own budgets. They may also attach restrictions, prohibitions, exemptions, waivers, and other provisions which specify how money may and may not be spent; these *limitation riders* generally begin with the words "no funds appropriated" and go on to specify the restriction. Recent examples include prohibitions on using federal funds for abortions or

Members of Congress from rural areas usually seek assignments to committees and subcommittees affecting farmers. By 1985 farm programs cost more than $30 billion annually. (*United States Department of Agriculture.*)

school busing. About forty or fifty such riders are adopted during each session. (Unlike regular statutes, a prohibition expires with the funding.)

Committees write bills so that they can build a majority coalition on the floor. They report measures that will result in particular and tangible benefits to the majority. These involve packages with many different projects or logrolls. Projects are funded on the basis of horse trades for votes rather than high cost-benefit ratios. Agencies must disperse their facilities into areas where costs are high and coordination becomes difficult. Funds for slum removal, public housing, and mass transit go to smaller towns that have little need for them, while large cities decay, so that the gravy can be spread.

Yet such budgeting makes political if not economic sense. Bills get the acquiescence, if not the strong support, of a majority. Rural areas vote for programs that benefit cities in return for programs that aid their interests. Research programs gain greater support when laboratories and clinics are located throughout the country, not in just a few centers. There are good reasons for having federal facilities located at the grass roots and not centered in Washington, especially at a time when mistrust of government is high. Programs which are paid for by all taxpayers but which benefit only a few are not as likely to be popular, and those voting for them are vulnerable; bigger packages with something for everyone help legislators with their constituents.

Committee conflict. Just as different units in the executive branch play games with one another, congressional committees try to influence the budget at the expense of their rivals. Conflict occurs when the budget committees face off against committees that report bills with excessive budget authority, as well as when attempts are made to put together deficit-reduction packages. Usually the result parallels the legislative process: it is not a case of the president versus Congress, but rather a matter of shifting alliances in order to pit some presidential agencies, departments, and committee majorities against others.

BUDGET RESOLUTIONS VERSUS BUDGET AUTHORITY. Bills providing budget authority are due to be passed into law on the seventh day after Labor Day. By September 15, Congress is also supposed to pass its *second budget resolution.* This timetable pits the budget committees, with their comprehensive "top-down" approach, against the legislative and spending committees, with their "bottom-up" approach. Conflict is virtually guaranteed. The Senate Budget Committee and the Armed Services Committee have squared off over the size of the defense budget, and the Finance Committee has fought the Budget Committee over backdoor spending measures.

Sometimes the second budget resolution is not reported or passed, either because of the crush of business near the end of the session (or in an election year when Congress recesses) or because the Budget Committee does not have the votes. (The House has a rule which provides that the first resolution substitutes for the second resolution.) Congress then simply passes the money bills reported by other committees. Other times the appropriations bills are not reported because they could conflict with budget ceilings, and Congress funds the government by *continuing resolution* (keeping spending at the existing rate). Sometimes a second budget resolution passes but simply ratifies what the spending committees have decided to do. The process is preserved, but hard choices are postponed to avoid conflict—what Louis Fisher refers to as "escapist budgeting."[26]

Occasionally the budget committees stand up to the spending committees and get a strong second resolution through Congress. This may be followed by a *reconciliation bill:* a proposed law which implements changes in other spending measures that have already been enacted. Such reconciliation is rare, although it remains the goal of the budget committees.

DEFICIT-REDUCTION BILLS. Yet another crunch occurs when the budget and taxing committees put together a package of proposed spending cuts and tax increases to cut the deficit, as they did in 1984 and 1985. With the participation of the White House, congressional leaders may put together a large package in one bill—as they did in 1981 and 1985—which short-circuits not only the regular budget process (and may even precede the adoption of budget resolutions) but also most appropriations measures. The deficit-reduction measure may contain multiyear "caps," or ceilings, on expenditures, which if enacted are taken as definitive directions to the spending committees.

PRESIDENTIAL BUDGET STRATEGIES

Thus far, this chapter has presented a pretty bleak picture of budget politics. Presidents present comprehensive budgets, but their own agencies and departments have an incentive to sabotage them and demand more. Congress has the power, through its budget resolutions and reconciliation bills, to implement a comprehensive program, but friction between committees, pressure from lobbyists, and escapist budgeting are the norm. Congress often undercuts its budget committees, and the result is "bottom-up" incremental increases rather than hard decisions.

Faced with the complexity of the budget process, presidents have adopted several different strategies. Looking at some of them provides a better understanding of relations between the legislative and the executive branches: how hard it is for presidents to get what they want and how wrong moves and missteps can backfire disastrously—but how well-thought-out strategies and bold maneuvers can yield great dividends.

The veto strategy

Presidents can threaten to veto any of the spending measures (such as the thirteen appropriations bills and the supplemental bills) which Congress passes, claiming that they will "bust the budget." For several reasons, such threats may not be very effective. For one thing, presidents lack the *item veto,* suggested by Eisenhower and Reagan, which would allow them to veto particular items in a spending bill rather than the whole measure. (Forty-three governors have such a power.) Usually Congress can design a bill which contains many things that the president wants and only a few that the president does not want, making it hard to veto.

Congress usually upholds the rare presidential veto. Sometimes more than one-third of the members of one chamber will pledge in advance to support a veto, giving the president some bargaining chips in negotiations with a spending committee. More than 144 Republicans, for example, sent a letter to Reagan making such a pledge in 1983.

Sometimes Congress can maneuver the president into casting an unpopular veto or accepting an unpalatable bill. In 1983 the Democrats wanted to put Reagan on the defensive; they hoped that he would veto public service jobs, extensions of unemployment insurance, medical insurance for the unemployed, and government assistance to prevent mortgage foreclosures so that they could charge "unfairness" in the next election. If Reagan had signed the measures, they could have taken the credit for them. Often legislators from the president's own party urge the president to sign election-year appropriations bills, especially the end-of-session supplemental bill, which usually contains expenditures designed to help members who are running in tight races.

The veto is a defensive weapon. It can keep Congress from funding at higher levels than the president would like, but not from giving less than the president wants—as in defense programs. The veto threat works best when the president wants to cut and Congress wants to increase; that has been the case for most nondefense programs since 1978.

The impoundment strategy

After Congress grants budget authority and the fiscal year has begun, on October 1, the president may use the ***impoundment*** strategy: have the Treasury and the OMB withhold funds from agencies. Congress never actually gives *money* to agencies when it grants budget authority; it simply authorizes the Treasury to honor checks written by them to cover their expenses. Therefore, it is impossible for Congress to prevent the OMB from telling an agency not to spend money or to prevent the Treasury from refusing to honor checks that go over its allotments.

In the past, presidents have relied on their constitutional powers as commander in chief and chief executive to impound money for weapons or funding for domestic programs in wartime as Roosevelt did with public works projects during the Second World War. Truman, Eisenhower, and Kennedy all stopped development of weapons systems which they opposed, and Truman refused to make a loan to the Spanish government which Congress had ordered.

Presidents have also used impoundment powers given to them by Congress. One law specifies that if an authorized activity can be carried out for less money than the amounts appropriated, the president need not spend the extra money. Other laws direct the president to impound money intended for state or local governments if they do not comply with federal laws, such as those prohibiting racial discrimination. Sometimes presidents ask Congress for special resolutions or laws which allow them to make across-the-board spending cuts or impose a spending freeze. Johnson and Nixon did so during the Vietnamese war to restrain inflation and redirect spending into defense. But Congress usually gives presidents less authority than they ask for, and it exempts so many programs that the "cuts" are symbolic; Nixon called one a "rubber ceiling" because it could stretch to accommodate any further spending mandated by Congress.[27]

President Nixon made the most use of impoundment powers. As of 1973 he had impounded more than $20 billion, and his budget for FY 1974 contained a list of 109 reductions that he intended to make, 101 of which he claimed would require no congressional action.[28] Nixon justified these cuts by arguing that Congress had implicitly given him the power to make them when it passed the Economic Stabilization Act of 1971 (which allowed him to control wages and prices and take related actions to cure runaway inflation and an international currency crisis, but which did not specifically mention impounding funds).

But Nixon was not impounding funds to stabilize the economy. Instead, he was making *policy impoundments;* he was cutting funds and even completely eliminating programs that he opposed, even though they had been given legislative and budget authorizations by Congress. Nixon targeted pork barrel programs—such as electrification of rural areas; antipoverty programs, including programs for community action, public housing, and urban renewal; and environmental programs—using impoundments as a substitute for getting Congress to pass laws reducing or eliminating these programs.

These impoundments struck at the heart of congressional politics. If the president could make them stick, he would control favors, side payments, pet projects, and logrolls. No committee could maintain its pattern of trades and its ability to forge coalitions if members thought that the deals could be undone and the funding terminated. And on the loftier plane of constitutional principle, as Senator Sam Ervin explained, "He has no authority under the Constitution to decide which laws will be executed, or to what extent they will be enforced. Yet, by using the impounding technique, the President is able to do just that."[29]

Interest groups, federal employees' unions, and state and local governments took the Nixon administration to court, where it lost about fifty federal cases. Judges ruled that Nixon had no legal authority to impound funds. Congress then passed the Budget and Impoundment Act of 1974, which provided that deferrals of spending to future fiscal years would go into effect after forty-five legislative days unless either chamber of Congress disapproved. Rescissions (in this case, funding cuts) would require Congress to pass a ***rescission bill*** in the regular legislative process.

The one-chamber veto was invalidated by the Supreme Court in 1983, and so Congress uses regular or supplemental appropriations bills to approve or disapprove of presidential requests for deferrals.[30] But Congress usually grants deferrals; in most years 90 percent are allowed. As for rescissions, that is a different story: approvals have ranged from 80 percent in 1979 to none in 1980, and usually a president winds up with fewer than half.[31]

The reconciliation strategy

In 1981 the Reagan administration dominated budget politics by temporarily changing the process. Reagan's program called for spending cuts of $41.3 billion from the proposals of the outgoing Carter administration and for a total of $130 billion in the first three fiscal years of his term. Ordinarily, new presidents present their program to legislative authorizing committees in piecemeal fashion. To cut budget authority, they must fight thirteen separate appropriations battles (one for each bill) and deal with backdoor spending and various committees that have jurisdiction.

If Reagan had fought his battles one by one, he would have dissipated his election mandate to cut spending. His proposals would have been stalled, gutted, or modified. Interest groups could have logrolled with one another, and congressional committees could have created majority coalitions against his cuts ("I'll vote against your cuts, and you vote against mine").

The fast track. Ordinarily, the first budget resolution sets goals for congressional committees, and the second resolution sets the actual ceiling on expenditures, with a reconciliation bill modifying committee authorizations that go above those levels. This timetable leaves hard choices for last. Reagan's supporters decided to reverse the process. Reagan decided to put his entire budget program—including all proposed cuts—into the first budget resolution and to follow it up immediately with a reconciliation bill.

The first budget resolution contained *binding* instructions to authorizing

President Reagan and his advisers planned a successful budget campaign in 1981. (*Larry Downing: Woodfin Group.*)

committees. They were required to report changes in laws necessary to conform to the budget totals within thirty days. These changes were then compiled by the budget committees into a single, omnibus reconciliation bill. Thus all Reagan's proposed budget shifts came early in the congressional session, all at one time, and on a single all-or-nothing bill.

The national agenda. The president used a national agenda strategy to win over public opinion before the important votes were cast. Public opinion about spending is usually uninformed and contradictory. Large majorities believe that the government consumes too much of the GNP and operates wastefully, and three-fourths of the public think that the size of government should be reduced. Around four-fifths support a constitutional amendment which would require a balanced budget (which they think would lower spending, not raise taxes). But large majorities favor increases for most specific government programs, including many social insurance programs that benefit the middle and working classes. With the exception of a few programs narrowly targeted at the poor, such as food stamps, welfare, and Medicaid, there was no support for cutting most domestic activities. Even in the case of programs for the poor, the public supports cuts to eliminate fraud and waste, not to deprive the truly needy. Conservatives try to win over the public by focusing on the general principle that spending should be cut. Liberals counter by talking about the effects that specific cuts will have on programs which the public supports.

Reagan hammered away on general principles. Just before the first budget resolution passed, a Gallup poll reported that 68 percent of the public approved of Reagan, 58 percent liked the way he was handling the economy, and 48 percent thought that they would personally benefit from his proposals. A Harris poll showed that 64 percent of the public thought that too much federal spending was the major cause of their own financial troubles. The White House organized closed-circuit television broadcasts to 15,000 Reagan supporters around the country to get them to sell the program at the grass roots, sponsored briefings for newspaper editors and publishers, arranged for press conferences and speeches around the country, and used other national agenda techniques. "We're facing a popularity issue," Tip O'Neill recognized, just before the vote on the resolution; "he's done the greatest selling job I've ever seen."[32]

The resolution passed the Republican-controlled Senate with ease. But the Democrats controlled the House. The White House Congressional Liaison Office created a bipartisan coalition of Republicans and conservative southern Democrats. The president held 69 meetings in the Oval Office, and more than 60 Democrats met with him during the three weeks preceding the vote. Reagan even telephoned members while the House was voting to round up support. Along with the carrot went the stick: the White House orchestrated a mail campaign to influence wavering southern Democrats, while Republican Party operatives told Republican moderates that unless they voted for it, they would face opposition in the primaries and would receive no funds from the party. The result: all 190 Republicans and 63 Democrats voted with the administration.

Next, the Senate Budget Committee reported a reconciliation measure to implement the resolution's cuts. The Senate quickly passed the measure. But House committees, controlled by liberal and moderate Democrats, ignored many of the first resolution's cutting instructions, and many of their changes were ploys which would salvage programs and prevent real cuts. So Reagan's supporters offered their own bill, and again the coalition passed it. Finally, 72 senators and 183 representatives attended a mammoth conference, which divided itself into 58 subconferences, and eventually reported out an omnibus reconciliation bill. As passed, it repealed or amended 436 laws and affected 266 of the 1310 spending accounts in the budget. Projected cuts in outlays in Reagan's first term totaled $140 billion, and his approval ratings soared to new highs, with 68 percent of the public supporting these cuts.[33]

Why early reconciliation worked. Reagan was able to dominate budget politics because he compressed the budget process, capitalized on his election mandate, exploited divisions among the Democrats, and retained public support during his "honeymoon" period. By putting together a single package, Reagan made the budget cuts highly visible and dramatic—susceptible to national agenda politics. This raised the stakes for his party, discouraged defections, and limited the negotiating room of his own leaders. Reagan created the equivalent of a parliamentary "vote of confidence": no member of his party could afford to undercut him on such an important bill so early in his first term.

The end of the process for one year: President Reagan signs the 1981 tax cut and budget bill at his California ranch. (*AP Photocolor.*)

The Democrats hoped to stretch out the process. They wanted to split the reconciliation bill into six separate measures, each of which would require a separate vote, so that different floating coalitions could be formed against the administration. Instead of casting a single vote for or against Reagan, they wanted Congress to cast many votes—on numerous amendments and on the final bills—which would put legislators on record about particular programs and keep them susceptible to pressures from interest groups and constituencies. Moreover, the Republicans would then be able to vote for Reagan on some issues but defect on others without being branded party traitors. The issue would turn from big government to a set of mini-issues: welfare, housing, transit systems, social security, and so forth. The House, controlled by Reagan's coalition, beat back all attempts to split up the omnibus bill, and its rules called for a single up or down vote with no amendments. "Do we have the right to meet our target, or can he in one package deregulate, delegislate, the things that have taken years to do?" Tip O'Neill asked before the crucial procedural votes were cast.[34] The answer came back: Reagan could and would.

Limits on early reconciliation. Presidents can rarely use the reconciliation strategy. When Reagan proposed $13 billion in cuts the following September, many southern Democrats and moderate Republicans defected from his coalition; he prevailed only after promising the "Gypsy Moth" Republican moderates that he would restore funds for some of their favored programs. Later they charged that he had not kept his promises, prompting Tip O'Neill to remark, "Republicans are fighting Republicans. My strategy is don't block the view."[35] The defeat marked the end of the Reagan budget coalition.

Congressional leaders of both parties refused to go along with early reconciliation the following year. And after the 1982 congressional elections, the conservative coalition no longer dominated the House, as a result of the Republicans' losses. In the Senate, Republican Party and committee leaders followed their own priorities on taxes and spending and began to distance themselves from the administration. By 1983 the budget process was completely out of presidential control.

Reagan decided to walk away from the entire budget process. He warned Congress that he would veto "budget-busting bills," but then did nothing as spending targets exceeded OMB totals. For the four years of Reagan's first term, spending increased by 41 percent, which hardly indicated much success for the "curtailer in chief." The president had learned that the organized constituencies favoring increased spending for programs could outlast his initial honeymoon period and his temporary successes with national agenda politics. The lesson was obvious: a new president should go for broke in the first two years with a large package of cuts and a national agenda campaign, because after that the presidential program faces legislative gridlock or reversal.

By 1985, having had three consecutive failures after one stunning initial success, the president was ready to exploit his second-term postinaugural honeymoon period. Again he introduced a package of large expenditures and tax cuts. Again he used national agenda politics to win public support for his program. But this time he was a lame-duck president, facing opposition from his own Senate Republicans, and the failure of his program to emerge intact once again demonstrates how hard it is for presidents to dominate the budget process.

FOCUS

THE REFORM AGENDA. Some reforms would increase presidential control, others would enable Congress to make more rational and comprehensive decisions, and still others would require both branches to observe certain limits.

Presidentialist reforms. Presidentialist reforms would allow the president to introduce the budget as a single bill, which would have priority on the congressional calendar. It would be voted on early in the session. A reconciliation measure, which would also have priority, could be introduced by the administration after the resolution passed. It would not be subject to amendment. These changes would give presidents an annual "vote of confidence" and would require them to conduct a national agenda campaign each year to obtain support for their budget. If they failed to do so, and if Congress passed a substitute budget based on its committee work, the lines would be clearly drawn between presidents and their opponents, which would make budget politics central to the following election and would promote a more responsible party system.

Congress could give the president greater discretion in deferring or rescinding spending during the fiscal year, or a constitutional amendment could give the president an item veto over appropriations. But Congress is not likely to pass any measures that give up its budget powers to the president.

Congressionalist reforms. Some reforms would strengthen the budget committees. The first budget resolution could establish binding ceilings rather than just suggest targets. The budget committees could give binding directions to taxing and spending committees. Conceivably, the work of the appropriations committees and their subcommittees could be transferred to enlarged budget committees. But because of the power of the taxing and spending committees, it is more likely that the top-down budget process will be weakened than that the committees, with their bottom-up approach, will lose their powers or have their functions consolidated. The budget committees and the budget resolutions are in danger of being reformed out of existence—not the appropriations committees.

IN CONCLUSION

Budget politics has always involved a free-for-all within the executive branch, as agencies have fought with departments to increase spending and as the OMB has fought with departments to lower it. The presidential budget then entered the legislative arena, where legislative and budget authority committees make their modifications. The result was a set of outcomes, based on the results of the legislative struggle, rather than budget policy. The system was suited for the legislative logroll and compromise.

The budget process was modified substantially in 1974 in the aftermath of the crisis over Nixon's impoundments. It was supposed to create top-down budgeting: Congress would have to make hard choices and formulate comprehensive policies. The Congressional Budget Office would give Congress the technical expertise to challenge the OMB and develop its own options. This might encourage a more responsible party system, since the majority party in Congress could formulate its own budget and take responsibility for it in the next election.

Sometimes the new process works as intended, with the two congressional parties confronting each other. On occasion the White House dominates budget politics by using early reconciliation during the honeymoon period. But often the process does not work. Bottom-up budgeting is still favored by legislators. Spending remains oriented toward district and state interests. Agencies spend on the wrong things—pet projects or services for the most highly organized and politically influential groups. Meanwhile, the government underfunds scientific research and social services, underpays its employees, and allows its facilities to deteriorate. Too little money is spent on management and program oversight.

Often budget resolutions are reported and voted on late. The second resolution may not even be enacted. Reconciliation has been used sparingly: in 1980 to trim $5 billion and in 1981 after the first budget resolution—and since then not at all. Sometimes Congress votes to suspend rules requiring the second budget resolution to be adopted before the final vote on appropriations bills, and instead considers the appropriations first (as it did in 1983 and 1984). At other times appropriations bills and other budget authority bills are not passed on time (except for the one funding Congress!), and as a result the fiscal year begins with the passage of a continuing resolution (providing funding at existing levels) until Congress acts. Sometimes that resolution serves for the entire year and no other authority is passed; continuing resolutions controlled the foreign aid program for several years, for example. The national government and the state governments cannot plan for the coming fiscal year when they do not know whether or when new funding levels will go into effect.

There are too many committees, and they get in one another's way. Budget committees issue targets and instructions which legislative committees ignore. Authorizing committees write backdoor provisions that circumvent appropriations committees, which in turn undercut the instructions of budget committees and infringe on other committees when they attach "riders." In most years, neither the president nor party leaders can control these committees; negotiation and compromise among them shape the final outcomes.

There are many reforms which could create comprehensive and rational budgeting, dominated by the president or by the majority party in Congress. Few are likely to be adopted, because they do not offer legislators any political advantages. "We want more government than we can pay for," observes Alice Rivlin, a former CBO director, "and no process can help solve that problem."[36] Proposing changes in the process without protecting the power stakes of the participants is putting the cart before the horse. Only when a coalition can be organized that insists on comprehensive, top-down budgeting and can win the battles with other congressional committees and then maintain itself through the subsequent midterm elections will fundamental change in budget politics occur.

NOTES

1. Kermit Gordon, "Reflections on Spending," *Public Policy*, vol. 15, p. 11; *The New York Times*, May 8, 1981.
2. *The New York Times*, Apr. 11, 1980.
3. Valerie Bunce, "Changing Leaders and Changing Policies: The Impact of Elite Succession on Budgeting Priorities in Democratic Countries," *American Journal of Political Science*, vol. 24, no. 3, August 1980, pp. 373–396.
4. *The New York Times*, Mar. 14, 1983.
5. Aaron Wildavsky, *The Politics of the Budgetary Process*, 1st ed., Little, Brown, Boston, 1964, p. 100.
6. Mark Kamlet and David Mowery, "The Budgetary Base in Federal Resource Allocation," *American Journal of Political Science*, vol. 24, no. 4, November 1980, pp. 804–808; Otto Davis, M. A. H. Dempster, and Aaron Wildavsky, "A Theory of the Budgetary Process," *American Political Science Review*, vol. 60, no. 3, September 1966, pp. 529–547.

7. Peter Natchez and Irving Bupp, "Policy and Priority in the Budget Process," *American Political Science Review*, vol. 67, no. 3, September 1973, pp. 951–963.

8. Lance T. LeLoup, "Agency Policy Actions: Determinants of Nonincremental Change," in Randall Ripley and Grace Franklin (eds.), *Policy-Making in the Executive Branch*, Free Press, New York, 1975, pp. 65–90.

9. W. Bowman Cutter, "The Battle of the Budget," *The Atlantic*, March 1981, p. 64.

10. William Greider, "The Education of David Stockman," *The Atlantic*, no. 247, December 1981, p. 30. This "close-up" was prepared with the assistance of Len Kreynin, Columbia College.

11. Ibid., p. 36.

12. *The Wall Street Journal*, Feb. 9, 1981.

13. *Newsweek*, Nov. 23, 1981, p. 41.

14. *The New York Times*, Nov. 22, 1981.

15. Louis Fisher, *Constitutional Conflicts between Congress and the President*, Princeton University Press, Princeton, 1985, p. 231.

16. Ibid., p. 229.

17. *The Federalist*, number 48.

18. LeLoup, op. cit., p. 126.

19. *Congressional Quarterly Weekly Reports*, vol. 41, no. 9, Mar. 5, 1983, p. 459.

20. John Ellwood and James Thurber, "The Congressional Budget Process Re-examined," in Lawrence C. Dodd and Bruce I. Oppenheimer (eds.), *Congress Reconsidered*, 2d ed., Congressional Quarterly Press, Washington, D.C., 1981, pp. 246–274.

21. Richard E. Fenno, *The Power of the Purse*, Little, Brown, Boston, 1966, pp. 311–312.

22. Ibid., p. 312.

23. Kenneth Shepsle, "The Failure of Congressional Budgeting," *Society*, vol. 20, May–June 1983, p. 5.

24. Bruce A. Ray, "Federal Spending and the Selection of Committee Assignments in the U.S. House of Representatives," *American Journal of Political Science*, vol. 24, no. 3, August 1980, p. 494.

25. Wildavsky, op. cit., p. 19.

26. Fisher, op. cit., p. 241.

27. James L. Sundquist, *The Decline and Resurgence of Congress*, Brookings, Washington, D.C., 1982, pp. 220–221.

28. Ibid., p. 205.

29. Sundquist, op. cit., p. 206.

30. Louis Fisher, "The Impact of *Chadha* on the Budget Process," *CRS Review*, 1983, pp. 12–14.

31. Ellwood and Thurber, op. cit., table 11–15, p. 266.

32. *The New York Times*, May 11, 1981; *The Gallup Report*, May 1981, p. 11.

33. *Congressional Quarterly Weekly Reports*, June 27, 1981.

34. Lance LeLoup, "After the Blitz—Reagan and the U.S. Congressional Budget Process," *Legislative Studies Quarterly*, vol. 7, no. 3, August 1982, p. 321.

35. Shepsle, op. cit., p. 8.

36. *The New York Times*, July 13, 1984.

FURTHER READING

Boskin, Michael, and Aaron Wildavsky (eds.): *The Federal Budget: Economics and Politics*, Institute for Contemporary Studies, Berkeley, Calif., 1982. Articles on trends in spending in the 1980s and on Reagan's budget strategies.

Fisher, Louis: *The Presidential Spending Power*, Princeton University Press, Princeton, N.J., 1975. A study of how the executive branch controls spending and avoids congressional mandates.

Ippolito, Dennis S.: *The Budget and National Politics*, Freeman, San Francisco, 1978. An overview of the modern budget process.

LeLoup, Lance T.: *Budgetary Politics*, Kings Court Communications, Brunswick, Ohio, 1977. A book about who wins and who loses in budget politics.

Schick, Allen: *Congress and Money*, Urban Institute, Washington, D.C., 1980. A comprehensive account of budgeting, emphasizing relations between different congressional committees.

Sundquist, James L.: *The Decline and Resurgence of Congress*, Brookings, Washington, D.C., 1982. An account of how Congress regained the power of the purse in the 1970s.

Wildavsky, Aaron: *The Politics of the Budgetary Process*, 3d ed., Little, Brown, Boston, 1979. A classic exposition of agency strategies in dealing with the OMB and the appropriations committees.

THE STUDY BREAK

Americathon. In this movie, made in 1979, the United States is so broke that only a telethon will save it from bankruptcy. A late-night bomb.

Greider, William: "The Education of David Stockman," *The Atlantic*, vol. 247, no. 12, December 1981. This article, containing the OMB director's admissions about what really went on in the first year of the Reagan administration, was a bombshell. Stockman was almost fired because of it.

USEFUL SOURCES

An Analysis of the President's Budgetary Proposals for the Fiscal Year, Congressional Budget Office, Washington, D.C., annually. The CBO's own projections for revenues and expenditures, as well as its analysis of presidential proposals. The CBO also issues a report in three volumes to the budget committees each February: *Part I, The Economic Outlook; Part II, Baseline Budget Projections for Fiscal Years____* (the years for which the budget is projected); and *Part III, Reducing the Deficit: Spending and Revenue Options.* These constitute alternatives to the administration's program.

The Budget in Brief, GPO, Washington, D.C., annually. Eighty pages summarizing important decisions, trends, and budget totals, including useful charts and tables.

Budget of the United States Government, GPO, Washington, D.C., annually. A volume consisting of more than 650 pages, half of which contain proposed expenditures for coming fiscal years.

Budget of the United States Government, Appendix, GPO, Washington, D.C., annually. This volume specifies, item by item, how much will be spent for each program, by each agency, and for what (salary, transportation, and so forth).

Budget of the United States Government, Major Themes and Additional Budget Details, GPO, Washington, D.C., annually. A publication covering many of the large program categories.

Special Analyses: The Budget of the United States Government, GPO, Washington, D.C., annually, 11 vols. Each volume deals in great detail with a particular function of government. One especially important volume covers the current services estimates, borrowing and debt management, federal credit, tax expenditures, and intergovernmental transfers of funds.

The Grace Commission, *President's Private Sector Survey on Cost Control, Final Report*, GPO, Washington, D.C., 1983, parts 1 and 2. A study of government waste and incompetence, containing materials on budgeting and financial controls.

Pechman, Joseph (ed.): *Setting National Priorities: The 1984 Budget*, Brookings, Washington, D.C., 1983. A Washington think tank assesses the presidential proposals and offers alternatives.

ORGANIZATIONS

Congressional Budget Office. House Annex 2, Second and D Streets, S.W., Washington, D.C. 20515. For more information telephone 202-226-2621.

House Budget Committee. Suite 214, Annex No. 1, Washington, D.C. 20515. For more information telephone 202-226-7200.

Office of Management and Budget. Executive Office Building, Washington, D.C. 20503. For more information telephone 202-395-3080.

Senate Budget Committee. Room 203, Carroll Arms Annex, 301 First Street, N.E., Washington, D.C. 20510. For more information telephone 202-395-3080.

The Constitution, signed in
1787, is housed today in the
National Archives. (*Howard
Chandler Christy, "Signing of the
United States Constitution,"
Granger Collection; Fred J.
Maroon.*)

The Constitution of the United States

The preamble defines the Constitution as a political compact of the American people and sets forth their goals. It is not an operative part of the Constitution and cannot be used to claim powers or assert rights.

We the people of the United States, in Order to form a more perfect Union, establish Justice, insure domestic Tranquility, provide for the common defence, promote the general Welfare, and secure the Blessings of Liberty to ourselves and our Posterity, do ordain and establish this CONSTITUTION for the United States of America.

ARTICLE I

Article I assigns all lawmaking powers to Congress, establishes qualifications for office and methods of election and impeachment, and enumerates and limits the legislative powers.

Members of the House need not be inhabitants of the districts they represent.

Section 1. All legislative Powers herein granted shall be vested in a Congress of the United States, which shall consist of a Senate and House of Representatives.

Section 2. The House of Representatives shall be composed of Members chosen every second Year by the People of the several States, and the Electors in each State shall have the Qualifications requisite for Electors of the most numerous Branch of the State Legislature.

No Person shall be a Representative who shall not have attained to the Age of twenty-five Years, and been seven Years a Citizen of the United States, and who shall not when elected, be an Inhabitant of that State in which he shall be chosen.

Representatives and direct Taxes shall be apportioned among the several States which may be included within this Union, according to their respective Numbers, which shall be determined by adding to the whole Number of free Persons, including those bound to Service for a Term of Years, and excluding Indians not taxed, three fifths of all other Persons. The actual Enumeration shall be made within three Years after the first Meeting of the Congress of the United States, and within every subsequent Term of ten Years, in such Manner as they shall by Law direct. The Number of Representatives shall not exceed one for every thirty Thousand, but each State shall have at Least one Representative; and until such enumeration shall be made, the State of New Hampshire shall be entitled to chuse three, Massachusetts eight, Rhode-Island and Providence Plantations one, Connecticut five, New-York six, New Jersey four, Pennsylvania eight, Delaware one, Maryland six, Virginia ten, North Carolina five, South Carolina five, and Georgia three.

This provision allows the national government to conduct a census of the population.

When vacancies happen in the Representation from any State, the Executive Authority thereof shall issue Writs of Election to fill such Vacancies.

The House of Representatives shall chuse their Speaker and other Officers; and shall have the sole Power of Impeachment.

Contrast election of representatives with provisions for senators in Section 3.

Section 3. The Senate of the United States shall be composed of two Senators from each State, chosen by the Legislature thereof, for six Years; and each Senator shall have one Vote.

Immediately after they shall be assembled in Consequence of the first Election, they shall be divided as equally as may be into three Classes. The Seats of the Senators of the first Class shall be vacated at the Expiration of the second Year, of the second Class at the Expiration of the fourth Year, and of the third Class at the Expiration of the sixth Year, so that one-third may be chosen every second Year; and if Vacancies happen by Resignation, or otherwise, during the Recess of the Legislature of any State, the Executive thereof may make temporary Appointments until the next Meeting of the Legislature, which shall then fill such Vacancies.

The Sixteenth Amendment provides for the popular election of senators.

Only one-third of the Senate seats are filled in each congressional election.

No Person shall be a Senator who shall not have attained to the Age of thirty Years, and been nine Years a Citizen of the United States, and who shall not, when elected, be an Inhabitant of that State in which he shall be chosen.

The Vice President of the United States shall be President of the Senate, but shall have no vote, unless they be equally divided.

The Senate shall chuse their other Officers, and also a President pro tempore, in the absence of the Vice President, or when he shall exercise the Office of the President of the United States.

The Senate shall have the sole Power to try all Impeachments. When sitting for that purpose, they shall be on Oath or Affirmation. When the President of the United States is tried, the Chief Justice shall preside: And no person shall be convicted without the Concurrence of two thirds of the Members present.

Judgment in Cases of Impeachment shall not extend further than to removal from Office, and disqualification to hold and enjoy any Office of honor, Trust, or Profit under the United States: but the Party convicted shall nevertheless be liable and subject to Indictment, Trial, Judgment, and Punishment, according to Law.

A Congress elected in November did not meet until thirteen months later, the following December, unless called into session after March 4 by the president. This provision has been superseded by the Twentieth Amendment.

Section 4. The Times, Places and Manner of holding Elections for Senators and Representatives, shall be prescribed in each state by the Legislature thereof; but the Congress may at any time by Law make or alter such Regulations except as to the Places of Chusing Senators.

The Congress shall assemble at least once in every Year, and such Meeting shall be on the first Monday in December, unless they shall by Law appoint a different Day.

Section 5. Each House shall be the Judge of the Elections, Returns and Qualifications of its own Members, and a Majority of each shall constitute a Quorum to do Business; but a smaller number may adjourn from day to day, and may be authorized to compel the Attendance of absent Members, in such Manner, and under such Penalties, as each House may provide.

Members of Congress may be expelled without impeachment or trial. Contrast this with the impeachment provisions regarding the executive and judicial branches.

Each House may determine the Rules of its Proceedings, punish its Members for disorderly Behaviour, and, with the Concurrence of two thirds, expel a Member.

Each House shall keep a Journal of its Proceedings, and from time to time publish the same, excepting such Parts as may in their Judgment require Secrecy; and the Yeas and Nays of the Members of either House on any question shall, at the Desire of one fifth of those Present, be entered on the Journal.

Neither House, during the Session of Congress, shall, without the Consent of the other, adjourn for more than three days, nor to any other Place than that in which the two Houses shall be sitting.

Section 6. The Senators and Representatives shall receive a Compensation for their Services, to be ascertained by Law, and paid out of the Treasury of the United States. They shall in all Cases, except Treason, Felony, and Breach of the Peace, be privileged from Arrest during their Attendance at the Session of their respective Houses, and in going to and returning from the same; and for any Speech or Debate in either House, they shall not be questioned in any other Place.

The separation clause prohibits members of Congress from being appointed department secretaries, thus preventing the possibility of a parliamentary government.

No Senator or Representative shall, during the Time for which he was elected, be appointed to any civil Office under the Authority of the United States, which shall have been created, or the Emoluments whereof shall have been increased, during such time; and no Person holding any Office under the United States shall be a Member of either House during his continuance in Office.

The Senate initiates its own tax bills in spite of this provision. Bills providing budget authority may be initiated in either chamber.

Section 7. All Bills for raising Revenue shall originate in the House of Representatives; but the Senate may propose or concur with Amendments as on other Bills.

Every Bill which shall have passed the House of Representatives and the Senate, shall, before it become a Law, be presented to the President of the United States; If he approve he shall sign it, but if not he shall return it, with his Objections, to that House in which it shall have originated, who

Bills become law if the president does not return them to Congress with a veto message within ten days. If Congress adjourns within ten days after presenting a bill to the president, it is pocket-vetoed if the president does not sign it.

Concurrent resolutions need not be presented to the president.

The two-thirds vote refers to a quorum, not the entire membership.

Section 8 contains seventeen enumerations of legislative power, which permit social programs, taxation, the regulation of currency, and interstate and foreign commerce (including manufacturing and service industries) and which enable the national government to manage the economy.

shall enter the Objections at large on their Journal, and proceed to reconsider it. If after such Reconsideration two thirds of that House shall agree to pass the Bill, it shall be sent, together with the Objections, to the other House, by which it shall likewise be reconsidered, and if approved by two thirds of that House, it shall become a Law. But in all such Cases the Votes of both Houses shall be determined by Yeas and Nays, and the Names of the Persons voting for and against the Bill shall be entered on the Journal of each House respectively. If any Bill shall not be returned by the President within ten Days (Sundays excepted) after it shall have been presented to him, the Same shall be a Law, in like Manner as if he had signed it, unless the Congress by their Adjournment prevent its Return, in which Case it shall not be a Law.

Every Order, Resolution, or Vote to which the Concurrence of the Senate and House of Representatives may be necessary (except on a question of Adjournment) shall be presented to the President of the United States; and before the Same shall take Effect, shall be approved by him, or being disapproved by him, shall be repassed by two thirds of the Senate and House of Representatives, according to the Rules and Limitations prescribed in the Case of a Bill.

Section 8. The Congress shall have Power To lay and collect Taxes, Duties, Imposts and Excises, to pay the Debts and provide for the common Defence and general Welfare of the United States; but all Duties, Imposts and Excises shall be uniform throughout the United States;

To borrow money on the credit of the United States;

To regulate Commerce with foreign Nations, and among the several States, and with the Indian Tribes;

To establish an uniform Rule of Naturalization, and uniform Laws on the subject of Bankruptcies throughout the United States;

To coin Money, regulate the Value thereof, and of foreign Coin, and fix the Standard of Weights and Measures;

To provide for the Punishment of counterfeiting the Securities and current Coin of the United States;

To establish Post Offices and post Roads;

To promote the Progress of Science and useful Arts, by securing for limited Times to Authors and Inventors the exclusive Right to their respective Writings and Discoveries;

To constitute Tribunals inferior to the Supreme Court;

To define and punish Piracies and Felonies committed on the high Seas, and Offenses against the Law of Nations;

To declare War, grant Letters of Marque and Reprisal, and make Rules concerning Captures on Land and Water;

To raise and support Armies, but no Appropriation of Money to that Use shall be for a longer Term than two Years;

To provide and maintain a Navy;

To make Rules for the Government and Regulation of the land and naval forces;

To provide for calling forth the Militia to execute the Laws of the Union, suppress Insurrections and repel Invasions;

To provide for organizing, arming, and disciplining the Militia, and for governing such Part of them as may be employed in the Service of the United States, reserving to the States respectively, the Appointment of the Officers, and the Authority of training the Militia according to the discipline prescribed by Congress;

To exercise exclusive Legislation in all Cases whatsoever, over such District (not exceeding ten Miles square) as may, by Cession of particular States, and the acceptance of Congress, become the Seat of Government of the United States, and to exercise like Authority over all Places purchased by the Consent of the Legislature of the State in which the Same shall be, for the Erection of Forts, Magazines, Arsenals, dock-Yards, and other needful Buildings;—And

The elastic clause adds a second dimension to the enumerated powers by broadening their scope. The clause allows Congress to legislate on the powers of all three branches.

To make all Laws which shall be necessary and proper for carrying into Execution the foregoing

These are limitations on congressional powers.

Powers, and all other Powers vested by this Constitution in the Government of the United States, or in any Department or Officer thereof.

Section 9. The Migration or Importation of such Persons as any of the States now existing shall think proper to admit, shall not be prohibited by the Congress prior to the Year one thousand eight hundred and eight, but a tax or duty may be imposed on such Importation, not exceeding ten dollars for each Person.

Slave trade was protected until 1808.

Habeas corpus requires officials to bring a suspect before a magistrate and give reasons for the arrest.

The privilege of the Writ of Habeas Corpus shall not be suspended, unless when in Cases of Rebellion or Invasion the public Safety may require it.

This prohibits acts of Congress that would result in punishment without a trial and also prohibits acts that would impose penalties retroactively.

No Bill of Attainder or ex post facto Law shall be passed.

No Capitation, or other direct, Tax shall be laid unless in Proportion to the Census or Enumeration herein before directed to be taken.

No Tax or Duty shall be laid on Articles exported from any State.

No Preference shall be given by any Regulation of Revenue to the Ports of one State over those of another: nor shall Vessels bound to, or from, one State, be obliged to enter, clear, or pay Duties in another.

No Money shall be drawn from the Treasury, but in Consequence of Appropriations made by Law; and a regular Statement and Account of the Receipts and Expenditures of all public Money shall be published from time to time.

No Title of Nobility shall be granted by the United States: And no Person holding any Office of Profit or Trust under them, shall, without the Consent of the Congress, accept of any present, Emolument, Office, or Title, of any kind whatever, from any King, Prince, or foreign State.

These are limitations on the states' powers. Those dealing with currency, credit, and contracts were directed against radicals and debtors in the aftermath of Shays's rebellion.

Section 10. No State shall enter into any Treaty, Alliance, or Confederation; grant Letters of Marque and Reprisal; coin Money; emit Bills of Credit; make any Thing but gold and silver Coin a Tender in Payment of Debts; pass any Bill of Attainder, ex post facto Law, or Law impairing the Obligation of Contracts, or grant any Title of Nobility.

The national government controls trade and diplomacy with foreign nations.

No state shall, without the Consent of the Congress, lay any Imposts or Duties on Imports or Exports, except what may be absolutely necessary for executing its inspection Laws: and the net Produce of all Duties and Imposts, laid by any State on Imports or Exports, shall be for the Use of the Treasury of the United States; and all such Laws shall be subject to the Revision and Control of the Congress.

Most interstate compacts are subject to congressional approval.

No State shall, without the Consent of Congress, lay any duty of Tonnage, keep Troops, or Ships of War in time of Peace, enter into any Agreement or Compact with another State, or with a foreign Power, or engage in War, unless actually invaded, or in such imminent Danger as will not admit of delay.

ARTICLE II

It is not clear what executive power means. Is it a title, referring to enumerated powers, or is it a separate grant of power?

Section 1. The executive Power shall be vested in a President of the United States of America. He shall hold his Office during the Term of four Years, and, together with the Vice President, chosen for the same Term, be elected, as follows:

Presidential electors need not be popularly elected.

Each State shall appoint, in such Manner as the Legislature thereof may direct, a Number of Electors, equal to the whole Number of Senators and Representatives to which the State may be entitled in the Congress: but no Senator or Representative, or Person holding an Office of Trust or Profit under the United States, shall be appointed an Elector.

This part of the Constitution was superseded by the Twelfth Amendment to avoid a recurrence of what happened in

The Electors shall meet in their respective States, and vote by Ballot for two Persons, of whom one at least shall not be an Inhabitant of the same State with themselves. And they shall make a List of all the Persons voted for, and of the Number of Votes for each; which List they shall sign and certify, the 1800 election, in which Jefferson, the presidential candidate, and Burr, the vice presidential candidate, received the same number of electoral votes from their supporters, which forced a contingency election in the House of Representatives.

and transmit sealed to the Seat of the Government of the United States, directed to the President of the Senate. The President of the Senate shall, in the Presence of the Senate and House of Representatives, open all the Certificates, and the Votes shall then be counted. The Person having the greatest Number of Votes shall be the President, if such Number be a Majority of the whole Number of Electors appointed; and if there be more than one who have such Majority, and have an equal Number of Votes, then the House of Representatives shall immediately chuse by Ballot one of them for President; and if no Person have a Majority, then from the five highest on the List the said House shall in like Manner chuse the President. But in chusing the President, the Votes shall be taken by States, the Representation from each State having one Vote; a quorum for this Purpose shall consist of a Member or Members from two-thirds of the States, and a Majority of all the States shall be necessary to a Choice. In every Case, after the Choice of the President, the Person having the greatest Number of Votes of the Electors shall be the Vice President. But if there should remain two or more who have equal votes, the Senate shall chuse from them by Ballot the Vice President.

This allows Congress to set a particular day on which presidential and midterm congressional elections are held.

The Congress may determine the Time of chusing the Electors, and the Day on which they shall give their Votes; which Day shall be the same throughout the United States.

No person except a natural-born Citizen, or a Citizen of the United States, at the time of the Adoption of this Constitution, shall be eligible to the Office of President; neither shall any Person be eligible to that Office who shall not have attained to the Age of thirty-five Years, and been fourteen Years a Resident within the United States.

This part of the Constitution was superseded by the Twenty-Fifth Amendment.

In Case of the Removal of the President from Office, or of his Death, resignation, or Inability to discharge the Powers and Duties of the said Office, the same shall devolve on the Vice President, and the Congress may by Law provide for the Case of Removal, Death, Resignation, or Inability, both of the President and Vice President, declaring what Officer shall then act as President, and such Officer shall act accordingly, until the Disability be removed, or a President shall be elected.

The President shall, at stated Times, receive for his Services a Compensation, which shall neither be increased nor diminished during the Period for which he shall have been elected, and he shall not receive within that Period any other Emolument from the United States, or any of them.

The oath does not specifically require the president to execute the laws; in a crisis the president may decide to dispense with their execution temporarily if it would interfere with higher constitutional obligations.

Before he enter on the Execution of his Office, he shall take the following Oath or Affirmation:—
"I do solemnly swear (or affirm) that I will faithfully execute the Office of President of the United States, and will, to the best of my Ability, preserve, protect, and defend the Constitution of the United States."

Section 2 enumerates the powers of the president. Contrast these few general terms with the many specific powers granted to Congress. The president is not given full executive powers. There is no removal power and no provision for issuing orders to heads of executive departments.

Section 2. The President shall be Commander in Chief of the Army and Navy of the United States, and of the Militia of the several States, when called into the actual Service of the United States; he may require the Opinion, in writing, of the principal Officer in each of the executive Departments, upon any subject relating to the Duties of their respective Offices, and he shall have Power to Grant Reprieves and Pardons for Offences against the United States, except in Cases of Impeachment.

The Senate consents to nominations by a majority vote and to treaties by a two-thirds vote of those present.

He shall have Power, by and with the Advice and Consent of the Senate, to make Treaties, provided two thirds of the Senators present concur; and he shall nominate, and by and with the Advice and Consent of the Senate, shall appoint Ambassadors, other public Ministers and Consuls, Judges of the Supreme Court, and all other Officers of the United States, whose Appointments are not herein otherwise provided for, and which shall be established by Law: but the Congress may by Law vest the Appointment of such inferior Officers, as they think proper, in the President alone, in the Courts of Law, or in the Heads of Departments.

Congress can give the power to appoint inferior officers to the president or the courts, but it cannot make appointments.

The President shall have Power to fill up all Vacancies that may happen during the Recess of the Senate, by granting Commissions which shall expire at the End of their next Session.

Section 3. He shall from time to time give to the Congress Information of the State of the Union, and recommend to their Consideration such Measures as he shall judge necessary and expedient; he may, on extraordinary occasions, convene both Houses, or either of them, and in Case of Disagreement between them, with respect to the Time of Adjournment, he may adjourn them to such Time as he shall think proper; he shall receive Ambassadors and other public Ministers; he shall take Care that the Laws be faithfully executed, and shall Commission all the Officers of the United States.

Section 4. The President, Vice President and all civil Officers of the United States, shall be removed from Office on Impeachment for, and Conviction of, Treason, Bribery, or other high Crimes and Misdemeanors.

ARTICLE III

Section 1. The judicial Power of the United States, shall be vested in one supreme Court, and in such inferior Courts as the Congress may from time to time ordain and establish. The Judges, both of the supreme and inferior Courts, shall hold their Offices during good Behaviour, and shall, at stated Times, receive for their Services, a Compensation, which shall not be diminished during their Continuance in Office.

Section 2. The judicial Power shall extend to all Cases, in Law and Equity, arising under this Constitution, the Laws of the United States, and Treaties made, or which shall be made, under their Authority;—to all Cases affecting Ambassadors, other public Ministers and Consuls;—to all Cases of admiralty and maritime Jurisdiction;—to Controversies to which the United States shall be a Party;—to Controversies between two or more States;—between a State and Citizens of another State;—between Citizens of the same State claiming Lands under Grants of different States, and between a State, or the Citizens thereof, and foreign States, Citizens or Subjects.

In all Cases affecting Ambassadors, other public Ministers and Consuls, and those in which a State shall be Party, the supreme Court shall have original Jurisdiction. In all the other Cases before mentioned, the supreme Court shall have appellate Jurisdiction, both as to Law and Fact, with such Exceptions, and under such Regulations as the Congress shall make.

The trial of all Crimes, except in Cases of Impeachment, shall be by Jury; and such Trial shall be held in the State where the said Crimes shall have been committed; but when not committed within any State, the Trial shall be at such Place or Places as the Congress may be Law have directed.

Section 3. Treason against the United States, shall consist only in levying War against them, or in adhering to their Enemies, giving them Aid and Comfort. No Person shall be convicted of Treason unless on the Testimony of two Witnesses to the same overt Act, or on Confession in open Court.

The Congress shall have power to declare the Punishment of Treason, but no Attainder of Treason shall work Corruption of Blood, or Forfeiture except during the Life of the Person attainted.

ARTICLE IV

Section 1. Full Faith and Credit shall be given in each State to the public Acts, Records, and judicial Proceedings of every other State. And the Congress may by general Laws prescribe the Manner in which such Acts, Records and Proceedings shall be proved, and the Effect thereof.

Section 2. The Citizens of each State shall be entitled to all Privileges and Immunities of Citizens in the several States.

A Person charged in any State with Treason, Felony, or other Crime, who shall flee from Justice, and be found in another State, shall on demand of the executive Authority of the State from which he fled, be delivered up, to be removed to the State having Jurisdiction of the crime.

Margin notes (left column):

The president does not execute the national laws, but rather oversees government officials; this justifies the president's claims to administrative powers.

The Constitution does not specify whether high crimes and misdemeanors involve offenses under federal laws or include a general pattern of abuse of power.

The judicial power extends to cases involving the Constitution, treaties, and federal statutory law.

The Supreme Court is the only court mentioned in the Constitution. The structure and jurisdiction of the federal court system are determined by Congress. *Good behavior* means life tenure for judges of federal constitutional courts. Judges of federal legislative courts serve fixed terms.

Section 2 specifies the jurisdiction of the federal courts. The original jurisdiction of the Supreme Court cannot be expanded by Congress.

The Seventh Amendment guarantees a trial by jury in most civil cases.

The Constitution limits the definition of *treason* and requires a judicial proceeding. This provision, along with prohibitions against ex post facto laws and bills of attainder, protects minority parties and factions.

Judgments in one state are enforceable in another state only by judicial decree obtained in the second state.

Fugitives are returned at the governor's discretion.

No Person held to Service or Labour in one State, under the Laws thereof, escaping into another, shall, in Consequence of any Law or Regulation therein, be discharged from such Service or Labour, but shall be delivered up on Claim of the Party to whom such Service or Labour may be due.

Section 3. New States may be admitted by the Congress into this Union; but no new State shall be formed or erected within the Jurisdiction of any other State; nor any State be formed by the Junction of two or more States, or parts of States, without the Consent of the Legislatures of the States concerned as well as of the Congress.

The Congress shall have Power to dispose of and make all needful Rules and Regulations respecting the Territory or other Property belonging to the United States; and nothing in this Constitution shall be so construed as to Prejudice any Claims of the United States, or of any particular State.

Section 4. The United States shall guarantee to every State in this Union a Republican Form of Government, and shall protect each of them against Invasion; and on Application of the Legislature, or of the Executive (when the Legislature cannot be convened) against domestic Violence.

ARTICLE V

The Congress, whenever two thirds of both Houses shall deem it necessary, shall propose Amendments to this Constitution, or, on the Application of the Legislatures of two thirds of the several States, shall call a Convention for proposing Amendments, which, in either Case, shall be valid to all Intents and Purposes, as part of this Constitution, when ratified by the Legislatures of three fourths of the several States, or by Conventions in three fourths thereof, as the one or the other Mode of Ratification may be proposed by the Congress; Provided that no Amendment which may be made prior to the Year One thousand eight hundred and eight shall in any Manner affect the first and fourth Clauses in the Ninth Section of the first Article; and that no State, without its Consent, shall be deprived of its equal Suffrage in the Senate.

ARTICLE VI

All Debts contracted and Engagements entered into, before the Adoption of this Constitution, shall be as valid against the United States under this Constitution, as under the Confederation.

This Constitution, and the Laws of the United States which shall be made in Pursuance thereof; and all Treaties made, or which shall be made, under the Authority of the United States, shall be the supreme Law of the Land; and the Judges in every State shall be bound thereby, any Thing in the Constitution or Laws of any State to the Contrary notwithstanding.

The Senators and Representatives before mentioned, and the Members of the several State Legislatures, and all executive and judicial Officers, both of the United States and of the several States, shall be bound by Oath or Affirmation to support this Constitution; but no religious Test shall ever be required as a qualification to any Office or public Trust under the United States.

ARTICLE VII

The Ratification of the Conventions of nine States shall be sufficient for the Establishment of this Constitution between the States so ratifying the same.

Done in Convention by the Unanimous Consent of the States present the Seventeenth Day of September in the Year of our Lord one thousand seven hundred and Eighty seven, and of the Indepen-

---

This is the fugitive slave provision, now an anachronism.

The Constitution does not refer to or forbid the acquisition of new territory. New states are admitted to the union on an equal footing with the existing states. Congress regulates the public lands of the United States within the territory of a state.

The president may use the armed forces or call a state militia into national service to maintain a state government or oust one that is not republican in form. This power has never been used against states that denied suffrage to a part of their citizenry.

Congress acts by a two-thirds vote of those present. It has never called a convention to propose amendments. It is not clear whether such a convention would be limited to subjects specified by Congress.

A state which has turned down an amendment may later ratify it, but a state which has ratified an amendment may not rescind its action.

The linchpin of the Constitution, the supremacy clause establishes the Constitution, the laws of Congress, and treaties as the supreme law of the land, which state as well as national officials must enforce.

State and local officials must take oaths to support the national Constitution.

Requiring that a person believe in a supreme being in order to qualify to hold public office is unconstitutional.

The ratification provision is inconsistent with the requirement under the Articles of Confederation that it be amended by unanimous vote of the state delegations to Congress.

dence of the United States of America the Twelfth. In Witness whereof We have hereunto subscribed our Names.

George Washington, President and Deputy from Virginia
New Hampshire—John Langdon, Nicholas Gilman
Massachusetts—Nathanial Gorham, Rufus King
Connecticut—William Samuel Johnson, Roger Sherman
New York—Alexander Hamilton
New Jersey—William Livingston, David Brearly, William Paterson, Jonathan Dayton
Pennsylvania—Benjamin Franklin, Thomas Mifflin, Robert Morris, George Clymer, Thomas Fitz-simons, Jared Ingersoll, James Wilson, Gouverneur Morris
Delaware—George Read, Gunning Bedford, Jr., John Dickinson, Richard Bassett, Jacob Broom
Maryland—James McHenry, Daniel of St. Thomas Jenifer, Daniel Carroll
Virginia—John Blair, James Madison, Jr.
North Carolina—William Blount, Richard Dobbs Spaight, Hugh Williamson
south Carolina—John Rutledge, Charles Cotesworth Pinckney, Charles Pinckney, Pierce Butler
Georgia—William Few, Abraham Baldwin
Attest: William Jackson, Secretary

Articles in Addition to, and Amendment of, the Constitution of the United States of America, Proposed by Congress, and Ratified by the Legislatures of the Several States, Pursuant to the Fifth Article of the Original Constitution.

AMENDMENT I [1791]

These prohibitions apply to all branches of the national government, and by the due process clause of the Fourteenth Amendment they apply to state officials as well.

Congress shall make no law respecting an establishment of religion, or prohibiting the free exercise thereof; or abridging the freedom of speech, or of the press; or the right of the people peaceably to assemble, and to petition the Government for a redress of grievances.

AMENDMENT II [1791]

This amendment guarantees the right to bear arms to the militias of the states but not necessarily to individuals.

A well regulated Militia, being necessary to the security of a free State, the right of the people to keep and bear Arms, shall not be infringed.

AMENDMENT III [1791]

This amendment provides protection against abuses like those committed by British troops before the Revolutionary War.

No Soldier shall, in time of peace, be quartered in any house, without the consent of the Owner, nor in time of war, but in a manner to be prescribed by law.

AMENDMENT IV [1791]

This amendment forbids the general warrant, which allows the police to go on a "fishing expedition" for evidence of crimes. It has been interpreted to require a judicial warrant for wiretapping and surveillance.

The right of the people to be secure in their persons, houses, papers, and effects, against unreasonable searches and seizures, shall not be violated, and no Warrants shall issue, but upon probable cause, supported by Oath or affirmation, and particularly describing the place to be searched, and the persons or things to be seized.

AMENDMENT V [1791]

This amendment guarantees due process in criminal and civil proceedings.

No person shall be held to answer for a capital otherwise infamous crime, unless on a presentment or indictment of a Grand Jury, except in cases arising in the land or naval forces, or in the Militia, when in actual service in time of War or public danger; nor shall any person be subject for the same offence to be twice put in jeopardy of life or limb; nor shall be compelled in any criminal case to be a witness against himself, nor be deprived of life, liberty, or property, without due process of law; nor shall private property be taken for public use, without just compensation.

AMENDMENT VI [1791]

Due process includes the right to knowledge of charges, free counsel for indigents, the right to effective legal representation, the right to a speedy and fair trail, the right to present witnesses and cross-examine hostile witnesses, and the right of appeal.

In all criminal prosecutions, the accused shall enjoy the right to a speedy and public trial, by an impartial jury of the State and district wherein the crime shall have been committed, which district shall have been previously ascertained by law, and to be informed of the nature and cause of the accusation; to be confronted with the witnesses against him; to have compulsory process for obtaining witnesses in his favor, and to have the Assistance of Counsel for his defence.

AMENDMENT VII [1791]

This amendment guarantees the right to a jury trial in civil cases unless waived by the parties.

In Suits at common law, where the value in controversy shall exceed twenty dollars, the right of trial by jury shall be preserved, and no fact tried by a jury, shall be otherwise re-examined in any Court of the United States, than according to the rules of the common law.

AMENDMENT VIII [1791]

For certain offenses specified by Congress, bail may be denied, and the accused detained before trial.

Excessive bail shall not be required, nor excessive fines imposed, nor cruel and unusual punishments inflicted.

AMENDMENT IX [1791]

In some judicial cases this amendment has been taken to create a "zone of privacy" for individuals into which the government may not intrude.

The enumeration in the Constitution, of certain rights, shall not be construed to deny or disparage others retained by the people.

AMENDMENT X [1791]

This amendment is rarely invoked today to prevent national action.

The powers not delegated to the United States by the Constitution, nor prohibited by it to the States, are reserved to the States respectively, or to the people.

AMENDMENT XI [1798]

This amendment limits the jurisdiction of the federal courts.

The Judicial power of the United States shall not be construed to extend to any suit in law or equity, commenced or prosecuted against one of the United States by Citizens of another State, or by Citizens or Subjects of any Foreign State.

AMENDMENT XII [1804]

The Electors shall meet in their respective States and vote by ballot for President and Vice-President, one of whom, at least, shall not be an inhabitant of the same States with themselves; they shall name in their ballots the person voted for as President, and in distinct ballots the person voted for as Vice-President, and they shall make distinct lists of all persons voted for as President, and of all persons voted for as Vice-President, and of the number of votes for each, which lists they shall sign and certify, and transmit sealed to the seat of the government of the United States, directed to the President of the Senate;—The President of the Senate shall, in the presence of the Senate and House of Representatives, open all the certificates and the votes shall then be counted;—The person having the greatest number of votes for President, shall be the President, if such number be a majority of the whole number of Electors appointed; and if no person have such majority, then from the persons having the highest numbers not exceeding three on the list of those voted for as President, the House of Representatives shall choose immediately, by ballot, the President. But in choosing the President, the votes shall be taken by states, the representation from each state having one vote; a quorum for this purpose shall consist of a member or members from two-thirds of the states, and a majority of all the states shall be necessary to a choice. And if the House of Representatives shall not choose a President whenever the right of choice shall devolve upon them, before the fourth day of March next following, then the Vice-President shall act as President, as in the case of the death or other constitutional disability of the President—The person having the greatest number of votes as Vice-President, shall be the Vice-President, if such number be a majority of the whole number of Electors appointed, and if no person have a majority, then from the two highest numbers on the list, the Senate shall choose the Vice-President; a quorum for the purpose shall consist of two-thirds of the whole number of Senators, and a majority of the whole number shall be necessary to a choice. But no person constitutionally ineligible to the office of President shall be eligible to that of Vice-President of the United States.

The House chooses from among the top three candidates for president, and the Senate from among the top two candidates for vice president. The date of March 4 was changed by the Twentieth Amendment.

AMENDMENT XIII [1865]

Section 1. Neither slavery nor involuntary servitude, except as a punishment for crime whereof the party shall have been duly convicted, shall exist within the United States, or any place subject to their jurisdiction.

Section 2. Congress shall have power to enforce this article by appropriate legislation.

This amendment supersedes Lincoln's Emancipation Proclamation.

AMENDMENT XIV [1868]

Section 1. All persons born or naturalized in the United States, and subject to the jurisdiction thereof, are citizens of the United States and of the State wherein they reside. No State shall make or enforce any law which shall abridge the privileges or immunities of citizens of the United States; nor shall any State deprive any person of life, liberty, or property, without due process of law; nor deny to any person within its jurisdiction the equal protection of the laws.

Section 2. Representatives shall be apportioned among the several States according to their respective numbers, counting the whole number of persons in each State, excluding Indians not taxed. But when the right to vote at any election for the choice of electors for President and Vice President of the United States, Representatives in Congress, the Executive and Judicial officers of a State, or the members of the Legislature thereof, is denied to any of the male inhabitants of such State, being twenty-one years

This is the first time the Constitution defines national citizenship. This section converted former slaves into citizens. All persons have the right to due process and equal protection of the law against state action.

The reduction in congressional representation mentioned in this section was never implemented, even after southern states disenfranchised blacks.

of age, and citizens of the United States, or in any way abridged, except for participation in rebellion, or other crime, the basis of representation therein shall be reduced in the proportion which the number of such male citizens shall bear to the whole number of male citizens twenty-one years of age in such State.

Section 3. No person shall be a Senator or Representative in Congress, or elector of President and Vice President, or hold any office, civil or military, under the United States, or under any State, who, having previously taken an oath, as a member of Congress, or as an officer of the United States, or as a member of any State legislature, or as an executive or judicial officer of any State, to support the Constitution of the United States, shall have engaged in insurrection or rebellion against the same, or given aid or comfort to the enemies thereof. But Congress may by a vote of two-thirds of each House, remove such disability.

Section 4. The validity of the public debt of the United States, authorized by law, including debts incurred for payment of pensions and bounties for services in suppressing insurrection or rebellion, shall not be questioned. But neither the United States nor any State shall assume or pay any debt or obligation incurred in aid of insurrection or rebellion against the United States, or any claim for the loss or emancipation of any slave; but all such debts, obligations, and claims shall be held illegal and void.

Section 5. The Congress shall have the power to enforce, by appropriate legislation, the provisions of this article.

AMENDMENT XV [1870]

Section 1. The right of citizens of the United States to vote shall not be denied or abridged by the United States or by any State on account of race, color, or previous condition of servitude—

Section 2. The Congress shall have power to enforce this article by appropriate legislation.

AMENDMENT XVI [1913]

The Congress shall have power to lay and collect taxes on incomes, from whatever source derived, without apportionment among the several States, and without regard to any census or enumeration.

AMENDMENT XVII [1913]

The Senate of the United States shall be composed of two Senators from each State, elected by the people thereof, for six years; and each Senator shall have one vote. The electors in each State shall have the qualifications requisite for electors of the most numerous branch of the State legislatures.

When vacancies happen in the representation of any State in the Senate, the executive authority of such State shall issue writs of election to fill such vacancies: *Provided,* That the legislature of any State may empower the executive thereof to make temporary appointments until the people fill the vacancies by election as the legislature may direct.

This amendment shall not be so construed as to affect the election or term of any Senator chosen before it becomes valid as part of the Constitution.

The provision in this section barring secessionists from holding office was widely ignored.

This section voids claims made by slaveholders and secessionists against the state governments and the national government.

This section did not prevent states in the 1890s from introducing literacy tests, levying poll taxes, or imposing other restrictions on blacks which did not explicitly mention race.

This amendment overturned an 1895 Supreme Court decision voiding an income tax.

This amendment replaced legislative election of senators with popular election.

AMENDMENT XVIII [1919]

This amendment, which legislated Prohibition, represents the only attempt that has ever been made to put a "social issue" into the Constitution.

Section 1. After one year from the ratification of this article the manufacture, sale, or transportation of intoxicating liquors within, the importation thereof into, or the exportation thereof from the United States and all territory subject to the jurisdiction thereof for beverage purposes is hereby prohibited.

Section 2. The Congress and the several States shall have concurrent power to enforce this article by appropriate legislation.

Section 3. This article shall be inoperative unless it shall have been ratified as an amendment to the Constitution by the legislatures of the several States, as provided in the Constitution, within seven years from the date of the submission hereof to the States by the Congress.

AMENDMENT XIX [1920]

This amendment guarantees the right to vote in federal and state elections. Many states had already granted women suffrage.

The right of citizens of the United States to vote shall not be denied or abridged by the United States or by any State on account of sex.

Congress shall have power to enforce this article by appropriate legislation.

AMENDMENT XX [1933]

As a result of this amendment, the president is inaugurated on January 20 rather than March 4. This amendment put an end to the situation in which a lame-duck president and Congress ran the government from November until the following March and in which the newly elected Congress did not convene for thirteen months. The new Congress now convenes on January 3, two months after the elections.

Section 1. The terms of the President and Vice President shall end at noon on the 20th day of January, and the terms of Senators and Representatives at noon on the 3rd day of January, of the years in which such terms would have ended if this article had not been ratified; and the terms of their successors shall then begin.

Section 2. The Congress shall assemble at least once in every year, and such meeting shall begin at noon on the 3rd day of January, unless they shall by law appoint a different day.

Section 3. If, at the time fixed for the beginning of the term of the President, the President elect shall have died, the Vice President elect shall become President. If a President shall not have been chosen before the time fixed for the beginning of his term, or if the President elect shall have failed to qualify, then the Vice President elect shall act as President until a President shall have qualified; and the Congress may by law provide for the case wherein neither a President elect nor a Vice President elect shall have qualified, declaring who shall then act as President, or the manner in which one who is to act shall be selected, and such person shall act accordingly until a President or Vice President shall have qualified.

Section 4. The Congress may by law provide for the case of the death of any of the persons from whom the House of Representatives may choose a President whenever the right of choice shall have devolved upon them, and for the case of the death of any of the persons from whom the Senate may choose a Vice President whenever the right of choice shall have devolved upon them.

Section 5. Sections 1 and 2 shall take effect on the 15th day of October following the ratification of this article.

Section 6. This article shall be inoperative unless it shall have been ratified as an amendment to the

Constitution by the legislatures of three-fourths of the several States within seven years from the date of its submission.

AMENDMENT XXI [1933]

As a result of this amendment, the experiment with Prohibition ended.

Section 1. The eighteenth article of amendment to the Constitution of the United States is hereby repealed.

Section 2. The transportation or importation into any State, Territory, or possession of the United States for delivery or use therein of intoxicating liquors, in violation of the laws thereof, is hereby prohibited.

This is the only amendment to be ratified by state conventions rather than by state legislatures.

Section 3. This article shall be inoperative unless it shall have been ratified as an amendment to the Constitution by conventions in the several States, as provided in the Constitution, within seven years from the date of the submission hereof to the States by the Congress.

AMENDMENT XXII [1951]

This amendment, which limits presidents to two terms in office (a proposal made by Republicans), first affected a Republican president, Dwight D. Eisenhower.

No person shall be elected to the office of the President more than twice, and no person who has held the office of President, or acted as President, for more than two years of a term to which some other person was elected President shall be elected to the office of the President more than once.

But this Article shall not apply to any person holding the office of President when this Article was proposed by the Congress, and shall not prevent any person who may be holding the office of President, or acting as President, during the term within which this Article becomes operative from holding the office of President or acting as President during the remainder of such term.

AMENDMENT XXIII [1961]

This amendment gives the District of Columbia representation in presidential elections equivalent to that of the least populous state.

Section 1. The District constituting the seat of Government of the United States shall appoint in such manner as the Congress may direct:

A number of electors of President and Vice President equal to the whole number of Senators and Representatives in Congress to which the District would be entitled if it were a State, but in no event more than the least populous State; they shall be in addition to those appointed by the States, but they shall be considered, for the purposes of the election of President and Vice President, to be electors appointed by a State; and they shall meet in the District and perform such duties as provided by the twelfth article of amendment.

Section 2. The Congress shall have power to enforce this article by appropriate legislation.

AMENDMENT XXIV [1964]

This amendment ended state poll taxes in federal elections.

Section 1. The right of citizens of the United States to vote in any primary or other election for President or Vice President, for electors for President or Vice President, or for Senator or Representative in Congress, shall not be denied or abridged by the United States or any State by reason of failure to pay any poll tax or other tax.

Section 2. The Congress shall have the power to enforce this article by appropriate legislation.

AMENDMENT XXV [1967]

This amendment supersedes informal arrangements about disability between presidents and vice presidents, such as those negotiated between Dwight Eisenhower and Richard Nixon. Filling a vacancy for vice president makes it unlikely that a double vacancy can occur. Gerald Ford, who was elected vice president by Congress and succeeded to the presidency upon the resignation of Richard Nixon, is the only American president ever to have come to office under this amendment.

Section 1. In case of the removal of the President from office or his death or resignation, the Vice President shall become President.

Section 2. Whenever there is a vacancy in the office of the Vice President, the President shall nominate a Vice President who shall take the office upon confirmation by a majority vote of both houses of Congress.

Section 3. Whenever the President transmits to the President pro tempore of the Senate and the Speaker of the House of Representatives his written declaration that he is unable to discharge the powers and duties of his office, and until he transmits to them a written declaration to the contrary, such powers and duties shall be discharged by the Vice President as Acting President.

Section 4. Whenever the Vice President and a majority of either the principal officers of the executive departments or of such other body as Congress may by law provide, transmit to the President pro tempore of the Senate and the Speaker of the House of Representatives their written declaration that the President is unable to discharge the powers and duties of his office, the Vice President shall immediately assume the powers and duties of the office as Acting President.

    Thereafter, when the President transmits to the President pro tempore of the Senate and the Speaker of the House of Representatives his written declaration that no inability exists, he shall resume the powers and duties of his office unless the Vice President and a majority of either the principal officers of the executive departments, or of such other body as Congress may by law provide, transmit within four days to the President pro tempore of the Senate and the Speaker of the House of Representatives their written declaration that the President is unable to discharge the powers and duties of his office. Thereupon Congress shall decide the issue, assembling within 48 hours for that purpose if not in session. If the Congress, within 21 days after receipt of the latter written declaration, or, if Congress is not in session, within 21 days after Congress is required to assemble, determines by two-thirds vote of both houses that the President is unable to discharge the powers and duties of his office, the Vice President shall continue to discharge the same as Acting President, otherwise, the President shall resume the powers and duties of his office.

AMENDMENT XXVI [1971]

This amendment lowered the voting age in most states from 21 to 18.

Section 1. The right of citizens of the United States, who are 18 years of age or older, to vote shall not be denied or abridged by the United States or any state on account of age.

Section 2. The Congress shall have the power to enforce this article by appropriate legislation.

The Declaration of Independence

In Congress, July 4, 1776:
The Unanimous Declaration of the Thirteen United States of America

When, in the course of human events, it becomes necessary for one people to dissolve the political bands which have connected them with another, and to assume, among the powers of the earth, the separate and equal station to which the laws of nature and of nature's God entitle them, a decent respect to the opinions of mankind requires that they should declare the causes which impel them to the separation.

We hold these truths to be self-evident: That all men are created equal; that they are endowed by their Creator with certain unalienable rights; that among these are life, liberty, and the pursuit of happiness; that, to secure these rights, governments are instituted among men, deriving their just powers from the consent of the governed; that whenever any form of government becomes destructive of these ends, it is the right of the people to alter or to abolish it, and to institute new government, laying its foundation on such principles, and organizing its powers in such form, as to them shall seem most likely to effect their safety and happiness. Prudence, indeed, will dictate that governments long established should not be changed for light and transient causes; and accordingly all experience hath shown that mankind are more disposed to suffer, while evils are sufferable, than to right themselves by abolishing the forms to which they are accustomed. But when a long train of abuses and usurpations, pursuing invariably the same object, evinces a design to reduce them under absolute despotism, it is their right, it is their duty, to throw off such government, and to provide new guards for their future security. Such has been the patient sufferance of these colonies; and such is now the necessity which constrains them to alter their former systems of government. The history of the present King of Great Britain is a history of repeated injuries and usurpations, all having in direct object the establishment of an absolute tyranny over these states. To prove this, let facts be submitted to a candid world.

He has refused to assent to laws, the most wholesome and necessary for the public good.

He has forbidden his governors to pass laws of immediate and pressing importance, unless suspended in their operation till his assent should be obtained; and, when so suspended, he has utterly neglected to attend to them.

He has refused to pass other laws for the accommodation of large districts of people, unless those people would relinquish the right of representation in the legislature, a right inestimable to them, and formidable to tyrants only.

He has called together legislative bodies at places unusual, uncomfortable, and distant from the depository of their public records, for the sole purpose of fatiguing them into compliance with his measures.

He has dissolved representative houses repeatedly, for opposing, with manly firmness, his invasions on the rights of the people.

He has refused for a long time, after such dissolutions, to cause others to be elected; whereby the legislative powers, incapable of annihilation, have returned to the people at large for their exercise; the state remaining, in the mean time, exposed to all the dangers of invasions from without and convulsions within.

He has endeavored to prevent the population of these states; for that purpose obstructing the laws for naturalization of foreigners; refusing to pass others to encourage their migration hither, and raising the conditions of new appropriations of lands.

He has obstructed the administration of justice, by refusing his assent to laws for establishing judiciary powers.

He has made judges dependent on his will alone, for the tenure of their offices, and the amount and payment of their salaries.

He has erected a multitude of new offices, and set hither swarms of officers to harass our people and eat out their substance.

He has kept among us, in times of peace, standing armies, without the consent of our legislatures.

He has affected to render the military independent of, and superior to, the civil power.

He has combined with others to subject us to a jurisdiction foreign to our constitution and unacknowledged by our laws, giving his assent to their acts of pretended legislation:

For quartering large bodies of armed troops among us;

For protecting them, by a mock trial, from punishment for any murders which they should commit on the inhabitants of these states;

For cutting off trade with all parts of the world;

For imposing taxes on us without our consent;

For depriving us, in many cases, of the benefits of trial by jury;

For transporting us beyond seas, to be tried for pretended offenses;

For abolishing the free system of English laws in a neighboring province, establishing therein an arbitrary government, and enlarging its boundaries, so as to render it at once an example and fit instrument for introducing the same absolute rule into these colonies;

For taking away our charters, abolishing our most valuable laws, and altering fundamentally the forms of our governments;

For suspending our own legislatures, and declaring themselves invested with power to legislate for us in all cases whatsoever.

He has abdicated government here, by declaring us out of his protection and waging war against us.

He has plundered our seas, ravaged our coasts, burned our towns, and destroyed the lives of our people.

He is at this time transporting large armies of foreign mercenaries to complete the works of death, desolation, and tyranny already begun with circumstances of cruelty and perfidy scarcely paralleled in the most barbarous ages, and totally unworthy the head of a civilized nation.

He has constrained our fellow-citizens, taken captive on the high seas, to bear arms against their country, to become the executioners of their friends and brethren, or to fall themselves by their hands.

He has excited domestic insurrections among us, and has endeavored to bring on the inhabitants of our frontiers the merciless Indian savages, whose known rule of warfare is undistinguished destruction of all ages, sexes, and conditions.

In every stage of these oppressions we have petitioned for redress in the most humble terms; our repeated petitions have been answered only by repeated injury. A prince, whose character is thus marked by every act which may define a tyrant, is unfit to be the ruler of a free people.

Nor have we been wanting in our attentions to our British brethren. We have warned them, from time to time, of attempts by their legislature to extend an unwarrantable jurisdiction over us. We have reminded them of the circumstances of our emigration and settlement here. We have appealed to their native justice and magnanimity; and we have conjured them, by the ties of our common kindred, to disavow these usurpations, which would inevitably interrupt our connections and correspondence. They, too, have been deaf to the voice of justice and of consanguinity. We must, therefore, acquiesce in the necessity which denounces our separation, and hold them, as we hold the rest of mankind, enemies in war, in peace friends.

We, therefore, the representatives of the United States of America, in General Congress assembled, appealing to the Supreme Judge of the world for the rectitude of our intentions, do, in the name and by the authority of the good people of these colonies, solemnly publish and declare, that these United Colonies are, and of right ought to be, FREE AND INDEPENDENT STATES; that they are absolved from all allegiance to the British crown, and that all political connection between them and the state of Great Britain is, and ought to be, totally dissolved; and that, as free and independent states, they have full power to levy war, conclude peace, contract alliances, establish commerce, and do all other acts and things which independent states may of right do. And for the support of this declaration, with a firm reliance on the protection of Divine Providence, we mutually pledge to each other our lives, our fortunes, and our sacred honor.

John Hancock [*President*]
[*and fifty-five others*]

Action-forcing process. A sequence of events which requires advance planning to meet a deadline.

Administration. A small unit of government (for example, the Welfare Administration) or the top officials appointed by the president (for example, the Reagan administration).

Affirmative action. Efforts to take into consideration characteristics such as race to improve the employment and educational opportunities of people who have been discriminated against in the past.

Agency. A unit of government (for example, the Agency for International Development).

Amendments. Proposed changes to a bill or constitution.

Amicus curiae brief. A legal argument filed by a group that is not itself a party to a case.

Anarchy. A society without government or law, based on the theory that government does more harm than good.

Anti-Federalists. The faction which opposed ratification of the Constitution. Also, the politicians in the 1790s who favored a weak central government. *See also* Federalists.

Appellate jurisdiction. The jurisdiction of the higher courts in reviewing cases from lower courts.

Appropriations. Funds requested in a bill which is reported by an appropriations committee and which provides budget authority. *See also* Budget authority.

Aristocracy. In theory, rule by the most talented. In practice, a term used by rulers to legitimize their power.

Articles of Confederation. The political compact of American states created by the Continental Congress in 1777 and ratified in 1781.

Authoritarian. Relating to nondemocratic rule by leaders who claim to know what is best for the people and who usually threaten or use force to maintain themselves in power.

Authority. The degree to which people accept a ruler's competence to govern.

Authorizing legislation. Laws which empower the government to act or set limits on governmental action.

Back channel. A person who channels communication between officials by bypassing normal procedures, especially in matters of diplomacy.

Ballot. A record of a voter's choice in an election. *Open* ballots involve a voice vote, a show of hands, or congregating in a location; *closed* or *secret* ballots involve a ballot box or voting machine; *party* ballot is a list of all the nominees for office of a single party which may be put in a *ballot box* (if one is used) by a voter to vote a straight ticket. A *party-column* ballot makes it easy to vote a straight ticket; an *office-column* ballot encourages voters to think about the candidate, not the party.

Bicameral. Consisting of two legislature chambers, which must pass identical bills in order for a measure to become law.

Bill of Rights. The first Ten Amendments to the national Constitution. Also, the provisions of state constitutions guaranteeing civil rights and liberties.

Bipartisan. Relating to or involving support by the two major parties.

Block grant. Funds distributed by one unit of government to another for a general purpose, such as law enforcement or housing.

Bond. A promise by a unit of government (or a corporation) to repay a loan at a specified rate of interest.

Borrowing authority. The authority of the government, established by law, to borrow money and incur obligations, usually by selling bonds.

Brandeis brief. A legal argument submitted to a court, consisting of facts that show the impact of laws or previous court cases on society.

Budget authority. The authority of government officials, established by laws passed by Congress, to spend money. *See also* Appropriations, Borrowing authority, and Contract authority.

Budget debt. The cumulative amount owed by the government in the form of Treasury bonds, bills, and notes.

Budget deficit. The amount in a fiscal year by which government spending exceeds budget receipts. A *stimulative* deficit is designed to boost the economy out of a recession or depression; a *structural* deficit is designed to run the economy at full employment.

Budget receipts. Money collected by the government in a fiscal year, including taxes, tariffs, fees, fines, sales of assets, and gifts.

Budget resolution. A congressional concurrent resolution (not subject to presidential veto) which sets targets or binding totals for budget authority and outlays.

Budget surplus. The amount by which budget receipts exceed outlays in a fiscal year.

Bureau. A small unit of government. *See also* Administration and Agency.

Bureau chief. The official who heads an administration, agency, bureau, or other small unit of government.

Business cycle. The period of time during which the performance of the economy goes from recession to recovery through boom and downturn.

Cabinet. A body consisting of the twelve secretaries and the attorney general, who run the executive departments; the vice president of the United States; and other officials with Cabinet status who meet as a group with the president.

Cabinet councils. Committees which consist of Cabinet secretaries and other top officials and which focus on government activities that cross departmental lines (for example, natural resources).

Candidate. A person who is running for an elective office.

Capital gains tax. The tax levied on the increase in value of an asset at the time of sale. Capital gains are usually taxed at a lower rate than income.

Casework. The help given by congressional staffers to people in their districts.

Categorical grant. Funds transferred from one level of government to another for a specified program (for example, highway construction).

Caucus. A meeting of the members of a political party at which they nominate candidates, discuss issues, and plan strategy. Until 1824 the congressional caucus was used to nominate candidates for president. Today, *precinct* caucuses in half the states choose delegates to district or state conventions, which send delegates to a national convention. At conventions delegates may caucus by geographic area, ideology, or issues. The Democrats and Republicans in the House and Senate meet in four separate *legislative party* caucuses.

Censorship. The suppression of information by the government.

Censure. A resolution condemning an official for a specific action or pattern of conduct.

Certification. A legal provision which requires officials to indicate that a specified circumstance exists before they act.

Certiorari (writ of). A petition to a higher court to review the decision of a lower court.

Chain of command. The channels through which orders are transmitted from superiors to subordinates.

Chamber seniority. Uninterrupted years of service in a legislative chamber.

Charismatic. Relating to the attributes of a ruler which lead people to believe that he or she has exceptional leadership qualities.

Checks and balances. The constitutional grants of power to the three branches of government enabling them to interfere with one another so as to prevent any one branch from accumulating all power or going beyond the bounds of the Constitution.

Chilling effect. The effect of a governmental action which leads people to believe that they will suffer adverse consequences if they exercise their civil liberties.

Civil liberties. The individual freedoms of speech, expression, assembly, religion, conscience, privacy, and due process of law, guaranteed by the national constitution and the state constitutions.

Civil service. The administrative service of the government consisting of permanently employed nonmilitary government workers. *See also* Political executives and Senior Executive Service.

Class. In politics, a large aggregate of people with similar social and economic characteristics.

Class action. A lawsuit which is filed by an individual but which seeks damages or relief for "all persons similarly situated."

Class polarization. Polarization that occurs when different classes support different candidates in elections or have different attitudes toward public policies.

Clear and present danger. The basis of a test advanced by Supreme Court Justice Oliver Wendell Holmes, Jr., specifying that the government may not abridge freedom of speech unless an illegal act is about to be committed because of a speech.

Clientele policy. A policy providing for costs to be widely shared, while benefits go to a clearly defined clientele group.

Closed rule. A rule permitting no amendments to a bill.

Cloture. A motion to end debate, usually requiring more than a simple majority to pass.

Coalition building. Bringing people into a temporary agreement until

the number necessary for action to be taken on an issue has been reached (usually a majority). A *partisan* coalition consists primarily of members of a single party; a *bipartisan* coalition brings in some members of the other party; a *conservative*, coalition combines most Republicans in Congress with many southern Democrats; a *liberal-labor* coalition combines liberal and moderate Democrats with urban or suburban Republicans from the northeast and the mid-Atlantic states.

Coattail effect. The positive or negative impact that a candidate running for a high office can have on candidates running for lower offices on the same party ticket. The *reverse* coattail effect is the impact of a candidate running for a lower office on candidates running for high offices.

Codetermination. Policy development and implementation by more than one branch of government.

Collective security. An agreement according to which each nation involved agrees to defend its allies against attack in return for similar pledges from them.

Committee hearing. A meeting of a committee to consider testimony on a bill by government officials and interested parties.

Committee leaders. The chair of a committee, the ranking majority member (next in line to be the chair), and the ranking minority member (who would be chair if his or her party had a majority).

Committee report. A document describing a bill that a committee wants Congress to pass. A *minority* report may urge defeat or amendments.

Committee seniority. Years of uninterrupted service on a congressional committee.

Concurrent power. Power that exists when more than one branch of government claims or has a constitutional power, such as the power to decide to go to war or conclude agreements with another nation.

Conditional delegation. The legislative authority to take action if certain conditions are met.

Confederation. A government in

which the constituent units retain their sovereignty and cede limited powers to national institutions.

Conference committee. A meeting of legislators from both chambers at which they reconcile their versions of a bill before final passage.

Conference report. The version of a bill returned to both chambers for final passage by the conference committee.

Congressional caucus. *See* Caucus.

Congressional coalitions. *See* Coalition building.

Congressional party. The members of a political party in Congress and the party committees which help them campaign.

Congressional roles. The routine ways in which legislators act. A *delegate* tries to "vote the district" and represent the wishes of the voters; a *trustee* "votes conscience" and tries to do what is in the best interest of the voters; a *politico* trades votes and tries to win influence.

Connecticut Compromise. An agreement consisting of compromises between the small and the large states at the Constitutional Convention involving equal representation of the states in the Senate.

Conscience rule. The proposal that delegates to national presidential nominating conventions be allowed to vote as they see fit, even if they are pledged to vote for a particular candidate.

Consensus. An agreement on what is to be done.

Conservative. In American politics, someone who believes in limiting the role of the national government in domestic affairs and in giving the states or the market more scope in allocating resources or solving problems. *See also* Liberal.

Constitution. The fundamental governing principles of a nation. It may be an unwritten collection of laws, customs, and usages (as in Great Britain) or a written document, like the American Constitution.

Constitutional Convention of 1787. The convention held in Philadelphia at which the Constitution was drafted.

Constitutional courts. The federal courts that deal with constitutional and statutory issues. Federal court judges are appointed for life. *See* Statutory courts.

Constitutional law. Decisions based on an interpretation of the Constitution in court cases. Commentary on constitutional law is found in law reviews.

Contempt of court. Failure to obey a judicial order. Persons found in contempt of court may be imprisoned or fined.

Continental Congress. The congress of representatives from the states which declared independence in 1776.

Contingency elections. Elections that are held when normal procedures fail. If the electoral college system fails to work, the House elects the president, and the Senate elects the vice president.

Continuing resolution. A law which provides budget authority to keep ongoing activities at their present level when one or more bills providing new budget authority have not been enacted.

Contract authority. The authority of government officials, established by law, to enter into contracts or incur other obligations in advance of congressional appropriations.

Convention. A meeting of delegates representing different territorial units at a single place. A *constitutional* convention creates or revises a state constitution or the national Constitution; a *nominating* convention (district, state, or national) selects party candidates for office.

Convention delegates. The representatives of a party's organization or primary and caucus voters. *Personalists* attend to nominate a candidate to whom they are pledged; *purists* are committed to particular issues or ideologies; *professionals* seek benefits for their state and local parties.

Corruption. The misuse of public office for personal gain.

Council of Economic Advisors (CEA). A presidential advisory unit which prepares the annual economic report of the president.

Counterforce. The targeting of an enemy's nuclear launchers.

Counterstrike. A retaliatory nuclear strike on enemy targets.

Countervailing targeting. The targeting of an enemy's political institutions.

County courthouse ring. A corrupt local party organization which controlled county judges, prosecutors, and sheriffs.

Covert action. An action involving the use of force against another nation without official acknowledgment or responsibility.

Critical election. An election in which the majority party retains office but loses support from part of its coalition.

Current services estimates. Estimates of receipts, outlays, and budget authority for coming fiscal years which assume no change in activities.

Dealignment. The detachment of electoral constituencies from traditional party identifications.

Debt. *See* Budget debt.

Deferral. An action or a lack of action by government officials that delays outlays to future fiscal years. Deferrals may be overturned by Congress.

Deficit. *See* Budget deficit.

Delegation of power. The designation of a unit of government by the executive, legislative, or judicial branch to implement policy.

Democracy. Government of, by, and for the people, who retain the right to choose their rulers and policies.

Demonstration grant. Funds provided by the government to try out new programs.

Department. A large unit of government, whose secretary sits in the Cabinet.

Departmental privilege. The claim that departmental business involving the White House may be kept from Congress and the courts.

Department secretary. *See* Cabinet and Department.

Depression. A period of economic decline, stock market collapse, and high unemployment.

Deregulation. The reduction or elimination of government economic controls.

Deviating election. An election in which the minority party wins but the majority party retains its advantage in terms of party identification.

Direct democracy. Government in which the people vote directly on the issues, as in a New England town meeting.

Distributive policy. A policy providing for costs to be broadly shared, while benefits are distributed to specific groups, usually those which have influence among decision makers in the bureaucracy.

Dual federalism. A constitutional interpretation which assigns powers strictly to either the states or the national government.

Due process of law. The requirement that the government not interfere with people's lives, liberty, or property without adhering to constitutional procedures and impartial administration of the laws. Due process of law is guaranteed by the Fifth and Fourteenth Amendments.

Dynamic factors. The influences on elections which change between one contest and the next, such as personalities and issues. *See also* Stable factors.

Elastic clause. Article I, Section 8, paragraph 18 of the Constitution, which states that Congress may make laws which are "necessary and proper" for carrying out the duties of all branches of government.

Election district. *See* Precinct.

Electoral college. A body consisting of the state electors who choose the president and the vice president of the United States.

Electors. The individuals chosen by the voters for the purpose of selecting one or more government officials. *See also* Electoral college.

Entitlements. Goods and services which government officials must provide to individuals who meet certain criteria set by law (for example, social security payments, welfare, and food stamps).

Equal protection clause. The Fourteenth Amendment to the Constitution, which provides that the states must guarantee all citizens equal protection under the laws. The courts use this clause to strike down laws which discriminate against people on the basis of race.

Equal Rights Amendment. A proposed amendment to the Constitution that would prohibit gender discrimination.

Equity power. The judicial power to effect a civil remedy which does not involve a monetary award to an injured party.

Establishment clause. The First Amendment prohibition of an official religion and of government funding of, and participation in, religious practices.

Exclusionary rule. A rule that makes evidence which was knowingly obtained by the government in violation of the Constitution or the legal rights of the accused inadmissible in judicial proceedings.

Exclusive power. Power assigned to a single branch of government. *See also* Concurrent power.

Executive branch. The president, the vice president, and the principal heads of the departments and other agencies accountable to the president. The term does not appear in the Constitution.

Executive Office of the President (EOP). The agencies which provide information, advice, and staff services to the executive branch. *See also* Council of Economic Advisors, National Security Council, and Office of Management and Budget.

Executive power. The power of the president, set forth in Article II of the Constitution, to make policy for the executive branch.

Executive privilege. The claim that the president's conversations with aides and departmental officials and the president's documents may be kept from Congress and the judiciary.

Executive supremacy. The claim that the president heads the government and that the other branches should cooperate with the president's policy initiatives.

Exploratory committee. A committee established by a contender for elective office before the official announcement of the candidacy.

Family assistance program. A proposed program that would have replaced the welfare system with grants to all families with children.

Favor. Patronage given by a politician in return for support of policies.

Favorite son. A home-state candidate who is put in nomination by a delegation to keep it uncommitted until it decides which contender to support.

Federalism. The division of powers between a national government (with sovereignty) and subordinate geographic units (such as states or provinces) which are guaranteed their powers by the constitution. *See also* Confederation.

The Federalist. A series of essays written in 1788 by Alexander Hamilton, John Jay, and James Madison. They were intended to persuade the New York convention to ratify the Constitution.

Federalists. The groups which favored ratification of the Constitution in 1788 and 1789. Also, the political party which formed in the 1790s around Alexander Hamilton and John Adams and which favored a strong national government and a national bank. *See also* Anti-Federalists.

Federal Reserve Board. The agency established by Congress to regulate the national banking system and currency.

Federation. A federal system. *See also* Federalism.

Filibuster. A prolonged debate in a legislative assembly, the purpose of which is to prevent a vote on a bill.

First strike. A surprise attack on an enemy's strategic nuclear forces, designed to eliminate its retaliatory capability.

First use. The use of tactical nuclear weapons to neutralize a conventional attack launched by a larger military force.

Fiscal equalization. The use of the national government's taxing and spending powers to redistribute national wealth from richer to poorer areas.

Fiscal federalism. The impact of the taxing and spending policies of the states on the national economy.

Fiscal policy. A policy of using taxing and spending powers to influence economic performance. A *compen-*

satory policy attempts to moderate the business cycle; a *propulsive* policy tries to achieve high rates of growth; a *corrective* policy is designed to alleviate a specific problem, such as high inflation.

Fiscal year. A twelve-month period used by the government to measure receipts and outlays. The calendar year begins on January 1, while the fiscal year for the national government starts on October 1 of the previous year.

Flexible response. The multiple targeting options and levels of retaliation in response to an enemy's use of strategic or tactical nuclear weapons.

Foreign Service. The career officials in American embassies, consulates, and the State Department.

Free market. An economic market in which the pricing and allocating mechanism for goods and services is based on supply and demand and in which neither sellers nor buyers combine to influence prices.

Gaffe. An inaccurate, offensive, or vulgar remark.

General revenue sharing. A program established by the national government to provide the states with funds for general government services.

Gerrymander. To draw district lines in such a way as to favor one party. Also, a district drawn as a result of gerrymandering.

Gold-plating. Providing features on military equipment that are unnecessary to carry out a mission.

Government. The institutions established by a society to make policies and enforce the laws. A government possesses a monopoly on the legitimate use of force. *See also* Legitimacy.

Grandfather clause. A legal provision stating that individuals who have rights or claims against the government do not lose them as a result of changes in the law. Grandfather clauses were used to guarantee whites the right to vote in southern states after literacy tests were introduced in the 1890s.

Grant-in-aid. Funds allocated by one level of government for programs carried out by another.

Habeas corpus, writ of. A constitutional provision requiring officials to bring anyone whom they arrest or detain before a magistrate and to state their reasons for the arrest. A writ of habeas corpus may be suspended in times of emergency.

Hearing. *See* Committee hearing.

Honeymoon effect. The tendency of legislators to cooperate with a newly elected executive official for a few months.

Impeachment. The constitutional method of charging presidents or judicial officials with high crimes or misdemeanors and of trying them for their misconduct in office. If convicted, they are removed from office. The House votes for impeachment, and the Senate conducts the trial.

Imperial presidency. A presidency such as those of post-World War II presidents who made war without congressional declaration and who vastly expanded their other powers. *See also* Executive supremacy, Prerogative powers, and Presidential powers.

Impoundment. An action or a lack of action by an official that precludes expenditures provided for by Congress. *See also* Deferral and Rescission act.

Incorporation. The judicial doctrine that extends some or all of the first Ten Amendments to the Constitution to state actions.

Incumbency effect. The tendency of voters to support the incumbent of the other party in an election.

Incumbent. A person who holds an office that is being contested in an election.

Independent agencies. Units of government that are not under the direct supervision of the president and whose officials are usually not subject to the president's removal powers, except for misconduct. These include independent *regulatory* agencies, *public corporations*, and many *authorities* and *boards*. *See also* Federal Reserve Board.

Independent expenditures. Funds spent on behalf of a candidate by a political action committee (PAC) which are not coordinated with the candidate's campaign and are not subject to federal limitations on contributions.

Indirect democracy. Government in which voters elect the representatives who make policies and the officials who carry them out. *See also* Direct democracy.

Industrial policy. A government tax, spending, and regulatory policy designed to influence investment in industrial enterprises.

Inflation. A general rise in prices.

Influence. The power to get others to do something of their own volition by convincing them that it is in their own best interest.

Initiative. A petition which puts a proposal on a ballot for decision by voters, bypassing the legislature. *See also* Direct democracy and Referendum.

Institutionalized presidency. A presidency in which the agencies and staff assistants help the president and the staff officials to whom the president delegates responsibility. *See also* Executive Office of the President and White House Office.

Interactive media. Media involving two-way communication, which allows viewers to transmit information back to a broadcasting studio or a central computer.

Interest group. An organization whose members have common goals and which attempts to influence government policy by helping candidates run for office, testifying before elected officials, and participating in the administration of programs. *See also* Pluralism.

Intergovernmental system. The system of administrative relationships between the national government, the state governments, and local units of government.

Internationalism. A government's participation in international agreements and organizations to promote national security and prosperity.

Interstate compacts. Agreements between two or more states. Most such compacts require the assent of Congress.

Interventionism. A government's protection of its national interests through involvement in the internal affairs of other nations.

Iron triangles. Alliances formed between bureau chiefs, lobbyists, and committee leaders.

Isolationism. A policy of defending the national interest by keeping foreign involvement and commitments to a minimum.

Issue networks. Groups of policy experts who communicate, leading to coalitions that attempt to influence policy. Issue networks have a broader range of participants than iron triangles.

Jim Crow. Laws and ordinances in southern states which segregated the races in the 1890s. Many were not overturned until passage of the Civil Rights Act of 1964.

Judicial activism. The tendency of some judges to use their understanding of the original constitutional principles to fashion judicial remedies for today's problems and to give less weight to previous judicial decisions. *See also* Judicial restraint and Stare decisis.

Judicial administration. The power of the judiciary to supervise state and national agencies in order to effect compliance with court orders, such as those ending racial discrimination.

Judicial branch. The federal district courts, the courts of appeals, the federal legislative courts, and the Supreme Court of the United States. The term does not appear in the Constitution.

Judicial orders. Orders requiring government officials or private parties to take or to refrain from taking specified actions.

Judicial restraint. The tendency of some judges to follow past precedents and defer to the policies of the other two branches. *See also* Judicial activism and Stare decisis.

Judicial review. The power of the courts to determine the constitutionality of the actions of the other two branches of government and to hold unconstitutional actions null and void.

Judicial supremacy. The doctrine that the judiciary is the final arbiter of what the Constitution means.

Laissez-faire. The doctrine that the government should not interfere with the allocation of resources by the marketplace.

Lame duck. An incumbent who is ineligible to run for reelection. A lame-duck Congress is an outgoing Congress that meets after the November elections.

Landmark decision. A Supreme Court decision that establishes important principles of constitutional law.

Legislative branch. The House of Representatives, Senate, and various congressional agencies, such as the Congressional Budget Office. The term does not appear in the Constitution.

Legislative courts. The federal courts (such as tax courts) established by Congress to try specialized cases involving specific statutes. Judges serve fixed terms. *See also* Constitutional courts.

Legislative party caucus. *See* Caucus.

Legislative party leaders. The Speaker of the House, the majority and minority leaders, and other legislators selected by the House and Senate party caucuses to hold important posts.

Legislative supremacy. The doctrine that Congress embodies national sovereignty and should set policy through its laws and appropriations.

Legislative veto. The provision of a law that allows a committee, a chamber, or the entire Congress to veto executive decisions or actions before or after implementation. The legislative veto was ruled unconstitutional in 1983 by the Supreme Court in *Chadha v. INS.*

Legitimacy. In politics, the perceived attribute of having a right to rule and of doing so justly.

Libel. A false written or recorded statement made knowingly and maliciously to damage someone. A spoken statement of this kind is called *slander*.

Liberal. In American politics, a person who believes that the national government should increase its role in domestic affairs, regulate the marketplace, and try to solve the country's economic and social problems. In European politics, the term refers to a person who relies more on the market than on the government. *See also* Conservative.

Literacy tests. Tests of a prospective voter's ability to read at a certain grade level or to interpret a section of the state constitution in order to register to vote.

Living Constitution. The Constitution as a set of principles guiding the solution of modern problems.

Lobbyist. A representative of an interest group who tries to influence government officials.

Lockean prerogative. The power claimed by executive officials to ignore or even violate the Constitution and laws if necessary to preserve the nation in times of extreme crisis.

Maintaining election. An election which is won by the majority party and in which the stable factors remain unchanged.

Majority. More than half. A *simple* majority is half plus 1; an *extraordinary* majority is anything greater than that.

Mandamus, writ of. A judicial order requiring officials to perform their duties.

Media politics. Campaigning which relies primarily on reaching voters through advertising rather than through the efforts of party workers.

Merit system. A system of appointment to office based on expertise and competence rather than political connections, quotas, wealth, or family background. The merit system is used for many appointments in the civil service.

Midterm convention. A convention held by a political party for the purpose of discussing issues rather than nominating a candidate.

Military-industrial complex. The close association that exists between the Pentagon, defense contractors, and congressional committees.

Military Keynesians. People who believe that military spending promotes employment and business prosperity.

Monetarists. People who believe that the most important economic factor is the supply of money and credit.

Monetary policy. A policy that attempts to influence economic conditions by influencing the supply of money and its cost.

Multiple advocacy. The presentation of different viewpoints on issues to decision makers by officials at the top levels of government.

Mutual assured destruction (MAD). The theory that if each superpower can retaliate against the other's first strike, a system of stable deterrence will be created.

National agenda politics. Politics aimed at influencing the outcome of a policy controversy by winning public support.

National command authority. The authority of the highest-level civilian officials who supervise the military chain of command.

Nationalism. The doctrine that a people should govern themselves. Also, the doctrine that the principal responsibility of a nation is to safeguard its own interests, even at the expense of other nations. *See also* Internationalism.

National Security Council (NSC). The advisory board that debates national security policies. The NSC consists of the president, the vice president, the secretary of state, the secretary of defense, and the chair of the Joint Chiefs of Staff (plus other officials invited to attend meetings). Its staff is supervised by the *national security assistant* to the president, one of the president's most important foreign policy advisers.

Necessary and proper clause. *See* Elastic clause.

Negative campaigns. Campaigns in which candidates attack the patriotism, character, or personal life of other candidates. Negative campaigns are often conducted by ideological and single-issue PACs. *See also* Independent expenditures and Political action committee.

Negative income tax. A proposed system that would give low-income people income from the government's tax agencies.

Negotiations. The processes by which parties try to resolve their differences on an issue. A *logroll* is a promise by each party to support a proposal of the other; a *package deal* puts all proposals in one bill; a *side payment* is something which is given to one or more of the parties but which has nothing to do with the issue; a *compromise* is an agreement according to which all parties modify their goals.

Neoconservatives. Democrats who remain liberal in domestic matters but who want strong national action in foreign affairs, including a military buildup.

Neoliberals. Democrats who have become skeptical about the ability of the national government to solve social problems and who believe that the size and scope of the bureaucracy should be reduced.

New Jersey Plan. Proposals put forward by the small states at the Constitutional Convention, calling for a weak executive and a Congress in which the states would have equal representation.

New patronage. Consulting contracts and professional retainers given to politically connected firms whose personnel have helped elect candidates to office.

New right. An alliance of conservatives who believe that a party can win elections only if it appeals to the broad mass of Americans on tax and social issues and of religious fundamentalists who believe that the government's policies should follow their interpretation of biblical precepts and prophecy.

Nightwatchman state. A government that restricts itself to maintaining domestic peace and providing for the national security. *See also* Positive state.

Nomination. The selection by a party of a candidate to run for office in the general elections, by *designation* of a party committee, by a *convention* representing party organizations, or by a *primary* that is open to the party voters and sometimes to independents.

Noncoordinated campaigns. Campaigns which are made without any communication with the candidate's organization and which are therefore exempt from the limits on campaign financing. *See also* Independent expenditures, Negative campaigns, and Political action committee.

Normal vote. The vote in an election if only party identification and the turnout rates of different groups determine the results. The normal vote is never the actual election results.

Nuclear winter. The condition that would exist (in the view of some scientists) after nuclear explosions produced enough smoke and dust to block out sunlight for a year or more, thus eliminating most life on earth.

Nullification. The doctrine that in a federal system a state may refuse to allow the enforcement of national laws which its legislature rules violate the national Constitution.

Obligations. Orders placed, contracts awarded, and other legally binding commitments made by government officials during a fiscal year. *See also* Outlays.

Office of Management and Budget (OMB). The presidential agency which prepares the budget and the budget message, determines whether departmental legislative proposals are in accord with the presidential program, and briefs the president on bills which contain provisions that the president might wish to veto.

Open rule. A legislative rule permitting a proposal to be amended.

Open seat. A seat in Congress for which no incumbent is running.

Original jurisdiction. Jurisdiction involving cases brought before a court for trial on the basis of both facts and law.

Outlays. Checks issued or cash disbursed to discharge obligations. Outlays also include interest on the public debt, even if not disbursed, such as interest credited to United States savings bonds.

Oversight. Legislative review of executive actions. Also known as *legislative, administrative,* and *congressional* oversight.

Parliamentary system. A system in which the majority party in the legislature chooses from its ranks the ministers, who run the principal departments, as well as the prime minister, who presides over the cabinet.

Party committees. Organizations that are responsible for the conduct of party business. These include the *national* committees, which represent the state parties; the *congressional campaign* and *senatorial campaign* committees, which assist candidates for Congress in fund-raising and advertising campaigns; and *state* and *local* committees.

Party government. The officials in government who act in concert to implement the program which their party presented to the voters in the preceding election.

Party identification. Voters' predisposition to consider themselves members of a party and to vote for the candidates of that party.

Patronage. Government employment or business received as a result of political connections.

Per curiam decision. An unsigned decision representing the opinion of a court.

Persuasion. *See* Influence.

Plebiscite. An election held to decide an issue. *See also* Direct democracy.

Pledge rule. A rule for a nominating convention that the delegates must vote for the candidates whom they pledged to support in the primary and caucus contests.

Pluralism. The decentralization of power and influence to autonomous public and private organizations, which can form temporary coalitions to influence public policy.

Plurality. The largest number of votes for a candidate or for a position in an election. A majority is always a plurality, but in a multichoice contest a plurality may be less than a majority.

Plutocracy. Rule by the wealthy.

Pocket veto. Presidents' power to veto a bill presented to them within ten days of the adjournment of Congress. Such a veto cannot be overridden by Congress. *See also* Veto.

Policies. *See* Clientele policy, Distributive policy, Redistributive policy, and Regulatory policy.

Political action committee (PAC). A nonparty organization which may legally raise and spend funds to influence elections by running noncoordinated campaigns and which may donate limited amounts directly to candidates' campaign organizations.

Political culture. The core beliefs about how politics is and should be conducted.

Political executives. The presidential appointees to the top positions in the government. They may be removed at the president's discretion. *See also* Administration.

Political party. A group of people who organize to control the government by electing public officials. A political party consists of the *party organization*, which recruits and elects candidates; the *party-in-government*, which consists of party members who hold office; and the *party-in-the-electorate*, which is made up of voters who identify with the party and usually vote for its candidates.

Political question. An issue designated by the judiciary for resolution by the president and Congress.

Political socialization. Education about politics gained in school or in the political arena.

Politics. The art of using power and influence to form coalitions or create a consensus, to manage problems, to allocate resources, and to resolve conflicts without resort to force.

Poll tax. A small fee charged by local officials for the right to vote. Poll taxes are now unconstitutional

as a result of the Twenty-Fourth Amendment, which was ratified in 1964.

Positive state. A government that deals with and solves economic and social problems. *See also* Nightwatchman state.

Poverty line. A measurement of income used by the Census Bureau. Families whose incomes are below the poverty line are classified as poor.

Power. The ability to get others to do things that they would not otherwise do. *See also* Influence.

Power elite. A permanent group which exercises the most power in society. A society with a power elite is the opposite of a pluralist society, in which many alliances form, all are temporary, and no group resolves all issues. Whether the United States has a power elite or is a pluralist society is a question on which political scientists are divided.

Power stakes. The factors in a situation that affect the power and influence of politicians.

Precinct. The smallest geographic unit in which votes are recorded by election officials. Also known as an *election district*.

Precinct captain. A local party official who mobilizes votes from supporters in a precinct.

Preferred freedoms doctrine. A judicial doctrine that emphasizes protection of the First Amendment guarantees against legislative action without due process.

Prerogative powers. Presidential powers exercised by virtue of the Constitution, sovereignty, international commitments and treaties, or the nature of an emergency. *See also* Lockean prerogative.

Presidential party. The party identifiers and committees which are oriented toward winning presidential (as opposed to congressional) elections. It includes the administration and most of the party's national committee.

Presidential powers. Powers that are assigned to the president by the Constitution, delegated by law, or established by custom and precedent. *Express* powers are mentioned in the Constitution; *inherent* powers are those which are exercised pursuant to the responsibilities of the office (that is, the president's responsibilities as the chief executive, the chief diplomat, and the commander in chief); *implied* powers are those which enable the president to perform the express and inherent duties of the office and which are not prohibited by the Constitution.

Presidential Republicans. Registered Democrats, located mainly in the south, who vote Republican in many presidential elections.

President pro tempore. The presiding officer of the Senate in the absence of the vice president of the United States, usually the most senior member of the majority party.

Primaries. Contests for party nominations that are decided by the party-in-the-electorate.

Prior restraint. The power to prevent a speech or a publication from reaching its intended audience.

Professionalization of reform. The initiation of social and economic reform by experts in issue networks.

Proportional representation. The apportioning of seats in presidential primaries or legislative elections on the basis of the percentage of votes received by a candidate or a party. *See also* Winner-take-all elections.

Protective legislation. Regulatory laws which single out women and children for special treatment.

Proxy. The power to act in the absence of another. The proxy rule permitted party leaders at nominating conventions to cast the votes of delegates from their states.

Pseudo event. An event staged solely so that it will be covered by the news media.

Realigning election. An election in which the minority party wins and gains the advantage in terms of party identification.

Recession. A downturn in business activity, corporate profits, and employment.

Reconciliation act. A law passed by Congress which brings budget and tax legislation into line with a congressional budget resolution.

Redistributive policy. A policy according to which costs are borne by all taxpayers to provide funds for cash payments or in-kind benefits to many people.

Redistricting. Changing legislative district lines.

Redundancy. In reference to weapons systems, the capability of completing a task in different ways, as a guard against a system malfunction.

Referendum. A popular vote on a proposal submitted to a state legislature. *See also* Direct democracy and Initiative.

Registrars. The public officials who register voters.

Registration. The process of legally qualifying to vote.

Regulatory policy. A government law or order designed to modify behavior by imposing costs or allocating benefits.

Reinforcing election. An election which is won by the majority party and which increases its advantage in party identification.

Reinstating election. An election, following a deviating election, which is won by the majority party.

Republic. A government in which the representatives of the people hold office and determine most public policies. *See also* Indirect democracy.

Reputation. A public official's overall character, as judged by the electorate. It may influence the official's calculations and conduct.

Reregulation. The restoration of regulations previously eliminated by Congress. *See also* Deregulation.

Rescission act. A law passed by Congress reducing or eliminating budget authority.

Responsible party. *See* Party government.

Responsible party system. A system of party competition in which each party takes a distinct position on important issues.

Retirement slump. The drop in electoral support of a party in a legislative district after its incumbent vacates a seat.

Retrospective voting. Voting based on a candidate's past performance.

Ripeness doctrine. The judicial rule specifying that a case should not be accepted for decision until the issues have fully evolved.

Runoff primary. A second primary held between the top two vote-getters if neither received a majority in the first primary.

Sedition. An attempt to overthrow the government by force. Seditious *speech* advocates the forceful overthrow of the government.

Self-regulation. The exercise of regulatory powers by private interest groups, without the interference of the government.

Senatorial courtesy. Presidents' practice of consulting senators from their party before nominating federal officials to positions in their states; soliciting the names of prospective nominees from these senators; and withdrawing the name of a nominee who a senator from the nominee's state says is "personally objectionable."

Senior Executive Service. The top-level managers of government programs who work under the political executives.

Seniority rule. A congressional rule which assigns members to committees partly on the basis of their *chamber seniority* and which determines their ranking on committees primarily on the basis of their *committee seniority*.

Separation of powers. The principle that legislative, executive, and judicial powers should be exercised by different institutions.

Shays's rebellion. A protest by farmers and former Revolutionary War soldiers in western Massachusetts in 1786 and 1787. It helped convince conservatives to organize the Constitutional Convention.

Social Darwinism. The theory that poverty and starvation improve the human species by eliminating the weak and promoting the "survival of the fittest."

Social insurance. Programs which spread the risk of unemployment or illness. Workers pay insurance premiums in the form of payroll taxes and receive benefits if they are ill or out of work.

Social issues. Issues such as busing to overcome racial segregation, prayer in schools, pornography, censorship in school libraries and textbooks, abortion, gun control, and other primarily non-economic issues.

Socialize risk. To implement programs by which the national government insures people or companies against risk (for example, flood insurance for individuals, export insurance, and insured loans for businesses).

Socioeconomic status (SES). A measurement of income, education, occupational prestige, and other social and economic characteristics for the purpose of ranking people and correlating these rankings with political behavior. *See also* Class.

Soft money. Funds used for voter registration and party building which are not subject to federal limitations on campaign financing.

Sophomore surge. The increased support that many incumbents receive from voters in their first bid for reelection.

Sovereignty. The condition that exists when a people are free to organize politically as they wish and are not subject to the will of any other political organization outside their territory.

Speaker of the House. The presiding officer of the House of Representatives. Formally chosen by the whole House, the Speaker is actually chosen by the majority party caucus. The Speaker is third in line for succession to the presidency.

Stable factors. Party identification, turnout rates among different electoral groups, and the tendency of groups to support one party or the other. These factors usually change slowly between one election and the next.

Stagflation. High inflation accompanied by low or negative economic growth and high unemployment.

Standing. The right to sue in court.

Standing legislative committees. Committees which may report legislation and which do not expire at the end of a session. There are approximately sixteen in the Senate and twenty in the House.

Stare decisis. The doctrine that judges should follow the reasoning and conclusions in previous cases and that they should be bound by previous rules of law when a case presents the same issue.

State. In European politics, a term that means considerably more than the term *government*. The state is the embodiment of the sovereignty of a nation, and its rights precede and are superior to those of the individual. The Constitution of 1787 did not create a state in this sense.

State action. Activities undertaken by private groups which are so regulated or supported by the government, or which perform such an important governmental function, that they may be considered the equivalent of actions taken by government officials. Party primaries are an example.

States' rights. The doctrine that all powers not specifically assigned to the national government are to be exercised by the states and that the powers of the national government should be strictly construed.

Statutory authority. The authority granted by laws passed by a legislature for public officials to act.

Statutory interpretation. A judicial or executive interpretation of the meaning of a law.

Subcommittees. Units which take initial action, including hearings, on legislation referred to the full committee.

Subsidy. A political allocation of funds from the government to private individuals or corporations.

Sunshine legislation. Laws requiring officials to allow the public access to administrative proceedings or files.

Super-PAC A political party which uses some of the fund-raising and campaign techniques developed by PACs.

Supply-side economics. An approach to economic problems that emphasizes stimulating the economy by cutting personal, corporate, and capital gains taxes; providing increased tax credits and depreciation for businesses; and deregulation.

Supremacy clause. Article VI of the Constitution, providing that national and state officials must enforce the Constitution, treaties, and laws of the United States over conflicting state constitutions or laws.

Suspect classification. A classification put into law based on race, religion, or ethnicity. Such classifications are considered "suspect" and are struck down by the courts unless there is compelling evidence that they achieve governmental purposes that cannot be achieved in any other way. Gender is not suspect classification.

Symbolic speech. Actions which are intended to communicate ideas but do not involve speech (such as wearing armbands) and which are therefore protected under the First Amendment.

Tariff. A tax levied by the government on goods imported from foreign nations. Tariffs are used to raise revenue or protect domestic companies.

Tax credits. Reductions in taxes owed due to an offsetting expenditure for a designated purpose.

Tax expenditures. The tax revenues lost to the government as a result of tax credits, deductions, income exclusions, exemptions, preferential rates, and deferrals of payments.

Totalitarianism. The concentration of all power, influence, and authority in the state. *See also* State.

Town meeting. An assembly of all the citizens of a community for the purpose of voting for candidates for office and deciding issues of local concern.

Trade association. An interest group consisting of companies engaged in the same kind of business.

Transformational leadership. Leadership that elevates the aspirations of the public and promotes the longer-term interests of the people, including their ability to act politically.

Treaty reservations. Stipulations accompanying the Senate's consent to a treaty, specifying the limits that the Senate puts on the terms of the treaty.

Turnout rate. The percentage of people who voted in an election. It is calculated by dividing the number of those who voted by the number of adults who are eligible to vote.

Tyranny. A system of government based largely on the concentrated power and influence of a small political elite, with no autonomous centers of countervailing power. Tyrannical rule may *usurp* power by displacing those who have a legitimate claim to rule, or it may *abuse* power by exercising it outside the rule of law.

Unanimous consent agreement. An agreement between party leaders in the Senate to facilitate the consideration of proposed legislation.

Uncoordinated expenditures. *See* Independent expenditures.

Unit rule. A rule providing that the majority of a state's delegation can determine how the entire delegation will vote at a national nominating convention.

Urban machine. A party organization in large cities which relied on patronage to gain control of city hall and which engaged in systematic graft and corruption.

Veto override. A two-thirds vote by both chambers of Congress by which measures previously vetoed by the president are enacted into law.

Veto power. The presidential power to prevent bills passed by Congress from being enacted into law.

Virginia Plan. A proposal made by the large states at the Constitution Convention for a strong national government and Congress. The states would be represented according to the size of their population. *See also* New Jersey Plan.

Waiver. A decision to exempt someone from the provision of a law.

Warrant. Judicial permission for the police or prosecutors to conduct a search, seize evidence, or make an arrest.

Watergate. The name given to the legal and constitutional violations that occurred during the Nixon administration. These included attempts to burglarize and wiretap the Democratic National Committee headquarters, seize confidential patient files of a psychiatrist, use the Federal Bureau of Investigation and other government agencies to harass "enemies" of the administration and conduct illegal surveillance of groups, play "dirty tricks" on the Democrats in the 1972 primary campaigns, raise illegal corporate funds for the presidential election, and reduce President Nixon's income tax liability. Several of Nixon's advisers went to jail because of their participation in these events, and Nixon himself resigned because of his attempts to cover up these crimes.

Welfare. Cash payments made by the government to categories of people (such as unmarried mothers) whose income is below a specified level.

White House Office (WHO). The collective name given to the staff assistants who perform personal and political tasks for the president, including scheduling, traveling, speech writing, planning political strategy, maintaining liaison with Congress and interest groups, and dealing with the media.

Winner-take-all elections. Contests in which the candidate who receives the plurality wins everything and in which the loser receives nothing. *See also* Proportional representation.

Wolfpack journalism. Journalism that focuses on candidates' gaffes and on scandals rather than on issues.

INDEX